A Guide for Student and In-Service Teachers

Successful Teaching
in Secondary Schools

revised

Sterling G. Callahan

Brigham Young University

A Guide for Student and In-Service Teachers
....

Successful Teaching
in Secondary Schools

revised

Scott, Foresman and Company
Glenview, Illinois   London

Preface

This textbook is designed to help beginning as well as in-service teachers sharpen the quality of their instructional techniques. To this end attention is focused on (1) teaching principles, (2) planning for teaching, (3) specific teaching procedures, (4) special teaching problems, and (5) recent developments in teaching. Major divisions of each chapter offer specific suggestions in the form of recommendations and cautions based on the careful examination of relevant principles. Care has been taken to insure that each major area selected for treatment contains illustrations of correct and incorrect uses. Footnotes, as well as the extensive bibliography, identify additional sources of current information for teachers who wish to engage in intensive study in a particular area.

The revised edition is characterized by a number of changes. With the exception of a few older references of enduring value, all of the bibliographical references and footnotes have been updated. A number of suggestions for modifications made by responsible students, teachers, and colleagues have been incorporated into the text. A survey of innovative instructional practices revealed novel techniques and challenging instructional approaches which have been identified and described at appropriate places within the existing framework of the book. Portions of chapters that appear to be less relevant than they were at the time of the first edition have been deleted. However, because instruction remains caught up in the whirlwind pace of educational change, two new chapters have been added. They focus attention on innovations of the past half decade—innovations that most strongly influence the performance of the superior teacher in the secondary school classroom.

Student teachers will find this volume valuable because of the examples provided and its pointed treatment of many troublesome areas. Experienced in-service teachers will find its content challenging, comprehensive, and practical. Further, its consistent concern for exposing readers to fresh, new instructional approaches is designed to serve the needs of all teachers, and the inclusion of a comprehensive table of contents and an extensive index serve to make the text a functional guide to effective teaching.

Contents

PART ONE
TEACHING PRINCIPLES

1. **Essential Principles: The Keys to Successful Planning and Teaching 2**

   Explaining Adolescent Student Behavior, 3.   Needs · Environmental influences · Expectations · Growth and development

   Helping the Teacher Plan, 8.   Types of objectives · Inseparables: objectives and procedures · The place of objectives · The place of procedures

   Forming and Using Clear Concepts, 10.   Experience and behavior · Differentiation and integration · Conceptualization and meaning · Levels of conceptual complexity

   Problems for Study and Discussion, 14.

2. **Essential Principles: The Keys to Meeting Instruction-Related Problems 16**

   Motivation, 17.   Intrinsic versus extrinsic motivation · Procedures as motivators · Interests as motivators · Immediate goals as motivators · Environment as a motivator · Success as a motivator · Need for different incentives · Reward or punishment? · Avoidance of frustration

   Interests, 20.   Superficial versus intense interests · Maturity and interests

   Readiness, 21.   Conceptual readiness · Physical readiness

   Individual Differences, 23.   Different rates for learning subjects · Generalized versus specific teaching · Differences within the learner

   Adjustment, 24.   Learning: the primary concern · Teacher-caused maladjustment

Classroom Control, 26. Purpose of classroom control · The teacher's responsibility · Teacher behavior · Clearly defined goals

Transfer of Learning, 28. Application and transfer · Demonstration of transfer

Problems for Study and Discussion, 29.

PART TWO
PLANNING FOR TEACHING

3. Planning Before Teaching 32

Planning–Forerunner of Effective Instruction, 33. Need for planning · Planning versus personality · Content plus methods · Criteria essential to planning

Planning for the Full School Year, 35. Examples of overall plans · Steps in developing overall plans

Planning for the Teaching of Units, 38. Unit defined · Subject-matter units and experience units · The teaching unit and the resource unit · Steps in developing a unit · The teaching unit and the overall plan

Determining Basic Information, 43. Specific information about the students · Information about the unit · Use of a seating chart · Examples of basic information

Problems for Study and Discussion, 51.

4. Objectives and Procedures in a Teaching Unit 53

Determining Enabling Objectives for a Teaching Unit, 54. Concepts · Memorization · Skills · Habits

Using Behavioral Objectives Efficiently in a Teaching Unit, 59. What are behavioral objectives? · Assumed limitations of nonbehavioral objectives · Specific uses · Specific suggestions

Determining Procedures for Achieving Enabling Objectives, 64. What procedures are best? · The teaching of concepts · The teaching of skills · The teaching of memorization · The teaching of habits · The teaching of positive tastes

Problems for Study and Discussion, 74.

5. Organizing Activities for Unit Teaching 76

Introductory Activities, 77. Sound activities · Variation in planning · Basic purposes · Unsound activities · Specific suggestions

Developmental Activities, 85. Sound activities · Recurring activities · Unsound activities · Specific suggestions

Concluding Activities, 92. Sound activities · Unsound activities · Specific suggestions

Problems for Study and Discussion, 96.

6. Materials, Resources, and Evaluation in Unit Teaching 97

Materials and Resources, 98. Purpose of materials and resources · Classification of materials and resources · Principles related to the selection of materials and resources · Use of aids in teaching specific subjects · Need for a comprehensive list · Recommendations

Evaluation Procedures, 108. Purpose of unit evaluation · Principles related to unit evaluation · Specific kinds of evaluation procedures · Categories of unit evaluation · Recommendations · Nonunit-related evaluation

Problems for Study and Discussion, 115.

7. Successful Teaching Units 117

Characteristics of Successful Unit Plans, 118. Basic information · Objectives · Procedures · Materials and resources · Evaluation procedures · Other general characteristics

Sample Teaching Units, 121. A teaching unit in biological science · A teaching unit in English

Successful Teaching Units in Review, 148.

Problems for Study and Discussion, 149.

8. Making a Daily Lesson Plan Effective 151

Essential Parts of the Plan, 152.

Daily Lesson Plan Forms, 154.

Practical Use of Specific Forms, 157.

Specific Suggestions, 165. Recommendations

Problems for Study and Discussion, 168.

PART THREE
SPECIFIC TEACHING PROCEDURES

9. Teacher-Centered Procedures 172

Use of the Lecture, 173. Principles related to lecturing · Correct and incorrect use · The lecture in special situations · Specific suggestions

Use of Questions, 179. Purposes of questions · Principles related to questioning · Specific suggestions

Use of Demonstrations, 184. Types of demonstrations · Demonstrations in special situations · Specific suggestions

Teacher-Centered Procedures in Review, 188.

Problems for Study and Discussion, 188.

10. Student-Centered Procedures 190

Use of the Textbook, 191. Principles related to the effective use of the text-book • Correct and incorrect use • Use in specific subjects • Specific suggestions

Use of the Assignment, 195. Characteristics of assignments • Principles related to the effective use of assignments • Correct and incorrect use • Assignments in specific subjects • Specific suggestions

Use of Homework, 199. Controversy and criticism • Principles related to the effective use of homework • Correct and incorrect use • Specific suggestions

Student-Centered Procedures in Review, 203.

Problems for Study and Discussion, 204.

11. Additional Student-Centered Procedures 205

Group Procedures, 206. Types of group procedures • Size of instructional groups • Principles related to group procedures • Correct and incorrect use • Specific suggestions

Individualized Instructional Procedures, 211. Types of individualized procedures • Recent individualization techniques • Principles related to individualized procedures • Correct and incorrect use • Specific suggestions

The Field Trip, 215. Principles related to the field trip • Incorrect usage • Use of the field trip in specific subjects • Specific suggestions

Additional Student-Centered Procedures in Review, 219.

Problems for Study and Discussion, 219.

12. Recurring Instructional Concerns 221

Continuous Study of the Student, 222. Special information about students • Devices used in the study of students • Principles related to the study of students • Specific suggestions

Use of Resource Persons, 227. Advantages of using resource persons • Principles related to the use of resource persons • Correct and incorrect use • Use in specific subjects • Specific suggestions

Use of Teacher-Prepared Materials, 231. Classification of materials • Special advantages • Principles related to the use of teacher-prepared materials • Use in specific subjects • Specific suggestions

Recurring Instructional Concerns in Review, 235.

Problems for Study and Discussion, 236.

PART FOUR
SPECIAL TEACHING PROBLEMS

13. Serving Instructional Purposes Through Discipline 240

Principles Basic to Effective Classroom Control, 241. The effect of the curriculum • The effect of planning • The effect of objectives and procedures • The effect of meaning • The effect of habits • The effect of growth and development · The effect of environmental influences · The effect of adolescent needs · The effect of expectations · The effect of readiness · The effect of motivation

Classroom Control in Practice, 252.   Unsound procedures · Sound procedures

The Role of the Teacher, 255.   Teacher-caused student misbehavior · Maintenance of specific routines

Classroom Control Practices in Different Subjects, 258.   Skill subjects · Concept-centered subjects · Social-centered procedures

Specific Suggestions, 259.   Recommendations · Cautions

Classroom Control in Review, 263.

Problems for Study and Discussion, 263.

14.   Readiness and Motivation   265

Effect of Readiness on Learning, 266.   Types of readiness · Readiness for a specific learning task · Principles related to readiness · Correct and incorrect use · Specific suggestions

Effect of Motivation on Learning, 275.   No learning without motivation · Motivational influences · Principles related to motivation · Correct and incorrect use · Specific suggestions

Readiness and Motivation in Review, 284.

Problems for Study and Discussion, 284.

15.   Individual Differences, Remedial Teaching, and the Reporting of Pupil Progress   286

Meeting Individual Differences, 287.   Advantages of knowing individual differences · Procedures for differentiating instruction · Principles related to differentiation · Correct and incorrect procedures · Use in specific subjects · Specific suggestions

Identifying a Sound Remedial Teaching Program, 301.   Goals of remedial teaching · Principles related to remedial teaching · Specific suggestions

Using Sound Marking and Reporting Procedures, 306.   Differences in marking and reporting · Principles related to marking and reporting · Current practices in reporting pupil progress · Specific suggestions

Individual Differences, Remedial Teaching, and Reporting Pupil Progress in Review, 315.

Problems for Study and Discussion, 315.

16.   Consistent Improvement in Instruction   317

Specific Practices for Improving Instruction, 318.   Identifying effective teaching · Gaining command of content · Evaluating methods · Improving the voice · Making use of personality · Using supervisory help · Using student opinion · Making the improvement program systematic · Affiliating with professional organizations · Pursuing graduate work

Principles Related to Instructional Improvement, 326.

Correct and Incorrect Practices, 328. Incorrect practices · Correct practices

Specific Suggestions, 331. Recommendations · Cautions

Problems for Study and Discussion, 334.

PART FIVE
RECENT DEVELOPMENTS IN TEACHING

17. Programed Instruction 336

Definition of Programed Instruction, 337.

History of Programed Instruction, 339. Early experiments · Mid-century interest · Current trends

Professional Reaction to Programed Instruction, 342. Limitations of programed instruction · Advantages of programed instruction

Basic Types of Programs, 345. Skinnerian programing · Crowderian programing · Programs for use in machines · Computer programs · Programed textbooks

Generalizations About Programed Instruction, 352.

Areas Using Programed Instruction, 356. The sciences · English · Mathematics · Foreign languages

Principles Related to Programed Instruction, 363.

Correct and Incorrect Use, 365. Procedures with limitations · Procedures with promise

Specific Suggestions, 369. Recommendations · Cautions

Programed Instruction in Review, 370.

Problems for Study and Discussion, 371.

18. Television and Team Teaching in the Modern Classroom 372

Television Instruction, 373. History of teaching by television · Approaches to teaching by television · Advantages of television instruction · Limitations of television instruction · New applications of television instruction · Principles related to teaching by television · Sound and unsound practices · Use of television in specific subjects · Specific suggestions

Team Teaching, 388. Development of team teaching · Definition of team teaching · Current variations in team teaching methods · Advantages of team teaching · Limitations of team teaching · Principles related to team teaching · Sound and unsound practices · Specific suggestions

Television and Team Teaching in Review, 401.

Problems for Study and Discussion, 401.

19. Recent Instructional Innovations 403

Individualization, 404. Programed instruction · Study carrels · Continuous progress programs · Self-directed learning · Reaction to teaching styles

Grouping, 410. Large groups · Small groups · Individualization · Grouping for special purposes

Problems for Study and Discussion, 413.

20. Additional Recent Instructional Innovations 414

Technology, 415. Computer-assisted instruction · Projection devices · Television

Flexibility, 421. Flexible scheduling · Flexible housing · Flexible procedures · Flexible use of instructional materials

Problems for Study and Discussion, 431.

BIBLIOGRAPHY 432

APPENDICES

Appendix A: Self-Scoring Instrument for Teaching Units, 441.

Appendix B: Confidential Evaluation of Self-Improvement Techniques, 453.

Appendix C: Innovations Awareness Checklist, 461.

Appendix D: Inventory of Student Unrest, 468.

Appendix E: How Relevant Is Your Curriculum for Students? 473.

INDEX 477

PART ONE

Teaching Principles

1. *Essential Principles: The Keys to Successful Planning and Teaching*

Effective secondary teaching methods are based upon sound psychology; thus, psychology becomes an essential tool in the basic equipment of any ambitious teacher who is willing to put forth the effort necessary to teach systematically. This chapter deals with some of the principles that have a direct bearing on the teaching-learning process:

Principles useful in explaining adolescent student behavior
Principles useful in helping the teacher plan
Principles useful in forming and using concepts

Chapter 2 will discuss principles useful in helping the teacher meet the most frequent instruction-related problems. Later chapters, devoted to the specific procedures involved in planning and teaching, assume an understanding of the principles discussed in these first two chapters.

EXPLAINING ADOLESCENT STUDENT BEHAVIOR

The adolescent's behavior is affected by his needs, by his environmental influences, by parental, peer-group, and teacher expectations, and by developmental changes resulting from his growth. If the teacher understands the effect of such influences upon the teenager and the learning process, his teaching tends to become systematic and gives him both interest and pleasure.

Needs

All students have basic needs.[1] The teacher's understanding of these needs heightens his ability to establish rapport and hence helps him communicate with his students. A superficial acquaintance with these basic needs, however, is not sufficient. The effective teacher must be able to identify such needs as they are expressed in individual behavior and to take action to help the student satisfy them in socially acceptable ways. Because the needs of the group are an extension of the needs of individuals, the identification of group needs must begin with a personal acquaintance with each pupil in the group.

Approval, Affection, and Security

Approval, affection,[2] and security are needs common to all human beings and are the first needs that must be understood by the thoughtful teacher. They are expressed in the desire to conform to peer-group customs (approval), to maintain close ties with home and family (affection), and to avoid physical harm (security). Because these universal needs exert a marked influence on the degree of receptivity to learning situations, an understanding of their effect on teaching and learning is essential.

Each learner responds readily to stimuli that he recognizes as closely related to his perceived needs. Understanding this fact, the well-trained

---

[1] Paul Henry Mussen, John Janeway Conger, and Jerome Kagen, *Child Development and Personality*, 3d. ed. (New York: Harper & Row, Publishers, 1969), pp. 181–184, provide a concise, useful discussion of physiological needs that must be satisfied if man is to survive.

[2] Lee J. Cronbach, *Educational Psychology*, 2d. ed. (New York: Harcourt Brace Jovanovich, 1963), pp. 113–121, discusses the need for approval and affection.

teacher can provide the stimuli for sound motivation. Ignoring the pupil's basic desires, or teaching in ways that run counter to his desires, may retard learning and inhibit pupil-teacher rapport.

Developmental Tasks

Adolescence, furthermore, is characterized by developmental tasks related to physical changes, emancipation from adult controls, and social adjustments.[3] Developmental tasks are essentially major problems related to growth, personal welfare, and individual adjustment. The changing voice in the boy and the breast development in the girl, occasional dissension between adolescent and adult, and the inability to relate oneself easily to the opposite sex are examples of such problems during adolescence.

The teacher who has a warm, human understanding of these development-related processes is in a favorable position to comprehend and deal effectively with adolescent behavior.

Environmental Influences

The effect of the surrounding world on pupil behavior must be recognized and understood in order to plan and teach with insight and effectiveness. Of particular concern to the instructional process are those environmental factors related to the home, the peer group, and the school.[4] Cultural forces act upon the basic biological inheritance of the individual to make him what he is. Environmental conditioning largely shapes his state of educational readiness or reticence, forming habit patterns that encourage or discourage effective study and attitudes that further or impede learning.

The Home

Classroom behavior is often related to circumstances in the home over which the individual student has little control. Extreme parental domination may result in teenage instability or aggression, the cause of which may not be recognized by the teacher. Frequent and heated parent-adolescent arguments feed the fires of domestic tension and may cause in-school behavior that is both baffling and disruptive. In addition, siblings may react differently to the same conditions,[5] thus confusing the

---

[3]See Robert J. Havighurst, *Human Development and Education* (New York: Longmans, Green and Co., 1953), pp. 111–158, for a complete discussion of developmental tasks.

[4]David P. Ausubel, *Educational Psychology: A Cognitive View* (New York: Holt, Rinehart & Winston, Inc., 1968), pp. 425–434, documents and discusses the exaggerated patterns of conformity within the adolescent peer group.

Influences of the home and the neighborhood as well as other cultural forces on personality development and classroom behavior are stressed by Herbert J. Klausmeier and William Goodwin, *Learning and Human Abilities: Educational Psychology*, 2nd. ed. (New York: Harper & Row, Publishers, 1966), pp. 8–9.

[5]Elizabeth B. Hurlock, *Adolescent Development*, 3d. ed. (New York: McGraw-Hill Book Company, 1967), chapter 15, discusses family relationships and the teenager.

teacher who hoped to have ready answers to questions about the behavior of youngsters coming from the same home.

The Peer Group

The effect of the peer group upon in-school and out-of-school behavior is pronounced and should not be underestimated by the instructor. The unwarranted assumption, by some teachers and parents, that teenagers generally are more responsive to adult wishes than to the wishes of their peers often creates problems. The formation of close-knit adolescent groups is both necessary for and typical of secondary-school youth. In an environment of their own creation teenagers are largely free of adult restraint. They behave—or misbehave—in conformity to the wishes of their peers, speaking, thinking, and dressing the way the group does.

The School

At the junior and senior high schools levels no less than one fourth of the student's total time is spent in the school or in school-related activities during the academic year. It is here that the teacher's influence is felt most strongly. But this influence must compete with all the other influences connected with the school—with after-school activities, with members of the peer group, with the administration, and even with the custodian.

In-school learning, therefore, can be no more efficient than the environment provided by the school for the promotion of learning. Students must have a feeling of security in an atmosphere where learning is the *dominant* concern, and the efficient teacher must know how to provide this feeling.

Expectations

The adolescent is also subject to the expectations of his parents, his teachers, his peer group, and himself. Keeping the pressures of these expectations within control is a challenge to any youngster, and for some it is overwhelming.

Parental Expectations

Parents often transfer their own thwarted ambitions to their children without realizing the negative effect such action may have upon the child's capacities, interests, and maturation. The relative instabilities of adolescence require a larger measure of parental love, understanding, and patience than is frequently given. Thus, where parental desires for their children are unrealistic, the teacher has the responsibility for making appropriate intercession.

Teacher Expectations

Because of this frequent necessity for teacher intervention, teacher expectations of students should be based upon an accurate knowledge of the child's capacity, past achievement, home environment, and personal motivation. The teacher's training and his access to confidential records place him in a position to determine what logically can be, and ought to be, expected of his students. On the basis of essential information in his possession, an effective teacher will realistically adapt assignments, make allowances for limited capacities, and give consideration to home problems that may affect a student's receptivity for learning.

Peer-Group Expectations

Peer-group acceptance is of vital concern to the secondary-school student, and he may cast aside parental and teacher expectations in an attempt to measure up to the expectations of his peers. A case in point is that of a bright student who may arbitrarily lower his academic achievement in order to maintain popularity with his peer group.

Self-Expectations

What the individual expects of himself is the result of concepts derived from personal experience. The image he holds of himself as an interactive person in an adolescent society will help determine his actual behavior.

The adolescent student's behavior will largely fall within the range of behavior viewed as acceptable by his contemporaries. Within this range he will identify the level at which he feels he can function with success. Viewing himself as an unskilled basketball player, for example, the adolescent will not participate in team play. On the other hand, his experiences in mathematics may lead him to believe that he is among the better students. In this field he will compete with enthusiasm.

The student's appraisal of his own ability, or lack of ability, is not infallible, however. He is often hampered because of his overappraisal or underappraisal of what he can do. Frequently estimations are based upon assumption only, without the benefit of experience. On the other hand, where the student has been fortunate enough to acquire a number of usable skills, his self-esteem will be enhanced, as will his mental picture of what he can do. Thus, the boy who has learned to dance has a definite social advantage. The student who has been taught effective study habits can, and probably will, study; self-expectation motivates him in this direction.

Growth and Development

As the adolescent moves along the developmental path, it is important that his instructors be professionally equipped to view him realistically in terms of his mental, physical, social, and emotional stature.[6]

---

[6]For a complete discussion of physical, emotional, social, and intellectual development, see George J. Mouly, *Psychology for Effective Teaching*, 2d. ed. (New York: Holt, Rinehart, & Winston, Inc., 1968), chapters 6–9.

Aspects of adolescent development relevant to the teaching-learning process are discussed by Nathan S. Blount and Herbert J. Klausmeier, *Teaching in the Secondary School*, 3d. ed. (New York: Harper & Row, Publishers, 1968), chapter 2.

Intellectual Growth

The behavior of the individual is limited by his mental ability, which grows at a rate unique to him and which grows more slowly as he advances in age. Although the teacher should have an accurate indication of mental ability, test scores may be prejudicial.[7] Culture-oriented intelligence tests frequently lack validity,[8] and unless they are interpreted with great care, such tests may harm the student's welfare by presenting a distorted picture. Consider, for instance, a case reported by Wellman and Pegram: Preschool orphanage children were enrolled in the University of Iowa Nursery School in the fall, at which time individual I.Q.'s were determined. By the time I.Q.'s were again measured in the spring, the children had made an average gain of seven points.[9] During the intervening months the teachers may have been able to present more difficult learning tasks yet hesitated for fear the children would be unable to grasp them.

Most psychologists recognize the effect of environment on certain intelligence test *scores*, yet they are somewhat unwilling to concede its effect on basic intellectual *capacity*.

Physical Growth

Like mental development, physical growth follows an orderly sequence during adolescence and gives rise to myriad social and emotional problems. There is marked variability in height, weight, and general body structure among members of the same sex of a given age. This is readily observable among eighth- and ninth-graders. In many cases the girls are a full head taller than the boys; heterosexual social adjustments are thus complicated. The inability of students to accept normal physiological changes with poise tends to accentuate the social ineptness of the teenager. Adding to the teenager's worries is the frequent occurrence of acne, poor posture, and other uncomfortable manifestations of growth.

Social Growth

With this rapid physical growth and continuing mental growth, the early teens are often characterized by a groping social insecurity, for it is during this period that the student must make his adjustment to the opposite sex within a framework of existing adult conventions and social taboos. Puberty brings the intensified interest of girl for boy and boy for girl, but without the needed social skills.[10]

---

[7]John P. De Cecco, *The Psychology of Learning and Instruction: Educational Psychology* (Englewood Cliffs, New Jersey: Prentice-Hall, Inc., 1968), p. 84, points out that intelligence tests have been criticized as being prejudicial to bright, nonconforming students as well as to race and social class.

[8]Morris L. Bigge and Maurice P. Hunt, *Psychological Foundations of Education*, 2d. ed. (New York: Harper & Row, Publishers, 1968), pp. 138–139.

[9]Beth L. Wellman and Edna L. Pegram, "Binet IQ Changes of Orphanage Preschool Children: A Reanalysis," *Journal of Genetic Psychology*, 1944, 65:239–263.

[10]Arden N. Frandsen, *Educational Psychology*, 2d. ed. (New York: McGraw-Hill Book Company, 1967), pp. 537–544, presents a long-range view of social development extending through childhood and youth.

The degree of social know-how exhibited by students during this period is highly variable. Adolescents of either sex who consistently withdraw from social contact with their peers frequently have problems that should be investigated by professional experts. Students with problems of extreme aggressiveness or of aggravated antisocial behavior will also benefit by referral to the school counselor.

Emotional Growth

The emotional behavior of secondary-school students varies from extreme self-consciousness to open rebelliousness. The psychologically oriented teacher understands that such behavior is not willful misconduct. The tendency to argue, typically found in adolescent boys, reflects growth toward self-directive adulthood. If the teacher shows an understanding of the nature and cause of socially disruptive behavior, youngsters may voluntarily channel their emotions into socially useful pursuits.

HELPING THE TEACHER PLAN

The understanding and use of principles to deal effectively with adolescent behavior find their counterparts in selected principles that aid the teacher in effective planning. To plan effectively the teacher should relate (1) his course to the total school curriculum and (2) his unit plans to the course. Furthermore, his unit plans should be so designed that they reveal the relationship of objectives to procedures. They must also reflect a genuine concern for materials and resources as well as for evaluation procedures.

Types of Objectives

Content areas in the school curriculum may be thought of as comprised of concepts, skills, symbols (memorizations), and habits to be learned.[11] Some of the concept-centered subjects are mathematics, chemistry, biology, and English grammar. Among skill subjects are found typing, physical education, and orchestra. But the need for memorization and for learning habits is common to all content areas.

An examination of a majority of secondary-school subjects reveals that the *concept* is the dominant type of objective. Through the acquisition of concepts (mental pictures), learners acquire the raw materials from which decisions are made and behavior is improved. Unfortunately the concept is often confused with the *symbol* (usually a word) that refers to the concept. A concept, by its very nature, can exist only in the mind.

---

[11]Asahel D. Woodruff, *Basic Concepts of Teaching; with Brief Readings* (San Francisco: Chandler Publishing Company, 1962), p. 72.

See Chapter 4 in the present text for a discussion of the kinds of objectives and their related procedures.

Skills and memorizations deserve curricular attention to the extent to which they are necessary to implement concepts.[12] For example, the motor manipulation of the typewriter (skill) is but a means of carrying out the pictures (concepts) of key placement that exist in the mind. One memorizes formulas in chemistry, not for the sake of memorization, but as a means of thinking and conveying thoughts systematically.

Concepts, similarly, deserve incorporation into the curriculum if they help meet the general aims of education. The concept a well-rounded diet helps promote physical health has justification for being taught to the extent to which it can be related to the general aim of health. The concepts related to the successful operation of a power saw have educational justification if they can be related to the general aim of increased vocational efficiency.

Inseparables: Objectives and Procedures

After acquiring a clear understanding of the aims of the curriculum, a teacher must develop an effective plan. The first concern must be to determine which objectives are appropriate to the students and to the subject to be taught. Attention should then be focused on the procedures necessary to achieve objectives. Evaluation must also be planned in terms of relevant stated goals, for evaluation is the process of determining the extent to which goals have been reached.

In planning effectively, the teacher must consider the procedures that are psychologically sound in terms of the enabling goals sought.[13] Each type of objective calls for its own unique procedures. A habit, for example, is not efficiently taught in the same way as a concept. For the conscientious planner, relating specific kinds of goals to appropriate procedures will be, in the beginning, a slow, painstaking process. But he will have the assurance that, with each succeeding carefully prepared plan, his ability to plan efficiently and systematically will improve.

The Place of Objectives

Improved behavior is the final goal of teaching and learning. This goal can be achieved only when smaller, intermediate goals that result in changed behavior have been identified and reached. For this reason the end-means relationship between objectives and procedures must never be forgotten. Procedures (methods) should be viewed as the means for achieving desired ends (objectives). Goal achievement, therefore, must be the primary instructional consideration, with activities, materials, aids, and evaluation procedures playing contributory roles. The teacher who

---

[12]Ibid., pp. 73–74.

[13]Ibid., p. 121.

Ausubel, Educational Psychology, pp. 514–515, expresses a preference for the idea of concept assimilation as opposed to concept formation. Acceptance of his point of view would give rise to many methodological implications.

permits students to engage in activities merely for the sake of activities is on a directionless treadmill.

The extent to which individual students are willing to accept teacher-formed objectives as worthy of pursuit will depend upon whether the objectives accomplish purposes that are of value to students.[14] For this reason goals not only must *be* attainable, but they must also be *considered* attainable by the learner. A budding junior high school athlete is less likely to be motivated by the distant promise of adult health than by the immediate and impressive need for playing a peer-group-approved game of softball—and playing it well.

For example, it is demoralizing and frustrating to students for their history teacher to state that acquiring a knowledge of United States history is the basic purpose of an eighth-grade course. The immensity of the task tends to discourage and defeat youngsters at the outset. A better procedure involves dealing with the content in terms of units and related unit divisions.

The Place of Procedures

Each kind of objective (concept, skill, memorization, or habit) calls for its own specific procedures if it is to be taught with efficiency.[15] The common practice of failing to select the procedures associated with the desired objectives accounts for much unsuccessful instruction.

The teaching of concepts, for example, involves bringing the student into direct contact with the referent of the concept (a smoothly planed board in a woodworking class, for example) or providing a substitute experience that approximates the real contact as nearly as possible (such as showing motion pictures of Europe during a unit on European geography).[16] The teaching of skills, on the other hand, calls for repeated practice under supervision, but only after one has a clear mental image of the skill to be performed.[17]

Although they are frequently treated separately in discussions on unit planning, instructional aids, materials, and resources, as well as activities aimed at evaluation,[18] may well be classified under the general category of *procedures*. Here again the purpose of these procedures is to serve as means to goal achievement, not as ends in their own right.

FORMING AND USING CLEAR CONCEPTS

Experience and Behavior

Learning is based upon experience, and perceptual experience is the

[14]Frandsen, *Educational Psychology*, p. 295.
[15]The different kinds of enabling objectives and their related procedures are illustrated in the sample units found in Chapter 7.
[16]Woodruff, *Basic Concepts of Teaching*, pp. 157–159.
[17]See Chapter 4, pp. 69–71, for examples of specific procedures for teaching skills.
[18]See Chapter 6, "Materials, Resources, and Evaluation in Unit Teaching."

beginning point of learning.[19] Such perception occurs when some form of energy (light, heat, sound, etc.) stimulates a sensory organ. Each percept (sensory awareness) thus formed results in an impression recorded in the brain. With the addition of other sensory impressions, meanings begin to form that give direction to the learner's behavior.

Deriving Meaning from Experience

The newborn infant, void of meaningful experience, is bombarded with a range of perceptual experiences—odors, pressures, and sounds. Gradually, as the infant develops and reacts to stimuli, these perceptual fragments are interrelated to form small clusters of meaning. It is this meaning that governs his controllable behavior.

Because of its relationship to meaningful experience, learning is entirely an individual matter. One learns only as he identifies the *meaning* in a given experience. It is evident that a teacher cannot do a student's learning for him, but *the teacher can manipulate circumstances so that the student will be encouraged to learn.*

Using Experience to Aid Learning

The cause of instruction is furthered when a learning experience can be related to a previous meaningful experience. The establishment of interrelationships between on-going and past experiences is limited or enhanced by the learner's background of meaning.

Concepts, however, are not the sole controlling factors in what an individual does. One's ability in skill performance and one's habits also play their role.[20] The patient confined to a wheel chair cannot play tennis; the student with bad study habits studies poorly. Furthermore, individual desires affect behavior. For example, the teenager who seeks teacher approval will exhibit conforming behavior in the presence of the teacher.

Differentiation and Integration

An essential concern of conceptual learning involves identifying the characteristics of a particular *referent* (the thing for which the concept stands) that set it apart from the other referents. This process of *differentiation* enables the young learner to arrive at meaningful conclusions with respect to his environment.[21]

Elementary-school youngsters learn to identify differences in social customs of different countries. More advanced learners make finer dif-

---

[19]Perceptual constancy and its relationship to learning is discussed by De Cecco, *The Psychology of Learning and Instruction*, pp. 214–216.

[20]A relevant, brief discussion of the importance of acquiring skills in this modern age is provided by De Cecco, *The Psychology of Learning and Instruction*, pp. 275–277.

Arthur T. Jersild, *The Psychology of Adolescence*, 2d. ed. (New York: The Macmillan Company, 1963), chapter 5, provides a useful discussion of teenage physical abilities and their psychological effect on the individual.

[21]Bigge and Hunt, *Psychological Foundations of Education*, p. 413.

ferentiations; students in a biology class, for example, learn to identify the fine-line differences that characterize various plants.

Determining how one referent relates to another is basic to the development of a well-rounded concept. Perceiving an object quite apart from other objects is important, but meaning is added when the object is viewed as having a particular function in relationship to other objects—as the relationship of the flower and the bee to pollination, of safe driving to good citizenship, and of a knowledge of parts of speech to effective communication. This functional relationship is called *integration*.[22]

Conceptualization and Meaning

Concepts tend to group themselves into meaningful, interrelated patterns.[23] Considered in isolation, they lose some of their meaning. The extent to which the learner is able to visualize relationships between and among the subdivisions of large concepts will determine the meaning the concepts convey to him. When he is able to visualize the existing relationships, the learner is said to possess *insight*.

It follows that learning by wholes is superior to the learning of isolated parts because of the importance of interrelationships and the understanding that results. Furthermore, recall is enhanced through such understanding.

When concepts are used in practical situations, they tend to become enlarged, modified, and clarified. The acquisition of useful concepts serves as motivation for the learner to acquire further concepts. This is particularly true when such concepts help him achieve his own ends.

Levels of Conceptual Complexity

It is not equally simple to acquire all different types of mental pictures, but all conceptual learning begins with concrete concepts. Furthermore, generalizations, abstractions, and the involved processes of analysis and synthesis rely on the concrete concept for their basic meaning.

Concrete Concepts

Concrete concepts are related to individual sensory impressions. The sights, sounds, and odors of the surrounding environment impose themselves upon the consciousness of the learner[24] regardless of his desire. When these impressions are meaningfully interrelated, mental pictures form that give direction to behavior.

Concrete concepts, those that result from direct sensory experience,

---

[22]Woodruff, *Basic Concepts of Teaching*, p. 181.

[23]Ausubel, *Educational Psychology*, pp. 506–507, describes the advantages to man of identifying concepts by categories; reception learning, problem solving, and communication are simplified and enhanced.

[24]Woodruff, *Basic Concepts of Teaching*, p. 125.

are the most vivid pictures the mind commands. Furthermore, they constitute the basic raw materials of which the more complicated concepts are comprised. Mental pictures (concepts) of chairs, animals, books, houses, plants, streets, and automobiles are easily acquired and are the essential parts in the formation of other mental pictures.

Generalized Concepts

Having at its disposal a large number of mental pictures that are particularly clear because of their closeness to the sensory process, the mind begins to classify. Concepts possessing similarities are placed in a common rubic. *Cans, dogs, desks, lights, men,* and hundreds of other items are subject to this process.

At the unsophisticated level of very early childhood, plants that are tall, have very thick stems, and produce leaves are categorized as *trees.* Similarly, creatures that possess four feet are classified as *animals.* This procedure, known as *generalization,* often takes place at the level of the subconscious. A great many generalized concepts are formed as soon as youngsters are able to identify similarities during their preschool years. (Examples: *Animals have four legs. All people do not dress alike. Birds can fly. Rocks are hard.*)

At all school levels extending from the primary grades through graduate study, generalizations are formed. This is true in all fields, but it is most apparent in the highly organized disciplines of the physical and biological sciences, mathematics, and English grammar.[25] In chemistry, elements may be grouped according to specific gravity; in botany, plants with certain characteristics are placed in the bean family; and in grammar, nouns with particular qualities are classified as common nouns.

Abstract Concepts

The formation of the abstract concept, like that of the generalized concept, is dependent upon the learner's mental pictures of concrete referents. After he has a range of experience with specific objects possessing a definite characteristic (hardness, goodness, carefulness, etc.), he finds that he is able to think of the characteristic quite independently of the object. Thus the learner is able to think meaningfully of *goodness* in the abstract without the necessity for relating it to a *good* person. He has now engaged in abstraction or has abstracted (removed) a particular quality from its concrete setting.[26]

The ease with which the learner is able to engage in abstraction will depend partially upon the clarity of his mental images of the qualities to be abstracted at the time they are still associated with concrete objects. Much of the haziness of abstractions can be traced to the lack of such vivid mental pictures. The learner who has contacted a *pleasant* butcher,

---

[25]See the unit objectives in the sample units of Chapter 7 for examples of generalizations.

[26]Ausubel, *Educational Psychology,* p. 505, provides a useful discussion of the relationship of generalization and abstraction to the world of physical realities.

a *pleasant* physician, a *pleasant* teacher, and a *pleasant* bricklayer without having strongly sensed the *pleasantness* of each person will suffer to some extent in an attempt to think abstractly about this particular quality. An abstraction can be no clearer than the quality of the referent on which it is based.

Having progressed through the steps of *differentiation* and *integration*, which help in the formation of concrete concepts, learners can undertake the conceptual tasks of *generalization* and *abstraction* with greater promise of success. The actual use of concept in real situations increases conceptual meaning and tends to fix mental pictures for subsequent use. As the junior high school student partakes of the privileges and responsibilities of democratic citizenship in a junior high school setting, his concept of democracy takes on expanded meaning. After repeated experiences with democratic school life, he is able to think about democracy in the abstract with some degree of insight. His acquired concept of democracy will serve a useful purpose in the tasks of citizenship that lie ahead.

Analysis and Synthesis

Beyond the level of generalization and abstraction lie the processes of *analysis* (pulling apart, mental disassembly) and *synthesis* (putting together, restructuring in a new way), which are essential to creative thinking in its more restricted sense.[27] The use of these processes by high-school students requires a level of experience and maturity. It should not be assumed, however, that analysis and synthesis offer too great a challenge to secondary-school students of particular talent. Knowing this, the perceptive teacher should identify capable students and give them special guidance in this type of thinking.

PROBLEMS FOR STUDY AND DISCUSSION

1. What would happen if teachers had to plan and instruct without a knowledge of educational psychology and human growth and development?

2. Define *developmental task* in your own words.

3. How do you account for the fact that truant, delinquent youngsters frequently come from middle-class homes where they have enjoyed untroubled relationships with their parents?

4. What are some of the typical forms of in-school misbehavior in which adolescents engage?

5. Describe the ideal in-school learning environment from the point of view of the psychologist.

6. Is learning really the *dominant* concern in American secondary schools? Should it be? Discuss.

7. If you discovered that the parents of one of your students were constantly urging him to achieve at a level above his capacity, what would you do? Be specific. Justify your action.

8. How do you explain, from a psychological point of view, the lack of regard many teenagers have for adult values?

---

[27]Woodruff, *Basic Concepts of Teaching*, pp. 143–144.

9. What is meant by the interdependence of mental, physical, social, and emotional growth? Discuss.

10. Relate several instances in which you have observed the marked relationship between social maturity and emotional stability in adolescents.

11. In your own words, define *concept* as it is used in this chapter.

12. Four types of objectives are listed in this chapter. Are there other types that you feel should be added? Discuss your point of view.

13. List some other concept-centered studies besides mathematics, chemistry, biology, and English grammar.

14. State in your own words the point of view of this chapter with respect to the relationship between objectives and procedures.

15. Do you feel that students should assist teachers in the formation of objectives? Why?

16. What is the relationship between perceptual experiences and concept formation? Explain in detail.

17. Why is learning entirely an individual matter?

18. Discuss in some detail the meaning of *meaning*.

19. State three meaningful generalizations. Tell why they are generalizations.

20. State three abstractions. What makes them abstractions?

2. *Essential Principles:*
The Keys to Meeting
Instruction-Related Problems

The teacher who aspires to a level of teaching above the commonplace must make advance preparation to insure his instructional competence. Such a teacher must be prepared to identify those difficulties that impede the teaching-learning process. Such difficulties are concerned with motivation, interests, readiness, individual differences, adjustment, classroom control, and transfer of learning. Essential principles related to these problem areas are identified and discussed in this chapter.

MOTIVATION

Because there is a *cause* for all student behavior, the teacher who wishes to understand behavior in order to improve instruction must study causation. With the few exceptions related to the functioning of the autonomic nervous system (nutritive, vascular, and reproductive responses), the individual behaves as he does because he is *moved*, or *motivated*, to do so.[1]

Intrinsic versus Extrinsic Motivation

Motivation may be either intrinsic or extrinsic.[2] As the biology teacher dissected the lungs of a dead cat, the members of the class gathered around his desk and observed in rapt attention. "Now," he said, "I believe you will want to read more about the respiratory system of mammals." The students not only *wanted* to read more, but they *did*, for they were *intrinsically motivated* (from within) by what they had seen.

On the other hand, the *extrinsically motivated* student is moved by outside pressures. Pat, for example, hated Algebra I, but she handed in her assignments every day. She knew that Mr. Culver would go over them in great detail and, furthermore, that he lacked compassion for the person who submitted a late assignment. Pat was motivated, but her motivation was extrinsic—that is, her incentive was external to the learning itself.

The student whose main concern is to get a high grade or to live up to his parents' expectations rather than to learn the subject is extrinsically motivated. However, a majority of educators view intrinsic motivation as serving a more useful educational purpose.

Procedures as Motivators

A teacher must understand how to motivate his students, and he must master the use of instructional devices, procedures, and materials in order to do so. He should, however, be aware of their limitations and strengths as motivators. Highly motivated learning results from directing the attention and desires of students toward goals with such force that the students are encouraged to persevere in the pursuit of these goals.

First-hand contact with the referent of a concept often results in positive motivation toward the goals set by teacher and student. The boy

---

[1]See Chapter 14 for a more extensive discussion of motivation.

[2]Morris L. Bigge and Maurice P. Hunt, *Psychological Foundations of Education*, 2d. ed. (New York: Harper & Row, Publishers, 1968), pp. 453–454, give a brief but clear explanation of extrinsic and intrinsic motivation.

in the woodshop class, for example, is asked to examine an expertly finished cedar chest and comes away with a strong desire to produce one just like it.

Such a strong desire cannot be fostered in the student unless he accepts the goal as his own. A teacher-imposed goal often misses the mark, largely because it fails to provide the pupil with intrinsic motivation. Each individual sees goal achievement in relationship to its effect upon himself. How strongly the student is motivated will determine his persistence and effort in reaching an objective.

Interests as Motivators

Motivation is closely related to the experiences, abilities, and needs of the individual. He will respond to a given learning situation to the extent that it is compatible with his subjective interests. This is simply another way of saying that meaning is fundamental to motivation—that if a student intensely desires something because he understands he will benefit from it, he will strive to achieve it. Because skill in playing popular music is a doorway to peer-group status, many youngsters are willing to spend hours acquiring this skill.

Immediate Goals as Motivators

Motivation is enhanced when students are able to relate immediate goals to remote, but meaningful, objectives.[3] Because the immediate goal is often viewed as easily attainable, it serves as a greater incentive than the more encompassing or remote goal. A student must be able to regard as attainable any educational objective—immediate or distant—that he is supposed to achieve. Otherwise he will develop a "why bother?" attitude.

Environment as a Motivator

The environment of every secondary-school student is comprised of a wide range of stimuli, all of which vie for attention. The student selects those stimuli that he perceives to be most closely related to his individual wants.

Students must learn to recognize the relationship between the desires created by their environment and the achievement of goals that will help fulfill these desires. The teacher has the responsibility of helping students in this frequently difficult task.

---

[3]Asahel D. Woodruff, *Basic Concepts of Teaching; with Brief Readings* (San Francisco: Chandler Publishing Company, 1962), pp. 50–51.

John P. De Cecco, *The Psychology of Learning and Instruction: Educational Psychology* (Englewood Cliffs, New Jersey: Prentice-Hall, Inc., 1968), pp. 33–42, finds that objectives stated explicitly in the form of terminal performances are more meaningful to student and teacher.

Success as a Motivator

Part of the teacher's role is to help the student achieve maximum motivation by helping him maintain the proper balance between his successes and failures.[4] The experience of success usually provides the highest motivation for gifted, average, or dull students alike. To be sure, circumstances may arise that warrant a temporary reversal of this balance for limited periods, particularly for bright students.

Motivation for the bright as well as for the dull student is also related to the self-concept of the learner. Having undergone specific experiences, students develop mental pictures of what they can and will do. A confident learner looks forward to success, and the student who consistently experiences success approaches new tasks with confidence. Successful experiences, therefore, are clearly related to motivation and to goal achievement.

Although psychologists and educators generally recognize the stimulating effect of success,[5] more attention should be paid to the fact that teacher-imposed reproof or blame gives rise to stronger student motivation than does a lack of interest on the part of the instructor. A knowledge of how one is progressing serves to stimulate the desire for improvement. If, therefore, grades satisfy the student's need to know his own progress, they will serve as motivators.

Need for Different Incentives

A teacher should carefully consider the incentives he is offering his students, remembering that specific incentives will not serve equally well in motivating all students. Students who vary individually with respect to intelligence, physical make-up, and emotional constitution will also vary with respect to potential for motivation. The teacher should learn to use different incentives in a variety of ways and to expect different results.

Competition, for example, often stirs the student to move with vigor toward a specific goal. Competition must be kept in proper balance, however, and should never be viewed as the goal itself. When a change in pace would add interest to his seventh-grade class, Mr. Willowby permits his students to play instructional games involving the use of teams. Experience has taught him, however, that youthful exuberance can easily carry such a procedure to excess. Therefore, all games are instructionally sound and are played under close supervision.

But Mr. Willowby and every good teacher must keep in mind that, in spite of stimulation from many sources, the learning process itself is an individual matter. *No one can learn for the student.* This he must do for

[4]See Arden N. Frandsen, *Educational Psychology*, 2d. ed. (New York: McGraw-Hill Book Company, 1967), pp. 296–298, for a helpful discussion concerning the effects of success and failure on learning.
[5]*Ibid.*, p. 296.

himself. The teacher at best can serve as an arranger of circumstances that will stimulate students to move in the desired direction.

Reward or Punishment?

To what extent should the teacher reward or punish the learner's behavior? No one can say with certainty. The cultural background, the personality, and the peer-group relationships of the learner must be examined before an answer to this question can be given. The proper course of action should be determined only in consideration of the specific needs of the individual pupils under given circumstances. Sensing a need for greater socialization on the part of a withdrawn youngster, Mrs. Young seated the shy student where he would be encouraged to converse with surrounding chatterboxes. The class clown, on the other hand, was seated at the rear of the class among well-behaved youngsters.

Avoidance of Frustration

The complete avoidance of frustration (goal blockage) in learning is impossible. For this reason the teacher must recognize frustration when it occurs and help the student cope with it effectively. Realistic goal-setting helps reduce the thwarting and enhances the ease of learning. Such goal-setting is important in encouraging achievement. Thus a short time after Mr. Thane permitted the twelfth-grade physics students to select their own individual class projects, he knew he was in for trouble. The least gifted students tended to choose the most difficult projects. But by helping them analyze specific procedures, the equipment to be used, and the conclusions to be drawn, Mr. Thane encouraged his students to set goals more in keeping with their capacities.

INTERESTS

Superficial versus Intense Interests

Certain adolescents, as well as certain adults, have superficial interests that are primarily limited to playing games, eating delicacies, watching television, and making light of others. Although such interests give direction to many student activities, intense, abiding, and worthy interests should be identified and harnessed to serve educational purposes. Continuing interest in good music and drama, effort to relate scientific advancements to international politics, and active participation in student body affairs are examples of student interests worthy of cultivation.

Inasmuch as learning (even that considered desirable by the teacher) does not take place without interest,[6] the teacher must examine the

---

[6]The general effect of interest arousal on the individual is examined by De Cecco, *The Psychology of Learning and Instruction*, pp. 135–136.

various forms and focuses of student interests. The content of a subject may be of interest to an adolescent, or his interest may be aroused simply because his friends enjoy the same activity. Where his immediate needs are being served, there will his interests lie.

Maturity and Interests

If the student possesses a measure of maturity, he may be interested in those things that relate to his post high-school needs and aspirations. For such a student, those activities classified as entertainment should not be allowed to monopolize the time and attention that ought to be given to his more basic interests.[7]

Unfortunately some teachers encourage shallowness by using sensational procedures to arouse student interest. But the best interest is evoked through direct contact with the referent of a concept when that referent will enable the student to relate what he perceives to his past experience.[8] The vividness of a child's experience when he first sees, hears, and smells an elephant at the circus bears this out. He relates the huge animal's size, motions, sounds, and odors to other farm animals he has observed, and these qualities take on additional meaning and, therefore, interest.

This interest arousal can be observed in the boy who dismantles a car motor (referent) in an auto mechanics class. Although he has heard about the parts of the automobile many times before, it is here that he is first able to perceive to his own satisfaction the interrelationship of spark plugs, carburetor, fuel line, and exhaust. Furthermore, the boy's first-hand contact also helps him avoid errors caused by a misunderstanding of words.

READINESS

A psychological state of readiness to act exists when the learner feels a need for new or different behavior.[9] When the need has been satisfied, the related behavior will cease. The student in general music who has learned the structure of a major scale is ready to formulate major chords. When he has learned how to make major chords, his desire for this information will abate.

It is helpful to divide readiness into two basic components: the *conceptual* and the *physical*. Other types frequently mentioned, such as *social* and *emotional* readiness, can be meaningfully related to conceptual readiness.

---

[7]Paul Henry Mussen, John Janeway Conger, and Jerome Kagen, *Child Development and Personality*, 3d. ed. (New York: Harper & Row, Publishers, 1969), pp. 703–706, discuss the traditional as well as the new alienations of adolescence. Both strongly interfere with interests and achievements held by adults to have particular value.

[8]Woodruff, *Basic Concepts of Teaching*, p. 266.

[9]See Bigge and Hunt, *Psychological Foundations of Learning*, pp. 456–458, for a brief but practical discussion of the relationship of readiness to learning.

Conceptual Readiness

The sequential arrangement of concepts in certain disciplines like mathematics makes it impossible for the student to advance to a higher conceptual level without having first acquired the more basic concepts. Effective curriculum planning is based upon the assumption that most students at a given grade level will have this readiness ("reaching out" or "need") for the content to be treated at that particular level. Typical ninth-graders are ready to study algebra. To the extent that students lack this readiness, they will have difficulty in acquiring course-related objectives.

Conceptual Deficiency

Similarly, the course content at given grade levels is frequently beyond the grasp of certain learners in the group not because they lack basic capacity, but because they lack an understanding of supporting concepts. This situation is often found in the close-knit, concept-laden fields of English grammar and physical sciences.

Social promotions in school represent a dramatic violation of the need for conceptual readiness. Knowing this, many curriculum workers have hailed the current emphasis on programed learning, which gives full support to the student's need to acquire one concept before he is permitted to move on to the next, more advanced concept.

Mental Maturity

Mental maturity is quite another matter. A youngster is ready to approach a problem with an excellent chance for successful solution only when his maturational progress has reached the point that will permit it. For example, the first-grader, because of limited capacity, cannot cope effectively with the complexities of geometry, and third-grade foreign-language students typically cannot comprehend the subjunctive mood.

Experience

Because mental pictures are the result of the learner's experiences, it is possible to speak of experiential readiness for learning. If students lack the experience essential for the formation of needed concepts (mental images), they must be exposed to it.

The foreign student who has not been exposed to American culture is not prepared to cope with the realities of the supermarket, highway traffic jams, unchaperoned dating during adolescence, and general casualness in personal behavior. The understanding of more complex concepts depends on the learner's acquaintance with a vast number of undifferentiated mental pictures.

Physical Readiness

If the student lacks neuro-muscular coordination, he is not able to undertake a task involving coordination even though he may fully possess the concepts necessary to carry it out. This is often the case with the child who has cerebral palsy: he may conceive of playing basketball, but his disease renders him helpless to do so.

In the majority of school subjects the learning of motor skills is inserted in the curriculum at that point when the physical development of students gives them the necessary coordination.[10] Typewriting, for example, is rarely offered at the elementary-school level. The grade placement of a specific subject is somewhat of a problem because of the differences in physical maturation at any given chronological age. Motor manipulations can never be taught successfully before the student is physically ready.

The teacher's identification of student readiness, both conceptual and physical, will provide him with part of the basic information essential to efficient instruction. If the teacher is unaware of the varying kinds and degrees of student readiness, the teacher as well as the learner is apt to lose time, energy, and patience.

INDIVIDUAL DIFFERENCES

No aspect of teaching calls for greater professional judgment than the necessity for dealing realistically with individual differences in students.[11] Among the most important differences with respect to the teaching-learning processes are those of intelligence, skills, habits, emotions, experiences, goals, interests, readiness, and adjustment. To be vaguely aware that differences exist in these areas is insufficient for the true professional. He must, instead, organize his teaching so that it reflects his acquaintance with the high degree of variation found among his students.

Different Rates for Learning Subjects

The rate of learning of a specific student may vary from subject to subject and from one division of content to another.[12] Furthermore, individual learners covering the same content will vary in their speed of learning and in their degree of retention. This is clearly seen in the case of Margo. She is one of the best students in her English literature class, but she acquires each concept in mathematics only after a struggle. In English grammar she does well, although she is not among the upper 20 percent. Her memory, however, is the envy of her classmates: whatever she learns she retains.

---

[10]See Chapter 4, pp. 56–57, for a discussion of the teaching of motor skills.
[11]See Chapter 15 for a more detailed coverage of individual differences.
[12]See Lee J. Cronbach, *Educational Psychology*, 2d. ed. (New York: Harcourt Brace Jovanovich, 1963), pp. 298–304, for a discussion of general individual learning rates.

Generalized versus Specific Teaching

Many teachers employ generalized teaching procedures and devote little attention to the separate needs of specific students. Jessie finds the class most challenging when the teacher lectures, but Merrill finds it boring and gets little from it. Because the teacher is wed to the lecture method, Merrill is placed at a disadvantage. Since methods suitable to a majority of the students may be quite unsuitable for a minority, the teacher must be continuously aware of the value of a variety of generalized as well as specific teaching procedures in trying to meet the needs of his students.

Because each learning experience serves as the basis for a further projection of content, complications arise when students arrive at different end results from an identical learning experience. Jessie, for example, learned from the geography lecture that West Germany is more populous than France, that it is highly industrialized, that it has very limited illiteracy, and that all sections of the country do not speak the same dialect. Merrill, on the other hand, intensified his dislike for the study of Europe and particularly for the lecture method. His learning was meager, and he was not in a position to derive much from the subsequent study of other German-speaking populations of Europe.

Differences Within the Learner

Even within the same learner more than one type of learning may be taking place simultaneously, although the instruction is focused in one direction only. Jessie not only learned about German culture, but she also gleaned a few facts about German topography as well as a few German nouns. Such concomitant learning is the rule rather than the exception, and it tends to intensify the variability of the range of what is learned. With Merrill, on the other hand, such beneficial learning on the side was naturally impossible.

ADJUSTMENT

The thoroughly adjusted student[13] is the one whose attention is free to move in any direction dictated by his interest.[14] It follows that a student cannot be intensely preoccupied and still remain properly adjusted for the purpose of learning.

The student cannot avoid being preoccupied if his basic needs are not properly satisfied. A home characterized by constant domestic strife

---

[13]Common sources of school stress that may lead to poor student adjustment are discussed at length by Thomas A. Ringness, *Mental Health in the Schools*, 1968 (New York: Random House, Inc., 1968), chapter 9.

[14]Woodruff, *Basic Concepts of Teaching*, pp. 255–256.

runs counter to the adolescent's basic need for security. His attention will be focused, in a large measure, on the home situation and its implications for himself. Emotional balance is the key to adjustment and requires the individual to be realistically but appropriately satisfied with himself in relationship to his environment. Such adjustment is crucial for proper learning.

Learning: The Primary Concern

The promotion of such adjustment, however, is a secondary concern of the school.[15] As an educational agency, the school is primarily concerned with teaching and learning. It should, therefore, undertake whatever measures are necessary to insure that the causes of instruction and learning are served. The teacher who envisions himself essentially as a "promoter of happiness" rather than as a "teacher of content" may deny his class needed instructional time. Time that should be devoted to teaching may instead be spent dealing with the aggravated adjustment concerns of students—ill health, domestic strife, or trouble with the police —for which they might well be referred to other professionals.

Adjustments, however, are enhanced when teachers assist their students in meeting developmental tasks. The search for and achievement of adult approval, peer-group approval, independence, and self-respect are basic to adolescent adjustment. Through "teaching content" the teacher may provide, perhaps unconsciously, a means for such adjustment.

To insure efficient learning, the school should aim at a satisfactory level of adjustment for all of its students. The student's appraisal of his school performance as successful or unsuccessful will promote or hinder adjustment. His adjustment will partially depend upon the relationship that he has established with his teacher, although conflicts that give rise to tensions are not confined to the school alone.

Teacher-Caused Maladjustment

Unfortunately, many cases of student maladjustment are caused by the teacher. The teenager who is humiliated by the instructor in the presence of his peers is a case in point. Inconsistency in the teacher's classroom behavior is another cause. A reduction in the frustration encountered in school should help promote the cause of learning.

Serious tensions brought to school or created in school serve as a bottleneck to free teacher-student communication. Often aggressive student behavior is the result of thwarted needs and is misinterpreted as antisocial or, at times, antiteacher behavior. Since such behavior frequently occurs at home, too, parents need assistance in understanding their offspring during the adolescent years. School counselors and guidance-minded teachers can reduce pupil frustration simply by talking matters over informally but purposefully with parents, students, or both.

---

[15]*Ibid.*, pp. 261–262.

The adjustment or maladjustment of a specific student should not be determined on the basis of scanty evidence. Careful, pointed observation over a period of time should reveal whether a student is in need of additional help. The matter of self-acceptance—whether the student feels he measures up to his own standards—provides the clue to many aspects of behavior.

CLASSROOM CONTROL

Like all human beings, the adolescent seeks approval of his behavior. Where there is a conflict between the approval of adults and members of the peer group, however, the teenager customarily responds to the value patterns of his companions. Such peer-group approval is constantly sought in the classroom, causing great concern for the teacher attempting to bring about and maintain an effective instructional environment. The teacher often becomes the butt of an adolescent's prank because the act has great peer-group appeal.

Purpose of Classroom Control

An effective classroom control situation may be defined as one in which *optimum learning takes place.*[16] Here again the means-end relationship of discipline and goal achievement must be kept in mind. The reason for imposing certain behavioral demands on students is to improve the possibility of efficient learning. Discipline for the sake of discipline is nonfunctional and empty.

The Teacher's Responsibility

The teacher, more frequently than the student, is held responsible for the quality of the control that exists in a given classroom. Although student participation may be encouraged, the teacher is basically responsible for the setting of goals. If the goals are too difficult or too easy, class morale and deportment suffer. In selecting such goals the teacher should display an intelligent realism, giving attention to the full range of abilities in his class.

The procedures used to establish objectives often give rise to student confusion that may erupt into aggressive resistance. Such resistance occurs when the teacher's preconceived notion of student achievement is arbitrarily imposed on the class without consulting students or giving careful consideration to what is *possible* for the students to achieve.

Because the teacher feels more comfortable using particular methods, he may use them repeatedly in spite of their negative effect on the

---

[16]Henry C. Lindgren, *Educational Psychology in the Classroom*, 3d. ed. (New York: John Wiley & Sons, Inc., 1967), pp. 364–370, gives a sound discussion of the purposeful control of the classroom environment.

general control of the class. Small-group discussions, frequently used by social studies teachers, often degenerate into gossip sessions with little or no academic value. Under such circumstances, students frequently take liberties and horseplay often ensues. The deportment of a group of students will be no better than the instructional procedures permit.

Teacher Behavior

Youngsters feel relaxed and happy in those school situations where the teacher's behavior is consistent.[17] When students cannot anticipate with some degree of accuracy what the teacher will do, they feel insecure. This insecurity is sometimes expressed in behavioral outbursts that are interpreted as misbehavior. The teacher may exhibit a cheerful, fun-loving, permissive personality on Tuesday, but on Wednesday the curtain has been drawn and gloom prevails. In the face of such personality vacillation, students may overtly express their displeasure.

Unfortunately, many *disciplinary* actions are taken by the teacher without first determining the cause of the apparent misbehavior. Punishments that are imposed in anger accomplish little in the way of rational analysis of problems and lasting solutions. Emotion-laden situations are further strained when the teacher acts in haste.

Clearly Defined Goals

Compatible classroom atmospheres are encouraged when students feel that the goals are clearly defined and understood.[18] If, in addition, they believe that the teacher is sincerely helpful and anxious to promote their success, students tend to accept the teacher in spite of minor dislikes. The youngster who is haunted by the fear of academic failure often displays classroom behavior that runs counter to the teacher's wishes.[19] Frequently such a student finds it easy to slip away to the shadowland of daydreams, where, in fantasy, he finds the success he is otherwise denied.

The adolescent has a range of needs that demand fulfillment but that may lead him onto paths incompatible with the learning environment the teacher hopes to maintain. Exhibitionism, which is so strongly tied in with the need for peer-group acceptance and heterosexual adjustment, is one of these paths. The disturbing need for emancipation from adult control is another. The tendency to repeat need-fulfilling behavior is encouraged

---

[17]Herbert J. Klausmeier and William Goodwin, *Learning and Human Abilities: Educational Psychology,* 2d. ed. (New York: Harper & Row, Publishers, 1966), pp. 146–147, presents a list of teacher characteristics that, in the opinion of students, distinguish "high" teachers from "low" teachers.

[18]Spurred by educational experimentation related to the development of small-step instructional programs, a substantial proportion of the current authors in the areas of education and psychology are urging that objectives be stated in behavioral terms. It is held that goals so stated are explicit and readily understood by students.

[19]Frandsen, *Educational Psychology,* p. 296.

each time an act satisfies such needs, regardless of its effect on acceptable classroom behavior.[20]

TRANSFER OF LEARNING

Application and Transfer

If the teacher wishes his students to make practical application of what he has taught them, he must consider the principles on which the transfer of learning is based. First of all, he must help his students identify facts that can be woven into meaningful generalizations. Students may, for example, discover that housing in colonial America was primitive, that white settlers were frequently in combat with Indians, and that many of these frontiersmen perished. From such facts a generalization may emerge—*Colonization of a frontier region is accompanied by many hardships.*

The teacher must then provide for the application of the generalization in a range of situations. Hardships of frontier life may be related to the westward movement, to the colonization of Alaska, or, with some modification, to space exploration. Finally, the teacher must instill an awareness of and a need for further applications.

Demonstration of Transfer

The student is also helped when the teacher demonstrates in a number of situations precisely how to make the transfer from original theory to practical application. Transfer is further enhanced when the materials or devices used for instructional purposes are similar to those that will be met both inside and outside the school.

Well-equipped mathematics classrooms frequently display a giant slide rule mounted above the chalkboard. This visual aid simplifies the teaching of the functions of the slide rule. Many biology teachers insist that specimens (plants, mammals, and insects) be brought into the classroom to provide examples of topics being discussed. Theory thus becomes meaningful. Teaching emphasis can also markedly help the learner recognize the relationship between the generalized concept and its practical application.

Most of the time the teacher should employ goal-related activities that the students feel have application in nonschool situations. In the shorthand class, dictation is confined largely to the type of correspondence that students will have to use on the job. In the sewing class, girls are required to work on projects that will have current value as well as serve a useful purpose after graduation. When the teacher uses goal-related procedures, the student is more likely to apply his acquired concepts and skills to sit-

---

[20]Lindgren, *Educational Psychology in the Classroom*, p. 217.

uations outside the classroom and to find satisfaction in their use. Further, objectives stated in terms of specific student behavior are of instructional value to the teacher and clarify for students the reasons for certain learning activities.

PROBLEMS FOR STUDY AND DISCUSSION

1. List and discuss the five instruction-related problems that you feel hinder the teacher the most in discharging his responsibilities.

2. Define *motivation* in your own words. Differentiate between intrinsic and extrinsic motivation.

3. From your past experience identify and discuss two student cases in which the balance between success and failure has not been maintained.

4. Cite an example in which the motivation of a slow learner has suffered because of his self-concept.

5. Write a paragraph explaining why no one can learn for the student.

6. Contrast superficial interests with deeper motivations and give examples of each.

7. How different should interest-arousing procedures be? Discuss.

8. Explain the difference between lack of capacity and lack of mental maturity. Give examples of each.

9. Single out the five most important student differences that affect the instructional process.

10. Describe at least one secondary-school student whose rate of learning is quite different in three different subject areas.

11. What does preoccupation have to do with adjustment? Discuss and give an example.

12. What do you find wrong with the following statement: Every teacher should be a guidance expert? Explain.

13. Explain what you feel is the proper guidance role of the teacher.

14. What is meant by an effective classroom-control situation? Discuss.

15. List at least five ways in which teachers often promote poor classroom control.

16. What are the possible results of hasty disciplinary action on the part of the teacher?

17. Indicate the relationship between goals and possible classroom misbehavior.

18. Cite four examples of adolescent student needs that may lead to undesirable classroom behavior.

19. Assuming that the basic purpose of education is to improve behavior, give examples of how behavior is improved as a result of instruction in biology, English literature, and history.

20. How is the transfer of learning assisted by the acquisition of meaningful generalizations? Explain.

PART TWO
Planning for Teaching

3. *Planning Before Teaching*

Since the need for a systematic approach to instruction became apparent in the first faltering attempts of man to communicate his thoughts, controversy over the nature and the extent of planning has tended to confuse well-meaning teachers. In the attempt to present a consistent point of view for such teachers, this chapter examines the need for planning, the purposes and advantages of long-range planning, and the nature of unit planning.

PLANNING—FORERUNNER OF EFFECTIVE INSTRUCTION

"Planning is a waste of time. Look at all the unexpected things that can happen in a high-school teacher's day. Besides, I happen to know that about half of the in-service teachers don't plan, and they ought to know what's good for them. So why should we spend so much time on planning? Let's get on with the teaching and forget the theory."

Such comments might be overheard in discussions in undergraduate planning and methods courses. There is much truth in such statements, but unfortunately the inexperienced teacher—and occasionally the experienced teacher—may draw untrue and unwise inferences.

Need for Planning

Highly successful teachers, who often give the impression of having done little planning, frequently *have* planned initially with unusual care.[1] In addition, they have had repeated practice in presenting specific material. The degree to which a teacher needs to engage in *detailed* planning will depend upon the effect planning has on his teaching. Student teachers and first-year teachers must realize that, as a general rule, it will be necessary for them to plan in considerable detail. The degree of detail will depend upon the presence or absence of certain teacher qualifications and characteristics:

1. Knowledge of content
2. Practical experience in the use of specific procedures
3. Degree of security
4. Organizational ability
5. Ability to anticipate with accuracy the likely classroom problems
6. Memory

In-service teachers frequently do not write out a plan, or they limit their written plans to only one kind. But this lack of planning encourages inferior teaching. There are teachers who rationalize that their experience in a particular subject has made it unnecessary for them to develop written plans; this argument hints strongly that such teachers are in an ever deepening rut. Since no two classes are ever identical, even where the same general content is taught at the same grade level for the tenth time, plans must be varied to meet the differing needs of new students.

Because the profession is constantly being upgraded, each group of new teachers should recognize the need to improve on the past. Of course, effective planning takes time. The need for time does not, however, relieve the

---

[1]Leonard H. Clark and Irving S. Starr, *Secondary School Teaching Methods*, 2d. ed. (New York: The Macmillan Company, 1967), p. 97, stress the advantages of effective planning.

General principles of planning and levels of planning are identified and discussed by Peter F. Oliva, *The Secondary School Today* (New York: World Publishing Company, 1967), pp. 145–146.

conscientious professional of his responsibility for doing what will improve his instructional success—developing a written plan.

Consistent planning and replanning of units hold the promise of improved instruction from year to year. The efficient teacher looks to the future by saving units for possible later use. Each specific unit should serve the following year as a resource in the preparation of the unit dealing with the same topic. Resource units,[2] consisting of reservoirs of related objectives, procedures, and materials, can be compiled by the teacher in this manner over a period of years. However, intensified interest in the use of new techniques serving the needs of differing students requires the necessity for careful planning.

Planning versus Personality

In this scientific age the concept of teaching as an *outpouring of personality* is being justifiably assailed from all sides. No one would deny that an interesting personality is an effective lubricant in the instructional process,[3] but one would also recall the many times he had been subjected to the conceptual emptiness of *all personality and no content.*

The teacher who is a sound and effective practitioner possesses a storehouse of well-organized professional knowledge that he employs wisely in planning and teaching. The poorly prepared teacher cannot transmit insights that he does not possess. The gifted student, particularly, is hampered by the instructor who is not in command of his subject, for the student's chance to advance commensurate with his capacity is handicapped by his teacher's inability to advance with him.

Content Plus Methods

With the emphasis on content mastery has come a growing criticism of the concern for methods from many unknowing persons. This attack is not without virtue, for it forces professional educators to reappraise the proper role of methods (procedures) in instruction. In the social studies class, for example, the dedicated, experience-unit enthusiast is encouraged to view activities as having value *only* as devices for helping achieve goals.

The frequent confusion of the relationship of means to ends[4] is felt strongly in this connection. Acquisition of lesson content, with few exceptions, must be viewed as the end goal, and methods must serve a subservient role as a means to goal achievement. The failure to define clearly the relationship of the two has encouraged criticism from knowledgeable and perceptive critics.

---

[2]See p. 41 for an explanation of the differences between the resource unit and the teaching unit.

[3]The effect of teacher personality, attitudes, and motives on students in low-income areas is discussed by William F. White, *Psychological Principles Applied to Classroom Teaching* (New York: McGraw-Hill Book Company, 1969), pp. 84–87.

[4]See Chapter 1, pp. 9–10, for a brief discussion of the necessary relationship of means to ends.

Criteria Essential to Planning

All planning must be concerned with practical limitations if it is to help improve instruction. Planning must observe the following criteria if it is to be of the greatest value:

1. *It must be practical and usable.* The practicality and usefulness of planning must be determined by the planner, not by a school-system supervisor or by an instructor in a methods class. The young teacher who has spent many hours in preparing written plans because course requirements so state may discard these plans as useless when confronted with the pressures of the real teaching situation. When he is free to chart his own course, the teacher will use those planning procedures *he views* as practical and useful.

2. *It must be economical in terms of time.* After examining the immensity of the teacher's task, one might assume that the competent teacher should spend at least six hours each day in planning. But this is an impossibility in view of the total range of professional responsibilities to be fulfilled. Plans should be as short as is compatible with the purpose of improved instruction.

3. *It should result in better teaching.* If the teacher is not able to teach better after having made careful plans, then his planning has served no useful purpose. Overly complicated plans frequently fall short of the mark; unnecessarily wordy plans sometimes inhibit rather than help in transmitting concepts. Planning for the sake of planning is but an academic exercise. Only when the teacher's classroom performance influences the lives of youngsters for the better does planning have practical justification. Planning is the means; goal achievement is the end.

PLANNING FOR THE FULL SCHOOL YEAR

Effective long-range planning calls for a realistic appraisal of what can be accomplished during the school year and what procedures will be most helpful. Furthermore, it involves understanding the relationships among different types of plans and knowing how these plans can be used to accomplish long-range goals.

Accumulated years of experience have led teachers to generally agree on the basic types of plans essential to effective teaching, but the terminology used to describe these plans varies widely. The three basic types of plans[5] that should provide an effective framework for successful instruction are:

---

[5] A brief but useful examination of the three types of teaching plans is provided by Leonard M. Douglas, *The Secondary Teacher at Work* (Boston: D. C. Heath & Company, 1967), chapter 11.

Homer Boroughs, Jr., Clifford D. Foster, and Rufus D. Salyer, Jr., *Introduction to Secondary School Teaching* (New York: The Ronald Press Company, 1964), pp. 129–134, differentiate long-range planning from short-range planning and provide several examples.

1. The Overall Plan (Semester or Year)[6]
2. The Unit Plan
3. The Daily Lesson Plan

Recent emphasis on individualized instruction has encouraged planners to reexamine the purposes of these three basic plans. Although modifications have taken place, the concern for establishing necessary relationships among concepts learned remains unchallenged. How this can best be brought about is much more open to challenge.

In structure, the Overall Plan is, perhaps, the simplest of the three. It has two essential characteristics: (1) it provides an overview of the course for the full year or semester by listing in sequence the units to be covered, and (2) it indicates the content and the time to be devoted to each unit. Certain planners encounter difficulty in developing overall plans by making them too lengthy or too complicated; neither type is appropriate.

Examples of Overall Plans

The following examples of secondary-school overall plans vary slightly, but they possess the same general characteristics.

Overall Plan for a High-School Physics Course

Unit	Time	Starting Date
1. What Physics Is About	4 days	Sept. 4
2. Gravitational Force in Fluids	8 weeks	Sept. 9
3. Force and Motion	4 weeks	Nov. 4
4. Basic Machines	2½ weeks	Dec. 2
5. Heat	6 weeks	Jan. 6
6. Power and Energy	4 weeks	Feb. 17
7. Electricity and Magnetism	5 weeks	March 17
8. Sound	2½ weeks	April 28
9. Light and Radiations	2½ weeks	May 16

The preceding Overall Plan for a physics course is comprised of units of varying lengths; the longest is eight weeks and the shortest is four days. No subdivisions within units are mentioned although unit planners often find this is helpful. Beginning dates for each unit are merely approximate, with the exception of the first brief introductory unit, but they provide a time check that usually proves to be of assistance.

---

[6]Peter F. Oliva and Ralph A. Scrafford, *Teaching in a Modern Secondary School* (Columbus, Ohio: Charles E. Merrill Publishing Co., 1965), pp. 25–31, provide a number of suggestions for making long-range plans.

Overall Plan for a Two-Semester High-School Biology Course

Semester I

1. Familiar Plants (two weeks)
2. Plants and Their Seasons (two weeks)
3. Useful Plants (two weeks)
4. Where Plants Live (one week)
5. The Structure of Plants (two weeks)
6. How Plants Adapt Themselves (one week)
7. Plants in Relation to Other Living Things (one week)
8. How Long Plants Live (two weeks)
9. Plant Diseases (one week)
10. How Plants Originated and Developed (one week)
11. Kinds of Plants (two weeks)
12. Sciences That Study Broad Aspects of Plant Life (one week)

Semester II

1. Familiar Animals (one week)
2. Useful Animals (one week)
3. Where Animals Live (one week)
4. How Animals Adapt Themselves (one week)
5. The Bodies of Animals (two weeks)
6. Animal Behavior (one week)
7. Community Life Among Animals (one week)
8. Animals in Relation to Other Living Things (two weeks)
9. Animal Diseases and Their Treatment (one week)
10. Animal Injuries to Man (two weeks)
11. How Animals Originated and Developed (two weeks)
12. Zoology (two weeks)

Steps in Developing Overall Plans

If the Overall Plan is to serve most usefully as an aid to unit planning, certain sequential steps should be observed.[7] The teacher should:

1. Without consulting outside sources, attempt to identify the units that he will teach during the full school year. (This step presupposes that the teacher has basic mastery of his content field. In the event this assumption is false, a satisfactory level of content mastery will have to be achieved before he may commence. Avoiding outside sources encourages the teacher to review and organize the concepts he currently commands.)
2. Indicate the sequence in which the units should be placed for most advantageous learning.
3. State the approximate amount of time to be devoted to each unit.
4. After exhausting his own thinking, consult three or four carefully selected secondary-school texts.
5. Compare tables of contents painstakingly with his own tentative outline of units.
6. Compare several textbooks.

---

[7]Organizing instructional tasks for a full year's work in tenth-grade English is discussed by Virginia Alwin, "Planning a Year of Units," *The English Journal,* 45 (September 1956), pp. 334–340.

7. Finally, consult again his own tentative outline, making appropriate adjustments in content, sequence, and time in the light of his new findings.

These steps are particularly helpful to the new teacher who may tend to place undue reliance on the text. If the individual entering the teaching profession has recently been exposed in some depth to the content of the subject he will be teaching, he should be prepared to think independently of the text. If his preparation has been lacking, however, he would do well to select the best possible text and follow it closely.

The alert, experienced teacher will constantly compare his own Overall Plan with the tables of contents in good textbooks. Minor adjustments should be made from year to year if they will assist in the instructional process.

To attempt to begin a year's work without first carefully identifying the major and minor topics to be covered is to invite misused time and misplaced emphasis. The amount of time devoted to a specific unit is a measure of the teacher's emphasis. Accurate timing is important; it is not uncommon to find teachers who have engaged in poor long-range planning (overall planning) entirely distraught toward the end of March because they have covered only half of the desired content of the course.

Fig. 1 Hierarchical arrangement of unit objectives.

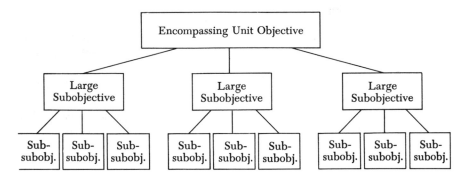

PLANNING FOR THE TEACHING OF UNITS

In order to possess *unity*, any subject or any topic must consist of strongly interrelated parts. This interrelationship is the most essential characteristic of a teaching unit. Not only must the objectives be related to each other, but procedures must be related to objectives.

Unit Defined

It may be helpful to think of the major and minor objectives of a unit as falling into a hierarchical arrangement as seen in Figure 1.[8] The large

---

[8]This hierarchical arrangement of objectives, and their close relationship to each other, can be identified in the sample teaching units in Chapter 7.

encompassing unit objective is comprised of smaller objectives. Because of the closeness of their relationship, these objectives can be taught more meaningfully in combination than as separate parts. Concepts, skills, symbols to be memorized, or habits to be acquired may be among the objectives.

A teaching unit may then be defined as *a plan for teaching carefully selected, closely related objectives to specific learners.* Included in the plan will be the appropriate use of learning procedures (activities), materials and resources, and evaluation procedures.

The unit centers attention on one major segment of a course. Below are typical examples of unit titles and their related subjects.

Unit Title	Subject
Mathematics in Taxes	General Mathematics
Central America	Geography
Polynomials	Algebra
Arthropods	Biology
Electricity and Magnetism	Physics
Nouns	English Grammar

The unit is comprised of related parts. For example, the unit in English Grammar listed above as *Nouns* will include the following large concepts (parts):

1. Nouns are most easily identified when more than one definition is understood.
2. Nouns may be classified in two groups: common and proper.
3. Nouns have two numbers: singular and plural.
4. Nouns make morphological changes only in the plural and genitive (or possessive) forms.
5. Nouns in English have three recognized genders: masculine, feminine, and neuter.

Each of these concepts in turn could be subdivided into meaningful smaller ideas for the purpose of teaching them more effectively.

Subject-Matter Units and Experience Units

An examination of the development of teaching plans reveals a wide range of attempts to organize and clarify teachable units.[9] Writings of recent years have focused attention primarily on two types—the *subject-matter unit* and the *experience unit.*[10] Variations of these basic types are frequently used.

---

[9]Marvin D. Alcorn, James S. Kinder, and Jim R. Schunert, *Better Teaching in Secondary Schools*, 3d. ed. (New York: Holt, Rinehart & Winston, Inc., 1970), pp. 87–88, contend that an unnecessary dichotomy is created through the attempt to contrast subject-matter units with experience units.

[10]William H. Burton, *The Guidance of Learning Activities*, 3d. ed. (New York: Appleton-Century-Crofts, 1962), pp. 327–328.

Subject-Matter Unit

In the subject-matter unit attention is directed toward teaching a major segment (unit) of the content. The objectives and learning experiences are most often predetermined by the unit planner. For example, a subject-matter unit might seek to teach students to solve mathematical problems that call for specific understandings; in literature courses the subject-matter unit might try to teach students to analyze a literary selection by applying certain concepts related to structure and form.

Experience Unit

The experience unit, on the other hand, directs attention toward pupil interests, needs, and problems. Learning procedures are selected on the basis of their social usefulness in solving student problems and meeting student needs. In this type of unit students are strongly involved in determining objectives and in selecting procedures.[11] Students might decide, under the direction of their civics teacher, that they want to "establish better relationships between the high school and the community." Learning activities and the assembly of information would be directed toward achieving this goal.

Some educators feel that the purposes of sound psychology are best served where unit emphasis is placed upon the acquisition of clearly identified content. They would, however, be quite unwilling to sanction the blind pursuit of subject-matter content at the expense of student interests and needs. This position argues for intelligent consideration of content as well as of procedures. In view of the emerging realism of the current educational scene, many teachers must give more thought to the serious tasks of planning and teaching. They cannot afford to identify themselves mostly with content or mostly with procedures, largely forgetting other essential instructional concerns.

Avoiding Confusion

Because of the tendency for unit-related terminology to confuse beginning teachers, some authors have pointed out that differences in types of units are matters of emphasis only.[12] To belabor the relatively small differentiations between teaching units, experience units, appreciation units, process units, and special-purpose units at the outset of the neophyte teacher's career when he is confronted with a range of other professional adjustments is unwarranted. Such differentiations can readily be made when other more pressing first-year teaching concerns have been resolved.

---

[11]See Jean D. Grambs, John C. Carr, and Robert M. Fitch, *Modern Methods in Secondary Education*, 3d. ed. (New York: Holt, Rinehart & Winston, Inc., 1970), p. 157, for a simplified discussion and description of an experience unit in operation.

[12]Clark and Starr, *Secondary School Teaching Methods*, p. 136.

The Teaching Unit and the Resource Unit

The *teaching unit* is essentially a plan to assist the classroom instructor in teaching a body of related ideas to *specific* students under *known* circumstances. The actual objectives and the implementing activities can be realistically determined only after the planner has an accurate indication of the composition of the group he will teach.

A *resource unit*,[13] although having the same general organizational structure as the teaching unit, serves as a reservoir of useful tools, procedures, and materials that the planner may draw on while developing a specific teaching unit. In the resource unit, for example, a great many more objectives are listed than can possibly be used in any one teaching unit.

The well-prepared resource unit serves as an excellent aid in the preparation of the teaching unit. A wise beginning teacher will surround himself with carefully selected resource units of known merit. He will find the preparation of units for his actual classroom instruction much less burdensome if he first surveys the range of ideas presented in the best of the available resource units.

Resource units may be developed as the result of group effort in which teachers of the same subject combine ideas,[14] or they may result from the cumulative planning (yearly additions) of an individual teacher. Frequently urban school systems of considerable size appoint committees of teachers from a given subject-matter area and grade level (tenth-grade English, e.g.) who are assigned the responsibility for developing resource units. Large city school systems throughout the United States have consistently engaged in the preparation of resource units through this process. Smaller school systems, where the development of such units is impractical, would do well to assemble a current file of these units.

Steps in Developing a Unit

In order to avoid the haphazard development of a unit, a certain sequence of steps should be followed systematically. Only when the first step is satisfactorily completed is the planner ready for the second. The proper order is reflected in the following topics:[15]

    I. Basic Information
    II. Objectives
    III. Procedures
    IV. Materials and Resources
    V. Evaluation Procedures

---

[13]Edgar M. Draper and Gordon Gardner, "How to Construct a Resource Unit," *The Clearing House*, 26 (January 1952), pp. 267–268, provide specific suggestions.

[14]Boroughs, Foster, and Salyer, *Introduction to Secondary School Teaching*, p. 142, briefly describe how a resource unit may be planned individually or cooperatively by teachers.

[15]Oliva, *The Secondary School Today*, chapter 7, provides useful illustrations of learning units accompanied by meaningful discussion. Although his use of the last four topics varies from that of the current text, their general intent is easily discernible.

Fig. 2. Diagramatic representation of the relationship of specific units to a full course in a United States history text for eleventh-grade students.

19 days	22 days	17 days	20 days
A New Nation Emerges from the Old	Beginnings of the New Nation	The United States and the Challenges of Domestic and Foreign Affairs	The United States Survives Strife at Home

When unit planners consider these basic steps in sequence, strong interrelationships and the essential cohesion of the unit will result. Chapter 7 and Appendix A are devoted to the presentation of examples of units structured in conformity to the five-step outline of unit divisions listed on the preceding page.

The Teaching Unit and the Overall Plan

The relationship of the unit to the course is comparable to the relationship of a single chapter heading to the full table of contents of a book.[16] The major divisions in a typical high-school history text are shown in Figure 2 as units of a school year. Note that the course in United States history is divided into ten units. Several other facts are also discernible:

1. Although the units are approximately the same length, they vary from thirteen to twenty-two days.
2. Units are based upon a chronological sequence of events, and important incidents that are closely related in time are grouped for instructional purposes.
3. In spite of the fact that each unit title represents a separate area, each one may be subdivided for more specific treatment.
4. The Overall Plan is a composite of the individual units.
5. The total time encompassed by all units is only thirty-five weeks (175 days), one week short of the typical school year. It is assumed that one week will have to be used in beginning and terminal activities.

It is not surprising that a good textbook can be related closely to an overall plan and to individual units, such as those in Figure 2. Today's publishers work in close cooperation with experienced teachers throughout the country to achieve this close relationship.

[16]A graphic treatment of the relationship between semester planning, unit planning, and daily lesson planning is found in Douglas, *The Secondary Teacher at Work*, pp. 120–121.

20 days	18 days	16 days	15 days	15 days	13 days
A Modern Nation Begins to Take Form	Reform in the Nation	The United States As a World Power	National Change Between Two Wars	The United States As a World Leader	Mid-Century Problems and Solutions

DETERMINING BASIC INFORMATION

Specific Information About the Students

Planning for a specific class will require that the teacher have an accurate indication of the following:[17]

1. Individual I.Q.'s as well as the range of I.Q.'s within the group
2. The approximate socioeconomic levels of individual pupils
3. The nature of academic as well as nonacademic difficulties faced by students
4. Potential offenders in terms of classroom control
5. The proportion of girls to boys
6. The range of background experiences of individual class members
7. The past subject-matter achievement of students as measured by course grades and standardized achievement test scores

Armed with this relevant information, the professionally prepared planner can visualize with considerable accuracy the nature of the students he will teach and what will be involved in teaching them most effectively.

If it can be assumed that *planning is preteaching*, the teacher should leave unexplored no avenue that will lead to a better practical understanding of the group. The success of the planning will be in direct proportion to its applicability to the class for which it was intended.

Capacity

In a heterogeneously grouped class where the I.Q. range is extreme, planning based upon inaccurate or incomplete information frequently results in unvarying general assignments, with little attention given to desired differentiation. The knowledgeable teacher realizes that the de-

---

[17]See Burton, *The Guidance of Learning Activities*, chapter 8, for an authoritative treatment of the effect of the family, the neighborhood, and the social class upon the learner.

gree of individual attention that should be focused on particular learners will depend, in some measure, on their capacities. Furthermore, information about the range of capacities of the students will alert the planner to the need for variation in procedures to conform to varying abilities.

Socioeconomic Status

In the planning of activities, a given unit may be entirely inappropriate when considered against the social and economic backgrounds of the pupils. A family living unit on food preparation that emphasizes light, expensive foods customarily served before the main course would have limited practical value for girls living in a slum area. They would benefit, instead, from a unit concerned with preparing substantial but low-cost meals.

Individual Problems

Efficient planning and teaching should give attention to the specific difficulties that confront students. In a class of thirty, these students may be found: a girl of normal intelligence with a cleft palate; a basketball star of average intelligence who has an inflated ego; two boys with marked withdrawal tendencies but high achievement records; a boy and two girls with measured I.Q.'s below 90; a boy who has had repeated encounters with the police; and a cerebral-palsied boy within the range of normal intelligence.

The competent teacher will consistently and consciously be aware of the demands these problems place upon him. Unless they are understood and dealt with at a professional level, such problems can conceivably create serious difficulty for individual students as well as for the class as a whole.

Probable Classroom Behavior

The early identification of students whose behavior is likely to result in poor classroom control is a great aid in planning.[18] More fundamental still is the determination of *why* misbehaving youngsters behave as they do. If this can be ascertained with accuracy, plans can be laid to entice students away from an undesirable course of action before it ever occurs.

Where it can be determined, for example, that a given boy is an inveterate attention-seeker, the teacher can plan socially acceptable procedures that will provide the desired attention. Gifted students in the class often prove to be troublemakers when they are not constantly challenged. Plans should be drafted for keeping such students meaningfully challenged, thus avoiding trouble.

In addition to these typical problems, adolescence is further fraught with problems related to boy-girl relationships.[19] The classroom provides an arena in which these problems may emerge with considerable force. In

---

[18]A number of causes of student misbehavior are discussed by Thomas A. Ringness, *Mental Health in the Schools* (New York: Random House, Inc., 1968), pp. 101–111.

[19]Elizabeth B. Hurlock, *Adolescent Development*, 3d. ed. (New York: McGraw-Hill Book Company, 1967), p. 503, briefly discusses boy-girl problems of adolescence.

early adolescence a certain amount of heterosexual antagonism usually develops, particularly among the boys who have lagged behind in physical development. In late adolescence the problem of dating couples who wish to sit together may prove to be trying.

Varied Backgrounds

Because of the diversity of socioeconomic levels and the increasing mobility of American families, students come to school with widely varying backgrounds. A child of a United States Army officer, for example, might have lived at least two weeks in every one of the fifty states by the time he was in the ninth grade. Contrast the ease of teaching such a student the geography of North America with the difficulties inherent in teaching the same subject to another student of comparable intelligence who had never been more than a hundred miles from his place of birth.

If planning is to be helpful, it must be undertaken with the realization that student experiences have varied considerably.[20] Experiences that are common to all and those that are uniquely individual in nature must be analyzed. The teacher must determine how these unique experiences can serve the purposes of instruction. Furthermore, if students are found to lack essential experiences, the teacher must find ways of providing them.

Subject-Matter Achievement

Somewhat related to the out-of-school experience of students is their subject-matter achievement. Extreme variability is noted among students in virtually all heterogeneously grouped classes. Substantial variation may be found even among students grouped according to some homogeneous measure. This is particularly borne out on the upper secondary level, where the range of reading achievement has been found to vary as much as seven years.

The frequently observed fact that *I.Q.* and *achievement* do not invariably bear a close relationship causes a great deal of difficulty for the novice planner. In order to avoid false assumptions, the planner should consider each factor separately before bringing this information together to determine the degree of relationship that actually does exist.

A twelfth-grade student of social problems may achieve at the eighth-grade level in United States history although his I.Q. is 115. Conversely, a ninth-grade pupil with an I.Q. of 98 may achieve at the twelfth-grade level in the area of English grammar. An eighth-grade mathematics teacher reports having given one of three A's to an over-achieving girl whose I.Q. was 101, although the average I.Q. for the class was 114. Some students who rank among the upper 25 percent of their

---

[20]See Morris L. Bigge and Maurice P. Hunt, *Psychological Foundations of Education,* 2d. ed. (New York: Harper & Row, Publishers, 1968), pp. 116–117, for a short treatment of culturally imposed differences.

classmates in music and art are sometimes known to have average or below-average intelligence test scores.

Information About the Unit

The basic information about the unit involves accurate recording of the proposed length, together with the time allotted for Introductory, Developmental, and Concluding Activities, and the relationship of the unit to the Overall Plan. Although there may be some error in these approximations, the necessity for recording this information will move the planner in the direction of realistically differentiating between the possible and the impossible, the practical and the impractical.

Increasing use of a wide variety of programed lessons and units designed essentially for student self-instruction has further reduced the emphasis for their completion within a specified period. Moving at his own pace, the student may complete his instructional task slowly or rapidly—but always at a speed that is compatible with his learning abilities and personal characteristics.

The student as well as the teacher should understand the relationship of the specific unit under consideration to other units in the Overall Plan. This should also be recorded as part of the Basic Information to help relate one unit to another in a meaningful way. The planner must constantly remember the need for interrelating the various course concepts in order to move smoothly from the simple to the more difficult.

Although all unit plans should contain this basic information, it is impossible to determine the detail needed in a unit unless one knows teacher needs and is acquainted with the students for whom the unit is planned. Inasmuch as a plan serves as an aid to the teacher, the need for restricted or lengthy plans will vary with the individual concerned. There is no doubt that the beginning teacher will need more extensive plans than does his seasoned colleague.

Use of a Seating Chart

Teachers have sought a device that would bring many facets of the desired basic information together in a concise, usable form. A coded seating chart,[21] like the one illustrated in Figure 3, is such a device. Since specific facts concerning individual capacities, achievement levels, and socioeconomic status must remain confidential professional information, such data must be kept in locked files or recorded in code form.

Advantages of a Code

The key to the code should never appear on the seating chart itself. As soon as it is memorized by the teacher it should be destroyed. Indeed,

---

[21]Clark and Starr, *Secondary School Teaching Methods*, chapter 2, stress the necessity for getting acquainted with students quickly. Suggestions for expediting the process are provided.

Fig. 3   Seating chart with a simplified code.

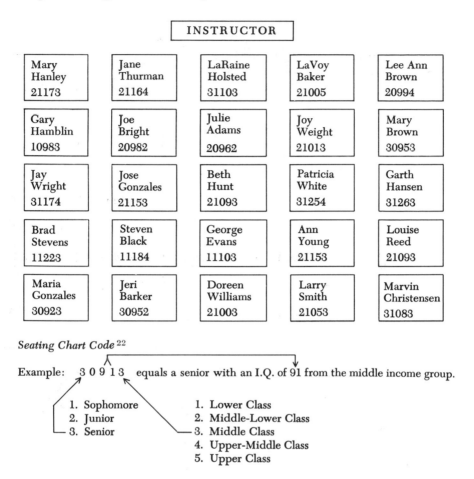

Seating Chart Code [22]

Example: 3 0 9 1 3   equals a senior with an I.Q. of 91 from the middle income group.

1. Sophomore   1. Lower Class
2. Junior   2. Middle-Lower Class
3. Senior   3. Middle Class
                      4. Upper-Middle Class
                      5. Upper Class

because of its simplicity, the code need not be written out at all. The key to the code appears here only for purposes of explanation.

The following advantages of this device may be noted:

1. It is simple in make-up and, therefore, usable.

2. It provides much of the essential basic information in a very concise form.

3. It keeps the information confidential.

4. It provides a picture of the exact location of each student together with relevant data pertaining to that student.

5. It encourages realistic planning.

---

[22]A strong case can be made for including in each student's code a numerical device indicating potential for self direction. Recent emphasis on independent study makes such a device particularly desirable.

Fig. 4   Seating chart with a complex code.

INSTRUCTOR					
Florence Graff 0992110.5731	Jerri Price 099907.2451	Bill Henlein 095019.0441	Sam Christensen 097908.8561	Elaine Purdy 096908.2451	Rebecca Turf 095019.6414
Ethel Weaver 092119.9541	Lamar White 094019.5451	Robert Gordon 098119.8431	Noel Roach 093019.2341	Blaine Noble 090019.1341	May Devenish 094018.9541
	Abe Silberstein 092018.8441	Lewis Shepherd 098908.2451	Bert Mecham 095019.8541	Helen Anderson 090119.4441	Reed Vincent 0943112.2431
Elsa Zeeman 093017.9541	Merl Vicklund 0911110.3441	Archie Bellows 096219.9541	Marlene Chadwick 094019.4451	Madeline + DeHart 097119.8541	Jo Ann Barlow 090018.5451

Key to Seating Chart Code

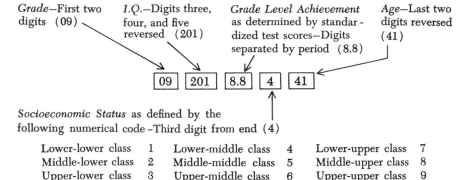

| *Grade*—First two digits (09) | *I.Q.*—Digits three, four, and five reversed (201) | *Grade Level Achievement* as determined by standar-dized test scores—Digits separated by period (8.8) | *Age*—Last two digits reversed (41) |

Socioeconomic Status as defined by the following numerical code –Third digit from end (4)

Lower-lower class	1	Lower-middle class	4	Lower-upper class	7
Middle-lower class	2	Middle-middle class	5	Middle-upper class	8
Upper-lower class	3	Upper-middle class	6	Upper-upper class	9

The number of separate bits of information to be coded for individual students will vary with the need and willingness of the teacher to assemble such information. When a teacher is teaching in the same small community in which he was born, it may be sufficient to have a coded indication only of student ages, I.Q.'s, and achievement levels. If his teaching situation, however, is totally new to him, he may need to have other specific items of information available in coded form.

A ninth-grade teacher of algebra found that her coded seating chart (Figure 4) served her purposes very well. She expanded, without sacrificing simplicity and intelligibility, the number of items of information coded.

Note that the "Grade Level Achievement" as it relates to mathematics can be of great assistance to the teacher in planning to meet the needs of students at varying levels. The numerical code defining socioeconomic status, however, may be too narrowly differentiated for practical use. A five-digit code would be sufficiently discreet and would be much easier to handle. The more sophisticated coding involving number reversals and a large number of digits will better protect the confidential nature of the information.

Realistic Planning Using a Code

Conscientious teachers agree that the planning of objectives and activities for a specific group of students should be undertaken only when the teacher has a clear mental picture of the students in the group. In addition, when the teacher can arrange a planning situation in which freedom from classroom pressures is insured, planning can take place at its best. An accurate seating chart with essential information about the students will thus help the teacher make realistic plans. He will find, for example, that he is less apt to plan procedures that are beyond the comprehension of a given student when the seating chart beside him indicates that the pupil's I.Q. is 94.

Examples of Basic Information

The Basic Information that follows was assembled by a social studies teacher concerned with teaching a unit on "The Low Countries" to a class in world geography.[23]

I. Basic Information
   A. Age and Grade Level
      1. The students are all in the tenth grade.
      2. The age range for the group is from fifteen to seventeen years.
   B. The unit will be approximately six days in length.
   C. This unit will be number twelve in a series of units.
      1. The preceding unit was on France, its history, its relationship to other countries, and its contributions to civilization.
      2. This unit is on the Low Countries (Belgium and the Netherlands), their history, their relationship to other nations, and their contributions to civilization.
      3. The next unit will be on Spain and will include the same general areas as the preceding units.
   D. The Nature of the Class
      1. The I.Q. range is from 86 to 127.
      2. The general social adjustments within the class are good.
      3. There are twenty-four girls and nine boys in the class.
      4. Most of the students come from lower-middle-class families. The majority of their fathers are employed in the local steel plant and maintain small farms on the side.

Although the teacher who assembled this information as a basis for effective planning probably felt that the information was adequate, a

---

[23]Additional examples of how Basic Information is used in the preparation of teaching units are found in Chapter 7.

beginning teacher might find it advantageous to have additional information. No mention was made of potential offenders in terms of classroom control, for instance, and there is little information about the students' backgrounds. An indication of general achievement in relationship to the world geography course also would help provide a more realistic picture.

A teacher of first-year Spanish assembled the same general information as that provided for the unit on "The Low Countries" but in a slightly different form and with a somewhat different emphasis. The content of this unit is concerned with vocabulary development; present, past, future, and imperfect tenses; and certain elements of Spanish history.

I. Basic Information
   A. Age: 15–18 years.
   B. Grades: Tenth and eleventh.
   C. I.Q.'s: Average—99.5, high—128, low—87.
   D. Background: Predominantly Protestant in belief. Six are Catholic The majority of students were born and reared in Sloacum Valley. Two come from Mexican families.
   E. Environment: Semirural.
   F. Socioeconomic Status: With two exceptions, students come from the lower-middle class. The two students come from the upper-lower class.
   G. Student Interests: Several of the boys in the class have considerable interest in farming. All students have expressed considerable interest in travel and languages, although this varies a great deal.
   H. Length of Unit: Four weeks—20 class periods of 50 minutes each.
   I. Number of Students: 25—10 girls and 15 boys.
   J. Purpose of This Unit as Related to the Course: It is expected that the students will have a broad overview of the Spanish language and its place in their lives by the end of this unit. Unit I (this unit) is, therefore, an introduction to the many phases of Spanish and will serve students as a frame of reference as later units are presented.
   K. Specific Information Concerning Certain Students:
      1. Mary and Manuel Larra have been in the country for two years, coming from Mexico with their parents. They are in the beginning Spanish class under special arrangements with their counselor. It is felt that helping their fellow students with Spanish will help them learn English more quickly and with less pressure. The class will also benefit. Special assignments will be given Mary and Manuel.
      2. Victor Lee has an extremely high linguistic rating. He has been placed between Mary and Manuel for maximum benefit.
      3. Delbert Tappia is deaf in the left ear. He is seated in the front seat for the best audio range.
      4. Richard Newberry is seated directly in front of the teacher's desk because of visual difficulty.

5. John Marks, Barbara Bestwick, and Reid Potter have high learning abilities and should be given outside work both by the instructor and by the Spanish Club.
6. Dee Huff and Alice Newman will need special help because of learning difficulties.
7. Mary Richfield will miss class each Wednesday so that she can visit her mother in Westbrook Hospital. Mary will need additional help in order to keep abreast of the class.

The Basic Information on which the Spanish I unit was based places particular stress on specific information about students. Instructional procedures will clearly have to be altered to meet the needs of these students. Admittedly the identification and recording of relevant, special information about students will take some time, but it should be rewarded with a greater measure of realism in planning and teaching than would be possible otherwise.

PROBLEMS FOR STUDY AND DISCUSSION

1. What leads the uninformed prospective teacher to doubt the necessity for planning?
2. Which of the following types of teachers need to spend the least time planning? Why?

> The fluent one
> The one with ten years of experience
> The one who organizes well
> The one with the pleasing personality
> The one who knows his subject thoroughly
> The one who likes students
> The inexperienced one

3. Why should the beginning teacher today be able to teach better than the beginning teacher of twenty years ago? Discuss.
4. What should be the proper role of teacher *personality* in instruction? Explain in some detail.
5. What should happen to a teaching unit after it has been used? Explain, giving necessary details.
6. What is the *basic* purpose of a teaching unit? Whose purposes are served through unit planning?
7. Why is the Overall Plan often described as the simplest of the three basic types of plans for teaching?
8. Without rereading this chapter, list briefly and in sequence the steps in developing an Overall Plan.
9. From your acquaintance with high-school courses, list at least one unit title not mentioned in this chapter for each of the following subjects:

English Literature	Business Arithmetic
Shorthand	Homemaking
Civics	General Science

10. What is the difference between a *teaching unit* and a *resource unit?* Indicate the two ways in which resource units are assembled.

11. Indicate the sequence of steps that should be employed in the development of a unit. Why is the matter of sequence of basic importance?

12. List, in the order of importance, the most essential information about class members needed by a secondary-school teacher if he wishes to plan effectively.

13. What are the implications for the teacher of the statement *planning is preteaching?* Discuss.

14. List ten difficulties that may arise in teaching when the teacher has planned on the basis of inaccurate or incomplete information about students.

15. Assume that you have in your tenth-grade English class students with the following problems: a girl with very poor vision; twin boys with I.Q.'s in the 90–95 range; an introverted girl with an I.Q. of 138; and a boy of average capacity who lost his right hand, the one with which he wrote, in a hunting accident the preceding summer. Indicate in general the classroom procedures you would employ in meeting the individual needs of these students.

16. Why should the teacher consider the I.Q. and achievement of given students separately?

17. How specific should the planner be in indicating the time to be devoted to introductory, developmental, and concluding activities? Explain.

18. What precautions should the teacher take in using a coded seating chart?

19. What specific advantages are provided when the teacher has an accurate indication of grade-level achievement of individual students in his particular subject and class? List and explain.

20. Exactly what information should be included under the caption *Basic Information* before one can plan a unit realistically? Would this vary from one class to another? Why?

4. *Objectives and Procedures in a Teaching Unit*

With few exceptions, activities are not justified unless they lead rather directly to a desired goal.[1] The responsibility of selecting appropriate objectives for a given unit and determining the most efficient procedures to achieve these objectives is one of the most formidable tasks confronting conscientious teachers.

---

[1]Leonard H. Clark and Irving S. Starr, *Secondary School Teaching Methods*, 2d. ed. (New York: The Macmillan Company, 1967), pp. 107–109, point out the strong need for relating activities to well-defined goals.

DETERMINING ENABLING OBJECTIVES
FOR A TEACHING UNIT

The size of the task involved in the selection and statement of unit objectives is vastly underestimated by the majority of unit planners. The most frequent difficulties encountered in evaluating unit objectives are the following:

1. No differentiation is made between *types* of objectives. It is the *type* of objective, however, that determines the procedure to be employed.

2. Objectives are not stated in their simplest form, with respect to either content or word usage.

3. Objectives are frequently too difficult or too easy for the average student at the particular grade level.

4. Minor objectives are not properly related to major objectives.

5. Concepts are listed in such a way that the development of thinking from the simple to the complex is *not* encouraged.

6. Objectives are not meaningfully interrelated.

7. Concepts to be learned are stated in topic form, thus encouraging vagueness on the part of the planner as well as the learner.

8. Objectives of limited value are often selected.

There are several types of enabling objectives with which all planners should be acquainted.[2] In the order of most frequent use they are: concepts, memorization, skills, and habits.

Concepts

The concept is a mental picture of an object, an event, or a relationship, derived from personal experience with the thing for which the concept stands (the referent). Typical concepts are: two and two are four; heads of state are in danger of assassination; diamonds are chemically comprised of carbon; a verb is often a word of action.

Planning Suggestions

Inasmuch as the majority of subject areas (English, mathematics, science, and social studies) in the curriculum are made up of mental pictures (concepts), it is wise to remember some of the problems unit planners encounter in listing concepts as objectives to be learned. Two suggestions should save the planner much time and distress:

1. Concepts are most meaningful to the students as well as to the teacher when they are written in full sentences and stated simply.

---

[2]Asahel D. Woodruff, *Basic Concepts of Teaching; with Brief Readings* (San Francisco: Chandler Publishing Company, 1962), pp. 119–120, lists five kinds of behavior that are closely related to the four basic types of objectives considered in this chapter.

See also John P. De Cecco, *The Psychology of Learning and Instruction: Educational Psychology* (Englewood Cliffs, New Jersey: Prentice-Hall, Inc., 1968), pp. 47–50.

2. An easily identified relationship must be established between major concepts and supporting minor concepts.

Specific Steps

1. List the concepts in the order they should be taught. For the time being do not focus undue attention on possible error of sequence or wording.

2. Review the list, inserting essential concepts that have been omitted and deleting nonessential details of fact.

3. Check the wording of the concepts. Avoid the use of difficult terms: be certain that concepts are presented in meaningful, complete sentences.

4. Arrange the sentences into a hierarchy of major and minor concepts.

    a. Place the unit objective that encompasses all minor objectives first.

    b. Place the first important minor objective next.

    c. Then list the subobjectives related to the first minor objective.

Memorization

Memorization involves the simple process of learning the symbols by which concepts are identified. For this reason it is frequently referred to as *symbolic learning*. There are many degrees of memorization, ranging from bare recognition of symbolic material to total verbatim recall.

Symbolic learning is not confined to the recalling of words and groups of words that are spoken or written. It may involve committing to memory signs, nonverbal symbols, configurations, and pictorializations like the following:

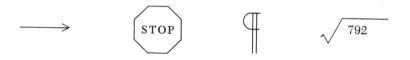

Understanding Concepts

Most symbolic learning (memorization) involves words. In every case the ease and speed with which memorization can take place is enhanced by a clear understanding of the concept for which the word or phrase stands.[3] Memorization without the comprehension of the underlying concept is a most inefficient, time-consuming, and trying procedure. Conscientious teachers in all subject areas are placing greater emphasis on conceptual clarity and are deemphasizing memory for its own sake.

---

[3]Morris L. Bigge and Maurice P. Hunt, *Psychological Foundations of Education*, 2d. ed. (New York: Harper & Row, Publishers, 1968), pp. 496–500, present a generally accepted discussion of the relationship between understanding and memorization.

Specific Steps

The symbol (either spoken or written) takes on meaning only in relationship to the concept for which it stands. This requires the following steps for the planner in listing symbols to be memorized:

1. Examine the concepts stated as objectives to be learned. Identify those terms that will have limited meaning for the students.

2. Place these terms in the order in which they are to be memorized once the related concepts are clear.

If a long poem or prose passage is to be learned thoroughly, it will be necessary to single out difficult words, first for conceptual attention and later for memorization.

Memorization in Foreign Languages

The identification and listing of symbols to be memorized are extremely important in foreign language study because of the necessary emphasis on vocabulary. Such a procedure leans rather heavily on "textbook" instruction, but it has greater justification in the teaching of foreign languages than in other fields. Foreign language texts are commonly organized into short two-day and three-day lessons. If such a text is followed rather strictly, planning units becomes difficult. Many teachers today are thus planning foreign language courses around groups of daily lessons rather than by units. Such daily plans must be closely related to an expanded Overall Plan.

Skills

A skill may be defined as the *coordination of nerves and muscles brought about either through practice or by virtue of natural endowment.* A skill may be developed to any desired level of proficiency, assuming that neural and physical equipment make this possible. The learning of skills requires two processes:[4]

1. Acquiring a clear concept of the motor action involved.

2. Practicing under supervision until the desired level of proficiency has been attained.

Skill Subjects

No subject is solely concerned with learning skills, to the exclusion of concepts, but several subjects are predominantly skill subjects—for example, typing, physical education, instrumental music, vocal music, indus-

---

[4]The essential relationship of concept formation to manipulative behaviors is discussed by Frederick J. McDonald, *Educational Psychology* (Belmont, California: Wadsworth Publishing Co., Inc., 1965), pp. 387–391.

The nature of the task of skill learning and specific suggestions for teachers are provided by Nathan S. Blount and Herbert J. Klausmeier, *Teaching in the Secondary School*, 3d. ed. (New York: Harper & Row, Publishers, 1968), pp. 96–101.

trial arts, and art. Certain subjects tend to be skill subjects although they are heavily dependent upon concept formation; homemaking and shorthand might be placed in this category.

Skills obviously play an important part in any physical education class. Note that each individual skill is essential to an effective total performance. It is basic, therefore, that a major skill be analyzed in terms of its component minor skills so that specific attention may be properly focused where needed.

A great deal of attention is currently being given to correct pronunciation in foreign-language classes. Inasmuch as physical manipulation of tongue, mouth, and lips is involved, such functional emphasis must be classified as skill learning. Skill learning is concerned with the coordination of nerves and muscles. A clear understanding of how this coordination is to take place (conceptualization) should precede the practice of any skill.

Habits

Habit formation—in addition to skill development, memorization, and concept formation—is another essential enabling objective that concerns teachers at all levels. Unfortunately it has been subject to widespread neglect, particularly at the secondary level. A habit has several characteristics:[5]

1. It is learned.
2. It is automatic.
3. It is set off by a cue or triggering stimulus.
4. It takes place without conscious control.
5. It is satisfying to the user.

Long-Range Objectives
The nature of the development of habits decrees that they must be thought of as long-range objectives.[6] They actually begin to function at the subconscious level only after a prolonged period of consistent repetition. For this reason it is more practical for the instructor to think of habits as related to the total yearly classroom operation rather than to a single unit that may be of relatively short duration. Once developed, habits can be of great value in helping the instructor and class members achieve certain goals.

Habit Categories
The teacher should consider several general categories of habits, under which specific habits might be listed—for example, routine, class-

---

[5]Woodruff, *Basic Concepts of Teaching*, p. 227.
[6]Homer C. Rose, *The Instructor and His Job* (Chicago: American Technical Society, 1966), p. 66, explains that the automatic nature of certain teachers' habits encourages the omission of explanations needed for full student comprehension.

room control, personal behavior, acceptable speech patterns, and study habits. Admittedly there will be considerable overlap among the specific habits attached to these categories, but they do provide a framework.

The following list shows the five general categories with related specific habits.[7] It will be readily noted that several items could logically be added to each group, but the enumeration is illustrative, not inclusive.

1. Habits Related to Routine:
    a. Abiding by efficient paper distribution procedures.
    b. Exercising personal tidiness around one's desk.
    c. Being in one's seat by the time the bell rings.
    d. Leaving the seats at the close of the class only when dismissed by the teacher.

2. Habits Related to Classroom Control:
    a. Giving consistent attention to the teacher and the instruction.
    b. Sharpening pencils only before and after class.
    c. Abstaining from horseplay during class.
    d. Using the classroom library only at times specified by the teacher.

3. Habits Related to Personal Behavior:
    a. Being consistently polite when addressing the teacher or class-mates.
    b. Avoiding running and yelling in the classroom.
    c. Being personally neat at all times.
    d. Avoiding rudeness under all circumstances.

4. Habits Related to Acceptable Speech Patterns:
    a. Using commonly accepted words for effective communication.
    b. Avoiding meaningless clutter words.
    c. Avoiding profanity completely.
    d. Avoiding *ain't* and other illiterate usages.

5. Study Habits:
    a. Getting down to study without unwarranted delay.
    b. Organizing the material to be studied in order to achieve maximum efficiency.
    c. Seeking the help of the teacher only when it is really necessary.
    d. Permitting no interference from classmates when expected to study.

---

[7]Specific habits identified here may sound dogmatic and authoritarian. Habits are by definition prescriptive in nature, giving direction to student behavior at the subconscious level. However, the teacher should encourage the learning of only those habits that complement the learning style of students and the teaching style of the instructor.

USING BEHAVIORAL OBJECTIVES EFFICIENTLY IN A TEACHING UNIT

Prior to 1960, limited attention was focused on the need for stating goals in such a way as to identify how a learner would behave as a result of having achieved the intended goal. However, for decades teachers have recognized the essential but frequently loosely-coordinated relationship between learning and behavior—without having discovered a device that would make this relationship meaningful to both student and teacher. The carefully-worded behavioral objective (sometimes referred to as the terminal objective) attempts to do this.

What are Behavioral Objectives?

During the 1950's psychologists and programmers became interested in the need for specific detail in constructing linear and branching programs. Spurred by the mounting influence of programed instruction on educational effort, Mager developed a brief programed text that presented the case for behavioral (performance) objectives in a simplified but convincing fashion.[8] He made no attempt to suggest how quality goals are to be selected; his central focus was on how a learner behaves when demonstrating the achievement of a particular goal. Emphasis was thus placed on observable performance.

Mager further contended that in order to achieve this behavioral emphasis, an objective should:[9]

1. Be stated as an intended outcome, not as a summary of content.
2. Meaningfully communicate the intent of the teacher by specifically identifying the terminal behavior expected of the student as evidence of his having achieved the desired goal.
3. State the relevant circumstances under which terminal behavior must be exhibited.
4. Specify the lower limits of acceptable performance.

Examples of behaviorally-stated objectives that conform to Mager's guidelines illustrate their restrictive and toning effect on loosely-structured, conventionally-worded objectives.[10]

Given a human skeleton, the student must be able to correctly identify by labeling at least forty of the following bones. There will be no penalty for guessing (list of bones inserted here).

The student must be able to reply in grammatically correct French to 90 percent of the questions put to him during an examination.

---

[8]Robert F. Mager, *Preparing Objectives for Programed Instruction* (Palo Alto: Fearon Publishers, 1962).
[9]*Ibid.*, pp. 43–45.
[10]*Ibid.*, pp. 45–50.

The student must be able to correctly solve at least seven simple linear equations within a period of thirty minutes.

Given twenty sentences containing a variety of mistakes in capitalization, the student is able, with at least 90 percent accuracy, to identify and rewrite correctly each word that has a mistake in capitalization.[11]

Assumed Limitations of Nonbehavioral Objectives

Repeated exposure to the deficiencies of traditional goals has accounted for a gradual conversion of experiment-minded teachers and educational institutions to the merits of stating goals in behavioral terms. Several such deficiencies as well as illustrative examples are identified below.

1. Traditionally-stated goals lack behavioral specificity. For example, the objective *to learn why Shakespeare occupies a position of pre-eminence among English writers* says little about what the learner should be able to do as a result of having achieved the goal.
2. Traditional appraisal frequently ignores the value of observable behavior. Because mental activity often does not result in observable behavior, it serves poorly as a device in the assessment of goal achievement. At the end of a unit concerned with mathematical equations, the teacher knows that when Johnny is able to balance 14 different equations of moderate difficulty with 95 percent accuracy within a ten minute period, he has achieved one of the major goals of the unit.
3. Teachers find it much easier and quicker to state generalized, non-specific objectives than to identify precise, behavior-oriented outcomes. For example, it is much simpler to identify the unit goal as:

To understand the causes and effects of World War II

than to specify what the student should be able to do when he has reached the goal by stating that

Allowed the fifty minutes of the regular class period, students should be able to pass, by 80 percent, a multiple-choice test consisting of forty carefully selected items dealing with the causes and effects of World War II.

4. Goals stated in nonbehavioral terms are relatively meaningless to students. To a physics class, a goal identified as *the study of direct current* can be baffling and lacking in motivation unless students

---

[11]Thorwald Esbensen, "Writing Instructional Objectives," *Phi Delta Kappan*, 48 (January 1967), p. 247.

perceive themselves as having responsibility for behaving in a different, specifically identified way as a result of goal achievement. Carefully worded behavioral outcomes enhance meaning.

5. Teachers seldom indicate the lower limits of acceptable performance, either in stated objectives or evaluation procedures. The goal *to be able to write a correct English theme* says nothing about the degree of correctness that is expected.

6. Program content and emphasis are not clear in traditionally-stated objectives. *To learn the major battles of the Revolutionary War* does not identify the real intent of the goal and may lead to false assumptions about emphasis.

7. Irrelevant activities are often pursued in the student's attempt to reach goals that are not spelled out in behavioral terms. For example, the biology student may engage in fruitless reading on assorted bugs in the attempt to meet a loosely-stated objective (*to learn the characteristics of beetles*) that might have been identified behaviorally as the *collection and labeling of three different kinds of beetles indigenous to the area.*

8. Traditional objectives give little consideration to the conditions under which a given behavior will take place. *To be able to solve quadratic equations* does not specify whether the problems are to be of a non-textbook, practical nature, selected from a text, or printed on a handout sheet to be solved at home.

9. The nonbehavioral goal focuses on goal identification alone; however, the behavioral goal combines the objective, terminal student activities, and specific evaluation procedures in one statement.

Specific Uses

Because of the relative recency of the emphasis on behavioral objectives, much of the work related to their uses must be classified as experimental. Unanswered questions include:

1. How can they best serve the purposes of long-range objectives?
2. Can they be employed equally well in unit planning and daily lesson planning?
3. Is all relevant goal-related behavior observable?
4. Can generalized or abstract conceptual objectives be stated in behavioral terms with as much meaning as concrete concepts or skills?
5. What is the most effective relationship between evaluation procedures and behavioral outcomes?
6. Do all subjects lend themselves equally well to the use of behavioral objectives?
7. Do carefully conducted research studies indicate that plans calling for the use of behavioral objectives are superior to plans that do not?

Extent of Use

Although the use of behavioral objectives in planning has increased dramatically since 1962, it would be unwise to generalize that even a sizable minority of secondary school teachers employ them. Their use is largely restricted to innovative schools and teachers. Many involved schools employ behavioral objectives in organizing and implementing programs of individualized instruction and continuous progress. During the 1968 fiscal year, fifteen projects involving experiments with behavioral objectives were funded by Title III of the Elementary and Secondary Education Act.[12] Undoubtedly many additional projects involving work with behavioral objectives are in the process of completion.

Stating Objectives

Each statement of objectives should:

1. Identify expected student behavior when demonstrating achievement of the objective.
2. Stipulate the conditions under which the behavior is to be exhibited.
3. Reveal the lower limits of acceptable performance.

Relationship to Enabling Objectives

The desirability of identifying both (a) concepts, skills, memorization, and habits (enabling objectives) as well as (b) behaviorally-stated objectives is questioned by certain teacher-planners who feel that the procedure represents an undesirable duplication of effort. However, a few perceptive, ambitious planners have indicated that the use of both categories has resulted in goal-oriented teaching and learning that has particular meaning for both instructor and student. They maintain further that the use of both categories results in higher student motivation, a more refined use of teaching techniques, and more carefully structured planning and teaching.

Examples of the advantages of this dual approach may be seen in the illustrations that follow. Each example has been taken from a different unit in which enabling objectives (consisting, with one exception, of large concepts and related subconcepts) are matched with expected behavioral outcomes.

Enabling Objectives *(Concepts)*	*Objectives Stated Behaviorally*
1. Use of the dictionary provides the most efficient means for finding the meaning of new words.	1. a, b. Using dictionaries, students will find the meanings of the following twenty unfamiliar words repre-

---

[12]*Pacesetters in Innovation: Fiscal Year 1968.* Title III, Supplementary Centers and Services Program, Elementary and Secondary Education Act of 1965 (Washington, D.C.: U.S. Department of Health, Education, and Welfare, April 1969), p. 4.

a. A good dictionary defines, indicates origin, and specifies the part of speech of different words.

b. Consistent use of the dictionary encourages speed and accuracy in its use.

senting different parts of speech. In columns to the right of the word list, students will indicate the meaning, origin, and part of speech. They will complete the test in class during a twenty minute period and must make no more than five of the 60 possible errors.

1. A noun is the name of a person, place, or thing.

1. Given a paragraph containing an equal number of different kinds of nouns (18 in all), students will be able to encircle at least 14 of them within a three minute period.

1. One of the basic rights of American citizenship is freedom of speech, which entails certain rights as well as responsibilities.

a. The citizen may tell others what he thinks and try to win them to his point of view.

b. He may listen freely to other points of view.

c. He has no right to say things that would aid an enemy, call for a forceful overthrow of the government, or harm other persons.

d. He has the responsibility for speaking out for democracy.

e. He has the duty to respect the right of others to voice their opinions.

1. a-e. At the conclusion of the semester, students in groups of five will be given one full class period to evaluate how effectively each member of the group has discharged his rights and responsibilities of free speech in the classroom. Evaluation will be based on ratings assigned on ten-point scales concerned with: (1) expressing personal ideas freely, (2) allowing others to express theirs, (3) avoiding the expression of harmful ideas about the country or school, and (4) effectively speaking out for democracy. Each student will rate every other student on each of the four points; an average rating of seven (ten is high) is the minimum acceptable standard.

Practical use of this dual approach has resulted in the identification of generalizations of particular value to teachers planning to use this pattern for the first time.

Like instructional procedures, enabling goals serve as a *means* to the end of changed student behavior. The learning of a specific concept, for example, is essential before the student can use the concept in a practical situation. Likewise, acquiring a mental picture of a specific motor skill is of little value if it remains a theoretical construct only. When the student relates the concept to reality through practical use, behavior is changed. The student can see this relationship with greater ease when he sees both categories of objectives organized or placed in such a way as to demand attention.

The use of two columns, in which the enabling objectives are placed in the first column and the corresponding behavioral objectives in the second column, simplifies relationships. Further, the portion of the written unit that lists the two types of objectives in adjacent columns provides a brief and meaningful overview of the unit for students as well as the teacher. Some teachers have found it desirable to distribute duplicated copies of matching objectives to all students in a given class.

The large inclusive unit objective (enabling in nature) is often not matched by a corresponding behavioral objective when a large number of complicated behaviors are involved. When matching of a corresponding goal is employed at this level, care must be exercised to be sure that the behavioral goal called for represents a careful sampling (or a composite) of relevant behaviors.

Specific Suggestions

The efficient matching of enabling objectives with corresponding behavioral objectives in a two-column arrangement requires the planner to give attention to particular steps.

1. State the nonbehavioral enabling objectives first.
2. Ask yourself if students have a reasonably good understanding of these objectives (concepts or skills), what behavior modifications (objectives) should result, and what form they should take.
3. State your behavioral objectives as simply and clearly as possible, incorporating (a) a description of the relevant circumstances under which the behavior will take place and (b) the lower limits of acceptable performance. It may be helpful to focus on quantity and time in describing acceptable performance.
4. Remember that each enabling subobjective does not require a stated behavioral objective. A behavioral goal usually is related meaningfully and easily to a cluster of related concepts and subconcepts or skills and subskills.
5. Be sure your behavioral goals can be observed and evaluated.
6. Eliminate methods from your statements of behavioral goals. Their focus should be on a description of terminal behavior, not on procedures for achieving them.
7. Determine whether your evaluation procedures unnecessarily duplicate your behavioral goals. Make adjustments when necessary.

DETERMINING PROCEDURES FOR ACHIEVING ENABLING OBJECTIVES

So great has been the preoccupation of teachers with the necessity for careful selection of teaching procedures that many have come to view methods as ends in their own right. This misplaced emphasis has had a detrimental effect upon the whole of American public education during the last half century. The relationship of *means* to *ends* must be clear to the teacher himself.

Unit procedures (methods) are the means for achieving unit goals. If procedures are poorly selected, efficient movement in the direction of the objectives is thwarted.[13]

The fundamental question that the teacher must, therefore, ask himself in determining procedures is *not:* "Should I use the lecture method, committee work, a field trip, or a resource person?" The basic question *is:* "Of the range of possible procedures that might be employed in achieving a given goal, which procedure will enable learners to achieve the goal most efficiently?" There are, of course, several relevant factors that must be considered:

1. Psychological soundness
2. Time considerations
3. Depth of learning
4. Type of learning
5. Nature of the class being taught
6. Effectiveness of the teacher in using given procedures

What Procedures Are Best?

The poor selection of procedures (means) gives rise to inefficiency in attaining objectives, to negative reaction on the part of learners, and to varying degrees of frustration for both teachers and learners. What procedures *are* best? Any specific response to this question would be shallow and irresponsible. *The best procedure is one that enables students to achieve goals with greatest efficiency.*

Objective Dictates Procedure

Perhaps the most relevant consideration in selecting procedures involves the determination of the *type of objective,* for the psychology of learning reveals that the kind of objective dictates the most effective learning procedures.

The ineffective, unscientific teacher is often known by his failure to identify correctly the types of objectives sought (whether concepts, skills, memorizations, or habits) and their corresponding procedures.[14] In a history class, which is essentially concerned with the teaching of concepts, such a teacher often requires the memorization of names and dates without first fitting them into a meaningful context. Or, a teacher of

---

[13]In this section the use of the term *objective* is confined to *enabling objectives classified by kind. Behavioral objectives,* on the other hand, will be specifically so designated. For the purpose of this discussion *enabling objectives* and *objectives classified by kind* are used synonymously.

[14]See William H. Burton, *The Guidance of Learning Activities,* 3d ed. (New York: Appleton-Century-Crofts, 1962), pp. 365–366, for an excellent treatment of the teacher's responsibility in the use of activities.

high-school chorus, essentially a skill subject, may spend a disproportion-
ate amount of time discussing the various aspects of vocal production.
The good teacher, then, needs to have a first-hand acquaintance with a
wide range of specific methods. If he has such personal experience, he
will be in a much better position to make a meaningful choice of unit
procedures.

Desirable Variety

A variety of procedures very often serves instructional purposes
better than the use of a limited number of sterotyped methods.[15] The
teacher should consider whether it would be desirable to use modifications of any or all of the following approaches to instruction:

Learning packages

Study periods under the teacher's
  supervision

Problem solving

Differentiated assignments

Game simulation

Modified lectures

Inquiry training

Frequent objective testing

Strong student involvement

Committee work under careful
  teacher supervision

Capitalizing on existing interests

Frequent bulletin boards prepared
  by students

Student self assessment

Carefully screened resource people

Role-playing and sociodrama

Pretests for diagnosis

Critical thinking

Guided self-activity

Extensive use of media

Thoroughly planned and supervised
  field trips

A systems approach to teaching

Application of concepts or skills
  to a practical situation

Diagnostic teaching

Carefully selected models, diagrams,
  or charts

Indirect (non-prescriptive teaching)

Student-made aids prepared under
  teacher supervision

Capitalizing on different learning
  styles

Teaching machines

Discovery learning

Team teaching

Thought questions

Teaching very large and/or very
  small groups

Quest programs

Television teaching

Use of subject-matter laboratories

Non-traditional evaluation
  techniques

Use of multiple texts

Creative teaching

Restructuring content for improved
  learning

Use of paraprofessionals

Interaction analysis

Programed learning

Independent study

Misused Variety

Of course, a wide variety of procedures is effective only if such

---

[15]Clark and Starr, *Secondary School Teaching Methods*, p. 161, emphasize the need for
the teacher to select methods that give consideration to the numerous individual differences
found in students.

procedures are justified in terms of goal achievement. Consider the case of Mrs. Whitney, who thinks of herself as a forward-looking teacher.

MRS. WHITNEY USES A VARIETY OF PROCEDURES

Every Friday students talked about current events in Mrs. Whitney's eighth-grade core class. On this particular Friday, Jane Berner reported on a newspaper article by the Director of the Federal Bureau of Investigation; Jimmy Wilson told about a murder in an adjacent city; and Sally Zimmer read an article about the President's vacation at his summer home. In all, some ten minutes were consumed in the reports. There was no class discussion afterward.

"We'll have to hurry along," the teacher announced. "Now we'll choose sides so that we can play the game of 'State Capitals.' Lowell, you be the captain of one team, and Louise, you be the captain of the other. When you have chosen your teams, line them up on opposite sides of the room."

After considerable commotion and a loss of seven minutes, the teams were chosen and faced each other from opposite sides of the room. The game lasted just eleven minutes, for the teacher had sensed an urgency to move on to another activity. Louise's team won, eliciting groans of dismay from the opposition as the participants took their seats.

"Now we are going to continue the four-minute reports that we started on Wednesday. We'll hear first from Margaret, then Susan, then Bob, and then Mary Jo."

The four-minute reports averaged more nearly two minutes and in one case just thirty seconds. Mrs. Whitney was disturbed, especially in view of her compulsive desire to keep the students active.

"You may select books or magazines from the classroom library and study for the rest of the period," she said. Because only seven minutes were left in the period at this point, there was a great deal more interest in anticipating the end of the period than in getting down to conscientious study. By the end of the period, the class was in a hubbub and the teacher felt frustrated.

Mrs. Whitney's emphasis had been on keeping students busy rather than on having them achieve certain goals. This emphasis had the following results:

1. The students engaged in a much wider range of activities than was desirable.

2. They were moved into another activity just as they were beginning to benefit from the on-going one.

3. They failed to derive the desired satisfaction from their activities.

4. They were subjected to miscellaneous, unrelated activities.

5. The students were unable to relate the activities to either an enabling or behavioral goal.

Thoughtful teachers will avoid such problems; effective planning, based upon an acquaintance with student behavior patterns, will enable conscientious teachers to rule out questionable procedures at the planning stage.

The Teaching of Concepts

Concepts may be taught most efficiently when the learner has a *meaningful, vivid* experience or series of experiences with the referent of the concept.[16] Consider what this means in a practical situation.

MR. SCHMIDT TEACHES A BIOLOGY CONCEPT

Mr. Schmidt, the tenth-grade biology teacher, planned that the understanding of the following concept would serve as one of the enabling objectives for the day: "Blood flows into the heart through the veins and out of the heart through the arteries."

To provide his students with a meaningful, vivid experience with the heart, arteries, and veins, Mr. Schmidt wheeled to the center of the classroom a plastic model exposing the simulated visceral organs of the body. The teacher asked Janice Peters to identify the heart. He made sure that all students—particularly the less gifted—had a clear picture of the location of the heart in relationship to the other organs of the body.

While making a simplified oral explanation, Mr. Schmidt used a pointer to trace the flow of blood into the heart through the veins and out through the arteries. Students were encouraged to ask questions, which they did. Willy Liston, a boy of average ability, was then asked to restate in his own words what the teacher had said. Willy was able to acquit himself rather well, so Mr. Schmidt assumed that a majority of his class had understood the concept. The model would remain in the room for some time for examination by those students who were still not sure of the concept.

Technical terms related to the phenomenon just observed were placed on the board. A large wall chart on which the heart and its parts were labeled was displayed, discussed, and related to the terms on the board. Part of the assignment for the next day included the memorization of the words on the chart. During the following days the concept of the flow of blood through the heart took on new meaning through discussion and use under varied circumstances, and the associated symbols became fixed in the minds of the students.

Specific Steps

An effective plan for teaching concepts (which incorporates the highly relevant elements of meaningfulness and vividness) involves four steps,[17] each of which was used by Mr. Schmidt in establishing the concept of blood flow in the heart:

1. Showing the referent of the concept.

---

[16]Woodruff, *Basic Concepts of Teaching*, pp. 155–156.
[17]*Ibid.*, pp. 209–210.

2. Discussing the concept until it has become clear.

3. Memorizing the symbols related to the concept.

4. Providing for the application of the concept in on-going life situations.

Showing. The first step, *showing the referent*, is fundamental but often neglected or thought unnecessary because it is assumed the students have prior knowledge. Difficulties arise when the referent (the thing itself) cannot be brought into the classroom or is quite some distance from the school. (Note how Mr. Schmidt solved this problem by using a model.) In such instances the instructor must provide substitutes for first-hand experiences.

Discussing. During this phase unclear and misunderstood aspects of the concept are exposed and made clear; fuzzy edges are brought into sharper focus. When properly conducted, the exchange of ideas among peers can have an illuminating effect upon the mental pictures being developed. Student questions can be brought up and resolved during class discussion.

Memorizing. After the concept begins to take form, the symbols identifying the concept itself should be introduced, and the process of *memorization* begins. If the concept has been well developed in the two preceding steps, memorization of essential terms will proceed without difficulty. Usually this step occupies little time and takes place simultaneously with the development and expansion of the concept.

Applying. The fourth step, *application*, poses particular problems because, in many cases, the classroom does not provide a satisfactory setting for the practical application of the concept. For this reason, the practical effect that comes from functional use will have to take place largely outside the school. This immediately raises a problem, because it is impossible for the teacher to know all that takes place in the out-of-school life of his students.

The Teaching of Skills

Although the teaching of skills has much in common with the teaching of concepts, essential differences in procedures should be noted. The acquiring of motor skills is best accomplished if the instructor makes sure that the learner:

1. Acquires a clear mental picture of the skill involved.

2. Practices the skill under competent supervision until the desired level of proficiency has been achieved.

Examples of motor skills in the process of being learned will illustrate these two processes.

MISS SIMONSEN TEACHES TYPING SKILLS

The beginning typing class was confronted with the task of learning to manipulate the keys of the typewriter with some degree of accuracy. Miss Simonsen, the instructor, properly identified the type of learning involved as that of a motor skill, knowing that the procedures to be used were dictated by the type of learning involved.

Acquiring the Concept. Miss Simonsen first directed the attention of the class to a large colored chart that provided a pictorial representation of the keyboard with the keys identified by letter. An outline of the two hands was superimposed upon the keyboard to indicate that certain fingers were to rest on certain keys.

When each student was seated before a typewriter with blank keys, the instructor said, "Please place your fingers on the second row of keys exactly as seen on the chart." Students attempted to comply, but some of them had minor difficulties that the teacher soon corrected as she circulated among the class members.

"Now, press the key with the little finger of the left hand." Students complied. "Note that this finger controls the letter 'a'. Now, press the key with the third finger of the left hand." Again students did as directed. "You will notice that this finger controls the letter 's'."

Each key and its controlling finger were identified in a similar fashion. Students stroked the key and noted the resulting letter. The teacher pointed out by means of the chart that it was not necessary to watch the keyboard if fingers were placed on the proper "home" keys.

Students were now encouraged to press each key, being sure to keep the fingers in the proper position while observing only the chart on the wall. Soon, a mental picture of the home keys and the position of the fingers on these keys began to take shape.

Practice. The development of proficiency in the use of these keys was yet another matter. In the following days Miss Simonsen assigned simple exercises involving the use of the home keys. Whenever she noted improper hand position in relationship to these keys, she was quick to correct it. If a problem proved to be of general concern, she stopped the class and commented on the nature of the difficulty.

SAMMY LEARNS A MUSICAL SKILL

As a first-year band student, Sammy Whipple had no experience in playing the trumpet when the school year began. According to his teacher the first skill he would have to develop would be that of producing a consistent, sustained tone on his instrument.

Acquiring the Concept. The first task was to provide Sammy with a clear mental picture of how to produce the desired tone. By way of illustration, the teacher first held the mouthpiece against his own lips, explaining why it was best to hold it in the center of his lips and why it was necessary to have certain lip tension. By means of a wall chart he next showed Sammy the position of the tongue while blowing the note.

Practice. The teacher now asked Sammy to put into practice what he had learned by blowing a clear, sustained tone. His first trial proved to be relatively fruitless, but the instructor gave him certain hints about how to improve the tone. Gradually, with the specific criticism of his instructor and consistent practice for a week, Sammy was able to produce a consistent, sustained tone on his instrument.

The Teaching of Memorization

Memorization takes place most efficiently and is retained longer when consideration is given to these two essential steps:[18]

1. The learner needs to understand the meaning of what is to be memorized.
2. The learner needs to drill on whatever is to be memorized until the desired level of memorization has been achieved.

Specific examples will illustrate the usefulness of these steps.

MR. BUSKIN TEACHES ABOUT A RADIO CONTROL PANEL

While Mr. Buskin's twelfth-grade English class was studying a unit on communication, students were faced with the need for knowing about the various parts of the radio control panel. Because of the nontechnical nature of the course, however, the students did not need to learn the functions of all the knobs on the panel; an acquaintance with six of the key ones would be sufficient.

Acquiring the Concept. During a field trip to the local radio station, the engineer explained in easily understood language the locations, functions, and names of the various control devices on the panel. The instructor then asked that information and names relative to the six key devices be repeated. Afterward students were encouraged to ask any questions about the control panel and the six devices in particular that they felt would be beneficial. Students were asked to make a diagrammatic sketch of the control panel, labeling the six major knobs.

Drill. The next day in class Mr. Buskin discovered that all the students knew the functions of the key control knobs and that all but four students could name the knobs correctly. A special drill on the names was assigned to the four students who were having difficulty. A brief check the following day revealed that two of the students had still not memorized the names of the knobs. Repeated drill was prescribed after the teacher checked again to be sure that these students really understood the functions of the knobs.

A typical violation of correct procedures for teaching memorization is reflected in a social science's class.[19]

MR. PULVER TEACHES ABOUT THE CIVIL WAR

The eleventh-grade class was just beginning a unit on the Civil War

[18]De Cecco, *The Psychology of Learning and Instruction,* p. 333, reemphasizes the need for meaningfulness in memorization.
[19]Arden N. Frandsen, *Educational Psychology,* 2d. ed. (New York: McGraw-Hill Book Company, 1967), pp. 377–381, discusses the need for meaningfulness in both content and teaching procedures in promoting efficient learning.

Mr. Pulver wrote twelve terms related to the Civil War on the board as follows:

Manassas	Jefferson Davis
Bull Run	Battle of Franklin
Gettysburg	Harpers Ferry
William T. Sherman	Emancipation Proclamation
Ulysses S. Grant	Robert E. Lee
Federalist	Appomattox

"You will memorize these words for tomorrow," he said. "They will help you a great deal in understanding the Civil War period."

During the class period that followed, a narrative background for the understanding of the period between 1860 and 1864 was laid, but only two of the terms listed on the board were mentioned.

It should have come as no surprise to this instructor that even the most conscientious students found considerable difficulty with the assignment because there was little or no context into which the names might logically fit. Recall would have been enhanced greatly if a series of properly interrelated and meaningful mental pictures had been provided before the memorization assignment was made.

The Teaching of Habits

The theory underlying the teaching of concepts, skills, and memorization is relatively uncomplicated, although the actual use of sound procedures to teach them is often violated. Similarly, the procedures that should be followed in forming a habit are relatively simple but often violated:

1. The learner must perform without variation the specific behavior or act (usually a motor function) that it is hoped will become a habit.

2. He must continue to repeat the behavior time after time, until the performance no longer demands conscious attention.

3. He must find the habit satisfying but not necessarily pleasant.

Conversely, the breaking of an undesirable habit calls for the use of the same general procedure:

1. The learner must consciously avoid performing the habit he wishes to break.

2. He must persist in avoiding the habit until doing so no longer requires his conscious attention.

3. He must find the new form of behavior satisfying but not necessarily pleasant.

The Teaching of Positive Tastes

To teach students how to develop a specific liking—positive taste or feeling—for a particular subject is a problem that confronts all teachers in varying degrees. As a general rule teachers should not attempt to teach positive tastes as such.[20] The reason for this is closely related to the nature of positive or negative tastes and how they are formed.[21]

As a concept begins to take form in the mind, the learner simultaneously appraises (either consciously or subconsciously) the effect of this concept upon his own welfare. If the effect is thought advantageous, the learner will have a positive feeling toward the concept. If the effect is thought disadvantageous, a negative feeling will result. The key, then, to the development of positive tastes lies in the teaching of clear concepts from which the learner draws his own conclusions about their value to him. A practical example involving the teaching of positive tastes should illuminate the preceding discussion.

MR. DAYHUFF CREATES A LIKING FOR MATHEMATICS

Andrew Dayhuff was greatly concerned that his eighth-grade general mathematics students should really like the subject. Repeated conversations with students, and parents as well, had indicated the distaste that many had for anything connected with mathematics. During the summer he took a course in educational psychology which was laden with information about how likes and dislikes are formed.

When school began in the autumn, Mr. Dayhuff decided that he would simply avoid the "preachy" sales talks of earlier years. He had repeatedly told his students of the necessity for learning mathematics and how much it would be to their disadvantage if they did not have a thorough mastery of the subject. This year instead, he followed certain steps that he felt were psychologically sound:

1. He made sure that every student understood not only how each problem was worked but why it was worked a given way.

2. No student was permitted to move to more difficult problems without first satisfying the teacher that he understood the essential concepts on which they were based. Care was exercised to make sure that students who were somewhat slow in developing clear mental pictures did not feel social pressure from either the group or the teacher.

3. No attempt was made to sell students on the subject of mathematics.

4. Practical applications were pointed out repeatedly with respect to virtually every problem assigned or discussed.

The actual carrying out of the proposed steps was no simple task; this was especially true of the first two steps. Mr. Dayhuff discovered after the first six weeks of school that, in spite of concerted efforts, the bright students were far ahead of the less gifted ones, creating serious problems in motivation and classroom control.

During the eighth week an anonymous questionnaire administered to students corroborated what he had assumed—that the less gifted

---

[20]Inasmuch as the development of taste has to do with emotional reactions, it should not be confused with analysis or conceptual examination. Nonconceptual feeling reactions (including tastes) are usually classified in the *affective domain*.

[21]See Woodruff, *Basic Concepts of Teaching*, p. 212, for an enumeration of points with respect to the modification of values.

students were liking mathematics, many of them for the first time in their lives. Mr. Dayhuff concluded that it was because they were achieving success; they were really understanding why certain things took place in mathematics.

But what did the questionnaire reveal about the more gifted students? They liked mathematics, yet they wanted to move at a faster pace. Because the class was very large (thirty-eight students) the principal gave the teacher permission to work out a plan for homogeneously grouping the students according to measured mathematical ability and past achievement. The plan was put into effect during the second semester.

Toward the end of the second semester, Mr. Dayhuff again administered an anonymous questionnaire to all students of both classes. The questionnaire was designed to determine to what extent students had developed a positive taste (liking) for mathematics. Responses were most revealing. Among slower students, only three of twenty-two students indicated a dislike for mathematics. Students among the more gifted group responded similarly, with only two indicating a mild dislike.

The proportion of students with a positive taste for a given subject is directly related to the clarity of their concepts and their appraisal of these concepts as having particular personal value.

In the main, the teaching of tastes should be approached indirectly through the teaching of concepts, but under particular circumstances there is psychological justification for teaching tastes directly. In so-called appreciation courses, such as Music Appreciation or Art Appreciation, which occur with relative infrequency in the secondary curriculum, the concern of the course and of the teacher is the creation of a liking (a positive feeling) for course content. Although it is impossible to have a feeling independent of a related concept, the emphasis in these courses would be upon the feeling rather than upon the concept itself.

PROBLEMS FOR STUDY AND DISCUSSION

1. What are the most frequent difficulties in selecting and stating enabling unit objectives? Which of these is most closely related to *your* personal weakness?

2. State a concept that might have been taken from a unit in tenth-grade biology. What makes it a concept? Explain.

3. List the types of enabling objectives in the order of the frequency of their occurrence.

4. Which type of enabling objective is found most frequently in your teaching major? Teaching minor?

5. Following the specific steps listed on page 55, list the concepts you hope to include in a brief four-day unit in your teaching major.

6. Do you feel there is justification for using different levels of memorization? Explain your reasoning.

7. Explain the relationship between comprehension and memorization.

8. Contrast the restricted definition of *skill* found in this chapter with the

definition commonly assigned to it in everyday usage. Give an example of a skill under each definition. Which definition is more helpful in planning a unit? Why?

9. Divide the large skill of *playing baseball* into its major divisions and subdivisions.

10. Define *habit* in your own words. Now see whether you have incorporated in your definition the characteristics of a habit listed on page 57.

11. Can the use of both enabling objectives and behavioral objectives be justified in the same unit? Defend your position.

12. Whose name is most frequently associated with behavioral objectives? Why?

13. A well-stated behavioral goal should contain what three basic elements? Why are all three necessary?

14. Identify and discuss at least five of the basic criticisms of nonbehavioral objectives.

15. Can you identify unanswered questions concerning the use of behavioral objectives in addition to those found on page 61? List them.

16. How do you account for the limited use of behavioral objectives? Explain.

17. Write three carefully structured behavioral objectives taken from a unit in your minor field. Have them criticized by a knowledgeable colleague.

18. What is meant by the following statement? *Enabling objectives, like instructional procedures, serve as a means to the end of changed behavior.*

19. Using two columns, insert in the first column five large enabling objectives and subobjectives taken from a unit in your teaching major. Then insert matching behavioral objectives in the second column.

20. If you felt it necessary to eliminate either enabling objectives or behavioral objectives from a unit, which would you omit? Why?

21. What is the basic question that a planner should ask himself as he ponders which procedure to use? Why?

22. List the particular problems involved in having students utilize learned concepts.

23. Tell exactly how you would teach the following concept in a class in Social Problems: *Racial strife is a nationwide problem in the urban centers of the United States.*

24. What is the best procedure to follow in teaching a positive taste (liking) for history? Explain your point of view.

5. Organizing Activities for Unit Teaching

The premise "goal achievement is of primary concern and procedures are secondary" should not be construed to mean that procedures are unimportant. They are rather the vehicles that enable the student to reach desired educational goals. Activities (procedures) should be so organized within the unit that they perform this function with maximum efficiency.

Conscientious educators have consistently sought a pattern within which unit activities could be meaningfully grouped, and in recent years they have tended to classify such activities under three headings: introductory activities, developmental activities, and concluding activities.[1] Although all unit activities are basically goal-related, such differentiation encourages planners to consider the essential characteristics of each classification.

INTRODUCTORY ACTIVITIES

Introductory activities are designed to *set the stage* so that the learning of unit objectives can move forward with optimum effectiveness.[2] Their common purpose is *not* to make a direct contribution to the achievement of unit goals (although this frequently is one of the side effects of well-planned introductory activities); rather, their main purpose is to expose students to the nature and content of the unit in order to awaken an intense and abiding interest.

Sound Activities

Specifically, introductory activities follow this sequence:[3]

1. A highly motivating, interest-arousing activity related to the unit is conducted in the classroom.[4]
2. A brief but interesting talk indicating the significance of the unit is given by the teacher.
3. The possible objectives of the unit are examined.
   a. Students are exposed to possible objectives previously identified by the teacher.
   b. Students react to the teacher's suggestions and give some of their own.
   c. Under the teacher's direction, students and teacher modify objectives and determine which are worthy of pursuit.

---

[1]Peter F. Oliva, *The Secondary School Today* (New York: World Publishing Company, 1967), pp. 150–172, provides examples of units in which different kinds of activities are employed.

[2]Nathan S. Blount and Herbert J. Klausmeier, *Teaching in the Secondary School*, 3d. ed. (New York: Harper & Row, Publishers, 1968), pp. 231–234, discuss introductory activities and give several practical examples.

[3]See Leonard H. Clark and Irving S. Starr, *Secondary School Methods*, 2d. ed. (New York: The Macmillan Company, 1967), pp. 138–141, for a detailed discussion of how a unit of work is introduced.

One author's concept of how a unit on the American Novel should be initiated is provided by John Walton, *Toward Better Teaching in the Secondary Schools* (Boston: Allyn & Bacon, Inc., 1966), pp. 136–137.

[4]Homer Boroughs, Jr., Clifford D. Foster, and Rufus C. Salyer, Jr., *Introduction to Secondary School Teaching* (New York: The Ronald Press Company, 1964), p. 148, identify some procedures used in arousing student interest in the unit theme.

      d. Students are encouraged to determine how each adopted unit objective is of personal value to themselves.

  4. The possible activities suitable for the achievement of stated objectives are discussed.

      a. Students are exposed to possible activities previously identified by the teacher.

      b. Students react to the teacher's suggestions and make additional ones.[5]

      c. Under the teacher's direction, students and teacher determine which activities are best suited to goal achievement.

      d. The role that each student will play in the stated activities is determined.

An example will illustrate the use of the above sequence in the introductory activities of a biology unit.

MR. SPEARS INTRODUCES A UNIT ON "FAMILIAR PLANTS"

1. Mr. Spears asked the students to gather around his desk so that they could observe with ease the oversized model of two plants—a sunflower and a rose. "After you have examined these models from all angles for at least five minutes," he said, "I want you to list several characteristics that make the sunflower different from the rose."

    a. Afterward, the teacher asked several students to read their lists aloud. Lists were compared, and the teacher wrote the differentiating characteristics on the board.

    b. Class attention was now directed to the large bulletin board that had been prepared during the past two days by three volunteers. It consisted of a variety of large pictures of roses and sunflowers, taken from various angles. Using a pointer, the teacher related the qualities of the sunflower to the characteristics on the chalkboard.

2. During the next few minutes, Mr. Spears explained in very general terms the nature of the total unit, focusing attention on the particular importance of plants to the welfare of man.

3. The understandings and information that the teacher and the students hoped to gain from the unit were discussed.

    a. The teacher wrote on the board the basic concepts he felt should emerge from a careful study of the unit.[6]

    b. Students were encouraged to react openly to the teacher's list. Explanations were made as he sensed student insecurities. Students were now asked to make their own suggestions, and when they differed from those of the teacher, they were listed on the chalkboard.

    c. During a class discussion the essential elements of the student objectives and teacher objectives were combined or resolved. When there were strong differences of opinion, the teacher patiently listened to objections and calmly explained his own point of view.

---

[5]With respect to the selection of procedures, students may be allowed considerable freedom as long as objectives are matched with psychological sound activities.

[6]These concepts were carefully worked out in a preplanned unit after careful consideration of the known composition of the class.

After considerable discussion, the final unit goals, acceptable to all, bore a remarkable similarity to those the teacher had preplanned.

    d. "Now," said Mr. Spears, "will you please list, on a clean sheet of paper to be handed in tomorrow, how the achievement of these goals will be of personal value to you."

4. The students and instructor then talked through the possible activities that might be employed in achieving the adopted goals.

    a. The teacher told of several interesting activities that he felt would lead to an understanding of the concepts (goals) sought.[7] These were listed on the chalkboard.

    b. Students were asked how they felt about the teacher's proposed activities; honest objections were solicited. Students were then encouraged to make their own suggestions. These were written on the chalkboard, and the class compared the two lists.

    c. After much discussion the students and teacher determined which activities would be followed. These activities were listed on the chalkboard and related to specific objectives.

    d. Each student was asked to think through briefly how each activity would personally involve him. There was a general exchange of ideas on this point.

In situations where unit content or procedures are fixed by law or administrative policy, there is little justification for going through the motions of "democratic selection." Furthermore, although a few teachers use democratic classroom procedures extensively, a substantial number of teachers allow students only a limited voice in determining either unit objectives or procedures. The psychological soundness of permitting students a limited voice in such matters had been both questioned and supported by educators holding different philosophical points of view. Many teachers, however, have taught with remarkable effectiveness under circumstances in which content as well as activities have been viewed as the province of the teacher and the school administration.

In the introductory activities of the "sunflower and roses" unit, for instance, one notes a measure of liberality in permitting students a rather strong voice in the determination of objectives and activities. Classroom behavior may be in danger unless the teacher can direct and control this strong student voice.

Where unit objectives and activities have been predetermined, introductory activities may be focused on arousing interest and motivation. This is the case with the introductory activities taken from a unit planned for use in an eighth-grade class in health.

INTRODUCING A UNIT ON "ALCOHOL AND TOBACCO"

1. On the opening day of the unit, students will bring news stories and pictures about alcohol and its use for display on the class bulletin board.

---

[7]Although he did not mention this to the class, the teacher was careful to relate each objective to correct procedures. Within the framework of sound psychological principles, he allowed students considerable freedom in the selection of activities.

    a. The teacher will read and discuss a few of the more relevant and interesting items for class benefit.

    b. After school a committee of students will arrange the clippings neatly on the bulletin board.

2. The day before the opening of the unit, students will be assigned the responsibility for counting the number of pages of advertising on alcohol and tobacco in several popular magazines and the number of television commercials on alcohol and tobacco seen in one evening during specified hours. Reports of individual surveys will be sampled briefly in class and written on the chalkboard.

3. The Blufftown Chief of Police will give a fifteen-minute talk on "My Experiences with People Who Drink and Drive." Students will be encouraged to ask him questions.

4. A ten-minute Coronet film, "Alcohol and Tobacco: What They Do to Our Bodies," will be shown. Students will be told what to look for before the showing, and afterward they will discuss the film briefly.

5. The teacher will write the predetermined course objectives on the board.

    a. The teacher will discuss the objectives and their relationship to individual student needs.

    b. Related general procedures will also be listed and discussed by the teacher.

    c. Students will be encouraged to ask questions concerning objectives, activities, or any other aspect of the unit.

Variation in Planning

There will, of course, be a high degree of variation in the planning of activities. Instructional procedures may be determined by the teacher alone; they may be subject to teacher-student planning at the beginning of the unit; or they may be determined as the unit progresses. This is true for all subject areas and for all teachers.

The introductory activities of the preceding unit on "Alcohol and Tobacco" clearly reflect the work of a conservative planner who feels that his function is to place unit objectives and activities ready-made into the hands of his students. Grambs, Carr, and Fitch, on the other hand, placed considerable emphasis on student participation in unit initiation. Exhibiting their preference for the experience unit, these writers suggest that introductory activities focus on the following key steps:[8]

1. Preliminary realistic diagnosis by the teacher of (a) curriculum requirements and (b) student interests, capacities, needs, and developmental tasks.

2. Tentative selection by the teacher of possible significant problems or areas of learning geared to the preliminary diagnosis.

3. Tentative preplanning by the teacher to clarify for himself the ways in which possible problems and areas may be approached most effectively.

4. Open, direct, and stimulating discussion with the class designed

---

[8]Jean D. Grambs, John C. Carr, and Robert M. Fitch, *Modern Methods in Secondary Education*, 3d. ed. (New York: Holt, Rinehart & Winston, 1970), p. 163.

to involve students in further diagnosis and choice of a problem
or area for further study in planning.

5. Sufficient preliminary exploration with the class to ensure that all
students understand the why and what of the unit enterprise finally
chosen.

6. Use of special materials, films, and activities (such as field trips)
that will both clarify understanding of the unit problem and focus
interest upon it.

7. Development of teacher-student plans adequate for the effective
completion of the unit.

Basic Purposes

Avoiding Stereotypes

In planning introductory activities, the teacher should attempt to find
a fresh, vital approach to the material. The teacher's lecture often fails to
elicit interest because it is part of the everyday instructional diet of
students. For the same reason, discussions in the social studies class
soon become old hat and, consequently, are not useful as introductory
activities.

Relating Objectives to Experiences

Students can understand unit objectives only when these objectives
are related to their own backgrounds. If the students lack essential
experiences, they will fail to catch the excitement the unit affords. If this
is generally true of the students, unit goals more in keeping with their
backgrounds should be sought, or those experiences must be provided as
a part of the unit so that the students will be able to approach the
objectives with understanding.

Stressing Vividness

Introductory activities should be so striking and vivid that the
students will want to identify themselves with the new unit's major
purposes. A boy who has watched a space flight, or a film of it, on
television is likely to be interested in rockets, thrust, space capsules, and
space travel.

Preparing the Room

The physical preparation of the room plays an important part in
beginning the unit because it stimulates student interest. An attractive
bulletin board may start the unit on a positive note; different seating
arrangements are often helpful.

In addition, special equipment and displays possess the potential for
motivating students. Use of individually prepared verb charts for foreign-
language classes, oversized slide rules for mathematics classes, and large
single-purpose maps of troublesome spots on the globe for a social problems class serve this purpose. Even the commonplace chalkboard may be
used in a new way to get the unit off to a good start. In the history or
literature class, for example, a neatly printed time line may be placed at the
top of or immediately above the chalkboard to lend emphasis to the chron-

ology of important events. The hidden chalkboard method, which calls for keeping the written material covered to enhance the surprise effect, can likewise be used to good advantage.

Relating Units to the Overall Plan

At times students fail to see the relationship between the various units of the overall plan. Thus, at the beginning of each new unit, its place in the total sequence of units must be pointed out to the learner so he will realize that the present unit is closely related to the preceding and following units.

Using Diagnostic Devices

The use of diagnostic devices is viewed by certain writers as an essential initiatory procedure.[9] The diagnostic device may take the form of a formal objective test, an informal written test, a class discussion, or even a game. Many subjects and units, however, would suffer through frequent use of diagnostic procedures. In a mathematics class, for example, if the teacher corrects student papers submitted at two- or three-day intervals, he is, in effect, conducting a continuing diagnosis; no further formalization of the diagnostic process is necessary.

Unsound Activities

The use of second best, unstimulating introductory activities gets many units off to a poor start. As a result students approach the study of such units with apathy, and sometimes they feel such units will be unavoidable drudgery. An examination of the unchallenging beginning activities for two units will illustrate this point. The following introductory activities were taken from a three-week unit on "Reptiles," prepared by the teacher of a tenth-grade biology class.

1. On the first day of the unit, the teacher will pass out a sheet of paper listing general activities.

2. Students will be asked to examine newspapers to discover articles of current interest concerning reptiles.

These two activities obviously fall far short of fulfilling the requirements of introductory activities as listed on pages 77–78:

1. There is little about either activity that would tend to stimulate interest, although the assignment to examine newspaper articles concerning reptiles points meekly in this direction. If this assignment were made two days before the beginning of the unit, its timing would be much better.
   a. Asking students to bring articles, pictures, or life specimens of the reptile class on the opening day of the unit would create specific interest.

---

[9]Clark and Starr, *Secondary School Methods*, p. 43, stress the necessity of initial diagnosis to be followed by continuing diagnosis.

      b. A carefully constructed bulletin board prepared by students under the direction of the teacher would elicit desired attention.

      c. A well-chosen, brief film might serve as a useful interest arouser.

  2. No attempt is made to indicate to students the importance of the unit or to relate it to other units in the course.

  3. The important consideration of unit objectives is totally neglected.

      a. The students are given no idea of the direction of the unit.

      b. No mention is made as to how these objectives relate to the personal values of students.

      c. What the students should be able to do as a result of having engaged in the activities of the unit is not clear.

  4. Activities are mentioned in a rather general way without relating them to unit goals or trying to involve the students.

Specific Suggestions

Any writer who makes definite recommendations without an exact knowledge of the details of the situations to which they might apply invites the possibility of considerable error. For this reason many of the recommendations and cautions throughout the book appear in the form of protective generalizations that have wide application. The specific help that such generalizations may provide for the inexperienced teacher, however, may be open to question, since many teachers find it difficult to apply theory to actual classroom situations.

Planners who wish to make the most effective use of introductory activities will find it helpful to examine the suggestions of competent teachers who have identified their own strengths and weaknesses in the use of such activities. A majority of the proposals listed here are positive recommendations, but several cautions are also included.

Recommendations

1. Gear interest-arousing activities to the specific level of the group being taught. It is well to remember that what interests one section of a given grade may not interest another.

2. Avoid the commonplace, the usual, the anticipated activity. This is especially important for those introductory activities that are mainly concerned with arousing interest. If a teacher has a tendency to use one particular procedure more frequently than others, he should avoid its use during the introductory phase of the unit.

3. Efficiently conducted and interpreted diagnostic testing will enable the teacher to plan realistically.

4. Be certain that students understand the objectives of the unit in terms of their individual experiences and backgrounds. Remember that when students are permitted to participate, they tend to establish objectives that they feel are attainable. What they assume to be attainable is related, in turn, to their previous experiences.

5. The extent to which students can be and should be involved in the planning of objectives varies greatly with the composition of the class being taught. Intelligent, well-behaved, mature, and largely self-directive students can be permitted a large measure of choice of objectives under the direction of the teacher. Those students, however, who lack maturity, capacity, self-direction, and the essential elements of classroom control may be incapable of making effective contributions to unit planning. In a large number of cases they will feel more comfortable if the teacher directs them in the identification of objectives.

6. Introductory activities should be so interesting and so attractive to students that they will want to identify themselves with the content of the unit. This identification involves a personal as well as a group acceptance of the values to be derived from the study of the unit.

7. Effective bulletin boards frequently add interest to the start of a unit. Timing, of course, is important in using this method, and the teacher must remember that, more frequently than not, his students should prepare bulletin boards under his supervision.

8. The rearrangement of flexible seating often serves a useful purpose in introducing a new unit.

9. Locating and bringing into the classroom reading materials, teaching devices, and special equipment are frequent steps in the initiation of a new unit. The assembly of maps, charts, and graphs is a basic concern, and the chalkboard is often used in a new and different way to get the unit off to an interesting start.

10. Certain activities may extend through the introductory, developmental, and concluding phases of the unit. When this is the case, they must, of course, be started during the introductory activities.

11. Inject enough detail into the written description of the introductory activities to avoid the need for later expansion or rewriting before the activities can be carried out. A sound question the planner might ask himself is: "Could another equally well-trained teacher read my plans and understand them sufficiently well to be able to carry them out?"

12. By the time the introductory activities are completed, students should sense a strong need for acquiring the content of the unit.

13. By the end of the introductory phase of the unit, students should understand the proposed range and depth of coverage of unit content as well as its significance.[10]

Cautions

1. Don't make the introductory activities too long. Although the proportion of the unit time spent on introductory activities varies a great deal, it generally occupies about one tenth of the total.

2. Don't fail to examine the introductory activities of similar units for ideas that might be incorporated into your own.

---

[10]Principles of value to the teacher in initiating unit activities are listed and discussed by Blount and Klausmeier, *Teaching in the Secondary School*, pp. 231–241.

3. Don't fail to use variety in your introductory activities.

4. Don't fail to differentiate clearly in your own planning between teacher activities, student activities, and activities that involve both.

5. Don't fail to arrange introductory activities in the most helpful sequence.

DEVELOPMENTAL ACTIVITIES

After the introductory activities have been successfully carried out, the teacher must focus class attention on the developmental activities. The major purpose of *developmental activities*[11] is to achieve the goals established during the preplanning and initiatory stages of the unit.[12] As the name implies, their chief concern is with the development of concepts, skills, and habits as well as with the memorization of related terms. So important are these activities that they usually occupy about four fifths of the unit time.

Sound Activities

In well-organized units developmental activities are characterized by the following:[13]

1. The activities reflect the type of enabling objective sought (concept, skill, memorization, or habit). The learning of a concept, for example, requires that the learner proceed through a series of steps quite different from those required for learning a habit.

2. The activities may consist of a wide variety of procedures, but *all* procedures must be appropriate to the type of enabling objective sought.

3. The activities are designed to help the learner achieve objectives through a step-by-step (inductive) progression. Activities, then, are arranged in a sequence that will provide for a gradual unfolding of concepts. Each succeeding experience aimed toward a given goal expands the concept or further develops the skill or habit.

4. Properly organized developmental activities are always directed toward a specific goal. Loosely organized activities reflect the uncertainty of the planner regarding the direction he should take.

5. The activities are planned, for the most part, in considerable

---

[11]Many examples of the use of developmental activities in unit plans are found in Chapter 7.

[12]Boroughs, Foster, and Sayler, *Introduction to Secondary School Teaching*, pp. 153–156, identify and discuss six purposes they feel should be served through developmental activities.

[13]Clark and Starr, *Secondary School Methods*, pp. 468–482, match understandings (concepts) with appropriate developmental activities in an illustrative seventh-grade resources unit, Enjoying animals.

An example of an eleventh-grade teaching unit in American Literature, The American Novel, is provided by John Walton, *Toward Better Teaching in the Secondary Schools*, pp. 134–139.

detail. A thoroughly planned unit often eliminates the necessity for detail in the daily lesson plan. This is particularly important for the beginning teacher.

6. The activities continuously motivate the students. Loss of student interest in the middle of a unit can prevent goal achievement.

7. Teacher ingenuity gives rise to a procedure or a combination of procedures that is, in some respects, different from any previously known to the teacher.

8. Flexibility is built into the timing of developmental activities to accommodate unforeseen accelerations or slowdowns.

The foregoing characteristics can be seen in the following examples of developmental activities.[14]

Developing a Unit on World War I

In an eleventh-grade history unit on "America and World War I," developmental activities were as follows:

Concepts (Objectives) to Be Developed	Activities Related to Objectives[15]
1. Although the United States tried to remain neutral, the country was forced into World War I. a. The United States joined the World Peace Movement. 　1) Roosevelt won the Nobel Peace Prize for mediating international disputes. 　2) Root and Bryan arbitrated many treaties.	The instructor will pick a panel of six students to represent the Hague Permanent Court of Arbitration. The instructor and the panel will decide beforehand which students will play which roles. Four of them will represent nations that have disputes, one will be a justice of the Supreme Court, and the other one will be Roosevelt, Root, or Bryan. The students will act out as best they can how disputes may have been arbitrated by one of the above mentioned Americans. This role playing should take no more than fifteen minutes. The instructor will then discuss the material on the World Peace Movement covered in the text.

[14]See Oliva, *The Secondary School Today*, pp. 151–153, for additional examples of specific developmental activities.

Blount and Klausmeier, *Teaching in the Secondary School*, pp. 242–245, provide examples of developmental activities from a unit of junior high school general science extending over a period of eight weeks.

[15]The column arrangement is used here to dramatize the necessary one-to-one relationship between objectives and activities. As a general rule, the author prefers that the objectives and related activities of the unit be treated in different sections. See the examples provided in Chapter 7.

b. In 1914 war engulfed Europe.
   1) Imperialism, nationalism, militarism, and alliances were the underlying causes of World War I.
   2) War started when Austria-Hungary declared war on Serbia.

Maps will be employed to show the political boundaries as they were in 1914. The teacher will then explain how the Central Powers and Allied Powers developed their alliances.

c. The United States tried to remain neutral.
   1) Wilson urged Americans to be neutral.
   2) The majority of the Americans sided with the Allies.
   3) The British interfered with our trade to Europe.
   4) German submarine warfare and the sinking of the *Lusitania* angered Americans.
   5) Wilson advocated a build-up of arms.
   6) Wilson tried in vain to negotiate a peaceful settlement of the war.

The instructor will discuss with the students the question of neutrality. He will use the example of thugs beating up an innocent victim while a bystander passively watches. The teacher will ask for student feelings on the subject.

d. The United States declared war on the Central Powers.
   1) Early in 1917 the Germans stepped up their submarine warfare.
   2) The Zimmerman Note and the sinking of American ships forced the Americans to change neutralist policies.
   3) On April 6, 1917, war was declared against the Central Powers.

Students will be asked to tell what they know about submarine warfare. The instructor will then explain why German submarine warfare and the Zimmerman Note changed Wilson's outlook on neutrality.

Developing a Unit on Health

The following developmental activities were taken from a unit titled "The Human Body and Digestion" intended for a tenth-grade biology class.

Enabling Objectives (Concepts)	Activities Related to Objectives[16]
3. The body is divided into three cavities.	The teacher will sketch a human figure on the board and ask the class to

---

[16]These developmental activities were taken from the middle of a unit; thus, other activities both preceded and followed those used here for the purpose of illustration.

a. The *cranial* cavity is in the head.
b. The *thoracic* cavity is under the ribs in the chest region.
c. The *abdominal* cavity is under the thoracic cavity; the diaphragm separates the abdominal and thoracic cavities.
4. Humans have an endoskeleton made up of bone and cartilage.

tell where the three body cavities are located. The students probably will not be able to differentiate between the thoracic and abdominal cavities without help.

Using a model of a human skeleton, the teacher will explain the term *endoskeleton* and the three uses of the skeleton.[17]

a. There are 206 bones in the body.

The teacher will ask for two or three guesses as to the number of bones in the skeleton model.

b. There are two types of cartilage in a baby's skeleton.
   1) *Temporary* cartilage makes up a large part of the skeleton.
   2) *Permanent* cartilage makes up the nose, outside ear, larynx, and trachea.

The teacher will point out the model's lack of nose and ears. The students will then be asked to feel their own nose and ears. What they feel is permanent cartilage.

c. The process of the temporary cartilage turning into bone is called *ossification*.
   1) Ossification is the depositing of calcium phosphate and calcium carbonate in the cartilage to make it hard.
   2) Ossification will continue throughout life. This is how broken bones heal.

The teacher will display a large X ray of a baby, pointing out the bone area and the temporary cartilage. He will explain to the class that ossification turns this cartilage into bones and that broken bones grow together in the same way.
The teacher will demonstrate the strength and hardness of an animal bone, formerly broken but properly healed, by hitting it with a rubber mallet.

d. Bones have several different parts.
   1) The outer surface of a bone is the *periosteum*.
   2) The main part of the bone has many channels called *Haversian Canals* that carry nourishment to the bone cells.

Using a cross-sectional chart of a human bone, the teacher will point out the periosteum and the Haversian Canals.

[17]Although all activities opposite the major objectives in step 4 tend to illustrate and clarify the basic concept that "humans have an endoskeleton made up of bone and cartilage," they are not necessarily matched with the sequential listing of subconcepts.

3) In the center of the bone are two types of marrow.
  a) Red marrow produces the red blood cells and also some white ones.
  b) Yellow marrow is usually inactive.

Animal bone marrow obtained through prior arrangement by a student will be shown to the class. The teacher will discuss the differences between red and yellow marrow.

e. The skeleton has three main purposes.
  1) The skeleton supports and forms the body.
  2) The skeleton provides for the attachment of muscles.
  3) The skeleton protects organs.

The teacher will again use the skeleton model to review the purposes of the skeleton.

Recurring Activities

In order to avoid relisting activities that are repeated throughout the unit, many planners have found that it saves time to identify and list such procedures under a subheading within the general category of developmental activities. The types of activities that lend themselves to this treatment are illustrated in the "Recurring Activities" of a United States history unit:

1. Each week the instructor will give brief quizzes at the beginning of three of the five class periods. They will cover the five most important concepts treated by the textbook material assigned for that day. Students will correct their own papers, and the instructor will discuss any questions that may arise during the correction period. Tests will then be collected so that the instructor can record the grades.

2. Each week three new volunteers will be asked to plan and assemble, under teacher supervision, a bulletin-board display related to the contents of the material to be covered in class during the week. Basic planning and related work will be done the week before the bulletin board is displayed. The display will be seen by class members on the first day of the unit.

3. On the days when quizzes are not given, students will give short oral reports during the first five minutes of the class. These spontaneous, informal reports will be related to outside reading for the preceding or current day. Students will be encouraged to read articles from periodicals and books other than the text.

4. With one or two exceptions, the last seven minutes of the class period will be devoted to a spirited teacher-led discussion related to the assignment for the following day.

5. During the course of the school year each student will have a chance to give a fifteen-minute report during one of the class periods. One such report will be given during this unit.

Unsound Activities

Developmental activities that are not effective frequently have one or more of the following characteristics:

1. They show little imagination on the part of the planner.
2. They lack a description of specific steps to be taken.
3. They are limited to two or three overused procedures.
4. They do not provide for a gradual unfolding of concepts.
5. They do not devote time to an activity in proportion to the benefit to be derived from it.
6. They are not practical for the class and the circumstances in which the activities must take place.
7. They do not maintain an appropriate balance among oral, written, and reading assignments; between first-hand and vicarious experiences; between long-range and short-range projects; between difficult and easy assignments; between teacher-centered and student-centered activities; and between individual and group work.
8. They fail to recognize the differentiation in assignment and teaching techniques needed to accommodate individual differences in students.
9. They bear little or no relationship to unit objectives.

Some of these deficiencies can be observed in the following brief excerpt taken from the developmental activities of a unit on "Speaking in Public":

Concepts (Objectives) to Be Developed	Activities Related to Objectives
1. An effective speaker captures his audience and keeps its interest.	Students will go over their speeches and cut out unnecessary sentences. The teacher will impress upon the class the idea that nothing ruins a speech more easily than a weak ending. Students will be encouraged to keep their voices loud and clear.

Specific Suggestions

A number of specific recommendations may help the planner in selecting developmental activities.[18] These activities should:

1. Be appropriate to the maturity of the class for which they are intended.
2. Keep students aware of what has been accomplished and what remains to be done.

---

[18]Leonard H. Clark, *Strategies and Tactics in Secondary School* (New York: The Macmillan Company, 1968), Part II, pp. 143–436, presents the challenging articles of a wide range of professionals addressing themselves to classroom strategies.

3. Be written out in considerable detail.

4. Be grouped, where practical, so that the approximate number of activities to be completed during a given day can be ascertained.

5. Indicate which activities are to be carried out by the teacher, which are to be the responsibility of the student, and which are to be joint responsibilities.

6. Conform to the steps appropriate to teaching the particular kind of enabling objective—concept, skill, memorization, and habit.

7. Be timed realistically in consideration of the total time available to the unit and of the value to be derived from a given activity.

8. Be described in terms of specific things to be done.

9. Keep the relationship between unit activities and unit objectives clearly established in the minds of students.

10. Be educationally sound as well as interesting.

11. Describe the preparation of the students or teacher essential to insuring the success of the activity.

12. Be flexible enough to accommodate unforeseen accelerations or slowdowns.

Certain suggestions with respect to the use of developmental activities apply to only a restricted number of units. A wide range of suggestions and possible activities should be considered, however, before the final selection is made. The unit planner might well ask himself these questions:

1. Have I provided for lengthy study periods where desirable?

2. Have I provided for appropriate use of group work?

3. After examining the results of the pretest, are students given a study guide to help them overcome deficiencies discovered through this test?

4. How desirable is it to use a wide range of procedures in this particular unit?

5. Does the unit provide for an appropriate amount of pupil activity?

6. Have I employed first-hand experiences where desirable?

7. When films, resource speakers, and special presentations are to be used in class, have I accurately indicated the time involved?

8. Have I made appropriate use of activities involving physical movement?

9. Have I planned unusual activities where they serve the best psychological and educational purposes?

10. Have I provided for guided self-activity?[19]

11. Have I planned a range of interrelated activities encouraging students to make continuous progress through the use of individualized procedures?

---

[19]Examples of the use of developmental activities in well-organized unit plans are found in Chapter 7.

CONCLUDING ACTIVITIES

Concluding activities are primarily designed to clinch basic unit concepts and skills. More frequently than not this is accomplished through procedures involving practical applications of what has been learned.[20] Concluding activities occupy roughly one tenth of the time devoted to the unit. However, the proportion of time devoted to specific kinds of activities will vary greatly depending on the nature of the particular unit.

Sound Activities

Some commonly used concluding activities are:

1. Papers, themes, or articles
2. Exhibits of items made by students
3. Practical problems that call for the application of several unit concepts
4. Application of newly acquired unit generalizations to new situations
5. Written or oral summaries of the unit by the students or the teacher
6. A teacher-conducted review of basic concepts and important relationships developed during the unit
7. A class project extending throughout the total unit[21]
8. Field trips
9. Unit examination
10. Movies
11. Resource speakers

These basic concluding activities may, of course, be modified, expanded, or combined for most effective use.

During the concluding (culminating) stage of the unit, activities should compel the students to interrelate the specific concepts they have acquired. As a result, concepts should be expanded, their meanings enlarged and stabilized. This, in turn, necessitates the use of procedures that will encourage this expansion of meaning. Concluding activities should effect a pulling-together of loose ends. Only a limited number of activities are suited to this task.

---

[20]Unit planners who wish to emphasize behavioral objectives will find that they tend to duplicate concluding activities. In order to avoid this duplication, planners must carefully analyze the function of each concluding activity and each behavioral objective, placing them in the proper category. Activities concerned with practical applications, testing, or student summaries may be assigned to the behavioral objective category; however, the teacher's summary, field trips, group discussions, and movies may be logically classed as concluding activities. Unwarranted and unnecessary duplication in planning gives evidence of loose thinking and adds to the teacher's confusion.

[21]Occasionally an instructor selects a learning activity that extends throughout the introductory, developmental, and concluding phases of the unit. Such an activity may, therefore, be classified as belonging to any one or all three of the categories.

A ninth-grade general science unit proposes the use of a limited number of concluding activities over a three-day period.[22]

CONCLUDING A UNIT ON "THE AIR OF THE EARTH"

1. The students will make a field trip to the local weather bureau.
   a. The trip will be scheduled for the third period and will extend into a portion of the lunch period.
   b. Students will be asked to list questions and also to be on the lookout for examples or evidence of material already studied.
   c. Prior arrangements will be made so that students can observe a weather map being constructed.
   d. Students will hear a weather report broadcast through the local radio station by Civil Aeronautics Administration personnel. Students have been listening to this daily broadcast for the past month.
   e. Before entering the bus for the fifteen-minute return trip, students will be handed a short list of questions designed to encourage a synthesis of what they have just seen and to encourage a review for the unit test.
2. Blank weather maps will be distributed to the members of the class.
   a. Students will be asked to place on the map information taken from previously monitored weather broadcasts and from information obtained from the local weather station.
   b. After plotting this information in code symbols, the students will draw the isobars and thermobars as best they can.
   c. They will be asked to study the maps they have drawn. On the basis of their drawings and their experience with local weather, they will be asked to make a forecast for the next day to predict what the weather instruments will indicate.
3. A final unit examination consisting of objective questions will be given.
   a. When the examination papers have been turned in, the teacher will distribute fresh copies of the same examination.
   b. Using this test as a guide, the teacher will give the correct responses and will answer any student questions concerning the test.[23]

Assuming that these activities are well conducted, one can easily visualize their clinching effect on unit concepts. Furthermore, such activities encourage the students to interrelate concepts and apply them in a meaningful situation.

During the concluding activities of a four-week unit in a twelfth-

---

[22]Concluding activities, like developmental activities, must be directed toward goal achievement. Because of their nature, however, they are frequently concerned with an expansion and reinforcement of the overall unit concept. For this reason no attempt has been made to establish a one-to-one relationship between each activity and its related goal. In their composite, concluding activities frequently represent the expected terminal behavior of students and—if successfully completed—indicate the achievement of behavioral objectives.

[23]With minor modifications, the achievement (or lack of achievement) of behavioral objectives for the unit on weather can be illustrated through steps two and three.

grade homemaking class, the teacher emphasized the clinching of concepts through practical application. Four days were devoted to this phase of the unit.

CONCLUDING A CHILD-CARE UNIT

1. Students will take an eighty-minute field trip to the children's ward of the general hospital.
   a. Arrangements will be made to make the visit immediately following school. The girls can walk the two blocks to the hospital.
   b. The head nurse will conduct a tour of the ward, explaining the problems of child care and illustrating with specific children.
   c. Each student will prepare ahead of time three practical and relevant questions that she hopes to ask the nurse if time permits.
2. Students will observe for two hours in a day nursery where the children of working mothers are cared for.
   a. Class members will identify prior to the visit twelve specific points to look for.
   b. A short paper on their observations will be prepared for the next day.
3. Under the direction of the teacher, class members will organize and conduct a nursery class for two hours at the close of one school day.
   a. Children of various ages (including siblings) will be brought in.
   b. Girls will be responsible for conducting appropriate play activities for a child who is not of their own family.
   c. Experiences will be discussed in class on the following day.
4. At the beginning of the unit, each girl will be assigned to make a case study of one child.
   a. Specific information will be assembled and recorded on forms prescribed by the teacher.
   b. The case study will be culminated and handed in during the concluding phase of the unit.

Unsound Activities

Students are generally unaware that they have moved from the developmental to the concluding phase of the unit. There is little reason for concern with this lack of pupil sophistication, but when the teacher is unaware of the need for culminating, clinching activities, students may be denied a desirable summarizing experience. This is what happened during the final two days of a unit on the "Biology of Heredity."

MR. BLOCKER CONDUCTS A UNIT ON BIOLOGY

Mr. Blocker's class proceeded as usual. For the first fifteen minutes he lectured on the assignment the students were supposed to have read the previous evening, and for the next fifteen minutes he discussed certain facts that he said were contained in the assignment for tomorrow. The last twenty minutes of the period were devoted to a study period.

During the last two days of the unit the teacher talked about (a) the discovery of fossils that trace genetic lineage to present-day species, (b) how to trace genetic lineage by various means, (c) evidence that supports the doctrine of evolution, and (d) how present-day embryos are related to ancient embryonic stages. Believing in rigid conformity to a time schedule, he terminated the unit on Friday, March 14, with another short lecture and an equally brief test on the assignments of the past three days.

Mr. Blocker was quite unaware that the identification and use of appropriate concluding activities would have added interest, motivation, and sound learning to his well-entrenched routine. He might have considered any of the following possibilities: a carefully selected motion picture, a resource person (probably the geneticist from the local college), a series of study questions aimed at integrating unit content, brief summarizing reports by students, or a carefully prepared unit examination quite different from his typical quiz.

Specific Suggestions

Careful consideration of these recommendations should reward the planner with improved teaching techniques and provide the student with more interesting experiences.[24]

1. Concluding activities, like introductory activities, should be of great interest to students.

2. They should consist of procedures that are markedly different from those to which the students have been exposed during the body of the unit.

3. Where possible, the students should in some way be brought into direct contact with the referent of the concept.

4. Students should be given the opportunity to make practical applications of the concepts learned.

5. Frequently students should be strongly involved in concluding activities through the use of brief reports, panel discussions, teacher-led discussions, and written exercises.

6. Important relationships between the basic concepts of the unit should be emphasized through new procedures.

7. As a general rule, concluding activities should consist of a range of activities, rather than merely one or two. Time limitations, however, may serve as a restriction.

8. Concluding activities that have been preplanned should be reevaluated, with student assistance, during the introductory phase of the unit.

---

[24]Additional suggestions related to concluding activities may be derived from an examination of questions 62–73 of Appendix A.

PROBLEMS FOR STUDY AND DISCUSSION

1. What is the basic reason for dividing unit activities into three categories?

2. Just how important to the success of the unit is the planning of activities? Explain your point of view.

3. List six specific purposes of introductory activities.

4. What is meant by the *preplanning* of a unit? Are there ever situations that do not involve preplanning? Explain.

5. In which phase of unit planning would you permit the most student participation: in the planning of objectives or in the planning of activities? Why?

6. Which types of introductory activities (field trip, resource speaker, movie, etc.) do you consider best suited to initiating a unit? List four activities in the order of their appropriateness to your teaching major. Why do you consider them particularly well suited?

7. Assumption: As an experienced teacher you have been assigned the responsibility of working with a new teacher in your subject-matter major. Because her greatest weakness lies in unit planning, you have decided to list several specific cautions about the planning of introductory activities. Which eight cautions would you list?

8. Should the developmental activity selected reflect the type of objective sought more accurately than the introductory activity? Explain your point of view.

9. Explain inductive progression and give one example taken from your minor field.

10. Give an example of developmental activities taken from your teaching major in which essential detail is lacking.

11. How far should the teacher go in attempting to provide varied activities? Discuss this within a psychological framework.

12. Give five examples of radically different but educationally sound procedures that you could use as developmental activities in teaching a unit in your minor field.

13. What is the purpose of listing recurring developmental activities separately? Give two examples of recurring activities not mentioned in this chapter.

14. Which unsound developmental activities are most likely to be used in your teaching field? Name three.

15. List five developmental activities that you would consider impractical for teaching students of a given grade in your subject-matter specialty.

16. According to this chapter, what is the fundamental purpose of concluding activities? Do you agree or disagree? Why?

17. List at least ten concluding activities that you might use successfully in teaching students of a specified grade in your teaching major.

18. List five concluding activities that would be appropriate in some other subject-matter areas but not in your teaching major or minor.

19. If you wish to emphasize behavioral objectives as described on pages 59 through 64, should you eliminate your concluding activities? Explain.

20. How would you go about selecting a concluding activity quite different from the activities you employed during the earlier sections of the unit? Explain.

21. Why is it better to involve students strongly in concluding activities rather than in developmental activities?

6. *Materials, Resources, and Evaluation in Unit Teaching*

In the preparation of the unit the planner focuses his initial attention on unit goals. The function of teaching materials and evaluation is the same as that of general procedures—assisting in efficient movement toward these desired goals. In reality the employment of materials, resources, and evaluation involves specific procedures (activities), and their use should be included in the description of unit activities.[1]

---

[1]Chapter 7 contains descriptions of unit activities in which teaching materials and evaluation procedures are combined in sequential order with other activities.

Because of the detail involved in the description of activities, many planners include only a token indication of the use of teaching materials and evaluation devices. When the written plans are translated into actual teaching-learning activities, however, teachers often discover that the materials and resources as well as the evaluation procedures have been neither procured nor adequately accounted for. In order to avoid this, several writers have suggested the use of major unit headings such as "Materials and Resources" and "Evaluation Procedures," under which proper lists can be compiled during the planning stage. In order to relate these two headings to the other unit headings, it is desirable to recall the five basic unit divisions that demand the planner's attention:

   I. Basic Information
  II. Objectives
 III. Activities
  IV. Material and Resources
   V. Evaluation Procedures

This chapter will be concerned with the last two divisions.

MATERIALS AND RESOURCES

In order to make varied, interesting, and sound use of teaching materials and resources, teachers must understand their purposes, how they are classified, how they can be used most advantageously in teaching a specific subject, and how mistakes in their use can be avoided. Furthermore, teachers need to have a working acquaintance with essential principles related to the selection and use of materials and resources.

Purpose of Materials and Resources

MR. WANDLESS SHOWS A MOVIE

When the eighth-grade United States history class saw that the movie projector was in place and that the windows were darkened, they knew from past experience that the time for fun had arrived. The film and the misbehavior began together. Although the students looked at the picture most of the time, their viewing had little educational direction. By the time it was over, Mr. Wandless wondered whether the film had served any useful purpose at all.

MRS. STRANG ENCOURAGES DIFFICULT READING

Mrs. Strang believed that students should read a wide range of difficult materials not required by most teachers of tenth-grade English. She reasoned that the students were living in a highly competitive age in which knowledge of the technical and the difficult was essential to progress. She felt that students should encounter difficult reading in the classroom, and she thus gave little attention to differentiating instruction.

A RESOURCE SPEAKER ENCOUNTERS RUDENESS

Terry Bacon, a forest ranger, was invited to talk to Mrs. Walker's tenth-grade biology class because he had a state-wide reputation for being able to communicate his vast knowledge about snakes to adolescent groups. Unfortunately his talk had been scheduled for the last twenty minutes of the period, just before the emotion-laden pep assembly that was to herald the football game with rival Southwest High School. Students were disinterested, unruly, and rude, and Mr. Bacon felt that he had lost his audience for the first time in several years.

The preceding examples tend to point up the basic problems of using teaching materials and resource persons in achieving unit goals. It is not sufficient that the materials and devices selected are potentially interesting to students; such materials and devices must move the students in the direction dictated by the established objectives. Furthermore, when such materials are employed, conditions must be controlled in order to encourage optimum learning.

Special teaching materials and resources have the potential of making both teaching and learning more interesting; however, this potential is often unfulfilled. Unless the teacher makes a careful appraisal of how the material or resource is to be used and of its effect upon pupil learning, he courts the danger of selecting an attractive activity for the sake of the activity alone.

Classification of Materials and Resources

The basic reason for the classification of teaching materials and resources is to help the unit planner quickly examine a range of possibilities in any one of several categories.[2] The classification is not intended to be inclusive, but it should provide help in identifying aids most suitable for use in a specific classroom situation.

Audio Aids

The teacher who uses his *voice* effectively has a marked advantage over his colleague who has never considered the voice an aid to learning. Variations in voice may be used to help create the excitement that results in student motivation, to arrest budding misbehavior, to provide the drama that creates a deep impression, to relieve student tensions, and to improve teacher-student relations.

---

[2]Nathan S. Blount and Herbert J. Klausmeier, *Teaching in the Secondary School*, 3d. ed. (New York: Harper & Row, Publishers, 1968), chapter 10, discuss how a range of audio-visual materials and devices may be used most effectively.

A second audio aid, the *record player*, provides recorded music, drama, or speech of high quality. Too often beginning as well as seasoned teachers are unaware of the large number of discs currently available for teaching purposes. There are any number of well-organized catalogs listing current audio-visual materials.[3] In every secondary school such catalogs should not only be made available but should be located so that their use is encouraged.

Because of extreme flexibility in the ways it can be used, the *tape recorder* has become one of the most popular teaching aids. It affords student or teacher the opportunity to record any sound that will serve an instructional purpose. This may be the recorded message of a public figure, the roar of a space vehicle streaking skyward, the talk of the high-school principal, or the first oral efforts of a beginning foreign-language student.

Visual Aids

Because 80 percent of the learner's readily recalled information is the result of his visual perception,[4] the unit planner must give particular attention to those devices that promote such perception. The student is constantly observing, both inside and outside the classroom. Thus it is the teacher's responsibility to direct his observation so that it best serves the purposes of instruction.

Technically speaking, everything the learner views may be classed as a potential visual aid to learning; however, common usage has restricted the meaning. Visual aids most frequently used in the classroom setting include the following:

The teacher	Projected pictures	Charts
Television	Movies	Maps
Models	Filmstrips	Relics
Chalkboard	Slides	Exhibits
Bulletin board	Microprojections	Specimens
Still pictures	Overhead projections	Collections

The teacher as a visual aid. The teacher should be consistently aware of the need for projecting the best possible teacher image to his students. This has strong implications for teaching techniques, teacher-student

[3]Catalogs listing materials available in school, district, or regional repositories should prove to be of immediate help. Free and inexpensive teaching-material catalogs that serve a nationwide range of users can also prove to be most rewarding. For this information see Walter A. Wittich, *Educators' Guide to Free Tapes, Scripts, and Transcriptions*, (Randolph, Wisconsin: Educators' Progress Service, 1969), and John W. Diffor and Mary F. Horkheimer, *Educators' Guide to Free Films* (Randolph, Wisconsin: Educators' Progress Service, 1969).

Free and Inexpensive Learning Materials (Nashville: George Peabody College for Teachers, Division of Surveys and Field Services), issued on an annual basis, provides suggestions for the use of many materials in a wide range of subjects.

[4]A. J. Foy Cross and Irene F. Cypher, *Audio-Visual Education* (New York: Thomas Y. Crowell Company, 1961), p. 6.

relationships, personality projection, and personal dress. The teaching unit can and will be no better than the teacher as an organizer of learning activities will permit it to be.

Projections. Assuming that students have the desired readiness, a well-chosen motion picture may provide a good approximation of first-hand contact with the referent. The use of projected movies, filmstrips, and slides, however, has become so firmly established in the thinking of the teacher-planner that it may tend to preclude the use of other worthwhile aids. Although their use often represents sound and desirable teaching, pictures serve only as substitutes for the real thing.

Models. Accurate models can, in certain situations, prove superior to the actual referent in providing vivid mental pictures. This is true, for example, of take-apart models of the inner ear or of the visceral organs of the body. If the average secondary-school pupil could have the first-hand experience of an astronaut in observing the Florida coastline, the vividness of such an experience would make the examination of a coastal relief map anticlimactic. However, because it is impossible to provide the first-hand experience, the teacher should make the substitute experiences as vivid as possible.

Overhead projector. Recent improvements in the quality of the overhead projector and the reduction in its cost have encouraged use of transparencies. Acetate transparencies can be prepared from the printed or typewritten page and from photographs or drawings. They can then be projected in a room of normal illumination. By means of transparent cell overlays, progressive sequences can be portrayed by superimposing one cell upon another. For example, a series of cells could be mounted for instructional use in a bookkeeping class. The first cell may contain a blank ledger sheet, the second cell a simple entry, and the third cell a more complicated entry. Each cell may be shown separately or in combination with others according to the purpose of instruction.

Television. Television has opened up a ready avenue of meaningful, interesting experiences that can be used to enrich unit teaching.[5] Television has application to virtually every secondary-school subject. Commercial television stations, educational stations with state-wide coverage, and closed-circuit stations with school-district coverage now provide a range of educational viewing from which wise planners may select those programs that best meet their objectives. Further, gradual reduction in the cost of television equipment—cameras, recorders, and monitors has encouraged forward-looking school districts to purchase such equipment for

---

[5]Marvin D. Alcorn, James S. Kinder, and Jim R. Schunert, *Better Teaching in Secondary Schools*, 3d. ed. (New York: Holt, Rinehart & Winston, Inc., 1970), pp. 280–289, identify the current growth and status of educational television.

closed-circuit use within individual classrooms. Thus by means of video tape, students may critically review a report they have completed a short time before.

For several years experiments were conducted in which closed-circuit educational programs were produced and simultaneously telecast to several states.[6] Because these programs were produced exclusively for classroom use, they were particularly adapted to the needs of students of a given age level and subject. Commercial stations, too, are anxious to provide teachers with suggested viewing programs that are correlated with content areas. The development of video tapes has encouraged actual classroom use of recorded programs that originate during out-of-school hours.

Inept use of visual aids. Unit teaching is limited to some extent by the inept or bungling use of certain visual aids. Misuse of the chalkboard is a prime example of such bungling. A substantial number of teachers use the board only when they are forced to; it never becomes a part of their calculated plan for teaching. Another example of unsuitable use of a visual aid involves the motion picture. Often the movie is shown without the necessary preview and identification of major points to be looked for. More often, class time is wasted while the mechanics of machine operation are solved.

Charts used in the classroom at times not only reflect poor workmanship but, worse still, are inaccurate. Occasionally maps are so small that they are not properly visible from the back of the room, or they are so full of detail that they are confusing. Specimens or collections may be so worn and aged that they actually convey incorrect impressions.

Audio-Visual Aids

A large proportion of helpful teaching devices are properly classified as both auditory and visual aids.[7] This is true of television, of the motion picture with sound track, and of the teacher himself. Many visual aids (models, charts, filmstrips, collections, and cell overlays) become excellent audio-visual aids when used by a skilled teacher who provides the sound track that brings the aids to life and illuminates their meaning. Conversely, many ingenious teachers have combined auditory aids with visual materials to effect a superior teaching situation. This is the case where the salient points from a tape-recorded message are mimeographed for the student to assist him in learning as he listens.

---

[6]The ambitious and complicated nature of the Midwest Program on Airborne Television Instruction (MPATI) is discussed by James W. Brown, Richard B. Lewis, and Fred F. Harcleroad, AV Instruction: *Media and Methods*, 3d. ed. (New York: McGraw-Hill Book Company, 1969), pp. 305–307.

[7]Robert W. Richey, *Planning for Teaching: An Introduction to Education*, 4th ed. (New York: McGraw-Hill Book Company, 1968), pp. 159–160, discusses the most important reasons for using audio-visual aids.

Printed Materials

Printed materials comprise the largest proportion of all teaching aids. Not only is there a wide range of textual materials, but supplementary materials are available through periodicals and newspapers. In order to make a wise choice, the teacher must understand these basic materials and their potential for effective teaching and learning and must keep up with the publication of new materials.

The textbook. The most frequently used of all printed educational materials is the textbook.[8] In the hands of a knowledgeable practitioner, the textbook becomes *one of many* aids to assist the student in acquiring clear concepts of subject matter. It is, perhaps, the student's best single academic friend, if he is taught how to use it correctly. Moreover, bright, self-directive students have often been known to move satisfactorily through the content of a course without the aid of a teacher by careful reading of a traditional or programmed textbook.

Textbook teaching has provided an escape hatch for the teacher who is unprepared, incompetent, overloaded with work, or instructing outside his own field of specialization.

Conscientious teachers must see that the textbook is not abused.[9] Improper use of the textbook involves using a text with a vocabulary level either too high or too low for the students; lack of instruction in how the text may best serve the student's purposes; unrealistic assignments with respect to length and difficulty; common assignments in which slow readers are expected to read as rapidly or with as much comprehension as fast readers; chapter-by-chapter treatment of course content where it is often assumed that all students read thoroughly and moderately well; and making a course so textbook-centered that the text, rather than the teacher, gives major direction to classroom activity.

Nontextbook materials. Other suitable types of course-related reading materials, when combined with the correct use of the text, can provide a richness in learning experiences that can be gained in no other way.[10] The general kinds of printed or duplicated materials useful in all areas are specific subject-oriented weekly newspapers; daily newspapers; encyclopedias and special reference books; workbooks; duplicated materials to be handed out; teacher-prepared study guides; pamphlets; and articles in popular and professional magazines. Each properly prepared unit will not only identify accurately the supplementary reading materials to be used but will indicate exactly how such materials fit into the sequence of learning activities.

---

[8]For a more complete discussion of the textbook, see Chapter 10, pp. 191–194.

[9]Homer C. Rose, *The Instructor and His Job* (Chicago: American Technical Society, 1966), pp. 136–137, provides a useful discussion of the selection and use of the textbook.

[10]Leonard H. Clark and Irving S. Starr, *Secondary School Teaching Methods*, 2d. ed. (New York: Macmillan Company, 1967), pp. 319–324, provide a useful discussion on sources of audiovisual materials including a section on homemade visual aids.

Special Aids

Although some aids must be made (or somehow procured) well in advance of their use, they often provide students with a class-related, after-school activity that is interesting as well as educational. Students who are otherwise difficult to motivate may take an active interest in this type of activity.

MRS. OLDS ACQUIRES A SHAKESPEAREAN STAGE

Mrs. Olds, a tenth-grade English teacher, found that it was almost impossible for her to teach Shakespeare properly without establishing a mental image of a Shakespearean stage for her students. Her drawings on the board and her verbal accounts proved relatively fruitless. Seizing the initiative, she asked two boys in the class who were gifted in woodwork but somewhat limited in English literature if they were interested in making a large but portable model of a Shakespearean stage. They were.

After explaining her need to the woodshop teacher, she solicited his advice and help. With Mrs. Olds serving as a consultant and with the help of the shop teacher, the boys produced a lifelike replica of the Globe Theatre, with a detachable roof, during a two-week period. Mrs. Olds no longer found it difficult to give students a meaningful picture of the original settings of Shakespearean plays.

Community Resources

Almost every community with a population of a thousand or more has many individuals, industries, or business concerns whose services may be marshaled free of charge in the interest of more effective unit teaching.[11] Teachers of specific subjects would do well to establish a file of resource persons and establishments. Such a file can be refined and expanded with each successive teaching of a given unit.

Each subject area requires a somewhat different use of individuals and establishments within a community. In searching for these community resources, teachers find it profitable to have students make suggestions that may then be incorporated into a file. The final selection of the resource person or of a field trip should be made by the teacher.

Customarily such files need not be related to a specific unit. If they are set up on a course-wide basis, they tend to be more practical. Although teaching as many as three different courses, some teachers have found it more feasible to include all resource persons in a single file. How this is done is largely a matter of individual teacher preference.

---

[11]William R. Lueck, Elwood G. Campbell, Leo E. Eastman, Charles W. Edwards, Clayton F. Thomas, and William D. Zeller, *Effective Secondary Education* (Minneapolis: Burgess Publishing Co., 1966), pp. 238–250, provide a comprehensive chapter treatment on using the community to serve instructional purposes.

Principles Related to the Selection of Materials and Resources

Effective selection and use of teaching materials and resources are enhanced by a working knowledge of relevant teaching principles.[12]

1. The initial learning of concepts is best accomplished by exposing the learner to the concrete referent, the actual thing for which the concept stands.

2. When a concrete referent cannot be used, the teaching of concepts is best accomplished by employing an aid that most closely approximates the referent of the concept. Exceptions to this statement are microscopic projections, oversized models of objects otherwise difficult to observe, slow-motion movies, and certain kinds of maps.

3. The best aids are those that promote taking the steps appropriate to the type of objective sought.

4. Since both efficient memorization and the efficient learning of motor skills require that concepts be acquired before drill or practice is undertaken, the teacher should employ materials and resources that are appropriate to the teaching of the underlying concepts.

5. When a concept of the coordination of movements in a skill is to be taught, a movie in slow motion frequently serves best.

6. In their beginning stages, habits are at the conscious level and thus are conceptual in nature. For this reason, the aids used for the teaching of habits should be appropriate for the teaching of concepts.

7. The use of printed material will only be meaningful to the extent that it recalls concepts associated with printed words.

Use of Aids in Teaching Specific Subjects

Vivid Referents for Concepts

In determining what aids are best suited to the teaching of a biology unit on "Reproductive Organs in Flowers," the planner must first ask himself what kinds of objectives are sought. In this case it can be assumed that the unit is almost totally concerned with the teaching of concepts and related names. The planner must then review the specific steps for teaching concepts. They are learned by (a) showing the referent of the concept or a facsimile, (b) telling about the referent, (c) memorizing related terms, and (d) using the concept in an applied situation.

The best aid in this situation would probably be the one that portrays most vividly the reproductive organs of flowers. A close-up motion picture in color would be very helpful because it provides an accurate approximation of the referent. This provides visual contact only, however, and always as seen by the eye of the camera. Because of size and the possibility of observation from any angle, a large, accurate plant model would serve as the best aid if used in conjunction with actual living flowers.

---

[12]A review of Chapter 1, pp. 8–10, will provide a broad basis for the understanding of principles related to the selection and use of teaching aids.

When a teacher is concerned with teaching concepts, he should use those aids that represent the referent itself or that are as similar to the referent as possible. In the descending order of their appropriateness, these aids are the referent itself, models, motion pictures, still pictures, and oral or written accounts.

If one can be sure that concepts are sufficiently vivid to elicit an accurate recall when the word (symbol) standing for the concept is seen in printed form, printed materials may then be used effectively as aids to instruction. (Seeing the printed word *statue*, for example, should give rise to a *mental picture* of a statue.) Where new concepts are being presented, however, the showing of the referent or a reasonable facsimile is highly desirable. The more abstract the content, the more difficult it becomes to portray such concepts through the use of concrete referents. This accounts for much of the difficulty involved in teaching abstractions.

Demonstration as an Aid

In teaching a skill subject, such as boys' physical education, efficient learning is promoted when the student acquires a clear concept of how a given skill is performed before he undertakes it. If, for example, he is concerned with learning to broad jump, the boy must first acquire a meaningful picture of the correct running approach and jumping form. The aid best suited for this purpose is a demonstration by someone who uses correct form. A motion picture would also serve as an effective aid, although it may not provide the same sensory impact as an actual demonstration. In some cases, a motion picture in slow motion has definite advantages over a demonstration.

Aids Clarify Concepts

Aids, then, serve the purpose of creating and clarifying concepts. They provide no help in the practice of skills except as they help improve the mental pictures that are basic to performance. This is true of typing, vocal production, sewing, or playing an instrument. Once the basic concepts have been acquired, the symbols (words) that stand for these concepts may be used in printed or spoken form to further clarify the concepts. Meaningful memorization, therefore, must first focus attention on the concept to which the symbol refers.

Need for a Comprehensive List

Unit planners will be able to save considerable time and plan with greater efficiency if they have access to a well-organized, comprehensive listing of materials and resources that are specifically related to the subject being taught.[13] Suggested lists may be readily compiled through the examination of a number of successful units in the subject area.

---

[13] Howard T. Batchelder, Maurice McGlasson, and Raleigh Schorling, *Student Teaching in Secondary Schools*, 4th ed. (New York: McGraw-Hill Book Company, 1964), p. 229, list a range of audio-visual aids. Use of extensive lists such as this one should prevent overlooking certain aids that might be particularly helpful.

Recommendations

Specific suggestions with respect to the identification, procurement, and use of aids may prove of great help to the beginning teacher. The following is a list of recommendations that have proven to be of practical benefit. Teachers should:

1. Use printed (symbolic) materials only after students have acquired the concepts that will make such materials meaningful; use time-consuming first-hand experiences only when students lack readiness for the use of books and printed materials; use models in preference to pictures or verbal materials where the experience of pupils makes this desirable; bring the concrete referent into the classroom if it is readily available and will serve a useful purpose; use audio or visual materials to help students understand abstract relationships.

2. Scan the range of possible aids before making a selection, and consider the teacher as only one of many possible audio-visual aids.

3. Select for class use an appropriate text in view of educational psychology, average reading level of students, interesting presentation, illustrations, and format; make sound use of encyclopedias and other specific references; provide students with a variety of nontextbook reading materials when such materials will assist in the acquisition of desired concepts; determine the extent to which workbooks and programed textbooks can serve a useful purpose; prepare and distribute useful materials; use a well-prepared study guide to assist students in their study.

4. List in unit plans only those materials that are available or that can be produced; employ students in the production and assembly of materials and in the operation of machines when the experience will prove rewarding and save valuable instructional time for the teacher; use students to gather instructional materials where this is practical; allow a sufficient amount of time for the preparation, procurement, or use of teaching aids.

5. Inject variety into the use of teaching aids; use aids as introductory and summary devices as well as for specific concept and skill development; become thoroughly acquainted with aids such as records, filmstrips, or movies before they are shown to the class.

6. Use maps in developing proper concepts of location, direction, relative size, and topography; but use only well-executed maps, charts, or models that leave accurate impressions.

7. Differentiate between the kinds of materials and aids that will be most helpful in teaching individual students; indicate specifically what class members are to look for in a filmstrip, movie, or field trip.

8. Select materials and resources for their educational rather than their entertainment value; coordinate educational radio and television programs with classroom work.

EVALUATION PROCEDURES

Unit evaluation will move forward with greater ease and efficiency if the teacher clearly understands the purpose of evaluation procedures, the principles related to unit evaluation, and the specific categories of unit evaluation. Furthermore, it is a great advantage to general instruction if the teacher is acquainted with a range of proven evaluation procedures that apply to his particular field of specialization.

Purpose of Unit Evaluation

The encompassing concern of all teaching and learning is improved student behavior. For this reason, these questions have become a matter of great concern: What change in behavior can one justifiably expect as a result of specific instruction? Under what circumstances should it take place? What degree of proficiency should one expect?

The basic purpose of unit evaluation is improved learning,[14] and improved learning, in turn, should be directed toward unit goals. Unit evaluation procedures, therefore, should aim at determining to what extent the objectives of the unit have been achieved.

Evaluation should help students learn more efficiently. Its prime concern, therefore, is not with defeating or frightening students but with identifying their learning difficulties so that appropriate help can be given. It should assist them in analyzing their weaknesses. It should set the stage for ready acceptance of teacher help based upon student self-understandings.[15]

Such frequently used evaluation techniques as personality appraisal, evaluation of oral and written English, or the analysis of study habits have little or nothing to do with unit goals. Such techniques are justified only if the teacher recognizes this lack of relationship and if they serve a long-range or nonunit-related purpose.

Principles Related to Unit Evaluation

Years of experimentation on the part of students, teachers, psychologists, and researchers have furnished helpful guidelines for those educators concerned with appraisal techniques. Before choosing specific devices for use in a unit, the teacher should consider the following general guidelines.[16]

1. The teaching-learning process consists of three basic facets: estab-

---

[14]William H. Burton, *The Guidance of Learning Activities*, 3d. ed. (New York: Appleton-Century-Crofts, 1962), pp. 480–485, presents a very useful list and discussion of frequently used evaluation devices.

[15]See Chapter 15, pp. 306–315, for a discussion of sound marking and reporting procedures.

[16]Peter F. Oliva and Ralph A. Scrafford, *Teaching in a Modern Secondary School* (Columbus, Ohio: Charles E. Merrill Publishing Co., 1965), suggest various non-testing evaluation procedures.

lishing objectives, engaging in goal-related activities, and evaluating to what extent goals have been achieved.

2. Evaluation, including marking procedures, should encourage the student to progress at his own level of capability and in relationship to his past achievement.

3. Diagnosis is one of the chief concerns of evaluation. This process should help the students direct their efforts toward academic areas needing improvement. Self-evaluation, an important adjunct of diagnosis, can be encouraged through various types of tests.

4. A simple indication of grade without additional explanation may do little to encourage self-improvement. The student should always be informed about evaluation procedures and their purposes.

5. After the student clearly understands the standards on which appraisal should be based, he should be encouraged to continuously appraise his own performance. Unit evaluation, in particular, should be organized to promote this type of self-appraisal.

6. When an evaluation procedure does not measure what it is supposed to measure, it is invalid.

7. The accuracy with which evaluation is carried out will help determine its usefulness.

8. Evaluation should be regarded as a continuous program in which attention is focused on balance between testing and nontesting, oral and written, and formal and informal procedures.

9. Emphasis should be on the appraisal of individual improvement rather than on comparison with members of the group.

10. Tests involving performance have greater validity than typical written tests.

11. Evaluation procedures should be arranged so that students do not feel that the learning or use of unit content is at an end when the test paper has been submitted.

12. Not all the objectives of a given unit need to be covered by test items.

13. Students tend to place too much emphasis on the written examination.[17]

14. The types of evaluation procedures employed in a given unit may vary considerably depending upon the needs of that unit. A range of different types of tests should also be employed to serve different purposes.

15. Both essay and objective tests have certain advantages.

16. It is false to assume that all students will exert maximum energy to achieve a high grade, although this is true of a substantial proportion.[18]

---

[17]The use, strengths, and limitations of teacher-made as well as standardized tests are discussed by Blount and Klausmeier, *Teaching in the Secondary School*, chapter 12.

[18]See James Rath, John R. Pancella, and James S. Van Ness, *Studying Teaching* (Englewood Cliffs, New Jersey: Prentice-Hall, Inc., 1967), pp. 161–193, for a thought-provoking series of articles on testing and evaluating by well-known authorities.

Specific Kinds of Evaluation Procedures

The range of evaluation procedures available for use in unit planning is broad.[19] Unfortunately this breadth is frequently not reflected in actual units. Written tests are too often used to the exclusion of other devices.

Among the specific kinds of evaluation devices, the following are most frequently used:

Written Work:	Tests and Examinations:
Unit papers	Diagnostic tests
Short reports	Preassessment
Chalkboard work	Unit examinations
Daily assignments	Mid-unit tests
	Short quizzes
	Oral examinations
	Class discussions
Oral Work:	Individual tests
Committee reports	Written tests
Class discussions	Essay tests
Debates	Objective tests
Brief individual oral	Miscellaneous:
reports	Projects
Teacher-student conferences	Case studies

An examination of the evaluation procedures used in specific units should prove helpful at this point.[20] The following evaluation procedures were taken from a tenth-grade unit on "Menu Planning." Note that in the absence of unit objectives, evaluation procedures appear somewhat vague.

EVALUATION IN A HOMEMAKING UNIT

1. Plan unit objectives cooperatively with students at the beginning of the unit. At the end of the unit have students indicate in written form how well they feel each of the objectives was achieved.
2. Keep brief anecdotal records of the attitudes that students express informally to note any changes or new attitudes that may have developed.
3. Maintain records of student progress through evaluating:
   a. Oral class responses
   b. Special assignments
   c. Tests, journals, and daily assignments
   d. Class interest, behavior, and attitude

---

[19]See John E. Horrocks and Thelma I. Schoonover, *Measurement for Teachers* (Columbus, Ohio: Charles E. Merrill Publishing Co., 1968), chapter 2, for a sophisticated discussion of measuring instruments.

[20]See Appendix A, questions 162–186. Questions listed in this appendix should suggest other evaluation possibilities that might be of help in unit planning.

4. Have each student evaluate herself through:
   a. Progress charts
   b. Daily check lists
   c. Her ability to put into practical use what has been taught in class
5. Have each student anonymously evaluate the unit and the teacher by responding on a five-point scale to a series of questions.

Although these procedures were designed for a unit in which behavioral objectives are not identified as such, several of them hint strongly at behavioral outcomes. Among them are 2, 3a-d, and 4a-c. If the second procedure, for example, were stated as a behavioral objective it might take on a somewhat different form.

2. Provided with dittoed rating sheets on which five basic attitudes are identified (interest in cooking, willingness to experiment, development of taste for variety in cooking, desire to participate in cooking at home, and willingness to participate in homemaking laboratory clean-up activities), students will rate themselves by encircling on a ten-point scale (1 low, 10 high) their positions at the (a) beginning and (b) end of the unit with respect to each attitude. Fifteen minutes will be allowed in class during the last day of the unit for this evaluation. The teacher will subjectively determine what represents a desirable change in individual attitudes for each student.

Note that these procedures do not include any major written examination on the content of the unit, but in view of the nature of the unit this may well be justified. Emphasis is placed on student self-evaluation as well as unsigned written evaluation of the teacher.

In the following tenth-grade English unit on "Modifiers Make Our Speech Live," evaluation procedures emphasize testing to the exclusion of other procedures.

EVALUATION IN AN ENGLISH UNIT

1. A diagnostic test will be given during the introductory activities.
2. Frequent quizzes will be given when they will serve a useful purpose.
3. All tests and quizzes will be reviewed orally in class.
4. A comprehensive unit test will be given as a concluding activity, together with a thorough test on adjectives.[21]
5. Fifty percent of the student's grade wll be based on his formal tests and quizzes, 10 percent on his theme, 25 percent on his participation in class, and 15 percent on cooperation, promptness (in class and with assignments), courtesy, and effort.

Informing students of the weighting of each general area of activity can serve as a helpful motivator and encourage self-direction on the part of students.

---

[21]Passing comprehensive unit tests is sometimes viewed as the equivalent of achieving behavioral objectives, although the specific circumstances of the examination and what represents a satisfactory grade are not detailed.

A twelfth-grade physics teacher included the following evaluation procedures in a unit on "Heat."[22]

EVALUATION IN A PHYSICS UNIT

1. Related to student self-evaluation:
   a. All student work will be graded and returned as soon as possible.
   b. The overall standing of each pupil will be indicated on returned work about four times during the unit.
2. Related to the teacher's evaluation of students:
   a. Oral reviews will be conducted at frequent intervals.
   b. Problems will be placed on the blackboard once each week for teacher and class criticism.
   c. A short time each day will be devoted to drill on new and old terms.
   d. Quizzes will be given as described in the developmental and culminating activities.
   e. Homework problems will be handed in every other day for correction and evaluation.
   f. The teacher will consistently observe the progress of class members.
   g. Written laboratory reports will be submitted at frequent intervals for teacher criticism.
   h. Two major tests will be given during the unit. In each case they will consist of (a) problems and (b) theory and definition.
   i. On a test related to another unit, questions from this unit will be included to determine pupil retention of basic concepts.

In each unit the planners must include in the introductory, developmental, and concluding activities a description of the exact evaluation procedures and the sequence in which they will take place.[23]

Much time can be saved in the selection of evaluation procedures to be incorporated into the unit if the planner will identify those procedures that have proved most successful in the past. Consultation with teaching colleagues in the same subject-matter field may also prove highly profitable.

Categories of Unit Evaluation

Evaluation of Student Knowledge

The category on evaluation of student knowledge includes those activities designed to determine to what extent unit goals have been achieved. Common activities are:

Tests	Board work
Themes	Projects
Reports	Homework
Discussions	Guided self-activity

[22]Evaluation procedures typically vary a great deal from one unit to another depending upon the characteristics of the unit and the teacher's preference.

[23]How evaluation procedures are incorporated into the development and concluding activities of the unit can be readily seen by examining the complete units in Chapter 7.

Student Self-Evaluation

Recent emphasis on student self-direction has pointed up the necessity for student self-evaluation. Thoughtful teachers have devised specific procedures that encourage students to appraise their own progress.[24] They often consist of:

1. Sequential lists of tasks that may be checked off by students when completed.

2. Special self-evaluation report cards on which are recorded the grades of work submitted to the teacher for correction and grading.

3. Descriptive statements of A, B, C, D, and E (or F) students.

4. Questionnaires that force the student to react to his classroom performances.

5. Self-directive programs that indicate whether the student has responded correctly to each frame.

6. Descriptive statements of behavioral objectives that enable students to determine readily whether they have achieved a minimum level of performance.

Evaluation of the Unit and the Teacher

Student appraisal of instructor competence has long been employed by teachers as a device for helping improve instruction as well as teacher-student relationships.[25] The most common device for this purpose has been the use of an anonymous student questionnaire or written response submitted at the end of a long unit or at the end of a semester or school year. Since the identity of the respondent is not known to the teacher, students feel free to air their grievances or praise. Such devices are admittedly highly subjective, but they do afford teachers the opportunity to know how students feel—information that is essential to continuous effective classroom operation. Any number of variations to this procedure can be found; some surveys ask for student reaction to the content and activities of the unit as well.[26]

Recommendations

The conscientious teacher should benefit from some specific suggestions about evaluation procedures. The use of such recommendations should not only save the teacher time and effort but also help him achieve success in unit evaluation.[27] Teachers should:

---

[24]A helpful discussion of the relationship between evaluation and school objectives is provided by Leroy H. Griffith, Nelson L. Haggerson, and Delbert Weber, *Secondary Education Today* (New York: David McKay Co., Inc., 1967), pp. 186–200.

[25]Horrocks and Schoonover, *Measurement for Teachers*, pp. 438–439, provide an example of a rating scale designed to determine the teacher's personal effectiveness. This device may also be used for self-evaluation.

[26]J. Lloyd Trump and Delmas F. Miller, *Secondary School Curriculum Improvement* (Boston: Allyn & Bacon, Inc., 1968), pp. 347–348, strongly recommend the need for individualization of evaluation.

[27]Clark and Starr, *Secondary School Teaching Methods*, Chapter 15, discuss a wide range of principles and techniques that should be considered in selecting and implementing unit evaluation procedures.

1. View evaluation as a series of related instructional procedures used by the teacher in helping the student improve academic achievement; view evaluation as a continuing activity that may well be a part of introductory, developmental, or concluding activities; extend evaluation procedures to several kinds of activities, avoiding unwarranted emphasis on the written test; attempt to determine through evaluation procedures (including behavioral objectives if used) whether students can apply what they are supposed to have learned; emphasize comprehension rather than memory in most evaluation procedures; include diagnostic procedures in the introductory activities where such procedures will serve a useful purpose.

2. Avoid an overriding preference for either subjective (essay) tests or objective tests, for each type serves a useful purpose; avoid the consistent use of a specific type of test if it is strongly disliked by a majority of students; recognize the strengths and weakness of each of the four types of objective tests—multiple choice, true and false, matching, and completion; give quizzes as often as they will serve a useful instructional purpose, but try not to antagonize students by giving quizzes with excessive frequency; review each test with class members after it has been corrected; prepare a well-organized examination that tests unit content and serves as an effective summary;[28] include difficult as well as easy test items to accommodate differing achievement levels.

3. Differentiate between formal and informal evaluation devices.

4. Include specific as well as general observations among evaluation procedures; give deserved attention to themes and written work in unit evaluation; view improvement of students' study habits as a part of evaluation; observe the undirected and out-of-class behavior of students as an indication of subject-matter acquisition and retention; make use of individual conferences with students as a part of the evaluation procedure.

5. Give consideration to the need for the student to keep accurate check on his own progress at all times; furthermore, make provision for the student to evaluate the instructor as well as the unit presentation.

Nonunit-Related Evaluation

Although this chapter has focused upon procedures designed to determine the extent to which unit goals have been achieved, not all evaluation procedures bear a close relationship to unit goals. Most of the nonunit-related evaluation procedures are aimed at appraising long-range objectives. For example, measuring the extent of habit formation that serves the purposes of effective study and classroom control is important in the teaching of all units. Determining the needed and actual improvement in teacher-student relationships is a continuing process that extends

---

[28]An encompassing unit examination (depending on its construction) may be used as a partial measure of the degree to which behavioral objectives have been achieved.

throughout the school year. This type of appraisal lends itself best to informal evaluation procedures such as teacher observation and student-teacher conferences, although more formalized techniques may be employed. Speed and comprehension in reading are important to all subjects and should be carefully appraised at specified times during the school year.

The administration and interpretation of standardized tests of mental maturity and subject-matter achievement are accepted procedures in accredited secondary schools.[29] These examinations call for the use of specifically prescribed procedures and are usually administered to large groups of students by school personnel who have had special training. Such tests permit interested teachers to compare meaningfully individual student scores with national or regional averages. Standardized examinations may be classified as evaluation procedures but have little direct bearing on the teaching of units.

PROBLEMS FOR STUDY AND DISCUSSION

1. What is the fundamental purpose of teaching materials? Explain.
2. Give three examples of the use of aids that do *not* move in the direction dictated by the established objectives.
3. Give five examples of poor usage of visual aids likely to be found in your subject-matter major.
4. List the advantages of the human voice over other auditory aids.
5. Under what circumstances does a model serve as a better aid than the referent itself? Explain.
6. Assumption: You are determined to make the best possible use of television in your teaching major. Describe the steps you would follow.
7. What is meant by *textbook teaching?* What does it mean in your particular field? Explain.
8. Identify the nontextbook printed materials that are of greatest use in teaching a particular course in your teaching minor. Be specific.
9. List the following aids in order of desirability for teaching concepts in your teaching minor: still pictures, narration, resource speakers, written accounts, and specimens.
10. When is the use of printed material as an aid to learning *not* justified? Explain.
11. What is the role of aids in teaching abstractions? Give two examples.
12. What is the basic purpose of evaluation? Explain.
13. How can one engage in a rigorous evaluation program without defeating students? Explain.
14. How would you use diagnostic procedures in teaching a unit? Explain specifically.

---

[29]During the past decade increasing and responsible criticism of culture-oriented tests has caused many school districts to re-examine the desirability of their use. Their lack of validity in testing students in minority groups is often the subject of negative comment.

15. Make several suggestions for helping the teacher avoid undue emphasis on written tests.

16. Which type of written work is most often neglected in your teaching major? Do you neglect it? Analyze your reasons.

17. Which type of test is best suited to student evaluation in your teaching minor? Defend your response.

18. What is the value of student self-evaluation? Explain.

19. Precisely how would you obtain an accurate indication of how much knowledge students had acquired in your subject-matter major?

20. Why should the teacher review the test with students once it has been corrected?

1. *Successful Teaching Units*

Occasionally one encounters an excellent teacher who apparently has made no written preparation. Usually, however, this teacher has, through the years, evolved a firm command of the subject matter and effective teaching procedures, and successful repetition of these methods has made a written plan superfluous. To assume that such a teacher has not done any careful planning is absurd. In reality years of planning have gone into the course, although it might be difficult for a substitute teacher to teach effectively the same unit in the manner carefully outlined in the experienced teacher's mind.

The real danger in failing to follow a written plan lies in the fact that many student teachers, beginning teachers, and teachers with a limited mastery of their subject matter assume that they can do likewise—and with equal success. Unfortunately poor quality teaching often follows such limited or hit-and-miss unit planning.[1]

Unit planning proceeds with greatest ease when the subject matter is developed along conceptual lines, as in units of mathematics, biological sciences, English grammar, and chemistry. In such subjects as the social sciences, English literature, and music, which are not as definitely structured, it is more difficult to make clear, interrelated statements of unit objectives.

In some subjects, however, substitutes for unit plans are successful. In the teaching of modern foreign languages, for example, careful and detailed organization of overall (yearly) plans from which daily lesson plans may be developed have proved effective. Most current foreign-language texts, therefore, are organized in short, daily lessons. The range of objectives that must be dealt with in foreign-language teaching (concepts, skills, memorization, and habits) complicates the organization necessary for effective instruction. Many successful teachers still insist on planned teaching units in teaching foreign languages, but the majority of teachers in this field are leaning toward the use of daily lesson plans based upon overall plans.

Recent emphasis on behavioral objectives and individualized instruction has further led to the modification of unit plans. Such modifications, however, do not alter the central concern for establishing necessary interrelationships among concepts and skills essential to unitary teaching.

CHARACTERISTICS OF SUCCESSFUL UNIT PLANS

All successful units must give attention to (a) *what* is to be taught and (b) *how* it is to be taught. This statement is obviously an oversimplification of all that is involved in unit planning, but these two concerns are fundamental to every unit.[2]

Most educators express a preference for five basic steps in unit planning:

1. Information basic to understanding the nature of the group to be taught must be assembled, organized, and recorded.

2. Appropriate major and minor enabling and behavioral objectives must be determined, carefully worded, organized, and written down.

---

[1]Howard T. Batchelder, Maurice McGlasson, and Raleigh Schorling, *Student Teaching in Secondary Schools,* 4th ed. (New York: McGraw-Hill Book Company, 1964), pp. 126–129, provide suggestions for unit preparation.

[2]Leonard H. Clark and Irving S. Starr, *Secondary School Teaching Methods.* 2d. ed. (New York: The Macmillan Company, 1967), p. 134, meaningfully discuss these two basic concerns, pointing out that the real learning products are changes that occur in students.

3. Procedures appropriate for the achievement of each objective must be determined and adequately described.

4. Teaching materials, resources, and devices necessary for the conduct of teaching procedures must be selected and listed.

5. Evaluation procedures that bear a direct relationship to unit objectives must be determined and listed.[3]

Although the core of the unit consists of the *objectives* and their related *procedures*, it is difficult to conceive of any well-planned and teachable unit that does not concern itself with all five of these steps. However, because each unit is devised by a particular teacher to assist him in teaching a specific group of students, one unit plan may not provide adequate help for another teacher in teaching a different group. By its very nature, unit planning is subjective. For this reason each of the units presented in this chapter might have been different if it had been prepared by a different teacher for use in another section of the same subject. A variety of detail is to be expected, but *all well-prepared units*[4] *should follow the same general outline.*

Basic Information

Encompassed in the Basic Information[5] of the unit plan will be the grade level and age range of students, the duration of the unit, and the relationship of the particular unit to other units in the Overall Plan. This section will also contain information about the nature of the class—individual I.Q.'s of students and the range of I.Q.'s, the socioeconomic status of the class members, students with particular problems, potential offenders in terms of classroom control, proportion of boys to girls, and the range of backgrounds represented by different students in the class. As much of this information as possible will be frequently recorded in code form on a seating chart that indicates diagrammatically the exact location of each student and relevant information pertaining to him.

Objectives

The unit objectives[6] will:
1. Identify all relevant unit objectives that can and should be treated during the unit.
2. Differentiate and group enabling objectives according to kind—concepts, memorizations, skills, and habits.

---

[3]Carefully stated behavioral objectives call for terminal outcomes, a special kind of practical evaluation.

[4]William H. Burton, *The Guidance of Learning Activities,* 3d. ed. (New York: Appleton-Century-Crofts, 1962), chapter 15, gives an analysis of a fifth-grade unit. His relevant comments apply to unit plans at all levels.

[5]See Chapter 3, pp. 43–51, for an extensive treatment of Basic Information.

[6]See Chapter 4, pp. 54–64, for an extensive treatment of Objectives.

3. List major objectives in proper relationship to minor objectives.

4. State objectives in the simplest form compatible with clarity and meaning.

5. Clearly differentiate between enabling objectives and terminal behavior when a dual approach to listing objectives is employed.

Procedures

Activities (procedures)[7] that are carefully considered along with Basic Information and Objectives will possess certain characteristics. They will be:

1. Frequently grouped according to introductory activities, developmental activities, and concluding activities.

2. Practical, in the sense that they can be carried out with a reasonable expenditure of time and energy.

3. Psychologically sound for the achievement of the specific objective involved.

4. Specifically related to the enabling objectives to be achieved.

5. Directed toward the cumulative achievement of changed behavior.

6. Selected only after a range of other possibilities has been considered.

7. Of general interest to students in the class.

8. Varied in consideration of student capacity, achievement, and maturity.

9. Described in sufficient detail to enable another teacher to obtain a clear picture of what is to be done.

10. Arranged in sequential order.

11. Flexible enough to permit unforeseen modifications.

Materials and Resources

In planning for the use of audio-visual aids, teaching materials, special devices, and resource persons,[8] the planner will:

1. Select and list the most effective teaching aids.

2. Avoid excess use of any one device.

3. Make certain aids when it is practical.

Evaluation Procedures

The procedures related to unit evaluation[9] should reflect the planner's effort to:

1. Insure that evaluation serves an instructional purpose.

2. Use a variety of evaluation procedures.

---

[7]See Chapter 4, pp. 64–74, and Chapter 5 for an extensive treatment of Procedures.
[8]See Chapter 6, pp. 98–107, for a detailed discussion of Materials and Resources.
[9]See Chapter 6, pp. 108–115, for a discussion of Evaluation Procedures.

3. Not overemphasize testing.

4. Relate all evaluation activities to unit objectives.

5. Assess the degree of behavioral change in students brought about through unit procedures.

6. Examine a wide range of possible procedures and their effect upon learning before making final selections.

Other General Characteristics

A number of general characteristics do not lend themselves to the preceding categorization. Good unit plans will:

1. Be practical and usable.

2. Be made up only after the examination of a wide range of usable resource materials.

3. Avoid the danger of undesirable brevity or unnecessary length.

4. Be planned in consideration of the teaching experience and subject-matter competence of the teacher who will use them.

5. Be consistent in form and make-up.

6. Possess a strong interrelationship of parts within the unit.

7. Give consideration to the instructor's teaching style and the student's learning style.

SAMPLE TEACHING UNITS

The unit plans presented in this chapter were prepared by first- and second-year teachers and taught in actual classroom situations. Because the units served the needs of specific teachers under particular circumstances, variation in specific detail is justified. The basic structure of each unit—Basic Information, Objectives, Procedures, Materials and Resources, and Evaluation Procedures—is the same. However, considerable leeway should be allowed each teacher within the framework of this structure in order to meet the needs of the specific students and teacher.[10]

The first unit differentiates a) enabling objectives and b) terminal behavior, using a two-column arrangement to clarify relationships. Further adjustments are made in concluding activities and evaluation procedures to avoid unnecessary duplication.

The second unit plan is soundly developed and illustrates the structure and characteristics of successful teaching units previously discussed.

---

[10]Peter F. Oliva and Ralph A. Scrafford, *Teaching in a Modern Secondary School* (Columbus, Ohio: Charles E. Merrill Publishing Co., 1965), pp. 27–31, indicate that if the unit plan is employed, students should have access to the instructional plans to be employed. An example of such a guide sheet for a junior high school unit on safety is provided.

A Teaching Unit in Biological Science

An experienced biology teacher who knows his subject matter and effective teaching methods should be able to teach the following unit with success. If he were without basic experience beyond the student-teaching level, he would probably need additional details before he could teach the unit.

Tenth-Grade Biology: "Root Systems"

I. Basic Information
   A. Age and Grade Level of Class
      1. The students are primarily sophomores but there are a few juniors.
      2. Their ages range from fourteen to seventeen.
   B. Length of Time for Unit
      1. The unit will be taught for three weeks (fifteen school days).
      2. Five days will be spent on the anatomy of roots and the types of roots.
      3. Two days will be spent sketching the anatomy of roots as part of laboratory work.
      4. Five days will be spent discussing the way a root absorbs minerals and water.
      5. One day will be spent in initiating the unit and two days in concluding it.
   C. The Position of This Unit in the Overall Plan
      1. This is the fourth unit taught in the year.
      2. The unit preceding this was "Introducing the Plant Kingdom."
      3. The unit following this is "The Use of the Stem."
   D. Nature of the Class
      1. There are seventeen boys and eight girls in this class.
      2. About half of the students were reared in a rural area, giving them a fair background for the subject.
      3. During the first unit on botany it was learned that four girls and five boys were not very interested in the subject. The girls are Sandra, Glenda, Lorna, and Margaret, and the boys are Wallace, Lewis, Gerald, Eldon, and Clarence. (For I.Q.'s and seating, see the seating chart.)
      4. Several of the class members have demonstrated a great deal of ability and interest in the subject.
   E. Seating Chart (see page 123)
   F. This unit is designed to help the students understand the way a plant gets food from the soil and also how the roots help hold the soil and moisture.

SEATING CHART

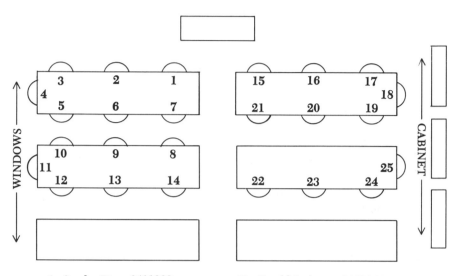

1. Sandra Bing, 0411239
2. Sally Peters, 5321517
3. William Oliphant, 7211426
4. Boyd Franks, 8921418
5. Melissa Williams, 3711421
6. Dean Patrick, 2911422
7. Robert Hill, 6131514
8. Wallace Rhone, 4190147
9. Lewis Grundig, 0590242
10. Herman Allred, 2201338
11. Charles Evans, 7001337
12. Willard Foss, 9980153
13. Gerald Jackman, 3990244
14. Ralph Clayson, 4301230
15. Eldon Ives, 1601337
16. Dale Seymour, 6121429
17. Milton James, 2101234
18. Clarence Holt, 5701346
19. Walter Jones, 3990332
20. Sammy Hinson, 0311431
21. Glade Healey, 7501438
22. Glenda Lee, 2290154
23. Lorna Brown, 0401246
24. Margaret Christen, 7701246
25. Aleen Markwell, 8790242

Key to Seating Chart Code

First number—*meaningless*
Next three numbers—*I.Q. reversed*
Next number—*General academic achievement:* High (5), Low (1)
Next number—*Socioeconomic status:* High (5), Low (1)
Last number—*meaningless*

II. Objectives[11]

Enabling Objectives

A. Concepts to Be Learned[12]
  1. Unit Concept: Two common types of root systems, possessing different characteristics, enabling plants to live under different conditions.

  2. Supporting Concepts
    a. There are two common types of root systems.
      1) A *fibrous* root system has many slender roots of equal size.
      2) A taproot system has a large primary root and many secondary roots attached to it. It acts as a storehouse for the plant.
    b. Plants are able to live under many different conditions because of these two systems.
      1) Fibrous roots cover a lot of area and bind the soil.
      2) Fibrous roots draw in available water very quickly.
      3) Taproots go down to deep water supplies.
      4) Taproots are important for absorption.
    c. Root hairs are important for absorption.
      1) They are one-celled outgrowths of the epidermis of the
      2) They grow only in the area behind the root tip, pushing out into new territory as the root grows.
    d. The root tip is the very end of the root and is made up of four regions.
      1) The *root cap* protects the root end and makes it possible for the root to push through the soil. CO_2 (carbon dioxide) is given off by the cap and mixes with H_2O (water) to form carbonic acid, which dissolves minerals and makes it easier for the root to push through the soil.
      2) The *embryonic* region is the growing point in the root. The cells are small and in a constant state of division.
      3) The *elongation* region is just back of the embryonic region.
        a) In this region cells grow in length to their full size.
        b) This growth pushes the root further out into the soil.
      4) In the *maturation* region the cells change to make special tissues.

---

[11]William R. Lueck, Elwood G. Campbell, Leo E. Eastman, Charles W. Edwards, Clayton F. Thomas, and William D. Zeller, *Effective Secondary Education* (Minneapolis: Burgess Publishing Company, 1966), pp. 99–101, give examples of specific unit objectives matched with teacher as well as student activities. Relationships are clearly maintained through the use of three columns.

[12]These conceptual statements (objectives) have been carefully prepared and stated.

Terminal Behavior
(Behavioral Objectives)

1. Allowed 50 minutes for its completion, students will be able to answer with 85 percent accuracy 30 completion, matching, and multiple-choice questions; one of two essay questions; and 11 questions involving identification of parts from a drawing in a unit examination concerned with the characteristics of the two most common root systems enabling plants to live under different conditions.

2. a-c. Given 10 minutes for its completion, students will be able to complete without outside help a short composition that describes with 100 percent accuracy the two common types of root structures, their purpose, and function.

2. d. Having access to several specimens of two basic root types, during a five-minute in-class exercise, students will list and define the four root regions. No errors will be allowed with respect to either listing or definition.

e. Under the microscope the five parts of the root can be seen.
   1) The *epidermis* is a single layer of brick-shaped cells on the outside of the root.
   2) The *cortex* is a large area of loosely packed cells under the epidermis and is the chief storage area for the root.
   3) The *endodermis* is a single layer of thick-walled cells.
   4) The *pericycle* is just outside the endodermis and consists of thin-walled cells one layer deep.
   5) The *central cylinder* is the chief conducting and strengthening region.
      a) Here is found the *xylem*, or water-conducting tissues, which take water from the root to the leaves and stems.
      b) The *phloem*, or food-conducting tissues, take food produced in leaves down to the root.
      c) *Cambium* is the tissue that lies between the phloem and the xylem.
f. Fleshy taproots become larger through the growth of the cambium. The cambium adds secondary phloem to the outside and secondary xylem to the inside. In the older taproots this growth can be seen in rings.
g. The automatic responses of a plant toward or away from a stimulus is called a *tropism*.
   1) Two types of tropisms influence roots the most.
      a) *Geotropism* is the growth of the root toward gravity.
      b) *Hydrotropism* is the growth of a root toward water.
   2) *Phototropism* (response to light) and *thermotropism* (response to heat) have a greater effect on the stem of the plant than on the roots.
h. Roots grow in many different environments.
   1) Soil roots are the most common.
      a) Decaying plants add organic matter to the soil.
      b) Organic matter holds water and makes the soil loose.
      c) Manure, leaf mold, and peat moss are soil conditioners, or *mulches*.
   2) Aquatic roots are found in water.
      a) They have no root hairs for absorption.
      b) They get minerals from the water in which they grow.
   3) Aerial roots are found only in very humid atmospheres.
      a) They get water from the atmosphere.
      b) They obtain minerals from debris that collects around them.
i. Some plants have *adventitious* roots, which develop from the stem or leaves. These roots are helpful to the plants in several ways.
   1) Prop roots help support the plant.
   2) Tip layering roots are for propagation.
   3) Climbing roots cling to the wall and allow the plant to grow upward.

2. e-f. Having access to root specimens and microscopes, students will draw
   and label the five parts of the root. All major parts must be correctly
   drawn and labeled, as well as three of the four subparts of the central
   cylinder. Students will be allowed 40 minutes for completion of this
   exercise.

2. g-j. In a brief talk with the teacher, students will correctly differentiate
   the four kinds of tropism, the kinds of environments in which roots are
   found, the purposes of adventitious roots, and at least three commercial
   uses for roots. Students found to be deficient will be assigned appropriate relearning tasks.

j. There are many commercial uses for roots.
   1) Certain roots, such as carrots and radishes, are crops.
   2) Some roots contain valuable drugs.
   3) Some roots are used for seasonings.
   4) Other roots are used to make dyes.
k. Molecules are always in motion and tend to move into areas of lesser concentration.
   1) The spreading of molecules is called *diffusion*. Diffusion involves the movement of molecules from a more dense to a less dense area.
   2) When molecules are evenly distributed, they are in a state of equilibrium.
l. A thin material that allows molecules to pass through is called a *membrane*.
   1) When a substance passes through a membrane, the membrane is permeable to the substance.
   2) When one substance goes through and another cannot, the membrane is semipermeable.
m. The passage of water through a semipermeable membrane is called *osmosis*. Water goes from a greater concentration to a lesser concentration of water.
n. The root hairs in the soil take in water by the process of osmosis.
   1) The cell of the root hair contains protoplasm, which is 70 percent water, and also contains solutions of minerals.
   2) The water in the soil contains minerals in solution.
   3) The concentration of water is greater outside the cell than inside; thus osmosis occurs.
o. Osmosis occurs from cell to cell in the root, moving the water to the upper parts of the plants. The cell-to-cell diffusion of water is called *successive osmosis*.
p. When water enters a cell, it builds up a pressure inside the cell. This is called *osmotic pressure*.
   1) This pressure causes the cell to become firm.
   2) The firm cells cause the plant to be stiff.
      a) This stiffness is called *turgor*.
      b) Turgor allows the plant to push through the hard ground.
q. Turgor in root cells creates root pressure.
   1) Root pressure can be so great that water is forced out of the leaves of plants.
   2) A loss of this excess water in plants is called *guttation*.
r. When osmosis works in reverse, water is taken from the cells.
   1) The loss of turgor in this way is called *plasmolysis*.
   2) Plasmolysis can occur when the concentration of water is greater on the inside of the cell than on the outside.
s. Absorption of water by a solid, resulting in swelling, is called *imbibition*. Imbibition is necessary to break open seed coats.

2. k-m. After a careful teacher demonstration and explanation (preceded by assigned reading) of diffusion of molecules through a membrane and passage of water through a semipermeable membrane (osmosis), during which student questions are encouraged, the demonstration will be repeated without explanation. Students will be required to give a brief written explanation of the scientific phenomena as the demonstration proceeds; they will be allowed to check their papers for five minutes before handing them in. Eighty percent accuracy will be required in the use of the following terms, all of which must be mentioned: molecules, diffusion, equilibrium, membrane, semipermeable, permeable, and osmosis.

2. n-p. Based on several days' observation of plants growing in water or soil and the dissection of these plants, students will write a short paper on how water and minerals are brought into the plant through successive osmosis, how osmotic pressure is created, and how plant stiffness is achieved. Papers must be written without help during a 20 minute period in class. They will be judged on the basis of 12 specific points, 10 of which are required to pass.

2. q-s. In the classroom students will display specimen plants they have procured in which turgor has reached a state of guttation, in which plasmolysis is evident, and in which imbibition breaks open seed coats. During an individual, two-minute teacher inspection of each display, students will explain each process and the reason for it. Any misunderstanding of the three basic processes and the terminology associated with them will be viewed as being below the limit of acceptable performance.

B. Terms to Be Memorized

1. Fleshy root	22. Phototropism
2. Taproot	23. Thermotropism
3. Fibrous root	24. Tropism
4. Root system	25. Aerial roots
5. Root cap	26. Aquatic roots
6. Root hair	27. Adventitious roots
7. Secondary root	28. Prop roots
8. Primary root	29. Tip layering roots
9. Embryonic region	30. Climbing roots
10. Elongation region	31. Membrane
11. Maturation region	32. Osmosis
12. Epidermis	33. Osmotic pressure
13. Cortex	34. Permeable
14. Endodermis	35. Semipermeable
15. Pericycle	36. Successive osmosis
16. Phloem	37. Plasmolysis
17. Cambium	38. Turgor
18. Xylem	39. Diffusion
19. Pith	40. Equilibrium
20. Geotropism	41. Guttation
21. Hydrotropism	42. Imbibition

C. Skills to Be Learned

There are no skills to be learned in this unit.

III. Activities Related to Unit Objectives
  A. Introductory Activities[13] (One class period)[14]
    1. The teacher will display several actual plant roots: fleshy taproot (carrot), long taproot (dandelion), fibrous root (grass), prop root (corn), climbing root (ivy), and tip-layering root (raspberry).
    2. The teacher will identify and tell a bit about each type of root.
    3. The teacher will ask the students which root would be best under certain conditions. *Example:* Which plant would grow best in a hardpan soil under shallow topsoil where rain is frequent but gentle? (*Answer:* fibrous roots.) This will demonstrate to the teacher how much knowledge of roots the students already have.

---

[13]Because these activities are largely introductory and motivational in nature, it is difficult to relate them to specific objectives of the unit. The experimental activities, however, can be easily related to the overall unit concept.

Nathan S. Blount and Herbert J. Klausmeier, *Teaching in the Secondary Schools,* 3d. ed. (New York: Harper & Row, Publishers, 1968), chapter 7, provide a useful and complete discussion of initiatory, developmental, and culminating activities as related to a teaching unit.

[14]The careful approximation and noting of time to be spent on each type of activity encourages more realistic planning.

B. 1-42. During a full fifty-minute period at the end of the unit, students will be expected to define correctly but in their own words the 42 terms listed under *Terms to be Memorized*. A maximum of six errors will be permitted.

4. The teacher will outline what is to be covered[15] in the unit.[16]
5. The teacher will inform the students of the evaluation procedures to be followed in this unit. The students will make and label several drawings of roots.
6. Under the teacher's direction, each student will set up two bean seeds on a wet nutrient agar. The seeds will be placed between two pieces of blotter paper or moss moistened with nutrient agar. The roots that grow will be studied during the developmental activities.

B. Developmental Activities[17] (Twelve class periods)
1. Recurring Activities
   a. When it is practical and useful, students will study twenty minutes of each class period under teacher supervision. This study period will be arranged so that it does not include the first or the last ten minutes of the period.

---

[15]It might be well to indicate more specifically *what* is to be covered and *how*.

[16]The illustrative units in this chapter were planned without any student participation in determining the objectives. If the teacher wishes to involve the students to some extent, he may have them help modify the objectives and activities during the introductory phase of the unit.

[17]Lack of detail in describing what specifically is to be done may result in teacher frustration when the unit is taught.

    b. Students will assist the teacher in making demonstrations.

    c. Each teacher demonstration will be accompanied by an oral explanation. Colored wall charts will be used to supplement this explanation.

    d. At the time of each demonstration, students will be encouraged to ask questions.

    e. With student help, large numbers of plant specimens will be obtained for classroom examination.

    f. Assignments for each day will be written in the upper right-hand corner of the chalkboard.

    g. Brief quizzes will be given at four-day intervals when appropriate.

2. Sequential Listings of Activities[18]

The daily breakdown of activities is as follows:

First Day[19]

    1. The teacher will take the roots that were on display the previous day and use them as the starting point in the discussion on the taproot.

    2. He will show the class that the taproot is long and will hold up a large plant.

    3. He will draw on the board a deep water supply and show how a taproot reaches it.

Second Day

    4. Using the fibrous root, the teacher will show how it covers a lot of area and binds the soil.

    5. He will explain with the aid of a chart how the many secondary roots draw in a great deal of water when it is available.

    6. He will illustrate at the chalkboard that the hair is one celled and is an outgrowth of the epidermis, or outer layer of the root.

    7. Using plant specimens he will explain that the hairs are located right back of the root tip and that as the root grows, the hairs are moved into new territory.

Third Day

    8. The teacher will use a modified lecture method to help the student understand the parts of a root tip.

---

[18]Note that many of the details essential to successful teaching have been omitted under the daily description of activities. For the beginning teacher this would be unwise. To assume that the spelling out of details should be left to the daily lesson plan is somewhat risky. In this plan, assignments, specific student involvement in activities, study period activities, and evaluation procedures have been given little or no attention, although they were mentioned in a general way under Recurring Activities.

[19]Indicating the precise developmental activities to be conducted on each day poses the risk of inflexibility. Adjustments can be made, however, through daily lesson planning. For the individual whose planning tends to be somewhat loose and inexact, this procedure has merit.

A chalkboard drawing will be used to explain the four different regions.

9. A twelve-minute movie will be shown: "Roots of Plants." It will be previewed by the teacher, and its most important parts will be pointed out before it is shown. The movie shows examples of tap and fibrous roots, their structure and function. It also shows the four regions of the root cap and introduces osmosis.

Fourth Day

10. The teacher will explain how to make a drawing and what format to use.

11. Ten demonstration microscopes will be set up with root caps under view. Ten students will draw root caps while the rest of the class members draw natural habitat pictures of taproots. When the first ten students are finished with the microscopes, the students will trade projects.

Fifth Day

12. Radish seeds will be examined both with the naked eye and under the microscope. The students will draw a sprouted radish seed as seen with the naked eye and then a detailed view of a root hair as seen with the microscope.

Sixth Day

13. Demonstration microscopes will be set up as on the fourth day, and students will follow the same procedures. Under the microscopes will be a cross section of a root. The different layers will be identified in a short lecture accompanied by a chalkboard drawing. Then the class will be asked to locate those layers on the microscope slide and make a labeled drawing of what they see.

Seventh Day

14. Using examples of plants in the room, the teacher and students will explain and demonstrate the different tropisms.

15. The students will be asked to indicate all the commercial uses of roots that they know of. A scribe (Sally will act as scribe) will record them on the board. To assure that all the uses are listed, the teacher will help where he feels it necessary.

Eighth Day

16. A teacher-led discussion of the different types of root environments will be held. Examples of all the different types mentioned will be called for. The

teacher will see that all the important forms are mentioned and given adequate attention.

17. Using the roots that were brought into the class the first day, the teacher will lead a discussion of adventitious roots.

Ninth Day

18. A drawing of a root cap and a cross section of a root will be given to each student. They will be asked to label all parts shown. This will be used as a short test.

19. A can of peppermint oil will be opened in the front of the room. As the students begin to smell it, the teacher will explain diffusion and equilibrium.

20. A glass of water and several cubes of sugar will be placed at the front of the class. One cube will be dropped into the water. As the sugar dissolves, the water will be tasted by students. They will then explain why the water is sweet. More cubes will be added until the sugar will not dissolve. The students will be asked to explain this.

Tenth Day

21. With a thistle tube, muslin, and a beaker of water, the teacher will set up a demonstration to show what a membrane is. (The muslin will represent a membrane.) The result will be explained by the teacher.

22. An animal bladder will be filled with syrup and placed in water. The water will permeate the bladder and fill it. This action will be explained by the teacher.

23. Using the full bladder as an illustration, the teacher will explain turgor.

Eleventh Day

24. A twenty-one minute movie entitled "Osmosis" will be shown. This movie illustrates the operation of osmosis in familiar forms.

25. With water in the bladder and syrup in the beaker, the teacher will demonstrate reverse osmosis, or plasmolysis.

Twelfth Day

26. A cutting of a plant will be placed in a concentrated salt solution. As plasmolysis takes place, the students will be asked to explain orally what is happening and why.

27. With the use of a water-logged stick, the teacher will explain imbibition and its uses.

C. Culminating Activities[20] (Two class periods)
   1. All the drawings that were made during the laboratory periods will have been corrected and graded by the teacher and will be returned to the students.
   2. With the help of the corrected drawings, the students will review the anatomy of a root. Such parts as the xylem and phloem will be stressed to make sure that the students understand their functions.
   3. The teacher, using the hidden chalkboard method, will review such terms as: diffusion, equilibrium, membrane, permeable, semipermeable membrane, osmosis, osmotic pressure, successive osmosis, turgor, guttation, plasmolysis, and imbibition. The teacher will selectively sample members of the class to find out whether or not the students understand the meaning of these words. If a student does not understand, one of the brighter students will be given a chance to answer. If none of the students know the answer, the teacher will explain and ask the question later.
   4. A unit test will be given. It will take about forty minutes for the slowest students to complete. (For details of this test, see the section on Evaluation.)
   5. Students who finish early will be given a mimeographed study help for the next unit on "Stems." They will be allowed to start studying.
   6. When all of the tests are in, the teacher will quickly go over the test, giving the answers and clearing up any questions.

IV. Materials and Resources
   1. Textbook: *Biology* by Elsbeth Kroeber, Walter H. Wolff, and Richard L. Weaver[21]
   2. Display of six types of roots made up of carrot, dandelion, grass, corn, ivy, and raspberry
   3. Twelve plates of nutrient agar
   4. Bean seeds
   5. Radish seeds
   6. Fifty pieces of blotter paper
   7. Peat moss
   8. Ten compound microscopes
   9. Slides and cover slips for everyone in the class
   10. Razor blades
   11. Students' own drawing paper and hard lead pencils

---

[20]Burton, *The Guidance of Learning Activities,* p. 368, discusses briefly the history and purposes of culminating activities. Specific errors to avoid are pointed out.

[21]It is important to include the authors of the text if this unit is to be filed as resource material for a later unit.

12. Movie "Roots of Plants," 12 minutes, $1.50 rental from T.M.U., A.V.A.
13. Movie "Osmosis," 21 minutes, $3.00 rental from T.M.U., A.V.A.
14. Movie projector
15. A semipermeable membrane (animal bladder)
16. A membrane (muslin)
17. A glass of water and several sugar cubes
18. A thistle tube and stand with clamp
19. Syrup
20. Large beaker of water
21. Cutting from a plant
22. Salt water in glass
23. College text: *The Plant World* by Harry J. Fuller (for the teacher's use)
24. A water-logged stick

V. Evaluation Procedures[22]
  A. Tests and Examinations (The weight given each item is shown.)
    1. After the anatomy of the root has been studied, a ten-minute test will be given in which a drawing of a root will be labeled by the students. (2/10)
    2. A comprehensive examination covering the completed unit will be given. This examination will contain completion, matching, and multiple-choice questions. There will be two essay questions of equal magnitude; students may choose one of the two questions to answer. They will also be asked to identify different parts of a drawing. (5/10)
  B. General Evaluation Procedures (The weight given each item is shown).
    1. The drawings that are made in the laboratory will be graded on completeness and neatness. (1/10)
    2. During the laboratory periods, the teacher will observe the students' work with the microscopes and make notes on their activities. (1/20)
    3. Personal teacher-student talks will indicate strengths and weaknesses. (1/20)
    4. The quality and extent of class participation will be recorded. (1/20)
    5. Teacher's evaluation of the students' abilities and the learning actually taking place will be noted. (1/20)
  C. Evaluation of Teaching
    1. After every class the teacher will evaluate the teaching done

---

[22]It is desirable to describe all evaluation procedures in the Developmental Activities.

that day in class.[23] He will note weaknesses and strengths.
2. After the unit is completed and the students have been evaluated, the teacher will examine the unit objectives to see whether they were reached.
3. The unit plan will be adjusted as necessary on the basis of the information gathered.

A Teaching Unit in English

The following English unit has the potential for considerable success if taught to the class described under Basic Information. Certain of the activities hold promise of making the dry bones of grammar take on new life.

Good Grammar Is an Aid to Communication[24]

I. Basic Information
  A. Statistics
    1. This is an eighth-grade class of thirty pupils.
    2. Ages range from twelve to fourteen. There are fourteen girls and sixteen boys.
    3. The I.Q. range is from 60 to 126.
  B. This unit will take about three and one-half weeks.
  C. Relationship of This Unit to Other Units
    1. The year's work on improving communications is divided into four sections.
      a. Development of abilities to speak well.
      b. Development of abilities to write well.
      c. Development of abilities to read well.
      d. Development of abilities to listen.
    2. This unit is the fourth in a series on improving communication by developing abilities to write well.
    3. This unit is preceded by a unit on "Aids to Better Spelling" and will be followed by a unit on "Punctuation."
  D. Nature of the Class
    1. The class contains two nonreaders and three very slow readers who read at about the third-grade level.
    2. One student is on probation from the Juvenile Court. He lives

---

[23]Interrelationships among concepts characterizing carefully-planned units of any kind are clearly evident in sound programed units or courses. Harry Huffman and B. June Schmidt, *Programmed Business Mathematics*, 2d. ed. (New York: Gregg Division, McGraw-Hill Book Company, 1968), provide a three-book series in which lesson, unit, and course planning are meaningfully interrelated.

[24]Wayne Dumas and Weldon Becker, *Introduction to Secondary Education: A Foundations Approach* (Scranton, Pennsylvania: International Textbook Company, 1968), pp. 262–263, present a brief but sound treatment of the essential characteristics of teaching units.

in a foster home but needs special attention. He is inattentive
and cannot concentrate on one thing for long.
3. Among the group are four bright students who have previously led in every class situation. Their behavior presents
a problem since a large proportion of the class sits by and
lets them lead in almost everything. Eighty percent of the
students are quite passive.
4. The degree of needed motivation will vary greatly because
of the wide range of abilities.
5. Students have all lived in the same area, and their experiences and backgrounds are about the same.
6. With four exceptions, students belong to the same religious
faith.

II. Enabling Objectives[25]
  A. Concepts to Be Learned[26]
    1. Unit Concept: An understanding of sentence construction
       and all of the parts of speech that make up sentences will
       aid students in better communication.
    2. Supporting Concepts
       a. All sentences have a subject and a predicate and convey
          a complete thought.
          1) The subject names the person, place, thing, or idea
             the sentence is about.
          2) The subject is a noun or another word or group of
             words used as a noun.
          3) Pronouns take the place of nouns.
          4) The complete predicate tells something about the
             subject.
          5) The simple predicate is the verb.
          6) The verb makes statements, asks questions, or gives
             commands.
             a) There are linking auxiliary verbs.
             b) There are transitive verbs, which transfer action
                from subject to object.
             c) Intransitive verbs may show action but do not
                transfer action to an object.
             d) There are verb phrases consisting of a main verb
                and auxiliary verbs.

---

[25]Objectives in this unit are confined to traditional non-behavioral objectives. Using
the double-column approach of the preceding unit on "*Root Systems*," behavioral objectives could be readily matched with corresponding enabling objectives.

[26]Because of the formalized approach to English grammar in this unit (with respect
to conceptual objectives as well as procedures), one should ask how much value it will
have for students somewhat below average in intelligence. Research studies of oral and
written application of grammar as well as teacher opinions emphasize the trend toward
a non-formalized approach at this level.

       7) Verbs have three principal parts:
         a) The first part shows *present* time.
         b) The second shows *past* time.
         c) The third shows *past* time with an *auxiliary verb* helper.
         d). Some verbs are more troublesome than others. They are *lie, lay, sit, set, rise,* and *raise.*
      8) Verbs have six tenses, showing present, past, future, present perfect, past perfect, and future perfect time.
      9) To conjugate a verb is to give in order the form of its several voices, tenses, numbers, and persons.
     10) Transitive verbs have voice.
         a) *Active* voice shows the subject as the actor.
         b) *Passive* voice shows the subject as receiver.
  b. A simple sentence conveys a complete thought and has a subject and verb, either or both of which may be compound.
    1) *Compound* means more than one.
    2) Compounds help improve choppy sentences.
  c. A compound sentence is composed of two complete sentences conveying two closely related thoughts.
    1) Compound sentences are connected by a coordinate conjunction: *and, but, or, nor.*
    2) Compound sentences may be connected by a semicolon.
  d. A complex sentence conveys one complete thought and is composed of one independent clause and two or more dependent clauses.
    1) A clause has a subject and a verb.
    2) A dependent clause relies on another clause to complete its meaning.
    3) An independent clause conveys a complete thought.
  e. Descriptive modifiers add meaning to words.
    1) Adjectives modify nouns and pronouns by telling kinds, colors, sizes, shapes, which one, and how many.
    2) Adverbs modify verbs, adjectives, and other adverbs by telling how, where, and when.
    3) A group of related words is called a phrase and may be used as a single adjective or a single adverb.,
    4) Adjectives and adverbs have three forms of comparison—positive, comparative, and superlative.

B. Terms to Be Memorized

1. Subject	5. Compound sentence
2. Predicate	6. Transitive verb
3. Simple sentence	7. Intransitive verb
4. Complex sentence	8. Active verb

9. Passive verb	15. Adverb
10. Linking verb	16. Adjective
11. Auxiliary verb	17. Conjunction
12. Independent clause	18. Positive
13. Dependent clause	19. Comparative
14. Phrase	20. Superlative

    C. Skills to be Learned

Note: Nothing classed as a skill is to be presented during this unit.

III. Activities Related to Unit Objectives

    A. Introductory Activities[27] (Two class periods)

        1. Reference will be made to the chart outlining the course for the year, which was developed by students and teacher during the first week of school.

        2. The need for the units in the second section of the year's work, "Improving Skills in Written Language," will be identified, written on the chalkboard, and discussed for a few moments. The list will be left on the board. After the film, students will add more reasons to the list.

        3. The film "How's Your English?" will be shown and followed by a discussion.[28] The film emphasizes the necessity for good word usage and explains how misunderstandings arise because of poor choice of words. The machine will be set up and run by the teacher with the aid of two boys, Kent and Roger.

        4. The students will be free to suggest desired activities concerning the unit. These will be listed and used if appropriate.

        5. The teacher will display two neat student notebooks and discuss their qualities. This will help establish a standard for neat notebooks and written work to be handed in.

        6. The teacher will explain why a vocabulary notebook is necessary and how it should be indexed and used. Each student will make one to be used for the rest of the year.[29]

    B. Recurring Activities[30]

        1. Oral reviews will be presented by the teacher each day.

---

[27]The importance of the teacher's role in introductory activities is stressed by Clark and Starr, *Secondary School Teaching Methods*, p. 141.

Lueck, et al., *Effective Secondary Education*, pp. 117–124, point out several techniques that can be employed in initiating a unit.

[28]Failure to indicate the length and source of a film means that this information will have to be determined later.

[29]There may be some doubt as to whether the students will have a clear idea of the nature of the unit by the time the Introductory Activities are completed.

[30]Peter F. Oliva, *The Secondary School Today* (New York: World Publishing Company, 1967), pp. 151–153 and 168–171, lists the developmental activities for two different units matched with desired outcomes.

This will last for not more than five or six minutes. Different methods and approaches will be used to keep interest alive.
2. Students will frequently use the chalkboard.
3. There will be supervised fifteen-minute work periods as often as possible. Some weeks they will occur about every day, and at other times less frequently.
4. Short quizzes to determine assimilation and understanding of material will be given each five or six days.
5. Worksheets will be distributed. All students will have a chance to air problems, get help, actually finish an exercise, and get the correct answers. This method will prove beneficial when the material and problems are rather difficult to understand.
6. The students will index a notebook for vocabulary building. As they meet and learn new words, the students will list these words alphabetically in the notebook. These lists will later furnish material for vocabulary tests and spelling lists.
7. Charts and flash cards will be used periodically.
8. Students will often refer to an eighth-grade literature book to find, in context, sentences for analysis and words for spelling lists and vocabulary building.
C. Sequential Listing of Activities[31]
1. The teacher will read several sentences and phrases, calling attention to the absence of complete thought and the lack of a subject or verb in the phrases.
2. The students will determine that some groups of words are not sentences because there is no subject or verb; all sentences must have a subject and a verb.
3. The students will eliminate all phrases from a list in the textbook. They will identify all the sentences by finding the subjects and verbs. They will classify them in two columns in their English notebooks, all verbs in one column and all subjects in the other.
4. Students will find and compile lists of nouns classified as people, places, ideas, animals, and things. They will get this information from books, observations, and experiences.
5. One student will read his list of classified nouns. If others in the room have new ones, they will be added to the list. The students will make sentences with a few of the nouns

---

[31]Activities have generally been carefully selected in consideration of the types of youngsters in this eighth-grade group. Occasionally, however, the planner wishes to use the textbook without specifically stating which exercise he is referring to. These activities have been consistently related to stated objectives. Furthermore, activities have been described well enough to permit a second teacher to get an accurate picture of what is to be done.

to be sure they see the relationship of the noun to the sentence.

6. A written exercise from the text will be assigned on finding, selecting, and classifying nouns in the four categories.

7. From examples of simple sentences on the board, students will detect that verbs are not always single words but may be two-, three-, or four-word verbs called *verb phrases*. They will clarify the word *phrase* if its meaning has been forgotten. This will be added to their vocabulary notebooks.

8. Students will work an exercise from their books on finding verb phrases.

9. The students will find sentences in their readers that contain action verbs. In order to save time, some of the verbs will be quickly written on the board. They will observe that some action verbs transfer action to an object and are called *transitive*. The prefix *trans-* will be defined, discussed, and written in the vocabulary notebooks. Students will observe that some action verbs and auxiliary (helper) verbs do not transfer action to an object; they are called *intransitive*. The prefix *in-* (not) will be defined, discussed, and put in the notebook. The two new words with their meanings will also be listed.

10. The students will work exercises from the textbook on finding verbs and classifying them as transitive or intransitive.

11. The students will complete work sheets on transitive and intransitive verbs, also finding subjects in the same sentences. This is to be an informal review.

12. The students will look at diagrams of sentences in the text containing transitive and intransitive verbs. They will try to diagram four or five sentences containing such verbs from the informal work sheet. They will then correct their own work, using the correct form the teacher puts on the board.

13. The teacher will give a short quiz on finding subjects and verbs (transitive and intransitive) and on diagraming a few simple sentences.

14. The students will refer to their texts for charts on the principal parts of verbs. *Principal* will be defined and added to vocabulary notes. Students will observe that many mistakes in usage can be eliminated if they know and understand when to use each of the three parts of verbs: the present part is for what happens now, the past part is for past time, and the third part also shows past time but always has a helper.

15. The students will review all three parts of the long list of verbs, saying them aloud in a sentence. They will discuss those parts that seem out of the ordinary or strange.

16. More work will be done on the troublesome verbs—*lie-lay, sit-set, rise-raise*—after it has been determined that students comprehend their principal parts.

17. The students will be given a dittoed chart with two verbs categorized in their six tenses.

18. The word *conjugate* will be defined and made meaningful as the teacher points out that the two words in the verb chart have been conjugated, or put in all of the different voices and tenses, using all of the persons and numbers.

19. Students will each select two verbs and, with the teacher's help, will conjugate them on their charts.

20. The students will do exercises on the three parts and six tenses of verbs. Work sheets will be completed in class.

21. The teacher will make assignments in the text on the parts of verbs and choosing the right verb.

22. A game called "Answer Me" will vary the "choose-the-right-verb" study. Fifteen troublesome verbs will be passed to half the class, fifteen members. Each student will ask a question using the past part of the verb he has been given. He holds the verb up while he is talking. Then the person next to him, without a verb, uses the same verb and answers back with the past participle and a helper. *Question:* I *saw* the circus last night. Did you? *Answer:* No, but I *have seen* one before.

23. A written test on the use of fifty verbs will be given.

24. The students will be asked to find some interesting descriptive sentences. These will be written on the board for analysis.

25. Students will observe that the most vivid words describe the nouns by telling the colors, kinds, sizes, shapes, how many, and which one. These words are called adjectives. The students will then be given a work sheet containing twenty sentences full of vivid adjectives. They will clarify all the adjectives in columns according to what they tell.

26. The teacher will diagram a couple of sentences on the board and then help the students diagram about six in order to see the relationship of adjectives to nouns.

27. The students will do some assignments on adjectives from the text, naming what they modify and what they tell about the word.

28. Students will be shown by the use of objects how to prop-

erly compare adjectives (for instance, *big, bigger,* when comparing two items; *big, bigger, biggest,* when comparing more than two items).

29. They will do an oral exercise on comparison. Each student will think of one adjective that can be compared and then by use of proper sentences will state it in the three degrees. Any mistakes will be corrected. New words will be added to the vocabulary notebook.

30. A short completion test will be given. The student will select the proper degree of comparison to fill in the space. There will be 25 sentences. *Example:* 1. Of the two boys, John is the _____ (thinner, thinnest).

31. A set of sentences from the text will be analyzed to find that how, when, and where words are called *adverbs.*

32. Students will classify adverbs from twelve to fifteen sentences into the three categories. They will determine what kinds of words they modify.

33. Work sheets will be given to the class. They will find all the adjectives and adverbs and draw arrows pointing to the words they modify. On the arrow they will write what the adjective or adverb tells about the word modified.

34. Some examples of simple sentences with compound parts will be analyzed from the book. The students will observe that the compound parts are connected by a conjunction and that conjunctions help relate the parts to each other.

35. The students will diagram several simple sentences with compound parts following examples given in the text. New words will be added to the vocabulary notebook.

36. Students will follow the text in analyzing compound sentences, noting that two closely related complete thoughts are connected by a conjunction or semicolon. Any new words will be defined and added to their notebooks.

37. Work sheets will be given to the class. They will find compound parts (subject and verb) and compound sentences, labeling each. Those who wish may try diagraming a sentence of their choice on the chalkboard. The class will criticize.

38. An assignment on simple and compound sentences will be given from the text. New words will be added to the vocabulary list.

39. An examination will be given on work covered this far. *Sample examination questions:*
    1. Tell if the sentence is simple or compound by putting S or C in the margin.
    2. Underline all subjects once, verbs twice.

   3. Write *1* above all adjectives, *2* above all adverbs.
   4. Write (*trans.*) or (*intrans.*) above all verbs.
40. After a short oral review, a test will be given on all terms and words in the vocabulary list. (Flash cards will be used to review words.) The test will be concerned with defining and filling in the blanks.
41. Before class, the teacher will write on the board two or three sentences that have complicated parts. By analysis the students will observe that there are phrases and clauses that depend on the rest of the sentence for their meaning.
42. The meaning of and differences between the words *clause* and *phrase* will be clarified and added to vocabulary notes.
43. From exercises in the text, the students will find clauses and phrases that act as adjectives, modifying nouns or pronouns. They will find clauses and phrases that act as adverbs, modifying adjectives, adverbs, or verbs and telling how, when, and where.
44. They will be encouraged to find clauses that act as nouns and may be used as subjects, predicate nominatives, or objects.
45. The students will be shown on the chalkboard how the clauses and phrases are diagramed. They will not diagram these yet
46. Work sheets will be given to the students. They will place parentheses around the clauses and phrases and draw an arrow to the words they modify. They will name the kinds of clauses and phrases.
47. Several exercises from the book on clauses and phrases will follow. There will also be chalkboard work.
48. An examination on complex sentences will be given. *Example:* Put parentheses around the dependent clause. Underline the complete independent clause. Circle the connecting link, and draw an arrow to the word to which the dependent clause refers; also tell what kind of clause it is.
D. Culminating Activities (Three or four class periods)
   1. A review in the form of an open-book test will precede an overall examination. Sheets of questions (underlining, matching, completion, or short essay) will be handed out. Questions on all material covered so far in the unit will be included in the questions. (The students won't know that this isn't a final.) Under a reasonable time limit the students will answer the problems. When the time is up, the students will be free to open their books and answer all questions that they omitted. Special help will be given

to those students with problems. Those who finish early and need no recheck may go to the library.

2. Each student will choose from a list of topics a subject upon which to speak for one or two minutes.[32] He will prepare the talk in school and record it on tape. This will be recorded before school and from 3:30 to 4:00 after school. These recordings will be played in the next class period. The students will criticize them on the following:
   a. Proper usage of words
   b. Content
   c. Correctness of subject matter
   d. Enunciation and voice

Examples of topics:
   a. How to use (1) in, into; (2) sit, set; (3) lie, lay.
   b. What do adjectives do?
   c. How do we use adverbs?
   d. What is a compound sentence?
   e. What is a verb tense?

3. The students will make a pen or pencil sketch to show some particular outstanding problem in the usage of words that they have overcome in studying this unit.[33] Or they may graphically portray some concept that has been especially interesting. These problems and concepts will be discussed very briefly by each student as he displays his visual object or sketch. These materials will be mounted on the bulletin board.

4. The students will take a final examination on all phases covered in this unit.

IV. Materials and Resources
   A. The following materials and teaching aids will be used during the teaching of the unit:
      1. Work sheets
      2. Extensive use of the chalkboard
      3. Charts
      4. Pictures for bulletin boards
      5. Colored pencils
      6. Drawing paper
      7. Indexed vocabulary notebooks
      8. Tests
      9. English notebooks
     10. Tape recorder
     11. Film projector

---

[32]Note the culminating nature of this activity. It calls for the practical use of much of the content of the unit in a real situation.

[33]Note the teacher's attempt to make the instruction personally meaningful for the student.

SEATING CHART

```
┌──────────────────┐
│     TEACHER      │
└──────────────────┘
```

Clifford X605	Lynn X705	Kathryn X801	James X961	Francis X904	Bill 01102
Susan X852	Bayle X1041	Todd 01053	Beth X1014	Sammy X891	Earl X965
Jay X993	Bonnie 01264	Kent 0854	Kay X1013	Jean 01185	Joan 01073
Linda X1205	Larry 01174	Laurel 01004	Vaughn 01095	Raylene X1022	Jimmy X974
John X913	Laura 01055	Roger 0904	Betty 01074	Wayne 0975	Claudette 0983

Seating Chart Code[34]

    X = Inattentive
    O = No problem
    101 = I.Q.
    1-5 = Discipline

    B. The following texts will be used during the unit:
        1. *Our English Language* by Matilda Bailey and Lalla Walker.
        2. Eighth Grade Literature Series.[35]

V. Evaluation Procedures
    A. Tests and Examinations[36]
        1. Both formal and informal tests will be given to measure the accuracy and extent of the students' learning.
        2. Short quizzes and a final examination will be given.
        3. Results of the exams and quizzes will be reviewed and evaluated.
        4. Open-book tests will be given periodically to teach the techniques of searching for certain facts, developing abilities in the use of the index, locating and recording important facts, combing out details, and reviewing important concepts.

---

[34]The seating chart might have been more appropriately included as a part of the Basic Information. Questions might be raised about the simplicity of the code and, therefore, the protection it offers in safeguarding confidential information.
[35]Inexact designation of the literature series tends toward haziness in planning.
[36]Evaluation procedures give evidence of the need for breadth and variation.

B. General Evaluation Procedures
1. Informative discussions, in which all of the students participate, will clear up hazy concepts in daily work.
2. The teacher will keep individual records of all the work
done by the students and will periodically review their status
with them in private conferences. Group relations and adjustment problems may also be discussed at this time.
3. Students will evaluate their own work while listening to
tape recordings of their own compositions. They will check
for incorrect usage, poor sentences, repetition, unnecessary
words, a good speaking voice, and general accuracy of information.
4. Students will rate their own written work according to a
chart set up for this purpose. They will check their own
notebooks for general appearance, margins, title, proper
spacing for paragraphs, completeness, and accuracy.
5. Any stories, sketches, objective material, or observations that
students bring in will be rated by the teacher and used for
instructional purposes where desirable.
6. Filmstrips will be used to reveal the art of communication
and how general principles must be employed to achieve
desirable social relations.
7. Teacher-made aids such as posters, pictures, sketches,
bulletin boards, and flash cards will be used to motivate
and provoke thinking.
8. Students will write questions for quiz games that will serve
as good motivation for an overall review.
9. The final grades will give attention to the student's progress
as well as his scholarship.

SUCCESSFUL TEACHING UNITS IN REVIEW

The earlier discussion on unit planning and the illustrative units suggest
several summary generalizations that explain the need for and the problems related to unit planning.

1. The best classroom instruction is based upon sound unit planning.

2. Unit planning developed from the need for teachers to group
related objectives in meaningful ways.

3. Unit planning encourages the establishment of close relationships
between objectives and the procedures (including the use of aids)
necessary to achieve these objectives.

4. Although unit plans may vary in detail depending upon the needs
of students and teachers, all plans must give consideration to basic
information about students, objectives, procedures, materials and resources, and evaluation procedures.

5. Behavioral objectives are viewed as essential by many unit planners, and a growing number of such planners prefer to relate enabling objectives to terminal behavior (behavioral objectives). Use of double columns encourages the meaningful matching of these two kinds of objectives.

6. Units of quality must be practical and usable, avoiding the danger of undesirable brevity or unnecessary length.

7. Activities may be advantageously grouped under three headings—introductory, developmental, and concluding—to meet the purpose of the unit.

8. Subject areas organized along conceptual lines lend themselves particularly well to unit planning. Teachers in skill areas have often elected to employ modified unit and daily lesson plans to fit their particular needs.

9. Unit planners may helpfully evaluate their own units through the use of special self-scoring devices.

PROBLEMS FOR STUDY AND DISCUSSION

1. Aside from the reasons teachers often give for not wanting to make written unit plans, what are their unstated reasons? Discuss.

2. Do you believe that no teaching of any sort should be undertaken without written plans? Explain.

3. List ten activities that are not related to unit content but that must be planned for.

4. Describe an individual who, as a first-year teacher, would not find it necessary to engage in writing unit plans. How closely do *you* approximate this individual?

5. Explain the following statement: Unit planning proceeds with greatest ease where the subject matter is well organized along conceptual lines.

6. What difficulties would you encounter in organizing a unit for teaching a foreign language when the major emphasis is on pronunciation and memorization? Explain.

7. If you were to limit your basic concerns with respect to unit planning to two areas only, what would they be? Why?

8. List the five basic steps that should be considered in unit planning. Of these, which steps are the most important? Why?

9. Describe the characteristics of students in a typical class to which you might teach your subject-matter minor. Give consideration to I.Q.'s, socio-economic status, student problems, potential troublemakers, and experiential backgrounds.

10. Do you believe that the objectives listed under "Concepts to Be Learned," pages 124–129, are too detailed? Explain.

11. What are the specific advantages of behavioral objectives? Specify.

12. Can you suggest a practical arrangement for relating enabling objectives to behavioral objectives that does not involve the use of parallel columns?

13. If your supervisor insisted that you use only one kind of objective—enabling or behavioral—which would you select? Why?

14. List five aids that are not commercially available for purchase but that you would like to make for teaching your subject-matter major.

15. What are the advantages of dividing developmental activities into *recurring* and *sequential* groups? Would this serve a useful purpose in teaching your subject-matter major?

16. How much detail is necessary in listing the objectives and activities of a unit? Explain.

17. Under what circumstances is it feasible to use a commercially produced film? Explain.

18. Assuming you have no other professional person to help you, name at least two practical ways for evaluating your unit other than by a self-scoring instrument.

VE: Word stress in Spanish is very uniform...
ertain rules.

uf LEARNING INVOLVED: Conceptual, memorization

WHAT (SUBJECT OUTLINE)	HOW (ACTIVITIES AND AI
enos días conversation.	A. Teacher-student resp B. Student-student resp teacher will ask for vo to come to the front of and repeat the conversa no one volunteers, she on two students that sh observed do it well. (and Bob)
view Spanish vowels pre- d yesterday.	A. Teacher will have th dents repeat the sampl words of the fourth da

8. *Making a Daily Lesson Plan Effective*

The daily lesson plan[1] is a device for keeping the teacher on the track of a carefully planned unit.[2] It should be prepared after class in anticipation of the needs of the class on the next day. The daily lesson plan is useful because:[3]

1. It encourages the planner to relate the objectives and procedures singled out for daily presentation to the overall objectives and procedures of the unit.

---

[1]William H. Burton, *The Guidance of Learning Activities*, 3d. ed. (New York: Appleton-Century-Crofts, 1962), pp. 322–324, provides a brief but stimulating discussion of the history and general nature of daily lesson plans.

Leonard M. Douglas, *The Secondary Teacher at Work* (Boston: D. C. Heath & Company, 1967), p. 124, emphasizes the need for detailed planning by the beginning teacher.

[2]A helpful discussion on how the daily lesson plan implements the unit is provided by Nathan S. Blount and Herbert J. Klausmeier, *Teaching in the Secondary School* (New York: Harper & Row, Publishers, 1968), pp. 219–225.

[3]Sidney L. Besvinick, "An Effective Daily Lesson Plan," *The Clearing House*, 34 (March 1960), 431–433, identifies and illustrates the characteristics of a daily lesson plan of quality.

2. It permits making the daily adjustments necessary for effective teaching.

3. It encourages a vivid and up-to-the-minute recall of the content of the unit.

4. It encourages specific planning needed to meet problems related to classroom control, motivation, and differentiated instruction.

ESSENTIAL PARTS OF THE PLAN

It would be misleading to infer that all daily lesson plans have identical organization; they are as varied as the teachers who use them. It is imperative, however, that the teacher give attention to the following:

1. Specific objectives (including the type of objective)
2. Specific procedures
3. Use of time
4. Materials and resources
5. Assignments
6. Evaluation
7. Relationship of a particular daily lesson plan to its parent unit

During the first year or two of teaching, the beginning teacher should experiment with different forms and plans to determine how these seven areas can best be covered.[4]

Examination of a range of daily lesson plans prepared by a number of different teachers for their specific needs discloses that these areas of concern are common to most planners. Such plans indicate (a) *what* is to be taught (the objectives) and (b) *how* it is to be taught (the procedures). In addition the time to be devoted to each activity is often indicated. More complete lesson plans mention the type of objective being taught (concept, skill, memorization, or habit) and the assignment for the day. In certain cases the objective for the day is related to a larger objective or to the encompassing unit objective.

The "Suggested Format for the Daily Lesson Plan"[5] on page 153 illustrates needed essentials. Designed to assist student teachers, this form contains brief explanatory statements about the type of information to be inserted under the various headings.

Some teachers have found it advantageous to use two or more different daily lesson plan forms, depending on the needs of a particular day. For example, when students must be reminded of a large number of details, ample space should be provided under *preliminaries* on the form.

---

[4]Arthur A. Delaney, "Lesson Plans—Means or End?" *The Clearing House*, 36 (January 1962), 295–297, examines the basic purposes of lesson plans.

William R. Lueck, Elwood G. Campbell, Leo E. Eastman, Charles W. Edwards, Clayton F. Thomas, and William D. Zeller, *Effective Secondary Education* (Minneapolis: Burgess Publishing Company, 1966), pp. 106–109, enumerate the major parts of a lesson plan.

[5]Ray T. Wilcox, *Handbook for Student Teachers*, rev. ed. (Provo, Utah: Brigham Young University, 1963), p. 21.

SUGGESTED FORMAT
FOR THE DAILY LESSON PLAN

Specific Objective: (Preferably one or a few concepts, symbols, skills, feelings, or habits from the unit plan that can be taught in one lesson.)

What to Teach	How to Teach	What Is Needed	Time
A statement of the few basic concepts to be taught and the related sub-concepts and/or the specific skills to be practiced and/or the symbols to be learned and/or the feelings to be developed and/or the habits to be fostered. (These should be related to the objectives in the unit plan.)	Procedures, methods, experiences, and questions designed to get the students to perceive this subject as clearly as possible and to organize and interpret the students' perception of the objects and events involved.	Needed instructional resources to portray the subject to students. This portrayal may include use of maps, books, papers, teaching aids, laboratory equipment, and so forth.	Rough estimate of the time involved for each phase of the lesson.

Assignment: (The assignment should be clear, definite, and stimulating. It should be within the pupils' ability to perform and varied to challenge all shades of ability in the class.)

Evaluation: (What is your reaction to the lesson after it has been taught? Are there points to be remembered that will help to avoid making the same errors when the lesson is taught again? What parts are good enough to repeat?)

On the other hand, it is often unnecessary for the teacher to give reminders, make announcements, and discuss long-range assignments. On such days the teacher may use a form that focuses full attention on objectives and related activities. Furthermore, the beginning teacher may find it helpful to use a form different from that which the experienced teacher would use. Two forms used with great frequency are represented in Example A and in Example I (pages 155 and 166).

DAILY LESSON PLAN FORMS

The five examples of daily lesson plan forms on pages 155–160 illustrate similarities as well as minor differences that may reasonably exist.[6] Look over the individual forms carefully before reading the discussion of each type.

Comments on Example A (See page 155.)

There may be some confusion about the difference between "Objectives Stated as Concepts to Be Learned" and "What to Teach." Both headings hint at objectives. Actually, under the first heading the teacher is concerned with general unit objectives. "Other Objectives" refers to other *types* of objectives and should have been so indicated. "Preliminaries" usually consist of announcements, reminders, and other noncontent-related details that often must be dealt with in a class. "Assignments" have been given a deservedly prominent position.

The column arrangement of "What to Teach," "How to Teach," "Time Used," and "Materials" encourages the establishment of a close relationship among these essential concerns. At the bottom of the page provision has been made for "Evaluation Procedures," which in this case refers to the teacher's evaluation of the preceding lesson in order to discover a basis for improvement.

Comments on Example B (See page 156.)

Information relating to subject, grade, date, and time may be helpful when a teacher has as many as three subject-matter assignments. The identification of the "Types of Learning" is useful in selecting procedures best suited to a given kind of objective. The "Objective" and "What to Teach" must be clearly established. The column concerned with "Time Use" would be more functional if placed next to the "How to Teach" column. A differentiation is made between the "Evaluation of Student Learning" and the "Evaluation of the Lesson." Since those two evalua-

---

[6]Leonard H. Clark and Irving S. Starr, *Secondary School Teaching Methods*, 2d. ed. (New York: The Macmillan Company, 1967), pp. 111–112, suggest the desirability of flexibility in lesson plan format to meet the preferences of individual instructors. Specific recommendations are made.

EXAMPLE A

Daily Lesson Plan for_____Date_____

Objectives Stated as Concepts to Be Learned:

Other Objectives:

Preliminaries:

Assignments:

What to Teach	How to Teach	Time Used	Materials

Evaluation Procedures:

EXAMPLE B

Subject_____Date_____

Grade_____   Time_____

Types of Learning_____

Objective_____

Time Use	What to Teach	How to Teach	Materials

Assignment   Evaluation of Student Learning

Evaluation of Lesson

tions seem to have a close relationship, this division may be questionable when one is attempting to confine the total lesson plan to one page.

Comments on Example C (See page 158.)

Use of a unit title or number may serve a useful purpose when individual lesson plans are to be filed away for later reference. The checking of the "Method" to be employed serves no useful purpose because this becomes obvious upon reading the "How to Teach" column. "What to Teach" seems to usurp the function of the "Lesson Objective" when the objective is confined to only the one lesson. The indication of time use is missing, making the plan less specific and useful. As in Example B, the "Evaluation" has been pointed toward the student and the lesson itself. However, these divisions and the small amount of space encourage a brief and general evaluation.

Comments on Example D (See page 159.)

Inclusion of the teacher's name takes needed space and does not contribute to the lesson plan. The listing of the "General Objective" followed by "Specific Objectives" has the advantage of establishing a clear relationship between the two. It is to be noted that because "Specific Objectives" are listed above, no attention is given to objectives among the column headings. "Teacher Activities" and "Student Activities" might well be combined into one column with an economy of space.

Comments on Example E (See page 160.)

Consideration is given only to goals (behavioral objectives and enabling objectives) and activities (preassessment and learning activities). Other details are assumed to be of limited value. Because the "Behavioral Objective" for a single daily lesson focuses typically on one terminal behavior, limited space is made available for needed wording. The "Preassessment" may be somewhat more detailed, requiring more space. "Enabling Objectives" often consist of a central concept or skill with supporting sub-concepts or sub-skills that may consume additional lines. Ample space is left for identification and sequential listing of "Learning Activities"; this is essential when use of materials, time use, and assignments must be incorporated in "Learning Activities".

PRACTICAL USE OF SPECIFIC FORMS

The five examples of daily lesson plans on pages 162–167 were designed to give direction to actual classroom presentations. They might have been quite different if they had been made out by different teachers. Note that they are brief, practical, and can be inserted on a prepared form of one

EXAMPLE C

                                        (Title)

Class_____Unit (No.)_____

Method:

  Discussion___ Illustration___ Demonstration___ Conference___ Lecture___

Type of Learning:

  Concept___ Skill___ Memorization___ Tastes and Preferences___

Lesson Objective:_____

_____

_____

What to Teach	How to Teach	Materials

Assignment:

Evaluation: Student   Lesson

EXAMPLE D

Class_____Name_____

Hour_____Date_____

General Objective_____

Specific Objectives_____

_____

Type of Learning_____

Time	Teacher Activity	Student Activity	Materials

Assignment:

Evaluation:

   1.

   2.

   3.

   4.

EXAMPLE E

Behavioral Objective:

Preassessment:

Enabling Objectives:

Learning Activities:

typewritten page.[7] Look over the individual forms carefully before reading the discussion of each type.

Comments on Example F (See page 162.)

The simplicity of the minor concepts in the "What to Teach" column is apparent, and they all bear a close relationship to the larger objective for the day at the top of the form. A primary concern is the teaching of these minor concepts at the start of the lesson. Concepts in the "What to Teach" column are stated as briefly as possible in the interest of saving space. "Check for squareness," concept 1, gives the false impression that it is an activity. If it were stated in its full conceptual form, however, it would be "The first step in sharpening a cabinet scraper is to check for squareness." This is clearly a concept. The development of the needed skill will come through the practice provided for in the assignment. Although little or no direct attention is focused on memorizing the chart of steps, recall is encouraged through proper conceptualization and use. Note that the teaching demonstration involves only ten minutes, with fifteen minutes devoted to the students' use of the concepts already learned. The majority of the class period will be devoted to supervised work on a project.

Comments on Example G (See page 163.)

Note that to facilitate teaching the larger goal has been broken down into two divisions. Several activities related to each of these two divisions tend to fix the concept in the students' minds. The space for "Reminders" at the top of the form and for "Unfinished Business" at the bottom gives evidence of practical concerns. Column arrangements of "Supporting Objectives," "Time," and "Procedures" clearly indicate the interrelationships.

Comments on Example H (See page 164.)

Numbers in the "What to Teach" column refer to the objectives in the unit plan. Use of this procedure would necessitate having the unit plan on the teacher's desk so that it could be easily correlated with the daily lesson plan. It would also be possible for the planner to write out the supporting objectives, listing in the adjacent column the number of the activity in the unit plan that corresponds to the given objective. In the main, the procedures used in the form in Example H should be used with extreme caution.

---

[7]Homer C. Rose, *The Instructor and His Job* (Chicago: American Technical Society, 1966), pp. 243–245, illustrates the use of a lesson plan in teaching a shop class how to tin a soldering copper. Analysis at key points in the lesson is stressed.

EXAMPLE F

Objective: The sharpening of a cabinet scraper involves several steps that must be followed in a given order.

Method: Discussion X   Illustration___   Demonstration X

Conference___   Lecture X

Type of Learning: Concept X   Skill X   Memorization X

Tastes and Preferences___

What to Teach	How to Teach	Min.	Materials
1. Check for squareness.	1. Show with T-square how light comes through where uneven.	2	1. Chart of steps to be used: scraper blade, T-square, saw vice
2. Remove old burr.	2. Demonstrate how file is held to remove burr.	1	2. Single cut mill file
3. File beveled edge.	3. Impress upon students that the file is to be used at a 45° angle to the blade.	3	
4. Hone filed blade.	4. Show the students how to hone on the flat side, then on the beveled side.	3	3. Oil stone
5. Burnish the edge.	5. Demonstrate how to properly hold and use burnisher. Stress the importance of burnishing at three angles: 45°, 67°, and 90°.	1	4. Burnishing tool.

Assignment: Have each student sharpen his own scraper, and have it checked by the instructor before the student resumes work on his project. (15 minutes)

Evaluation:

1. Student Learning   2. Lesson Presentation

EXAMPLE G

Subject: U.S. History   Time: 2:00 P.M.

Reminders: No school Friday; P.T.A. meets tonight; buy lunch tickets

Lesson Objective: The rapid growth of cities after the Civil War caused
  many problems.

Supporting Objectives	Time	Procedures
		Briefly review yesterday's class. Quickly outline on the chalkboard questions to be answered in today's lesson. Remind students to look for important questions they would like to have answered or to learn more about.
A. Cities grew rapidly after the Civil War. Examples: New York City, Chicago, Los Angeles, Salt Lake City, Provo.	10	A. Show pictures of large cities. Discuss: world metropolis, largest city in the Midwest, largest city in the West, largest city in Utah, largest city in Utah county. 1. How large does a community have to be to become a city? (Use the chalkboard to show different kinds of people coming to cities.) Make graphs to show the increase in the size of cities between 1790 and 1950: Row 2--New York; Row 3--Chicago; Row 4--Los Angeles; Row 5--Salt Lake City; Everyone--Provo. 2. Are some Western cities growing at a faster rate today than some Eastern cities?
B. The growth of cities brought many problems. 1. Much construction was needed: sewers, water purification plants, firehouses.	10	B. Discuss: 1. Does Provo City have sewers? Does Provo City have water purification plants? Does Provo City have firehouses? Why? (Assign special reports on the above three topics.)
2. Graft and corruption became problems all through the nation. (Boss Tweed & Tammany Hall; Thomas Nast; U. S. Grant)	15	2. Cite an example: School's student-body president elected by a small group asking special favors. School's principal helps man become Superintendent who gives the principal free reign. Ask pupils for examples--Look in newspapers, etc. Tell story of Boss Tweed, Thomas Nast, and U. S. Grant.
3. City slums grew.	10	3. Relate the report of the Board of Health. Do we have slums today? Show picture.

Assignments: 1. Special reports on sewers (John & Sam); Provo Water Department (Jack & Bill); Provo Fire Department (Mary & Betty).
  2. Graphs as assigned in A above.
  3. Collect news articles about graft. (Did crime pay?)

Unfinished Business: 1. We did not get a chance to discuss whether cities
  today have solved their problems or what kind of problems they still have.
  2. Should cities be abolished?
  3. Questions the students still want answered:
     a. What is the difference between a city, a town, and a village?
     b. Are city children smarter than those who live in small towns?
     c. Does it cost more to live in a city?

EXAMPLE H

Subject: Music Fundamentals (Grades 7 through 9)

Kind of Objective: Concept___, Memorization___, Skill___, or Habit___

Objective: The great staff is made up of the treble and the bass clefs,
and the line between them is known as Middle C. Notes placed on a
specific line or space can be read and played and have the same meaning to all musicians.

What to Teach	How to Teach	Materials
II, A, 4	Teacher will lecture, using the permanent staff on the chalkboard.	Chalkboard
II, A, 5	Students at board will insert notes on staff at request of teacher. Students at seats will check board work.	
	Students will draw treble and bass clefs at seats and fill in notes at the request of the teacher. Students will locate and fill in notes for each of the following sequences in the treble as well as the bass clef: B-C; F-A-C; D-F-A; G-B-D. The class will be organized into pairs. They will check each other's paper.	Paper
	The teacher will then insert the proper notes on the permanent staff at the chalkboard.	
II, A, 6	The teacher will play the notes on the piano. The students will hum them lightly.	
II, A, 4, 5, and 6	Again students will be asked to insert specific notes on the clefs drawn at their seats: C-E-G; D-G-B; A-C-F; A-C-E; A-D-F; B-D-F. Student pairs will again check each other's paper. The teacher will insert the proper notes on the permanent staff and play the notes on the piano.	

Assignment: For tomorrow, students will write the correct letters (A, C,
E, etc.) beside the notes on the dittoed copy of "Silent Night," in the
key of C.

Evaluation:

Special Concerns: Have a private chat with Martha; see Douglas about his
missing assignment; praise Wilma for her excellent board work yesterday.

Comments on Example I (See page 166.)

This form may well serve the purposes of a thoroughly experienced teacher who has taught the same unit a number of times. It would *not* serve the needs of the beginner. Note, for example, that this planner does not explicitly designate objectives and activities. Emphasis in this case is placed on activities.[8] If a teacher does not have a clear picture of the objectives he hopes to teach, he will encounter difficulties.

This lesson plan does have these advantages, however. It is very simple, consisting of four basic headings—"Routine and Preliminaries," "Subject-Matter Treatment," "Assignment," and "Miscellaneous Concerns." Ample space is provided for listing routine and preliminary procedures, but a minimum of space is devoted to subject-matter treatment because of the limited need of the seasoned teacher. At the bottom of the page the planner may insert notes to help him conduct a better lesson.

Comments on Example J (See page 167.)

Emphasis on behavioral objectives has the advantage of indicating what the student should be able to do by way of terminal performance when the lesson has been completed, a concern that has not been given consideration in the preceding lesson plan forms. Most frequently this emphasis is related to a cluster of enabling unit objectives requiring more than one day for treatment.

Preassessment—a determination of how much students know about what is proposed to be taught—is likewise most often reserved for a full unit or unit segment. However, under certain circumstances it may be employed effectively in a single daily lesson plan. Enabling objectives (what to teach) are treated much as they would be in the preceding daily lesson plan forms. When assumed to be essential, indications of materials to be used and timing considerations are incorporated as a part of the description of learning activities.

SPECIFIC SUGGESTIONS

Specific suggestions for the preparation and use of daily lesson plans can be of great practical benefit, particularly to the beginning teacher or to the teacher who wishes to improve the efficiency of his planning. The following recommendations and cautions are aimed at providing such teachers with positive direction and with suggestions for avoiding the errors that often beset the novice.

---

[8]See Peter F. Oliva, *The Secondary School Today* (New York: World Publishing Company, 1967), pp. 192–196, for illustrations of daily lesson plans with accompanying explanations.

EXAMPLE I

Subject: French I   Date: November 21st

Routine and Preliminaries:

    1. Call roll. Students respond in French.
    2. Collect assignments.
    3. Reassign seats for Jean, Paul, Terry, and Millie.
    4. Ask for three volunteers to work on the bulletin board for next week.

Subject-Matter Treatment:

    1. Introduce the verb etre. Conjugate the verb on the board. Give one
       or two examples of the verb used in sentences.
    2. Give examples of the verb in its various conjugations (present tense
       only). Have students work at the chalkboard for this exercise. Help
       the students having difficulty. Make constructive criticism as stu-
       dents put examples on the board.
    3. Review the French vocabulary by having the students participate in
       a spelling match. Students are to spell in French as the words are
       dictated by the teacher from page 37 of the text.

Assignment:

    1. Students will complete the exercises related to etre on page 39 of
       the text.

Miscellaneous Concerns:

    1. Promote the French Club meeting to be held on Tuesday.
    2. Stimulate Tonya Wilkes' desire to learn French.
    3. Send Harry and Hilda to the library to work on special reports
       during the study period.

EXAMPLE J

Behavioral Objective: Given a dittoed sheet on which the
poem <u>A Wanderer's Song</u> is printed, during a five-minute
period students will underline the separate words,
phrases, and passages that illustrate the use of literal
imagery. An acceptable level of performance will be
represented by a score of 17 of the 22 to 25 possible
underlinings.

Preassessment: Subject to no time limit, students will be
asked to underline the words, phrases, and passages in
the poem <u>October's Bright Blue Weather</u> by Helen Hunt
Jackson illustrating the use of literal imagery. If
students on the average underline 23 of the 32 to 34
desired passages, the lesson will be assumed to be
unnecessary.

Enabling Objectives (Concepts): Literal imagery signifies
vivid and particularized passages in poetry that evoke
mental pictures of concrete objects or sensory experiences.
In contrast to figurative imagery, literal imagery does
not call for a change or extension of the obvious meaning
of words.

Learning Activities:
1. Without further explanation, the teacher will read
aloud the first two stanzas of the poem <u>Elegy Written
in a Country Churchyard</u> by Thomas Gray, which contains
much literal imagery. In a class discussion, students
will be asked to tell what makes the poem concrete and
vivid.
2. A second poem, <u>My Luve Is Like a Red, Red Rose by</u>
Robert Burns, will be read aloud. Students will again
participate in a discussion, having access to the poem
in their text.
3. The teacher will now slowly and meaningfully read
aloud twice the <u>Requiem</u> by Robert Louis Stevenson.
Students will be asked to write individually on scratch
paper the words, phrases, and passages that evoke
pictures of real objects or sensory experiences. Passages
judged by the teacher to fall most nearly in the desired
category will be written on the blackboard. The teacher
will now discuss and define literal imagery, using the
passages on the board to serve as examples.
4. Students will be given a dittoed sheet on which three
short poems (<u>Boy at the Window</u> by Richard Wilbur, <u>Fear</u>
by Hart Crane and <u>Suicide in the Trenches</u> by Siegfried
Sassoon) appear. They will be asked to underline words,
phrases, and passages that represent literal imagery.

Recommendations

1. Be sure that the daily lesson plan will enable you to teach the content of the unit.[9]

2. Determine through tryout whether a combination use of behavioral objectives and enabling objectives is preferred to the use of adjacent "What to Teach" and "How to Teach" columns in preparing a daily lesson plan.

3. After deciding which forms best serve your purposes and individual tastes, have a supply duplicated for consistent daily use.

4. Organize the daily lesson plan form so that desired attention can be given to major objectives, supporting objectives, procedures, materials and resources, evaluation of the lesson and pupil learning, assignment, and routine.

5. The basic concerns of objectives, procedures, time devoted to procedures, and materials may advantageously serve as headings for adjacent vertical columns. With this organization, corresponding items can be placed in parallel columns.

6. Keep the lesson plan as simple as is compatible with usefulness, clarity, and completeness.

7. Establish the relationship between activities occurring on successive days.

8. Establish the relationship of small concepts to large concepts through daily planning.

9. Use the daily lesson plan to make day-to-day adjustments that cannot be anticipated in advance.

10. Single out for treatment on any given day only those objectives (usually supporting enabling objectives) that can be taught effectively. The attempt to cover ground encourages superficiality.

PROBLEMS FOR STUDY AND DISCUSSION

1. What are the essential differences between the unit plan and the daily lesson plan? Discuss each briefly.

2. What are the essential parts of a daily lesson plan? Discuss each.

3. List and discuss three basic justifications for using a daily lesson plan.

4. Are daily lesson plans unnecesary in some subject-matter areas? Explain your thinking.

5. Which daily lesson plan form would be most helpful in teaching your subject-matter major? Why?

6. What is the advantage of placing objectives and related activities in adjacent columns?

---

[9]James S. Kinder, *Using Audio-Visual Materials in Education* (New York: American Book Company, 1965), chapter 5, provides repeated examples of the use of auditory materials in improving the quality of instruction.

The role of the daily lesson plan as a device for implementing the details of a well-planned teaching unit is discussed by Blount and Klausmeier, *Teaching in the Secondary School*, pp. 219–224.

7. Is it always advisable to indicate the approximate time to be devoted to each activity? Why?

8. Indicate a subject in which the listing of materials would be of limited value. Indicate one in which it would be of great value. Where does your subject-matter major lie with respect to the need for listing materials?

9. If a teacher states the daily objective at the top of his plan, is it really necessary to list supporting objectives below? Why?

10. How important is it to have a specific place on your daily lesson plan form for evaluating student learning? Why?

11. Is the inclusion of a time column in the daily lesson plan form essential? Discuss.

12. What values do you see in using two or three different daily lesson plan forms on different days? Explain.

13. Under what conditions would you prefer the combination use of behavioral objectives and enabling objectives to the use of adjacent "What to Teach" and "How to Teach" columns? Explain.

14. List six recommendations that should be helpful to the new teacher in preparing and using daily lesson plans.

15. Give five examples of day-to-day adjustments that cannot be considered in the unit plan but that should be covered in the daily lesson plan.

16. Can you use another teacher's daily lesson plan forms? Why?

PART THREE

Specific
Teaching Procedures

9. *Teacher-Centered Procedures*

Certain procedures are by their very nature teacher-centered.[1] It is the purpose of this chapter to discuss three of these procedures—lectures, questions, and demonstrations—and their effect upon the teaching-learning process. Although other procedures might be identified as teacher-centered, the three mentioned here are particularly important because they are used so frequently.

---

[1]J. Lloyd Trump and Delmas F. Miller, *Secondary School Curriculum Improvement: Proposals and Procedures* (Boston: Allyn & Bacon, 1968), pp. 388–391, identify four imperatives aimed at improving teaching methods, the first of which is "to change the nature of teacher presentations."

A range of teacher-centered patterns of instruction are discussed by Peter F. Oliva and Ralph A. Scrafford, *Teaching in a Modern Secondary School* (Columbus, Ohio: Charles E. Merrill Publishing Co., 1965), pp. 78–83.

Fig. 1   Types of Lectures.

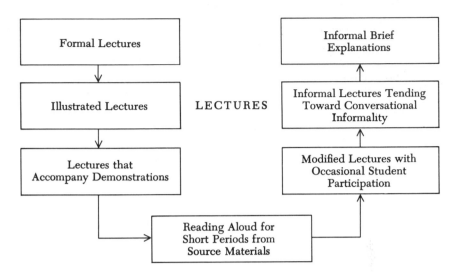

USE OF THE LECTURE

The lecture is commonly described as a teaching procedure in which there is a one-way channel of communication. Under this definition the instructor makes an oral presentation of information to which the student reacts by silently listening and taking notes. Such a definition, however, imposes certain restrictions on the usefulness and flexibility of the lecture —restrictions that are best avoided.[2]

It is instructionally helpful to think of the lecture as encompassing a range of related procedures in which the one-way flow of ideas is the dominant characteristic. Because of the variations that are labeled "lecture," it is desirable to think of lectures on a continuum, extending from the highly formal to the highly informal. The diagram in Figure 1 illustrates this continuum and lists the various types of lectures.[3]

Principles Related to Lecturing

Planning for the use of the lecture should rest on a solid platform of relevant psychological principles. Difficulties can be avoided if the planner evaluates lectures by means of the following criteria.

[2]Leonard H. Clark and Irving S. Starr, *Secondary School Teaching Methods*, 2d. ed. (New York: The Macmillan Company, 1967), pp. 210–214, discuss the strengths and limitations of the various kinds of lecture.

[3]Wayne Dumas and Weldon Beckner, *Introduction to Secondary Education: A Foundations Approach* (Scranton, Pennsylvania: International Textbook Company, 1968), pp. 238–239, point out that the lecture technique has many disadvantages but that teachers should understand its potential as an effective method. Specific suggestions and cautions are provided.

1. The lecture in its pure form is subject to criticism as a classroom procedure. Long formal lectures that present difficult content are unsuited for the average secondary-school classroom.

2. Learning is an active, not a passive, process. For this reason, classroom learning calls for the learner's meaningful reaction to stimuli; if there is no reaction, there is no learning. Passive students frequently lose interest and become inattentive.

3. Individual instructors should identify the types of procedures best suited to their subject, to their personality, and to their class. The lecture, perhaps as much as any teaching procedure, needs modification. The teacher should realize that students have basic needs that must be recognized and reflected in the use of any method. Not all students are equally interested in the same kind of lecture. Similarly, the lecture that is interesting and valuable to the teacher may not be equally interesting and valuable to students in the class. Students are interested in specific methods only to the extent that those methods lead them where they want to go.

4. The lecture, which is comprised of spoken symbols (words), can be only as meaningful as the mental pictures attached to these symbols in the mind of the learner. Thus, students tend to be more interested in the lecture that is specifically related to content already known and liked. Their attention span varies, depending on the individual student's experiences and native capacity, as well as on the communicative ability of the speaker.

5. Language usage (vocabulary level, meaningful examples, fluency, and freedom from speech idiosyncrasies) helps determine how students will react to a lecture.

6. Students may be challenged to work hard to grasp the content of a difficult lecture, but the right kind of humorous comment will ease the strain on them.

7. The teacher who talks too much without really saying anything is recognized as phony by the class.

8. Certain types of subjects (English literature and history, for example) lend themselves to the use of the lecture more readily than others, and specific variations of the lecture (illustrated lectures, informal brief explanations, etc.) tend to be well suited to certain subjects.

9. The successful lecture is held in a setting where competing stimuli are excluded.

10. The teacher should be realistic in judging how much the class will get out of the lecture.

Correct and Incorrect Use

The experienced teacher may identify in the following examples some reflections of his own use of the lecture. The purpose of these illustrations, however, is (1) to provide a meaningful picture of variations in the use of the lecture and (2) to point out that each variation has strengths as well as limitations, depending on the circumstances surrounding its usage. The marked limitations of the formal lecture, for example, are perhaps most apparent as they relate to secondary-school classroom instruction. Although the merits of the lecture variations illustrated in these examples are not discussed, some of the advantages of each type will be obvious. Furthermore, the specific, practical suggestions for using the lecture (pp. 177–179) will be more meaningful against the background of varied examples.

MR. ROBBINS GIVES AN ILLUSTRATED LECTURE

Students are always delighted when Mr. Robbins decides to give another illustrated lecture in their tenth-grade geography class. Because of his long period of military service in the Orient and his very practical hobby of photography, he has acquired several hundred slides of unusual beauty and interest. For each picture, Mr. Robbins has carefully woven together a narrative explanation that capitalizes on the natural interests of teen-agers and is factually sound. The only time that Gerald Riding is interested enough to avoid making a disturbance in the class is during these illustrated lectures.[4]

MR. SIMMONS USES A DEMONSTRATION WITH HIS LECTURES

Lloyd Simmons has an enviable reputation among the senior high school chemistry teachers in his school district. This is largely based on the ease with which he explains certain chemical phenomena to his students in the laboratory. His rule for teaching is: Never lecture without showing. His concern for "showing" apparently works very well, for his students encounter little difficulty in coping with the rigors of college chemistry.

When he gives a demonstration for class benefit, Mr. Simmons asks the students to gather around the teaching area, encircling him and the apparatus. As chemical reactions begin to take place, he points out what is happening and encourages students to identify the reason for the phenomenon. He is careful to be sure that his oral explanations do not obscure or substitute for perceptive observation on the part of students.[5]

MISS DONAKER READS ALOUD FROM SOURCE MATERIALS

For more than a decade, Miss Donaker, the speech teacher at the Thomas Jefferson Senior High School, has assembled and carefully classified an extensive file of supplementary materials. To illustrate particular points, she often reads aloud short essays, speeches, monologs, and dialogs from her collection. On special holiday occasions she may, to the delight of her class, read certain short poems or readings of particular charm and interest.

[4]Five steps required in the formal lecture of today are identified and discussed by John E. Coleman, *The Master Teachers and the Art of Teaching* (New York: Pitman Publishing Corp., 1967), chapter 3. A brief history of the use of the lecture is also presented.

[5]Practical suggestions for humanizing the lecture are listed by Leonard M. Douglas, *The Secondary Teacher at Work* (Boston: D. C. Heath & Company, 1967), pp. 131–132.

PASTOR WOODCOX SUCCEEDS WITH A MODIFIED LECTURE

Pastor Woodcox had learned a great deal about fourteen-year-old ninth-grade boys and girls because his church responsibilities in working with youth groups had brought him into contact with all kinds of youngsters. Of one thing he was certain: Their willingness to listen to long speeches was limited.

Pastor Woodcox was invited to the Woodrow Wilson Junior High School to talk to a ninth-grade civics class about the operation of the local city government. His recently expired term as city commissioner provided him with essential background information. The teacher who contacted him had outlined the basic areas to be covered but left the method of presentation to the discretion of the speaker.

For the first fifteen minutes of his talk, interest remained extremely high. Within five minutes, however, the pastor noted a mild uneasiness among his listeners. It was time, he felt, to involve them actively in the discussion.

"Which one of you," he said, "can tell me the steps that the citizens of this community must go through in order to select the mayor?" After looking around the group and giving each one the impression that he might be called on, the pastor finally selected a student whose hand was raised. Group interest was rekindled, and he continued with his lecture.

Whenever he again felt that interest was beginning to wane, Pastor Woodcox solicited student comments, asked questions, or injected humor into his lecture. At the end of the class one of the students made a statement somewhat representative of the thinking of the group: "Boy, I really believe I know something about city government now. And it was interesting, too."

MR. BRIAN LECTURES INFORMALLY

The thing that students liked most about his class was that Mr. Brian didn't seem to be lecturing to them. It was more as if he were talking to them on their own level. Moreover, students were learning algebra in the bargain.

Although Mr. Brian did most of the talking, students had the impression that they were active participants in the thinking that was taking place. Every now and then he would ask, "Is this reasonable, Bill?" or "Sally, what's wrong with this thinking?"

Even when students posed questions without the formality of raising their hands, the teacher did not seem to object. It was as if his main concern was to keep the path of easy communication open. When students abused their privileges, he had a quiet talk with them after class.[6]

---

[6]E. Dale Davis, *Focus on Secondary Education: An Introduction to Principles and Practices* (Glenview, Illinois: Scott, Foresman and Company, 1966), p. 242, suggests that "teachers can improve their lectures by considering the instructional objectives they have set for their students, presenting the material from the pupil's point of view, using good illustrations and demonstrations, outlining important parts of the lecture on the chalkboard, and talking fluently with little reference to notes or actual reading of materials. . ."

The Lecture in Special Situations

Because illustrated lectures closely approximate first-hand contact with the referent, they provide unusual help for students with limited experiences. For this reason illustrated lectures serve well in teaching geography and foreign cultures. If students are concerned with learning new concepts or correcting erroneous concepts, the use of pictures accompanied by an adequate explanation provides a meaningful learning experience.

Demonstrations[7] are frequently combined with an informal lecture to round out student comprehension. As long as the student is acquiring proper concepts through observation, oral explanations may not be necessary. In some cases they actually distract from the more important concern of observing the cause and effect of a given phenomenon. In most situations, however, the teacher will need to accompany a demonstration with an explanation.

Perhaps the most commonly used modification of the lecture involves the encouragement of student questions and reactions as the instructor proceeds with his discussion. This method has the advantage of promoting consistent student attention. Teachers often intersperse relevant questions in their lectures to good advantage. Informality is thus encouraged, and the potential monotony of the straight lecture is frequently averted.

It may be useful to think of the content of a textbook as comprising a very long, formal lecture. Although students sometimes react meaningfully to such content, often they do not. When they do not, they become bored and apathetic. Knowing this, psychologists and educators developed a technique (programed instruction) for presenting content in small, progressively more difficult segments to which the student must react before he is permitted to move on to the next segment. Using such programed materials, the teacher is able to avoid the most distressing negative characteristic of the formal lecture by encouraging the student to react to each minute parcel of information. (See pages 337–339).

Computer-assisted instruction (CAI) supplements the basic frames (steps) of a program by presenting carefully correlated and automated audio-visual materials. Thus, the boredom of the straight lecture is dealt a double blow.

Specific Suggestions

Knowing how to use any teaching method effectively calls for a broad acquaintance with underlying psychological principles. The use of the lecture is no exception. Examination of these principles leads to specific suggestions that give direction to the beginning teacher's—as well as the more experienced teacher's—use of the lecture.

---

[7] See pages 184–187 for a discussion of demonstrations.

Recommendations

All of the following recommendations are applicable to each variety of lecture method, but some of them have greater applicability to specific types. For example, the encouragement of questions and comments has limited application to the formal lecture, but it may be of great advantage in a modified lecture.[8]

1. Know your subject.
2. Organize your materials thoroughly.
3. Get the attention of the class before you start.
4. Encourage students to take notes.
5. Indicate the relationship of one topic to another.
6. Adapt your lecture to specific listeners; consider their individual differences.
7. Use a vocabulary that is easily understood; be concise but adequate.
8. Speak clearly and fluently; be sure everyone can hear what is said.
9. Experiment with different modifications of the lecture, carefully analyzing how they can best be employed.
10. Use teaching aids to assist in clarifying meanings.
11. Use meaningful, illustrative stories.
12. Emphasize the important points.
13. Be sure the lecture helps achieve established objectives.
14. When appropriate, plan the lecture to develop critical thinking.[9]
15. When practical, and to avoid monotony, encourage student questions and comments.

Cautions

The above list of positive recommendations does not focus attention on many of the specific errors frequently made in using the lecture. The following cautions should help teachers avoid common pitfalls.

1. Don't use the lecture too frequently or to the exclusion of other methods.
2. Don't assume that students have understood all that was said.
3. Don't introduce irrelevant ideas or materials.
4. Don't extend the lecture beyond the pupils' attention span.
5. Don't use the lecture just to cover the material rapidly.
6. Don't spend unwarranted time on unimportant aspects of the lecture.
7. Don't follow your notes or the textbook verbatim.

---

[8]A useful list of cautions and concrete suggestions for the use of the lecture are provided by Douglas, *The Secondary Teacher at Work*, pp. 131–132.

Several specific suggestions for the improvement of the lecture method are identified and discussed briefly by Nathan S. Blount and Herbert J. Klausmeier, *Teaching in the Secondary School*, 3d. ed. (New York: Harper and Row, Publishers, 1968), pp. 265–266.

[9]Oliva and Scrafford, *Teaching in a Modern Secondary School*, pp. 79–80, point out the tendency of beginning teachers to use the lecture. Whether the lecture should be employed, according to them, depends in part upon the skill of the speaker and the maturity of the listeners.

8. Don't lecture so rapidly that students cannot follow your thinking.

9. Don't use a monotonous tone in delivering the lecture.

10. Don't use annoying or distracting mannerisms.

11. Don't appear listless and bored.

A careful re-examination of his own lecture habits will reveal to the conscientious teacher many other cautions that should be recorded for further reference.

USE OF QUESTIONS

Questioning can be an aid to instruction—depending upon the skill with which it is employed by the teacher.[10] It has much in common with the lecture, for it is essentially a teacher-controlled device for promoting thought, making appraisals, and moving students toward desired goals. Although the teacher is chiefly responsible for questioning related to subject-matter content, he also is responsible for providing the setting in which students will feel free to ask relevant questions.

Purposes of Questions

Questioning is correctly employed to:[11]

1. Stimulate analytical thought.
2. Diagnose student difficulties.
3. Determine progress toward specific goals.
4. Motivate students.
5. Clarify and expand concepts.
6. Encourage new appreciations and attitudes.
7. Give specific direction to thinking.
8. Relate cause to effect.
9. Encourage student self-evaluation.
10. Encourage the application of concepts.

A brief look at each of these purposes will point up the importance of thoroughly understanding the use of the question.

Stimulating Analytical Thought

Getting students to think intensively about subject-matter content and its importance to society is a recurring problem for teachers. The

---

[10]William H. Burton, *The Guidance of Learning Activities*, 3d. ed. (New York: Appleton-Century-Crofts, 1962), chapter 18, discusses the improvement of questioning.

Clark and Starr, *Secondary School Teaching Methods*, pp. 217–223, provide another sound discussion on questions and questioning techniques.

Illustrations of questions to be avoided in the classroom and questions used to achieve given instructional purposes are provided by John Walton, *Toward Better Teaching in the Secondary Schools* (Boston: Allyn & Bacon, 1966), pp. 153–155.

[11]See Burton, *The Guidance of Learning Activities*, pp. 438–439, for a similar discussion of the purposes of questions.

Matters of concern to the teacher skilled in the art of questioning are discussed by Peter F. Oliva, *The Secondary School Today* (New York: World Publishing Company, 1967), pp. 254–258.

thought-provoking question serves well in this connection if effectively employed; this calls for proper timing and a meaningful statement of the question. Emphasis is not upon a recall of facts but upon thinking about facts in a meaningful, interrelated way. Some nonoral questions—such as the essay and, at times, multiple choice and matching—can be used to help stimulate thought.[12] More frequently, however, the thought-provoking question is asked orally as a part of the class discussion.

Tenth-grade English grammar: Why is it important for the college-bound student to understand English grammar?

Ninth-grade civics: What is likely to happen to individual citizens of a city the size of ours if the local government is dishonest?

Twelfth-grade physics: What are the practical applications of the concept that the transmission of sound waves varies with the media through which it is transmitted?

Note that the student is encouraged to provide a response that has been carefully thought out. The quick answer is out of place.

Diagnosing Student Difficulties

All of the various types of questions may be helpful in determining the academic trouble spots of students. In fact, to obtain a valid appraisal, it is desirable to use a wide range of question types. The following examples may be directed toward groups or individuals in written or oral form:

Ninth-grade literature: Describe the character of Lady Macbeth.

Tenth-grade biology: Define *taxonomy* in your own words.

Tenth-grade world history: Indicate when Pericles lived and what his major contributions were.

Determining Progress Toward Goals

Various kinds of questions can be used in determining progress toward goals. Objective questions, for example, have the advantage of extensive sampling. Specific weaknesses can thus be discovered, permitting appropriate remedial steps to be taken. Story problems give students the opportunity to exhibit their subject-matter strength in applied situations.

Motivating Students

Student interest can be awakened and perpetuated through the effective use of questions. This is often accomplished during the initiation of the unit, but it may take place at other times as well. For example, the teacher in a twelfth-grade physics unit concerned with motivating the

---

[12]Dumas and Beckner, *Introduction to Secondary Education*, pp. 245–246, briefly discuss the need for designing the question to stimulate thinking.

class to study a unit on "Waves and Sounds" may pose this question: "What is the relationship between sound waves and waves caused by dropping a pebble into a tub of water?"

Thought questions are typically viewed as having good potential for motivation. A series of rapid-fire, short-answer questions, however, may also motivate by opening up new possibilities or revealing weaknesses previously unknown to students. Other motivating questions accompany demonstrations during which students are asked to explain the phenomena taking place.

Clarifying and Expanding Concepts

Once a student has formed a partial concept, the teacher may further clarify the concept by posing questions that impel student reactions. This is a case in point: During the study of an eleventh-grade unit on "World War II," students had been highly interested in the details of the conflict, but the teacher wanted them to relate these details to the current world scene. "What is the relationship of the U.S.S.R.'s participation in the defeat of Germany to present world tensions?" he asked.

The use of probing counterquestions in response to student questions may help the student answer his own inquiries—if the counterquestions do not offend or aggravate.

Encouraging Appreciations and Attitudes

To the extent that appreciations and attitudes are comprised of concepts, they are subject to modification. If the teacher wishes to help students think more rationally about race relations, for example, he may wish to modify, clarify, or expand underlying mental pictures. One of the more frequently used techniques for accomplishing this is a thought question, such as, "If you were a member of a racial minority in a small city, how would you approach your fellow citizens with respect to schooling, housing, and social relations?"

Directing Thinking

Class discussions, if permitted to wander, may become quite unrelated to the central theme of a lesson. An inoffensive way to redirect the thinking of class members is to pose an arresting question that will turn their thinking in the direction the teacher wishes it to go.

Relating Cause to Effect

The *why* question is typically used to relate cause to effect. Its prime concern is to avoid the meaningless repetition of facts without a real understanding of their relationships. Examples of sound questions of this type are:

Why was Ulysses S. Grant considered to be a weak President?
Under what circumstances can the atom be split? Why?
Why is the nitrogen cycle essential to the maintenance of life?

Encouraging Self-Evaluation

Students tend to be receptive to criticisms that come from within. Herein lies the value of self-evaluation. If the teacher has had experience and possesses tact, he can pose questions that encourage self-examination. Such questions might include some of the following:

Was your reasoning correct or faulty in this case? Why?
What is the correct answer to the question you missed?
What can you do to make a better score on the next test?
Why did you make a higher score on the last test?

Promoting Application

Questions that call for the application of known ideas are used to good advantage in certain subjects. Story problems, for example, are often helpful in teaching mathematics; concluding activities in mathematics units may be comprised, in part, of such problems. In the typewriting class the question "How do you type a simple business letter?" calls for a specific applied response. In the civics class the question "What specific steps must a foreigner follow in obtaining citizenship?" confronts students with the necessity for recombining facts in a practical way. "How is the carburetor cleaned in a Ford automobile?" calls for application in the auto-mechanics class. Each time students write a paper or theme for any class there is always the implied question "What constitutes a correctly written English composition?"

Principles Related to Questioning

It is helpful to identify how questions can be employed effectively in clarifying concepts, encouraging appreciation, relating cause to effect, and encouraging self-evaluation. Maximum long-range help is provided, however, when minute bits of information derived from the successful use of questions are distilled into sound generalizations.[13] The following are based upon broad principles of education.

1. Questions provide one means of assisting instruction.
2. Questions are means, not ends.
3. Questioning is only profitable when the student has a background that will enable him to react intelligently.
4. A sequence of questions should lead progressively to specific understandings.
5. There is a close relationship between the teacher's ability to use questions and his knowledge of content.
6. The teacher's ability to use questions effectively is aided by his intelligence and successful experience.[14]

---

[13]Techniques of good questioning are provided by Clark and Starr, *Secondary School Teaching Methods*, pp. 220–223.

[14]Burton, *The Guidance of Learning Activities*, p. 437, emphasizes the need for native ability in questioning.

7. Specific types of questions should be used to achieve desired purposes.

8. Teachers should not specialize in one particular type of question to the possible exclusion of other types.

9. Ingenious teachers develop interesting and helpful modifications in the use of the question-answer technique.

10. Questioning should aim at fitting fragments of information into meaningful wholes.

11. The quality of questioning is limited by the teacher's quality of thinking.

12. The form and wording of a question is only secondary to its basic purpose of assisting the teaching-learning process.

13. An essential part of the question-answer technique involves encouraging students to ask questions.

Specific Suggestions

The following suggestions should serve as pointed reminders of certain things to remember or avoid in the use of questions.

Recommendations

1. Use specific kinds of questions to serve specific purposes.[15]

2. Use thought-provoking questions frequently.

3. Use quick, random questions for review.

4. Use related questions that become progressively more difficult if you want students to acquire concepts in depth.

5. Ask questions only when you have a definite purpose for doing so.

6. Ask questions that are within the pupil's own range of experience and knowledge.[16]

7. Ask questions that are free of confusing parenthetical elements.

8. Word questions as simply as possible without distorting meaning.[17]

9. If you wish to have a question answered in a certain way (compare, classify, outline, define, etc.), indicate this clearly.

10. Only accept student replies that are reasonably complete and meaningful.

11. If students do not answer your questions with reasonable completeness and accuracy, make sure the class is not left with false concepts.

12. As a general rule, use some portion of a student's answer if only to encourage him and keep him interested.[18]

---

[15]Howard T. Batchelder, Maurice McGlasson, and Raleigh Schorling, *Student Teaching in Secondary Schools*, 4th ed. (New York: McGraw-Hill Book Company, 1964), pp. 173–175, provide an excellent but brief discussion of the types of questions.

[16]Oliva, *Secondary School Teaching Today*, pp. 255–258, lists and discusses fifteen practical suggestions designed to help the teacher interested in polishing his questioning technique.

[17]Burton, *The Guidance of Learning Activities*, pp. 442–445, gives specific hints for the wording and form of questions.

[18]Clark and Starr, *Secondary School Teaching Methods*, p. 221, discuss how student answers should be treated.

13. Establish a classroom climate in which students will feel free to ask questions.[19]

14. Before asking for a response to a thought question, allow students time to think about it.

Cautions

1. As a general rule, don't ask obvious questions.[20]

2. Don't react emotionally if the student fails to answer a question correctly.

3. Don't ask "Are there any questions?" as a device for determining whether students have understood the lesson. Usually you will get no response even when students do not understand.

4. Don't allow the questioning procedure to lead you and your students away from the planned subject.

5. Don't ask ambiguous questions.

6. Don't direct your questions to a few isolated students. Include as many students as possible in your questioning.

7. Don't attempt to bluff if you are not sure of the answer to a student's question. Say "I don't know" and then find out.

8. Don't discourage student responses to student questions.

9. Don't ask catch questions.

10. Don't ask questions that call for two different and confusing reactions to the same question.

11. Don't ask questions that contain words not understood by students.

12. As a general rule, don't repeat questions. Insist that students listen to what you say.

USE OF DEMONSTRATIONS

By definition a demonstration is concerned with *showing*.[21] Because showing often involves the learner's first-hand contact with the referent of the concept, its sensory impact is extremely vivid. Demonstration, therefore, becomes a very helpful instructional tool in the hands of a knowledgeable teacher.

---

[19]Oliva and Scrafford, *Teaching in a Modern Secondary School*, p. 80, believe that questioning is still the major instructional activity of many classroom groups and that teachers sometimes underestimate the skill needed for effective questioning.

[20]Vincent McGuire, Robert B. Myers, and Charles L. Durrance, *Your Student Teaching in the Secondary School* (Boston: Allyn & Bacon, 1959), p. 158, list a number of specific cautions. Characteristics of good questions and positive suggestions for questioning are presented on pages 157 and 159.

[21]A highly useful discussion of demonstration as it relates to preparation, conduct, and discovery learning is provided by James W. Brown, Richard B. Lewis, and Fred F. Harcleroad, *AV Instruction: Media and Methods*, 3d. ed. (New York: McGraw-Hill Book Company, 1969), pp. 485–492.

Types of Demonstrations

A majority of current secondary methods texts do not give specific attention to the use of demonstration. Many writers prefer to accord it only token attention as an aid to the lecture method. Demonstration has, however, certain psychological advantages that warrant its separate treatment:

1. It provides sensory impact that the written or spoken word cannot match.
2. It is basically interesting to students.
3. It affords freedom from the boring repetition of lectures.

It is useful to classify types of classroom demonstrations in terms of how closely they approximate the lecture. Note the varied ways in which demonstration may be used:

Pure demonstration with no explanation
Demonstration with a few explanatory comments
Half demonstration—half lecture
Lecture with some demonstration

Pure Demonstration

Occasionally the observation of a given phenomenon requires such attention that any spoken word serves as a distraction. This is the case in an auto-mechanics shop where the instructor is demonstrating the assembly of close-fitting mechanical devices. Comments during a laboratory demonstration in a chemistry class may at times cause the students to miss an important chemical reaction.

Although no comment is made during certain demonstrations, it is desirable for the teacher to indicate in advance what the student is to look for. Similarly, when the sensational portion of a demonstration is finished, a discussion of what has occurred and why is highly desirable.

Demonstration with Comments

In a typing class the teacher often demonstrates the correct position of the fingers on the keys, using a typewriter mounted on a high stand. He insists that students observe carefully the exact position of his hands as he makes a few explanatory comments. The dominant concern, however, is their observation. In a geometry class the teacher illustrates (shows) various geometric patterns at the chalkboard while he briefly explains them. Here again, the instructor is less concerned with his oral explanation than with the visual impact of his drawings.

Half Demonstration — Half Lecture

In the woodwork shop the teacher tells his students why it is necessary to prepare oak in a given way before finishing it. His explanation accompanies the actual *showing* of how the preparation is done. The homemaking teacher shows students how to use the pinking shears as she explains the reason for their use. The algebra teacher explains how to balance an equation while he demonstrates the process on the chalkboard.[22]

Lecture with Demonstration

A French teacher may explain in some detail about life along the Mediterranean Coast. Later, students are briefly shown a large map and two pictures. Students in a shorthand class take dictation for the major portion of an hour. When the teacher discovers some students using incorrect forms, she stops the class long enough to demonstrate the correct form at the board. Dictation then continues.

A majority of classroom demonstrations take place in the science courses or in skill-related subjects. But many students in other subject areas would benefit from greater emphasis on *showing*. This is particularly true of less gifted students who have limited ability to think abstractly.

Demonstrations in Special Situations

Teachers of skill subjects frequently use the demonstration to good advantage.[23] Demonstration is particularly helpful in foreign-language classes because of the current emphasis on oral use. The teacher says a phrase or sentence, and the students mimic him. In the orchestra or band class, the teacher repeatedly finds it necessary to illustrate how to make the tone he wants his players to reproduce. If he is unable to give a proper demonstration, his chances of getting the right response from the students are limited.

The teacher of home economics often follows a sequence of showing, telling, supervising student practice, and then repeating the sequence as needed. All forms of shop instruction rely heavily on demonstration to give students a correct and vivid impression of a given skill to be performed. Demonstration in combination with other methods is probably the best and most frequently used procedure for providing students with clear mental pictures of skills to be learned in physical education classes.

In addition, demonstrations are often useful when concepts are being developed. Certain mental processes, such as those involved in algebra, are best explained by example—thus through showing. If the teacher relies solely on the spoken word to teach such processes, he frequently does not get his point across. Analysis of sentence structure may be accomplished in several ways, but many English teachers have employed diagraming for this purpose because it lends itself nicely to demonstration.

---

[22]Oliva and Scrafford, *Teaching in a Modern Secondary School*, p. 79, emphasize the need for using audio-visual aids.

[23]A range of specific "tips for effective demonstrations" are provided by James S. Kinder, *Using Audio-Visual Materials in Education* (New York: American Book Company, 1965), pp. 137–138.

Specific Suggestions

Thoughtful teachers rely on a broad acquaintance with educational principles to give direction to their use of specific methods. The following suggestions relate to the use of demonstration as a teaching technique.

Recommendations

1. Re-examine the exact objectives of the lesson before you give a demonstration.

2. Practice the demonstration as many times as necessary to do it effectively.

3. Satisfy yourself that all needed materials are available before starting the demonstration.

4. Be sure that all students can easily observe the demonstration. This may call for reseating students or having them stand in a semicircle around the demonstrator.

5. Exclude all distracting influences before the demonstration is started.

6. Before beginning the demonstration, explain what you are about to demonstrate and the purpose of the demonstration. Tell the students what to look for.

7. Speak clearly and distinctly.

8. Use a vocabulary understood by all.

9. To assure yourself that students are understanding the demonstration, pause at intervals to ask questions or to allow students to ask questions.

10. Face the students as much as possible.

11. Briefly review the key points of the demonstration as soon as it is completed.

12. Employ good safety practices under all circumstances.

Cautions

1. Don't prolong the demonstration. It should usually not exceed twenty-five minutes.

2. Don't present the demonstration so fast that students fail to grasp the key ideas.

3. Don't squeeze too many concepts into one demonstration. Make it as simple as possible.

4. Don't draw attention away from the demonstration by a lengthy explanation unless it is justified.

5. Don't use unfamiliar trade or technical terms without explaining their meaning.

6. Never give a demonstration without first having a trial run. There is always the possibility that it may not work.

TEACHER-CENTERED PROCEDURES IN REVIEW

Under specific circumstances, teacher-centered activities achieve unit goals more effectively than do activities requiring maximum student involvement. Three teacher-centered activities—lectures, questions, and demonstrations—have been discussed in this chapter. Each has unique advantages when employed efficiently by a trained teacher.

The several variations of the lecture all serve useful instructional purposes. Of these variations the formal lecture is the least practical for secondary-school instruction.

Questions, too, may be used to achieve a range of purposes. They may be used to stimulate thought, diagnose difficulties, determine progress, motivate students, clarify and expand concepts, encourage new appreciations, give direction in thinking, relate cause to effect, encourage self-evaluation, and encourage the application of concepts.

The prime purpose of the demonstration is to *show*, an essential step in the teaching of concepts. Demonstration provides the learner with first-hand contact with the referent, effecting a vivid sensory impact. Among the variations in demonstration are pure demonstration, demonstration with few comments, half demonstration and half lecture, and lecture with demonstration.

PROBLEMS FOR STUDY AND DISCUSSION

1. What are the disadvantages of the formal lecture? List at least five.

2. Give an example in which the use of the formal lecture would be appropriate in teaching your subject-matter major.

3. Describe at least three different situations in which the illustrated lecture would be appropriate in your teaching minor.

4. List several general situations in which reading aloud to the class for a short period is justified.

5. What advantages does the formal lecture have over the modified lecture? Give specific examples.

6. Do you believe that it would be appropriate to permit conversational informality in teaching your minor field? Why?

7. Identify ten situations in which informal brief explanations are warranted.

8. If you were lecturing to a group of students who had widely varying abilities and interests, how would you go about meeting their varied needs? Explain.

9. Explain precisely how thought can be stimulated through asking questions.

10. Give three examples of thought-provoking questions that you might logically ask in teaching your major field.

11. Indicate the advantages of the story problem.

12. What kinds of questions would be most helpful in encouraging students to expand partially formed concepts? Give one example.

13. How can cause be related to effect through questioning? Give two examples of cause-and-effect questions appropriate to your subject-matter minor.

14. Do you tend to use one type of question much more frequently than other types? Is its use justified? Explain.

15. Describe one ingenious and different questioning procedure that you can use in teaching your major field.

16. What are the psychological advantages of demonstration as a method?

17. Which variation of the demonstration do you prefer for teaching your minor field? Give your reasons.

18. Give a description of a teaching situation in your major field in which half demonstration and half lecture would serve a useful instructional purpose.

19. What steps should be taken to eliminate competing stimuli during a demonstration?

20. If a demonstration is carried out well, is it necessary to repeat the main points? Why?

10. *Student-Centered Procedures*

All learning requires the meaningful reaction of the learner, but some procedures demand student participation in order to promote learning. The uses of three such procedures are discussed in this chapter: the textbook, the assignment, and homework. The following chapter will cover additional student-centered procedures.

USE OF THE TEXTBOOK

The textbook is a systematic arrangement of subject material designed to assist the instructor in teaching particular content to students at a specific grade level.[1] In no other one place can the teacher—or the student—find an equivalent concentration of course-related materials.

One of the most commonly used teaching aids, the text may also be one of the most helpful aids to the effective teacher.[2] However, if the teacher selects a poor text or uses a good text poorly, unsatisfactory learning may result.

The well-organized textbook contains some of the best teaching materials, provides suggestions for specific points worth considering, and suggests a possible range and sequence of units for the course. By carefully examining a good textbook before completing unit and yearly plans, the teacher can often save valuable time.

The reading of a text by all students establishes a common background that is essential to certain teaching procedures. In addition, a well-organized text helps the student understand how various parts of the course content are interrelated and provides him with an easy means of review. The use of high quality photographs, drawings, and charts—many in color—can help clarify difficult content.

Principles Related to the Effective Use of the Textbook

Effective use of the textbook is based on the following proven principles.

1. Effective planning is assisted by a sound text that helps identify course objectives.

2. The textbook is only one of many devices to help students achieve educational goals.[3] Furthermore, no one text is suitable for all students. Since they vary in intelligence, background, and subject-matter achievement, different individuals will benefit from the use of different textual as well as nontextual materials. Similarly, the student's liking for a given text will depend upon how well it serves his individual purposes.

3. The vocabulary in a general textbook will help determine its usefulness. The need for variation in vocabulary levels is met by assigning carefully selected supplementary textbooks for students with high as well as with low reading abilities.

---

[1]See Roland C. Faunce and Carroll L. Munshaw, *Teaching and Learning in Secondary Schools* (Belmont, California: Wadsworth Publishing Co., Inc., 1965), pp. 245–246, for an enumeration of the strengths and weaknesses of textbooks.

[2]Leonard H. Clark and Irving S. Starr, *Secondary School Teaching Methods*, 2d. ed. (New York: The Macmillan Company, 1967), p. 272, describe three types of developmental reading programs for junior and senior high school students.

[3]Wayne Dumas and Weldon Beckner, *Introduction to Secondary Education: A Foundations Approach* (Scranton, Pennsylvania: International Textbook Company, 1968), p. 394, believe that "subject content of tomorrow will be drawn from many material sources, only one of which will be the textbook."

4. Because students learn concepts through both verbal and graphic symbols, it is essential that textbooks be well illustrated.

5. A student derives meaning from the printed page only to the extent that the printed words (symbols) are related to meaningful concepts. Such concepts can be expanded when the textbook is interesting to the student.

6. A student is ready to use a text if he has (a) general knowledge of its content, (b) mastery of the basic concepts, (c) adequate vocabulary mastery, and (d) proficiency in reading.

7. Use of the textbook to the exclusion of other teaching materials and aids is an unsound teaching practice.[4]

8. Effective textbook use is impossible in classrooms where student behavior is not carefully controlled.

9. Students who are preoccupied with nonschool problems and interests are unable to use the textbook effectively.

Correct and Incorrect Use

Incorrect uses of the textbook are illustrated in the following narrative accounts.

MRS. RYDEN DEMANDS A RIGOROUS PACE

Mrs. Ryden had been given to understand that the educational climate had changed, that students were now expected to accomplish more. So, in her class, The History of California, Mrs. Ryden required students to cover a chapter every three days in spite of the fact that the vocabulary level of the text was roughly one grade beyond them. Students protested, parents complained, and the teacher became disgruntled; but the students were still kept to their rigorous pace.

MR. HULL RELIES ON THE TEXT

W. R. Hull had some traditional ideas about teaching; the text was his Bible. If the students knew the text, they knew the course and, according to him, deserved high grades. Mr. Hull was never known to make assignments outside the text or to use supplementary materials. If students chose to seek additional information, they did it on their own. There were occasional class discussions, but never for very long, and invariably the students were sent back to study their texts.

In Mrs. Ryden's class unrealistic requirements with respect to textbook assignments soon created unfavorable feelings about the text as well as about the course content. Frustration—from having to cope with a vocabulary that was too difficult—served only to defeat the students. Mr.

---

[4]Clark and Starr, *Secondary School Teaching Methods*, p. 276, emphasize the need to have a range of reading materials easily available to students.

Hull, the second teacher, had fallen into the pattern of textbook teaching and had no intention of being jarred out of this rut.[5]

These difficulties were avoided by Mrs. Willmot, who used the textbook as only one aid among many for teaching a tenth-grade American literature class.

MRS. WILLMOT BUILDS FROM THE BASIC TEXT

At the beginning of the year Mrs. Willmot again ran an inventory of her classroom library. She found books containing selections of varying difficulty, in content as well as in vocabulary. Gifted and below-average students could all be given reading assignments in keeping with their capabilities.

During the first few days, Mrs. Willmot demonstrated the use of the basic text. Brief assignments were worked out involving the use of footnotes, the table of contents, and the index. After several of these assignments, the students were able to use the text efficiently. The teacher also identified course objectives that required the dominant use of the basic text. However, students were also required to read other sources available in the school library as well as in the classroom library.

Student reading assignments were differentiated to accommodate reading level, interests, and intelligence. While students read during the study period, Mrs. Willmot, seated at the back of the room, held brief diagnostic conferences with students about their own reading problems.

Use in Specific Subjects

In classes where the teaching of concepts is the main concern, textbooks are employed in a variety of ways. Biology teachers often make excellent use of the text's colored plates and cell overlays. In mathematics classes, teachers often find it profitable to discuss the basic ideas to be covered; these same ideas are then reinforced through reading the text. Literature texts are usually anthologies in which students read widely to fulfill varied assignments.

Specific Suggestions

The following recommendations and cautions are closely related to the principles underlying the sound use of the textbook presented earlier in this chapter. These specific suggestions are based upon the experience of individual teachers.

---

[5]Peter F. Oliva and Ralph A. Scrafford, *Teaching in a Modern Secondary School* (Columbus, Ohio: Charles E. Merrill Publishing Co., 1965), pp. 14–15, describe traditional textbook teaching and some of its implications.

Focusing on the weaknesses of textbook teaching, Raymond H. Muessig, "Bridging the Gap between Textbook Teaching and Unit Teaching," *The Social Studies*, 54 (February 1963), pp. 43–47, offers specific suggestions to social studies instructors.

Recommendations

1. Investigate the various ways in which a textbook may be used.[6]
2. Evaluate the text in terms of course goals.
3. Be sure that the vocabulary and content of the text are appropriate to the class for which they are intended.[7]
4. Use a text that is current.
5. Use the text to help achieve the objectives of the unit and the course.
6. Supplement the textbook with other materials and procedures. Use the reading of the text to stimulate other activities.
7. Discover how other teachers in your subject-matter area have used the textbook advantageously. Adapt the best of their procedures to your own use.
8. Adapt the textbook to the class, not the class to the textbook.
9. Become thoroughly acquainted with the text before giving assignments in it.
10. Teach students how to use the table of contents, the index, headings, topic sentences, marginal notations, and charts.
11. Make allowances for individual differences among the students. Make available three or four supplementary texts that deal with the same content at different vocabulary levels.
12. Identify students with reading difficulties, and provide remedial help for them.
13. Conduct textbook exercises that will enable students to learn how the text can help them understand course content.
14. Explain difficult passages, charts, and illustrations.
15. Encourage intelligent student reaction to textbook discussion.
16. Arrange for appropriate checks to determine that textbook reading has been done consistently and well.
17. Be imaginative, varied, and experimental in the use of the textbook.
18. If some part of a chapter of the text has been unusually well prepared, use this particular portion to advantage.

Cautions

Although many cautions can be inferred from the preceding recommendations, a few pointed admonitions may be helpful.

1. Don't view the text as an end in itself.
2. Don't let the textbook become the course.
3. Don't use the text in a mechanical fashion.
4. Don't rely as strongly on the text once you have gained experience and security in teaching.
5. Don't forego the planning necessary for efficient teaching because textbook teaching appears easier.

---

[6]Specific suggestions for the proper use of the textbook can be found in Howard T. Batchelder, Maurice McGlasson, and Raleigh Schorling, *Student Teaching in Secondary Schools*, 4th ed. (New York: McGraw-Hill Book Company, 1964), pp. 175–177.

[7]Eighteen relevant questions concerned with textbook selection are posed by Clark and Starr, *Secondary School Teaching Methods*, p 274.

USE OF THE ASSIGNMENT

One of the most important procedures requiring strong student participation is the assignment. It may be long or short; difficult or easy; general or differentiated; and related to a single lesson, to a unit, or to a full school year.[8] Because of this extreme variety, writers have emerged with a score of different classifications to serve their individual purposes. Asssignments are often described in terms of contrast: daily or unit assignments; oral or written assignments; textbook or nontextbook assignments; and individual or group assignments. More important than the classification of the assignment is the careful understanding of its purpose—to encourage and assist students to reach specified goals.

Characteristics of Assignments

The assignment may be viewed by students as the teacher's device for imposing school-sanctioned punishment upon learners. In the hands of a wise professional, however, it can be the means of providing students with exciting new opportunities for self-directed learning.[9]

Vague, uninteresting, unmotivated assignments can have a strong negative influence on many students. Yet, they can be and are made into exciting challenges when the classroom teacher relates them to individual student needs, provides the necessary background, and arouses student interest.

Recent emphasis on individualized instruction has encouraged knowl edgeable teachers to tailor assignments to meet the unique needs of specific students. Ideally, in a class of thirty students no two assignments would be identical. Because teaching circumstances are not ideal, teachers tend to limit the number of differentiated assignments made in such a group.

Principles Related to the Effective Use of Assignments

Because teachers frequently err in their use of the assignment, they need the assistance of principles that will give direction to their planning.[10] The following principles apply to all types of assignments.

1. Assignments are unjustified unless they relate to specific goals.

[8]Leonard M. Douglas, *The Secondary Teacher at Work* (Boston: D. C. Heath & Company, 1967), p. 143, feels the assignment should be clear, flexible, appropriate in length, important enough to motivate students, and reasonable in consideration of pupil load.

William H. Burton, *The Guidance of Learning Activities*, 3d. ed. (New York: Appleton-Century-Crofts, 1962), chapter 12, discusses the assignment against the background of "The Improvement of Assign-Study-Recite Procedures." His comments are challenging and sound.

[9]Peter F. Oliva, *The Secondary School Today* (New York: World Publishing Company, 1967), pp. 260–264, presents eleven recommendations that should characterize the effective assignment.

[10]Specific suggestions for making the assignment are provided by Oliva and Scrafford, *Teaching in a Modern Secondary School*, p. 201.

2. Assignments may serve a range of purposes.

3. The extent to which a student will work hard on an assignment will depend upon the degree of his motivation.

4. The learner will work conscientiously to accomplish an assignment when he realizes that it will serve *his* purposes as *he* sees them.[11]

5. Students study conscientiously to complete assignments that they have helped plan. Assignments that evolve naturally from unit activities have a good chance of being accepted by students.

6. A student cannot successfully pursue an assignment unless he understands the concepts on which it is based.

7. An assignment can be completed only when students have the readiness essential for its completion. Students must possess adequate reading skills, have a grasp of essential background concepts, and be motivated.

8. Conscientious work on assignments requires a measure of student self-discipline.

9. The assignment is only one of the essential procedures in teaching and should not be used exclusively.

10. Assignments must be differentiated in order to meet the individual needs of students.[12]

11. The use of special devices (study questions and study guides) gives helpful direction to certain types of assignments.

12. Stereotyped assignments tend to reduce interest in school work.

13. Carefully worded assignments are fundamental to effective planning and teaching.

Correct and Incorrect Use

Perhaps the most ineffective and commonplace assignment is undifferentiated and must be completed by the following day. For such an assignment all students are required to do the same amount of work.[13]

MRS. DAWSON GIVES A HASTY ASSIGNMENT

During the last two minutes of the ninth-grade literature class, Mrs. Dawson became somewhat alarmed. She had not finished her discussion of **Silas Marner** as she had hoped, and the assignment was yet to be given.

Hastily she thumbed through the pages of the text. "You will all read pages 39 through 49 for tomorrow," she said. "I'm sure it will be interesting." Just then the bell rang, and the students filed out of the room.

---

[11]An example of a short, differentiated assignment is given by Clark and Starr, *Secondary School Teaching Methods*, p. 168.

[12]Burton, *The Guidance of Learning Activities*, pp. 294–295, identifies several specific difficulties confronting the teacher in making assignments.

[13]John Walton, *Toward Better Teaching in the Secondary Schools* (Boston: Allyn & Bacon, Inc., 1966), pp. 293–294, indicates that the failure of students to complete assignments may be related to the fact that they compete poorly with nonschool interests.

Mrs. Dawson violated several principles related to giving assignments properly:

1. She made the assignment under pressure without considering its appropriateness.

2. She failed to interest the class in the assignment.

3. She failed to differentiate the assignment by providing for varying abilities among students.

4. She did not permit questions about the assignment.

5. She did not write the assignment on the board.

Increasing awareness of the use of and demand for auto-instructional materials and procedures have encouraged many alert teachers to experiment further with techniques involving student self-imposed assignments.

MISS VERD ENCOURAGES SELF-DIRECTION

The logic of increasing student self-direction and its potential for carryover into adult life appealed strongly to Miss Verd. Realizing that each student's ability to manage his own affairs does not always bear a close relationship to age or intelligence, she decided to assign a Self-Directive Quotient (SDQ) to each student in her eighth-grade history class. Over a three month period individual students were observed carefully; the degree of self-direction involved in past academic achievements was analyzed; and finally a reasonably accurate SDQ for individual students (written in pencil and subject to change) was inserted on the seating chart under each name.

Two of her twenty-nine students were judged to require a minimum of teacher direction. They were allowed freedom to go to the library at will; to read at the rear of the classroom even when lectures were being given; to pursue individual teacher-approved, course-related projects; and to work on programed materials either in the classroom or the library. No specific assignments were given; however, an individual conference was held each week with both students and problems were discussed, progress was appraised, and a general student outline of work to be accomplished for the following week was examined and modified as assumed desirable by both parties. Nine additional students were found to be moderately self-directive. Miss Verd altered differentiated assignments to give consideration to her recent assessment. Further, students with very limited self-directive ability were given special kinds of assignments.

Assignments in Specific Subjects

Assignments can and should be used to aid instruction in every well-organized class. The difficulty, length, type, and circumstances of each assignment should vary, depending on its effectiveness in reaching a desired educational goal.[14]

---

[14]The common assignment, the achievement-level assignment, and the self-management potential of students are discussed by Nathan S. Blount and Herbert J. Klausmeier, *Teaching in the Secondary School*, 3d. ed. (New York: Harper & Row, Publishers, 1968), pp. 280–281.

Large written assignments related to and extending through an entire unit are common in history and English composition classes. Concept-centered courses, such as geography, English literature, history, biology, and the physical sciences, frequently call for assignments involving library work. In these cases gifted students are often sent to the library to engage in self-directed research. Some of the skill subjects are the only areas in which the short reading assignment is not frequently employed.

To infer that one type of assignment should be associated with a specific subject imposes an unwarranted restriction on teacher ingenuity. Variations in assignments are desirable if they help achieve educational goals and simultaneously maintain student interest.

Specific Suggestions

The conscientious teacher can be sure that he is using the assignment correctly if he is aware of the principles listed on pages 195–196 and observes the related recommendations and cautions enumerated below.

Recommendations

1. Be sure that unit as well as daily assignments bear a close relationship to the unit.

2. Be sure the assignment is understood by all. Permit students to participate in planning certain assignments, and make sure students understand *why* they are undertaking a given assignment. Encourage them to ask questions.

3. When necessary, give students specific help in completing the assignment.

4. Use various kinds of assignments.

5. Assess each student's ability to be self-directive; then allow him reasonable freedom under teacher supervision to carry out self-imposed assignments.

6. Make the assignment meaningful in terms of its perceived value to the student.

7. Be sure that daily assignments fit in logically and consistently with other learning activities.

8. When homework is assigned, allow students time to start it during the supervised study period.

9. Write assignments on the chalkboard if this serves a useful purpose.

10. When students lack background information essential to the completion of an assignment, plan experiences that will provide the necessary background.

11. Use study guides to assist students in fulfilling assignments.

12. Make assignments to promote the continuity of learning. Remember that they are an essential part of a long-range (unit) learning experience.

13. Plan assignments that will make it possible to determine the achievement level of individual students with relative ease.

14. Help students develop adequate study habits through the use of the assignment.

15. Give the assignment when interest has reached a high peak.

Cautions

1. Don't make individual assignments without considering differences among class members.

2. Don't always make the assignment in terms of pages to be read.

3. Don't make the assignment sound as if it were being done for the teacher.

4. Don't threaten students with assignments.[15]

5. Don't give the assignment after the bell has rung.

6. Don't give day-to-day assignments that tend to fragmentize subject matter.

7. Don't make assignments that interfere with major out-of-school activities.

USE OF HOMEWORK

It is common practice to label as *homework* any class-related preparation that is done outside of class. Although homework is a type of assignment, it deserves special consideration because it poses particular problems that make its effectiveness as a teaching procedure highly variable.[16]

Controversy and Criticism

Because home study is typically undertaken without the benefit of teacher supervision, it is often subject of criticism.[17] The value of homework in the total educational program of the adolescent is being seriously questioned on the basis of research evidence. The statement of one authority in the field is worthy of examination:

> The few statistical studies show that home study is not a significant factor in affecting the achievement of pupils. Results are about the same with or without home study.
>
> There is, however, one aspect of this topic which must not be overlooked. Home study of the traditional formal sort may be dispensed with as far as the evidence now shows; however, as we move toward

---

[15]Clark and Starr, *Secondary School Teaching Methods*, p. 89, differentiate between having students redo unsatisfactorily completed assignments and assigning school tasks as punishment. The latter may result in negative conditioning.

[16]The issues, problems, strengths, and limitations of homework are thoroughly examined in a full volume treatment by Grace Langdon and Irving W. Stout, *Homework* (New York: The John Day Company, 1969).

[17]How much homework should be required of differing secondary-school students under varied circumstances is usefully discussed by *Ibid.*, pp. 258–260.

modern teaching which identifies study with learning and which utilizes not one or two but a large number of varied study activities, a different situation emerges.[18]

The increased space-age emphasis on academic rigor in all subjects has encouraged many teachers, administrators, and parents to use any device for increasing academic productivity. As a result, homework has received added impetus in some school districts. In practice the use of home study is being expanded and intensified in certain areas and restricted in others. Unfortunately, controversy among teachers and administrators in the same schools and districts is often in evidence, causing undue student confusion.

Principles Related to the Effective Use of Homework

The following principles suggest a middle-of-the-road approach, designed to assist the teacher in using homework as one device among many for promoting learning.[19]

1. As an educational device, home study is of value only to the extent that it improves learning.

2. Research studies on homework provide a much more reliable basis for homework policies than the anxious admonitions of parents, lay persons, and misinformed educators. The value of homework, however, has not been conclusively proved or disproved through research evidence.

3. A home study program is more likely to be successful if it is related to the total school program. Homework should be viewed as a supplement to the work of the school day.

4. Students can study well only when the environment is conducive to study.

5. The emergence of carefully prepared and tested programed materials (lessons, units, or full textbooks) promises to make certain kinds of homework more productive as well as interesting.

6. The results derived from homework are often directly related to the effectiveness of the teacher's planning for homework assignments.

7. The time required by individual students to complete specific assignments will influence the success of the homework program. Well-informed teachers are realistic in what they expect of students.

8. An increase in the amount of work required of students may not improve the quality of their education.

9. Students often react negatively toward home study on the basis of their previous experience.

10. Students become confused if there is controversy among their teachers about the value of homework.

---

[18]Burton, *The Guidance of Learning Activities*, p. 313.

[19]Clark and Starr, *Secondary School Teaching Methods*, pp. 258–261, provide a helpful general discussion as well as specific suggestions about homework.

Correct and Incorrect Use

A number of questionable practices can be identified in the home-work assignment of the eleventh-grade United States history teacher described below.

MISS COUSINS ASSIGNS WEEKEND HOMEWORK

Miss Cousins was firm in her resolve that there would be homework over the weekend in spite of the basketball game. In addition, she felt that it was only appropriate that the assignment be somewhat heavier than usual because students would have two days free. As a matter of fact, she thought, the class had been particularly unruly that Friday afternoon and needed to be punished.

Several unsound procedures can be observed here:

1. Students were encouraged to develop negative feelings toward homework because it interfered with something they really wanted to do.
2. The assignment was excessive and partially based on retribution.
3. The teacher gave little thought to student motivation.

Note the contrast between Miss Cousins' homework assignment and that of Mr. McGruder.[20]

MR. McGRUDER PROVIDES INTERESTING HOMEWORK

Fred McGruder, eighth-grade teacher of Iowa History, believed that homework should be limited in quantity as well as in type. By common consent, no teacher in his school made a take-home assignment over the weekend. On Monday, students were assigned the individual responsibil-ity for a brief two-minute oral report to be given the next Monday. As a basis for the reports, the students were to contact any person over seventy years of age who had spent his childhood in Iowa in order to find out what life was like during their childhood. The reports were to focus attention on transportation, housing, communication, and industry. The teacher motivated the assignment by pointing out the range of interest-ing facts that might be uncovered.

In this situation the assignment was nonbookish, it was carefully related to the course content, it was reasonable, it was interesting, and it could be carried out without teacher supervision. However, with the exception of the trait of nonbookishness, programed textbook assignments may possess these same positive characteristics. Observe how one teacher made effective use of the programed text.

---

[20]"Homework is a practice and habit-fixing device—not an evaluation device," ac-cording to Douglas, *The Secondary Teacher at Work*, p. 112.

MR. NYMAN EMPLOYS THE PROGRAMED TEXTBOOK

Because Mr. Nyman had followed with interest various attempts to produce effective programed textbooks for Algebra I over the period of a decade, he was well aware of their strengths and limitations. He had identified three such texts, published by different firms, that seemed to have unusual merit. When certain students encountered a particularly troublesome area, he would suggest that they work through that portion of one of three programed textbooks known by him to deal effectively and simply with the topic of concern. Inasmuch as these texts were organized for self-directive study the teacher often suggested that students spend extra time in home study until he indicated that they had acquired satisfactory comprehension. Mr. Nyman was generally pleased with the results of his procedure.

Specific Suggestions

Many of the desirable and undesirable practices in the use of the homework assignment are reflected in the recommendations that follow.[21]

Recommendations

1. Closely relate homework assignments to in-school study.
2. Work with other teachers in the school to establish a homework policy that is educationally sound and understood by all.[22]
3. Differentiate between what can best be accomplished under supervised study and what can best be accomplished through home study.
4. Be careful about assigning homework just because you feel that it is expected.
5. Make certain types of homework optional for students.
6. Use parent conferences to promote better home study conditions.
7. Consider the possibility of group projects during after-school hours.
8. Emphasize homework that does not involve the study of the text.[23]
9. Help students view home study as an added opportunity to learn.
10. Motivate students by saving some of the more interesting assignments for home study.
11. Assign activities that can be effectively carried out without teacher supervision.
12. Become acquainted with a range of programed textbooks in the

---

[21]Dumas and Beckner, *Introduction to Secondary Education,* p. 256, point out the dilemma represented by a situation in which many teachers feel that homework should be reduced because of related correctional work while at the same time college professors are insisting that student work in basic areas (writing, for example) must be intensified.

[22]*Ibid.,* p. 256, stress the need for continuous evaluation of the effectiveness of homework.

[23]Blount and Klausmeier, *Teaching in the Secondary School,* pp. 282–285, indicate that library work, auto-instruction, laboratory work, and discovery learning can serve effectively in making flexible, individualized assignments.

area of your teaching major; they may prove to be invaluable in making homework interesting and understandable.

13. Be sure that homework assignments are clearly understood.

14. Be sure that students understand the purpose of homework and relate it to their personal needs.

Cautions

1. Don't assign homework every evening.

2. Don't assume that home circumstances are equally conducive to study for all students.

3. Don't assign homework as punishment.

4. Don't neglect the possibility of group work as desirable out-of-class study.

5. Don't expect the impossible of students.

6. Don't make homework a routine chore.[24]

7. Don't assign busy work for home study.

8. Don't assume that homework will be self-motivating.

STUDENT-CENTERED PROCEDURES IN REVIEW

This chapter has focused attention on three instructional procedures that require a large measure of student participation—the use of the textbook, the assignment, and homework. Each has its own specific contribution to the teacher's storehouse of effective teaching methods, but each may prove to be of limited value if used poorly.

Although subject to frequent abuse, the textbook is one of the basic instructional tools, for in no other place can the student find the same concentration of relevant materials. Furthermore, the well-organized textbook, particularly the programed text, provides the student with a means of effective, self-directed study during the school day and after school hours.

The assignment serves a range of purposes, and if it helps the student achieve his *personal* purposes, he will work hard to complete it. In order to serve most effectively, assignments should be wisely differentiated to meet the needs of individual students and thus provide essential motivation.

Homework has value to the extent that it improves learning, but its efficiency as an instructional device is subject to much criticism. Research evidence does not conclusively support the value of homework, although academic emphasis has increased its use. There is general agreement, however, that a home study program must be closely related to the total school program if it is to be successful.

---

[24]Robert D. Strom, *Psychology for the Classroom* (Englewood Cliffs, New Jersey: Prentice-Hall, Inc., 1969), pp. 63–64, strongly indicts both parents and teachers for equating lack of homework with pupil failure—or great quantities of homework, faithfully completed, with success.

PROBLEMS FOR STUDY AND DISCUSSION

1. List ten student-centered teaching methods commonly used in your teaching major.

2. List five reasons for the frequent misuse of the textbook.

3. Write a short paragraph defending the following statement: The well-chosen textbook is the most helpful aid available to the knowledgeable teacher.

4. Describe how a textbook might best be used in your minor field.

5. Describe the role of the textbook in unit planning.

6. If you were responsible for selecting the textbook to be used by all teachers of your subject-matter major in a large school district, what qualities would you look for? List them.

7. How is it possible to meet the needs of students with high reading abilities and the needs of students with low reading abilities through the use of textbooks? Explain.

8. Explain the circumstances under which a programed text might be more effectively used than a traditional text.

9. Identify four or more procedures for making a general assignment interesting to students.

10. Give an example of how you propose to differentiate a major unit assignment in your subject-matter specialty in order to meet the needs of heterogeneously grouped students.

11. Discuss the following statement: The assignment is a means, not an end.

12. Describe five errors commonly made in giving assignments.

13. How effective do you feel the average student would be in assigning himself goal-related learning tasks? Why?

14. Suggest three or more procedures for motivating assignments in your minor field.

15. How can you make sure that the assignment is understood by all students?

16. Why is the value of homework being seriously questioned at the present time? Discuss.

17. How do you propose to use homework in your teaching major? Defend your position.

18. How much time can average students be expected to spend on homework in your teaching major? Explain.

19. Identify five practices that you are going to avoid in the use of homework during the school year.

20. Suggest a procedure that will enable teachers in a given school to make homework assignments without interfering with those given by other teachers.

11. *Additional Student-Centered Procedures*

Three additional teaching methods that demand student participation are group procedures, individualized instruction, and the field trip.[1] Each one, by its very nature, is subject to wide variation in classroom use. This chapter focuses on several of these variations and presents the principles and suggestions related to each method.

---

[1]Roland C. Faunce and Carroll L. Munshaw, *Teaching and Learning in Secondary Schools* (Belmont, California: Wadsworth Publishing Co., Inc., 1965), pp. 171–172, stress the need for students to learn from each other, especially peer-group interaction.

GROUP PROCEDURES

Types of Group Procedures

Different types of group procedures serve specific instructional purposes. The major types are identified here.[2] The entire class functions as a single unit in a *whole-class discussion*.[3] The teacher informally directs the discussion to achieve understanding of a given topic, and the students make comments and respond to questions posed by their fellow students as well as by the teacher. This large-group discussion is occasionally used as an introductory activity for later and more intensive small-group work within the class.

In a *forum discussion* a small number of students (usually from three to five) present prepared statements on a given topic to a large group or the entire class. After the presentation the speakers may ask questions of each other, and the forum moderator then solicits questions from the audience directed to a given speaker. Classes may also be divided into *panels*, usually four to eight students, that are responsible for obtaining, discussing, and finally presenting findings on a specific topic to the total class.

Informal role playing[4] (unrehearsed dramatization) is employed in social science and literature classes to encourage students to develop greater insight into the characters they are studying. Since they have no script, students must rely on information derived from their reading and from class discussion. *Small study groups*[5] of three or four students are often employed by the classroom teacher for different purposes. Although such groupings are typically based on common interest, they may be developed along various lines.

Debate provides one means of small-group as well as large-group activity in which opposing points of view can be expressed. Usually members of two teams alternate in making five- to eight-minute presentations. After the members are finished, rebuttals are allowed. Other forms of debate call for teacher-directed class discussion following the formal presentation or questions directed to team members.

Size of Instructional Groups[6]

The influence of team teaching during the decade of the sixties focused attention on instructional groups of different size. Although terms

---

[2]*Ibid.*, chapter 8, provide a useful discussion of the problems and processes of learning in groups. Specific examples are included.

[3]See Nathan S. Blount and Herbert J. Klausmeier, *Teaching in the Secondary School*, 3d. ed. (New York: Harper & Row, Publishers, 1968), pp. 261–264, for a useful presentation of whole-class discussion.

[4]The purpose and value of role playing are discussed by Leonard H. Clark and Irving S. Starr, *Secondary Teaching Methods*, 2d. ed. (New York: The Macmillan Company, 1967), pp. 238–240.

[5]Blount and Klausmeier, *Teaching in the Secondary School*, pp. 256–273, present the advantages of different types of small-group activity.

[6]See J. Lloyd Trump and Delmas F. Miller, *Secondary School Curriculum Improvements: Proposals and Procedures* (Boston: Allyn & Bacon, Inc., 1968), chapters 18, 19, and 20 for a discussion of independent study, large-group discussion, and small-group discussion.

used to identify such groups are approximate at best, instructional advantages gained from the wise use of varied groups are much in evidence.

Large-group instruction is characterized by one-way communication in which the teacher lectures to a group ranging in size from 50 to 300 students. Because the team teacher assigned to make the large-group presentation is often released from other instructional responsibilities, and because he feels the necessity for teaching particularly well before the large group, he plans with unusual care. A large number of aids including television, tape recordings, overhead projections, and especially prepared visual materials are used during a single presentation, often with the assistance of one of his team colleagues.

Class-size instruction, employed by teaching teams as well as conventional teachers, lends itself to a variety of instructional techniques. Although teacher-student interaction is possible, it often succumbs to traditional one-way communication in which the teacher assumes the dominant role. The tendency for teachers to lecture has encouraged educators to seek groupings and techniques in which the domination of one person appears strangely out of place.

Small-group instruction calls for varied procedures involving student groups ranging in size from four or five to fifteen. Essentially student-centered, such groups encourage a maximum of participation by all students. Occasionally the teacher becomes involved in discussions for brief periods, but more frequently he prefers to allow students to direct the exchanges leading toward well-defined goals.

Individualized instruction represents the antithesis of large-group instruction; during the past decade it has made massive gains, not only in the development of techniques for its practical implementation but also in the proportion of teachers willing to use them. The improvement of linear and branching programs, computer-assisted instruction, and self-directive programs not involving stimulus-reinforcement sequences has contributed to the accelerated use of individualized instruction.

Principles Related to Group Procedures

The following principles will give direction to the use of group procedures.[7]

1. A worth-while group activity must have an educational purpose.

2. Effective group participation is based upon common needs and interests and is focused on the solution of a recognized common problem. Students are eager to discuss topics that they feel are of vital importance to themselves.

3. Basic concepts necessary for effective group work must be developed before the work begins.

---

[7]John P. De Cecco, *The Psychology of Learning and Instruction: Educational Psychology* (Englewood Cliffs, New Jersey: Prentice-Hall, Inc., 1968), pp. 16–20, describes the procedures employed by Flanders in analyzing teacher-student interaction in the classroom. This technique has attracted widespread attention as a means of analyzing classroom communication and group procedure.

4. In group activities calling for student direction, immature students are strongly influenced by their immediate interests and by peer-group demands.

5. It is the teacher's responsibility to determine that group work is best suited for achieving the desired objective and to help the students plan group activities effectively.

6. Careful advance identification of appropriate topics gives positive direction to group discussions.

7. Discussion in the absence of relevant information is meaningless.

8. During a well-conducted discussion,[8] all students are mentally alert, even those who do not participate vocally.

9. Effective group work calls for assigning responsibilities to individuals.

10. Students learn to work cooperatively in a group through supervised practice.

11. Cooperative group work calls for the use of democratic procedures in using resources and resolving conflicts.

12. A friendly atmosphere encourages student participation in discussion.

13. At the end of a discussion, the teacher should identify and stress specific conclusions.

Correct and Incorrect Use

Teachers encounter many difficulties in conducting class discussions.[9] Note that the majority of the difficulties in the following narrative could have been avoided through careful consideration of the preceding principles.

MISS LEFTWICH CONDUCTS AN UNPLANNED DISCUSSION

Miss Leftwich was tired on Monday morning and, like her students she had failed to do her homework. The social problems class, however, was one in which class discussion could always serve as a stop-gap method, she reasoned.

"James," she asked, "what was the most significant news item to appear in the newspaper over the weekend?"

"I don't know."

"Mary Lynne, can you tell us?"

"There was a train wreck in New York State."

---

[8]A helpful treatment of group discussions including cautions and limitations is provided by Ben M. Harris, Wailand Bessent, and Kenneth E. McIntyre, *In-Service Education: A Guide to Better Practice* (Englewood Cliffs, New Jersey: Prentice-Hall, Inc., 1969), pp. 253–260.

[9]Robert D. Strom, *Psychology for the Classroom* (Englewood Cliffs, New Jersey: Prentice-Hall, Inc., 1969), p. 135, points out that the orientation of many teachers leads them to view the school as a coercive institution in which obedience to authority is a dominant concern. Overemphasis of authority can serve as a strong deterrent to a response-evoking classroom discussion.

A note of interest had been touched, and one after another students commented on this particular train wreck, train wrecks they had read about, train wrecks their families had known about, and finally, automobile accidents. Miss Leftwich made no effort to stem the tide, and the discussion ran its course without direction.

William Donovan, a social problems teacher in an adjacent town, also made a practice of having a class discussion on Monday covering the most important current event that had taken place over the weekend. His preparation, however, was in marked contrast to that of Miss Leftwich.

MR. DONOVAN LEADS A WORTH-WHILE DISCUSSION

As soon as the bell rang, Mr. Donovan announced that the class would spend the first ten minutes talking about an event of major political significance that had occurred in South America over the weekend.

"What was it?" he inquired. Mr. Donovan paused for a moment to give all students time to react; then he called on Sally Brandt.

"An uprising took place in La Paz, Bolivia," she responded.

"And why is this of concern to the United States?" he probed further. Before Sally could answer four other hands shot up. He gestured to Sally to remain quiet while other students thought about the problem.

Gradually, nearly all of the students gave evidence of mental activity. Only then did he permit student response. First, Jean Bennett gave her opinion, followed by Willis Morgan. Several others spoke up without the formality of the raised hand; the teacher did not object as long as the students observed proper etiquette by not speaking while others were speaking.

During the next five minutes a number of students mentioned three major ideas, but in slightly different ways. Mr. Donovan asked Chris Randle if he could identify these basic points and write them on the board in his own words. He could and did. Making minor modifications, the teacher used these points to summarize the discussion.

Specific Suggestions

The recommendations and cautions below, drawn from the principles stated earlier in this chapter, should provide a basis for effective use of group procedures.

Recommendations

1. Be sure that class discussions are goal-oriented and that they move continuously toward the desired objective.[10]

---

[10]Howard T. Batchelder, Maurice McGlasson, and Raleigh Schorling, *Student Teaching in Secondary Schools*, 4th ed. (New York: McGraw-Hill Book Company, 1964), pp. 154–158, list and discuss specific suggestions related to group discussion.

2. Use the discussion method as a means of identifying, analyzing, and solving problems.[11]

3. Be sure the topic for discussion can be developed through an exchange of ideas.

4. Make sure that students are well enough versed on the discussion topic to participate effectively. If students do not have the information necessary, help them find it. Culturally disadvantaged students, poor readers, and students from minority groups are often erroneously judged to have limited capacity.

5. Set up safeguards to prevent the discussion from wandering, but learn to guide without dominating.

6. Conduct the discussion in such a manner that all class members are encouraged to participate; recognize the effect that differences in ability will have upon the students' group participation. Help students develop skill and ease in class discussions.

7. Stimulate thinking by asking thought questions; at the same time, encourage each student to do his own thinking.

8. Before permitting student-directed group activities, make sure the students understand the purpose of the activity and exactly how it is to be accomplished.[12]

9. See that the class discussion is more than a response to the teacher's questions.

10. Encourage students to evaluate the progress of their group work.

11. Use a different and interesting procedure for stressing conclusions reached in the discussion.

12. Be sure that the physical arrangement of the room is conducive to the type of discussion held.

13. Form small discussion groups when this method will serve a useful purpose.

14. Consider using informal role playing as a classroom procedure.

15. Consider the advisability of concluding a unit with a panel discussion.

Cautions

1. Don't allow group discussions that do not serve the purposes of unit objectives.

2. Don't call for the response of star pupils to the exclusion of the less gifted.

3. Don't be satisfied with the use of one stereotyped discussion or group procedure.

4. Don't allow controversy and resulting emotionalism to bring productive discussion to a standstill.

5. Don't allow ineffective student discussion to continue for a prolonged period.

---

[11]Circumstances under which the whole-class discussion proves to be the most effective instructional approach are examined by Blount and Klausmeier, *Teaching in The Secondary School*, pp. 261–264.

[12]According to *Ibid.*, p. 270, "small group activities sometimes meet the varying abilities, interests and needs of students better than do large group activities . . ."

6. As a teacher, don't dominate the class discussion if its primary purpose is to encourage students to arrive at their own conclusions.

7. Don't lose control of the situation while directing class discussions.

8. Don't use group activities to the exclusion of individualized instruction; the probable merit of each procedure should be carefully appraised before use.

INDIVIDUALIZED INSTRUCTIONAL PROCEDURES

Instructional activities may be classed in terms of the participants as whole-group activities, small-group activities, and individual activities. The last category consists of those procedures that are undertaken without the assistance of other members of the class.

Types of Individualized Procedures

Composition—including the writing of themes as well as creative writing—is, obviously, a learning task that lends itself to individual work. *Reading*, the most important and most frequently used learning activity at the secondary and college levels, is essentially done by the individual. Although *laboratory work* and *experimentation* frequently take the form of teacher demonstration or joint student endeavor, they are often carried out by a single learner.

General assignments are given to the entire class with the usual understanding that they are to be completed by individual students. *Individual projects*[13] take the form of a major task to be performed or something to be constructed: making a cedar chest, caring for a farm animal, assembling and preparing an English journal, etc. They call for the use of definite skills in solving specific problems.

Individual contracts, although infrequently used at the present time, are written descriptions of specified unit-related work to be completed by individual students within a certain time. Students are frequently given the option of taking one of three or four contracts, all of which vary in difficulty. In *supervised study*[14] the teacher gives assistance only on request. Although similar to supervised study, *library study*[15] usually calls for a greater measure of self-direction on the part of the student.

---

[13]Clark and Starr, *Secondary Teaching Methods*, p. 171, indicate that conducting the class as a laboratory is an effective means of providing for individual differences. "Here the pupils can work on their various tasks individually or in small groups under the teacher's guidance."

[14]Wayne Dumas and Weldon Beckner, *Introduction to Secondary Education: A Foundations Approach* (Scranton, Pennsylvania: International Textbook Company, 1968), pp. 241–242, point out the advantages of supervised study for the student with limited self-directive abilities—but only if the supervision is undertaken by the teacher in his subject-matter specialty.

[15]Peter F. Oliva and Ralph A. Scrafford, *Teaching in a Modern Secondary School* (Columbus, Ohio: Charles E. Merrill Publishing Co., 1965), p. 85, point out that "the newer independent study programs provide full utilization of school resources to assist a student to engage in independent research."

Recent Individualization Techniques

Responding to the mid-fifties' emphasis on individualized learning, educators and psychologists busied themselves with the improvement of instructional techniques to be used self-directively by individual students. The most extensive of these new efforts has taken place in the area of *programed learning*. Two basic types—linear and branching programs— have been subject to widespread experimentation. During the past fifteen years of consistent improvement, many early programs have been replaced by newer, more carefully developed and tested ones.

Computer-assisted instruction, which relies heavily on the principles of programed learning, calls for the electronic correlation of several components—programs, audio-visual aids, cathode ray tube, electric typewriter, and printout sheet—to achieve a highly sophisticated approach to automated self-instruction. Although computer-assisted instruction is being tried out on a very limited scale in public secondary schools, it holds the promise of accelerating the rate of learning for students fortunate enough to have access to the necessary equipment.

Self-directed learning may make use of a range of procedures—programed learning, computer-assisted instruction, individual projects and contracts, and independent library study. Of particular interest have been recent experimental efforts to allow bright, self-directive students almost total freedom in the selection of project objectives and the procedures used to achieve them. Usually designated as *quest programs*, such approaches are typically reserved for gifted students to extend their studies in course-related areas of unusual interest not covered by the course outline.

Principles Related to Individualized Procedures

The following list of general principles (which are thoroughly treated in textbooks on educational psychology and educational theory) give direction to the sound and effective use of individualized procedures.[16]

1. The most efficient learning is often brought about through individualized procedures since all learning—although it may be stimulated by group activities—is ultimately an individual process.

2. Effective teaching involves knowing whether individualized or group procedures will best serve the needs of specific learners. The choice of group or individual activities should be determined by their efficiency in helping the student achieve desired goals. All learning procedures, regardless of the type, should be related to specific goals.

3. Individualized as well as group learning procedures vary in their motivational effect upon the student. When the learner sees that a

---

[16]A full chapter treatment of individual student experiences as related to the secondary-school classroom is provided by Faunce and Munshaw, *Teaching and Learning in Secondary Schools,* chapter 9.

learning activity is of personal value, however, he will be strongly motivated.

4. Programed learning and computer-assisted instruction have contributed substantially to the improvement and acceleration of self-directed learning.

5. Individualized learning procedures place major responsibility on the student and promote the development of independent study and work methods. Special skills can be learned only through individual effort.

6. Individualized learning procedures help the teacher meet the varying needs ot students.

7. Combinations of individual activities and group activities provide many possibilities from which the teacher can select the methods most appropriate for a certain situation.

Correct and Incorrect Use

Two contrasting examples of the use of individualized instruction in the form of creative writing are provided here. In the first example several of the preceding principles have been violated.

MR. BENTON RESTRICTS STUDENT THEMES

T. H. Benton was an English teacher of the old school. His retirement was imminent, and he looked back with nostalgia on the days when students were told what to do and were expected to do it. A portion ot one unit in his tenth-grade class was grudgingly devoted to creative writing.

Students were permitted to select and develop any one of three topics written on the board. Themes were to be two thousand words in length and, according to the teacher, were to reflect good thinking as well as good English usage. Although students were permitted to consult grammar handbooks, little personal assistance was available. Furthermore, compositions were to be completed within a one-week period.

The limitations imposed by Mr. Benton's assignment tended to stifle motivation. Students were restricted not only to certain topics but also to a specific length. Many themes of intense personal interest would, therefore, have to be ruled out. Because creative writing was an area in which the students had very limited experience, they needed the personal attention of the teacher—a need that was not met.

MISS WILTON ENCOURAGES INDIVIDUAL THEMES

Miss Wilton had only three years of teaching experience, but her ideas about ninth-grade English composition were interesting and motivational. Before the creative writing assignment was mentioned, she read the best student theme of the preceding year to a keenly interested class. She then asked students what subjects they would like to write about; several responded with specific topics. Students were requested to list three theme topics of particular interest. During the study period Miss Wilton conferred briefly with individual students, and they jointly decided which of the three topics would be the most appropriate.

Miss Wilton did not believe in imposing a specific theme length on students, but she usually indicated that the longer themes should be between one and two thousand words. During the study periods in which the students worked on their themes, she moved from student to student, providing suggestions and praise as needed.

Miss Wilton recognized that creativity cannot flourish in a highly restricted environment. She also realized that students need help without teacher domination in the selection and development of topics. Part of the help Miss Wilton provided took the form of motivation.

Advantages of a quest program are to be seen in the self-directive efforts of students described below. Although only a limited number of students can qualify for this kind of program, the innovative instructor should determine that those who do qualify are not denied the experience.

MR. WILLIAMSON BELIEVES IN QUESTING

Mr. Williamson soon reached the conclusion that his ninth-grade biology class was the brightest one he had been exposed to in his six years at Dover Junior High School. Three boys consistently led the class, not only in test scores and quality of work completed but also in interest and motivation. To keep Ward, Henry, and Jeb working to capacity posed a troublesome problem.

When the teacher read an account of a self-directive quest program used to individualize instruction for bright chemistry students in a New Jersey high school, he felt this was the answer to his problem. Asking the three boys to come by after school, he explained the possibility of their undertaking separate, individual, biology-related projects. They would be given a great deal of freedom to use special equipment; to use laboratory facilities before school, after school, or on Saturdays; to use the instructor's professional library; and to visit the school library during class periods as long as these privileges were not abused. One additional condition had to be met: they must exhibit the same competence in course content as students not involved in the quest program.

The boys were exuberant; this held the promise of providing room for intellectual expansion. Mr. Williamson instructed the students to return one week later with fully developed written plans for their individual projects. Consideration must be given to the specific problem to be solved, to the exact procedures to be followed in solving it, to the careful scheduling of time to be spent on the new effort as well as on the course work required of all, and to how the final reports were to be written up. The teacher felt that with rigorous advance student planning approved by him, consistent teacher interest, and a brief, individual, weekly progress report, the projects would enjoy the probability of success.

Specific Suggestions

Specific suggestions relating to individualized procedures are based largely on the assumption that each student is different and, therefore, requires varied instructional treatment.[17]

Recommendations

1. Give the student engaged in an individualized learning activity essential guidance without denying him the desired experience of planning, executing, and evaluating.

2. Provide the types of resources that will encourage individual study.

3. Allow for flexibility in making individual assignments.

4. Recognize that immature students struggling with the problems of self-direction may falter frequently in the pursuit of an educational goal. Help them become efficiently self-directive.

5. Select learning activities that are suitable for meeting the challenge of individual differences in intelligence, achievement, and interests.[18]

6. Encourage students to be self-directive while working on individualized special interest projects.

THE FIELD TRIP

A field trip is, in reality, an educational journey, usually designed to supplement and expand concepts already discussed in class. On a field trip the entire class visits a point of instructional interest, such as a museum, art gallery, factory, industrial center, or government installation. The field trip has the following advantages as a teaching procedure:

1. It provides first-hand experience.

2. It is pleasurable because of the vivid learning experience.

3. It is more interesting for a majority of students than many other learning experiences.

4. It provides a common experience upon which meaningful discussions can be based.

Principles Related to the Field Trip

An examination of generalizations related to field trips is profitable for all teachers and provides a type of insurance against mistakes for the

---

[17]E. Dale Davis, *Focus on Secondary Education: An Introduction to Principles and Practices* (Glenview, Illinois: Scott, Foresman and Company, 1968), pp. 251–252, shares the feeling of many authors of the past decade that independent study is an effective means of caring for the individual needs of students.

[18]William H. Burton, *The Guidance of Learning Activities*, 3d. ed. (New York: Appleton-Century-Crofts, 1962), pp. 239–243, discusses instructional and administrative provisions for individual differences. Specific suggestions are given.

beginner.[19]   The following principles have developed from the experience of various teachers.

1. The field trip is educationally valuable to the extent that it meaningfully relates phenomena observed outside the school to subject matter taught in school.[20]

2. The student is more likely to understand a concept if he has had direct experience with its referent.

3. Because field trips call for the use of more than one sense organ, they provide an impact that is rarely found in the classroom.

4. Field trips may serve a number of different purposes, including original discovery, verification, and motivation.

5. Field trips should be taken only to fulfill specific goals.

6. Field trips provide the opportunity for students to observe the functional relationships of objects and processes.

7. Field trips encourage students to be aware of their environment.

8. Because of their experience and maturity, secondary-school students derive greater benefit from the field trip than do younger pupils.

9. The planning essential to the efficient conduct of a field trip provides excellent opportunities for cooperative work. For this reason, class members should make advance preparation under the direction of the teacher. Furthermore, definite follow-up procedures should be planned and carried out.

10. If a field trip is desirable, the school administration should be actively concerned with its implementation.

Incorrect Usage

The problems encountered by a first-year English teacher on a field trip to Washington, D.C., are representative of difficulties that might largely be avoided through detailed planning.[21] Her troubles were unfolded to a sympathetic colleague the day after the trip.

A POORLY PLANNED TRIP

Mrs. Willowby, I didn't know whether we would ever make it back with all students intact. If you have time, I'll tell you the whole story.

We had been studying **Julius Caesar** in my ninth-grade English class. It seemed like a good idea to clinch a number of the points about

---

[19]Clark and Starr, *Secondary Teaching Methods,* pp. 340–341, identify areas that should be given consideration in conducting educationally sound field trips.

[20]A helpful list of community resources that might be profitably visited during a school-planned trip has been assembled by Faunce and Munshaw, *Teaching and Learning in Secondary Schools,* pp. 260–261.

[21]An excellent series of suggestions on planning a field trip is provided by James W. Brown, Richard B. Lewis, and Fred F. Harcleroad, *AV Instruction: Media and Methods,* 3d. ed. (New York: McGraw-Hill Book Company, 1969), pp. 395–396.

Blount and Klausmeier, *Teaching in The Secondary School,* p. 269, identify the risks involved in failure to engage in detailed planning before taking a field trip.

Shakespeare's life and writings by taking my twenty-nine students on a field trip to the Folger (Shakespearean) Library, just a short distance from the Library of Congress. As you know, it contains an authentic replica of the Shakespearean stage. When I mentioned the possibility to the students, they were wild about the idea.

I suppose everyone has to stumble through the first year of teaching. Next year I'll know better. Well, I found that you have to make special arrangements for transportation by either hiring a bus from the local bus company or waiting two weeks for a time when a school bus would be available. We ended up chartering a bus for a three hour period and charging each student fifty cents. I finally had to pay the fare for two students who came without their money. I suspect they really couldn't afford it.

You know, I thought that I had remembered everything, but now I wonder whether I remembered anything. For one thing, I forgot to have students obtain written permission to take the trip from their parents. Furthermore, one of the girls ran right in front of a car while we were getting off the bus. I thought for sure that she would be hit—but miraculously she escaped. I wonder if her parents could have sued me if she had been hit?

We waited at the west entrance to the school for ten minutes before the driver showed up. Actually, he had come to the front entrance and waited for us there. I suppose I was at fault by not telling him where to pick us up.

I've never seen my students as rowdy as they were on the bus. You would have thought they had just been released from long prison terms, they acted as if school were out for sure. They yelled back and forth, walked up and down the aisle, and even tossed books around the bus. I tried to get them quieted down, but I couldn't do a thing with them. Finally some of the boys started to rock the bus; I actually thought it might tip over. Just about that time the bus driver pulled over to the curb, stopped the bus, and demanded that everyone get off. He opened the door, and the kids knew he meant business. It took some mighty fast talking to get him to continue the trip without making three of the boys get out. After that they behaved very well.

Most of this teacher's troubles were related to the lack of specific plans. If she had worked out the details of the trip with students two weeks ahead of time, school transportation could have been provided, written permission from the parents could have been obtained and checked, and proper student conduct could have been discussed. She also might have reviewed appropriate control procedures in the event misbehavior did occur.

According to the English teacher's account, little or no time was spent in pinpointing exactly what students were to look for, how they were to make notes and report the evidence of their observations, and what would be expected of them in the way of a follow-up. What took place at the Folger Library itself is not told, but one may assume that the visit was not nearly as profitable as it might have been.

Use of the Field Trip in Specific Subjects

There is no subject in the secondary curriculum that could not be effectively served by some type of field trip.[22] This is true of concept-centered as well as skill areas. Variation in type, length, and purpose is to be expected, but no trip is justified unless it proves to be a more efficient teaching procedure than others that might be chosen.

Specific Suggestions

Helpful suggestions have been passed from one teacher to another in the attempt to improve class-related field trips. The following suggestions apply to almost every field trip.

Recommendations

1. Be sure all students know the purpose and destination of the field trip. Help them identify what they are supposed to learn from such an experience.[23]

2. Plan essential details with students before the trip.[24] Have students gather specific advance information about the subject of study and help them prepare a series of questions to be answered while on the field trip.

3. Be sure that students understand the relationship of what is seen on the field trip to what has been discussed in class.

4. As a part of effective planning, with the students' help establish standards of conduct to be observed while on the field trip. Encourage students to think of the trip as a carefully planned learning experience, not as a pleasure excursion.

5. Be aware of legal responsibilities in conducting field trips.

6. Be sure the field trip serves an educational purpose.

7. Solicit the help of the administration and other faculty members in planning and carrying out the field trip. Be sure the trip is adequately supervised, even if it requires the assistance of other teachers or, in some cases, parents.

8. Help students derive maximum benefit from the trip by subsequent pupil appraisals, teacher-led discussions, and class reports.

9. Consider the possibility of short as well as long field trips and of field trips outside of school hours.

10. Permit small groups within the class to take field trips for different reasons if you can be sure that they will serve educational purposes.

---

[22]James S. Kinder, *Using Audiovisual Materials in Education* (New York: American Book Company, 1965), pp. 138–140, discusses the field trip as one of the educational devices made possible through the use of community resources.

[23]Evaluative questions to be asked by the teacher following the field trip are listed by Brown, Lewis, and Harcleroad, *AV Instruction: Media and Methods*, pp. 396–398. Examples of evaluative comments by different teachers are provided.

[24]Kinder, *Using Audiovisual Materials In Education*, pp. 139–140, indicates that "there are at least five important steps in planning and executing a successful field trip." These steps are discussed.

Cautions[25]

1. Don't assume that the field trip is essentially a device for teaching elementary-school children.

2. Don't use the field trip to teach concepts that can be taught just as well through less complicated and less time-consuming procedures.

3. Don't overlook the possibility of a short trip that may involve only walking.

4. Don't allow the students' excitement to be expressed in misbehavior.

5. Don't allow minor breaches of conduct to grow into major disruptions while on a field trip.

ADDITIONAL STUDENT-CENTERED PROCEDURES IN REVIEW

Three procedures requiring student participation—group procedures, individualized instruction, and the field trip—have been discussed in this chapter. Because of their marked differences, these procedures provide the effective teacher with instructional flexibility in helping students achieve desired goals.

Group procedures may range from whole-class discussions to small study groups. Capitalizing on student interests, the teacher may utilize such activities to encourage goal-oriented learning. In directing group activities he must develop the concepts on which effective group work is founded and be consistently vigilant in determining that such activities serve the purposes of education.

Individualized instructional procedures include compositions, reading, laboratory experimentation, general assignments, individual projects, and library study. Each of these procedures may have a different motivational effect on the learner, and it is the teacher's responsibility to determine how each method can best be employed.

The field trip is an educational journey designed to expand class-related concepts. It provides learners with the advantages of vivid first-hand knowledge, intense interest, and common experience. Although not all field trips are educationally justified, they are valuable to the extent that they meaningfully relate phenomena outside the school to subject matter taught in the school.

PROBLEMS FOR STUDY AND DISCUSSION

1. Define *forum discussion*.
2. List five basic values of group activities. Discuss each briefly.
3. Why must all group discussion procedures be directed toward the achievement of goals? Explain.

---

[25]Brown, Lewis, and Harcleroad, *AV Instruction: Media and Methods,* p. 398, suggest that teachers should be aware of liability in connection with field trips.

4. Describe a large-group discussion in which you participated or observed that accomplished little. Identify the reasons why little was accomplished.

5. List three cautions to be observed in planning and conducting group activities.

6. Describe individual projects in three different subject-matter areas.

7. Expand and clarify the following statement: Learning is entirely an individual matter.

8. Under what circumstance is reading the most economical device for learning? Explain.

9. Identify the advantages to be gained through a quest program. What are its limitations?

10. It has been said that effective study of any sort should be based upon a knowledge of essential techniques and habits. Identify three of each.

11. Name at least two modern aids to self-directed learning.

12. What characterizes efficient teacher supervision of study? Explain.

13. State in your own words three psychological principles that justify the use of the field trip.

14. Specifically, what kind of planning is necessary to insure the success of a field trip?

15. Describe a field trip in which you participated as a secondary-school student. What problems arose that threatened to nullify the educational value of the trip? Knowing what you know now, how would you have handled these problems?

16. Which of the following group procedures is best suited to effective teaching in your subject-matter major: whole-class discussion, forum discussion, panel discusion, unrehearsed dramatization, small study group activities, or debates? Why?

17. Assuming that you are teaching your subject-matter major, list five field trips you might promote.

12. *Recurring Instructional Concerns*

Many instructional problems arise almost every school day, while others occur with varying degrees of frequency. Although some of these concerns are relatively trivial in nature, others are basic to effective instruction. This chapter is addressed to three of these basic concerns—continuous study of the student, the use of resource persons, and the use of teacher-prepared materials.

CONTINUOUS STUDY OF THE STUDENT

The study of students, so important to efficient, scientific teaching, is something much more fundamental than "being nice" to students, giving and correcting assignments, or maintaining an atmosphere conducive to study. It is the procedure whereby the teacher uses scientifically proven as well as less sophisticated devices to determine the mental, physical, social, and emotional status of his students.[1] Because the individual's status in all of these areas is subject to variation, the study must be a continuing one if it is to provide current information. Furthermore, the acquisition of this information must precede planning and teaching if it is to serve most helpfully in improving instruction.

Special Information About Students

In acquiring up-to-date knowledge of the student, the teacher needs to be particularly aware of certain important areas.[2]

Capacity

Although some research evidence shows that I.Q.'s have been influenced through environment, most psychologists support the assumption that one's basic capacity remains relatively stable. A real problem arises, however, when a teacher draws false conclusions about the student's capacity, regardless of what it may be. For this reason, it is important that the teacher corroborate his subjective evaluation of a student's intelligence by examining the results of standardized tests of mental maturity. When the teacher has reason to doubt the reliability of a student's score on a group test, he may wish to recommend that the student be given an individually administered examination.

Subject-Matter Achievement

Because it largely depends on student effort and teaching skill, student achievement in content areas is subject to considerable variation. The teacher, therefore, should be aware of the academic standing of individual class members in most subject areas. This need requires the use of specific evaluation procedures to inform the teacher as well as the student, and calls for the establishment of accurate, flexible, and practical record-keeping procedures.

Experiences

During a few short months a student may be exposed to a number of major experiences that have a marked influence on his academic perform-

---

[1]Peter F. Oliva, *The Secondary School Today* (New York: World Publishing Company, 1967), pp. 282-287, identifies and discusses specific information needed by the teacher to understand individual students. Brief, illustrative case studies are provided.

[2]Several proven procedures for learning about the pupil are pointed up by Leonard H. Clark and Irving S. Starr, *Secondary School Teaching Methods,* 2d. ed. (New York: The Macmillan Company, 1967), chapter 2.

ance and his attitude toward school.[3] It is possible, for example, that one student may take a trip across the country and into Canada, suffer the loss of a parent, and receive his first failing grade in school. If the teacher neglects keeping pace with such events, his planning and teaching may result in academic injury for that particular student.

Family Status

The student may have a very pleasant relationship with his parents during the early years of adolescence;[4] then, a sudden eruption into overt rebelliousness during middle adolescence leaves parents, teacher—and student—stunned. If this happens, academic performance, classroom behavior, and general attitude toward teachers and school may be affected. Because there is marked variability in personality development, a teacher's best insurance against the unexpected is to maintain consistent contact with those factors in a student's life that affect his personality.

Peer-Group Status

Conformity or lack of conformity to the values of peers can have an overnight effect on the popularity of a student. Since the teacher is rarely invited into the intimate council of the peer group, he may be entirely unaware of the status of its members. As a result, he must be particularly observant to determine the current degree of peer-group acceptance of the members of his class, for acceptance or nonacceptance can have a marked effect on a student's behavior and classroom activity.[5]

Self-Concept

How a student views himself will, to some degree, affect his peer-group relationships, his behavior at home, and his performance in the classroom. Major events in his life may dramatically alter his self-concept and give rise to rejection or approval. In attempting to help the student acquire and maintain the mental health essential to effective study and learning, the teacher should keep abreast of student successes and failures in academic, nonacademic, and peer-group settings and of their effect upon student behavior. Because of their changing nature, interests may also give new direction to student desires and activities, and the teacher must be aware of such changes.

---

[3]The social system within the school and its effect upon the individual student's social position and behavior are discussed by Frederick J. McDonald, *Educational Psychology*, 2d. ed. (Belmont, California: Wadsworth Publishing Co., Inc., 1965), pp. 557–565.

[4]Well-illustrated causes of student misbehavior originating with the home and community are provided by Oliva, *The Secondary School Today*, pp. 344-346.

[5]John E. Horrocks, *The Psychology of Adolescence*, 3d. ed. (Boston: Houghton Mifflin Company, 1969), chapter 4, discusses widening social contacts, changing roles as a result of development, the importance of contemporaries' opinions, and the adolescent's concept of his own role.

Devices Used in the Study of Students

Cumulative Records

A majority of well-administered schools currently maintain permanent records on which essential information relating to individual students is recorded from year to year.[6] Such records customarily contain standardized I.Q. and achievement test scores and the student's final marks in different subjects. Frequently, major disciplinary infractions as well as police records are also noted. Although there is considerable variation in the types of cumulative records kept, they always provide confidential information to help the teacher understand his students as individuals.

Teacher-Student Conferences

The informal conference is one of the better devices for helping the teacher become more fully acquainted with his students. Often these conferences take the form of a private conversation at the teacher's desk or at the pupil's work station. A somewhat more formal situation is the private before-school or after-school chat. If the teacher has an office, private conferences are also possible during the school day. Because of the frequency with which they may take place, teacher-student conferences afford advantages not found in other procedures.

Teacher Conferences

Information about students obtained from other responsible teachers may save a great deal of time. In certain circumstances a meeting of several teachers who have relevant information about a specific student or situation may be desirable.[7] The subjective nature of this type of information should be recognized, however; in some cases it will be necessary to discount certain information because of the teacher's emotional involvement.

Parent-Teacher Conferences

Much light can be shed on classroom behavior through a parent-teacher discussion. Domestic tensions may be aired, evidence of parental domination may come to light, or problems of concern to parents may be reviewed. Occasionally, when it will serve a useful purpose, the student is included in such conferences.

---

[6]See Wayne Dumas and Weldon Beckner, *Introduction to Secondary Education: A Foundations Approach* (Scranton, Pennsylvania: International Textbook Company, 1968), p. 274, for a brief discussion of cumulative records.

[7]The necessity for maintaining communications among teachers and the nonteaching supportive staff (guidance counselors, nurses, social workers, librarians, etc.) as a means of encouraging student progress is stressed by Robert D. Strom, *Psychology for the Classroom* (Englewood Cliffs: Prentice-Hall, Inc., 1969), p. 116.

Thomas A. Ringness, *Mental Health in the Schools* (New York: Random House, 1968), p. 292, feels that certain information about a given student must be interpreted to the teacher by the nonteaching specialist as a matter of protection to the pupil.

Sociometric Devices

Specific techniques have been devised for measuring the feelings that group members have for each other. One of the most common and useful devices is the *sociogram*, which attempts to measure the pattern of friendships in a class.[8] Because sociograms can assist the teacher in identifying friendless students (isolates), popular students (stars), and students with specific social problems, they, too, can serve a useful purpose—if they are employed with care.

Purposeful Observation

A good share of the teacher's classroom time is spent observing students under varying circumstances.[9] This observation, if not directed toward particular ends, may be of limited value in providing or confirming information about students. If, however, the teacher observes student behavior to determine changes in social adjustment, such observation becomes specific and can be of great help.

Autobiographies

Themes and autobiographies in which students are given freedom to write of their experiences, successes and failures, likes and dislikes, personal points of view, and self-concepts often reveal heretofore unknown aspects of their personality that can be valuable to the teacher. Such information can be utilized in more effectively organizing teaching procedures and materials to meet the individual needs and desires of students.

Procedures for Recording Information

Once relevant information has been obtained, it should be organized and recorded in the manner best suited for future use. Incorporating such coded information as a part of a seating chart enables the teacher to have before him relevant confidential information about students (I.Q., socio-economic status, subject-matter achievement, etc.) to which he can refer at will. Some teachers write relevant bits of information on five-by-eight cards, which are then filed alphabetically. Remarks concerning rate of progress, student problems, and study habits are sometimes included. A similar procedure involves using an individual folder for each student in which the teacher from time to time inserts notes or anecdotal accounts concerning classroom behavior. As long as subjectivity can be minimized in this type of reporting, the accumulation of such accounts over a period of time may be very helpful in interpreting student behavior.

---

[8]An example of a sociogram is found in Clark and Starr, *Secondary School Teaching Methods*, p. 35.

[9]Systematic observation—used as a technique for studying individual behavior—is thoroughly explored by Robert L. Thorndike and Elizabeth Hagen, *Measurement and Evaluation in Psychology and Education,* 3d. ed. (New York: John Wiley & Sons, Inc., 1969), pp. 471–483.

Principles Related to the Study of Students

Generalizations about student behavior and its causes contribute to the understanding of specific acts that comprise in-school behavior. Several of these principles are identified here.[10]

1. Each student is a composite of the biological and environmental factors that make him what he is. Therefore, student behavior varies depending on the environmental factors that give direction to behavior.

2. Because of the changing nature of the student's environment, the student is constantly changing. Thus, continuous study of the student is necessary to keep abreast of changes that might influence teaching and learning.

3. Better teacher-student rapport is established when the teacher gives evidence of consistent interest in all aspects of the student's welfare.

4. The choice of teaching methods should be directly related to the characteristics of the students to be taught;[11] similarly, the changing composition of a student group may make it necessary to modify teaching procedures.

5. Student attitudes toward academic achievement will vary, depending on peer-group and home influences and on student maturity.

6. The student reacts to learning stimuli as a unified whole, not as a physical, social, or emotional entity only.

Specific Suggestions

Recommendations

1. Study students systematically. Set aside a specific time for studying a particular student or students.

2. Record essential information in permanent form so that it will be useful in the future. Devise a practical procedure for making anecdotal records of relevant student behavior, and use the cumulative records in the front office to supplement basic information.

3. Be continuously aware of the factors that tend to affect personality development in students, and establish organized procedures for discovering additional information.

4. Become familiar with standardized tests that provide pertinent specific information. Compare students in terms of one characteristic at a time, such as I.Q. Later compare them in terms of another trait, such as subject-matter achievement.

5. Recognize your own limitations in analyzing student behavior and prescribing treatment for students with deep-seated problems. Seek the

---

[10]William H. Burton, *The Guidance of Learning Activities*, 3d. ed. (New York: Appleton-Century-Crofts, 1962), pp. 150–151, presents a useful set of principles concerned with the growth processes of the learner.

[11]Clark and Starr, *Secondary School Teaching Methods*, pp. 184–185, point out that verbal teaching methods are frequently not suited to teaching poor learners. For such students they suggest the use of concrete, simple activities.

assistance of guidance experts, administrators, psychologists, and, at times, psychiatrists in your work with disturbed students.

6. Have parent-teacher conferences at least once each year and more often if needed.

7. Make periodic checks on the academic standing of all students in the class.

8. Recognize the subjective nature of observations.

Cautions

1. Don't jump to hasty conclusions about the cause of student behavior.

2. Don't assume you know all about students after a limited number of personal contacts.

3. Don't forget that the physical health of individual students is not always obvious.

4. Don't use lack of time as an excuse for not knowing your students better.

5. Don't allow your emotions to sway your appraisal of student behavior.

USE OF RESOURCE PERSONS

The use of resource persons, like the continuous study of students, is a basic instructional concern. Nearly all communities afford many resources on which the alert teacher can call to enrich his teaching. Among community-related learning activities are visits to museums, concerts, lectures, industrial and government installations, newspapers, television and radio programs, legislative assemblies, and special exhibits. One of the most frequently used resources of the community, however, is the individual specialist who is brought into the classroom to supplement the teacher's instruction.[12]

Advantages of Using Resource Persons

Resource individuals often expose students to the activities and functions of the community in a meaningful and helpful way. The police chief who is invited to talk to students about the incidence of crime in their own city will probably leave a lasting impression. Not an infrequent advantage is the impression of the school that the resource person takes back to the community. If the impression is a negative one, however, it can prove to be a great disadvantage.

If the teacher has taken the trouble to assemble a file of carefully

---

[12]A few of the outstanding people in the community on whom the teacher can call are listed by Howard T. Batchelder, Maurice McGlasson, and Raleigh Schorling, *Student Teaching in Secondary Schools*, 4th ed. (New York: McGraw-Hill Book Company, 1964), p. 183.

selected resource persons, he may be in a position to identify and invite to his class the most useful individual from a range of possibilities. Furthermore, the teacher is in a position to exercise selectivity in terms of established criteria: degree of specialization, current experience, and the ability to communicate effectively. In larger communities people of national prominence have been known to give of their services willingly if it can be demonstrated that students will benefit from their presentations.[13]

Contact with a person who is immersed in an important enterprise related to the course content is a real and exciting experience for students. For example, a local FBI agent may be invited to talk to an American problems class or combination of classes about the dangers of foreign espionage in our missile industry. Class members tend to look with considerable respect upon such an individual; as a result, they listen attentively.

Principles Related to the Use of Resource Persons

An understanding of the role of resource people in the total range of possible teaching procedures will help the teacher use such individuals most effectively. The general principles below are applicable to many specific teaching situations.

1. The classroom teacher often lacks the degree of specialization that enables him to teach a particular portion of his subject with insight and enthusiasm; resource persons, on the other hand, frequently possess the desired specialized knowledge. Individuals with a particular competence are frequently glad to share their knowledge with student groups, and there are few communities that do not contain at least a few prominent specialists who might profitably be used to enrich instruction.

2. All possible procedures, including the use of the resource person, should be examined to determine which one will be most helpful in moving students efficiently toward a particular goal.

3. Student motivation is often enhanced by hearing a subject explained by a person who has an intimate acquaintance with it and thus can be expected to provide authentic information.

4. Poorly selected resource people may prove to be instructionally undesirable. For example, if the vocabulary used by a resource speaker is over the heads of students, the authority's speech will serve a no more useful purpose than an overly difficult reading assignment.

5. Students often know persons in the community (frequently relatives) who may advantageously be used to supplement instruction. An invitation to such specialists gives students the opportunity to make proper arrangements, under the direction of the teacher, for the person's appearance in school.

---

[13]Oliva, *The Secondary School Today*, pp. 250–251, describes the advantages enjoyed by students involved in the Higher Horizon's Program through use of the extensive and diversified resources of New York City.

Correct and Incorrect Use

Some teachers have good intentions with respect to teaching but make errors in implementing certain procedures. The case of Mr. Adkins, the senior high school foreign-language teacher who wished to use Mr. Fritz Neumann as a resource person in the first-year German class, is a good illustration.

POOR PREPARATION FOR A RESOURCE PERSON

Mr. Adkins, the instructor, asked Sally Venable to invite Mr. Fritz Neumann, an immigrant who had been in the country for three years, to come to the German class on Tuesday, November 12. Arriving at the school at the designated hour, the visitor reported to the front office. After some delay, it was decided that he was to go to the German class. When he finally found the room, he was embarrassed because he was late. Not knowing what he was expected to say or do, Mr. Neumann launched into a discussion of German agriculture, and the students soon became bored.

A marked contrast is seen in the procedures followed in Mr. Hillman's visit to a high-school chemistry class.

MR. BING CAREFULLY PREPARES FOR AN OUTSIDE SPEAKER

During a casual encounter on the street, Mr. Bing, the chemistry teacher, had an opportunity to renew his acquaintance with Mr. Hillman, a well-known chemical specialist employed in the local steel industry. Mr. Bing was singularly pleased when the chemist indicated his willingness to serve as a resource person for Mr. Bing's high-school chemistry class.

A short time later the teacher asked two student volunteers to contact the proposed guest about the details of his presentation. They were given specific instructions that they were to relay tactfully to Mr. Hillman: (1) He was to come on Tuesday morning, March 14, at 10:35 A.M. (2) He would be met at the main door of the school and shown to the classroom by Dave Small, one of the volunteers making the original contact. (3) He would occupy the last twenty minutes of the period, from 10:40 to 11:00 A.M. (4) His demonstration and discussion were to be concerned with "Acids and Their Effect on Different Metals."

Mr. Hillman was asked by the student volunteers precisely what materials and equipment he desired for the purpose of his demonstration; these materials were provided and placed in usable order before his visit. Billy Southall, one of the volunteers, assumed responsibility for introducing the guest and extending appreciation when the presentation was completed.

Use in Specific Subjects

In the attempt to motivate students to consider scientific fields as career possibilities, industry has in recent years encouraged cooperation on the part of schools and industry to improve secondary-school science instruction. As a result, specialists actively engaged in scientific pursuits are frequently invited into the schools to give demonstrations and lectures in physics and chemistry classes.

Foreign-language classes lend themselves very well to the use of the native who can illustrate exact pronunciation and conversational fluency. Skill subjects—including vocal and instrumental music, typing and short-hand, physical education, homemaking, and shop courses—are particularly adapted to the use of demonstration and, therefore, to the use of specialists from both inside as well as outside the school.

The majority of resource people who are invited into the school give talks on their specialty; this is typical in such classes as English, history, and mathematics. Unfortunately, qualified speakers are not used as frequently as warranted by their abilities and their effect upon pupil learning. The individual who has something to say about a subject, who communicates with ease and at the level of the learners involved, and who views his talk to students as a community service can be an interesting and helpful aid to the teacher. The use of a carefully selected outside person has the advantage of novelty and, furthermore, often provides a desirable change of pace for the teacher and the students. All subjects in the secondary curriculum would benefit from the occasional use of such resource specialists.

Specific Suggestions

Recommendations

1. Keep a current file of the resource persons in your community who can and will contribute effectively to your teaching.

2. Select only the individual whose work, knowledge, skill, or experience enables him to make a contribution of high quality. Select a person who is able to express himself with fluency and ease and who will not talk over the heads of students. (It is possible for an individual to be so highly specialized that students cannot understand his particular message.)

3. Contact the resource person in time for him to prepare his contribution.[14] Let him know exactly what is expected of him in terms of subject-matter treatment and the timing of his presentation. Encourage the resource person to contribute his own ideas for improving the presentation. (Given an opportunity, he may offer a service not previously considered or suggest an improvement that has merit.)

4. Show consideration and courtesy to the resource person from the time of the original contact until he leaves the school building.

5. Allow students the opportunity to express their appreciation to the resource person for his visit to the class. Personally thank him for his

[14]Roland C. Faunce and Carroll L. Munshaw, *Teaching and Learning in Secondary Schools* (Belmont, California: Wadsworth Publishing Co., Inc., 1965), pp. 259–264, identify and discuss community resources and projects that might be advantageously used by the school.

assistance. (This may take the form of an oral expression of thanks as well as a written "thank you.")

Cautions

1. Don't ignore the possibility of using parents and recent graduates as resource persons.[15]

2. Don't forget to provide the resource person with all essential information necessary to make his presentation successful.

3. Don't stifle the originality of the resource person by insisting on rigid conformity to established procedures.

4. Don't fail to establish procedures for limiting the time spent by a given resource person and for keeping him on the subject.

5. Don't forget to prepare students for the visit of a resource person.

6. Don't fail to publicize the resource person's visit if students from other classes, or the public, are to be invited.

7. Don't fail to enlist the cooperation of other teachers in making a resource visitor's presentation successful if students from their classes are to be in the audience.

USE OF TEACHER-PREPARED MATERIALS

The range of usable prepared materials is limited only by the teacher's ingenuity. Virtually all teachers, regardless of the quality of their instruction, make many of their own tests, and teachers of average ability often produce course outlines, study guides, and reading lists. Superior teachers, however, are known for their use of wide varieties of teaching materials to accomplish course objectives and for their inventiveness in producing their own materials and devices to serve the needs of specific students.

Classification of Materials

In order to survey the types of materials commonly produced by secondary-school teachers, it is necessary to assign these materials to certain arbitrary categories.[16]

Duplicated Materials

The most frequently used teacher-made instructional aids fall into the category of duplicated materials. The following guides, aids, and supplements are some of the materials commonly duplicated:

---

[15]*Ibid.*, pp. 375–376, list a number of resource persons and the topics they might discuss most profitably for students.

[16]See Chapter 6, pp. 98–107, for a discussion of the general use of materials and resources in unit instruction.

Clark and Starr, *Secondary School Teaching Methods*, pp. 326–328, provide a useful discussion of printed and duplicated materials.

Course or unit objectives
Course or unit outlines
Sequential list of unit
    activities
Unit assignment sheets
Study questions
Reading lists
Examples of correct or
    incorrect student work

Drawings, charts, or graphs
Subjective and objective tests
Evaluation checklists
Self-appraisal devices
Supplementary materials not
    found in the text or library
Important announcements
Messages to parents
Study hints

Collected Materials

Many teachers have made effective use of certain types of materials that have been assembled over a period of time. Such collections include:

Relevant newspaper and magazine articles
Course-related stories
Course-related pamphlets
Textbooks of differing interest and reading levels
Student work of good and poor quality[17]

Materials for Meeting Individual Differences

Many teachers produce special materials in order to provide adequately for individual differences in their students. Unit contracts, typically calling for a three-step differentiation in work required of students—*difficult, average, or easy*—and many modifications of the basic contract idea are currently being used. Often years of experience have taught the teacher the value of using specific written help to assist less gifted students with their more difficult study problems. Study guides, reading lists, and self-evaluation checklists serve helpfully in this connection.

Materials to Aid in Student Self-Direction

Although quality teachers have consistently encouraged students to be self-directive, the recent emphasis on the importance of student self-direction has led inventive teachers to develop several different devices. They have developed self-evaluation report cards that encourage students to maintain an accurate record of their grades and progress in a given course; they have worked out checklists to be employed by students in the self-correction of themes, grammar usage, and subject-matter content; and they have adapted or developed study guides that give direction to efficient study.

Miscellaneous Materials

Much of the teacher's time and ingenuity are devoted to producing materials and aids that, because of their diversity, are best grouped under the miscellaneous heading:

---

[17]Student anonymity must be maintained whenever such collections are used.

Displays (Dioramas, woodwork
   exhibits, etc.)[18]
Collections (Rocks, artifacts,
   best student themes, etc.)
Specimens (Pressed flowers,
   stuffed animals, etc.)[19]
Scale models (House,
   Shakespearean stage, etc.)
Simple maps[20]
Relief maps

Charts
Graphs
Flat pictures[21]
Personal photographs
Color slides[22]
Transparencies
Filmstrips
Microscopic slides
Teaching machines
Programed learning materials

Special Advantages

When the teacher goes to the trouble of preparing his own materials, it is usually because he feels strongly that they will serve the needs of the teaching-learning situation better than conventional materials. One of the basic advantages of teacher-made devices is that they are prepared with specific students in mind and are intended to serve particular purposes. The "Study Hints" sheet prepared for distribution to students who find it difficult to study effectively is a good illustration of the individualized use of a teacher-prepared device. If the teacher prepares such an aid for specific students, he usually considers their unique interests. When interest is present, students are motivated, and motivation encourages learning.

The teacher has the chance to exercise individual ingenuity whenever he makes or prepares his own materials and devices. He also has the opportunity to involve students in the production. This participation can have a positive effect on student learning as well as on interest arousal.

Principles Related to the Use of Teacher-Prepared Materials

An examination of the following principles, which apply to all teacher-made instructional materials, should help provide a foundation on which the teacher can base the production and use of his own teaching aids.

---

[18]James W. Brown, Richard B. Lewis, and Fred F. Harcleroad, *AV Instruction: Media and Methods*, 3d. ed. (New York: McGraw-Hill Book Company, 1969), chapter 15, provide examples of effective instructional displays.

[19]Three-dimensional teaching materials are discussed by Walter Arno Wittich and Charles Francis Schuller, *Audio-Visual Materials: Their Nature and Use*, 4th. ed. (New York: Harper & Row, Publishers, 1967), chapter 6.

[20]Brown, Lewis, and Harcleroad, *AV Instruction: Media and Methods*, chapter 7, provide an extensive discussion of the use of maps, charts, and graphs.

[21]The use and purpose of flat pictures is thoroughly examined by James S. Kinder, *Using Audiovisual Materials in Education* (New York: The American Book Company, 1965), chapter 3.

[22]A brief but pointed discussion concerned with providing, improvising, and adapting audio-visual aids is found in Leonard M. Douglas, *The Secondary Teacher at Work* (Boston: D. C. Heath & Company, 1967), pp. 152–156.

1. The production and use of teacher-prepared materials may take any form that serves the needs of instruction. How effective such materials will be as teaching devices depends upon their significance to the students, which, in turn, depends upon the extent to which they are related to the students' past experiences.

2. Teacher-prepared materials and devices can expand and strengthen course-related concepts, skills, memorizations, and attitudes.[23] At the same time, these materials may be used to meet the individual needs of students.

3. Teacher-prepared materials should be designed to help students achieve unit objectives. Unless other prodedures better serve the educational purpose, teacher-prepared materials should be used frequently.

4. The duplication of written materials provides one device for supplementing basic oral or written materials. When duplicated materials are employed, their relationship to unit objectives must be clear to the learner. Although duplicated materials serve most frequently as supplements, they may also be used to present basic information to the class.

5. The occasional use of well-prepared hand-out materials can add interest to routine instruction.

6. The effectiveness of teacher-made materials should be appraised each time they are used.

Use in Specific Subjects

Certain subjects lend themselves well to the use of specific aids. The teaching of Spanish, for example, calls for the use of teacher-collected items that reflect Spanish culture as well as provide effective motivation for vocabulary drill. In the interest of effective instruction, the teacher might develop flash cards with words on one side and equivalent drawings on the other, assemble pictures portraying different aspects of the culture, or record native speech on tapes.

The mathematics teacher should continuously seek to develop means for simplifying difficult concepts. An ambitious teacher of geometry might build various shapes (spheres, cubes, triangles, circles, parabolas, cones, etc.) that he could employ in class with a high degree of success. The teacher of physics can find a helpful supply of teaching materials in radio and television repair shops. Such items are often available at no cost to the teacher if their purpose is explained.

Duplicated music is used effectively in vocal and instrumental classes. Choral groups at times are asked to learn a certain selection when only a single copy of the music is available. The needed music can be reproduced from a single copy with a minimum expenditure of time and effort if the necessary equipment and facilities are available.

In social studies classes, teachers make excellent use of acetate

---

[23]E. Dale Davis, *Focus on Secondary Education: An Introduction to Principles and Practices* (Glenview, Illinois: Scott, Foresman and Company, 1966), p. 255, points out that the alert teacher will have little difficulty in obtaining a variety of instructional materials to meet the differing needs of students.

pockets in which a map can be inserted, leaving it visible to the class. By means of a grease pencil the teacher may then trace out a certain route, encircle an area of particular importance, or pinpoint a given spot without injury to the map itself.

Specific Suggestions

Recommendations

1. Be sure that each teacher-made device serves a specific instructional purpose, and give careful consideration to the *type* of objective it is designed to help achieve. Furthermore, make sure that students understand the relationship of teacher-developed materials to the unit and to the course.

2. Use teacher-devised materials to help meet the individual needs of students by providing motivation for students with special problems, helping gifted students work to their capacities, and encouraging student self-direction.

3. Organize duplicated materials attractively and simply so that their purpose is clear, and be sure that the vocabulary in such materials is readily understood by a majority of students. Give an easily understood oral or written explanation of how these hand-out materials should be used.

4. Use teacher-prepared materials to serve a range of instructional purposes. Think of different ways of using such materials to promote learning.

5. Prepare materials to meet student interest as long as a useful instructional purpose is served. If humor is introduced through the use of these materials, take steps to see that it, too, serves an instructional purpose.

6. Encourage school administrators to provide physical facilities, equipment, and clerical help so that all teachers will be able to produce their own instructional materials.

7. Reproduce the best materials and aids made by your colleagues if such devices will help you teach better. Duplicate noncopyrighted materials of particular value to instruction if they are not easily accessible to students.

Cautions

1. Don't overlook the possible value of student-prepared materials.

2. Don't view duplicated materials as the only teacher-prepared aid to instruction.

3. Distribute hand-out materials *only* when this is the best instructional procedure.

RECURRING INSTRUCTIONAL CONCERNS IN REVIEW

Three recurring instructional concerns—continuous study of the student, the use of resource persons, and the use of teacher-prepared materials—

have been examined in this chapter. Employed effectively by a well-organized teacher, each has a unique contribution to make to the teaching-learning process.

A continuous study of the student provides the teacher with a basis for the effective use of content and methods. The information gained involves an acquaintance with the mental, physical, social, and emotional status of students, all of which are subject to variation. Several devices are used in acquiring and keeping this information current—cumulative records, teacher-student conferences, parent-teacher conferences, sociometric devices, and purposeful observation.

The resource person may be used by the alert teacher to enrich his instruction. With the aid of a carefully assembled file of resource persons, such a teacher can invite to his class the most helpful individual from a range of possibilities. Thus, specialists within the community can be employed to add variety and to serve particular instructional needs.

Superior teachers consistently exercise ingenuity in planning, assembling, and producing materials that serve the purposes of student learning. Among these materials are duplicated items, collections of various types, and a wide range of miscellaneous devices—displays, specimens, models, maps, charts, pictures, slides, and simple teaching machines. The production and use of such teacher-prepared materials may take any form that serves the needs of instruction.

PROBLEMS FOR STUDY AND DISCUSSION

1. Explain fully the following statement: Improved student behavior is the basic concern of education.

2. Why is the *continuous* study of students repeatedly emphasized in this chapter?

3. If you found that students in your teaching major were achieving in a range extending over three grade levels, how would you alter procedures to meet the students' needs? Be specific.

4. Suggest three procedures that the teacher can follow to keep up-to-date on the changing relationship of students to their peers. Be specific.

5. How does the cumulative record aid in the continuous study of students? Explain.

6. Assumption: You have discovered there are three social isolates in your class of thirty students. Would this affect your teaching procedures? How?

7. Give an example taken from your own experience as a high-school student or from your friends' experiences in which your teacher used incorrect procedures in the continuous study of his students.

8. In the order of their importance, list the traits that should characterize the effective resource person.

9. In what specific area of your teaching minor do you have weaknesses that might be partially compensated for by the use of a resource person? List two or more weaknesses.

10. Why are interest and motivation said to be aroused by the use of well-chosen resource persons? Be specific.

11. Assumption: As an experienced teacher you have been approached by a new teacher for suggestions relating to the use of the resource person. List the cautions you would propose.

12. List seven types of duplicated materials that are frequently produced and used by teachers in your teaching major.

13. Indicate the types of teacher-made collections that serve the most useful educational purpose. Which one will be most helpful to you in teaching your subject-matter major?

14. Identify at least three practical devices the teacher might use to help students become self-directive.

15. Which three of the following teacher-made or student-made devices will be of greatest help in teaching your subject-matter minor: specimens, displays, models, relief maps, charts, personal photographs, flat pictures, and transparencies? Why?

16. Which specific subjects lend themselves best to the use of teacher-made materials? Why?

PART FOUR
Special Teaching Problems

13. *Serving Instructional Purposes Through Discipline*

Sound classroom control may be defined as *the intelligent manipulation of all circumstances and factors in the schoolroom to serve the purposes of instruction.* Effective discipline is closely related to classroom control. The end result of successful discipline is *intelligent self-direction.*[1] Teachers who help students toward meaningful, conscious self-direction also achieve sound classroom control.

---

[1]Arden N. Frandsen, *Educational Psychology,* 2nd. ed. (New York: McGraw-Hill Book Company, 1967), pp. 637–638, states that the teacher's basic concern in assisting students toward social development is to encourage rational self-discipline as an end result.

The negative implications of the term *discipline* worry the future teacher, and the in-service teacher is frequently concerned because his attempts to maintain discipline have been unsuccessful. Anxiety is justifiably felt by a large proportion of teachers, for several studies have reported that the inability to control the classroom behavior of students is the number one cause of teacher failure.[2]

The experienced teacher knows that if he is unable to create and maintain an effective but tension-free classroom environment, the efficiency of his teaching will be markedly diminished.[3] Batchelder, McGlasson, and Schorling propose a useful breakdown for considering the many facets of classroom control: (1) constructive discipline, (2) preventive discipline, and (3) remedial discipline.[4] Others view discipline from four somewhat varying philosophical points of view. These differences are apparent in the following statements.[5]

School One: The term *discipline* is not recognized as a problem of classroom operation. The teacher who is teaching effectively and well will have the full cooperation of his students.

School Two: A traditional approach to discipline is a sound one. All infractions result in punishment, sometimes severe.

School Three: Although students occasionally engage in disruptive behavior, this is understandable and normal. It will be necessary to exercise a measure of control at times to protect the rights of other students, but severe punishment in the traditional sense of the word is not sanctioned.

School Four: Misbehavior in the classroom is symptomatic of some problem. Proper classroom control consists of identifying the causes and taking whatever steps are necessary to remove the causes.

PRINCIPLES BASIC TO EFFECTIVE CLASSROOM CONTROL

Although it is possible to cite numerous examples of disciplinary situations that were effectively or ineffectively handled, it will serve a

---

[2]W. R. Flesher, "The Beginning Teacher," *Educational Research Bulletin,* 24 (January 1945), 14–18.

Wayne Dumas and Weldon Beckner, *Introduction to Secondary Education: A Foundations Approach* (Scranton, Pennsylvania: International Textbook Company, 1968), p. 250, discuss studies of discipline-related teacher failure as well as teacher anxieties generated by inability to control classroom behavior.

William E. Amos and Reginald C. Drem, *Managing Student Behavior* (St. Louis, Missouri: Warren H. Green, Inc., 1967), p. 10 "are convinced that failure to gain and maintain effective control in the classroom accounts for more teachers leaving public school classrooms than all other investigated causes put together."

[3]Lee J. Cronbach, *Educational Psychology,* 2nd. ed. (New York: McGraw-Hill Book Company, 1967), p. 502, speaks out for a middle-of-the-road approach between teacher domination and total lack of teacher control.

[4]Howard T. Batchelder, Maurice McGlasson, and Raleigh Schorling, *Student Teaching in Secondary Schools,* 4th ed. (New York: McGraw-Hill Book Company, 1964), p. 81.

[5]Adapted from Norma E. Cutts and Nicholas Moseley, "Four Schools of School Discipline; a Synthesis," *School and Society,* 87 (February 1959), 87.

more useful purpose if the principles that underlie sound solutions to classroom behavior problems are first identified.[6] A discussion of all the principles related to classroom control is impractical, for there is hardly a principle in the field of educational psychology that does not have some bearing on student classroom behavior. Those that have particular relevance are singled out here for brief mention.

The Effect of the Curriculum

Classroom control becomes easier when the curriculum is geared to the students' achievement and interests. Youngsters who find the course too difficult are frequently uninterested, discouraged, and, therefore, disruptive. Those who find the course too easy are similarly affected, so that both groups have the potential for creating situations that adversely affect discipline. The student who feels that the curriculum will further his personal interests is likely to engage in goal-oriented activities and, therefore, is not inclined to misbehave.[7]

The Effect of Planning

Planning should meet the varied needs of all students in the group.[8] A knowledge of the range of ability, background, achievement, and desire to learn will help the teacher plan realistically and, therefore, achieve sound classroom control. Individual differences among students include variation in intelligence, aptitude, achievement, training, and motivation. Failure to deal intelligently with these factors means that poor teaching and, hence, poor discipline will probably result.[9]

The Effect of Objectives and Procedures

Goals that seem unachievable to the learner may cause behavior

---

[6]Principles for governing student behavior together with procedures to be used in the development of self-control are listed and discussed by William H. Burton, *The Guidance of Learning Activities*, 3d. ed. (New York: Appleton-Century-Crofts, 1962), pp. 557–559.

Four basic democratic principles and related subprinciples essential to effective classroom discipline are presented by George V. Sheviakov and Fritz Redl, *Discipline for Today's Children and Youth*, rev. ed. (Washington, D. C.: National Education Association, 1956), pp. 10–16.

[7]*Ibid.*, pp. 494–495.

[8]Three different methods of planning and control—undirected activities, teacher-controlled activities, and group-controlled activities—are illustrated and discussed by Cronbach, *Educational Psychology*, pp. 499–502.

Louis E. LaGrand, *Discipline in the Secondary School* (West Nyack, New York: Parker Publishing Co., 1969), p. 15, suggests the necessity for effective planning in encouraging student involvement in democratic classroom procedures.

A helpful treatment of essential teacher preparation for the first day of school is provided by Burton, *The Guidance of Learning Activities*, pp. 542–544.

[9]Sheviakov and Redl, *Discipline for Today's Children and Youth*, pp. 46–47, relate problems of discipline to dissatisfactions in the work process.

difficulties.[10] Large objectives should be approached step by step, and the student should advance to the next step only after he has understood the preceding ones.[11] Furthermore, when the teacher selects an inappropriate procedure for achieving a specific goal, he is hindering the child's desire to be attentive.

The Effect of Meaning

When meaning is emphasized in preference to rote memorization, students tend to be less resistant to learning. Sound study patterns and desirable classroom behavior are by-products of situations in which comprehension is a dominant concern.[12] A case in point is the enthusiasm of a class whose English teacher is able to read Shakespeare and make it meaningful to the students at their own level of understanding.

The Effect of Habits

Habits of misbehavior can result in poor classroom conduct.[13] For this reason, the teacher who is concerned with creating and maintaining effective classroom control should devote considerable attention to helping students develop habits that will facilitate learning. Among such worthwhile habits are politeness in personal relationships, listening thoughtfully to classroom discussions, and studying effectively alone when it is expected.

Habits, both good and bad, resist change and can be perpetuated through only occasional repetition. The habit of rudeness within the classroom will be reinforced by an occasional outburst, even if the student does not exhibit rudeness all the time in dealing with his classmates.

The breaking of habits harmful to effective classroom behavior calls for repeated avoidance of the habit. Each time the students show a desire to follow a wrong habit pattern, they must meet the teacher's firm insistence that they behave otherwise. No variation, no compromise should be allowed until a new habit is well established.

The Effect of Growth and Development

Changes that occur in students during the adolescent years underlie

---

[10]A brief but helpful examination of the relationship of classroom goals and motivation for learning is provided by Cronbach, *Educational Psychology,* pp. 525–526.

The danger of imposing adult goals upon immature learners is pointed out by George J. Mouly, *Psychology for Effective Teaching*, 2nd. ed. (New York: Henry Holt, 1968), p. 493.

[11]See the discussion of the hierarchial nature of objectives by Asahel D. Woodruff, *Basic Concepts of Teaching; with Brief Readings* (San Francisco: Chandler Publishing Co., 1962), pp. 71–73.

[12]*Ibid.*, p. 247, reviews the role of concepts in the control of behavior.

[13]The strength of the habit motive as a matter of educational significance is described by Mouly, *Psychology for Effective Teaching*, p. 78.

LaGrand, *Discipline in the Secondary School*, p. 31, cautions against the teacher's habitual employment of instructional skills and techniques that are outmoded. He suggests the reevaluation of such skills at regular intervals.

many of the so-called disciplinary difficulties in the classroom. A teacher who does not understand the nature and cause of these changes is severely handicapped in dealing intelligently with related classroom behavior problems. For example, a teacher who is not aware of the reason for the lack of emotional control in a pubescent girl may jump to faulty conclusions, such as the assumption that she is basically unstable.

Mental Ability

One, but only one, of the factors that determine the individual student's behavior in the classroom is intellectual capacity. A student can achieve no more than his natural ability will permit. When teachers consistently pressure students to overachieve, emotional reactions may arise that, in turn, create an unfavorable bias toward study and a continuing aversion to learning.

Because students vary a great deal in the rate at which mental ability grows, uninformed teachers often make unjustified comparisons of student capacities, effort, or achievement. Normal students of the same chronological age may differ markedly in their ability to be attentive to classroom procedures because of the rate of growth of their mental abilities. Misbehaving Walter, slow in maturing, may find it quite impossible to become interested in the teacher's lecture on city government.

If subnormal capacities are indicated by recently administered intelligence tests and are corroborated by personal observation, the teacher may find it desirable to refer students with such marked intellectual limitations to special agencies within the school district or community. Often these agencies can provide better educational opportunities for these youngsters than can the school. Such youngsters with subnormal capacities can be a consistent distraction to other students and may retard general class progress.

Since studies during the past few years have revealed that intelligence test scores are influenced by environmental factors,[14] it is wise for a teacher to withhold judgment about the capacity of a misbehaving youngster (or any youngster) until he has had an opportunity to observe the child's behavior under a range of circumstances.

Physical and Social Maturation

Because girls achieve physical maturity more rapidly than boys, social problems frequently develop during adolescence. These problems can affect the study climate of the classroom and give rise to misbehavior. Certain socially aggressive girls, for example, are known for their constant classroom chattering, a practice pursued without regard for its effect on the class.[15]

The change in attitude toward the opposite sex that comes with the onset of puberty is reflected in classroom behavior. The teacher must see

[14]See Mouly, *Psychology for Effective Teaching*, pp. 264–267.
[15]Frandsen, *Educational Psychology*, p. 637, stresses the need for "self-disciplined conformity to the regulations required for efficient and happy classroom work. . . ."

that the newly intensified interest does not interfere with the main function of the school. He must realize, however, that this interest is a normal outgrowth of biological development and will play an increasingly important role in personality development.

A physical problem may be the source of a student's academic failure. Such problems as poor vision, poor hearing, limited muscular coordination, heart disease, or lung ailments may result in extensive or limited academic failure, which, in turn, may lead to misbehavior. Students who are at a physical disadvantage because of inadequate nourishment often suffer social and cultural disadvantages because they come from economically marginal or submarginal homes.

The explosive physical energy of the teenager may give rise to horseplay within the classroom in the form of scuffling, throwing books, or running. When provision is made for extensive and vigorous exercise during the school day, the tendency for horseplay is diminished.

The Effect of Environmental Influences

The conditioning influences of the home, the peer group, and the teacher help determine the classroom behavior of each student. Each of these factors plays a unique and varied role in furthering or inhibiting individual adjustment, personal attitudes, and academic success.

The Home

Students who come from democratically oriented homes tend to be more disobedient, although they are more self-directive and inquisitive than youngsters from autocratic homes. The autocratic teacher may find that the child from the democratic home will have difficulty adjusting to teacher expectations.

Certain forms of adolescent instability may be related to earlier rigid controls in the home.[16] The tendency to be argumentative, a habit often characteristic of certain adolescent periods, is encouraged in an authoritarian home environment and may be transplanted to the school setting. Paul, for example, viewed his father as a tyrant with whom he was always in conflict. When he discovered that his teacher also insisted on having his own way, Paul exhibited his argumentative nature in the classroom.

The youngster whose home life has encouraged emotional stability will tend to exhibit mature behavior in the classroom. Conversely, emotional outbursts, such as aggressive behavior, excessive argumentation, displays of temper, and frequent crying, may be related to unstable home environments.

Culturally deprived environments impose restrictions that may be reflected in certain types of classroom misbehavior. Barney not only misused the English language through gross violations of standard gram-

---

[16]Gail M. Inlow, *Maturity in High School Teaching* (Englewood Cliffs, New Jersey: Prentice-Hall, Inc., 1963), p. 347, describes three home situations that make it difficult for an adolescent to adjust to a properly conducted classroom situation.

mar, but he also abused it through a constant torrent of profanity. Knowing Barney's family background, his teacher could see that it was difficult for the boy to speak otherwise.

Students often come to school after mistreatment and abuse at home. Winifred found it impossible to focus on her studies at school because her thoughts were on the beating her father had given her the night before. In some instances when restraining home influences are discarded in the more permissive atmosphere of the school, students tend to misbehave.[17] Janet was reared in a lower class home where she was dominated by her father, four older brothers and sisters, and an unmarried aunt. As a result, Janet used every opportunity to exert her own authority in the classroom with domineering, ungracious behavior toward her peers and her teacher.

Another factor to remember is that siblings subjected to the same home influences may exhibit quite different traits in the classroom. Because Lorna has been classified by her teachers as a discipline problem, these teachers will be inclined to think of her brother Arthur as posing the same sort of problem. Judgment, however, should be withheld, pending first-hand experience, since Arthur may be a different type of individual altogether.

The Peer Group

A student's acceptability to a peer-group clique may be related to the social status of his family. Many classrooms contain students who are ostracized because of poverty, poor dress, or socially unacceptable manners or speech resulting from cultural impoverishment. When such a situation exists, the teacher must shape the classroom environment so that the needs of the class as well as those of the individual may be met.

Social adjustments essential to adolescent development are encouraged in the informality of play situations involving other members of the peer group. Denied opportunities for such desirable activities under school sponsorship, students tend to compensate through horseplay and social exchanges in the classroom. A well-organized school activities program will benefit classroom control.

Language usage among adolescents, freed of conformity to adult standards, may be evidence of the existence of a new culture—a subculture—unique to them. The slang, the tendency for vulgar speech and profanity, and the disregard for correct grammar all point in this direction. Even a determined effort on the part of the teacher may not stem the tide, but it may exert a moderating influence.

The Teacher

The teacher should try to establish a personal relationship with each student in his class, a relationship that will aid the cause of instruction. Ideally, the teacher will attempt to create an environment in which the

---

[17]LaGrand, *Discipline in the Secondary School*, p. 105, finds "that conflicting views on behavior between home and school are a major source of confusion in the student's life."

student feels confident and secure but in which he views the classroom as a place where learning is promoted.[18]

The Effect of Adolescent Needs

The fulfillment or lack of fulfillment of adolescent needs will strongly influence the type of behavior that is exhibited in the classroom.[19] Adolescents need to be understood by a teacher who strives to help them meet their unsatisfied needs in socially acceptable ways; they need freedom from absorbing preoccupations; and they need affection, both at home and at school.

Teacher Understanding

Teachers who basically understand why students behave as they do are in a position to give positive direction to student behavior. Youngsters who engage in loud, boisterous, and sometimes coarse talk may be appraised by such teachers as adolescents who are ineptly and unskillfully reaching out for adult independence. Knowing that such behavior is transitional, these teachers can inoffensively guide student behavior to less extreme forms.

Students from minority groups who fail to conform either individual-ly or as a group to middle class standards are simply exhibiting condi-tioned behavior over which they sometimes have little control. Such behavior, which often takes the form of overt rebellion in certain urban high schools, may evoke calls for heavy-handed justice from certain teachers as well as school patrons. Under such circumstances the wise teacher must be guided by a refusal to be stampeded into thoughtless retaliation, by an unwillingness to allow irrational student behavior to trigger irrational teacher behavior.

Pressures from Unsatisfied Needs

When an adolescent's basic needs are not satisfied, pressures build up that may erupt into nonconforming or socially undesirable behavior. Denied peer-group approval, for example, teenagers will brave adult wrath to gain such approval. Students often ride roughshod over the values of their teachers if they can thus win the praise of other students. Making light of the teacher's methods or personal mannerisms is a common device for winning the praise of adolescent peers.

Age-related developmental tasks are of such absorbing concern to most teenagers that such tasks frequently overshadow academic concerns. When the teenage boy is confronted with a situation in which he must choose whether he will attend a basketball game or go unprepared to his

---

[18]Frederick J. McDonald, *Educational Psychology*, 2d. ed. (Belmont, California: Wadsworth Publishing Co., Inc., 1965), pp. 521–525, provides a useful explanation of the influence of classroom environment on student behavior.

[19]*Ibid.*, p. 504, points out that the means employed by students in satisfying needs are not always compatible with the goals of a learning situation.

English class the following day, the decision is most often in favor of going to the game with his peer group. Teenagers know that peer-group approval comes through participation in common endeavors.

Freedom from Preoccupations

Optimum adjustment presupposes a balanced satisfaction of basic needs. The well-adjusted student is one who is free of persistent absorbing preoccupations, who is accepted by his peers and by members of the opposite sex, and who has sound and rewarding associations with adults. As a result, he is secure and self-confident. Optimum adjustment, however, does not mean that a student's classroom behavior will conform to what an autocratic teacher assumes to be the ideal.

Need for Affection

All adolescents need affection, although the behavioral manifestations of this need often take strange forms.[20] This was the case with Evan. At sixteen his relationship with his stern, inflexible father had reached the point where Evan felt that the easiest solution was to leave home. Evan's reactions to his father's demands were violent, profane, and abusive. He needed the approval of understanding parents who were willing to give tangible evidence of their affection during the unstable adolescent years. Furthermore, Evan would have benefited from the patient understanding of his teachers, who instead tended to view him as a discipline problem.

Ridicule and loss of prestige are extremely distasteful to the teenager, especially when they take place in the presence of his peers. Repeated studies of why students dislike certain teachers have revealed that ridicule is one of their most objectionable traits. In most cases, the wise teacher avoids punishing a student in the presence of his friends.

The Effect of Expectations

Realistic expectations on the part of parents, teachers, the peer group, and the student himself encourage consistent student effort that, in turn, promotes sound classroom behavior.

Parental Expectations

Parents at times impose upon their children unrealistic ambitions that run counter to the aptitudes, interests, and wishes of the children. The thwarted desire of a parent to complete medical school, for example, may cause the parent to select medicine as a desired professional goal for a son without considering his son's ability and desire. The teacher who finds a youngster bearing the burden of someone else's ambitions often finds a rebellious and frustrated youngster who presents a difficult behavior problem.

---

[20]Frandsen, *Educational Psychology*, pp. 603–608, describes how an aggressive, defiant, maladjusted child is guided toward mental health by a knowledgeable teacher. An analysis of the steps taken is also provided.

Teacher Expectations

The teacher's expectations should reflect a realistic acquaintance with student capacities, academic achievement, and personal desires. Teachers, like other adults, may err by expecting too much or too little of students.[21] To err either way is to invite the possibility of overt or covert rebellion.

Peer-Group Expectations

An adolescent who wishes to join or who is a member of a particular peer group will usually exert great effort to conform to the expectations of the group. If the peer group expects a member to be a troublemaker, he will try to conform in spite of the teacher's wish to the contrary.

Self-Expectations

What a student expects of himself will be the result of his past experience and the concepts he has learned from these experiences. If he has found that he has mechanical aptitude, a student is likely to develop an interest in mechanics and acquire some competence in this area. If he suffers one social defeat after another, his self-image as a social person will suffer, and he may exhibit withdrawal tendencies. When his teachers have given him the impression that he is a troublemaker, he may conform to their picture of him.

The possession of a range of skills promotes self-confidence and heightens one's self-expectations. Desirable behavior is more often exhibited when the student feels he is a person of merit. The teacher can be of great assistance in helping the adolescent create a healthy and psychologically sound self-image. Each youngster, regardless of capacity, should encounter some measure of success to build his self-image, and it is the teacher's responsibility to help him succeed. The student will not, as a general rule, violate his belief that he is a person of worth and that he deserves respect.

The Effect of Readiness

Teachers often overlook how certain types of readiness affect the individual student's willingness and ability to engage in goal-oriented behavior.[22] Careful analysis of readiness factors can be useful to teachers in promoting an effective classroom study climate.

Readiness for a Voluntary Change

Gaining a clear mental picture of the need for behavioral change underlies the actual change. Before misbehaving students are willing to change their own disruptive behavior, they must understand that it is in

---

[21]Problems caused by unrealistic teacher expectations are discussed by Nathan S. Blount and Herbert J. Klausmeier, *Teaching in the Secondary School*, 2nd. ed. (New York: Harper & Row, Publishers, 1968), pp. 482–484.

[22]David P. Ausubel's discussion of readiness of culturally deprived students, *Educational Psychology: A Cognitive View* (Holt, Rinehart & Winston, Inc., 1968), pp 269–271, contains several implications for classroom discipline.

their interest to do so. Voluntary change comes after proper insights have been acquired. The mathematics teacher would have paid almost any price if Dean would stop making those semiaudible, deprecating remarks in the back of the room. They served Dean's ego needs, and he was not ready to give them up.

Mental Maturity and Conceptual Readiness

Immaturity is the cause of a lack of conceptual readiness in many students. Mental maturity is related to the process of maturation and should not be confused with slow learning.[23] Students not sufficiently mature to grasp specific concepts will feel great frustration if pressed for impossible achievement. Although the placement of course content at a given grade level presupposes that students are ready to learn it, this supposition is frequently false—as the failure of students at all grade levels attests.

The teacher should try to recognize the moment of optimum readiness for the introduction of a new concept, because premature exposure to difficult concepts may result in negative reactions and student inattention.[24] When the physics teacher introduced concepts that a large majority of the class could not understand, the students concentrated for a while, but their minds soon began to wander. Some students began to converse.

Physical Readiness

Physical readiness, related to neuro-muscular coordination, can impose restrictions on learning that are just as severe as those imposed by conceptual readiness.[25] The would-be typist who has poor muscular coordination will never be able to type at a high rate of speed unless, through the process of maturation, better coordination is achieved. Similarly, if the physically immature seventh-grade boy is thrust into athletic competition where he consistently fails, strong disruptive antagonisms may assert themselves. Motor skills can never be taught successfully before the student is physically ready to learn them.

The Effect of Motivation

How well a student responds to classroom procedures will depend partly on his motivation.[26] If his motivation is weak, he will probably seek more interesting pursuits. Frequently this takes the form of misbehavior. Norma was so highly interested in biological science that the teacher found it difficult to provide her with challenging reading materials. Yielding to his responsibility to the total group, the instructor left Norma

---

[23]See the discussion of the growth of mental ability on page 244.

[24]Lack of readiness as a possible cause of disinterest is discussed by Frandsen, *Educational Psychology*, pp. 81–82.

[25]See Woodruff, *Basic Concepts of Teaching*, p. 285.

[26]Ausubel, *Educational Psychology*, p. 393, presents a series of motivation-related recommendations that are of particular value to the student of classroom control.

to her own devices. Because her teacher neglected to help her and because she was not sufficiently motivated to find materials on her own, she became a troublemaker in the class.

The assumption that learners are equally motivated by the same set of circumstances is false. A teaching procedure that proves particularly interesting for one student may be quite boring for other students. And bored students tend to cause behavior problems. Competition in the classroom[27] is a form of aggression, while committee and small-group work may help satisfy the need for affiliation.

Motivation Through Self-Interest

Each individual relates all perceived occurrences to his own person and evaluates them in terms of their assumed effect on him and his environment. Reactions to classroom situations are, similarly, related to their assumed effect upon the student. If he feels that it will be advantageous for him to misbehave, he will misbehave. Thus Donna cut class and went to a movie with a girl friend because she knew that Mr. Bogg's lecture would be uninteresting.

When the learner places great value on certain goals, he will expend tremendous energy to achieve them. If the valued goal is to make an impression on a certain member of the opposite sex, motivation may be strong, and the adolescent may expend a great deal of effort to achieve this goal. Classroom convention and teacher-imposed rules standing in his way may simply intensify his effort.

Motivation Through Successful Experiences

Motivation may be held at a desirable level by providing the learner with a proper balance between successes and failures. Unwise use of either praise or blame may also affect motivation and, consequently, classroom control. Successful experiences tend to strengthen the student's self-concept and his desire to achieve higher goals. The person whose attention is centered on unit goals is seldom troublesome.

The desirable amount of praise or blame given by an instructor will vary with the student and the circumstances in which it is given. Lavish praise from a teacher, for example, can prove humiliating to a fifteen-year-old boy if given in the presence of his peer group. Teacher-student rapport may thus be disturbed. Mrs. Jex, another teacher, makes a policy of discovering the strong points of below-average students so that she can legitimately praise their work. On the other hand, she limits the praise given to gifted students—success is often its own reward.

When the teacher quickly rewards desired behavior with praise that results in satisfaction, there is a good chance that this behavior will recur. Therefore, teachers who wish to perpetuate certain behavior should praise it. Mr. Parris took advantage of the P.T.A. meeting to tell Mr. and Mrs. McIntyre how much improvement their son Blaine had shown in his

---

[27]The advantages and disadvantages of competition are discussed and illustrated by Frandsen, *Educational Psychology*, pp. 299–301.

last English theme. The teacher was aware that Blaine had received considerable pressure from home to improve and anticipated that this praise would free Blaine from undue parental pressure as well as stimulate him to further improvement.

Motivation Through Realistic Goal Setting

If goals are not carefully selected in consideration of student abilities, it is quite probable that students will meet with great frustration, and the stage will be set for disruptive behavior. Hoping that it might have a helpful influence, the physical education instructor placed Lindsey on a basketball team consisting of boys who played much better than he did. Because he could not measure up to team expectations, Lindsey became antagonistic and abusive.

Motivation Through Attention and Interest

Learning cannot take place if the learner is inattentive. Whether inattention leads to disruptive behavior or to daydreaming (overt and covert expressions of inattention), the net instructional result is negative. Leslie was preoccupied with thoughts of going away to college next year, and for her the Latin II class might just as well have been omitted.

Students focus attention on what interests them. A basic aspect of effective teaching involves identifying individual student interests and using them to achieve a high degree of motivation. The interested person is the attentive person, and the attentive individual usually does not create discipline problems.

Motivation Through Contacting the Referent

The extent to which the student makes first-hand contact with the referent of the concept or a realistic facsimile will largely determine his interest in the concept. Vivid, real experiences promote interest and thus promote acceptable behavior. Students in the civics class were enthusiastic about their visit to the city hall, where they had an opportunity to meet the city manager personally and hear him tell about the problems of city government.

CLASSROOM CONTROL IN PRACTICE

There can be no substitute for a knowledge of the principles underlying so-called discipline problems, but knowledge alone is not enough. One must have sufficient practice in the application of principles so that fumbling, trial-and-error attempts are replaced by a degree of sophistication in maintaining classroom discipline. Specific examples of discipline practices will help the beginning and experienced teacher alike to relate the preceding principles to actual practice.[28]

---

[28]Thomas A. Ringness, *Mental Health in the Schools* (New York: Random House, Inc., 1968), pp. 95–96 and 127–128, provides a helpful description of school discipline and morale as it existed under the administration of a traditional iron-fisted principal and later as it was changed under the leadership of a knowledgeable new administrator.

Unsound Procedures

Questionable classroom control practices are a matter of great concern to conscientious educators. The following examples point out different manifestations of unsound behavior.

MR. FOLKNER REACTED EMOTIONALLY

J. J. Folkner was a nervous teacher. Minor student infractions that should not have upset him gave rise to extreme reactions. When he observed that students were chewing gum, he stopped the class for a five-minute lecture on the social evils of gum chewing. If he discovered that students were whispering during the study period, he lost his temper. Occasionally, when students submitted late papers, he reacted violently before the entire class, although only a small minority of the class was at fault. His tenth-grade biology class was tense and lacking in warmth.

MISS INGRAM ACTED ON IMPULSE

Sally Ingram was a first-year teacher, fresh from a secondary methods class in which she had become acquainted with the necessity for maintaining discipline at all costs. On her first day on the new job she was put to the test by Bill Whitley, age fifteen. Seated in the rear of the class and being somewhat bored with the classroom procedures, Bill tossed his ninth-grade geography book to his friend two aisles to his right. Miss Ingram decided that this type of behavior must be stopped at once.

"Bill Whitley, leave the room and go to the principal's office immediately," she called loudly.

The boy hastily complied, confused and thunderstruck at the abruptness of his new teacher. Miss Ingram wondered what procedures she should follow from this point.

MR. BRINKS MADE AN ABRUPT CHANGE

Throughout the school year, the eleventh-grade United States history class had been permitted a measure of freedom customarily denied students in many other classes. They were allowed to talk freely at their seats. Even during the study period the instructor made no attempt to stifle this informal exchange of ideas, unless the noise reached unusual proportions.

It was only when Mr. Brinks made an exchange visit to the history class of a teacher of excellent reputation in another city that he realized his class was too noisy for study purposes. Shortly afterwards, Mr. Brinks was informed of his supervisor's imminent visit to his classroom. Panicked by the news, Mr. Brinks tried to impose a decree of total silence on his boisterous students. Overt rebellion was the result, since the students had become used to his laxity.

Sound Procedures

Certain teachers in every secondary school are known for their ability to deal effectively and inoffensively with classroom control problems by using preventive as well as remedial discipline. Specific practices of such teachers are described in the following narrative accounts.[29]

MR. MOON COLLECTED INFORMATION ABOUT STUDENTS

From the first day of school Mr. Moon seemed to be entirely in command of his students, even his troublesome eighth-grade general mathematics class. The students liked him, and he was fond of them. When a new teacher asked him to explain his success in promoting desirable classroom behavior, he replied that he felt it was related to his study of each student as an individual.

"As soon as I can," he said, "I begin to collect information about each student. I talk to them about their interests; I determine what their likes and dislikes are. It is a wise practice, I feel, to form an opinion about the student's capacity based upon careful observation and first-hand experience before looking at the test-determined I.Q. They're not always in agreement, you know.

"As soon as I have a substantial amount of information, I try to put it to good use in my teaching. If a student has a limited capacity, he may not be able to acquire certain concepts, and his limitation has to be taken into account. This approach is realism in teaching. Students with specific interests should be encouraged to relate these interests to the classwork as much as possible. Youngsters with culturally impoverished backgrounds are not responsible for many of their academic difficulties, and it should not be inferred that they are. They need, of course, consistent, step-by-step assistance to bring them up to the desired level of competence."

MR. HONE EMPLOYED QUIET FIRMNESS

Two minutes before the final bell was to ring, the smoldering quarrel between Homer and Lynn erupted into a bona fide fist fight. There were several exchanges of blows before Mr. Hone could separate the boys. The teacher spoke quietly and firmly.

"I will not tolerate this in my room. Homer, you sit on this side of the room, and, Lynn, you sit on the opposite side until the bell rings."

After the bell rang, Mr. Hone called both boys to his desk.

"I want to talk to you individually about this before I decide what is to be done."

In separate talks with the boys the cause of the difficulty came to light. Then, in joint discussion, Mr. Hone and the two boys reached an agreement and determined appropriate classroom behavior. Nothing was

[29]Staten W. Webster, *Discipline in the Classroom: Basic Principles and Problems* (San Francisco: Chandler Publishing Co., 1968), part two, presents a description of ten cases involving student behavior problems. Solutions to these problems are provided by teachers of high quality known to maintain effective classroom control.

said to the class about the outcome of the incident. Inasmuch as the instructor assumed that no useful purpose would be served through punishment, none was given.

MISS KNELL KEPT UP-TO-DATE IN HER SUBJECT

Two girls were conversing as they left Miss Knell's eleventh-grade English literature class.

"She keeps things moving all the time, doesn't she?" said Jennie. Mary said, "It's more fun to listen to her lessons than it is to talk to the other kids. I don't know how she does it. She's the first teacher I ever had who kept me so interested I didn't want to cut up."

The principal, who had overheard the conversation, could have told them the answer. It was the basic subject-matter preparation of the teacher. She knew her subject thoroughly—keeping up with the journals, attending workshops, and taking advanced courses at the university.

Although vigorous disciplinary action may be warranted under extreme circumstances, knowing one's students, being relaxed in one's control of them, and keeping current in one's own subject all help maintain an atmosphere in which optimum learning can take place. The practices of Mr. Moon, Mr. Hone, and Miss Knell lend support to this conclusion.

THE ROLE OF THE TEACHER

Few teachers will admit that most disciplinary problems are caused by the teacher. It is quite true that directionless teenagers will frequently take over a classroom situation where teacher leadership is lacking.[30] However, it is the teacher's responsibility to give positive direction and control to the goal-oriented behavior of students. It is not his role to stand idly by, assuming that the native goodness of adolescents will somehow induce them to want to conform to the teacher's desire.[31]

Teacher-Caused Student Misbehavior

A substantial share of teacher-caused student misbehavior originates with a *lack of planning*.[32] Effective planning for classroom control begins

---

[30]Cronbach, *Educational Psychology*, pp. 534–535, views "disciplinary problems as a failure of leadership."

[31]Edwin J. Brown and Arthur T. Phelps, *Managing the Classroom*, 2nd. ed. (New York: The Ronald Press Company, 1961), pp. 125–129, discuss (1) increasing pupil activity, (2) improving school morale, and (3) improving personal attitudes as procedures for helping achieve effective classroom control.

The principles of behavior modification are discussed by Webster, *Discipline in the Classroom*, pp. 52–57.

[32]Many of the advantages of group planning are identified in a case study presented by Cronbach, *Educational Psychology*, pp. 506–510.

with an analysis of the individual students that compose the group to be taught.

Several different behavior patterns of the instructor are harmful to teacher-student relationships and tend to encourage student misconduct.[33] *Inconsistency* in the teacher's dealings with the class leaves students somewhat frustrated and without a basis for predicting the teacher's reactions. The resulting insecurity is expressed in an unwillingness to follow the teacher's suggestions, in general tension, and in attempts to anticipate the teacher's next move.

Another form of teacher behavior that promotes student misconduct is the *failure to communicate* to class members the desirable standards of classroom conduct and the *failure to insist that such standards be maintained.* Students and teachers should come to a working agreement about desirable standards of classroom behavior, such as consistent politeness, not interrupting the teacher, and listening when others are speaking. The teacher must, of course, be responsible for determining that the desired behavior is consistently carried out until proper habits are formed.

The teacher who consistently *threatens students* with punishment[34] for infractions is encouraging misbehavior—unless the threat is carried out. Because each unfulfilled promise of disciplinary action creates an impression that the teacher will never carry through with a threat, the student's subsequent behavior is geared to what he believes will or will not happen, not to what the teacher *says* will happen.[35]

Emphasis on individualized, self-directive learning poses a number of problems for the conscientious teacher who wishes to maintain an appropriate classroom climate for study. Not all bright students have acquired skills in self-direction; further, not all students of average and below average capacity are lacking in such skills. For this reason, the teacher has the responsibility for determining the extent to which individual students can be profitably self-directive and for determining the privileges that should be permitted such students in the self-directive pursuit of educational goals. Teacher error in this critical area can spell defeat for a program of student self-direction.

Maintenance of Specific Routines

The establishment and maintenance of specific routine procedures is one of the neglected areas of classroom control. The teacher must, of necessity, assume responsibility for initiating these procedures and for

---

[33]According to McDonald, *Educational Psychology*, p. 543, "a teacher may be predisposed to attend to certain kinds of pupil behavior and to ignore other kinds. In this way the teacher's perceptions of a pupil's characteristics are limited to the kinds of behaviors that the teacher sees as desirable or undesirable in the classroom setting."

[34]See Fritz Redl and William W. Wattenberg, *Mental Hygiene in Teaching* (New York: Harcourt Brace Jovanovich, Inc., 1959), pp. 365–367, for a helpful treatment of threats.

[35]McDonald, *Educational Psychology*, p. 542, finds that "teacher control of pupil behavior is related to the kinds of expectations pupils have about patterns of control."

seeing that they are continued or modified as necessary. Failure to give adequate attention to these routines can spell disciplinary defeat in classrooms that are otherwise well conducted.[36]

A classroom situation in which many aspects of effective routine are violated will illustrate the harm possible.

MR. SCHILLING NEGLECTS ROUTINE

When Mr. Johnson, the supervisor, paid an unexpected call on Sam Schilling, he found a most revealing situation. Seated in the back of the room at an empty desk, he was able to observe the entire operation of the class.

After the bell rang, students were still conversing in the hall. When all except two students were finally in their seats, the teacher began to call the roll. A murmur ran through the class as he spoke each name and received in return the unfailing "Here" or "Present."

"Now, pass in your homework for today," said Mr. Schilling. Everyone began to talk, and somehow one fourth of the papers did not arrive at the front of the class. In desperation the teacher moved swiftly along each row of seats, picking up the missing assignments from the desks.

Toward the middle of the period, Mr. Johnson noticed that the room was unusually warm. The wall thermometer beside him registered 80 degrees. Several students were obviously drowsy, and three of them had their heads down on their desks. Finally the boy nearest the windows threw open two of them, letting in a chilling blast of sub-zero February air.

"Close those windows right now," snapped Mr. Schilling. Reluctantly the offender did so.

After a prolonged lecture and discussion period, the teacher declared that the remaining ten minutes would be a study period. As soon as the teacher had made his announcement, three boys went to the pencil sharpener, where they stood in line, waiting their turn. They were soon joined by four other students who playfully sauntered over.

During the so-called study period, one student came to Mr. Schilling's desk to ask a question. Before the student could get the answer, another student stood at the desk waiting for her question to be answered. Within five minutes several more students crowded around the teacher's desk, seeking help and obscuring the teacher's view of the class. Just when it appeared that the class might get completely out of control, the bell rang and the class members filed out without a final word from their teacher.

[36]LaGrand, *Discipline in the Secondary School*, pp. 167–168, finds that the establishment of classroom routines is essential to an effective instructional program. However, he points out that procedural changes on a temporary basis after habits have been formed can have a motivational effect on students.

Burton, *The Guidance of Learning Activities*, p. 537, identifies several elements of classroom management that can become routine.

Robert Sylwester, *Common Sense in Classroom Relations* (West Nyack, New York: Parker Publishing Co., 1966), chapter 3, provides a thorough and useful discussion on developing sound daily routines.

Mr. Schilling failed to control several aspects of classroom routine: Students were not ready to start work when the bell rang; papers were not handed in systematically; temperature control was neglected; students were not required to study during the study period; and the procedures employed in responding to student questions aggravated the already existing confusion.

CLASSROOM CONTROL PRACTICES IN DIFFERENT SUBJECTS

Must the art class be as quiet as the mathematics class? Should students in a shop class avoid loud conversations just as their friends in an English class are expected to do? A generalization will be useful: *Classroom control is sound if it promotes efficient instruction.* In this statement nothing is said about the intensity of noise. Instead, attention is focused upon learning and sound instruction, not upon discipline-oriented teaching procedures.

Most teachers today realize that there need not be absolute silence in order for learning to take place. Instead, students learn best in a tension-free atmosphere where they are highly motivated to achieve goals known to be educationally sound. Effective education, however, does require a sensible and serious attitude.

Skill Subjects

Some teachers conduct a classroom in which there is little semblance of order and in which learning moves forward at a reduced pace. Teachers often justify their lack of control by rationalizing that stricter discipline would stifle creativity and represent unwarranted rigidity. The tendency for this laxity is sometimes found in classes involving motor manipulations and physical skills.

Music classes concerned with instrumental or vocal work can get out of hand very easily, unless students are required to behave in a way that promotes instruction and learning. In physical education classes, students may view games and exercises as pure play. Although composing a substantial proportion of the activities in such a course, play must be so directed or restricted that it serves the specific purposes of instruction. Because of the noise occasioned by the nature of the activity, typing classes encourage loud talking among students unless the teacher takes appropriate steps to avoid it. Classes concerned with painting and drawing serve as ready-made temptations to the less self-directed students,[37] because free movement of students about the room is normally essential to the conduct of the class. When students are permitted to abuse this

---

[37]An interesting case study in which an art teacher discovers the strengths and limitations of undirected class activities is told by Cronbach, *Educational Psychology*, pp. 503–506.

necessary privilege, however, disorder soon prevails. Shop classes involving auto mechanics, woodwork, and metalwork pose many of the same control problems. If the nature of the class leads students to misbehave, the teacher must plan in advance to counter this tendency.

Concept-Centered Subjects

Concept-centered classes, which are basically concerned with mental rather than physical activities, present a different type of classroom control challenge. In the algebra class, for example, even a moderate amount of noise may interfere markedly with the students' concentration during a study period. In an English class, the teacher's reading of a particular literary selection may require the undivided attention of every member of the class if maximum benefit is to be derived. For less gifted students, the mastery of some of the concepts of English grammar may require a great deal of uninterrupted concentration. Each instructor must determine for himself the extent to which given elements in the classroom environment interfere with, or promote, the cause of learning.

Social-Centered Procedures

A wide range of social activities are employed in teaching. Among them are committee work, working in pairs, and large-group discussions. Because of the students' tendency to use these class projects for promoting their own social life rather than the teacher's proposed goal, some teachers feel that such activities are not sufficiently productive to warrant more than occasional use.

SPECIFIC SUGGESTIONS

Listed here are a number of specific hints that should be of pointed assistance to the beginning teacher as well as the seasoned instructor who is still encountering difficulties in the general area of discipline.[38]

Recommendations

1. Set up desirable standards of classroom behavior and insist that the students maintain these standards.[39] Be firm in your dealings with

---

[38]Herbert J. Klausmeier and William Goodwin, *Learning and Human Abilities: Educational Psychology*, 2nd. ed. (New York: Harper & Row, Publishers, 1966), pp. 195–197, view the sound teacher as a helpful person regardless of the type of leadership he exercises.

Sheviakov and Redl, *Discipline for Today's Children and Youth*, pp. 62–64, make eight basic recommendations that provide help to teachers who encounter classroom behavior problems.

[39]According to Redl and Wattenberg, *Mental Hygiene in Teaching*, pp. 361–362, instructional needs are served when the teacher defines, reasonably and unemotionally, the limits of classroom behavior.

students, especially during the period when habits are being formed for the school year.[40]

2. Indicate to the misbehaving student that although you dislike the infraction you do not dislike him.

3. Put classroom suggestions on a positive rather than a negative basis.

4. Encourage your students to respect other students and adults; insist that students treat you with respect at all times.

5. Identify as quickly as possible the students whose behavior might give rise to classroom control problems. Learn how to use group leaders in solving such problems, and use social pressure to encourage misbehaving students to conform to group standards.[41]

6. Always be fair in your dealings with the entire class as well as with individual students.

7. Be appropriately friendly with students, especially with those who have adjustment problems.[42]

8. When students have deep-seated problems with which you are not qualified to cope, refer them to appropriate professionals within the school or community.

9. Create an atmosphere of general pleasantness and scholarship in which students will not want to disturb others. Smile frequently, particularly when it is necessary to establish an atmosphere of general warmth.

10. Develop a sincere sense of humor that has student appeal, but make it serve the cause of instruction.

11. Make a practice of carefully reviewing and appraising your classroom control problems at the end of the school day. Incorporate into your daily lesson plan appropriate action for the next day.[43]

12. Free yourself of personal idiosyncrasies and annoying mannerisms.

13. Use correct and appropriate English.

14. Take a keen interest in student activities and in current events, relating them to your classwork where possible.

15. Plan interesting, informative, and varied activities for your students, but be sure these procedures are psychologically sound. Know when and when not to involve students in planning; but if student ideas are sound, use them.

---

[40]Blount and Klausmeier, *Teaching in the Secondary School,* pp. 479–481, discuss the necessity for the teacher to establish himself as the figure of authority in the classroom.

[41]Redl and Wattenberg, *Mental Hygiene in Teaching,* pp. 348–353, suggest several devices for providing supporting self-control for the child with tendencies for misbehavior.

[42]Leonard H. Clark and Irving S. Starr, *Secondary School Teaching Methods,* 2nd. ed. (New York: The Macmillan Company, 1967), pp. 79–80, point out that the personality of the teacher has much to do with creating a desirable classroom atmosphere. Further, both teacher personality and the nature of the classroom climate strongly influence classroom control.

[43]Redl and Wattenberg, *Mental Hygiene in Teaching,* pp. 354–358, suggest restructuring the learning situation as a means of assisting learners to cope more effectively with specific problems.

16. Know each student's name, his friends, and his interests; then consider the effect of differences in age, maturity, interests, and intelligence upon classroom control. Furthermore, recognize the effect that adverse home environments may have upon an individual's classroom behavior.

17. Use the seating plan to help maintain order by separating students who would create a disturbance if they were seated together.

18. Establish and maintain well-understood, definite procedures for distributing and collecting papers and materials.

19. Be sure that each student feels that he is important and that he has accomplished something worth while. Moreover, help him feel that he is accepted by the teacher as well as by other students.

20. Try to make each student aware that it is possible for him to improve and that it is important for him to do so.

21. Indicate that you have confidence in what students can and will. do.

22. Be sure that classwork is not too difficult or too easy for individual students.

23. Talk privately with students about severe infractions. Once remedial disciplinary action is started, follow through with it, but keep the nature of any such action confidential.[44]

24. Under certain circumstances, conferences with teaching colleagues and administrators may prove to be helpful.

25. In cases of marked misbehavior, it may be helpful to encourage the offending student to compose and sign an agreement whereby he promises to improve. The signatures of parents and counselors may also be warranted in certain cases. At times, a telephone call to interested parents may prove to be the most helpful and efficient way to improve student behavior. Parent-teacher conferences may be most informative and rewarding in attacking specific discipline-related problems.

26. Students change their behavior voluntarily when they see it is in their interest to do so.

27. During teacher presentations, learn to make eye contact with students, particularly with those tending toward misbehavior. When the attention of particular students begins to waver, call on them.

28. In handling disciplinary infractions be calm and dignified as well as firm.

29. When misbehavior begins to assume large proportions, it may be wise to isolate the offender from the group until the situation has been resolved.

30. Allow a student time for meditation before discussing his misbehavior with him.

---

[44]The limitations of punishment as a classroom control procedure are examined by Cronbach, *Educational Psychology*, pp. 492–494.

A carefully documented treatment of the advantages and disadvantages of punishment against the background of motivation is provided by John P. De Cecco, *The Psychology of Learning and Instruction: Educational Psychology* (Englewood Cliffs, New Jersey: Prentice-Hall, Inc., 1968), pp. 152–156.

31. When property is damaged or destroyed, restitution is essential. This may be sufficient punishment in many cases.

Cautions

1. Don't raise your voice as a means of maintaining order.
2. Don't become belligerent in attempting to be firm.
3. Don't resort to force as a solution to a discipline problem.
4. Don't display your emotions in the presence of the class.
5. Don't allow small infractions to grow to a point where they become generally disruptive.
6. Don't threaten students, but take action, if necessary, after thinking through the situation.
7. Don't expect more of students than their capacities, interests, and motivation will permit.
8. Don't convey the idea that you are functioning only as a policeman to keep everybody in line.
9. Don't send students to the principal's office for minor infractions.[45] Unless a problem is particularly severe, solve it yourself.
10. Don't allow students to move around the room unless it serves the purpose of teaching and learning.
11. Don't discuss personal matters of great concern to students in the presence of other students.
12. Don't place yourself in the position of arguing with the class or individuals within the class.
13. Don't hesitate to change the seats of students if this will serve a useful purpose.
14. Don't willfully antagonize students.
15. Don't be pointlessly autocratic.
16. Don't use a laissez-faire approach to classroom control.[46]
17. Don't be tactless in your dealings with students.
18. Don't waste time unnecessarily in changing from one activity to another.
19. Don't make snap judgments with respect to what remedial action is best.
20. Don't hold a grudge against a student.
21. Don't "allow yourself to be fooled by the surface appearance of a discipline problem."[47]

---

[45]Mouly, *Psychology for Effective Teaching*, p. 233, states that although classroom control measures should emphasize the positive, ". . . teachers occasionally have to punish children as a means of helping them toward self-discipline."

Key elements that effect discipline are identified and discussed by LaGrand, *Discipline in the Secondary School*, chapter 5.

[46]Klausmeier and Goodwin, *Learning and Human Abilities*, pp. 182–186, discuss research related to authoritarian, democratic, and laissez-faire leadership and point out implications for classroom behavior.

[47]Sheviakov and Redl, *Discipline for Today's Children and Youth*, p. 57.

CLASSROOM CONTROL IN REVIEW

The best classroom environment is one that results in efficient learning. Discipline involves employing guidance and teaching techniques to encourage students to become self-directive and thus to create an atmosphere conducive to learning.

Sound classroom control is achieved most efficiently if the teacher is equipped with a theoretical and working knowledge of relevant principles that underlie classroom behavior—principles related to curriculum, planning, objectives and procedures, activity and experience, meaning and behavior, habits, growth and development, environmental influences, adolescent needs, expectations, readiness, and motivation. Only when the teacher has acquired genuine skill in relating such principles to the classroom behavior of students is he free to focus his attention on the other concerns of instruction.

PROBLEMS FOR STUDY AND DISCUSSION

1. Why is the ultimate goal of discipline often described as self-discipline? Discuss.

2. Define discipline as the traditionalists of fifty years ago would have defined it. Why is it defined differently today? Explain.

3. Identify at least ten reasons why more teachers fail because of poor class discipline than for any other reason.

4. Are superintendents justified in placing so much emphasis on the teacher's ability to control the class? Explain your reasons.

5. What is the advantage of a knowledge of basic principles of classroom behavior as opposed to an acquaintance with very specific suggestions?

6. List ten common classroom disciplinary problems that might be avoided through effective planning.

7. Should the teacher plan for meeting disciplinary problems in his daily lesson plan, in his unit plan, or in his yearly plan? Why?

8. Describe three typical classroom situations in which the inefficient use of audio-visual aids tends to promote misbehavior.

9. Example: Ninth-grade Florence (I.Q. 103) had gradually ceased to try in her English I class. In addition, her classroom behavior during the past month had been very disturbing to the teacher. She held frequent loud peer-group chats during class and was prone to show off. On the basis of this scanty evidence, indicate (1) possible causes for her misbehavior and (2) the desired action on the part of the teacher for each possible cause. List the most likely cause first, the next most likely cause second, etc.

10. Assumption: An eleventh-grade boy has a tendency to swear occasionally in your classroom. Describe the steps you would take to meet this situation.

11. Is the teacher ever justified in employing punitive discipline? Discuss, giving examples.

12. If you wanted the students in your class to form five basic habits that would encourage effective classroom control, what would they be?

13. What is the effect of peer-group acceptance on classroom behavior?

14. Discuss the relationship of heterosexual adjustment to classroom behavior.

15. Give several examples taken from your teaching major in which objectives assumed to be of particular value by teachers are rejected as personal goals by the students.

16. It is generally held that all adolescents need affection. How is this need expressed in classroom peer-group relationships?

17. In what ways may students attempt to adjust their academic and social behavior to make it acceptable to their peers? Discuss, giving examples.

18. Give several examples taken from your teaching minor in which lack of readiness promotes classroom misbehavior.

19. Identify the procedures you would employ in encouraging students to be self-directive without violating appropriate individual or classroom control.

20. A substantial share of teacher-caused misbehavior originates with lack of planning. Give several examples that lend support to this statement.

21. How quiet should a class in art be? In social science? In orchestra? Explain.

14. *Readiness and Motivation*

Beginning teachers soon learn what experienced teachers have consistently observed—that readiness and motivation profoundly influence the learning process. This chapter is devoted to a discussion of principles, practices, and specific suggestions aimed at enabling the teacher to make more effective use of readiness and motivation in classroom situations.

EFFECT OF READINESS ON LEARNING

The absence of readiness affects the learning process in one clear-cut manner: the student simply cannot learn.[1] Students at any grade level usually possess some degree of readiness for the study of that year's curriculum content, although students with limited achievement, ability, and motivation may be far below the desired level for optimum learning. The eleventh-grade boy of average intelligence who reads with the comprehension and speed of an eighth-grader is only partially ready to read the eleventh-grade United States history text. He is not, however, totally lacking in readiness.

The learner is said to be *ready* to undertake a given learning task when he has reached the point in his mental, physical, social, and emotional development where the accomplishment of that task is possible as well as desirable. Unfortunately, uninformed laymen and teachers often view physical readiness as the sole determiner of the readiness to learn.[2] The same error is committed when the student's readiness is determined solely on the basis of his social, mental, and emotional maturity. This oversimplification is responsible for many basic errors that impede the learning process.[3]

Types of Readiness

Physical Readiness

The learning of skill subjects, such as typing, instrumental music, or physical education, requires neuro-muscular coordination. Students excelling in these areas are customarily those who are physically ready to learn the basic techniques and who are willing to practice to achieve the necessary coordination.

In a typing class one occasionally finds a bright and apparently physically normal senior high school student whose coordination does not enable him to achieve beyond a bare minimum in typing skill. If he is not ready, no amount of effort on his part will result in his typing at a high rate of speed. Similarly, the physical education teacher is often aware of the clumsiness of certain students in his class, a clumsiness that cannot be overcome through practice. If this lack of coordination is related to slow

---

[1]Asahel D. Woodruff, *Basic Concepts of Teaching; with Brief Readings* (San Francisco: Chandler Publishing Co., 1962), p. 278.

[2]William H. Burton, *The Guidance of Learning Activities*, 3d. ed. (New York: Appleton-Century-Crofts, 1962), p. 160, points out that there are many forms of readiness.

[3]Henry C. Lindgren, *Educational Psychology in the Classroom*, 3d. ed. (New York: John Wiley & Sons, Inc., 1967), p. 299, points out that during the past few years, concepts of readiness for undertaking certain kinds of learning experiences (reading, for example) have been sharply modified.

Some authors have elected to substitute the phrase *entering behavior* for *readiness* in order to avoid confusion with the term *biological maturation*. John P. De Cecco, *The Psychology of Learning and Instruction: Educational Psychology* (Englewood Cliffs, New Jersey: Prentice-Hall, Inc., 1968), pp. 61–63, defends this usage.

maturation, there is little that the teacher can do except wait for physical growth to provide the desired readiness.

Intellectual Readiness

Three factors contribute to intellectual readiness—neural growth, native capacity, and experience. For example, the preschool child, regardless of native capacity, cannot hope to cope with the complexities of nuclear physics, because the physical development of his brain and nervous system is not sufficiently advanced to permit his understanding. Similarly, the possibility that a twelve-year-old can function as a business executive is restricted by neural growth, in spite of his I.Q. or experience.

Students with limited mental capacities will never be ready to undertake certain intellectual tasks. The dull youngster, for example, may flounder in second-year algebra and in the physical sciences. Because his inability to think abstractly restricts his mental activity, he is able to solve only relatively simple problems. The above-average student, on the other hand, can learn progressively more difficult and complex ideas because he is able to grasp the basic concepts necessary to his understanding.

Experience also affects a student's intellectual, or conceptual, readiness,[4] since concepts can be acquired only through meaningful experiences. The individual who has had the opportunity for extensive travel has a great advantage over the nontraveler in a geography course. Similarly, the readiness of any given student to understand national and world problems comes as a direct result of wide reading and experience gathered from talking to many people.

Conceptual readiness to learn a certain task or a more complex concept also relies on the knowledge of the necessary basic concepts. The beginning clarinet player who aspires to play in the school band must learn tone production and fingering, as well as how to play in a small group, before he is ready to participate in the full band. If a typical seventh-grade student were suddenly confronted with the task of learning quantum physics, a subject for which he had no prerequisite training, he would lack essential readiness. Although he might have the study skills, emotional stability, coordination of hand and eye, and essential social skills, he would still lack the basic concepts necessary for an understanding of the new subject. He could progress no more rapidly than the acquisition of the supporting concepts would permit.

Social Readiness

Forced participation in a large class is a frightening experience for students who tend to be introverted. The wise teacher, however, may induce the timid youngster to participate to some extent by asking

---

[4]Benjamin S. Bloom, ed., *Taxonomy of Educational Objectives: The Classification of Educational Goals; Handbook I: Cognitive Domain* (New York: David McKay Co., Inc., 1956), pp. 17–20, presents a classification of conceptual objectives that has found wide acceptance. Consisting of six major categories, the taxonomy is arranged in hierarchical order.

carefully selected questions. Such questions should enable the student to experience success and should build up his image as a competent class participant in his own mind as well as in the minds of his peers. Once his confidence is built up, the student may be able to answer more difficult questions and to share his ideas more freely. Later he may participate with enthusiasm in discussions that are of real interest to him.

Emotional Readiness

Emotional adjustments have a close relationship to the social readiness of a student. Few problems are of more pressing and real concern to the teenager than peer-group acceptance. An eleventh-grade girl who is excluded from membership in a cliquish group to which she very much wants to belong is preoccupied with her rejection and its assumed impact on her personal welfare. During this period she may lack emotional readiness for serious study.

Another serious form of emotional unreadiness is found in the junior high school student who comes from an overprotective home. Having been denied contact with a realistic world and the toughening effect of occasional failure, the student finds it difficult to get along with his peers and is unequipped to meet the rigorous competition without severe emotional discomfort. When he receives a grade lower than he had anticipated, he responds emotionally; if he is then deservedly scolded by the teacher, he sulks and feels unjustly treated.

A Range of Readiness

A ninth-grade social dancing class presents a picture of varying degrees of readiness. Because the girls have matured physically more rapidly than the boys, their movements are well coordinated and, in many cases, skilled; with few exceptions they are physically ready to participate in social dancing. Among the boys, however, only those who are considerably above average in physical development have the neural and muscular control necessary to dance with ease and grace.

Inasmuch as dancing is a social as well as a physical activity, varied heterosexual social adjustments complicate the already great problem of differences in physical readiness among the boys and girls. At this age girls often express a strong, overt interest in boys. They are socially *ready* for this type of activity. Boys, on the other hand, possess a covert interest in girls, which is infrequently expressed in actual social contact. Given their choice, boys of this age often avoid heterosexual social contact altogether. It should be noted, however, that there is wide variation in the degree of readiness of members of the same sex.

Still another aspect of readiness is observable in the dancing class. Girls generally have acquired a conceptual readiness for dancing, have learned the latest steps, and have gained a measure of proficiency in performance that is matched by few boys.

Readiness for a Specific Learning Task[5]

Determining Physical Readiness

It is advisable for students to have a physical examination by a competent physician at regular intervals throughout their school years. If physical difficulties are discovered that may influence in-school behavior, the teacher should be informed so that he can help the student either overcome his difficulty or achieve within the framework of his limitations. Unfortunately, youngsters do not have physical checkups very frequently after early childhood.

Specialists in the field of physical education have played a key role in developing instruments that measure the various elements of motor ability —agility, sensory and motor coordination, and steadiness.[6] Specific tests have also been designed to measure the degree of athletic skill as well as the muscular strength and organic fitness of individual students.[7] However, in skill areas other than physical education—band, orchestra, typing, shorthand, and shop—means of appraising needed readiness, as represented by muscular coordination, are not so fully developed.

Determining Intellectual Readiness

Nearly all secondary schools throughout the United States have organized programs of standardized testing in which intelligence testing is the dominant concern. Currently available are numerous group tests that have demonstrated both a high degree of validity and reliability.[8]

However, within the past few years, conscientious professionals have repeatedly drawn attention to the lack of validity of many culture-oriented tests used to measure the intelligence of disadvantaged students, particularly those in minority groups. Although intelligence tests are administered to groups as a general rule, many school systems have the personnel and facilities to administer individual intelligence tests as well, thus providing a more accurate measure of the capacities of students with varying backgrounds.

---

[5]Herbert J. Klausmeier and William Goodwin, *Learning and Human Abilities: Educational Psychology*, 2d. ed. (New York: Harper & Row, Publishers, 1966), pp. 591–617, identify and discuss the most frequently used standardized tests of achievement and academic aptitude, often employed to determine student readiness for pursuit of an academic task.

Several approaches to the diagnosis of learning problems are provided by Wayne Otto and Karl Koenke, *Remedial Teaching: Research and Comment* (Boston: Houghton Mifflin Company, 1969), part 4.

[6]A complete discussion of the measurement of motor abilities is provided by H. Harrison Clarke, *Application of Measurement to Health and Physical Education* (Englewood Cliffs, New Jersey: Prentice-Hall, Inc., 1967), chapter 12.

[7]*Ibid.*, pp. 266–276, also identifies many of the better known tests used in measuring specific motor abilities.

[8]A thorough, instruction-related discussion of validity and reliability is provided by Robert D. Strom, *Psychology for the Classroom* (Englewood Cliffs, New Jersey: Prentice-Hall, Inc., 1969), pp. 285–303.

Standardized achievement tests in each of the content areas have received a great deal of attention in recent years. In the social studies field, for example, several standardized tests are available for measuring recall and understanding, and a few tests have been produced that evaluate the skills needed for studying social studies.[9] Similar tests have been developed for appraising mastery of subject matter in other basic areas of the secondary curriculum. Of greater flexibility, however, is the teacher-made test designed to measure achievement. If valid, reliable. complete, and well administered, such a test provides a useful indication of whether the student is ready to take the next academic step.

Determining Social Readiness

The many facets of social readiness make any measurement in this area very difficult. Sociometric techniques (procedures for measuring the social structure of a given group)[10] have been of considerable help to teachers in assaying social readiness for learning, but the validity and reliability of these tests may be seriously challenged. When the evidence they provide has been corroborated by careful observation, however, the teacher has a basis for planning classroom social situations that will promote learning.

Determining Emotional Readiness

Emotional readiness for learning must be largely inferred from the results of tests designed to measure academic adjustment, personal social adjustment, and social status. Although such tests are being improved, their validity and reliability still leave much to be desired.

As in other areas, thoughtful classroom observation by the teacher reveals many individual emotional problems. Occasionally the help of other specialists in the school system (counselors, psychologists, and psychiatrists) is needed to determine the emotional status of such students, and it may be desirable to refer students to such specialists for individual help.

Determining Readiness for Self-Direction

Increasing emphasis on individualization of instruction has been accompanied by a corresponding emphasis on student self-direction. Readiness for self-direction is compounded of many factors—study habits, relevant experiences, family background and expectations, and self-expectations. Although intelligence is also a component of effective self-direction, the experience of educators has led them to believe that it is not as important as once assumed. On the basis of long-range varied experience

---

[9]Frank J. Estvan, *Social Studies in a Changing World: Curriculum and Instruction* (New York: Harcourt Brace Jovanovich, Inc., 1968), pp. 291–293, provides examples of standardized achievement test items used to evaluate spatial orientation.

[10]Frederick J. McDonald, *Educational Psychology*, 2d. ed. (Belmont, California: Wadsworth Publishing Co., Inc., 1965), pp. 631–637, presents a brief discussion of the measurement of the social structure of a class.

with students in which the teacher assesses their potential for self-manag-
ment, he must determine the degree of their readiness to launch out on
their own.

Principles Related to Readiness

The psychological principles that have a close relationship to readiness are so numerous that this chapter can list only those that seem to
have the greatest relevance.

1. Many kinds of readiness are essential to efficient learning. Furthermore, "each subject has its own unique set of readiness factors,"[11] and
each student possesses varying degrees of readiness.

2. Readiness factors for an individual student can change rapidly.
Bearing this in mind, the teacher should continuously check to determine
the student's readiness for schoolwork.

3. Readiness for learning should be one of the criteria for grouping
students. The content for a particular grade level is selected on the
assumption that students are ready to learn that content. Effective classroom teaching, however, involves identifying *if* and *when* each learner is
ready for a given learning task.

4. An individual's readiness for learning is partially dependent upon
his physical, mental, social, and emotional status. A student is not in an
optimum state of readiness when he is physically ill, when he lacks
essential concepts, or when he is preoccupied with pressing problems. On
the other hand, a student is ready for a learning task when he has the
mental maturity to cope with the task, and he is ready to engage in a
motor skill when he has the required coordination of nerves and muscles.

5. The student is conceptually ready to take the next learning step
when he understands the prerequisite concepts, and he cannot succeed in
learning tasks for which he is not conceptually ready. Thus the learner is
ready to memorize when he understands the meaning of the symbols to
be memorized, and he is ready to undertake difficult social tasks when he
has mastered the basic tasks on which the more difficult ones rely.

6. Postponing the introduction of concepts beyond the point of
optimum readiness may be as harmful as premature introduction. The
teacher, however, can determine whether readiness has been achieved by
assigning students a learning task and by observing the results.[12] The alert
teacher should quickly identify the state of readiness and adjust the
learners' task to meet this condition.

7. If the learner wants something that he feels has great value, he is
ready to behave in ways that he feels will meet this desire. Therefore,

---

[11]H. Orville Nordberg, James M. Bradfield, and William C. Odell, *Secondary School
Teaching* (New York: The Macmillan Company, 1962), p. 72.

[12]Citing an earlier study, De Cecco, *The Psychology of Learning and Instruction*,
p. 74, points out that the performance of certain children classified as retarded exceeded
the performance of certain of their peers classified as gifted. Caution in preperformance
assessment is thus encouraged.

readiness to study (not to be confused with readiness to be curious) depends upon how useful the study appears to the individual learner.[13]

8. Effective study habits help develop readiness for learning. When students are known to have study problems, readiness factors should be considered as possible causes.

9. Although readiness factors are typically given greater attention in the elementary school than in the high school, they are equally applicable to learning situations at both levels.

10. Interests, needs, and motivation may be considered aspects of readiness.

11. Opportunity and encouragement are important in promoting readiness for learning.

Correct and Incorrect Use

The violation of the need for conceptual readiness is apparent in all school systems that automatically promote poor achievers and dull students with the rest of the age group without regard for subject-matter comprehension. This factor alone accounts for much of the distaste for arithmetic and mathematics that students feel during their elementary- and high-school days and that they carry over into their adult life. The same factors are at play in the English grammar course when students are required to keep in step with the class, although they may understand very little of what has been taught. As a result, there are senior high school students who make errors in punctuation and spelling in every line they write, and English teachers are faced with reteaching, year after year, those elements of grammar that students have only partially learned. The unfortunate payoff for the student who has been consistently but undeservedly promoted may come when he undertakes his first paid position. In the harsh competition of the nonschool world, such a student is forced to face reality.

Although curriculum planners attempt to place specific educational activities at grade levels where a majority of students will be ready for them, problems still exist.[14] One such problem is described below.

NORMAN'S READINESS TO LEARN IS INCONSISTENT

Norman Dudley was a bright boy, a fact that his teachers, the administration, and his parents readily admitted. At the insistence of his

---

[13]According to *Ibid.*, pp. 138–139, curiosity may be related to boredom.

Ibid., p. 147, points out that motivated students do not invest great effort in achieving goals that they have little chance of attaining.

Ibid., p. 234, stresses the need for capitalizing on the curiosity and tendency for exploration among disadvantaged children.

[14]A well-documented, insightful discussion on the problems associated with determining student readiness for a given learning experience and making appropriate use of this information in the school setting is provided by J. Galen Saylor and William M. Alexander, *Curriculum Planning for Modern Schools* (New York: Holt, Rinehart & Winston, Inc., 1966), pp. 217–218.

parents he moved through the three years of an ungraded primary unit in two years and at the age of twelve found himself in the eighth grade. Academically, Norman was maintaining pace with his peers very well, but in the physical education class and in social contacts with schoolmates of both sexes he was left far behind.

Because his physical development was slow, because he came from a family of physically small persons, and because he was advanced by one year, Norman's performance in the gym class was among the poorest in the group. He simply did not have the neuro-muscular development that would enable him to compete effectively with his peers. The physical education instructor realized that in another two years Norman's physical development would probably enable him to keep pace with the class. Unfortunately, there was no provision for holding Norman back for this desired period.

The case of Norman illustrates the impossibility of providing optimum educational opportunities for all youngsters under an inflexible grade placement. Even if a student is socially ready for a learning experience, he may not be physically and mentally ready. Such cases point to the desirability of reorganizing the secondary curriculum in a way that will more effectively serve the varying needs of individual students.[15] There is reason to doubt whether this can be done without disrupting the present graded arrangement.

Recent experimental developments, however, have given a bright new outlook for certain secondary schools that have been searching for a means of more effectively meeting the individual needs of students.

SAMMY USES A PROGRAMED TEXT

At the beginning of the school year, tests showed that Sammy Pitkin was a full year ahead of his classmates in mathematics aptitude and achievement. Mr. Waltham was determined to find some way to develop Sammy's potential. After he had examined several available programed texts for first-year algebra, he chose the one that seemed to be most carefully worked out in detail, sequential placement of concepts, and ease of usage. He also made sure that programed texts in the same series were available for second-year algebra, trigonometry, and elementary calculus.

The teacher, the student, and his parents jointly decided that Sammy would work independently of the class. Under Mr. Waltham's supervision Sammy began work on the first-year algebra book, moving as rapidly as he felt he could.

The use of the special text forced Sammy to react immediately and meaningfully to the concepts presented. Furthermore, it was structured so that he could not proceed to the next concept until he had a satisfactory comprehension of the preceding ones. Troublesome concepts

[15]Klausmeier and Goodwin, *Learning and Human Abilities*, pp. 95–124, discuss six characteristics of the individual student that strongly influence his readiness for efficient learning.

that remained unresolved after careful reading and reacting to the frames of the programed text were discussed with the teacher. When Sammy was ready for the more difficult concept, he was able to move along at his own speed. He was intensely interested.

Around the first of December, Sammy announced that he had completed the first-year algebra book. When Mr. Waltham administered a comprehensive examination covering the content of first-year algebra, he discovered that Sammy scored among the upper 25 percent of the students who had taken a full year to complete the course. Together they re-examined the errors made on the test and decided that Sammy was ready to begin studying second-year algebra. Although he did not progress as rapidly as he had in the first course, by the end of May Sammy had completed second-year algebra.

Specific Suggestions

Because readiness is composed of so many facets, teachers often tend to focus attention upon only a few of these facets to the exclusion of others. A helpful device for avoiding this omission is for the individual teacher to prescribe for himself a series of specific recommendations and cautions that take into consideration the major facets of readiness. The starting point for such a list is presented here.

Recommendations

1. Help students develop the readiness essential to effective study.

2. Continuously check on the students' mental, physical, social, and emotional readiness for learning.

3. Be sure that standardized tests of mental maturity (I.Q. tests) are given at regular intervals, and use the results of these tests as a source of information about the intellectual readiness of the students.

4. Insist that culturally disadvantaged students be given tests that yield valid measures of their intelligence. Often this calls for administering individual intelligence tests.

5. Be aware of in-school and out-of-school factors that may influence the students' emotional readiness to learn.

6. Use standardized tests as well as teacher-constructed tests to determine achievement levels in various subject areas.

7. Carefully observe students to determine their readiness for specific school-related tasks.

8. Remember that even under ideal teaching-learning situations readiness factors impose limits to accomplishment.

Cautions

1. Don't forget that readiness consists of many facets.

2. Don't oversimplify your thinking about any type of mental, physical, emotional, or social readiness.

3. Don't forget that readiness comes as a result of a long series of related preliminary developments.

4. Don't assume that readiness for undertaking a given task is present without investigating.

5. Don't assume that a student is ready for specific learning tasks just because he has reached a given chronological age.

6. Don't require students to become involved in learning tasks for which they are not ready.[16]

7. Don't ignore the influence of study habits on readiness.

8. Don't forget that readiness to be self-directive is made up of many factors of which intelligence is only one.

9. Don't overlook the value of stimulation, opportunity, and experimentation as means for encouraging certain types of readiness.[17]

EFFECT OF MOTIVATION ON LEARNING

Readiness and motivation are closely related concerns of the instructional process, and both must be present if serious, goal-oriented learning is to take place. Because motivation plays such an important role in the teaching-learning process, writers of responsible methods textbooks devote considerable attention to it, and educational psychologists feel that an understanding of its principles is basic to sound teaching. The use of motivational devices has become so much a part of the instructional process that many teachers go about this aspect of their teaching somewhat mechanically. A good case, however, can be made for careful, conscious, frequent reevaluation of motivational teaching procedures.

When a learner identifies a goal that has personal value for him, he tries to reach that goal.[18] *Motivation* may thus be described as the personal, internal process that determines the strength and direction of a person's behavior or line of action. Motivation may also involve a second person (for example, the teacher) trying to arouse the first to greater effort.

According to McDonald,[19] motivation consists of three elements: (1) an energy change takes place in the neurophysiological system of the learner; (2) feelings (psychological tensions) about the goal are aroused; and (3) the learner makes those responses that will lead him to the desired goal. For example, the college-bound tenth-grade student of English grammar may (1) begin his course with a general desire to learn grammar; (2) discover that he is particularly weak in subject-verb

---

[16]Saylor and Alexander, *Curriculum Planning for Modern Schools*, p. 216.

[17]*Ibid.*, pp. 216–217.

[18]J. Lloyd Trump and Delmas F. Miller, *Secondary School Curriculum Improvement: Proposals and Procedures* (Boston: Allyn & Bacon, Inc., 1968), pp. 22–23, stress the advantages of individual pupil goals, indicating that a curriculum designed to implement such goals is frequently different from many existing curriculums.

The relationship of individual goal setting to school-related motivation is discussed by Klausmeier and Goodwin, *Learning and Human Abilities*, pp. 436–443.

[19]McDonald, *Educational Psychology*, pp. 112–113.

agreement, an area of major emphasis in the college entrance examination he hopes to pass; and (3) concentrate his attention for a prolonged period on meeting this deficiency. The wise teacher should be aware of such a need and help the student accomplish his goal.

It is often useful to differentiate between extrinsic and intrinsic motivation.[20] *Extrinsic* (external) forces exist outside of the learner and tend to press him into a given course of action. Among these external forces are rewards, punishments, physical circumstances, and the desires of others. The teacher's praise, the teacher's rebuke, a fire alarm in the school building, and parental ambitions may thus be viewed as extrinsic motivators.

Intrinsic (internal)[21] forces, on the other hand, originate within the individual and impel him to seek a given goal. Such forces include attitudes, needs, and anxieties. An interest in music, an attitude toward a racial minority, the need for food, and the fear of failing the chemistry test are all expressions that motivate certain behavior.

No Learning Without Motivation

Few students have escaped the boredom of an unmotivated class. Such a class is characterized by the teacher who leaves his students with half-formed and hazy concepts; by the teacher who makes no attempt to select procedures that will be interesting to students; by the teacher who criticizes students negatively rather than constructively; and by strained personal relationships between students and teacher. In such a classroom, student desires are not considered, and the teacher assumes total responsibility for establishing instructional goals. No attempt is made to surround students with new and different teaching devices to arouse their interests. Furthermore, the teacher is not sufficiently well acquainted with individual members of his class to employ motivational techniques to best advantage. Little attempt is made at individualizing instruction.

Student motivation is often at a minimum in required courses, as teachers of English, history, and general mathematics are well aware. As a result, such courses pose difficult problems of motivation. The instructor is faced with the necessity for encouraging learners to see personal value in course objectives even when the students' personal inclinations run in the opposite direction.[22] How, for example, does one motivate a youngster from a lower-class rural family to study United States history?

---

[20]*Ibid.*, pp. 145–153, presents a useful discussion of motivation and instructional strategies that are closely related to intrinsic as well as extrinsic motivation.

A range of motives classified as intrinsic or extrinsic are discussed by William F. White, *Psychosocial Principles Applied to Classroom Teaching* (New York: McGraw-Hill Book Company, 1969), pp. 6–27.

[21]The values and problems of both intrinsic as well as extrinsic motivation are examined by J. Charles Jones, *Learning* (New York: Harcourt Brace Jovanovich, Inc., 1967), pp. 63–67.

[22]A great leap forward in injecting meaning into instructional goals has been accomplished for both student and teacher through recent emphasis on behavioral objectives. Robert F. Mager, *Preparing Objectives for Programmed Instruction* (Palo Alto: Fearon Publishers, 1962), states the case for such objectives simply and with force.

To achieve motivation, the teacher can make the course content as meaningful as possible by (1) carefully selecting and using textbooks and supplementary reading materials, (2) including interesting narrative accounts in class lectures, (3) relating certain aspects of the course content to the life of the student, and (4) using course-related projects geared to the student's interests. Furthermore, the teacher can permit a degree of student participation in establishing unit goals, in devising and using interesting aids to convey concepts, and in providing experiences in which the student can succeed.

Motivational Influences

Student Interests and Desires

What interests a student will motivate him.[23] Marvin, the son of an electrical engineer, developed a sizable technical vocabulary and an abiding interest in the field of engineering. By the time he reached high school, Marvin was reading most of the popular and some of the technical articles related to his special interest. He was motivated to choose any subject that seemed related to engineering.

Although teachers have always known that student interests and desires play an important role in motivation, they frequently fail to make practical use of this truth. The mathematics teacher knows of Darrell's interest in farming; yet, though Darrell is failing, the teacher refuses to adapt the story problems in mathematics to the boy's interest. On the other hand, Darrell's English teacher permits her students to write on any topic that interests them, as long as she feels it serves an educational purpose.

If a student perceives a subject or a unit as having particular value for him, he will study to achieve its goals; if he finds little relationship between subject-matter goals and his personal desires, he will respond apathetically or negatively. Kathy has always viewed her role in life as a domestic one; thus she loved her homemaking course and worked hard in it. When she became engaged during her senior year, she had an additional incentive to learn as much as possible about sewing, cooking, child care, and general household management. Her teacher said she had never seen a girl work so hard.

A somewhat similar case is that of Warren Sutter. Since he had previously been a C student in English, Warren realized that his chance for making a respectable score on the freshman English examination at the state university next year would depend largely upon how much information he could acquire during the current year. To enter the university was the most important goal in his life right now. As a result Warren studied English as he had never studied before. After school he often sought the help of the teacher, and he spent between one and two

---

[23]Klausmeier and Goodwin, *Learning and Human Abilities,* pp. 433–436, provide a relevant discussion of student interests as related to motivation.

hours every evening on English. But his supreme sacrifice came when he decided that going out for the basketball team would consume too much of his time. His desired goal determined his motivation and effort to learn English.

Environment

Every individual views all environmental factors in terms of their effect on his personal welfare. This applies to all curriculum- and instructional-related situations as well as to the actual physical environment.

The biology laboratory equipped with numerous specimens, individual study stations, and an adequate number of microscopes; the English classroom with displays of effective student themes, a well-equipped classroom library, and adjoining small rooms for special study projects; the social studies classroom with a large moveable globe, a plentiful supply of retractable maps mounted above the chalkboard, and an extensive file of photographs of historical events—all are representative of a desirable physical environment to motivate learning.

Some students view certain subjects as threats to their personal well-being. The poor achiever in mathematics who is suddenly thrust into a class situation in which he cannot hope for even a small measure of success is subject to frustration. Similarly, the physically underdeveloped youngster who is expected to compete effectively with his peers on the gym floor may feel that his inability is detrimental to his personal status. Before these students can be adequately motivated, the impediments to their achievement—mathematics background and physical development—will have to be resolved.

Success

Students are motivated if a proper balance between successful and unsuccessful experiences can be maintained. A major responsibility of the teacher is to assist the student in achieving success, for success often serves as an effective motivator. The student who has a past record of achievement develops the confidence necessary for undertaking more difficult tasks.

Below-average and retarded youngsters in classes composed largely of average students are continually confronted with defeats. Instruction geared to the average student does not and cannot meet the needs of the slower students. As a result, few of them achieve even what their limited capacities would permit. For this reason, a homogeneous grouping of students helps provide a setting in which youngsters can achieve success most of the time. However, it is neither necessary nor desirable for students to achieve success under *all* circumstances. The bright student who finds himself in an average group may gain success with limited effort. His motivation becomes dulled, his interest wanes, and poor habits are formed. He is, therefore, denied the challenge he deserves.

For self-directive students, success is enhanced by the use of carefully selected programed materials. Designed to provide a continuing series of successful experiences, such materials reinforce correct student responses. Moreover, through the use of computer-assisted instruction (an electronically refined process using the principles of programed instruction), the essential steps of stimulus, response, reinforcement, and concept acquisition are accelerated; hence, motivation reaches a high point.

Goals

If a student sees that an established instructional goal lies in the same direction as his personal desires, he will be motivated.[24] The course goals for a class in auto mechanics, for example, may aim to give students a detailed acquaintance with engine parts and enable them to diagnose and, finally, to repair mechanical difficulties. Students often register for this elective course because their personal goals and the course goals are identical.

Any goal that students view as unattainable hinders motviation. This is often true for below-average students, but it may be true for above-average and bright students as well. A teacher who requires students to complete a full week of assignments in two days stifles motivation, for students react to assignments in terms of what they believe can or cannot be done. In such a situation, defeat is probable from the start.

Incentives

No one incentive will motivate all students equally.[25] Beginning teachers often assume that a threat of low grades will stimulate all students to greater effort. Experienced teachers, however, readily agree that one can expect highly variable reactions to such a threat. Similarly, the promise of higher pay and better job opportunities in the future for students who consistently work hard will motivate only a portion of the class members.

Principles Related to Motivation

The proper use of motivation to promote learning calls for a knowledge of readiness, individual differences, adjustment, and learning theory. Hence, principles directly related to motivation are numerous,[26] but only those that provide the greatest help to the teacher are listed below.

1. All behavior (except that governed by the autonomic nervous system) is motivated.

---

[24]Nathan S. Blount and Herbert J. Klausmeier, *Teaching in the Secondary School*, 3d. ed. (New York: Harper & Row, Publishers, 1968), pp. 81–84, provide a useful discussion of the relationship between goals and student motivation.

Burton, *The Guidance of Learning Activities*, p. 54, makes a strong plea for student involvement in goal identification.

[25]The classroom use of incentives is covered by McDonald, *Educational Psychology*, pp. 148–149.

[26]Blount and Klausmeier, *Teaching in the Secondary School*, pp. 81–89, list and discuss eight useful principles of motivation.

White, *Psychosocial Principles Applied to Classroom Teaching*, pp. 27–29, lists fifteen motivation-related recommendations of particular value to the classroom teacher.

2. The mind may be stimulated by an external force, but it is the learner's reaction to the stimulus that results in learning.

3. Motivation is best viewed as a tool to assist instruction, not as an end in itself.

4. Each individual views environmental factors in terms of their assumed effect on his personal welfare. If the individual is lacking something he views as essential to the maintenance of his way of life, he is ready to take whatever action he believes will supply that lack.[27]

5. Since each learner sees only what his experience and ability enable him to see, his motivation will result partly from what he sees in a particular situation.

6. Interests motivate students, and, in the absence of interest, learning does not take place. It is easy, however, to confuse superficial interests with deeper motivation.

7. When a student recognizes a goal to be of personal importance to him, he is motivated.[28] Conversely, if he believes that what he is learning will not help him achieve his desired goals, his responsiveness will be limited. A student who is strongly committed to a goal will exert great effort to achieve that goal.

8. Learning that brings reward and satisfaction to the student acts as a motivator for further learning.

9. The student's level of aspiration is the result of experience from which he develops a concept of what he will be able to do.

Correct and Incorrect Use

Many teachers achieve a degree of student motivation by chance. Although they teach in traditional ways and without any specific intention to motivate, their instruction still results in some movement toward goals. The pronounced inefficiency with which this movement takes place, however, often differentiates the unskilled teacher from the skilled. The examples below point out this difference.

MR. BOWDEN HAMPERS MOTIVATION

The eleventh-grade United States history class was known to all the students because Mr. Bowden, the teacher, was unrelenting in his demand for strict discipline. Since he was an authoritarian, he placed ready-made course and unit objectives into the hands of students. The daily procedure consisted of a class lecture for the first twenty minutes, followed by a half-hour study period in which students studied from their

---

[27]Maslow's theory of human motivation, useful in explaining student behavior both inside and outside the classroom, is examined by Klausmeier and Goodwin, *Learning and Human Abilities*, pp. 425–428.

[28]The inconsistency of an instructional system in which teachers exercise greater authority at the same time learners are seeking independence from external authority is discussed by William M. Alexander and Vynce A. Hines, *Independent Study in Secondary Schools* (New York: Holt, Rinehart & Winston, Inc., 1967), pp. 2–4.

texts and answered study questions prepared by the teacher. There was no variation from this procedure. Mr. Bowden paid no direct attention to individual differences among his students; however, he did tell them that they could read supplemental material outside of class if they wished.

This teaching situation emphasizes the fact that there is much more to motivation than stern classroom control. Because students were given no voice in determining objectives or were not encouraged to ask questions about them, they found it difficult to accept the course objectives as their own. A lecture procedure in which student participation is severely restricted is not conducive to learning.

There are, fortunately, many teachers whose professional knowledge enables them to use motivational techniques effectively. Look, for example, at Mrs. Kapp.

MRS. KAPP ACHIEVES MOTIVATION

Mrs. Kapp was determined to get her tenth-grade world geography unit on the Middle East off to a good start. Although she devoted a good deal of time to preplanning class objectives, she discussed them in detail with members of her class and asked for their suggestions. The teacher insisted that students not only understand the objectives, but that they personally accept them as being important.

A diagnostic test given at the beginning of the unit revealed approximately what each student knew about the Middle East. Mrs. Kapp could plan realistically from this point on, giving consideration to individual differences in achievement and ability. Assignments were often differentiated to take this into consideration, and students were thus kept interested.

Mrs. Kapp frequently showed and explained colored slides during this unit. Two attractive bulletin boards were prepared by students under the teacher's direction, and special oral reports, which supplemented textbook study, were given by student volunteers.

During the supervised study periods, which were held when Mrs. Kapp felt they would serve a useful purpose, the teacher moved among the members of her class, helping, suggesting, and, in many cases, praising. Students were encouraged to be realistic in what they expected of themselves.

Mrs. Kapp knew how to motivate students. She was aware of the basic motivational need for students to personally accept course objectives as their own. Furthermore, she planned realistically for the teaching of content on the basis of an up-to-date knowledge of student achievement.[29] Desirable stimuli were provided through interesting teaching aids, and she helped establish and maintain effective rapport with her students through assistance given during the supervised study period.

---

[29]Motivation as an outgrowth of effective teacher-pupil planning is discussed by Leonard H. Clark and Irving S. Starr, *Secondary School Teaching Methods*, 2d. ed. (New York: The Macmillan Company, 1967), pp. 126–131.

MR. HAYMOND'S ENTHUSIASM MOTIVATES

Students were not quite sure why they liked Mr. Haymond so much, but his supervisor could have identified the reason very quickly: Mr. Haymond knew how to motivate students. There were several significant factors that the supervisor noticed when he visited Mr. Haymond's ninth-grade English class.

Mr. Haymond was enthusiastic whenever he talked about English literature; it was as if he were discussing the most important thing in the world. But he didn't stop there. When he assigned a literary selection, he carefully identified, with student help, the most difficult words; he then explained and wrote them on the board. Students were told to look for specific subtle meanings. With interest, dramatic flourish, and meaning, Mr. Haymond read aloud the first page of the selection. The students soon began reading enthusiastically on the strength of their own motivation and interest.

When general student interest began to diminish, Mr. Haymond held a brief discussion in which he asked specific questions designed to reveal the real reasons for this lack of interest. The students were then willing to get back to their reading. During the study period Mr. Haymond talked briefly and informally with individual students about what they were reading and its meaning to them. In order to make the material meaningful, he related his explanations to the students' background. He also used the information he had gained during the question-and-answer period to reawaken their interest and help meet individual needs.

Through his observation of the class, the supervisor singled out the reasons for Mr. Haymond's unusual skill in motivating students. The teacher was intensely interested in the content he was teaching and was well prepared to teach it. This interest was, in turn, communicated to his students.[30] He was realistic in understanding that all students would not be equally interested, and he made a conscious effort to keep alive the interest of the less gifted students. The identification and explanation of difficult terms and subtle meanings helped solve difficulties in comprehension before they could arise and aided in sustaining interest.

Specific Suggestions

For both beginning and experienced teachers, the following recommendations and cautions should serve as helpful guidelines for the effective use of motivational procedures.

Recommendations

1. Identify, through experimentation, the incentives that motivate different students in your class. Use direct contact with natural phenome-

---

[30]The positive relationship between the teacher's enthusiasm for his subject and student appraisal of his quality as a teacher is discussed by Klausmeier and Goodwin, *Learning and Human Abilities,* pp. 143-150.

na as a means of motivation.[31] Employ teaching procedures that are interesting to students.

2. Help students identify the personal value that specific academic goals will have for them, and also help them establish realistic and educationally sound goals for themselves.[32]

3. Be aware of the motivational effect of grades; then use them sparingly for this purpose. However, as a basis for motivation, keep students informed about their academic progress.[33]

4. Provide students with a sound balance between successful and unsuccessful experiences. Arrange for successful experiences that will build their self-expectations, and help students achieve good grades where possible.

5. Maintain a desirable balance between approval and disapproval while helping bring about optimum student motivation. Constructive criticism is preferable to negative criticism in dealing with students, but occasional negative criticism is better than no criticism at all.

6. Find means for establishing and maintaining rapport with students. Help the individual student manage his tensions and his emotions.

7. Make your lessons meaningful so that students will be stimulated. Help the student interpret what is desirable performance for himself in consideration of his unique characteristics.

8. Learn to identify the physiological, social, and emotional deficiencies in the lives of students. Their attempts to meet these problems may explain certain kinds of student behavior.

9. Surround students with stimuli that will help make course content more interesting and desirable.

10. Teach your subject so well that students will develop a liking for it and for all that is related to it.

Cautions

1. Don't forget that all behavior is motivated.

2. Don't assume that each student will accept the stated goal of the class as his own personal goal.

3. Don't assume that one incentive or one kind of incentive will motivate all youngsters.

---

[31]The necessity for having the student make repeated contact with the referent of the concept to be learned or with a carefully contrived facsimile is examined by James W. Brown, Richard B. Lewis, and Fred F. Harcleroad, *AV Instruction: Media and Methods*, 3d. ed. (New York: McGraw-Hill Book Company, 1969), pp. 29–30.

[32]Howard T. Batchelder, Maurice McGlasson, and Raleigh Schorling, *Student Teaching in Secondary Schools*, 4th ed. (New York: McGraw-Hill Book Company, 1964), p. 146, stress the importance of relating academic goals to the needs and interests of students.

Blount and Klausmeier, *Teaching in the Secondary School*, pp. 83–84, provide a useful discussion of goals and goal setting. Examples are provided.

[33]"The most significant contribution of programed instruction and automated teaching is the technique of providing the learner with knowledge of results as he proceeds from one item or problem to another" according to Robert A. Davis, *Learning in the Schools* (Belmont, California: Wadsworth Publishing Co., Inc., 1966), pp. 159–160.

4. Don't use competition as an end in itself, but only as a supplementary form of motivation.[34]

5. Don't use rewards and punishments unless you are sure that they will serve as desirable motivators.

6. Don't emphasize the failing aspects of a student's performance even though he is academically weak or limited in capacity.

7. Don't confuse educationally justified, interesting activities with entertainment.

8. Don't assume that all students will be equally interested in the same activity.

READINESS AND MOTIVATION IN REVIEW

This chapter has been concerned with the examination of two fundamental instructional concerns—readiness and motivation. Efficient learning would be impossible if either one were absent.

Several kinds of readiness may simultaneously influence the effectiveness of learning; however, each kind of readiness can exert its own effect. Physical readiness, for example, is essential for learning skill subjects, such as typing, instrumental music, and physical education. Neural growth, native capacity, and experience—the three aspects of intellectual readiness—determine whether a student can undertake complex mental tasks. Similarly, social experience provides essential knowledge and self-assurance that result in social readiness.

Motivation may be described as a state of arousal in which an individual wishes to achieve a specific goal and exerts effort to do so. Therefore, motivation is of fundamental concern to all teachers in helping promote efficient learning. How responsive a learner is to an instructional situation and how hard he will work to achieve a goal will depend upon his motivation. If a student sees that instructional objectives parallel the direction of his personal values, he will be strongly motivated.

PROBLEMS FOR STUDY AND DISCUSSION

1. Describe in some detail the characteristics of the student who would be ready to study effectively in the area of your teaching major.

2. How does I.Q. affect readiness? Discuss. Give examples that support your discussion.

3. Assumption: Two boys of the same chronological age (15) live in the same neighborhood. One is a slow learner (I.Q. 89), and the other boy is bright (I.Q. 132). In what respects and under what circumstances may the slow learner be more nearly ready than the bright boy to undertake learning tasks in a ninth-grade English class?

---

[34]Blount and Klausmeier, *Teaching in the Secondary School*, pp. 486–489, describe three different categories of competitive climate.

4. Discuss the relationship of concept formation to intellectual readiness.

5. Assumption: You have a girl in your tenth-grade class who is academically above average but who is excessively shy and lacking in social confidence. Describe the specific steps you would take in helping her achieve social readiness.

6. Describe three classroom situations in which students exhibit lack of emotional readiness for learning.

7. Explain the following statement: In the absence of readiness the student cannot learn.

8. Discuss the effect of unearned promotion on the student's readiness to learn.

9. Is the intelligence test an accurate measure of the student's intellectual readiness to undertake a given learning task? Explain.

10. Describe a classroom situation related to your teaching major in which motivation is at a minimum. How closely does your teaching approximate this situation?

11. Differentiate between teacher goals and student goals. Why should the teacher be concerned with student goals?

12. Indicate how you would motivate a group of slow learners to learn general mathematics. Be specific.

13. Give three examples, from your own experience, in which strong motivation has caused students to work unusually hard.

14. What is the relationship between failure and motivation? Discuss and provide illustrations.

15. Explain the relationship between the use of programed learning materials and individual student success. Are such materials motivational? Why?

16. Assumption: The teacher views the unit goals as attainable, but students in the class believe the goals cannot be attained. Whose will should prevail? Discuss.

17. Discuss the relationship between the student's level of aspiration and his past experiences. What does this relationship have to do with motivation?

18. Give five examples of intrinsic motivation that can be used to good advantage in your teaching major.

19. Explain the following statement: All behavior (except that governed by the autonomic nervous system) is motivated.

15. *Individual Differences, Remedial Teaching, and the Reporting of Pupil Progress*

This chapter presents a discussion of three of the basic instructional responsibilities that are of continuing concern to the conscientious teacher: meeting the individual differences of students, providing remedial instruction, and reporting the progress of the students.

MEETING INDIVIDUAL DIFFERENCES

Because learning is an individual matter, the consideration of individual differences among students heightens learning efficiency.[1] When the selection of methods, rate of content coverage, teacher expectations, and so forth are geared to the individual's level, the student can achieve success. This is often the case when slow learners in a heterogeneously grouped class are regrouped according to ability and procedures and expectations are modified to meet the needs of the new group.[2]

Fortunately, psychologists and educators largely agree about the characteristics that are most significant to education. Those most frequently mentioned are intelligence,[3] emotional stability, physical health, social adjustment, experiential background, aspirations, interests, school achievement, attitudes, temperament and disposition, readiness, and specific skills, including reading skills. The sensitive teacher will be aware of these and other factors in the classroom situation when he attempts to improve instruction.

Advantages of Knowing Individual Differences

Instruction geared to the individual pupil has many advantages that are missing in group instruction. The very nature of our current school organization, however, rules out the possibility of large-scale tutorial instruction, so that the teacher must find some practical means of differentiating instruction for individuals in his class. An accurate appraisal of the characteristics that make the individual different from his classmates is necessary to establish a basis for careful, individualized teaching.

When the teacher has this basic information, he can employ a range of activities geared to the interest and comprehension levels of different students, or groups of students, instead of using one learning activity suitable for only a small portion of the class. His instructional plans are more apt to succeed because they will be geared to meet the specific needs of individuals. Because he knows that Carolyn is gifted in art work but socially insecure, the teacher can ask her to help decorate the bulletin boards rather than give an oral report before the class—an assignment doomed to defeat. If Carolyn's work on the bulletin board is good, the teacher will have an opportunity to give her deserved praise, which will help Carolyn develop self-confidence.

---

[1]Lee J. Cronbach, "How Can Instruction Be Adapted to Individual Differences?" in *Learning and Individual Differences*, ed. Robert M. Gagne (Columbus, Ohio: Charles E. Merrill Publishing Co., 1967), pp. 23–39, stresses the relationship between a studied consideration of individual differences in students and effective instruction.

[2]The problems of underachievers are examined within a psychological framework by Henry C. Lindgren, *Educational Psychology in the Classroom*, 3d. ed. (New York: John Wiley & Sons, Inc., 1967), pp. 478–482.

[3]John P. De Cecco, *The Psychology of Learning and Instruction: Educational Psychology* (Englewood Cliffs, New Jersey: Prentice-Hall, Inc., 1968), pp. 113–121, discusses differences in intelligence and their relationship to the teaching-learning process.

Using Materials Effectively

Effective use of materials and equipment requires specific as well as general knowledge of the students in a class. The teacher is aware, for example, that gifted Lynn Wesley will be bored if he is required to read the text used by a majority of students in eleventh-grade United States history. As a result, Lynn is assigned a college-level text and given freedom to study in the library. Similarly, the shop teacher has discovered through experience that Theron Heaps does not exhibit the same degree of responsibility in the use of power tools as do other students. As a result, the teacher plans to allow Theron to use the power saw only under teacher supervision. Furthermore, the teacher insists that Theron rigidly observe all safety precautions when using any power tool.

Improving Socialization

The teacher may plan to group students in order to improve socialization. Ethel Hill, for example, a girl with high social aspirations and marked cliquish tendencies, never associates with students below the upper-middle class from which she comes. Mr. Angus changed her seat so that Ethel was surrounded by lower-middle class students who were quite socially acceptable to the others in the class.

Planning Assignments

More realistic assignments can be planned if the teacher knows the academic strengths and weaknesses of his students. The biology teacher knows that Dean Cook is limited in interest and intelligence. As a result, the specific assignment planned for Dean is less demanding than that required of the average student, although it provides the essential concepts. In the same tenth-grade class is a student of average capacity who is intensely interested in biology but who reads at the sixth-grade level. Assignments planned for this boy involve the use of special materials and the exchange of course-related ideas with a group of interested and bright youngsters.

Increasing Motivation

The steps taken to motivate students often bear a direct relationship to what the teacher knows about his students.[4] He may know, for example, that although Ralph hopes to become an attorney, his oral English is hardly what one would expect to find in the courtroom and must be improved if he is to achieve his goal. At appropriate times and under the desired circumstances, this fact is called to Ralph's attention. Eleanor Van Leuven, a student in the same class, hopes to become a newspaper reporter. At the suggestion of the teacher, Eleanor makes several contributions to the local paper as well as the school paper, but

[4]Ben M. Harris, Wailand Bessent, and Kenneth E. McIntyre, *In-Service Education: A Guide to Better Practice* (Englewood Cliffs, New Jersey: Prentice-Hall, Inc., 1969), pp. 95–106, provide insightful suggestions concerning essential information about students that teachers should possess before attempting to group them.

only after the articles have been examined by her instructor. She is also given the assignment of clipping out class-related newspaper articles to display on the bulletin board.

Developing Rapport

The development of rapport between student and teacher, so essential to effective instruction, is enhanced through the teacher's personal acquaintance with each student. Max Underwood, the band director, made it a policy to find out about the musical as well as the nonmusical, out-of-school activities of his students. Before and after school, before and after class, and whenever he met students in the hall, he would make such friendly comments as "I heard that you played very well in the young people's meeting last night, Glen" or "Lucy tells me that you have decided to form a string ensemble." To convey through teaching procedures the unmistakable attitude that students are nothing more than members of the crowd inhibits rapport and promotes antagonism. Students should be regarded as individuals at all times and dealt with on an individual basis whenever possible.

Gearing Methods to Learners

Learning efficiency is enhanced by the selection of those methods that are best suited to the specific characteristics of the students. Slow learners, for example, respond poorly to a straight lecture method. They may, however, learn effectively from a carefully planned informal discussion geared to their own interest and vocabulary level. Gifted students, on the other hand, often profit from procedures involving intensive self-directed reading. Furthermore, the learner who is preoccupied with a serious personal problem will require a different instructional procedure than the student who can focus his conscious attention in any direction.

Procedures for Differentiating Instruction

Literally dozens of techniques are currently employed in the attempt to meet the individual needs of students effectively.[5] These techniques may be helpfully categorized as (1) administrative provisions and (2) instructional provisions. Those listed and discussed below represent procedures that have received varying degrees of emphasis from teachers and specific school systems.

Administrative Provisions

Administrative provisions for differentiating instruction are under the direct control of the school superintendent or principal.[6] Teachers are

---

[5]Leonard H. Clark and Irving S. Starr, *Secondary School Teaching Methods*, 2d. ed. (New York: The Macmillan Company, 1967), p. 426, stress the need for an extracurricular program organized to guide all students into valuable and interesting activities that serve their individual needs.

[6]See *Ibid.*, pp. 163–165, for a useful, brief exposure to administrative provisions for meeting individual differences.

also, of necessity, strongly involved in helping implement these procedures. Some of the most frequently used administrative provisions are:

Grouping by sections according to ability

Variation in number of subjects a student may take

Exploratory courses aimed at vocational guidance

Special classes for slow learners and retarded pupils

Special classes for the gifted

Team teaching

Provision for individual progress in a subject without regard to grade level

Mid-year promotions

Accelerations

Nonpromotion or elimination

Special guidance services

Modular scheduling

Grouping According to Ability. One frequently used administrative procedure is that of grouping students in sections according to ability. Although there has been considerable fluctuation of educators' willingness to group students homogeneously, the post World War II emphasis on science and international competition has exerted force in this direction. Currently few sizeable, forward-looking secondary schools throughout the nation have withstood the pressure to engage in ability grouping of some sort; in many schools it takes different forms.

Academic Load Related to Ability. Some schools restrict or expand the number of subjects a student may take on the basis of his past performance.

Exploratory Courses and Special Classes. Secondary schools offer a number of exploratory courses aimed at vocational guidance. Among these are shop courses of various types, homemaking, and business courses.

Large school systems frequently provide special classes for slow learners and retarded pupils. Such classes, however, pose very real difficulties for small school districts in terms of staff, housing, and financial support. Although special classes for the gifted have long existed in large metropolitan areas, they are now being developed with increasing frequency in smaller cities. National pressures and resulting public support have encouraged this movement.

Team teaching. Team teaching, which involves the use of two or more professionals or para-professionals in an instructional situation, has received widespread attention during the past few years.[7] Varieties of teaching teams have been assembled and used with varying degrees of success at all levels of the secondary school. The classes taught range from very large groups to small and homogeneous groups.

---

[7] See Chapter 18, for a more detailed discussion of team teaching.

Modular Scheduling. Administrative use of uniform blocks of time (modules) is now commonplace among many new, large schools. Used singly or in combinations, the module enables the administrator to schedule a given class for a short period or for a very long period determined by instructional needs. Making and explaining an assignment may require only one fifteen-minute module, but taking a field trip may call for the use of twelve such modules. The flexibility of modular scheduling can be used to serve the needs of students of varying ability found in different sections of the same course or groups of students in the same section with different problems. Further, a limited number of sophisticated attempts at modular scheduling involving the use of the computer possess the potential for changing each student's schedule every period of every day for several days—although in practice this is never done.

Specially Prepared Materials. Many secondary schools throughout the United States are experimenting with programed learning. Specially prepared materials permit step-by-step and largely self-directed progress in learning a particular subject. Students may move slowly if limited by academic ability or poor past achievement, or they may move rapidly from one step to another if their comprehension permits. Infrequent but increasing experimentation with computer-assisted instruction calls for the electronic coordination of audiovisual aids with carefully programed materials. Utilizing the advantages of step-by-step progression, this approach also capitalizes on the speed, flexibility, and storage capacity of the computer.

In order to encourage differentiation in instruction, administrators in forward-looking school systems often encourage the collection of a range of specially prepared units gathered from many sources. This material can thus be readily available to all the teachers in the system. When necessary materials are not available, administrators—particularly in large, well-financed districts—sometimes activate committees to undertake the production of such materials on an extra-pay or released-time basis. During the past few years in a growing number of schools, emphasis has been placed on producing units whose central focus has been behavioral objectives.

Promotions. Mid-year promotions serve a useful purpose by permitting slow students who are one semester behind their age group to advance in grade without waiting a full year. Similarly, bright students who have taken extra courses may in a few years earn sufficient credits to warrant a promotion at the mid-year mark. Neither practice is typical, however.

Accelerations and nonpromotions, so frequent in the 1930's, are now largely a matter of history, because they violated the need for gradual step-by-step advancement. Although the desirability of having students proceed at rates suitable to their capacities and achievement is well recognized, other provisions serve these needs much more effectively. One such provision is a special guidance service that provides specific help in the areas of vocational, social, academic, and personal adjustment.[8]

Instructional Provisions

The procedures employed by teachers to differentiate instruction for students are numerous and varied. Differentiation frequently takes place at the level of unit planning when three kinds of activities are listed— those suitable for slow, average, and fast learners. Objectives may be similarly differentiated. The daily lesson plan may pinpoint specific procedures for students with special problems. Some of the most frequently used instructional provisions are:

Differentiation in unit planning	Remedial teaching
Supervised study	Out-of-school projects
Differentiated assignments[9]	Differing student contracts[10]
Self-directed study	Use of practical problems
Informal grouping	Nonacademic guidance
Subject-matter enrichment	as needed
Differentiated questions	Referral as needed[11]
Consideration of interests	Laboratory instruction
Modification of content	Special marking and
Use of varied texts and other	reporting procedures
teaching materials	Tutorial help

Supervised Study and Assignments. Supervised study permits the teacher to identify students with academic problems and to give them appropriate help. During a full study period, a range of students may receive such assistance. Frequently this help is focused on in-class assignments that have been designed to meet the needs of individual students. Although many teachers yield to the work-saving approach of making one assignment to all members of the class, more knowledgeable instructors recognize the need for differentiating assignments realistically in terms of student achievement and ability.

---

[8]Lindgren, *Educational Psychology in the Classroom*, chapter 17, discusses guidance services as a means of providing individualized help for the learner.

[9]Clark and Starr, *Secondary School Teaching Methods*, pp. 166–169, discuss and give examples of differentiated assignments.

[10]Ronald C. Faunce and Carroll L. Munshaw, *Teaching and Learning in Secondary Schools* (Belmont, California: Wadsworth Publishing Co., Inc., 1965), pp. 224–225, relate programed learning to the use of individual student contracts as a device for promoting independent study.

[11]Wayne Dumas and Weldon Beckner, *Introduction to Secondary Education: A Foundations Approach* (Scranton, Pennsylvania: International Textbook Company, 1968), pp. 273–274, point out the need for student referral when classroom teachers determine that professional counselors are better equipped to assist students. Willingness to make needed referrals is said to be a mark of professionalism.

Self-directed Study. Total individualization may be combined with self-direction through the use of programed materials. Realizing the unique capacities and learning styles of individual students, a growing number of experimental teachers are turning to techniques that enable the student to move meaningfully at his own pace, quite independent of class progress. The most useful and frequently employed devices for accomplishing this have been linear and branching programs, although a number of different, self-directive programs have been tried out by ingenious teachers.

Grouping. Within the individual classroom, informal groups may be established to serve many useful purposes—committee work, review, demonstrations, and work on projects. Although in-class grouping is more common at the elementary-school level, it deserves much wider experimentation and use at the secondary levels.

Questioning. Skillful use of the question is another effective way of meeting student differences in ability and achievement and of relating subject matter to student interests. Because of its extreme flexibility, the question may be used in connection with many instructional procedures and provides one of the most effective means for bringing student, subject matter, and teacher together.

Modification of Content. Modification of course content through deletion or addition of material is often desirable. For slow learners, one possibility is to delete one or two difficult units during the school year. For rapid as well as slow learners, the use of textbooks of varying difficulty is common practice among better teachers. This practice may be extended by providing students with a wide range of nontextbook materials of varying difficulty. Newspapers and magazines serve well in this connection.

Tutorial Help. If rapport between student and teacher is solidly established, tutorial help may be effectively given during study periods and before and after school. The limitation of this procedure is the time the teacher can devote to the task. Remedial teaching often involves tutorial help that may be provided by the teacher or by another student under teacher supervision.

Programed Materials. During the past decade linear and branching programs that present the content of a single lesson, a unit, or a full course have been greatly refined and improved. (See Chapter 17 for a detailed discussion of programed learning.) Used by a wise instructor, such programs encourage student self-direction, release the teacher for other needed tasks, and permit the student to move as rapidly or as slowly as he should to acquire needed concepts and skills.

Learning Packages. The past few years have seen the development of a new variety of units and single lessons aimed at encouraging student self-direction. Known by different names—learning packages, unipacks, and self-instructional packages—their chief concern is to have students complete a series of sequentially placed learning tasks that may involve diagnostic testing, goal identification, conventional study, reading, composition, audiovisual aids, programed materials, consultation with the teacher, small group study, and examinations. The *Learning Activity Packet* (LAP) currently in use in the Nova (Florida) Project requires students to proceed through a series of well-defined steps.[12] In the preparation of each LAP, the teacher (1) starts by determining the scope and sequence of a given subject to be covered; (2) prepares a pretest to determine how knowledgeable the student is about content; (3) acquires a general picture of what is to be presented; (4) determines what subconcepts are to be taught; (5) selects a title for the LAP; (6) lists concept-related behavioral objectives stated in terms of performance; (7) checks to determine that objectives are so stated that they can be measured and rewrites them if necessary; (8) prepares assignments and activities to be followed by students in achieving LAP goals using a variety of materials; (9) rechecks to determine that materials are appropriate to goals sought; (10) prepares a student self-test that calls for recycling in the event the student fails to pass the test; and (11) prepares a final examination based upon content covered which permits recycling to include needed learning activities for students who fail to pass. Students who pass the final examination are allowed to proceed to the next LAP.

Computer Assisted Instruction. Use of the computer for the purpose of individualizing instruction has occupied the dreams of educational experimenters during the past few years; however, actual attempts to combine programing techniques with the speed and flexibility of the computer have been limited to a small but increasing number of well-financed, carefully-structured investigations using the resources of a major university, a research center, or a large public school system.[13] Institutions noted for their continuing interest in this field include the University of Illinois, Stanford University, the University of Texas, the University of Michigan, the University of Pittsburgh, Florida State University, and the University of California.

A high degree of variability is found among computer-based instructional programs, both with respect to purpose (drill-and-practice, tutorship, or dialogue) and instructional materials (software) as well as hardware needed to implement them. A typical program calls for the use

[12]"Title Three Tales," Widefield School District No. 3, Security, Colorado, October 1969.

[13]Don D. Bushnell and Dwight W. Allen, eds., *The Computer in American Education* (New York: John Wiley & Sons, Inc., 1967), pp. 92–107, provide helpful brief descriptions of a range of projects involving computer-assisted learning.

of student terminals linked electronically to a computer (often remotely located) of adequate size and capability. Usually the student console (terminal) is equipped with a cathode ray tube (CRT), an attached electric typewriter, and a filmstrip projection system containing the sequentially placed frames of the program. Students seated at such a console are exposed to stimuli (frames, pictures, diagrams, or statements) to which they respond.

Most teaching stations (terminals) possess audio-visual capability permitting visual displays, which appear on the CRT screen like a television picture, with voiced clarification or comment. An integral part of this complicated procedure is the information retrieval system whereby desired visuals, audio tapes, or printed information may be presented in a desired sequence as programed. Although few such terminals exist, a fully equipped computer-terminal combination calls for the use of audio as well as visual tape banks, a random-access slide projector, an audio playback unit, an oscilloscope with light pen facility, and computer-controlled lights for indicating feedback in addition to the hardware and software identified earlier.

Principles Related to Differentiation

It is important for the teacher to be able to determine the value of specific instructional procedures designed to meet the individual needs of his students. If he is to do this consistently and effectively, he must be able to relate specific procedures to generalizations that have wide application.[14] An acquaintance with the following principles is therefore basic.

1. Students vary in many ways that influence teaching and learning. For this reason the teacher must consider the individual differences of each student if teaching and learning are to be realistic. There is little value in recognizing individual differences unless the teacher uses this information to promote effective learning.[15]

2. Differences among students that have the greatest effect on the teaching-learning process are related to intelligence, achievement, goals, interests, skills, habits, emotions, abilities, readiness, adjustment, socio-economic status, personal health, and past experiences. Although intelligence is frequently singled out as the most important, it is only one of many factors.

3. Certain kinds of differences affect specific types of learning.

---

[14]Herbert J. Klausmeier and William Goodwin, *Learning and Human Abilities: Educational Psychology*, 2d. ed. (New York: Harper & Row, Publishers, 1966), pp. 495–501, list and discuss eight principles of particular relevance in providing for individual instruction.

[15]Harris, Bessent, and McIntyre, *In-Service Education: A Guide to Better Practice*, pp. 96–103 provide a "Worksheet for Analyzing Individual Differences" among students and describe how it can be employed in helping teachers to group students effectively.

4. Because both heredity and environment play a marked role in determining individual differences, teacher expectations should be based on the careful appraisal of the abilities and backgrounds of the students.[16]

5. Adolescents do not go through the developmental tasks in the same sequence and at the same rate.

6. A student's academic behavior is not consistently the same under all circumstances, and his behavior may vary within a generally consistent pattern of development.

7. The gifted child may be generally bright or bright in one area primarily. Exceptional talent and severe retardation are easily discernible, but the variations between these two extremes are less obvious and thus often receive limited attention. The fact that students may be handicapped in one area but gifted in another further complicates effective instruction.

8. Students must first be understood as individuals *apart* from the group and later as individuals functioning *within* the group.

9. A highly trained school staff is needed to insure that maximum learning takes place in spite of individual differences among students.[17]

10. Students grouped homogeneously according to one measure will exhibit differences with respect to other measures.

11. Individual guidance should be used as a device for helping the student achieve the most he possibly can.[18]

Correct and Incorrect Procedures

Differentiation of instruction to serve the needs of specific learners is universally recognized by teachers as imperative, but many of them do not exhibit adequate techniques of differentiation in the actual classroom.

Incorrect Procedures

The following examples point out certain teacher weaknesses in differentiating instruction.

MR. PICKETT HAS DIFFICULTY MEETING STUDENT DIFFERENCES

Arlo Pickett believed in heterogeneous grouping, but he admitted that he had a serious problem keeping all members of his mathematics class

---

[16]Clark and Starr, *Secondary School Teaching Methods*, chapter 2, discuss a range of special techniques that can be of assistance in helping teachers become acquainted with their students.

[17]See Klausmeier and Goodwin, *Learning and Human Abilities*, p. 499, for a brief discussion of the need for a competent school staff to provide for individual differences.

[18]William Marshall French, *American Secondary Education*, 2d. ed. (New York: Odyssey Press, 1967), p. 345, states that "the teacher who knows the individual pupils as individual personalities, who knows their background, their interests, their strengths and shortcomings is the most important person in a sound counseling program."

The need for selecting those instructional activities most appropriate for individual learners is stressed by Nathan S. Blount and Herbert J. Klausmeier, *Teaching in the Secondary School*, 2d. ed. (New York: Harper & Row, Publishers, 1968), p. 250.

together because the I.Q.'s in the group ranged from 87 to 129. Instruction was geared to the middle one half of the class; as a result the brighter students were often bored during discussions and finished their assignments in half the time required by below-average students. In order to keep these brighter students occupied, Mr. Pickett required that they work on enrichment materials. If they finished this assigned work early, they performed clerical tasks for the teacher or prepared bulletin boards instead of working on additional challenging problems.

MRS. McCOARD WORKS WITH A SLOW SECTION

Mrs. McCoard had taught eleventh-grade English for six years without ever teaching one of the slow sections. When she was inevitably assigned a slow group, she was crushed. She had high academic standards and was determined to see that these students measured up to her expectations. Assignments were difficult and long. Even when students failed to comprehend an idea after what she assumed was an appropriate explanation, Mrs. McCoard felt justified in moving to the next point. Gradually students became apathetic and began to misbehave; Mrs. McCoard declared that it was impossible for these students to cope with the course.

Serious errors or omissions in differentiating instruction can be identified in each of the preceding examples. Mr. Pickett attempted to assist the bright students through the use of enrichment materials, but additional work on more difficult content was denied them. Lack of realism is reflected in the teaching of Mrs. McCoard, who tried to force students to learn beyond what their capacities and past achievement would permit.

Correct Procedures

Effective use of teaching techniques, devices, and a school staff is illustrated in the cases below.

MISS MANSFIELD PLANS FOR DIFFERENTIATION

Hillsdale Consolidated Senior High School was made up of students from a range of social and economic circumstances. The administration and faculty members, however, had cast their lot in favor of heterogeneous grouping, realizing that teachers would have to exhibit considerable skill in meeting the individual differences of their students.

Miss Mansfield viewed her two classes of active and highly varied tenth-graders as an instructional challenge. Knowing there was a wide range of differences among her students, she assembled specific information on each student with respect to I.Q. and achievement in world history, the subject she was teaching. As the class progressed, she experimented with in-class grouping in order to (1) aid social adjustment, (2) assist with classroom control, and (3) serve the academic needs of students.

In her unit plans the teacher described assignments with three levels of difficulty. Further adjustments were often made during the study periods after the basic assignments had been given. No one was allowed to loaf in Miss Mansfield's classes, but she made sure that the less gifted students were not asked to do work that was beyond their capacities and their level of conceptual readiness. Gifted students, on the other hand, were directed to more difficult reading and were encouraged to work on individual projects that provided genuine challenge.

MR. WHITTED MAKES USE OF PROGRAMED MATERIALS

The principal at the new and well-furnished Brownell High School had stressed the need for individualization of instruction in a number of faculty meetings. He pointed out the availability of numerous movable carrels, small committee-size rooms adjacent to classrooms, and a wide range of programed materials as requested by teachers.

Bill Whitted, now in his third year of teaching mathematics, had been assigned responsibility for both the first and second year algebra classes. Seeking the approval of the principal, he decided to totally individualize his algebra classes through the use of programed materials. After a full year of examining such materials in mathematics, he felt that he was in a position to select the most effective ones. A series was chosen that permitted uninterrupted and coordinated progression through the content of first year algebra, second year algebra, trigonometry, and beyond.

First and second year classes (fifty-four students) were scheduled at the same hour in a spacious room containing sixty student stations and fifteen additional study carrels located along the walls and at the back of the room. A noncertificated teacher aide (competent in mathematics) and a mathematics student-teaching major were assigned to Mr. Whitted to provide students with individual help. Although materials were designed to be totally self-directive, the team members soon discovered that students tended to find difficulty with certain problems and at different stages of progression. Before a month of the new program had passed, it was obvious that a sizable range in the ability of both first and second year algebra students existed; their accomplishments extended from very little achievement to what would normally be expected of students during the middle of the second year.

Students who tended to cluster at specific levels of understanding were often given small group instruction in one of the small rooms. Distractable individuals who found it difficult to concentrate at their seats were encouraged to use study carrels, and students were told to seek instructional help after reasonable effort failed to produce desired comprehension.

After the first six months of the school year, Mr. Whitted was able to make several generalizations about the new program:

—Students varied in their ability to be self-directive.

—Used under supervision, carefully selected programed materials would enable students to move at their own speeds with good comprehension.

—Although a few students had not completed more than the equivalent of three months work, roughly 50 percent of the students were beyond the achievement level expected of students in a traditional program, and two of the students were nearing the completion of second year algebra.

—Instructional techniques of team members used in the new program improved with experience.

—Small-group discussions combined with the use of self-directed programed materials and occasional tutorial help proved to be an effective teaching combination.

Use in Specific Subjects

Concept-Centered Subjects

Learners who have limited general intelligence will have academic difficulties, particularly in areas demanding abstract thinking—such as mathematics, chemistry, physics, biology, English grammar, and certain areas in the social sciences. Confusion often arises, however, because of the failure to differentiate between the lack of capacity and a record of poor achievement. It is possible for a bright student to do poorly in mathematics for many reasons, including poor teaching, lack of motivation, limited reading ability, or conceptual gaps in his learning. To conclude that the poor achiever is necessarily a dull student is an unwarranted and shallow assumption.

Skill Subjects

Poor neuro-muscular coordination can inhibit performance in any skill subject, such as typing, band, orchestra, shorthand, and physical education. Difficulties may arise when this lack of coordination is not immediately recognized or when poor performance is attributed to a lack of effort or a lack of motivation. No amount of instructional effort can bring about efficient muscle coordination if the student is not physically ready.

Subjects Requiring Some Prior Experience

Work experiences and incidental experiences related to the student's environment often provide the background essential to success in specific subjects. A student's interest in farm mechanics, for example, is often related to his farm background. It is unrealistic to assume that the occasional city-bred youngster who gets into a farm mechanics class will have the same experience-related concepts as a farm youth, although his interest may be as high. Similarly, the youngster of low socioeconomic status who has been brought up in an impoverished language environment can hardly be expected to show the same interest in correct speech as the student from more favored circumstances.

Specific Suggestions

Recommendations

1. Create learning situations in which students are encouraged to work to their capacity, learning situations that are not too difficult but that provide challenge for all.

2. Explore the possibility of grouping students according to academic ability and achievement.[19] Students may also be grouped informally in the classroom to serve social, instructional, or classroom control purposes.

3. Provide special groups for students whose differences are extreme. Make case studies of students with special problems.

4. Use a variety of procedures to differentiate instruction in view of student interests. Use the best programed materials available to implement this instruction.

5. Teach the same content in a shorter period than usual as one means of keeping the bright youngster challenged. Encourage carefully selected bright students to enter college early.

6. Do not deny promotion to slow-learning students.[20] Modify the curriculum to meet their needs;[21] involve them in class activities; and develop an atmosphere of understanding to help these students achieve their potential.

7. Make assignments flexible in consideration of differing interests and abilities. Individualize instruction through the use of special assignments and contracts.

8. Experiment with different means of meeting individual needs.

9. Encourage students to make continuous vertical advancement even if it is at the expense of horizontal enrichment.[22]

10. Plan units and daily lessons carefully for the differentiation of instruction.

11. Use the supervised study period to evaluate student effort and achievement and to redirect student efforts as needed. Give students individual help to the extent that time will permit.

12. Rephrase or reword questions to serve the needs of individual students.

13. Use a range of textbooks and other materials of varying difficulty.

[19]J. Lloyd Trump and Delmas F. Miller, *Secondary School Curriculum Improvement: Proposals and Procedures* (Boston: Allyn & Bacon, Inc., 1968), chapters 18, 19, and 20, present a strong case for independent study, large group instruction, and small group discussion. Maximum individual achievement within the school setting is thus encouraged.

[20]Homogeneous grouping, multi-track curriculums, and several types of individualized instruction may be employed to insure consistent, earned promotion for students without violating conceptual readiness.

[21]The disadvantages of requiring slow-learning students to repeat grades or to be denied promotion are discussed and documented by Lindgren, *Educational Psychology in the Classroom*, pp. 514–515.

[22]William H. Burton, *The Guidance of Learning Activities*, 3d. ed. (New York: Appleton-Century-Crofts, 1962), p. 242, voices strong opposition to "busy work" as a means of providing for individual differences.

14. Remember that students seek different personal goals and that their goals may be different from those the teacher has in mind.

15. Explore the possibility of using team teaching.

Cautions

1. Don't overemphasize the individual I.Q. as a measure of ability.

2. Don't expect all students to learn at the same rate.

3. Don't permit double promotions unless the school system has no better means of providing for the educationally gifted child.

IDENTIFYING A SOUND REMEDIAL TEACHING PROGRAM

Remedial teaching is a special type of instruction aimed at helping students overcome academic difficulties not caused by a marked limitation in general capacity.[23] The teaching of the mentally retarded is not included under remedial teaching, although slow-learning youngsters often need remedial teaching and are frequently found in such programs.[24]

Most remedial teaching is currently being carried on in heterogeneous classes in which extremes of student ability and achievement are pronounced. Less common are homogeneously grouped classes in which attention can be focused on the individual learning problems of the students. Perhaps a majority of the attempts to provide special help are made through individual contacts with students during the study period or before and after school.

If several students in a class display the same difficulty, a special in-class group, small or large, may be formed to economize the time and effort spent on reteaching. If the teacher discovers that a particular concept simply has not been comprehended by his students, the entire class may require special help. However, judicious use of carefully selected programed materials often well serves the needs of individual students with particular problems.

In large secondary schools standardized examinations may reveal common marked deficiencies among a substantial portion of the student body. In this case, remedial classes may be established as part of the curriculum. Some large schools have classes that are comprised of students who have previously failed a particular course; such classes essentially provide remedial instruction geared to the level of the class.

One recognized impediment to effective learning is poor reading ability, a problem that affects a substantial portion of the total secondary-

---

[23]Poor learners and culturally-deprived youth are listed among the types of students who would benefit from remedial help according to Clark and Starr, *Secondary School Teaching Methods*, pp. 180–194.

[24]*Ibid.*, pp. 184–188, provide several concrete suggestions for teaching poor learners.
See Burton, *The Guidance of Learning Activities*, p. 235, for a description of the characteristics of the dull pupil.

school population. Classes in remedial reading are, therefore, common in large schools and are frequently found as noncredit courses in college curriculums.

Goals of Remedial Teaching

If effectively carried out, remedial teaching helps students identify the specific academic problems that are causing difficulty. It is, therefore, diagnostic in nature. Once the difficulty is pinpointed, a definite course of action must be charted to improve learning. Remedial teaching thus has the advantage of permitting a direct attack on the individual problems of students.

Mistaken concepts are a frequent source of difficulty. A budding typist, for example, may wrongly assume that a rhythmic pattern is basic to the acquisition of high speed. Remedial teaching can correct such false concepts. Remedial teaching also seeks to supply missing concepts essential to academic progress. An understanding of the Civil War depends upon a comprehension of events prior to the war; in a program of remedial teaching, such events can be identified and taught.

If the interrelationship of concepts is not clear to the learner, remedial teaching can again correct the difficulty. A student in a grammar course, for instance, may not see the connection between dependent clauses and effective written composition. Such relationships must be grasped before the student can make satisfactory progress in the course.

If the teacher can assist the student in overcoming persistent academic problems before they result in general disappointment, defeat, and decreased motivation, he is teaching effectively. A remedial teaching program aims at early diagnosis of the individual learner's problems and at teaching him what specifically can and should be done to overcome his difficulties.

Principles Related to Remedial Teaching

The teacher concerned with remedial teaching needs to identify guidelines that give direction to his instruction. Several of these guidelines are listed below.

1. Academic difficulties requiring remedial teaching may stem from culturally impoverished environments, poor teaching, poor study habits, lack of interest, and limited capacities. Students may also need special help with a range of problems not directly related to academic performance. The sympathetic, helpful teacher exerts a positive influence on the student who is encountering multiple difficulties.

2. Emotional difficulties, like academic difficulties, can be helped through remedial teaching.[25] Indeed, self-concepts may be enhanced if remedial teaching enables students to achieve success often.

---

[25]Lee J. Cronbach, *Educational Psychology*, 2d. ed. (New York: Harcourt Brace Jovanovich, Inc., 1963), pp. 646–651, discusses the need for and effect of remedial effort on learners with emotional difficulties.

3. Many kinds of remedial groups may be established—for example, groups of high-achieving students whose performance and achievement are below their potential, groups of average students who are deficient in one specific area, and groups of slow learners. Although many average and some brilliant children need remedial help, they need help less frequently and with a smaller range of problems than do below-average students.[26]

4. Published standardized tests provide a sound means of helping diagnose student problems preparatory to undertaking a remedial program. Remedial teaching itself often requires other special instructional materials and facilities.

5. Remedial teaching should only follow an accurate diagnosis of learning difficulties.

6. Teaching procedures effective for most students may be ineffective for students in a remedial program. In such a program, standards need to be adjusted realistically to meet student capacities, interests, and personal goals.

7. If a student is lacking basic skills, it may be necessary to call in a remedial teaching specialist. Special training is highly desirable for any teacher who has a major responsibility for remedial teaching.

8. Inability to read at the desired level has an adverse effect on academic achievement in nearly all subjects. Special work in this area may be needed by students at all levels of achievement and capacity.

9. Professional attention to physical difficulties can help improve learning.

10. Remedial assistance should continue until the recipient has reached the desired level of achievement.

Correct and Incorrect Procedures

Teachers with limited experience often provide inadequate remedial instruction or neglect such instruction entirely. This is borne out in the illustration that follows.

MISS SYMONS NEGLECTS LOW ACHIEVERS

Bessie Symons enjoyed her first year of teaching Algebra I to ninth-graders. Her students—twenty-seven in all, with I.Q.'s ranging from 97 to 136—were grouped heterogeneously, and she was finding it difficult to keep them all progressing at the same rate.

By the end of November the teacher realized that students were separating themselves largely into two groups—the high achievers and the low achievers. Division of the class into two sections would have helped her teaching, but the administration was opposed to it. Miss Symons chose an easy solution to her problem: Her teaching was directed to the high achievers, and the low achievers were left to

---

[26]Provisions for dealing with slow-learning children are discussed by Klausmeier and Goodwin, *Learning and Human Abilities*, pp. 517–519.

flounder. Occasional help was given to slower students during the study period, but Miss Symons reasoned that the brighter students had just as much claim to her help as the less gifted. By the end of the semester the low achievers were thoroughly discouraged and near the point of open rebellion.

Miss Symons exhibited neglect of her students; her few efforts to institute remedial teaching procedures were half-hearted at best.

Successful use of remedial teaching procedures is reflected in the work of the teacher described below.

MR. TATE USES EFFECTIVE REMEDIAL PROCEDURES

As soon as the principal informed Frank Tate that he would have the responsibility for the 10B's, the slow group that two teachers had already declared unteachable, he knew that his ingenuity would be challenged. There was one thing in his favor, however: Students were more or less homogeneously grouped—their I.Q.'s extended only from 86 to 103.

Mr. Tate began by readministering the history achievement test that had been given at the end of the previous school year. Scores were recorded in code form on a seating chart that also contained a coded I.Q. He gained permission from the administration to move as slowly as he thought advisable for the group being taught. The first week was devoted largely to corroborating what achievement test scores had revealed and to establishing rapport with the group.

Mr. Tate found that students hated a straight lecture but that they were most responsive in an informal situation. The teacher used this knowledge to great advantage. As the school year advanced, a range of diagnostic procedures was used to determine the nature of learning difficulties. A reading test, for example, revealed what the teacher had assumed—that only a very small proportion of his group was reading at the tenth-grade level. He therefore used a range of simplified texts geared to the individual reading abilities.

Once rapport had been established, Mr. Tate concentrated on having students acquire effective study habits, and he spent time looking into the home backgrounds of specific students. Praise was used effectively in motivating students. If a student completed a learning task that had been simplified to provide him with a successful experience, he was praised. No one was made to feel that he was failing.

The teacher employed methods that were known to make subject matter meaningful to students. Narration accompanied by dramatics proved successful. Carefully selected resource persons were well received, and field trips provided meaningful learning experiences. Several students indicated that they were enjoying school for the first time in their lives.

Examination of Mr. Tate's teaching procedures reveals that he was realistic in his expectations. Furthermore, these expectations were based upon careful assembly and weighing of the facts. He established rapport with his students, creating the impression that he was their ally. Methods and materials were adjusted to what the students could and would accept. Because he realized that the students did not possess effective study habits, the teacher directed attention to establishing such habits.

Use in Specific Subjects

All courses demanding student achievement may result in partial failure and academic problems. Students frequently encounter their greatest academic frustrations in highly organized, concept-centered subjects. For this reason, the need for remedial teaching is greatest in such subjects as mathematics, English grammar, biology, bookkeeping, chemistry, and physics. The study of other, more loosely structured subjects, such as history, geography, and homemaking, may give rise to difficulties, but they are usually less pronounced and less frequent. Usually the skill subjects are less dependent on conceptual content; therefore, student frustrations are minimized. The study of a subject like shorthand, however, in which a high degree of motor skill is required in addition to a thorough knowledge of the meaning and use of symbols, may cause severe academic distress and necessitate remedial teaching.

Specific Suggestions

The following specific suggestions for conducting programs of remedial teaching bear a close relationship to the principles presented earlier.[27]

Recommendations
1. Use a range of procedures to diagnose learning difficulties.
2. Determine the reading level of students in your classes at least once each year.[28]
3. Maintain close personal contact with the academic achievement of each student.
4. Establish rapport with students and encourage them to seek your help when they need it. Make the student feel that you are always sympathetic to his problems, regardless of their cause.
5. Remember that students can achieve only what their capacities permit them to achieve. Determine what these capacities are.
6. Experiment with the use of different procedures in providing remedial help for students.
7. Devise means for improving the study habits of students.
8. While seeking the possible causes of poor learning, determine the relationship of physical, social, and emotional factors to the need for remedial work. Ascertain whether environmental influences have been responsible for problems that affect learning.

---

[27]A useful treatment of poor learners, their characteristics, and the teaching techniques most helpful in meeting their needs is presented by Clark and Starr, *Secondary School Teaching Methods,* pp. 180–188.

[28]Robert D. Strom, *Psychology for the Classroom* (Englewood Cliffs, New Jersey: Prentice-Hall, Inc., 1969), p. 50, identifies several reading-related problems encountered by secondary school teachers. Possible solutions are also suggested.

9. Identify questionable teaching procedures that make it necessary to reteach content.

10. Procure and use the facilities and materials necessary for conducting an efficient remedial teaching program.

11. Call in remedial teaching specialists as needed to solve particular problems.

Cautions

1. Don't assume that the student in need of remedial work is necessarily dull.

2. Don't assume that bright students never need remedial help.[29]

3. Don't attempt to engage in remedial teaching without first having diagnosed a student's difficulties.

4. Don't make a public point of the fact that certain students are engaged in remedial work.

USING SOUND MARKING AND REPORTING PROCEDURES

Broadly conceived, the fundamental purpose of assigning grades and reporting these grades to parents is to help students achieve desirable educational goals. More specifically, however, marking and reporting help:

1. Determine student progress toward specific objectives.
2. Stimulate students to continued effort or to greater effort.
3. Keep students informed of their individual progress.
4. Acquaint students with their deficiencies.
5. Indicate students' standing in a given class or with respect to national norms.
6. Provide an administrative record of student achievement.
7. Inform parents of pupil progress.
8. Maintain contact with the home.[30]

Several writers have noted that the purpose of marking has been in a state of transformation, moving away from merely assigning and reporting marks to improving pupil learning.[31] In spite of this change, current practice still emphasizes the reporting of marks.

[29]Specific suggestions for helping the academically talented student to achieve his potential are provided by Clark and Starr, *Secondary School Teaching Methods,* pp. 197–201.

[30]Relationships between home and school are improved through the effective use of a carefully prepared report form. See Blount and Klausmeier, *Teaching in the Secondary School,* pp. 423–427.

[31]Norman E. Gronlund, *Measurement and Evaluation of Teaching* (Toronto: Macmillan Co. of Canada, Ltd., 1965), p. 373, states that "the main reason for reporting to pupils and parents is to facilitate the learning and development of the pupils."

De Cecco, *The Psychology of Learning and Instruction,* pp. 170–172, describes educational studies and conflicts among educators as related to the use of grades as incentives to learning.

Controversy with respect to marking on a competitive basis is strong. Although elementary schools tend to discount competitive marking, high schools are reluctant to give it up because grades are useful in gaining admission to colleges. A general trend toward rigor in assigning grades for secondary-school students has received strong support from the current emphasis on international competition in the sciences and on education in general.

That marks are considered lacking in validity and reliability is borne out by several research findings. One writer[32] concluded that marks are based in part upon intelligence as well as upon achievement and that girls receive higher grades than boys. Another discovered a positive relationship between marks received and most-liked and least-liked students.[33] Still a third writer found that most teachers differ in their interpretations of achievement and that the value assigned to a given mark differed from school to school and even from teacher to teacher in the same school.[34] In spite of these problems, the marking and reporting of pupil progress serve an important purpose in education and deserve serious attention.

Differences in Marking and Reporting

During the past half century many different types of grading systems have made their appearance. At the present time three basic systems are being used: numerical grades, letter grades, and descriptions of progress.[35] In a few cases, combinations involving two or more systems are employed.

Numerical Grades

The numerical grade may take the form of a percentage score, a percentile rank, or numbers ranging from one to five or one to ten. Because of its flexibility, the percentage score is frequently employed by teachers. A given percentage score on a test, however, may be relatively meaningless to parents in the absence of information about test difficulty, the group tested, and instructions that preceded testing. The percentage system is, nevertheless, traditionally entrenched, and many parents prefer it because of its assumed ease of interpretation.

Percentile rank is a statistical measure that indicates the percentage of the class above and below a particular student. In a class of one hundred, for example, a student with a percentile rank of sixty-four would have achieved a higher mark than sixty-four (or 64 percent) of his classmates. A percentile rank mark is infrequently employed because it requires an involved explanation and extensive computation by the teacher.

---

[32]Robert S. Carter, "How Invalid are Marks Assigned by Teachers?" *Journal of Educational Psychology*, 43 (1952), pp. 218–228.

[33]S. Trevor Hadley, "School Mark—Fact or Fancy?" *Educational Administration and Supervision*, 40 (1954), pp. 305–312.

[34]Frederick B. Davis, *Educational Measurements and their Interpretation* (Belmont, California: Wadsworth Publishing Co., Inc., 1964), p. 307.

[35]A useful brief discussion of marking systems currently employed is provided by Clark and Starr, *Secondary School Teaching Methods*, p. 380.

Simple number scores are also seldom used in secondary schools, although they permit a quick computation of grade-point averages. A grade-point average of 3.0, for example, means that all grades received by a given student have averaged 3.0, or the equivalent of B on the following five-point scale: E = 0, D = 1, C = 2, B = 3, and A = 4. Often this scoring procedure is modified to encompass numbers one through ten.

Letter Grades

Letter grades have been and still are the most popular means of reporting student progress.[36] A system of five letter grades, usually A, B, C, D, and E, is most frequently employed. (Occasionally the letter F is substituted for E as the lowest mark.)

Descriptive words such as *Excellent, Good,* and *Poor,* together with their letter equivalents *E, G,* and *P*—are still to be found, but the use of this system is diminishing. *S (Satisfactory)* and *U (Unsatisfactory)* probably represent the most simplified use of letters for grading purposes. The words *Pass* and *Fail* (*P* and *F*) also serve the same purpose. The two-letter systems, however, have been severely criticized by parents.

Because parents are acquainted with the use of a four- or five-letter procedure in grading, they often prefer it to other schemes involving the use of letters. Although letter grades are inherently no more meaningful than a percentage system, many parents are accustomed to them and feel that letters can be interpreted more accurately.

Descriptive Statements

During the past two decades, descriptive statements have been employed with increasing frequency in secondary schools as a means of reporting student progress to parents. Originating in the elementary schools, descriptive statements were slow to be adopted at the more conservative secondary levels. Although such statements have many different forms, the following examples, taken from report cards of students in an eleventh-grade United States history class, indicate the general nature of the descriptive method:

> Although Jim's capacity is good, he seems to be more interested in sports than in history. His present achievement is below the class average.
>
> Tanya is a consistently good student. Her study habits are excellent, and she works hard. Improvement in her reading speed and comprehension would be of great help to her.
>
> Sammy did an outstanding job of helping prepare his committee's bulletin board, but his test scores have placed him in the lower 25 percent of the class. He finds it hard to pay attention and has a tendency to show off. I believe that a parent-teacher conference may be helpful.

---

[36]Richard H. Lindeman, *Educational Measurement* (Glenview, Illinois: Scott, Foresman and Company, 1967), pp. 145–150, points out the inadequacies of A-B-C reporting and suggests useful alternatives.

Shanna is now able to discuss meaningfully the causes and effects of the Civil War, their relationship to the Reconstruction Period, and their effect on current racial strife as well as typical students in the upper 25 percent of her class. She received fourth to the highest grade (92 percent) on the examination given at the end of the semester.

The descriptive statement has many advantages: It usually conveys a more meaningful message to the parent than the letter or number grade; it enables the teacher to mention specifically those strengths or weaknesses about which parents should be informed; and it can be used as an explanatory supplement to a letter or number grade. Further, it is often employed to indicate the achievement of desired behavioral objectives. Although this is true to some extent of all examples cited above, it is particularly true in Shanna's case.

Descriptive statements of A, B, C, D, and E students can be worked out by the teacher or jointly developed by students and the teacher. Such statements tend to make the percentage or letter grade more meaningful for students as well as parents. The following paragraph describes the A pupil in a junior high school:[37]

"A" Pupil (95-100 Percent, Superior Work): One (1) whose work consistently shows an intelligent comprehension of the subject matter through his ability to retain facts and principles learned; (2) who is able to apply subject matter learned to new problems, (3) who organizes his work well; (4) who speaks clearly and forcibly in discussions; (5) who presents neat, well-arranged, accurate, complete work on time; (6) who performs required skills with a high degree of techniques; (7) who completes both the average and the enriched assignment; (8) who has good study habits; (9) who has the power of analyzing his own work to discover his strong and weak points; (10) who shows marked initiative, industry, and attention.

The marking procedures described above do not cover the many possible combinations that are used widely and successfully by school systems. In some systems, for example, a letter grade is rarely given without a descriptive word or statement intended to clarify its meaning, and a descriptive statement of student progress is often accompanied by a letter grade.

Principles Related to Marking and Reporting

General principles giving sound direction to marking and reporting practices of both beginning and experienced teachers are presented here.[38]

[37]Burton, *The Guidance of Learning Activities,* p. 512.
[38]Five guidelines of value to educators responsible for the establishment of grading policies are identified by Lindeman, *Educational Measurement,* pp. 143–145.

1. The home and school must work cooperatively in furthering the cause of learning, and meaningful reporting of pupil progress helps serve this purpose. Parents want to know about the strengths and weaknesses of their children, and as a basis for understanding student grades, parents should understand the objectives students are trying to achieve.[39]

2. Symbols used to report student progress may be interpreted differently by students, teachers, and parents. Because parents are generally not professionally trained in the field of education, reporting devices should be easily understood and reasonably complete. Parent-teacher conferences and descriptive reports to parents are more helpful devices for reporting student progress than the traditional report card.

3. Report-card grades and comments should be recorded only after a careful examination of the quality of student performance on all class-related activities. A single report-card grade is a relatively meaningless and subjective composite of several grading factors. Meaningful evaluation and reporting require differentiation in grading for achievement, effort, and citizenship.

4. Each marking system has specific advantages and disadvantages.[40] All grades, however, are relative. A mark given for specific academic performance may vary from teacher to teacher, from subject to subject, from circumstance to circumstance, and from school to school. In addition, grades frequently lack reliability and validity.

5. The students, as well as their parents, need to know how they are doing in school. Thus, a basic purpose of marking is to provide students with a definite indication of their performance. A corollary purpose is to provide them with an incentive for improving that performance. Unfortunately, grade-conscious students work for high grades rather than for the mastery of content.

6. An overemphasis on marks can seriously interfere with specific aspects of the learning process. The teacher's development of a wholesome attitude toward marks is a primary step in establishing a worthwhile grading system.

7. Students who are encouraged to become actively involved in helping to determine their own grades and the form used to report them tend to view report card grades as less threatening. Further, they become more interested, knowledgeable participants in the grading process.

8. Differences in student abilities should be reflected in the evaluation, marking, and reporting of student achievement.

9. Teachers have the responsibility for devising procedures to accurately measure and appraise the extent to which students have attained desired school goals.

---

[39]An example of an inclusive report card in which attention is focused on performance in subjects and subareas within subjects, on classroom attitudes, and on attendance is provided by De Cecco, *The Psychology of Learning and Instruction*, p. 652.

Gronlund, *Measurement and Evaluation of Teaching*, p. 377, presents the facsimile of "a comprehensive report form that combines dual marking and checklists of objectives."

[40]*Ibid.*, p. 375, singles out several of the shortcomings of the traditional marking system.

10. Teachers tend to discriminate against certain types of students in determining grades.

11. The use of curves in assigning a given letter grade to a definite proportion of students is indefensible in many cases and should be used with extreme caution.

Current Practices in Reporting Pupil Progress

If report-card grades are to provide an accurate indication of achievement, the quality of student performance must be determined and recorded quite frequently. Ideally, marks should be assigned on a daily basis, but, in view of the clerical work required by such a procedure, this is usually impossible. For a marking procedure to be acceptable, however, marks must be assigned as frequently as possible in view of the teacher's work load and the psychological effects on the student.

Knowing Areas to Be Evaluated

The teacher must know in advance the areas to be evaluated, and he must plan his teaching so that he will have a number of marks in each of these relevant areas by the time the report-card period is at an end. Although his main concern will be academic achievement, he should also note progress with respect to citizenship and effort.[41] When several scores are accumulated in each area, the task of computing averages is relatively simple. Unfortunately, teachers often rationalize that they do not have the time to properly systematize their marking and grading procedures. The result is an incomplete and perhaps unreliable grading system.

Misusing the Inclusive Grade

Well-administered schools and school districts assign different marks for academic achievement, effort, citizenship, and other relevant factors. The interpretation of grades is thus enhanced, and students who rank low in one area may be above average in another. In the past there has been a particular temptation on the part of well-meaning teachers to allow consistent strong effort and excellent classroom behavior to overcompensate for low academic achievement. In the composite one-letter grade, true academic achievement can be disguised or hidden. Differentiated grading helps overcome this.

"Shall I mark the group of low ability on the same basis as the group of high ability?" This troublesome question has not been adequately answered.[42] When evaluated in relationship to a fixed standard in a large

---

[41]Referring to a study involving twenty-nine sections of an English composition course, Davis, *Educational Measurements and Their Interpretation*, p. 313, found that the marks given students revealed to a low relationship to their scholastic aptitude. He concluded that marks were to a large extent based on factors other than skills and knowledge in English composition.

[42]Robert L. Ebel, *Measuring Educational Achievement* (Englewood Cliffs, New Jersey: Prentice-Hall, Inc., 1965), pp. 396–399, elaborates on three basic reasons why marking is a complex and difficult problem.

A sound approach to assigning marks in differing homogeneous groups is presented by Burton, *The Guidance of Learning Activities*, p. 516.

school, low-achieving students, although grouped together, would receive consistently low grades. Conversely, high-achieving students would receive high grades. In developing a marking procedure, the teacher should consider its effect on student motivation, teacher-student rapport, and student learning. Of these factors, student learning is the most important.

Marking on a Relative Basis

Some schools have adopted a policy of marking students in relationship to other students in the same homogeneously grouped class. In order to provide an honest picture of student achievement with respect to a fixed standard, however, coded symbols on the school transcript may indicate the nature of the homogeneous group in which the mark was received. Such a procedure provides help for the college admissions officer faced with the decision of whether to admit a student on the basis of his academic achievement.

Some teachers assign students relative numerical ranks according to academic performance. The student who receives the highest average is designated as student number one, while the student with the lowest average is identified as number twenty-nine in a class of that size. Letter grades may then be assigned according to numerical rank: The top four students may receive A grades, the next six B's, etc.

Rank-order grading and competitive marking are viewed by most educators and psychologists as running counter to known facts about learning.[43] Under such a system differences in rate of learning, ability, interests, and background are not considered. As a result, motivation suffers. Undue attention is focused on achievement for the sake of achievement. Furthermore, the slow but conscientious learner feels defeated and discouraged.

Reporting to Parents

Many different procedures are followed in reporting grades to parents. Report cards are now usually issued on a quarterly (nine weeks) basis, although some school districts issue them only at the end of the semester. The more frequent approach is much more desirable because it tends to maintain a more constant contact with the home. A six-week report-card period is still employed by some school systems.

Simplicity Essential. A simplified but meaningful reporting procedure is to indicate on the report card whether the student is above grade level, at grade level, or below grade level in academic achievement. Because it avoids many of the dangers implicit in the rank-order system, this procedure enables students and parents to make broad comparisons with other learners in the class.[44] As the student approaches the final years of his secondary schooling, he needs to be realistically aware of his

---

[43]*Ibid.*, p. 519.

[44]Blount and Klausmeier, *Teaching in the Secondary School*, pp. 430–431, stress the importance of indicating comparative achievement to parents.

general standing in the class. Parents need this same information as a means of guiding their children through difficult decisions concerning their future.

Multiple Reports. Although the single report card is feasible and practical in the elementary school, the involvement of many teachers per student at the secondary level makes this somewhat impractical. When employed in secondary schools, the single report card necessitates the transfer of grades submitted by different teachers to a single card—a clerical burden for the teacher charged with compiling grades. An attempt to reduce this clerical load has led to experimentation with new punch-card systems, data processing procedures, and computer-based systems that may provide an easier means of sorting, compiling, and mailing report cards.

Supplementary Reports. Many teachers have found it helpful to send home an informal report from time to time as a supplement to the regularly issued report card. But teacher commitments restrict rather markedly the time that can be devoted to this extra reporting. A more frequent practice is to send home with the report card duplicated or printed letters that provide a general explanation of the nature and meaning of the report card and its contents.

Parent-Teacher Conferences. The need for parents to understand report-card grades has been so pronounced that many secondary schools have adopted the elementary-school procedure of setting aside a specific block of time for parent-teacher conferences. Because of the much larger number of students per teacher in the secondary schools (150 as opposed to 30, for instance), the parent-teacher conference has severe limitations. It is often used, however, in the attempt to solve aggravated student problems.[45]

Descriptive Statements. Perhaps the reporting method least susceptible to misunderstanding is the descriptive statement. Although it is admittedly subjective, there is little chance that parents will misinterpret a statement such as "Polly needs help with her reading." Many schools are using this procedure in combination with other grades, but the practice is not as widespread as it might be.

Information Provided by Parents. Parents may play a vital role in providing teachers with essential information about their adolescent children. Although such information is seldom sought or provided with the regularity of a report card, printed or duplicated forms occasionally are used to obtain needed information. Habits, health status, out-of-school

---

[45]*Ibid.*, pp. 434–437, discuss the need for the conduct of parent-teacher conferences. Gronlund, *Measurement and Evaluation of Teaching*, p. 376, describes the advantages of the parent-teacher conference.

activities, personality traits, and emotional concerns are typical of the kinds of information that parents can and should provide in helping the school help the child.

Specific Suggestions

The specific suggestions listed below are derived from general principles and may be of particular help to the beginning teacher or the teacher with limited experience.[46]

Recommendations

1. Help develop a marking system that will be understood and supported by parents, teachers, administrators, and students alike.

2. Review marking procedures at regular intervals and make appropriate modifications where desirable.

3. Base the report-card grade on a range of relevant grades.

4. Make simplified, meaningful, descriptive statements of student progress to supplement number or letter grades.

5. Use a marking system that enables students to see their standing in relationship to other students in the class.

6. Establish a procedure for frequently recording a mark for daily classroom performance.

7. Mark on other relevant factors in addition to academic achievement.

8. Solicit parents' opinions with respect to the form and use of the report card.

9. Keep parents aware of what the school is trying to achieve.

10. Be sure that parents and students know what each mark means.

11. Arrange for parent-teacher conferences at least once each year and more often as occasion demands.

12. Encourage students to work for the acquisition of subject-matter content rather than for high grades.

13. Keep students informed of their own progress.

14. Encourage students to practice self-evaluation.

Cautions

1. Don't wait until the report card is issued to contact parents about problems of unusual concern.

2. Don't stifle student motivation through marking procedures.

3. Don't permit the report card to be the only teacher contact with the home.

---

[46]Ebel, *Measuring Educational Achievement*, pp. 439–441, lists twenty-seven extremely helpful generalizations related to marking and reporting.

Howard T. Batchelder, Maurice McGlasson, and Raleigh Schorling, *Student Teaching in Secondary Schools*, 4th ed. (New York: McGraw-Hill Book Company, 1964), pp. 284–288, cover some of the newer appraisal techniques.

A helpful discussion concerning report cards, accompanied by numerous examples is found in Clark and Starr, *Secondary School Teaching Methods*, pp. 390–400.

4. Don't overemphasize marks.[47]

5. Don't use a marking system to force students to bend to your will.

6. Don't use the same standard for marking groups of students with different abilities.

7. Don't use the unmodified normal curve as a basis for apportioning marks.

8. Don't combine several grading factors (achievement, effort, etc.) into one composite grade.

INDIVIDUAL DIFFERENCES, REMEDIAL TEACHING, AND REPORTING PUPIL PROGRESS IN REVIEW

This chapter has focused attention on the role of teaching to meet individual differences, on remedial teaching, and on reporting pupil progress.

Although students differ in literally hundreds of ways, educators have devoted their attention to those differences that exert the greatest influence on teaching and learning: intelligence, emotional stability, physical health, social adjustment, experiential background, aspirations, interests, school achievement, attitudes, temperament and disposition, readiness, and skills. Techniques currently employed in the attempt to meet the individual needs of students may be classified as administrative provisions and instructional provisions.

Remedial teaching is a special type of instruction aimed at helping students overcome academic difficulties. Academic problems requiring such teaching may stem from limited cultural environments, inefficient teaching, poor study habits, or lack of interest.

Although the basic purpose of grading and reporting is to help students achieve desirable educational goals, a range of more immediate goals is also served. Three types of grading systems are currently being used: numerical grades, letter grades, and descriptions of progress.

PROBLEMS FOR STUDY AND DISCUSSION

1. List the ten individual differences among students that you feel have the greatest effect on the teaching-learning process.

2. Assumption: In your tenth-grade world history class you have the following students: Sandra, who is socially withdrawn; William, who is very bright; Sara, who is totally disinterested; James, who is thoroughly conceited; and Tina, who is culturally impoverished. Describe how you would plan to teach world history and still meet these students' individual differences.

3. Describe how you would realistically differentiate unit assignments in your subject-matter major to meet the individual differences likely to be found in a typical class.

---

[47]Faunce and Munshaw, *Teaching and Learning in Secondary Schools*, pp. 350–351, expand on the need to not make marks ends in themselves.

4. List five procedures that should be avoided in teaching slow learners. Explain your reasoning.

5. List five important administrative provisions for meeting individual differences among students.

6. Do you believe that students in your subject-matter minor should be grouped homogeneously? Defend your position.

7. Describe five different ways in which you could use in-class groupings to differentiate instruction.

8. Assumption: Patty has an I.Q. of 125 but poor muscular coordination. In which subjects is she most likely to be successful. In which will she be likely to encounter difficulty? Why?

9. Is remedial teaching necessary in a homogeneously grouped class of bright students? Explain.

10. In you teaching major, which concepts are most likely to require remedial teaching?

11. What is the relationship between a culturally impoverished environment and the need for remedial teaching?

12. Describe the special materials you would need in conducting an effective program of remedial teaching in your subject-matter major.

13. Assumption: You are teaching a student whose reading level is three grades below that of the average student in the class. How would this probably affect his achievement? What steps would you take to help this student?

14. What is the fundamental purpose in grading students? Explain.

15. List five advantages of using descriptive statements in reporting student progress.

16. Write a brief paragraph that summarizes your philosophy about marks and marking.

17. Explain each of the following statements: (1) All grades are relative. (2) Teachers tend to discriminate against certain types of students in grading. (3) Different ability groupings within the same school complicate marking.

18. What grading factors in addition to academic achievement should be considered in reporting progress to parents? Defend you position.

19. Assumption: You have the responsibility for teaching two homogeneously grouped classes, one of low ability and one of high ability. Should students in these classes be marked in relationship to a fixed standard or in relationship to other students in their individual groups? Explain.

16. *Consistent Improvement in Instruction*

The knowledgeable instructor is aware of the need for consistently and specifically improving instruction as a means of upgrading student achievement. The beginning teacher generally has a particular need for bettering himself, and the conscientious experienced teacher is often plagued by a vivid awareness of his own deficiencies. However, the type of improvement occasioned by intermittent guilt feelings at not having done a better job or characterized by sporadic attempts to improve is not the kind of improvement that produces the true professional.

Attaining instructional excellence is a complicated process. The teacher must have a basic command of his subject matter. He must keep abreast of his field and be able to communicate his knowledge effectively to others at their level of comprehension. He must have a thorough acquaintance with psychological principles and be able to make practical use of them in teaching. Above all, the teacher must desire to improve. He would do well to devise, then follow, a carefully constructed plan for improvement. In a quest for betterment, consistency is a key concern. Without consistency, the teacher will soon find that the cumulative effect of his efforts is diminished, continuity is thwarted, and improvement moves forward at an unsteady pace.[1]

The individual instructor can develop his own program for self-improvement by:

Identifying what comprises effective teaching[2]
Identifying personal weaknesses in teaching
Establishing a systematic program of self-appraisal
Devising and identifying procedures that will lead to improvement
Using the suggestions of other professionals—teachers, supervisors, and administrators
Making effective use of student opinions
Identifying and using rating scales and other devices in self-appraisal
Appraising his subject-matter competence
Carefully analyzing his personality[3]
Appraising the effectiveness of his methods
Evaluating student-teacher relationships
Analyzing the effect of membership and participation in professional organizations
Recognizing the benefits of additional graduate work
Recognizing the benefits of additional types of in-service training

SPECIFIC PRACTICES FOR IMPROVING INSTRUCTION

Although most sincere teachers are interested in improving their instructional competence, only a minority of them, unfortunately, are willing to pay the price of *planned* improvement that calls for systematic evaluation by others; honest, structured self-appraisal; and consistent effort. This minority, however, has developed a wide range of successful improvement practices. An examination of several of these will be useful.

---

[1]Stressing the necessity for maintaining competence and becoming a better teacher, Robert D. Strom, *Psychology for the Classroom* (Englewood Cliffs, New Jersey: Prentice-Hall, Inc., 1969), chapter 3, provides a convincing chapter discussion on instructional improvement.

[2]Leonard H. Clark and Irving S. Starr, *Secondary School Teaching Methods*, 2d. ed. (New York: The Macmillan Company, 1967), p. 4, indicate that the central concern of instruction is to make desirable changes in student behavior.

[3]Robert W. Richey, *Planning for Teaching*, 4th ed. (New York: McGraw-Hill Book Company, 1968), pp. 57–62, describes the characteristics of the well-adjusted teacher.

Identifying Effective Teaching

The attempt to discover with scientific exactness what comprises effective teaching is a never ending quest.[4] During the past few years, for example, there have been repeated attempts to analyze teaching in order to establish a justifiable basis for merit pay. None of these efforts has resulted in a conclusive scientific statement concerning the precise nature of effective teaching. There is, however, general agreement among teachers and people concerned with teacher appraisal that certain characteristics are indispensable for an effective teacher:[5]

He is intelligent.
He is in command of his subject.
He knows how to communicate his subject to students.
He is able to establish and reach objectives.
He uses methods effectively.
He is able to modify student behavior.
He varies instruction to hold student interest and to allow for individual differences.
He understands and likes students.
He is able to motivate students.
He can accurately appraise student readiness for learning.
He plans effectively.
He has an effective teaching personality.

The relative importance of these traits poses a dilemma for those wishing to make an objective appraisal of instruction. Is it more important, for example, that a teacher be highly intelligent or that he be in command of his subject matter? Does a teacher's outgoing personality have a greater effect on student learning than does his careful planning? Although the relative importance of such characteristics is still to be discovered, *all* are important for effective teaching.

Inability of teachers and administrators to reach an agreement with respect to criteria employed in teacher evaluation has lead certain researchers to redirect their efforts. Circumventing personality and procedural approaches, they have employed a single criterion—pupil growth—as the measure of teacher effectiveness. At the University of California, Los Angeles, for example, a series of performance tests of teacher competence were developed.[6] One week prior to the evaluation teachers were given

---

[4]Renato Mazzei, "Desirable Tarits of Successful Teachers" *Journal of Teacher Education*, 2 (December 1951), pp. 291–294, provides a well-documented review of attempts to identify desirable teacher traits up to mid-century.

[5]The relationship between teacher characteristics and pupil learning is examined thoroughly in a careful treatment by Herbert J. Klausmeier and William Goodwin, *Learning and Human Abilities: Educational Psychology*, 2d. ed. (New York: Harper & Row, Publishers, 1966), chapter 5.

[6]W. James Popham, "The Performance Test: A New Approach to the Assessment of Teaching Proficiency," *Journal of Teacher Education*, 19 (Summer 1967), p. 218.

prespecified objectives and a range of activities from which plans for two weeks of instruction were developed. Pre- and post-testing of the pupils of specific teachers enabled researchers to determine pupil advancement toward goals sought during the period involved; no attempt was made to determine the relationship between teaching procedures and achievement gains.

Gaining Command of Content

Knowing that he can do relatively little to improve his basic capacity, the improvement-minded teacher turns to specific areas in which he can progress. A United States history teacher, for example, may discover that he is only partially in command of his subject. Identifying areas of weakness (the westward movement, for instance) will enable him to set up a specific program designed to round out his knowledge.

Occasionally teachers are confronted with the necessity for teaching subjects for which they have had limited preparation. In such cases, taking the necessary college courses is highly recommended. If this is impossible, a rigorous schedule of reading and self-instruction is indispensable.

Evaluating Methods

In order to determine whether he is communicating subject matter effectively to his students, the teacher is forced to examine his methods. He may find it helpful to ask himself the following questions:[7]

Do I use methods that move students directly toward desired educational goals?

Is my basic instructional concern the improvement of student behavior?

Do I use procedures that are varied to meet the needs of individual students?

Do I plan effectively for the use of specific methods?

Are the methods used appropriate to the type of goal sought?

Are too many or too few activities used?

Is there an appropriate balance between individual and group activities?

Are activities conducted in the most productive sequence?

Are the methods interesting to the majority of students?

When specific weaknesses in methodology are discovered, equally specific countermeasures should be taken. Reminders can be helpful in

---

[7]Alvin C. Eurich, *Reforming American Education: The Innovative Approach to Improving Our Schools and Colleges* (New York: Harper & Row, Publishers, 1969), chapter 5, discusses the "Innovative Approach to Teaching."

See Appendix B in the present text for an extensive list of questions to evaluate the adequacy of specific procedures.

meeting these weaknesses. For example, a talk with his supervisor made a teacher of junior high school English aware that a majority of his questions were directed to the upper 10 percent of his class. Acting in good faith, the teacher wrote a note to himself on a three-by-five card in large block letters: EQUAL TIME FOR ALL. This was kept on his desk for the next month as an ever present reminder of his deficiency.

Methods that are used most frequently should be subject to searching reappraisal. Because the teacher becomes subjectively attached to certain procedures, he may need the help of his colleagues in making an accurate appraisal. Five mathematics teachers in a large high school on the East Coast worked out, with the approval of the school administration, a reciprocal arrangement in which they observed the instruction of one other colleague for a full period at least once each month. Following each observation, the observer and the observed teacher met for a helpful exchange of ideas, many of which were directed toward improving methods.

Improving the Voice

The teacher's voice is often less effective than it could be.[8] Unattractive voices and speech patterns can result from speaking too loudly or too softly, using a monotonous tone, displaying speech idiosyncrasies, and using faltering speech.

Frequently the teacher has a high-pitched voice or a voice with a nasal quality that proves annoying to students and sets the stage for student mimicry. Occasionally a voice-conscious teacher speaks so softly or uses such deep tones that students think his speech affected, and communication is inhibited. The tone of some teachers' voices consistently implies criticism of the students and reveals unwarranted defensiveness. Student-teacher relationships cannot help but be negatively affected under such circumstances. Moreover, the teacher who raises his voice so that he can be heard in an unruly classroom is encouraging continued student misbehavior.

The ideal teacher's voice is one that serves as a useful aid in the instructional process. It is a voice that generally exudes warmth, friendliness, and enthusiasm but can, when occasion demands, project force and firmness that evoke student respect. It is a voice that is varied. But more than anything else, it is a voice that communicates enthusiasm for the subject and a general liking of and respect for students.

Many teachers have benefited from the analytical review of tape recordings of their class presentations, a device that can be both revealing and helpful. Others have learned to use their voices more effectively by taking speech classes in which they are encouraged to inject variety and color into their speech. Still others have solicited the criticism of an interested and competent fellow professional—usually another teacher or

---

[8]Richey, *Planning for Teaching*, pp. 58–59, makes specific recommendations for the improvement of the voice.

the supervisor—to make constructive comments after observing a class presentation. A combination of all three procedures has many advantages.

Making Use of Personality

Personality may be viewed as the dynamic organization of those traits and characteristic patterns of behavior that are unique to the individual. The effective use of a teacher's personality is essential in conducting most classroom activities. Personality projection aids teaching, for communication takes place between persons—even in the absence of the spoken word.

The teacher whose personality helps create and maintain a classroom environment in which students feel comfortable and want to learn is said to have a desirable teaching personality. Scientific examination of the teacher's personality, however, does not warrant the statement that the effective teacher possesses specific personality traits to a definite, known degree.[9] There is often a marked variation in personal characteristics among the many teachers rated as excellent. The teacher's adjustment to individual circumstances, the school, and the community may further modify his personality.

Numerous attempts have been made to provide personality checklists, rating scales, and other devices to assist the teacher in improving his personality.[10] Wellington and Wellington,[11] for example, provide a series of ten basic questions and subquestions aimed at helping the teacher discover his personality type. The authors assume that if the teacher is aware of the type of person he is, he can then employ his unique characteristics to the best advantage in teaching.

Many devices have been developed to enable the teacher to rate himself on such personality characteristics as helpfulness, approachability, friendliness, fairness, sincerity, etc. Batchelder, McGlasson, and Schorling[12] provide a checklist of ten basic questions, each with accompanying descriptive statements, that may be checked by the teacher. Other checklists might consist of several basic divisions of traits on which teachers can grade themselves.

---

[9]Myron Lieberman, *Education as a Profession* (Englewood Cliffs, New Jersey: Prentice-Hall, Inc., 1956), p. 255, criticizes the assumption that there is only one effective type of teaching personality.

[10]A useful "Self-Rating Scale for Determining Fitness for Teaching," is provided by *Ibid.*, pp. 134–135.

Wayne Dumas and Weldon Beckner, *Introduction to Secondary Education: A Foundations Approach* (Scranton, Pennsylvania: International Textbook Company, 1968), pp. 366–368, provide a "Guide for Teacher Appraisal" that may be used for teacher self-evaluation or for supervisory purposes.

[11]C. Burleigh Wellington and Jean Wellington, *Teaching for Critical Thinking: With Emphasis on Secondary Education* (New York: McGraw-Hill Book Company, 1960), pp. 311–312.

[12]Howard T. Batchelder, Maurice McGlasson, and Raleigh Schorling, *Student Teaching in Secondary Schools*, 4th ed. (New York: McGraw-Hill Book Company, 1964), pp. 289–291.

In spite of limited progress made in attempting to relate teacher personality to effective teaching,[13] few educators would deny that such a relationship exists. Consideration of others, ability to react quickly in emergencies, creativeness, intelligence, and willingness to defer judgment are qualities that should be periodically reappraised by the conscientious teacher. Admittedly, current research evidence may not enable the teacher to know the precise traits he should concentrate on, but those characteristics generally accepted as influencing teaching effectiveness will justifiably serve as the objects of attention until such evidence is presented.

Using Supervisory Help

The supervisor's role is a difficult one, because it involves both giving positive suggestions and encouragement and supplying essential criticism.[14] Many times, because of the delicate nature of his relationship to in-service teachers, the supervisor visits only at the teacher's request. Unfortunately, some conscientious teachers find it difficult or embarrassing to invite the supervisor in for a visit, even if they stand to derive considerable benefit. Supervisors as well as principals, who often engage in supervisory functions, respect the teacher who asks for assistance when it is needed. It is highly desirable to establish rapport that will enable such visits to be made without undue strain.

Another possible source of help is informal teacher discussions directed toward matters of common instructional concern. If rapport that permits an uninhibited exchange of ideas can be established, much practical benefit can be derived from frequent, frank discussions about methods, classroom control, teacher personality, and general classroom operation. New teachers, in particular, stand to benefit from the exchange of ideas with a helpful, experienced, and competent teacher.

Using Student Opinion

Secondary-school students are generally willing to comment uninhibitedly on the quality of the teacher's classroom performance if anonymity can be assured.[15] In six related minor studies in the Washington, D.C. area, students were asked to identify the characteristics of their most disliked secondary-school teachers.[16] Participants in the six studies seemed

---

[13]Lieberman, *Education as a Profession,* p. 239, correctly indicates that "the scientific study of personality is still in its infancy."

[14]Dumas and Beckner, *Introduction to Secondary Education,* pp. 334–335, identify some of the advantages of supervision as a means for improving instruction. Related problems are also singled out.

[15]Harry N. Rivlin, *Teaching Adolescents in Secondary Schools,* 2d. ed. (New York: Appleton-Century-Crofts, 1961), pp. 437–438, discusses different ways of using student opinion to help improve instruction.

[16]Sterling G. Callahan, "A Comparative Study of Student Dislikes Found in Teachers with Special Reference to the Secondary Level" (unpublished master's thesis, George Washington University, 1947).

to feel that a weak personality is the most typical characteristic of the poor teacher. The following negative traits, listed in order of frequency, were mentioned by students as characteristic of their most disliked teachers:[17]

Ridiculed, was sarcastic
Was partial to certain
   students
Was unsympathetic toward
   students
Had disagreeable personality
Unreasonable
Narrow-minded
Threatened and frightened
   students
Unkind

Impatient, always wanted
   to hurry students
Did not understand the
   problems of students
Did not make students
   want to do more
Old-fashioned in appear-
   ance and thought
Was domineering
Had no sense of humor
Rude

Useful Procedures

Many different procedures are used to obtain students' opinions about the teacher's strengths and weaknesses. Checklists covering a range of possible teacher traits (fairness, scholarship, ability to put subject over, likableness, effectiveness in use of methods, and interest in students) are often provided students at the end of a semester or long unit of work. The students are asked to rate the teacher's traits as outstanding, very good, satisfactory, poor, or very poor. Some checklists also have a number of blank spaces in which students may insert additional teacher traits or make specific comments.

Another appraisal device is less elaborate. Students are asked to list on a blank sheet of paper what they liked most about the teacher and the class instruction. On a separate sheet they are asked to enumerate the teacher characteristics and instructional procedures most disliked. Be cause of the extreme diversity of responses, however, this procedure does not lend itself easily to tabulation. The combination of a checklist and free response appears to have the greatest advantage, especially if responses are tabulated and processed so that they can be of maximum use to the teacher.

Because anonymity must be assured to encourage honest responses, students are told not to sign their names and are encouraged to disguise their handwriting so that individuals cannot be identified. Some teachers have found it advisable to ask for responses only after report cards have been made out as a guarantee that responses will not reflect the students' hopes for higher grades.

Advantages of Tabulation

When tabulation of student responses is possible, a helpful picture of major likes and dislikes emerges that may be used advantageously by the

[17]*Ibid.*, pp. 208–209.

teacher to improve his personality and his classroom instruction. Because they have similar values, students tend to think alike about teacher traits. For example, when a teacher has asked students in his five sections of English (approximately 150 students) to give him the benefit of their reactions to his teaching and personality, he may discover that over one hundred of them feel that he is *unfair*. What *he* may personally feel about his being unfair is of secondary importance in establishing student-teacher rapport, for a large majority of his students honestly feel that he is unfair. The teacher could help establish better rapport by taking steps to improve his image in the eyes of his students.

Making the Improvement Program Systematic

The pious desire to improve is a far cry from the fulfillment of that wish. Although the wish itself is a beginning, it must be followed by a period of conscientious planning and implementation of plans. Of basic concern is a systematic program. The following questions related to improvement should be answered specifically:

Exactly what self-appraisal can I and should I undertake? How often should I evaluate specific procedures?

Which of my fellow professionals are best suited to provide the type of criticism I need? Can I establish specific times to avail myself of their help?

How can I employ student opinions in a practical way to help me improve? How often and under what circumstances should student opinions be sought? What devices should be used in obtaining their opinions?

Which professional organizations afford the greatest promise of helping me improve?

What type of in-service help is offered by my school district? How and when can I obtain this help?

What graduate courses do I need to round out my professional and subject-matter competence?

When these inquiries have been answered through careful study, the teacher is in a position to outline the precise steps he should take in his improvement program.

Affiliating with Professional Organizations

Many organizations in professional education were established for the prime purpose of helping teachers improve,[18] and they often cater to special needs and interests. Every subject-matter area in the secondary-school curriculum is at present represented by one or more national

18The advantages of professional affiliation, especially for beginning teachers, are stressed by E. Dale Davis, *Focus on Secondary Education: An Introduction to Principles and Practices* (Glenview, Illinois: Scott, Foresman and Company, 1966), p. 275.

organizations. With few exceptions these organizations function as departments within the National Education Association. Among these are the Music Educators National Conference, National Council for the Social Studies, National Council of Teachers of Mathematics, National Science Teachers Association, and the Speech Association of America.

Each of these organizations publishes its own periodical, usually at monthly intervals throughout the school year, and many of them also publish a yearbook that reflects current findings in their own particular field. Professional growth is encouraged through consistent reading of such national publications.

At the national conventions held by these professional groups, members have the opportunity to hear from leaders in their respective fields and to exchange ideas in small groups. The state and local organizations often afford the opportunity for active participation in stimulating projects. Many teachers hold membership in professional organizations at the national, state, and local levels and maintain a degree of activity at all levels.

Pursuing Graduate Work

Any honest self-appraisal reveals some teacher weaknesses in methodology, personal behavior, and subject-matter competence. Fortunately, these deficiencies may be overcome through effective study in carefully selected graduate courses.[19] So great has been the faith of state boards of education in the value of additional graduate work that the renewal of teaching certificates is generally granted only upon completion of a specified number of graduate hours.[20]

A desirable procedure in selecting graduate work involves first identifying the areas of greatest deficiency and then selecting those courses that provide the needed help. Although course work can help the teacher keep informed of current developments in his subject matter and methodology, certain teachers have unfortunately rejected this opportunity and have selected classes that afforded easy credit.

PRINCIPLES RELATED TO INSTRUCTIONAL IMPROVEMENT

Because the principles related to the improvement of instruction are so numerous, only the most relevant ones are singled out for discussion here.

1. A well-planned program of self-appraisal, which calls for the systematic examination of instructional practices at specified intervals, is

---

[19]Dumas and Beckner, *Introduction to Secondary Education*, p. 346, point out that several states now require the completion of a fifth year of professional study as a basis for receiving the standard secondary school teaching certificate.

[20]Certain state boards of education will accept undergraduate credit toward certificate renewal but usually with the stipulation that the undergraduate hours exceed the graduate hours otherwise required.

superior to general, haphazard self-evaluation. The competent teacher views himself as a learner who must identify his own weaknesses and take positive action to correct them. He employs various devices, such as carefully constructed scales, in his self-evaluation.[21] Furthermore, the teacher makes use of frank student appraisal of his instruction and personality as clues to self-improvement.

2. Development of skill in the evaluation of learning is essential in improving teaching. By improving his instruction the teacher improves his ability to help students reach educational goals.[22]

3. The generally accepted minimum level of instructional competence is far from the ideal,[23] and the conscientious teacher continuously seeks to surpass this minimum level.

4. The conscientious study of how other teachers have improved their teaching serves as a great aid to an instructor. Because he is professionally oriented, he learns how to make the most effective professional use of his supervisors, administrators, and fellow teachers. Such a teacher is also aware that the basic concern of in-service training is the improvement of instruction. He knows how to take advantage of well-organized and well-conducted faculty meetings, and he attends workshops that enable him to investigate specific instructional problems under the supervision of specialists. Informal study groups composed of teachers often provide practical assistance. Similarly, demonstrations by other teachers evoke interest and encourage professional growth.

5. Maintaining currency with respect to innovative instructional practices cannot be achieved through reading alone. Forward-looking teachers identify promising new practices throughout their states, regions, and the nation. If opportunities for visiting the scenes of experimental projects are lacking, they organize groups of similarly interested teachers to make such trips possible. Here they can view and hear firsthand information about the strengths and weaknesses of specific programs.

6. Teachers cannot teach effectively unless they possess a thorough knowledge of their subject matter. Reading carefully selected books and periodicals helps them keep abreast of developments in their fields and related methods. Active membership in professional organizations can provide encouragement for improved teaching, while graduate study serves as a helpful aid to professional growth, especially if it follows or accompanies teaching experience. Professional writing based upon experience or research promotes individual growth.

7. Skill in the use of teaching procedures is fundamental to teaching

[21]John D. McNeil, "Antidote to a School Scandal," *Educational Forum*, 31 (November 1966), pp. 69–77, identifies several problems in the tendency of evaluators to react to instruction in terms of their own value systems. From the point of view of subjectivity, self-evaluation is doubly vulnerable.

[22]Clark and Starr, *Secondary School Teaching Methods*, pp. 98–102, discuss the close relationship between effective goal selection by the teacher and goal achievement by the student.

[23]John Walton, *Toward Better Teaching in the Secondary School* (Boston: Allyn & Bacon, Inc., 1966), pp. 60–62, stresses the wide variety in social, academic, and economic backgrounds a beginning teacher may expect to find among his colleagues.

success. Continuous improvement in the selection, production, and use of materials thus contributes to better instruction.

8. Efficient teacher growth is related to intellectual alertness; a constantly improving teacher maintains good mental health.

9. The teacher can evaluate progress toward instructional efficiency only if he is well informed about the qualities that compose such efficiency.

10. Desired improvement in teaching does not necessarily come as a result of experience.

11. Employing superintendents tend to stress the prospective teacher's personality.[24] Thus it is important to be aware of certain traits that need improvement.

12. The effective teacher is interested in and expresses concern for individual students.

13. Carefully organized classroom experimentation designed to improve instruction may motivate students as well as the teacher.

CORRECT AND INCORRECT PRACTICES

Incorrect Practices

The following examples describe a range of ineffective practices aimed at instructional improvement.

MISS NATHAN ESTABLISHES UNREALISTIC GOALS

Afton Nathan was a perfectionist. When she completed college and took a position in a large urban junior high school, she vowed that she would be the best teacher in the school before the year was over. After she had had an opportunity to survey the qualities of the fifty-five teachers in the school, she realized that she had established a formidable goal for herself.

Miss Nathan planned her program for self-improvement with great care and carried it out as effectively as she could. She selected and used self-evaluation devices, solicited student opinions, and sought the help of her professional colleagues.

By the end of the school year, she was quite a different person from the neophyte teacher who had undertaken her first paid teaching position just nine months before. She had made substantial gains in self-confidence and in her ability to teach; but, as she evaluated the classroom

---

[24]Robert D. Strom and Charles Galloway, "Becoming a Better Teacher," *Journal of Teacher Education*, 18 (Fall 1968), pp. 285–292, stress the assumption that the attempt to identify the "good" teacher has failed because a single set of criteria has been employed. They find the use of multiple criteria giving consideration to the unique characteristics of individual teachers to be more in keeping with current teacher-competency research trends.

performances of the four or five teachers with reputations for outstanding teaching, she realized that she fell far short of their achievement.

MR. STORRS FAILS TO PLAN FOR IMPROVEMENT

For the third time in seven years of teaching, Arthur Storrs found himself in a new teaching situation. He was aware that he had many deficiencies as a teacher, for his infrequent contacts with supervisors and supervising principals had left him with the definite impression that his classroom performance was below average. Furthermore, many students made no attempt to hide their dislike for Mr. Storrs and his teaching procedures.

But Mr. Storrs was a stubborn individual; he refused to be driven out of teaching. After all, he had his pride, and no principal or supervisor was going to tell him how to run his class. He knew that it was absolutely essential that he improve his classes and he wanted to improve, but what could he do?

MR. SEARLE VIOLATES STUDENT ANONYMITY

Shortly before grades were issued at the close of each semester, John C. Searle asked his students to evaluate him and his teaching. Students were simply told to write a paragraph about the teacher and a paragraph about his teaching techniques, indicating what they liked or disliked. All statements were signed.

Mr. Searle was most gratified with student responses. Only a few widely dispersed statements hinted at deficiencies. He was particularly pleased that the four boys in the third-period class who were consistent troublemakers had so many fine things to say about him.

Although Miss Nathan's desire to make rapid improvement was commendable, her perfectionism was unrealistic. The process of ripening into a mature, thoroughly efficient teacher is not accomplished in one or two years; it requires continuing effort over a long period of time. Mr. Storrs accomplished little by his defensive approach to his problems. With the active help of well-meaning supervisors, he could have charted a gradual, yet practical approach to the improvement of his teaching. Desire alone was not sufficient. Mr. Searle could not hope for honest responses from his students without insuring anonymity, and because of the varied nature of student comments, it was impossible to tabulate them effectively for more efficient use. Furthermore, students were asked to evaluate the teacher at a time when they might feel that their responses could have a bearing on their forthcoming grades.

Correct Practices

Some more promising procedures used by teachers in attempting to improve their teaching are illustrated in the following examples.

MR. MELVIN PLANS EFFECTIVELY

At the close of his second year as a mathematics teacher at Richards High School, Mr. Melvin made several disconcerting observations with respect to his professional achievement. His growth was at a standstill, and he wondered for some time whether he should remain in teaching. His grasp of subject matter was entirely inadequate. Furthermore, he felt lost when other teachers began to talk about the values of programed learning, team teaching, and the newer developments in education.

After considerable introspection, Mr. Melvin decided that he would stay in teaching but that, in order to make it interesting for himself and beneficial to his students, he would have to make some marked improvements. Over a period of several weeks, he thought through and spelled out a specific program that he felt would lead to continued betterment:

1. He would go to the state university during the summer term, and he knew precisely which three courses he would take: Programed Learning, Behavior Problems in the Secondary School, and a rigorous undergraduate course in mathematics.

2. For the next school year he would plan his units and daily lessons with particular care. At the completion of each lesson and unit he would write an informal appraisal, pointing out strengths and weaknesses.

3. He would join the National Council of Teachers of Mathematics and read **The Mathematics Teacher** regularly for useful hints. Furthermore, he would take an active part in the work of his own local professional organization.

4. He would ask the district supervisor, Mr. Burnham, to visit his classes approximately once each month and to set aside time to discuss various problems that arose in the classroom.

5. He would ask Mr. Long, the principal, to make an occasional visit to his class and to then react privately to his teaching methods and effectiveness.

6. He would attempt to get the three other mathematics teachers to set aside one hour each week to discuss common problems related to the teaching of mathematics.

7. Toward the end of September he would use an extensive checklist to rate himself with respect to characteristics essential to successful teachers. This process would be repeated again in April as a basis for comparison.

8. He would administer a standardized mathematics achievement test to all students during the first two weeks of the school year. During the final week of the school year he would administer another form of the same test. Grade level gains—or losses—in mathematics would be evidence of his competence or lack of competence as a teacher.

9. As a continuing check on his teaching efficiency, Mr. Melvin would use a range of evaluation devices to determine the progress made by students during the development of each unit.

10. At the end of each nine-week report-card period, he would ask students to rate him anonymously on twenty-three teacher characteristics. Each successive student rating would be compared with earlier

ratings. He would rate himself and compare his evaluation with those of his students.

11. At the end of each day, he would analyze his teaching performance by means of a duplicated checklist and assign himself a letter grade.

Mr. Melvin charted a rigorous program of improvement for himself, but he realized that if his carefully laid plans were not carried out, his professional advancement might be thwarted.

MR. OSTLER'S TEACHERS VISIT A LARGE SCHOOL

Over a period of three years Alton Ostler, a rural secondary-school supervisor, had established a rapport with his teachers that was the envy of surrounding school districts. Through joint discussion, he and his teachers decided that a visit to a large high school located in a city thirty miles away would be both interesting and rewarding. As a result, arrangements were made to observe the instruction of competent teachers in the large school.

Scheduled visits were made during seven months of the school year. English teachers observed English teachers, mathematics teachers observed mathematics teachers, etc. Provision was also made for the visiting teacher to have an opportunity to discuss classroom procedures with the observed teacher. By the end of the school year, every teacher in the rural school had at least one opportunity to observe excellent teaching by his subject-matter counterpart in the large school. A rich accumulation of ideas was taken back to the school to share with other teachers.

Next year Mr. Ostler hopes to visit innovative junior and senior high schools throughout the state with separate groups of teachers. Traveling in one car, interested colleagues may find pre- and post-visitation discussions most useful. On the tentative agenda are visits to eight different progressive schools where among other innovations the following can be observed: Use of PLATO, the University of Illinois contribution to computer-assisted instruction; use of student help in televising and recording tapes for immediate instructional benefit; use of a three-teacher team to teach mathematics to a large group of nongraded senior high school students using a range of programed materials; and the use of several subject-matter library-study centers supervised by librarians with a teaching major in the subject of concern.

SPECIFIC SUGGESTIONS

Although the conscientious teacher may be equipped with a storehouse of principles related to instructional evaluation, he is still confronted with this question: "What specific steps can I take to improve my teaching?" The suggestions below are designed to help answer this question.

Recommendations

1. Find out how respected educational psychologists define effective teaching; then evaluate yourself according to their standards.

2. Start improving your instruction as soon as you begin to teach, and continue to improve throughout your teaching career.[25]

3. List in specific, written form the steps you will take to improve your teaching; then carry them out.

4. Identify your most pronounced instructional weaknesses and work on overcoming them.[26] Make use of carefully constructed rating scales in identifying your weaknesses.

5. Recognize your strengths as well as your weaknesses. Using a personality inventory of known validity and reliability, analyze your own personality. Determine the frequency with which you should use such a device.

6. Identify the people who can be of greatest assistance to you in improving your instruction; then seek their help. Have frequent and frank chats with your supervisor and principal about your instructional competence. Establish a friendly relationship with colleagues who teach the same subject, and discuss professional problems with them often.[27]

7. Promote and support in-service training that will lead to professional improvement. Help organize and participate in informal study groups within your school, and arrange to see demonstrations of superior teaching.[28]

8. Be inventive in developing and implementing procedures for keeping up-to-date with respect to attractive, promising methods such as programed learning, computer-assisted instruction, interaction analysis, and the various forms of individualized instruction.

9. Devise specific procedures for making the most effective use of student opinions about your personality and teaching competence. If written opinions are solicited, student anonymity must be assured.

---

[25]Nathan S. Blount and Herbert J. Klausmeier, *Teaching in the Secondary School,* 3d. ed. (New York: Harper & Row, Publishers, 1968), p. 556, emphasize the need for experimenting with recent innovations as a means of professional improvement.

[26]According to Roland C. Faunce and Carroll L. Munshaw, *Teaching and Learning in Secondary Schools* (Belmont, California: Wadsworth Publishing Co., Inc., 1965), p. 423, self-evaluation is the first step teachers should take on the road to professional improvement.

[27]In no teaching situation is the necessity for the exchange of professional ideas more pronounced than in the instructional team. David W. Beggs, III, ed., *Team Teaching: Bold New Ventures* (Indianapolis, Indiana: Unified College Press, Inc., 1964), chapters 4, 5, and 11, provides a number of examples that point up the need for this exchange.

[28]Leroy H. Griffith, Nelson L. Haggerson, and Delbert Weber, *Secondary Education Today* (New York: David McKay Co., Inc., 1967), pp. 273–274, stress the value of district-level and school-level meetings as playing a vital role in a continuing teacher education program.

Ben M. Harris, Wailand Bessent, and Kenneth E. McIntyre, *In-Service Education: A Guide to Better Practice* (Englewood Cliffs, New Jersey: Prentice-Hall, Inc., 1969), pp. 245–252, provide a thorough discussion of the value of demonstrations in an in-service education program.

10. Examine carefully your own subject-matter competence in your teaching major and minor. Take a graduate course aimed at professional improvement at least once every other year.

11. Evaluate the methods you use in terms of their helpfulness in moving students toward desired educational goals. Use a carefully planned checklist to measure the effectiveness of your teaching procedures. In the attempt to improve, experiment with assignments, grouping, testing techniques, and programed learning.[29]

12. At least once very six months read a challenging new professional book.[30] Become active in the national and local professional organizations most closely related to your teaching major.

13. Write a brief evaluation of each unit taught. Determine the effectiveness of your use of teaching aids as a part of this evaluation. Provide a space on your daily lesson plan form for evaluating how well the lesson was taught and how improvements could be made.

14. Appraise your enthusiasm for teaching, particularly for units in areas of limited preparation. Be aware of how the learner will be affected by your attitude toward the unit.

15. At the close of each day ask yourself: "How well did I teach today? What did I do wrong that I can improve tomorrow?"

16. Evaluate your personal relationship with each student at least once during each report-card period.

17. Make a systematic evaluation of your mental health yearly.[31]

18. Compare the picture of the teacher you are with the picture of the teacher you feel you should be.

Cautions

1. Don't postpone establishing and following a personal, well-planned program of instructional evaluation and improvement.

2. Don't view a single aspect of instructional evaluation as comprising a program.

3. Don't make plans that cannot be carried through.

4. Don't seek the help of incompetent teachers.

5. Don't spend an unjustified amount of time in worrying about your instructional deficiencies.

---

[29]Walton, *Toward Better Teaching in the Secondary School*, pp. 105–106, suggests that the prime consideration in the selection of any method is its potential for helping students achieve goals efficiently. However, beyond this point, he states that opportunities for the exercise of teacher preference exist.

Sidney P. Rollins and Adolph Unruh, *Introduction to Secondary Education* (Chicago: Rand McNally & Co., 1964), pp. 181–182, indicate that freedom to experiment is an essential part of a sound in-service training program.

[30]Clark and Starr, *Secondary School Teaching Methods*, pp. 459–460, stress the need for professional reading as one means of keeping abreast of the profession.

[31]Lieberman, *Education as a Profession*, pp. 234–238, provides a well-documented discussion of the mental health of teachers.

PROBLEMS FOR STUDY AND DISCUSSION

1. Describe the difference between a carefully constructed plan for the improvement of instruction and a general desire to improve. Give examples.

2. How important is consistency in improving instruction? Give two examples of teachers who were inconsistent in attempting to improve.

3. Suggest five ways to identify personal weaknesses in your teaching.

4. In fifteen to twenty brief statements, describe the qualities that you feel are characteristic of the effective teacher.

5. Describe in some detail a systematic and practical program for instructional improvement that would extend throughout a full school year.

6. Identify and assign rank order to four innovative procedures you feel would help you to improve your teaching.

7. Assumption: You are teaching in a consolidated high school in which there are fifteen teachers. Indicate exactly how you would make use of your school principal in attempting to improve your instruction during your first year of teaching.

8. If you had to choose between excellence in subject-matter knowledge and excellence in the use of instructional procedures, which would you choose? Why? Explain in detail.

9. List six practical procedures for helping you gain better command of your subject.

10. Without consulting the text, list ten relevant questions to use in appraising your teaching methods.

11. Assumption: You teach in a school district that has a general secondary-school supervisor. Although you have not encountered particular difficulty in your teaching, you are anxious to accelerate your rate of improvement. Tell exactly how you would use the supervisor to accomplish this end.

12. Describe in a brief paragraph the ideal voice for teaching. Now rate your own voice, using the descriptive paragraph as a measuring device.

13. Appraise your teaching personality by means of one of the checklists or devices mentioned in this chapter. What are your chief personality weaknesses? What steps can you take to overcome them?

14. What are the advantages of teacher self-evaluation as opposed to evaluation by others? Explain.

15. Name ten cautions to be observed in the use of student evaluation of the teacher.

16. Describe at least three different devices that could be used for student evaluation of teachers. Which do you find most helpful? Why?

17. What is the advantage of being able to tabulate student reactions to the teacher?

18. List the three professional organizations at the local, state, or national levels that would be of greatest help in furthering your professional growth.

19. Identify five professional and subject-matter courses that you can and should take in order to insure growth and overcome deficiencies.

20. Outline a specific program of professional reading aimed at your instructional improvement.

PART FIVE

Recent Developments in Teaching

17. *Programed Instruction*

Few educational developments throughout history have captured the fancy of professional educators and the general public as has programed instruction. Its promise of accelerating learning, its relationship to mechanization, its fascinating novelty—all have invested programed learning with an allure that makes an objective appraisal especially difficult. However, use of programed textbooks is outdistancing any other educational innovation, and the school not using some form of programed materials will soon be the exception. Currently over 5,000,000 schools are using programed materials.[1]

DEFINITION OF PROGRAMED INSTRUCTION

A definition of programed instruction generally acceptable to psychologists and educators a decade ago is no longer relevant. A current

---

[1]Allen D. Calvin, ed., *Programmed Instruction: Bold New Venture* (Bloomington, Indiana: Indiana University Press, 1969), p. 37.

definition must give broad consideration to several possible teaching media: the teacher himself, a programed text, a tape-slide offering, a teaching machine using microfilm, a carefully planned series of self-directed student activities, a computer-assisted presentation, or skillfully combined procedures representing an instructional system. Reflecting needed breadth, authors of a popular text define programed instruction as "a planned sequence of experiences, leading to proficiency, in terms of stimulus-response relationships."[2]

Although instructional experiences may consist of a human voice, a recorded message, a photograph, a motion picture, or a typewritten message; the most frequently used learning experience associated with programing takes the form of a printed frame—usually a short paragraph or sentence containing a brief instructional message and a related question (often placed in a rectangular box) calling for student response. A series of such interrelated frames is called a *program*. The program—presented by book, teaching machine, or computer—leads the student through a body of materials in small steps.[3]

The learner sees a stimulus (frame), responds to it, and receives an immediate indication of whether his answer is correct or incorrect. Thus the psychological concerns of *stimulus, response,* and *reinforcement* are an integral part of programed instruction.

During the past few years programs have been adopted with increasing frequency in schools concerned with individualizing instruction, and the term *programed instruction* has become widely used in the educational community. *Automated teaching, auto-instruction, machine teaching,* and *computer-assisted instruction* (CAI) are variant terms, all referring to instruction that requires the use of programed (systematically organized and presented) materials. The tendency to use the phrase *computer-assisted instruction* as synonymous with programed instruction is misleading; presentation by computer is by no means essential to programed instruction. It represents only one of several devices and procedures adapted to help students achieve proficiency through sequentialized, stimulus-response-reinforcement learning.[4]

Programed learning that follows the procedures introduced by B. F. Skinner has several characteristics:[5]

---

[2]James E. Espich and Bill Williams, *Developing Programmed Instructional Materials: A Handbook for Program Writers* (Palo Alto, California: Fearon Publishers, 1967), p. v.
James W. Brown, Richard B. Lewis, and Fred F. Harcleroad, *AV Instruction: Media and Methods,* 3d. ed. (New York: McGraw-Hill Book Company, 1969), p. 111, state that "programed instruction is coming to be regarded as a means of allowing students to achieve important instructional objectives *without* the teacher's intervention as a 'dispenser of knowledge.'"
[3]Several examples of partial programs and related frames are illustrated in this chapter.
[4]*Innovation in Education: New Directions for the American School* (New York: Committee for Economic Development, 1968), pp. 55–57, describes the nature of programed instruction and computer-assisted instruction.
[5]Although non-Skinnerian programs are widely used (see pages 346–349), Skinner-type programs account for a large majority of those currently in use.

Fig. 1.   Sample frames on the nature of programing.

1. In a programmed text, the educational material is broken up into small portions called <u>frames</u>. If you read these carefully you will be able to fill in any gaps in the <u>frames</u>. You are now reading the first fr_____ of a specimen program.   (fr)ame

2. Each frame involves some question, or several questions, or blanks to fill in. The whole collection of frames makes up the program or _____med text.   program(med)

3. If all students of a programmed text have to go through all the _____ , we call this a <u>linear program</u>. The other kind of program is called a <u>branching program.</u> When some students read different parts of a program from others, we call this a _____program.   branching
linear/branching

4. The contents of a programmed text, which we call the _____ , could be put onto a film or paper strip. A device for presenting this, one frame at a time, is called a <u>teaching machine.</u> This teaching machine is then, technically speaking, using the same _____ as a programmed text.   program

   program, material

5. Is this true or false: "A teaching machine in which all the students go through all the frames is using a <u>linear</u> program, by contrast with a <u>branching</u> program."   true

1. The content to be learned is organized in a sequence designed to promote optimum learning.

2. The learner is required to respond actively to the content presented.

3. He is given an immediate indication of whether his response is correct or incorrect.

4. He advances by small steps through the content.

5. The content is organized to provide a preponderance of correct responses.

6. The learner starts at his own level of comprehension and moves gradually and systematically toward the desired objectives.

A five-frame illustrative linear program concerned with teaching students a limited number of basic programing concepts is presented in Figure 1.[6] The column on the right-hand side of the page should be

---

[6]From *Programmed Instruction: Bold New Venture*, edited by Allen D. Calvin. Copyright © 1969 by Indiana University. Reprinted by permission of Indiana University Press.

covered with a card or paper until the student has read and responded to each frame. After student response, the card should be moved down until the correct answer is revealed. Immediate reinforcement is thus provided.

Psychologists generally restrict the definition of programed instruction to include those materials and devices that (a) provide a stimulus, (b) call for the learner's response, and (c) provide for reinforcement of the response. This definition has been helpful in establishing precise and meaningful communication among educators. According to this definition certain mechanical devices and printed materials—for example, the reading pacer and the workbook—cannot be categorized as programed instructional materials, since, while they possess some, they do not have all of these characteristics.

Recent emphasis on behavioral outcomes has encouraged programers to intensify efforts to design programs leading to measurable increased proficiency. Further, educators have often indicated that without the evidence of improved student behavior, one method is no better than another. Therefore, some educators have insisted upon reference to behavioral gains in the definition of programed instruction.

HISTORY OF PROGRAMED INSTRUCTION

The assumption that experimentation in programed learning originated during the 1950's belies the facts. Teaching by machine—one aspect of programed learning—began prior to the Depression.[7]

Early Experiments

Sidney L. Pressey, a noted psychologist, is credited with having focused attention on the possibility of teaching through the use of machines during the late 1920's. He produced a machine that called for student responses to multiple-choice items. The student was required to press answer buttons numbered to correspond to multiple-choice test items. If the correct response was selected, the machine automatically moved to the next question; if an incorrect response was selected, the error was mechanically noted, and the student had to make additional responses until he selected the correct one.

Pressey noted that devices such as this could actually teach, since the student was provided with an immediate knowledge of correct and incorrect responses. In addition, students of varying abilities and achievement could move at their own pace. Although Pressey's early enthusiasm did not result in an immediate move toward the mechanization of

---

[7]A list of patents for educational devices issued by the U.S. Patent Office from the turn of the century until 1930 is provided by I. Mellan, "Teaching and Educational Inventions;" *Journal of Experimental Education*, 4 (March 1936), pp. 291–300. Although patent numbers are listed, the devices are not described.

instruction, it helped point the way. In 1932, after suffering several defeats in his attempts to obtain adequate financing and engineering assistance, Pressey announced that he was abandoning further work on his project.[8]

Mid-Century Interest

In 1954 B. F. Skinner redirected attention to the possibilities inherent in the use of teaching machines.[9] His ideas circulated widely among psychologists and educators, reawakening interest in systematic self-instruction. From that time on, programed instruction received widespread publicity, both in professional journals and in popular magazines, and inspired experimental effort directed toward basic research as well as the production and use of teaching materials.

The initial favorable reaction led to many rash claims, including statements that:

1. The use of programed material would greatly reduce or do away with the need for teachers.

2. Conventional textbooks would be replaced by programed textbooks.

3. Students would be able to learn several times faster than the normal rate through the use of programed material.

Entranced with the possibility of relief from the drudgery of classroom drill, teachers grasped hopefully at the idea of mechanized instruction; and the military and private industry at home and abroad were quick to anticipate the possibility of accelerating training programs through the use of teaching machines. Various companies fed these hopes by hurrying unproven and improperly tested programs and devices into production. Even those who were sincerely interested in serving the cause of education through the new medium lost some of their objectivity in their zeal. "Ironically," as Schramm pointed out,[10]

> it might have been better for programed instruction if, at times during the beginning years, it could have been delivered from its friends. Its friends were sometimes too friendly, too full of enthusiasm to be critical, too absorbed in their own work to take a broad look at what was happening to programs, too close to developments to be good guides either for educators or for the public.

---

[8]B. F. Skinner, "Teaching Machines," *Science*, 128 (Oct. 24, 1958), pp. 969–977, provides an interesting account of Pressey's early contributions and the reasons for their limited acceptance.

Of significance is a more recent Pressey position in which he criticized both the theory and practice of programed learning. See Sidney L. Pressey, "A Puncture of the Huge 'Programing' Boom," *Teachers College Record*, 65 (1964), pp. 413–418.

[9]Skinner, "Teaching Machines," pp. 970–977, discusses in some detail the principles and implications involved in bringing about behavioral changes in experimental subjects.

[10]Wilbur Schramm, *Programed Instruction Today and Tomorrow* (New York: Fund for the Advancement of Education, 1962), p. 15.

Current Trends

The initial flurry of rash claims for programed instruction has given way to more careful examination of the facts. From the first, of course, experiments were carried out to test the validity of assumptions about the new teaching tool. Indeed, Schramm reported that approximately one hundred experiments had been conducted by November 1962.[11] But many of the early claims for programed instruction were based on experiments of short duration and limited coverage. Recent experiments tend to be longer, more solidly based, and more sharply focused.

The amount of repetition employed in programs is a matter of considerable controversy, and several studies have been set up to establish guidelines. Concern with the size of the learning step from one frame to the next has also led to extensive research, though conclusive answers have not yet been obtained. Another area of experimentation has centered on the question of whether overt responses produce results demonstrably superior to those achieved through covert responses. Of equal concern is the question of whether the *constructed* response, in which the student fills in a blank, or the *selected* response, in which he marks a multiple-choice item, is preferable as a learning method. Although immediate reinforcement is generally accepted as an essential feature of programed instruction, researchers thus far disagree as to what kinds and how much reinforcement are desirable.

Because of intense public interest, both the Federal government and national foundations have granted substantial sums for research on programed instruction. Much of this funding has been directed in recent years to one area—computer-assisted instruction (CAI). However, all branches of the military service have been active in encouraging general research on self-instructional devices. Unfortunately, much of this current effort is reported only in mimeographed form to a selected number of interested persons, and there is often a disturbing lapse of time before the results of such research appear in the professional journals and receive general distribution. Communication among researchers in the field has improved greatly, and with pointed reading nonspecialists are able to maintain partial currency.

Meanwhile, although the proliferation of "hardware" that accompanied the programing boom of the late 1950's has subsided, the production of programed materials can still be termed exploratory. This fact is evident in the development of several different kinds of programed texts and in the manufacture of a range of devices for presenting programs. Some programs are now available in text form and for use in machines, both with and without branching. In brief, there has been no commercial decision as to the "best" method of programing or of presenting programs.

---

[11]*Ibid.*, p. 11.

PROFESSIONAL REACTION TO PROGRAMED INSTRUCTION

Because of the impact of programed learning on the educational scene, questions are being asked that point up the hopes as well as the anxieties of teachers:

1. What are the strengths and limitations of programed instruction?
2. Will the emphasis on programed instruction influence curriculum structure and the involvement of teachers in curriculum development?
3. How can programed materials best be combined with conventional materials to promote optimum student learning?
4. To what extent will the use of programed instruction add to the impersonalization of teaching?
5. Can the use of programed materials be made to serve the needs of students with different characteristics—the dull as well as the bright, the nonself-directive as well as the self-directive?
6. How much influence will the computer have on the use of programed materials and what direction will it take?
7. What modifications in physical plant facilities are necessary to encourage efficient use of programed instructional materials?

The answers given by those most actively engaged in producing and using programed materials reflect the growing pains of more than a decade. Because past claims of unusual gains in student achievement were often made without adequate research or documentation, many educators developed a skepticism that programed instruction advocates found highly disturbing. Sensitive to criticism, these proponents have now developed a restraint more in keeping with objective research.

Limitations of Programed Instruction

Van Til, Vars, and Lounsbury enumerate several disadvantages to programed learning identified by classroom teachers:[12]

1. Despite the large and steadily increasing number of programs currently available, really effective ones are still relatively rare. Too many are dull, lifeless, uninteresting. Branching programs and those treating the same content on different levels of difficulty still are few in number. Moreover, manufacturers have only recently begun to publish the detailed information research and field testing that is needed to judge the suitability of a program for particular students.

---

[12]From *Modern Education for the Junior High School Years* by William Van Til, Gordon F. Vars, and John H. Lounsbury, copyright © 1961 and 1967 by The Bobbs-Merrill Company, Inc., reprinted by permission of the publisher.

2. Much time and money is required to develop programed materials. Few schools can afford to develop their own, and the purchase of commercially produced items likewise may be prohibitively expensive.

3. Heavy demands are placed upon the teacher who works with students studying individually via programed materials. At one moment he may be called upon to help a student with an elementary concept of arithmetic; five minutes later another student in the same room calls for help with a complex problem involving the theory of functions . . . .

4. Curriculum revision may be stimulated as a staff considers possible use of programed instruction. However, when once adapted, programed materials may have the opposite effect . . . .

5. By their nature, programs are closed systems of thought; creativity and divergent thinking are severely restricted. Even in branching programs, provision is seldom made for a student response that has not been anticipated by the programer . . . .

Oliva suggests the knowledgeable, restricted use of programed instruction:[13]

. . . Exclusive reliance on programed instruction runs the same risk as mass instruction or ill-used educational television. It makes the false assumption that the imparting of knowledge is all there is to education. It would be devastating and pedagogically unsound to subject learners to entire schedules of courses taught only by means of programed instruction.

Teachers should be wary of the programs which they purchase for use with students. The idea of self-instruction or automated learning has caught on with the public, who see in this an easy way, they believe, for their children to get a quick and painless education. The quality of programs runs from very poor to superior. Some are turned out in quick fashion to earn a fast dollar while the market is hot . . .

The writings of a substantial number of educators reflect the need for caution before blanket approval is accorded programed instruction. Their contention is that programed learning in its varied forms is only a tool to assist the instructor in more effective teaching. To impute magic to programed learning reveals an ignorance of what it is all about. It is a means, not an end; it is a device that has promise only when used knowledgeably and with care. Further, if the tool is poorly constructed, its potential for helping learners is limited at the outset.

---

[13]Peter F. Oliva, *The Secondary School Today* (New York: World Publishing Company, 1967), p. 118.

Advantages of Programed Instruction

Guarded optimism seems to characterize the thinking of many specialists currently working in this field. Other psychologists and educators, specifically less involved, have, however, maintained a critical awareness of new developments. The general feeling of this latter group is to withhold unqualified endorsement until research provides definitive answers to the many existing questions. Viewing programed instruction as one of several instructional strategies worthy of examination, McDonald supports Lumdaine's opinion "that the development of programed instruction is a useful model of an effective instructional strategy, which, if carefully studied, can be made more effective."[14]

The optimistic assumption of the early sixties that, under given circumstances, all segments of the curriculum might be programed, is now heard less frequently. Wide-ranging attempts to prepare programs in a large number of content areas have met with limited success in the less structured areas of literature and social studies. Highly successful programing has been largely restricted to compact, well-structured areas.

> Experimentation has established that programed techniques can be effective in teaching logic, mathematics, and languages; improving the capacity to recognize distinctions and alternatives; teaching reasons and explanations as well as conditioning for correct responses; providing for student independence in the choice of subject matter and goals as well as in the determination of learning speed; and cultivating high learning motivation in the student.[15]

Many other writers believe that programed instruction will help increase the efficiency of learning. They feel that the mounting complexity of modern education and industrial training requires the use of the most effective instructional procedures and devices to provide thorough education for an ever increasing number of students. The development of auto-instructional materials, based upon proven psychological principles, is an essential step in achieving this goal.

Readily admitting that a majority of teachers are less than enthusiastic about programed instruction, Gleason states that ". . . the overwhelming majority of teachers who try programed instruction are generally enthusiastic. The author has worked with hundreds of classroom teachers who have used programed instruction. In almost every instance, they expressed positive reactions to the *technique*, although not always to the particular program or the way in which it was used."[16]

---

[14]Frederick J. McDonald, *Educational Psychology*, 2d. ed. (Belmont, California: Wadsworth Publishing Co., Inc., 1965), p. 99.

[15]*Innovation in Education: New Directions for the American School*, p. 55.

[16]Gerald Gleason, "Will Programed Instruction Serve People?" *Educational Leadership*, 23 (1966), p. 477.

A helpful enumeration of the advantages of programed instruction is provided by Van Til and associates.[17]

1. Routine instruction, such as drill in spelling, foreign language vocabulary, or number combinations, may be provided by programs, freeing the teacher for the more creative aspects of teaching, especially those that require personal interaction between teacher and students.
2. As a tutor, a programed device is objective, impartial, and exhibits endless patience. (Yet criticism or a pep talk may be inserted if desired . . .)
3. The student's errors are made in private, not open to ridicule by his peers.
4. Each student goes through a program on his own, providing individualization in *pace* with linear programing, in both pace and content with branching programs. . . .
5. Appropriate programs may facilitate enrichment for the advanced student and remedial work for the less capable. . . .
6. Some programed devices maintain a continuous record of student performance. This gives the teacher information on which to base further individualized instruction. . . .
7. Before he can write a program or select from those already published, the teacher must formulate his teaching objectives in precise terms and analyze content in considerable detail. . . .
8. The importance of student success and immediate knowledge of results, stressed in programed instruction, may carry over into other instruction provided by the teacher. . . .

While still anticipating the possibilities of important changes, other proponents of programed instruction express the need for caution in predicting its effect on the total school operation. Although they are firm in their contention that significant changes in classroom procedures and teacher responsibilities will take place as a result of programed learning, they admit that it is difficult to predict how extensively this method will influence the procedures, staff, and plant facilities of school systems.

BASIC TYPES OF PROGRAMS

Two basic types of programs (linear and branching), bearing the names of their chief proponents, B. F. Skinner and Norman A. Crowder, have been used most frequently by educational programers. Each type appears to have particular advantages and should be examined separately.

[17]From *Modern Education for the Junior High School Years* by William Van Til, Gordon F. Vars, and John H. Lounsbury, copyright © 1961 and 1967 by The Bobbs-Merrill Company, Inc., reprinted by permission of the publisher.

Skinnerian Programing

The majority of programs currently being produced are developed according to the principles identified and used by B. F. Skinner.[18] It is his belief that progress toward specific goals should be made in very small steps in order to reduce the possibility of error and provide for a preponderance of successful responses. This belief is explained by one of Skinner's co-workers:[19]

> It is intended that the student be led through a series of carefully graded steps, none of which is too difficult to answer, yet each of which is slightly more difficult than the preceding one. This procedure, leading an organism to emit a response which is initially at low strength in his repertoire by reinforcing responses which more and more closely approximate the required one, is known in many laboratories as the reinforcement of successive approximations.

The use of small steps is illustrated in the frames in Figure 2, taken from a program based upon the principles employed by Skinner.[20] Notice that each successive correct response moves the student one step forward, in linear fashion, toward the ultimate desired comprehension of irregular verbs.

In these frames it should be observed that (1) the stimulus appears in the form of sequentially placed, numbered frames; (2) student response (inserting a word, checking a verb form, or matching verbs with one of two possible letters) is called for; and (3) reinforcement is provided by the correct answers in the right-hand column, exposed by a sliding shield after response.

Crowderian Programing

Norman A. Crowder has developed certain programed instructional techniques that vary somewhat from those of the Skinnerians. Crowder believed that individual differences in rate of progress and the optimum size of learning steps were not being adequately provided for in Skinnerian programs, and, like Pressey, he rejected the Skinnerian view that multiple-choice items were pedagogically unsound because they exposed

---

[18]A useful discussion of linear programing, its assertions and variations, is presented by Nathan S. Blount and Herbert J. Klausmeier, *Teaching in the Secondary School*, 3d. ed. (New York: Harper & Row, Publishers, 1968), pp. 304–317.

[19]Lloyd E. Homme, "The Rationale of Teaching by Skinner's Machines," in *Teaching Machines and Programmed Learning: A Source Book*, eds. Lumsdaine and Glaser (Washington, D. C.: National Education Association, 1960), p. 133.

[20]Reproduced with permission from *How to Use Programmed Instruction in the Classroom* by Dr. Robert E. Silverman, © 1967 by Bolt Beranek and Newman, Inc., Cambridge, Massachusetts.

Fig. 2.   Sample frames from a lesson on irregular verbs.

	Example A
6. In this program you will see why some verbs are more difficult to use than others, and you will learn to use some of the difficult verbs correctly.	NO ANSWER NEEDED
To begin, however, let's review some things that you probably already know about verbs.	

7. Most verbs have a number of different *forms*.	FIGHT
JUMPED is a form of the verb JUMP.	
SWAM is a form of the verb SWIM.	
FOUGHT is a form of the verb	

8. Different forms of a verb are used to show action at different times.	present
BOUNCE . . . BOUNCED . . . HAVE BOUNCED	past
BOUNCE shows (present/past) .... time.	
BOUNCED and HAVE BOUNCED show (present/past) .... time.	

9. There are names for the forms of verbs.	present
Present Past Past Participle	
BOUNCE BOUNCED HAVE BOUNCED	
The form that shows present time is called the	

	Example A
10. *Present Past Past Participle*	past
BOUNCE BOUNCED HAVE BOUNCED	past participle
The form that shows past time all by itself is called the	
The form that shows past time by using some form of HAVE or BE is called the	

11. *Present Past Past Participle*	ED
BOUNCE BOUNCED HAVE BOUNCED	are
JUMP JUMPED HAVE JUMPED	
These verbs have two things in common:	
1. The past and past participle forms of each verb end with the letters	
2. The past and past participle forms of each verb (are/are not) .... spelled the same way.	

12.
Verbs (like BOUNCE and JUMP) whose past and past participle forms end with ED are called *regular verbs*. Which of these is a regular verb?

Present	Past	Past Participle
DRINK	DRANK	HAVE DRUNK
CALL	CALLED	HAVE CALLED

CALL

13.
Verbs whose past and past participle forms do not end with ED are *irregular verbs*. Which of these is an irregular verb?

Present	Past	Past Participle
THINK	THOUGHT	HAVE THOUGHT
LOVE	LOVED	HAVE LOVED

THINK

Example A

14.
Make an R in front of the regular verbs in this list and make an I in front of the irregular verbs.

Present	Past	Past Participle
BREAK	BROKE	HAVE BROKEN
HURT	HURT	HAVE HURT
BARK	BARKED	HAVE BARKED
SWING	SWUNG	HAVE SWUNG
FILL	FILLED	HAVE FILLED

I. BREAK

I. HURT

R. BARK

I. SWING

R. FILL

5

the student to error. The following passage is his own description of "automatic tutoring by intrinsic programing":[21]

> The student is given the material to be learned in small logical units (usually a paragraph, or less, in length) and is tested on each unit immediately. The test result is used automatically to conduct the material that the student sees next. If the student passes the test question, he is automatically given the next unit of information and the next question. If he fails the test question, the preceding unit of information is reviewed, the nature of his error is explained to him, and he is retested. The test questions are multiple-choice questions. and there is a separate set of correctional materials for each wrong answer that is included in the multiple-choice alternative. The technique of using a student's choice of an answer to a multiple-choice question to determine the next material to which he will be exposed has been called "intrinsic programing."

---

[21]Norman A. Crowder, "Automatic Tutoring by Intrinsic Programming," in *Teaching Machines and Programmed Learning: A Source Book*, eds. Lumsdaine and Glaser (Washington, D. C.: National Education Association, 1960), p. 286.

The use of Crowder's techniques to individualize instruction according to student response is illustrated in the following passage, designed to acquaint students with certain concepts related to tests:[22]

> Scores on a test are usually referred to as "raw" scores, and each raw score is simply the number of correct answers. A raw score of 34 means that a certain student answered 34 questions correctly. A percentage score is slightly different, since a raw score of 34 could mean 100%, or 50%, or any percentage between 1 and 100. If there were only 34 items on the test, a raw score of 34 would be 100% correct, and if there were 68 items on the test, a raw score of 34 would be 50% correct. A percentage is easily calculated by dividing the raw score by the total number of items on the test. If a raw score of 15 is 25% correct, how many questions were there on the test? 60, of course. If there were 30 items on the test, and the highest score is 27 items correct, and the lowest raw score is 15, the highest raw score is what percentage correct?

If your answer is:	Turn to:
27%	page 2, top half of the page
81%	page 7, bottom half of the page
90%	page 11, bottom half of the page

Programs for Use in Machines

Both the Crowderian (branching) and the Skinnerian (linear) types of programs may be adapted for use in machines. Devices that make use of the principles adopted by Crowder have certain general characteristics: Subject-matter content to be presented is placed upon microfilm as individual frames or content steps to which the student may react. (As many as 10,000 or more frames may be used in teaching a given program.) The student using the machine begins with frame one of the sequence. He reacts by pressing a button that is numbered or lettered to correspond to the multiple-choice item he selects. If his answer is correct, a new frame appears that so informs him, and then new material (a frame) is presented to which he is supposed to react by again pressing the correct button. If his answer is incorrect, however, he is instructed to press a button that automatically brings correctional material to the viewing screen. After the student has reacted with the desired response to the correctional material, he is directed to press another button that

---

[22]William A. Deterline, *An Introduction to Programmed Instruction* (Englewood Cliffs, New Jersey: Prentice-Hall, Inc., 1962), p. 84.

returns him to the mainstream of sequentially placed frames. As long as he responds correctly, he is given progressively more difficult material.[23]

The introduction of correctional materials for students who have responded incorrectly marks one of the essential differences between Crowderian and Skinnerian programing. Skinnerians contend that if steps are kept sufficiently small and related to preceding steps, no correctional teaching is necessary. Crowderians, on the other hand, feel that if remedial or correctional branching is built into a program, large steps may be taken until difficulties are encountered, at which time remedial frames may be logically introduced.

Computer Programs

The past few years have seen a marked increase in the willingness of educators, federal agencies, and commercial concerns to experiment with computer-assisted instruction (CAI). Capitalizing on needed experience gained through the use of both linear and branching programs in the teaching machines of the late fifties and early sixties, experimenters sought to link the amazing capabilities of the computer to the problems of instruction.

Because the computer is a highly sophisticated electronic machine, earlier machine programs could be adapted to their use. Moreover, a range of additional advantages could be utilized, assuming that specially designed programs and hardware were available. For example, through the use of the cathode ray tube, visual materials could be programed to appear on the screen in a given sequence, serving the needs of individual learners. Communication between student and computer could be effected through the use of the electric typewriter and the printout sheet. Branching programs—one aspect of the computer capability—could be utilized to accommodate the needs of widely different students. A record of correct or incorrect student responses to given frames could be stored in the memory bank for instant retrieval by teachers.[24]

The instructional promise of the computer remains great. Unfortunately, up to the present time relatively few major experiments focusing on CAI have attracted national attention. Among them are the PLATO project at the University of Illinois, the Stanford University Elementary Arithmetic Program, and the experimental efforts at the University of Texas.

---

[23]For an older comprehensive review of the status of machine- and computer-based teaching, see Lawrence M. Stolurow and Daniel Davis, "Teaching Machines and Computer-Based Systems," in *Teaching Machines and Programed Learning, II: Data and Direction*, ed. Robert Glaser (Washington, D. C.: Department of Audiovisual Instruction, National Education Association, 1965), pp. 162–212.

[24]Patrick Suppes, Max Jerman, and Dow Brian, *Computer-Assisted Instruction: Stanford's 1965–66 Arithmetic Program* (New York: Academic Press, Inc., 1968), chapter 2, provide a useful description of the students, hardware, curriculum materials, program logic, procedures and evaluation techniques employed in teaching arithmetic to elementary school youngsters.

Reasons for the slow introduction of CAI into the public schools may be narrowed to a limited few. Riding on the shoulders of programed instruction, CAI has found it necessary to move with caution. Specialists in the development and use of CAI needed several important supporting competencies: understanding of subject-matter content, knowledge of sound methodology, an acquaintance with programing techniques, and knowledge of computer capabilities. Individuals with such competencies were difficult to find and assembling a team of such individuals was still more difficult. Needed skills had to be developed as professional insights grew. Further, financing necessary to the production of sound programs by highly skilled technicians suitable for and utilizing the capabilities of the computer called for large expenditures, often beyond the reach of many interested individuals and experimental laboratories. The research and development phase of a major undertaking such as CAI can be expected to occupy a span of several years before it is seriously considered for extensive adoption in the public schools. Accompanying such development must be a gradual acceptance by the tax-paying public.

Programed Textbooks

Although a great deal of interest has been focused on the use of teaching machines, the programed textbook has been used more frequently. After the first excitement engendered by the hope for mechanization of instruction, advocates of programed instruction began to examine cost factors and review the available research on the use of machine teaching as opposed to a programed text. Many concluded that the teaching machine provides no basic advantage.

The programed text, which affords the great advantage of economy to a school district, appears in a variety of forms depending upon subject matter and student needs. In the Crowderian text, sometimes referred to as the scrambled text, the student reads and reacts to a single stimulus item that is printed on a given page. Deterline explains the organization of the scrambled text as follows:[25]

> The pages of the book are numbered sequentially, but the material is assigned to pages randomly and the student is directed to turn to a page number which is determined by his choice of an answer to each question. For example, on page one he may read several short paragraphs and then a multiple-choice question that has a different page number printed beside each of the answer choices:
>
> | If your answer is: | Turn to page: |
> |---|---|
> | Choice a | 5 |
> | Choice b | 23 |
> | Choice c | 10 |
> | Choice d | 19 |

---

[25]Deterline, *An Introduction to Programmed Instruction*, p. 44.

Suppose that the correct answer is Choice b, and that the student turns to page 23. He is told that his choice is the correct answer, and is then told to continue reading the rest of page 23 and to answer the next multiple-choice question at the bottom of that page. Each of the incorrect alternatives on page 1 sends the student to a different page where he is informed that his choice is not correct, told why it is not correct, and provided with more information designed to help him answer the question correctly. Then the student is told to return to page 1 and to select the correct answer. The correct sequence is from page 1 to page 23, with three alternate routes to handle students who don't select the correct answer. Page 23 contains another multiple-choice question which has only one correct answer and three incorrect answers, each of which leads to its respective correcting branch. An errorless route through the first seven frames might follow this sequence: 1–23–7–25–12–3–18. It is assumed that the student who follows this sequence has adequately learned the material on each page in the series, and it is further assumed that the alternate response-determined branches have adequately corrected any misconceptions or misunderstanding on the part of the students who have made errors, but who have eventually also reached page 18.

Structure of Arithmetic, a text designed to help students strengthen their computational skills and to acquire a better comprehension of the nature of *number* and *operation*, is classified as a linear program. It is intended to serve as the text for a one-semester course in general mathematics or for students wishing a refresher course preparatory to taking algebra. It may also serve as an introduction to modern mathematics.

The introduction and instructions for the use of the 3700-frame text are programed by way of illustration; contents of the full volume are presented in thirty chapters. The first six frames of the 32-frame introduction are reproduced in Figure 3.[26]

Illustrative frames from the final chapter, "Measurement," are printed in Figure 4.[27] In order for these frames to be meaningful to the learner, he must have learned the content of the preceding chapters.

GENERALIZATIONS ABOUT PROGRAMED INSTRUCTION

Several generalizations that have been widely accepted by psychologists and educators should prove helpful at this point.

---

[26]P. 1 in *Structure of Arithmetic* by John H. Minnick and Raymond C. Strauss. (Harper & Row, 1968.) Used with permission of the publisher.
[27]Pp. 485–486 in *Structure of Arithmetic* by John H. Minnick and Raymond C. Strauss. (Harper & Row. 1968.) Used with permission of the publisher.

Fig. 3. Sample frames from a programed arithmetic text.

1. Since this is a programmed text, you must actively participate while studying it. At intervals a word is omitted, and it is your responsibility to supply the missing word. Then you should have a pencil handy, and whenever a blank appears, fill in the missing _____ .

WORD

2. After filling in the blank, you should check your answer by comparing it with the correct response, which is provided at the end of the frame. Each frame tries to convey a particular idea, and you can best learn that idea by responding whenever a blank appears, and comparing that response with the correct one, which is found at the _____ of the frame.

END

3. It is important that you understand clearly the idea presented in each frame before proceeding to the next. If your response to the blank does not exactly match the answer given at the end of the frame, you have probably misunderstood something and should re-read the frame to see why your response was incorrect. Do not go on to the next frame until you are certain that you have learned the _____ which was presented.

IDEA

4. If your answer to the frame exactly matches the one given at the end, you have probably understood the idea completely and should feel ready to go on to the next frame. It is your active response to a missing word and the immediate reinforcement of the response by comparing it with the _____ one given at the end of the frame which best insures that you will learn.

CORRECT

5. Naturally, you will want to avoid reading the correct response until after you have made your own. It will be a good idea for you to hold a small card over the correct response while reading the frame, so that you will not accidentally read the answer before making your _____ .

RESPONSE

6. Remember, you will learn more if you make your response _____ reading the correct one given at the end.

BEFORE

1. Although programed instruction is not new, it is still in the experimental stage. Effective teachers have employed and still employ the principles on which programed learning is based, even if they are not always aware of it.

2. Programed instruction may or may not involve the use of teaching machines or computers, and it may appear in a variety of different forms.

3. Teaching machines and programed materials afford the promise of helping the teacher as well as the student make more economical use of his time, but they do not serve as a substitute for the teacher. Programed instruction provides some but not all of the advantages of tutoring. It is essentially concerned with individualizing instruction.

4. Subjects that are highly structured (mathematics and science) lend themselves more readily to programed instruction than do less systematic subjects (history or literature). Programed instruction tends to emphasize the science of teaching. Although the use of programed materials is largely limited to fields in which there is a fixed, correct

Fig. 4.   Sample frames from the last chapter of a programed arithmetic text.

1. We have constructed the real number line. We began by choosing a line and one point on it. We called this point the _____ .

ORIGIN

2. ... _____ ...
                0

The origin was labeled with the number zero, and we called zero the _____ of the origin.

COORDINATE

3. ... _____ ...
                0

We next chose a line segment

x———y

and used it to locate other points both to the left and right of the origin.

... _____ ...
    -2 -1 0 1 2 3 4 5 6

The points thus determined had coordinates which are numbers that form a set called the _____

INTEGERS

4. ... _____ ...
        -2 -1 0 1 2 3 4

But some points on the line had not been given coordinates. The rational numbers enabled us to give coordinates to many other points.

... _____ ...
    -2 -1 P 0 ½ 1 4/3 2   3   4

What coordinate is given to the point labeled P?

– (2/3)

5. ... _____ ...
    -2   -1   0   1   2   3 Q 4

But there were still points on our line to which no rational number could be assigned as a coordinate. The point Q, above, was such a point. We used an _____ number as a coordinate for Q.

IRRATIONAL

6. ... _____ ...
    -3 -2 -1 0 1 2 3 π 4

Many other points on our line had coordinates which were irrational numbers. Indeed, between any two points with rational number coordinates are an _____ number of points with rational number coordinates and an _____ number of points with irrational number coordinates.

INFINITE;   INFINITE

7. And between any two points with irrational number coordinates were an infinite number of points with _____ number coordinates and an infinite number of points with _____ number coordinates.

RATIONAL;   IRRATIONAL (either order)

8. The union of the set of rational numbers and the set of irrational numbers is the set of _____ numbers.

REAL

9. Hence every point on our line had a coordinate which was a real number, and we called our line the _____ _____ line.

REAL NUMBER

10. ... _____ ...
        -2 -1 0 1 2 3 4 5

The segment

x———y

which we used to construct our real number line played a very important part. The coordinate of every point (other than the origin) depended on our choice of segment XY. We shall call XY a UNIT SEGMENT, or simply a "unit."

11. It would have been quite correct to construct our real number line using a *different* unit segment. Thus, if our choice of unit had been

w———z

we could still have constructed a real number line.

_____
    -1   0   1   2

and each point on this line would still have had a _____ number for its coordinate.

REAL ,

12. ... _____ ...
        -1   0   1   2
           w   z

But the coordinate of every point (other than the origin) on the number line which uses segment WZ as a unit is _____ _____ the coordinate of that point on the number line which uses segment XY as a unit.

... _____ ...
    -2 -1 0 1 2 3 4
           x   y

DIFFERENT FROM (not LESS THAN!)

answer, many concepts are not of this nature and, therefore, cannot be programed with the same success.[28]

5. Some programs are worked out to redirect the student's attention to areas in which he has shown a weakness. In such cases the student's response is used to determine the material he will cover next. These branching programs redirect learning once errors have been made. Computer use provides for immediate access to branching frames, a definite advantage over textbook programs.

6. Programed materials, like other teaching materials, should be selected to meet the individual needs of learners as nearly as possible. The same program may not be equally helpful for all students; the better student may need to take fewer steps to reach a goal than the slow or average student. Individual differences among students and variation in content among different subjects necessitate differentiation in spacing of material, speed of presentation, and method of programing. Programed learning provides needed opportunities for individual instruction in schools where advanced courses or courses of limited difficulty are not part of the curriculum.

7. Reacting to the recent suggestions of teachers, publishing houses have produced many varieties of programed materials. Popular among these different approaches has been the programed single chapter or unit. Further, the programing of individual lessons or series of concepts has met with considerable favor.

8. Programed instructional devices should be evaluated in terms of goals achieved and not in terms of inherent or potential value. All the programed device can do is to present the available content in a way that facilitates learning.

9. The use of programed devices and automated teaching machines (including computers) is influencing and will continue to influence curriculums at all levels.

10. Certain units of a course may be taught by conventional materials, while other units are taught with programed materials. A few experimental teachers may elect to use conventional as well as programed materials in the same unit.

11. Subject-matter content that is carefully programed encourages the student to see relationships between the segments of content he is learning.

12. Programing is a technical task that requires a thorough acquaintance with the content to be programed as well as an understanding of the techniques of programing.

13. Development and use of programed materials in their varied forms are not sufficiently well advanced to permit a sound prediction of

---

[28]Continuing efforts to program materials suitable for use in relatively unstructured courses are reflected in the study by Sidney J. Parnes, *Programming Creative Behavior* (Albany, New York: State University of New York Press, 1966).

the precise role they will play in education. Many of the hasty assumptions of the past decade have been modified or recast to conform more with the practice.

AREAS USING PROGRAMED INSTRUCTION

An examination of the subject areas for which programs have been produced reveals the greatest number in mathematics, general science, English grammar, and other structured subjects. These subjects were the first to attract the attention of trained programers. Since then, however, a wide range of programs have been produced for less well-structured subjects such as history and literature. Of a total of 352 programs listed by the United States Office of Education in 1963, 35 percent were concerned with mathematics, 20 percent with the sciences, 7 percent with grammar usage and spelling, 7 percent with the language arts, and 5 percent with social studies.[29]

The Sciences

As early as 1948 a modified Pressey punchboard (one of the first teaching machines) was reported being used to teach chemistry at Syracuse University.[30] Results of this study indicated that learning is significantly enhanced if the student is provided with immediate knowledge of examination results—as was the case when using the punchboard device.

Programs '63 identified sixty-nine programs available in the fields of applied science, general science, biology, chemistry, physics, and psychology.[31] Although information concerning the number of secondary programs in specific subjects is not available, there is little doubt that the science areas—with the exception of front-running mathematics—have the next largest number of programs. Sample frames from an elementary experimental science course concerned with pupil self-discovery of differences between vertebrates and invertebrates are presented in Figure 5.[32]

---

[29]*Programs '63, A Guide to Programed Instructional Materials* (Washington, D. C.: Center for Programed Instruction, 1963), p. vi. Riding the crest of widespread professional enthusiasm, this publication appeared annually for a few years; however, a number of factors (publishing house losses and unfulfilled promises among them) contributed to its demise, and it did not appear after 1963.

[30]George W. Angell and Maurice E. Troyer, "A New Self-Scoring Test Device for Improving Instruction," *School and Society,* 67 (Jan. 31, 1948), pp. 84–85.

[31]*Programs '63*, p. vi.

[32]Jerry Short and Betty E. Haughey, *An Experimental Study of Sequencing Strategies* (Pittsburgh, Pennsylvania: The American Institutes for Research, 1966), p. B-3.

Fig. 5. Sample frames from an elementary science lesson.

1. What do all invertebrates have in common?

2. What do all vertebrates have in common? _____

3. Circle the animal that lays soft eggs in water.

4. Circle the animal that lays eggs with hard shells.

5. Circle the animal that lays soft, jelly-like eggs.

6. Circle the animal that has young that are born alive.

7. Circle the animal whose inside body temperature depends on the outside temperature.

8. Circle the animal whose inside body temperature does not depend on the outside temperature.

English

Because of the structured nature of formal grammar, it has often been programed without the difficulties that accompany the programing of social studies. Recent successful attempts have been made to respond to the emphasis on composition through the use of programs that have been carefully organized and class-tested. Further, several programs concerned with the presentation of sentence structure are also available.

Variations in linear programing are commonplace. An example (Figure 6) of this variation is seen in the following frames taken from the first of twenty-two lessons on structural and transformational grammar.[33]

Mathematics

The greatest number of programs currently available in any one field deal with teaching mathematics. Perhaps the basic reason for this fact is that mathematics is a highly structured subject in which there can be definite answers.

One extensive program in business mathematics (see Figure 7) calls for constructed (written) responses in each frame.[34] Correct responses appear in small print below the heavy, double line at the bottom of each frame. Answers may be hidden by using a sliding shield (cardboard or paper). At anytime the student wishes, he may expose the correct answer, although he is cautioned not to do so until he has made his own response. Teachers who have used this and similar programs report that the tendency to cheat by prematurely exposing correct answers is minimized when learners become aware of the thorough, teacher-administered testing procedure employed as a part of the program.

Foreign Languages

Seeking to accelerate the learning of their students, foreign-language teachers have enthusiastically turned to a wide variety of stimulus-response devices. Introductory programed courses for seven different foreign languages—French, German, Hebrew, Italian, Japanese, Russian, and Spanish—are identified and illustrated in *Programs '63*. The largest number of these have been developed as aids for teaching Spanish.

French

At Hamilton College the content of a French course was programed,

---

[33]Pp. 306–308 in *Teaching in the Secondary School* by Nathan S. Blount and Herbert J. Klausmeier. (Harper & Row, 1968.) Used with permission of the publisher.

[34]From *Programmed Business Mathematics, Book 2* by Harry Huffman and B. June Schmidt. Copyright © 1968 by McGraw-Hill. Used with permission of McGraw-Hill Book Company.

Fig. 6. Sample page from a programed modern grammar text.

1. The English language has nine types of very simple sentences. These are called BASIC SENTENCES. They may be used alone, or they may be combined. All more complicated sentences which you read and write are combinations of these nine _____ sentences.

2. < Some pianists are women. > is an example of one of the _____ types of basic sentences.
   (How many?) — basic

3. < The umbrella is black. > is also a basic s_____. — nine

4. < Turkeys gobble. > is another _____ _____. — sentence

5. < The umbrella + is black. >
   < Turkeys   + gobble. >
   These basic sentences have _____ main parts.
   (How many?) — basic / sentence

6. How many main parts does this basic sentence have?
   < Our team + won the match. > — two

7. < The umbrella + is black. >
   < Our team   + won the match. >
   All English sentences, whether they are basic or not, have two main parts. In < Most rabbits eat carrots. > we would put a + after _____ to show the two main parts. — two

8. To show the two main parts of
   < Don looked happy. >, we would put a + after _____ . — rabbits

9. < The chicken + seemed sick. >
   This basic sentence, like all English sentences, has _____ main parts. — Don

10. We would save a lot of words and time if we could refer to the two parts by single terms, instead of saying "the part to the left (or right) of the + sign." — two

Let's call the part to the *left* of the + sign the SUB-JECT GROUP.
In < Two mice + were behind the stove. > *Two mice* is the _____ group.

11.	< Some of my books + are at home. > Here *Some of my books* is the subject _____ .	subject

---

12.	We will be using the term *group* in a very special way. You are used to thinking of a group as having two or more items, but here a group may have only one word. For instance, in < Joan + was upset. > the subject group has only _____ word. <div align="center">(How many?)</div>	group

---

13.	In the basic sentence < Those chairs + are antique. > the subject group is *Those chairs* because it is the part of the sentence to the _____ of the + sign.	one

---

14.	In < Skunks + are friendly. > *Skunks* is the _____ _____ .	left

---

15.	The term we use for the second part of the sentence is PREDICATE GROUP. < Skateboards + are fun. > In this basic sentence *are fun* is the _____ group.	subject group

---

16.	The predicate group is that part of a sentence to the (left/right) of the + sign. [Choose one]	predicate

---

17.	What is the predicate group in this sentence? < These oysters + are raw. >	right

---

18.	A predicate group may also have only one word. For example, in < Someone sneezed. > *sneezed* is the _____ _____ .	are raw

---

19.	The subject group is to the left of the + sign, and the predicate group is to the _____ of the + sign.	predicate group

---

20.	< My goldfish is dead. > After what word would you put a + to separate the subject and predicate groups?	right

---

21.   < My goldfish + is dead. >   goldfish
      What is the first word in the predicate group?

---

22.   The first word in the predicate group of   is
      < Two anteaters + are in the zoo. > is _____ .

---

23.   *Is* and *are* are forms of the word *be*. Here is a list   are
      of all the forms of *be: am, is, are, was, were, been,*
      and *being*.

      Which of these basic sentences has a form of *be*?
      (Write only the letter of the sentence.)
               a. < Two hawks shrieked. >
               b. < The stranger was a doctor.>
               c. < John hit his sister. >

---

24.   Let's look more closely at these sentences.   b.
               < My goldfish + is dead. >
               < Two anteaters + are in the zoo. >
               < The stranger + was a doctor. >

---

with 35 visual units of sixty frames each, 35 corresponding audio units,
and 35 units in a workbook. Results showed that students taking the new
programed course averaged about 20 percent higher on standardized tests
of written French, grammar, and translation than did students who had
taken the old course.[35] Such evidence encourages the use of programed
materials for other language courses.

German

The programed device for a beginning German course (see Figure
8)[36] reflects the current audiolingual emphasis. Students are required to
use a combination of questions or statements reproduced by tape recorder
or in written form. Exact procedures used in this program vary markedly
from those confined to the printed word; however, the essential elements
of effective programing are present—stimulus, response, and reinforcement.

In the frames shown in Figure 8 the star at the end of a sentence indicates that the student is to listen to the tape associated with the program.
The equal sign calls for the student to say orally the English equivalent of
the German sentence he has just written; this serves as a check for comprehension. Where appropriate, correct responses are written at the bottom
of the frame so that they can be covered to prevent premature exposure.

---

[35]Schramm, *Programed Instruction Today and Tomorrow*, p. 47.
[36]From *Programmed Instruction: Bold New Venture*, edited by Allen D. Calvin. Copyright © 1969 by Indiana University. Reprinted by permission of Indiana University Press.

Fig. 7.   Sample frames from a programed text in business mathematics.

1

Read the following statement carefully. Be sure that you understand it before proceeding.

On January 1 of this year, Mr. Shaffer agreed to pay $500 at the end of each of 10 years to settle a debt. He wants to know how much cash would be required if he paid cash in a lump sum on January 1 instead of spreading the payments over 10 years. Assume that the "going rate of interest," determined by business conditions, is 5% compounded annually.

Refer to the statement above to answer the following.

(a)   On January 1, did Mr. Shaffer agree to settle a debt? _____

(b)   How was Mr. Shaffer to settle the debt? ....

....

(c)   The payments were to be made at the (beginning/end) _____ of each year.

(d)   How much cash would it take over a period of 10 years to settle the debt?

$_____

(e)   As an alternative to settling the debt by spreading payments over a 10-year period, what other method of settling the debt is Mr. Shaffer considering?

....

(f)   Would you expect that it would take more or less cash to settle the entire debt

on January 1 of this year?   _____   Why? ....

....

(a) yes   (b) by paying $500 at the end of each of 10 years   (c) end   (d) $5,000   (e) paying cash in a lump sum   (f) Less, because the creditor will accept less in order to have use of his money without waiting.

2

Mr. Shaffer's alternate plan of paying cash immediately involves calculating the *present value of an ordinary annuity.*

Present value refers to value (today/in 10 years). _____

An *annuity* frequently involves making payments yearly, or an_ _ _ _ _ _ _ .
(*Write in the letters of a word.*)

Mr. Shaffer's alternate plan involves a/an _____ annuity.
                                                (what kind?)

---

today   annually   ordinary

3

What kind of annuity is involved in Mr. Shaffer's agreement to settle the debt?

---

ordinary

4

An annuity is a series of equal payments made or received regularly over a period of time. Check all of the following that represent annuities.

_____(a) Receiving $100 each month during the next 10 years

_____(b) Paying $100 the first year, $80 the next, $60 the next, $40 the next, and so on

_____(c) Paying $100 at the end of each year for 20 years

(a) Receiving $100 each month during the next 10 years   (c) Paying $100 at the end of each year for 20 years

---

5

Check all of the following that represent annuities.

_____(a) Receiving $200 quarterly for 5 years

_____(b) Paying $100 semiannually for 10 years

_____(c) Receiving varying amounts annually

_____(d) Paying $100 at irregular intervals

(a) Receiving $200 quarterly for 5 years   (b) Paying $100 semiannually for 10 years

---

6

Does an annuity have to be paid or received yearly? _____ Why?

. . . .

. . . .

No. Annuities involve equal payments or receipts at regular intervals; these payments may be made monthly, quarterly, semiannually, or yearly.

PRINCIPLES RELATED TO PROGRAMED INSTRUCTION

The psychological principles that constitute the basis for programed instruction are relatively simple and are generally familiar to the qualified teacher. Stimulus, response, and reinforcement must be understood by all who are concerned with the production and use of programed materials.

Stimulus:

1. Every response is the result of a stimulus. Programed instruction involves providing appropriate stimuli to which the learner can make the desired response.

Response:

2. Programed learning prevents passivity on the part of the learner, since it calls for student response to specific segments of information.

3. Response to questions or other stimulus items keeps the student in a state of continuing mental activity.

4. Programed materials provide the student with an opportunity for giving correct responses.

Fig. S.   Sample page from a programed German text.

454.

You will hear a question about each picture. Select the picture to which the question applies and write your answer under the picture.★

1. _____   2. _____

3. _____   4. _____

1. Ich singe ein Lied.   2. Ja, der Schuh ist nass.
3. Das Kind hat ein Glas.   4. Ich lese ein Buch.

455.

Repeat the new form of the verb singen. ★

456.

The word you have just repeated means SINGS or IS SINGING.
It is written singt.
Pronounce singt and check. ★

457.

Write the sentence. ★

_____

Der Mann singt. =

The man is singing.

Reinforcement:

5. Programed materials keep the student continuously informed of his progress.

6. The student is motivated when he gets an immediate indication of whether his response has been right or wrong.

7. Immediate reinforcement adds to the speed, efficiency, and interest of learning.

8. The learner benefits by being able to move immediately to the next item of content if he has responded correctly or by being immediately referred back to misunderstood or partially understood content for restudy.

9. When learners are immediately apprised of errors, they can make the necessary corrections before repeated use has tended to reinforce their mistakes.

General:

10. Individuals may learn effectively, and without the aid of a teacher, by responding to sequentially placed items.

11. Motivation to learn may in some cases be aided by programed learning because many of the negative elements of interpersonal teacher-student relationships are absent.

12. In programed learning the student may start at his own level and proceed toward the desired goal by acquiring carefully graduated concepts.

13. When using programed materials, the learner may proceed as rapidly or as slowly as he wishes.

CORRECT AND INCORRECT USE

The chance for teacher error in the selection and use of programed instructional materials is great because of their experimental nature. Therefore, the teacher who proposes to use such materials would do well to read a number of relevant current articles, to discuss the nature of programed materials with teachers who are successfully using such material, and—only then—to proceed, with appropriate caution.[37]

---

[37]Phil G. Lange, ed., *Programmed Instruction: The Sixty-Sixth Yearbook of the National Society for the Study of Education,* Part II (Chicago: University of Chicago Press, 1967), pp. 253–254, provides a sound discussion of the conditions that contribute to effective programed instruction.

Procedures with Limitations

The desire to keep abreast of the new instructional practices has led many teachers and administrators to make hasty and somewhat unsound decisions. This danger is inherent in the use of programed materials. Look, for example, at the cases of William Addison and Phyllis Vance.

MR. ADDISON'S ENTHUSIASM MEETS WITH DIFFICULTY

After his visit to the ASCD Convention in Chicago, Principal William Addison was an enthusiastic convert to the idea of computer-based programed instruction. As he wandered from one display to another in the exhibition hall, he imagined how the learning process in his own consolidated high school could be streamlined. He visualized row after row of students seated at computer terminals responding to instructional frames presented by the machine.

Upon his return Mr. Addison lost no time in voicing his enthusiasm to his superintendent and the members of the school board. In the face of his persistent eagerness, funds were finally made available for the superintendent, one school board member, and three teachers to visit the computer center at the University of Illinois.

Discussion with experienced specialists involved in computer-assisted instruction soon punctured Mr. Addison's hopes and those of his colleagues. He discovered that in Chicago sales-oriented representatives of commercial firms had not given him an accurate picture of cost factors involved in the installation and operation of CAI programs. He also learned that Title III funds for experimentation in this area had been markedly reduced and that few local school districts were able to carry on such programs without financial help from the federal government. Moreover, tested programs of high quality were simply not available in the quantity necessary for the presentation of a range of subjects by computer.

Several conclusions were jointly reached during the homeward journey: CAI was a fascinating but expensive approach to teaching; although much had been accomplished, many of its problems remained to be solved; small school districts like their own would have to forego CAI until such time as federal assistance was more plentiful. In the meantime, educators in Mr. Addison's district would do well to maintain currency by pointed reading and visitation of CAI programs already well established.

MISS VANCE ACQUIRES NEEDED INFORMATION

Miss Phyllis Vance was always determined to be the first one in her school district to try new innovations in education. She was the first of the "life adjustment" advocates—and the first to discard it when the hard-core curriculum bandwagon passed her way. She pushed for the cause of television instruction but shortly thereafter declared it to be impractical and undesirable.

In a similar manner Miss Vance expressed an immediate preference for machine teaching when she heard about it. According to her, machine teaching would soon relieve teachers of their burdensome routine tasks and elevate them to the level of instructional engineers who could flip the switch and watch learning take place. But Miss Vance's principal insisted that much careful thought, study, and cautious experimentation precede the endorsement of a new procedure.

Under his direction Miss Vance was encouraged to read widely about programed instruction, and he made it possible for her to attend a workshop in which the theory underlying the new medium was exposed. Finally, he encouraged her to talk to several teachers in an adjacent school district who had experimented with programed instruction. Only then did he feel that it was time to ask Miss Vance to appraise carefully how their high school could make the most effective use of programed instruction.

Failing to exercise needed caution, both Mr. Addison and Miss Vance fell prey to the fascination of the new. Without adequate knowledge of the principles on which programed instruction and its computer counterpart are based, they made hasty professional commitments. Their chances for success were thus limited at the outset. Fortunately Miss Vance received the type of guidance she needed; however, Mr. Addison lost a measure of his colleagues' respect in acquiring the information he needed.

Procedures with Promise

Recognition of the many problems related to the introduction and use of programed instructional materials has led other teachers and administrators to exercise varying degrees of caution. Two such educators are Mary Bacon and Thomas Dalley.

MRS. BACON PREPARES FOR SUCCESSFUL PROGRAMED INSTRUCTION

Mary Bacon, known to her teaching colleagues and administrators as a stable, conscientious, hard-working, and successful teacher, was asked by her principal to investigate the possibility of using programed instruction in teaching ninth-grade English grammar. When she accepted the responsibility, she indicated the need for allowing adequate time for study and examination of programs already in operation.

Taking her job seriously, Mrs. Bacon acquired the latest available bibliography on programed instruction and began to learn about this new field. She found that an increasing number of textbooks provided helpful illustrated information; much of her reading, however, was confined to periodical literature. Gradually she identified the major strengths and weaknesses of programed instruction. Early in her reading she became convinced that the quality of professional work that had gone into developing a program greatly determined its potential for success.

Mrs. Bacon had several informative discussions with teachers in other districts who were using programed materials in teaching English grammar. She discovered that programed materials could be used to serve a variety of instructional needs; not only could they be used to provide accelerated learning, but they could also be used to serve the needs of the slower learner. Furthermore, they could serve as remedial aids and as devices for review. After investigating the feasibility of using computer-connected terminals and other machines for presenting English grammar programs, she decided that programed texts would provide essentially the same experience at a fraction of the cost. She reported back to her principal that she would like to experiment on a limited scale with the use of programed materials during the next semester. Further use, she indicated, should be based upon the evaluation of the limited experiment.

MR. DALLEY DISCOVERS PROGRAMED INSTRUCTION THROUGH COURSE WORK

The graduate course in programed instruction that Mr. Dalley took at the state university proved to be an eye opener. He returned to his teaching determined to use programed instruction in his own classes. Armed with his course-acquired knowledge and following the move-with-caution procedure stressed by his professor, Mr. Dalley set up a program for himself.

In March he approached his principal about the possible use of programed instruction in his algebra classes. The principal was much better informed than Mr. Dalley had assumed he would be; he expressed interest in the possibility and promised the necessary administrative backing, providing that this experiment did not disrupt the already existing curriculum.

Mr. Dalley then wrote to the publishers of elementary-algebra programed textbooks, asking them to send him examination copies. From the range of texts he selected the one that he felt most nearly served his purposes. Permission was granted to order ten of these texts for use in his two beginning algebra sections starting in September.

He decided he would experiment by having the top eight students in the two sections move through the programed text as rapidly as possible. Tests would be given at frequent intervals, and Mr. Dalley would have a personal interview with each student at least once every week. Further, students using programed materials would be encouraged to seek the teacher's help after reasonable effort had been spent unsuccessfully in trying to grasp needed concepts.

If his early experimental efforts proved to be satisfactory, he would include more students in the program during the second semester. If the efforts proved to be unsatisfactory, however, he would restrict the use of programed materials until he thoroughly analyzed the causes of the poor results.

Programed materials would also be used experimentally to provide a self-directed review of course segments found to be causing students difficulty. Mr. Dalley would obtain the latest bibliography on programed instruction issued by the National Education Association and keep abreast of the latest developments in the field.

If the results of the first year proved to be singularly successful, he would consider using programed texts for teaching all first-year algebra students the following year.

Mrs. Bacon approached the investigation of programed instruction with desirable caution. She read the relevant literature until she had a firm basis for whatever action was to be taken. In addition, she discussed the use of programed materials with other teachers who had employed them successfully. Finally, she suggested that experimentation in her own school be initially conducted on a limited scale. Mr. Dalley, likewise, systematized his movement into programed instruction. Each successive step he took in this direction was carefully identified and analyzed; little was left to chance.

SPECIFIC SUGGESTIONS

Conscientious teachers, with the best of intentions, sometimes meet with limited success in using programed materials to promote learning. The possibility of effective use of such materials is increased if detailed planning, continued reading, and an alert appraisal of the role of programed learning in the total educational process precede the actual use of the materials. Recommendations and cautions for the use of programed instruction are provided below.

Recommendations

1. Become acquainted with the advantages and disadvantages of programed instruction before you try it out; profit by the experience of other school districts. Also become acquainted with programed materials and teaching machines that have been used successfully in your area of specialization.

2. Remember that the potential for success of any programed course or unit is directly related to the quality of the professional work that has gone into the program.

3. Select programs that best promote your course objectives.

4. Use programed materials to help meet the individual differences of students.

5. Determine the specific points that characterize an effective programed course before you select the material to use in your teaching.

6. Be willing to experiment with programed materials on a limited scale in your classroom.

7. Keep up to date with respect to the use of computer-assisted instruction, especially in the area of your specialty.

Cautions

1. Don't assume that programed material will serve as a substitute for the teacher.

2. Don't confuse the commercial zeal exhibited in selling an automated teaching device with the educational value of the product.

3. Don't avoid experimentation with the newer approaches to programed instruction—programed units, programed lessons, learning packages using programing techniques, and computer-assisted instruction.

PROGRAMED INSTRUCTION IN REVIEW

Programed instruction refers to the use of systematically organized materials and calls for the application of the psychological principles of stimulus, response, and reinforcement. Items (frames) in sequence may be presented in a programed text or prepared for use in a machine or a computer. Computer-assisted instruction (CAI) is a sophisticated extension of the principles of programed instruction in an electronic setting.

Two major types of programs are currently being used—Skinnerian, or linear, programs and Crowderian, or branching, programs. Skinnerian programs call for advancement by very small steps with content structured to provide a preponderance of correct responses. In a Crowderian program the student who makes an incorrect response does not proceed with the program until he has successfully completed a remedial frame or loop. Both types of programs have strong proponents, but the majority of those programs currently in use falls into the Skinnerian category.

Although most of the statements concerning programed instruction made by responsible psychologists reflect cautious optimism, statements may range from sweeping denunciation to unqualified endorsement. For this reason it is highly desirable for the prospective user of programed materials to become fully informed about such materials before attempting to use them. To become knowledgeable the teacher must read current descriptions of programs, discuss the strengths and weaknesses of such programs with teachers who have used the materials, and cautiously experiment with the materials only after careful plans have been made.

PROBLEMS FOR STUDY AND DISCUSSION

1. Define programed learning in your own words.

2. What are the basic psychological principles involved in programed instruction?

3. Differentiate between Crowderian programing and Skinnerian programing.

4. Name five advantages claimed for programed instruction.

5. Define the following terms as they relate to programed instruction:

Reinforcement	Intrinsic programing
Step	Linear programing
Frame	Branching
Scrambled textbook	Loops

6. Differentiate between programed instruction and machine teaching.

7. What is the relationship between computer-assisted instruction and programed learning? Explain.

8. Why have computers not been used more extensively as aids to instruction?

9. Describe Pressey's contribution to programed instruction.

10. How do you account for the skepticism of many of the critics of programed instruction? Explain.

11. Write a careful, one-paragraph statement about the future of programed instruction based upon a consideration of its current status.

12. Name three extensively used programed texts suitable for secondary schools.

13. What are the advantages of a programed text as opposed to a teaching machine?

14. What are the advantages of taking large steps in programed materials? What are the disadvantages? Explain.

15. At what grade levels has programed instruction been tried?

16. Identify the areas in the secondary curriculum in which programed materials have been used most frequently up to the present time. How do you account for this?

17. Discuss several different ways in which programed textbooks can be used by the classroom teacher.

18. About how many programs are currently available in the United States at all educational levels?

19. List in order the steps you would take to inaugurate the use of programed materials in your teaching major or minor. Assume that programed materials have not been used in your school before.

20. List in you own words at least five cautions that should be of particular value to the new teacher who wishes to use programed instructional materials.

18. *Television and Team Teaching in the Modern Classroom*

Television instruction and team teaching (often combined) have been two of the most influential and durable post-World War II teaching developments. Both have undergone dramatic improvements; furthermore, current widespread experimentation should lead to continued improvement. The conscientious teacher should be a front-line participant in this experimentation.

TELEVISION INSTRUCTION

As a result of past research, the question of whether television can serve as an effective instructional medium for large groups of students is no longer an issue. Studies indicate that students taught by means of television make gains in achievement comparable to, and in some cases exceeding, gains made by students taught by conventional procedures.[1] In a comprehensive early study, Schramm reported that

> instructional television is at least as effective as ordinary classroom instruction, when the results are measured by the usual final examinations or by standardized tests made by testing bureaus. . . . We can say with considerable confidence that in 65 percent of a very large number of comparisons [393] between televised and classroom teaching, there is no significant difference.[2]

In spite of these and other findings, much carefully controlled research is being conducted to find a defensible answer to the question of how television can best be used in education. Responsible educational specialists have evinced an abiding interest in television and its innovative uses in serving the needs of learners at all educational levels.

History of Teaching by Television

The history of television instruction is relatively brief. Utilizing the technical know-how acquired piecemeal during the thirties[3] and early forties, commercial television made its debut in the years immediately following World War II. It was not until commercial television had reached considerable stature, however, that attention was seriously focused on the new medium's potentials as an instructional device.[4]

Experiments of the Mid-Fifties

In the mid-fifties the schools of Pittsburgh became the first of many educational institutions to become involved in television instruction. Programs were telecast to assist in teaching arithmetic, French, and fifth-grade reading. These programs were so successful that one educational television station was not enough, and a second was started in 1957. At

---

[1]*Teaching by Television*, A Report from the Ford Foundation and the Fund for the Advancement of Education, 2d. ed. (New York: The Ford Foundation, 1961), p. 7.

[2]Wilbur Schramm, "What We Know About Learning from Instructional Television," in *Educational Television in the Next Ten Years* (Stanford: Institute for Communication Research, 1962), p. 53.

[3]One of the early sustained efforts at providing educational television is recounted by E. B. Kurtz, *Pioneering in Educational Television, 1932–1939* (Iowa City: State University of Iowa, 1959).

[4]Dave Chapman, *Design for ETV: Planning for Schools with Television* (New York: Educational Facilities Laboratories, 1960), pp. 21–22, provides a brief, readable history of educational television up to 1960.

the present time, educational television is widely employed in Pittsburgh's elementary and secondary schools and adult education programs.

Hagerstown, Maryland, is the seat of one of the oldest and best-known closed-circuit instructional television projects. In September 1956, when the project started, 5300 students received one full lesson each day by television. A year later 12,000 students were being taught by television; three years later, 16,500 of the 18,000 students enrolled in the elementary schools in Washington County, Maryland, were being instructed through the new medium. "Today the completed system links forty-five schools to the Hagerstown studios. It can send out six lessons simultaneously by cable to more than 800 TV sets throughout the country. Fifty-six courses are now televised."[5]

Use in College and Adult Education

The advantages of television instruction for college and adult education were quickly recognized. In 1954 Pennsylvania State College became the first college-level institution to employ educational television. Other institutions, such as the Chicago City Junior College, have made extensive use of television to reach a large adult audience. Since 1956 this Chicago college has been broadcasting a home educational television program that by 1960 had an estimated viewing audience of between 30,000 and 50,000 adult students with a median age of thirty-five. "Chicago's experience has . . . aroused great interest and brought a stream of observers. A number of junior colleges are currently making use of TV and others have plans to do so . . ."[6]

By 1960 coast-to-coast educational programs were appearing over commercial networks.[7] *Continental Classroom*, one such program, reportedly had 414,000 viewers for an early morning course in "Modern Chemistry." However, after a few short seasons the course was dropped.

According to Chapman,[8] in early 1960, 569 school districts throughout the nation were regularly using televised instruction, 117 colleges and universities were giving credit for televised courses, 144 closed-circuit television systems were in operation in educational institutions, and 45 educational television stations were in use.

Multi-State Cooperative Use

The most extensive single project involving the multi-state use of television solely for educational purposes was in operation for several years and served schools in Illinois, Indiana, Kentucky, Michigan, Ohio, and parts of Wisconsin as well as Ontario, Canada.[9] Known as the

---

[5]Alvin C. Eurich, *Reforming American Education: The Innovative Approach to Improving our Schools and Colleges* (New York: Harper & Row, Publishers, 1969), p. 238.
    [6]*Ibid.*, p. 229.
    [7]An accurate picture of the status of educational television as of August 1961 is presented in *Teaching by Television*, pp. 1–8.
    [8]Chapman, *Design for ETV*, p. 22.
    [9]James W. Brown, Richard B. Lewis, and Fred F. Harcleroad, *AV Instruction: Media and Methods*, 3d. ed. (New York: McGraw-Hill Book Company, 1969), p. 305.

Midwest Program on Airborne Television Instruction (MPATI), this project helped to enrich the educational offerings in 17,000 schools and colleges enrolling 13 million students. An airplane flying at an altitude of 23,000 feet over Montpelier, Indiana made it possible to telecast prerecorded lessons to schools within a 400-mile radius, some of which otherwise could not be reached by television.

Over 300 carefully selected teachers prepared, taught, and recorded lessons for use in the MPATI program. Moreover, by 1966 university television studios had produced for MPATI the largest library of instructional tape materials in existence.[10] Because of its success, this project was expanded every year. Elementary schools in particular, as well as secondary schools, colleges, and universities took advantage of this unusual service. A wide range of courses were transmitted at various times throughout the day, including courses that were difficult to teach as well as conventional courses.

Denied the request for six UHF channels, leaders in this ambitious project undertook conversion to the 2,500 megacycle system, Instructional Television Fixed Service (ITFS). Financial problems related to the testing of the new system proved to be discouraging; participating schools gradually withdrew from the program. As a result, "MPATI was rendered economically unviable, and at the close of the 1967–68 school year it ended its transmitting function . . ."[11]

Unwilling to allow the extensive gains of this forward-looking project to come to naught, a number of interested educators (including some of its founders as well as individuals representing sponsoring organizations) formed a new corporation bearing the MPATI name. The chief purpose of the new organization was to increase the availability of high quality ITV materials to educational groups at the lowest possible cost using the extensive production and library facilities of the parent organization. Membership support was sought from 1) state departments of public instruction and/or ETV network authorities, 2) community school systems, and 3) founders and/or sponsors.

Approaches to Teaching by Television

Ever since television captured the public fancy during the late forties, educators have expressed keen interest in its possible use in education. There have been repeated attempts to make commercial television conform to desired educational standards. Profit-minded telecasters, however, have exerted strong opposition to any educational innovations that might reduce the viewing audience, although they have been willing to recognize the need for a general cultural elevation of most commercial programs. Educators, desiring to use television specifically in behalf of education, supported the establishment of television channels used exclusively for educational purposes.

---

[10]*Ibid.*, p. 305.
[11]Eurich, *Reforming American Education*, pp. 228–229.

Four major types of broadcasting can be used within or in conjunction with the schools: public (educational) television stations, commercial educational programing, closed-circuit production, and Instructional Television Fixed Service (ITFS).

Educational Television Stations

In order to protect the educational interest of television viewers in the United States, the Federal Communications Commission (FCC) has reserved over 600[12] television channels in the very-high-frequency and ultra-high-frequency ranges for the exclusive purpose of telecasting non-commercial (essentially educational) programs. Further, the number of such allocations has doubled since 1963. Commercial stations are not permitted to use these channels. Most states have one educational television station at the present time, and several states have two or more. As of January 1, 1970, there were 77 VHF and 105 UHF stations for a total of 182 authorized educational television stations in operation.[13] Because they are under the control of the FCC, these stations are committed to operate on a nonprofit basis, and the programs they present must be educational. Furthermore, they must make their facilities available to a range of nonprofit agencies within the community, such as service clubs and public service agencies.

Because of their singleness of purpose, these stations provide the largest proportion of television viewing that is pointedly educational. Public-school systems frequently present programs at specifically desired times, usually during school hours. During nonschool hours, well-established stations present a range of cultural offerings that compete with commercially sponsored programs. Many of these programs are interesting and entertaining as well as educational, but the proportion of the total viewing audience that they attract is relatively small.

Evidence of the growth of educational television (ETV) is readily observable in the rapid expansion of National Educational Television (NET), which now numbers well over 100 stations among its affiliates. Its central objective is to provide "a television program service of substance and quality . . . to the American people through the nationwide network of noncommercial ETV stations . . ."[14] State, university, and local ETV stations have relied heavily on the range and educational quality of television materials made available through NET. Further, regional networks (the Eastern Education Network and the Western Education Network, for example) have proved to be of unusual help in serving the ETV needs of educational institutions in specific regions of the country.

---

[12]*1970 Broadcasting Yearbook*, pp. A–86–A–89.

[13]*Broadcasting: The Business Weekly of Television and Radio*, 78 (February 2, 1970), p. 5.

[14]Allen E. Koenig and Ruane B. Hill, *The Farther Vision: Educational Television Today* (Madison: The University of Wisconsin Press, 1967), pp. 88–89.

Commercial Educational Programing

Although frequently criticized by educators and interested lay groups for not devoting a larger proportion of their total time to educational programing, all commercial television stations produce a wide variety of programs that have educational value. Movies about historical events that are technically and factually sound or movies about science have been shown on commercial channels. Many other programs of public interest, such as the moon landing or the national political conventions, have educational merit. Commercially sponsored news broadcasts are daily events, and on several programs students have the opportunity to see and hear prominent national and international figures.

Many educational television programs originate as commercial network presentations (NBC's "First Tuesday," for example), but a substantial number are produced and telecast by local stations. Limited statewide telecasts provide students with the opportunity to hear official pronouncements of the governor, to see and hear members of the state legislature discuss critical issues, and to view cultural programs of particular merit presented by universities within the state.

Closed-Circuit Production

Closed-circuit television affords the opportunity of showing phenomena or presentations that are of interest only to a restricted audience.[15] This type of television is not "broadcast" in the conventional sense of the term; it is rather sent out over wires or by means of microwaves to specially equipped receiving sets.

Some of the uses of closed-circuit television include observation of certain processes when immediate contact with the phenomenon could entail danger to the viewer—such as steel production—and observation of group processes and behavior both with and without the knowledge of the group. Because of its unique flexibility and relative economy, closed-circuit television is used more frequently for instructional purposes than are the other telecasting procedures.

Instructional Television Fixed Service (ITFS)

Much experimentation is currently being conducted on the use of low-power transmission over channels far above the highest UHF range. Officially designated as Instructional Television Fixed Service (ITFS), such broadcasts are transmitted at frequencies in the 2500–2690 megacycle range. ". . . ITFS signals have a service range of 5–20 miles, depending upon terrain. These short-range ITFS signals are broadcast in the same manner as VHF and UHF transmissions, but reception of ITFS requires special equipment. Thus, ITFS becomes, in effect, a private TV

---

[15]Two well-known closed circuit ETV projects in Hagerstown, Maryland and in the state of South Carolina are described by D. A. de Korte, *Television in Education and Training* (Netherlands: Philips Technical Library, 1967), pp. 39–42.

distribution system, available only to receiving points with ITFS receiving capability. It is not intended for reception by the general public."[16]

Exercising its broad regulatory function, the FCC has authorized the use of a large number of channels for educational television in the 2500–2690 band. The Commission specified that these high-frequency channels were to be used for the transmission of "instructional and cultural material to schools and other selected receiver locations."

Differentiating ETV and ITV

With the growth of the use of television for a wide range of educational purposes has come the necessity to differentiate between educational television (ETV) and instructional television (ITV). ETV refers to the equipment and transmissions of educational stations granted special channel allocations by the Federal Communications Commission. ITV, on the other hand, refers to the use of television for classroom instruction. It may call for the use of broadcast television to serve parts of courses or to demonstrate specific skills. It may also involve innovative teacher-student use of portable TV cameras and recorders in different classes as well as use in large group instruction.

Advantages of Television Instruction

A review of the advantages of instructional television reveals several reasons why its proponents have become increasingly enthusiastic about its prospects for improving education.[17] Repeated studies indicate that it is as effective as conventional instruction when objective comparisons involving measurement of student gains are made.

Presenting Real Events

Because television makes use of both sight and sound, it can present the natural phenomena of the world in actual form. The noisy excitement of a large steel mill, remote corners of the globe, or even outer space itself may be brought forcibly and realistically to the attention of the learner. Televised moon landings and exploration provide vivid contact with reality for space-oriented students. Many aspects of the problems of human relations can be effectively portrayed, and incidents of racial unrest in Africa, China, or Washington, D. C., may be shown while still fresh or even while happening.

Building on the success of Early Bird and Telstar, separate series of INTELSAT communications satellites were placed in service under the direction of COMSAT (Communications Satellite Corporation). By December 31, 1968, "COMSAT was leasing to its customers 941 full time

---

[16]"ITFS, A New Concept for ITV Distribution: A Guide for Administrators," Maryland Public Broadcasting Commission, 1969.

[17]Brown, Lewis, and Harcleroad, AV Instruction: Media and Methods, pp. 295–297 provide a compact listing of the special advantages of broadcast television as well as meaningful illustrations.

circuits. . . ."[18] Commercial use of such circuits enables the public to see events on other continents as they take place, and the possibility of additional global television programs specially adapted to educational use affords great promise.

Revealing Specialized Photographic Views

Microscopic forms of life can be magnified, photographed, and presented on television to unlock secrets hidden from the naked eye. Slow growth processes can be accelerated. Thus stages in the development of a rose, which actually extends over several hours or days, may take on new and vital meaning when seen in a few seconds. Conversely, rapid activity —such as combustion within a cylinder, the performance of a mile runner, or the flight of a hummingbird—can be shown in slow motion with marked educational advantages. Further, accurate close-up views of the moon beamed back to earth by superbly trained astronauts are now available to excite the imagination of learners.

Portraying Past Events

Past events can be brought to life and made meaningful through dramatizations on television. These dramatizations may be live plays or recorded on film. The effect of the Depression on human lives and values, the way of life peculiar to the colonial period, and the major battles of the Civil War have been accurately re-created and recorded on film and made available for television viewers. Carefully selected films and other forms of dramatization provide impact possible through no other medium.

Teaching Large Audiences

Television affords the opportunity for large audiences in the same auditorium or in different locations to view clearly a demonstration or a lecture that may be given in the next city, in another part of the country, or on the other side of the world. Television also provides a ready means for showing students valuable material that may be one of a kind (a specific document, painting, or play) or available in limited supply (rare breeds of animals or exotic plants).

Offering Needed Courses and Programs

Through television students can take courses that are not offered by their school. Both commercial and educational television stations present early morning classes in mathematics, physical sciences, foreign languages, and other subjects, and some courses are given for academic credit. In the main, these courses are intended for adult audiences. Evidence of continuing interest in such offerings is reflected in the 1970 programing of certain commercial stations. CBS, for example, presents a 6:00 a.m. daily (except for Saturday and Sunday) series called

---

[18]*COMSAT: Report to the President and the Congress for the Calendar Year 1968* (Washington, D. C.: Communications Satellite Corporation, 1969), p. 2.

Sunrise Semester in which nationally known professors present lectures on foreign cultures.[19]

Television also provides the opportunity for curriculum enrichment that could not possibly be found otherwise. Commercial channels, for example, provide excellent news coverage of significant events throughout the world as well as interpretation of news by nationally known commentators.

Using Educational Facilities More Efficiently

Proponents of educational television believe that this medium is economically advantageous. Very large classes are made possible, space in a building can be better utilized, special teachers and particularly valuable outside lecturers and resources can be used efficiently, and teaching presentations of unusual quality can be filmed for re-use.[20] Shortages of teachers in special subjects (languages, music, and science), inadequate facilities (laboratories and demonstration devices), and space limitations may be partially overcome through the use of television.

Improving Preparation and Distribution of Tapes

Preparation of educational video tapes for national distribution has improved their quality and effected substantial savings over locally produced and distributed tapes. Among the organizations most active in producing and disseminating ETV materials are the National ITV Center, the Great Plains Instructional TV Library, and the National Center for School and College TV.

Making Use of Immediate Replay

During the past decade the shrinking costs of television equipment have had a positive influence on the classroom use of television cameras and video recorders. Frequently students are trained to use them, relieving the school of the necessity of employing technicians.

Because the camera-recorder combination affords the opportunity of immediate playback, teachers have been delighted with the opportunity to show students their strengths and limitations when the immediacy of audio-visual recall via the tape has maximum impact. Using this technique, teachers can reexpose students to a range of needed educational experiences minutes after they have been involved in them. Among such experiences are giving a talk, participating in a committee report, helping with a demonstration, displaying a new technique or article, participating in a dramatic presentation, or directing a class discussion.

Limitations of Television Instruction

Although television has instructional advantages, it also has limitations, especially when compared with the versatility of a competent

[19]TV Guide, January 31, 1970, p. 33.
[20]Walter A. Wittich and Charles F. Schuller, *Audiovisual Materials: Their Nature and Use,* 4th ed. (New York: Harper & Row, Publishers, 1967), p. 466.

classroom teacher. As yet there is no conclusive evidence to indicate that television instruction is superior to well-planned, effective classroom instruction.[21]

Although television can present demonstrations or lectures of high quality, live presentations may not be available at the specific time needed to provide maximum instructional help for the teacher and students. Programs recorded on video tape, however, may be telecast at any time that serves the needs of the school district.

Because televised lessons move at a fixed rate of speed and teach specific content in a predetermined sequence, the individual needs of students cannot be easily met. If a student, although attentive, has failed to comprehend a particular concept, there is no opportunity for the teacher to reexplain. Television instruction does not permit the exchange of ideas between the teacher and his students; generally it provides for one-way communication only.[22] The individualization of instruction must, therefore, be cared for through other procedures.

The use of educational television is limited by the availability of facilities in the schools and by the trained staff needed to present the programs effectively. If programs are telecast from a central studio in a large school system, a great deal of expensive electronic equipment is essential. This equipment must be either controlled or supervised by technicians who usually demand sizeable salaries. Moreover, full or part-time artists are frequently employed to prepare visual materials.

Some school systems have found it necessary to reduce the nature and extent of their educational television offerings because of budgetary considerations. The cost of television instruction for small, isolated school districts precludes the possibility of its use in most cases. In large school districts with a sizeable capital investment in television facilities, even the cost of video tapes can be substantial. Such tapes, however, can be stored for further use or erased and reused at will.

Some highly effective teachers do not want to televise their presentations; others strongly object to the many hours they must spend planning and preparing materials for educational telecasts, because they feel that the time thus spent would have been better invested in conventional teaching. The most frequent complaint of television instructors, however, is that they miss the satisfaction that comes from personal contact with students. The total impersonalization of teaching an unseen audience robs many television teachers of the enthusiasm that is maintained spontaneously in the conventional classroom.

---

[21]Examination of several hundred research studies focusing on the comparison of measured learning resulting from 1) direct instruction, and 2) television instruction revealed a dominant finding of no significant difference. See J. Christopher Reid and Donald W. MacLennan, *Research in Instructional Television and Film* (Washington, D.C.: U. S. Government Printing Office, 1967), p. 4.

[22]A few educational television experiments involving the oral participation of students located in a different building from the lecturer have been tried with varying degrees of success. Most television instructors, however, teach classes in which there is no possibility for student response.

New Applications of Television Instruction

During the past decade the video tape recorder has been widely used by commercial television to provide flexibility in programing, in meeting time-zone related problems, and in the use of television personalities and technical staff. Likewise, the use of taped recordings has been gradually embraced by specialists in educational television in order to encourage flexibility. Educational television stations with statewide coverage, school district closed-circuit transmissions, and students and teachers focusing on informal classroom presentations are currently making consistent and effective use of the video tape recorder. Further, the expanding use of the video tape recorder for home and amateur use will undoubtedly influence its employment in educational situations.

Using special equipment, television studio technicians and teachers may project conventional films or slides to supplement their learning presentations. Moreover, equipment is now available for the projection of opaque materials (objects, nontransparent cards, or small facsimiles), although such equipment is typically found only in the television studio.

It is now possible for an instructor to write or sketch on a perspex plate beneath which a television camera is mounted. Written images are reproduced on the monitor's picture tube; functions of the chalkboard are thus simulated.

Electronic communications satellites have been orbited in such a way as to retain the fixed position most favorable for international or trans-oceanic television transmissions. Simultaneous viewing of many important foreign events (particularly those in Western Europe) at the time they are taking place is now possible for American television audiences. The widely publicized use of Telstar, Early Bird, and Comsat has perpetuated a keen interest in such broadcasts. Further, because many such events have historical and political significance, educators have found it convenient to have students view them either as live broadcasts or taperecorded replays.

Principles Related to Teaching by Television

A number of principles related to television have found widespread acceptance and are currently giving strong direction to educational practices in this relatively new area. Additional experimentation may lead to some modification of these principles.

1. Although television is a useful instructional tool, its precise role in American education has yet to be defined conclusively.

2. Educational television involves the two senses that most strongly influence the learning process—sight and hearing.

3. The coordinated teamwork of many people goes into the production, transmission, and final classroom consumption of educational television.

4. Educational television is best suited for certain kinds of teaching

procedures—especially demonstration and lecture—and is subject to the limitations of these procedures. Although a wide range of concept-centered subjects may be taught effectively by television, it does not provide a general solution to all learning problems.

5. All students are not equally receptive to television instruction. Because of its emphasis on showing, television may be particularly helpful to poor readers. In addition, students who find it difficult to learn from lectures may find television demonstrations vivid and stimulating.

6. All teachers are not equally suited to serving as television instructors. Only those individuals who are suited by disposition, preparation, and personal preference should be encouraged to engage in such instruction.

7. The quality of television instruction may vary from teacher to teacher, from district to district, and from school to school. In order to use this medium most effectively, the teacher and the administrator should constantly seek to identify the components of quality television instruction wherever they find it. They should also keep abreast of current research on the problems of television viewing and conduct their own research comparing the effectiveness of television instruction with other types of instruction.[23]

8. Television is a means, not an end; it is one of many highly useful devices for improving education. In general, this medium should be employed only in situations where it is superior to other possible teaching procedures. The purpose of educational television is to teach with efficiency; if this goal is not achieved, another method should be sought.

9. Commercial television has a strong impact on the unstructured education of children and youth during their out-of-school hours.[24] Teachers and parents share the responsibility for determining that students make the most effective educational use of this commercial medium, which has great potential for good or harm.

Sound and Unsound Practices

Because television instruction is a relatively new field, teachers are not always acquainted with the most effective ways it can be used. Several common mistakes are reflected in the descriptive accounts below.

SUPERINTENDENT GOULD UNDERESTIMATES TECHNICAL NEEDS

Superintendent A. William Gould has always viewed himself as being in the forefront of educational progress. During the early fifties he read about exciting experiments that were being conducted with the new

[23]Continuing interest of the United States Office of Education in comparing the effectiveness of educational television with other instructional procedures is reflected in Reid and MacLennon, *Research in Instructional Television and Film.*

[24]Kimball Wiles, *Teaching for Better Schools,* 2d. ed. (Englewood Cliffs, New Jersey: Prentice-Hall, Inc., 1959), p. 264, supports the assumption that television has a greater impact on boys and girls than does radio.

medium of television in some of the larger cities. Although he administered a school district of only 6000 elementary- and secondary-school students, he felt that it was mandatory that he move into the area of television instruction.

Since there was no educational television station in his state, he decided that the best use of the new medium would be to project closed-circuit programs to schools in his district. Acting on his insistent and enthusiastic requests, the school board finally agreed to provide $75,000 for the initial experiment. Although Superintendent Gould had done a great deal of reading on educational television and had visited two districts in which it was operating, he soon found that there were technical concerns to be resolved that he knew virtually nothing about.

He hired technical personnel to place the closed-circuit station in working order, but as the work progressed, he discovered the need for additional technical help. Plans for extending the coaxial cables from the high school to two elementary schools had to be abandoned in the interest of economy. It was finally decided to confine the original experiment to the high school.

Before the first pictures were projected into the high-school auditorium for student viewing, the original appropriation had been spent, and the superintendent found it necessary to explain his miscalculations to the school board and ask for additional funds.

PRINCIPAL JARMAN FINDS TEAMWORK ESSENTIAL

When Principal J. Willard Jarman disclosed his plans for the use of closed-circuit television in his high school of 2000 students, the teachers were generally enthusiastic. Their enthusiasm waned, however, as they began to encounter the hard realism of television production, even on a small scale.

They soon discovered that although the twenty-five or fifty-minute presentations were not long, each one required many hours of painstaking planning. Charts and aids had to be prepared with particular care because of the larger number of viewers, and possible teacher errors in presentation had to be identified in advance.

The necessity for functioning as a team soon became apparent. Teacher-monitors who were not on camera had to insure that students were giving the program their complete attention and that televised presentations were related to the unit. Answering questions, evaluating and recording progress, and maintaining classroom control were a part of their responsibility.

After two scheduled presentations had to be canceled because of technical difficulties, it was obvious that the engineering personnel played an essential role. Mr. Jarman finally decided that interested students with limited knowledge and backgrounds could not serve as adequate substitutes for individuals with the desired technical training.

MRS. SWINBURNE FAILS TO USE COMMERCIAL TELEVISION

Mrs. Margaret Swinburne taught high-school English in a district that, because of size and economic factors, did not have closed-circuit television. Furthermore, reception of the one educational television station in the state was impossible. By means of a booster, however, commercial television was very good on two channels.

Although Mrs. Swinburne was an avid television viewer, she never once made an outside viewing assignment related to the course work. Shakespeare's **Macbeth, Hamlet,** and other excellent dramatic presentations were shown on commercial channels at about the same time they were being discussed in class. It was by chance alone that several students saw the shows.

Conscientious, alert teachers who wish to keep pace with the latest educational developments have attempted to make the most effective use of television in promoting instruction. Television is most likely to be employed successfully in urban areas where closed-circuit educational programs, educational channels, and commercial telecasts provide a range of possibilities to choose from.

MR. SNARR USES MPATI PROGRAMS

Donald H. Snarr was a beginning eleventh-grade history teacher in a large Cincinnati high school. After reading about some of the research in education, he had become fascinated with the possibilities of using television teaching. It was the opportunity for using television instruction that had made him want to teach in Cincinnati rather than in a rural district. In the city he found that he could make effective use of the MPATI lessons broadcast over an ETV station. Because of widespread acceptance of educational television by schools in the region, enthusiasm for its use was at a high level, and programs of high quality and variety were frequently available. In addition, commercial channels provided a number of history-related programs, many of which were sufficiently authentic to be used as educational supplements.

Mr. Snarr used the MPATI programs frequently. He found that the written instructions prepared to enable classroom teachers to make the best use of these programs were most helpful. From the major commercial television networks he obtained a list of programs for the school year that were reported to have particular value for students of United States history. After carefully examining these lists, he selected those programs that he felt were authentic, interesting, and educational.

The well-coordinated efforts of the large number of teaching and technical personnel involved in preparing and broadcasting MPATI programs often result in productive educational tools that the classroom teacher may use as an integral part of the total classroom learning situation. Close cooperation on the part of all members of the team concerned with the preparation and presentation of television lessons for use in a single school district is also essential if success is to be achieved. This fact is illustrated in the following case.

PRINCIPAL PARKER VIEWS TELEVISION TEACHING AS TEAM EFFORT

Principal Claude W. Parker of McKinley Junior High School decided to make a team endeavor of television teaching. At Christmastime his teachers were informed that during the next school year the school district would be sending its own educational programs over coaxial cables into each of the schools and that McKinley would present programs as well as receive them.

After considerable discussion, the school board decided that for the first year the experiment would focus on ninth-grade English. All six of the ninth-grade English teachers thus became a team to work out the problems of teaching in the new medium. Throughout the second semester Mr. Parker held semiweekly meetings to analyze the content to be stressed, the aids to be employed, and the teaching presentation itself. By March 15 certain conclusions were reached:

1. Each teacher would take his turn before the camera, teaching the content he felt he could present most effectively.

2. During the ten days prior to a presentation, all teachers would serve as a team to help prepare content, make aids, and provide suggestions. The teacher who was to give the presentation would serve as team chairman.

3. Prior to the actual telecast two trial runs would be made. Two members of the team would criticize these trial runs by using a checklist and making appropriate written comments.

4. All team members would observe the actual telecast, and each teacher would rate it on a checklist.

5. All six sections of ninth-grade English (180 students) would receive television instruction at the same time. During the first semester television instruction would occupy no more than one fifth of the total instructional time. Each teacher would be responsible for teaching his particular section when they were not viewing closed-circuit television.

6. It would be highly desirable to hire a part-time employee to do lettering, charts, and other artwork that might be necessary.

At the suggestion of the teaching team, team members would be allowed to return a month earlier, with salary, to insure that the details of preparation would be adequately cared for.

Use of Television in Specific Subjects

The teaching of all subjects in the secondary-school curriculum can benefit from the use of television.[25] It is misleading, however, to assume that television instruction serves as an equally valuable aid for teaching all subjects.

Skill Subjects

Conceptual aspects and techniques of skill development may be presented visually. For example, it might be helpful to film the hand position and finger mechanics of a world-famous pianist for a television

---

[25]A number of recent public school practices involving the use of educational television are described by Brown, Lewis, and Harcleroad, *AV Instruction: Media and Methods*, pp. 305–310.

program. Similarly, the slow-motion performance of championship high jumpers might provide a clear picture of how the skill is performed. The student, however, cannot develop a particular skill without practice. In addition, only through personal contact between teacher and students can the imperative needs of skill development (teaching of concept—student trial—correctional coaching—retrial—and recoaching) be met. Television alone does not permit direct contact or provide actual practice.

Concept-Centered Subjects

Those subjects that are predominantly concerned with acquiring understanding (mental pictures)—such as mathematics, physics, chemistry, biology, English grammar, and the social studies—lend themselves best to television teaching. The social studies class, for example, can learn from exposure to social phenomena, narrative accounts, historical events, and current happenings. Commercial television programs are largely concerned with this type of content. Some producers of such programs yield to the temptation for sensation, with the result that much of the content is not authentic and thus is unsuitable for instructional purposes. Under the persistent goading of educators and an alert press, however, commercial television has produced, and is continuing to produce, some programs of social and historical significance that are factually sound and interest-arousing, sometimes to its own financial disadvantage. The knowledgeable social studies teacher can use television programs effectively by carefully selecting the specific viewing assignments and by following through with related in-class discussions.

Specific Suggestions

A number of specific suggestions will help promote the effective use of television for instructional purposes.[26]

Recommendations

1. Ask commercial television stations to provide you with a list of course-related programs, and make assignments that involve viewing these programs.

2. Remember that television is only one of a range of audio-visual media that can be used to further the cause of instruction.

3. Use television in combination with other needed procedures to help you reach sound educational goals.

4. Become thoroughly acquainted with the programs being offered by the educational television stations in your area.

5. Determine which areas in your teaching field best lend themselves to television instruction. In addition, while planning your teaching units, give specific attention to the possibility of using television for enrichment.

---

[26]Koenig and Hill, *The Farther Vision*, pp. 197–207, present a meaningful discussion on "Trends in Station Programing."

6. Experiment with the use of immediate replay of in-class, student-produced videotapes as a means of improving instruction. Train volunteer students in the essential operation of the TV camera and the videotape recorder.

7. Volunteer to help produce an educational television program related to the subject you are teaching. Make arrangements for recording teaching presentations of unusual merit for future use.

8. Visit a high school in which closed-circuit educational telecasting has been used successfully for some time. Determine the feasibility of closed-circuit telecasting within your own school district if it is not currently available.

9. Identify the most successful teachers in your subject area within the school district. Inquire how they use educational television.

10. Visit the nearest educational television station with some of your professional colleagues.

11. Keep up-to-date on the research findings related to educational television.

12. Make a survey of the television viewing habits of students in your classes. Determine to what extent these habits serve an educational purpose.

13. When the students are to watch a televised program, be sure a classroom teacher is supervising the viewing. Encourage intelligent reaction to what is seen through note-taking, a follow-up discussion, testing, and related problem solving.

Cautions

1. Don't neglect the use of commercial television programs in helping students achieve educational goals.

2. Don't forget that in television instruction concepts must be taught to all viewers at a fixed rate.

3. Don't attempt to appear before the television camera without adequate preparation and rehearsal.

4. Don't forget that many necessary types of instruction do not lend themselves to television presentation.

5. Don't forget that television instruction is relatively expensive when it is transmitted to a limited number of students.

6. Don't be suspicious of educational television; try it out.[27]

7. Don't forget that television instruction is limited to those procedures that can be televised.

TEAM TEACHING

Team teaching, like educational television, encourages the use of teachers of particular competence for instructing large numbers of stu-

---

[27]Judith Murphy and Ronald Gross, *Learning by Television* (New York: The Fund for the Advancement of Education, 1966), pp. 11–12, review difficulties encountered by educational television in finding public school acceptance.

dents. Both procedures claim to have effected a general improvement in instruction as well as a more efficient use of the superior teacher. School administrators have also been concerned with the most efficient use of all faculty members. They have expressed particular interest in the possibility of reaching educational goals efficiently through cooperative staff effort.

Development of Team Teaching

In the elementary schools two or more teachers have worked effectively together to improve instruction for several decades; the secondary schools have been much slower to see the merits of combined teacher effort. During the mid-fifties the Commission on the Experimental Study of the Utilization of the Staff in the Secondary School—established by the National Association of Secondary-School Principals and supported by the Ford Foundation—initiated a number of studies concerned with staff utilization in the secondary schools. The most prominent of these investigations involved team teaching.[28]

The concepts underlying this method are not new; one need only examine earlier plans for grouping children and providing an atmosphere for sound instruction to catch glimpses of its inception. The Lancastrian Plan, the Dalton Plan, the Winnetka Plan, Wirt's Platoon System, Hosic's Cooperative Group Plan, and finally the ungraded school contained varying traces of what has come to be known as team teaching.[29] Burton reports that

> the new development probably started in the Franklin School at Lexington, Massachusetts, in 1957, as part of the joint program of research and development sponsored by the Harvard Graduate School of Education and certain public school systems.[30]

Since that time the growth of experimentation in team teaching has attracted national attention. A large number of team teaching projects have been tried in every section of the country, and the results have been reported in professional journals. For example, the January issues of the *National Association of Secondary-School Principals Bulletin* from 1958 through 1962 were devoted to the review of staff utilization practices, primarily team teaching.

Definition of Team Teaching

In team teaching two or more teachers cooperatively formulate a plan, carry it out, and evaluate its effectiveness as it relates to a specific

---

[28]Leonard H. Clark and Irving S. Starr, *Secondary School Teaching Methods*, 2d. ed. (New York: The Macmillan Company, 1967), pp. 131–132, provide a brief discussion of the development of team planning.

[29]William H. Burton, *The Guidance of Learning Activities*, 3d. ed. (New York: Appleton-Century-Crofts, 1962), p. 286.

[30]*Ibid.*, p. 286.

group of students. Although many varieties of teaching teams are being experimented with throughout the United States at this time, most of them have certain common features.[31]

1. Several sections, usually two to four, of a given class (ninth-grade English, for example) meet at the same hour.

2. Teachers of the respective sections usually constitute the teaching team. The librarian or a clerical person may be considered a team member and occasionally an administrator or an audio-visual specialist is also included.[32]

3. Sometimes the team leader is the one who most nearly qualifies as a master teacher. Other times there is no designated chairman, and the team members assume the leadership role depending upon their degree of involvement in large-group presentations.

4. Frequently, perhaps once or twice a week, all sections meet together for a teacher-centered presentation. Most of the time, however, they meet individually under the direction of their particular teacher.

5. When the sections meet in one large group, seating facilities other than the typical classroom are required. Sometimes the students meet in specially constructed facilities, but frequently they meet in the library, the cafeteria, or the auditorium.

6. Specific teaching presentations to the combined sections are usually made by the team member who is best qualified in terms of preparation, personality, and preference. Teachers are thus given the opportunity to capitalize on their strengths and avoid embarrassment in their weak areas.

7. In each individual section teachers are free to use whatever methods they wish, as long as the methods are appropriate to the goals sought. Usually there is a close relationship between the content covered in the large and in the small groups.

8. Planning for team teaching is frequently carried out under the direction of the team leader during a period set aside for this purpose. Such planning may be a joint responsibility, or it may be delegated to a single member of the team, depending upon specific needs.

9. Special materials and audio-visual devices are used extensively, especially during the large-group presentations.

---

[31]Gail M. Inlow, *The Emergent in Curriculum* (New York: John Wiley & Sons, Inc., 1966), pp. 288–298, presents an insightful description of the characteristics of team teaching.

Another meaningful discussion related to the definition of team teaching is provided by the person whose name is most often associated with the term. See J. Lloyd Trump, "What is Team Teaching?" *Education* (February 1965), pp. 327–332.

Harold S. Davis and Ellsworth Tompkins, *How to Organize an Effective Team Teaching Program* (Englewood Cliffs, New Jersey: Prentice-Hall, Inc., 1966), pp. 13–14, identify two broad team categories—hierarchic and synergetic.

[32]William Van Til, Gordon F. Vars, and John H. Lounsbury, *Modern Education for the Junior High School Years*, 2d. ed. (Indianapolis: The Bobbs-Merrill Co., Inc., 1967), pp. 210–211, identify different possible team organizations and their strengths and limitations.

Current Variations in Team Teaching Methods

A look at several current team teaching practices will indicate their similarities as well as their differences.[33]

Team Teaching Within a Single Discipline

At the Geneva, New York Junior High School a seventh-grade science team teaching program was carefully discussed and finally initiated. Three science teachers (one without experience) and the librarian formed the team. Two science sections (56 students) were combined, and the schedule was adjusted to permit students to meet in the school museum and resource center at the same time during the twenty weeks of science instruction.

Different members of the team were assigned responsibility for specific large-group presentations after which students were divided into three smaller groups working under the direction of team teachers.[34] One group remained in the museum where experiments were performed; the second group went to the library for research; and the third group reported to a third member of the team for further exploration and discussion. After a specified period of time—usually one or two days—students rotated stations. The team member responsible for the large-group presentation worked with one of the three groups or as a general consultant as the need was felt.

Different Team Specialties Related to One Course

At Meadowbrook Junior High School in Newton Center, Massachusetts, a Theater Arts course was designed by a faculty committee calling for the use of teachers from different disciplines. In its final form the instructional team consisted of "an art teacher, who taught scene design and organized the construction of sets; two music teachers who did the orchestration, managed the costumes and make-up; one English teacher who dealt with acting, directing, and dancing; one social studies teacher who dealt with acting, directing and lighting; and a math teacher who handled the financial problems."[35]

After an initial exposure of nine weeks to the skills of play production, the 150 students enrolled in the course were subdivided into groups of thirty. Each group took in turn those course segments related to play

[33]Robert H. Johnson and John J. Hunt, *Prescription for Team Teaching* (Minneapolis: Burgess Publishing Co., 1968), pp. 38–39, identify the nature and location of three somewhat different secondary school team teaching programs.

Using the expertise of a range of specialists, David Beggs, III, ed., *Team Teaching: Bold New Venture* (Indianapolis: Unified College Press, Inc., 1964), provides a remarkably comprehensive and timely description of variations on the team teaching theme in spite of the publication date of his book.

[34]According to Trump, about 40 percent of the student's time should be spent in large-group instruction, about 20 percent in small-group instruction, and about 40 percent in individual study. See J. Lloyd Trump, *Images of the Future* (New York: National Association of Secondary-School Principals, 1959), p. 9.

[35]"Team Teaching in Theater Arts," Meadowbrook Junior High School, Newton Center, Massachusetts, pp. 1–3.

production—music and dance, acting, directing, costumes and make-up, and scene design. During the third of the four school terms, the course was open only to those students cast in a play or to those selected to make the costumes and construct the scenery.

Combining Team Teaching with Related Innovations

The Los Alamitos High School, Anaheim, California combines several new practices in its varied approaches to team teaching. Further, separate disciplines within a subject area are taught by a teaching team assigned the responsibility for developing instructional procedures. Students electing to study a particular subject are referred to a specific team, evaluated, and placed in an appropriate unit of study. The individual student's unit grade is determined through joint evaluation by teachers who have worked with him.

Among the innovative features incorporated in the schoolwide team teaching are: nongraded classrooms designed to eliminate grade-level barriers; individualized study packets for each discipline, concerned with maximizing the continuous progress of individuals and groups; daily demand flexible scheduling, permitting teachers to call specific students to classes for certain purposes and for a desired length of time as determined by student needs; student determination of unit goals to be reflected in changes in behavior; and a flexible school plant designed after repeated teacher-administrator-architect conferences to make provision for large-group, small-group, and individualized instruction.[36]

Planning for Team Teaching

Great stress is placed on the need for effective planning in order to insure team teaching success in the Tupelo, Mississippi High School. Under the direction of the district superintendent, the school board helped plan needed renovations; the guidance staff became involved in checking the schedule for flexibility; each area team was scheduled to meet at a common time to plan instructional procedures and to evalaute the success of team efforts; and the skills of clerical personnel were made available to team members.

Flexible scheduling enhances team effort by making large-group, small-group, and independent study as well as self-instruction and quest programs possible. Resource centers staffed by a teacher and a paraprofessional were set up in major academic areas. Further, a range of subject-related laboratories promotes individualized learning.[37]

Interns as Members of the Teaching Team

The eighth-grade social studies team teaching experiment at the Judson Junior High School, Salem, Oregon, has been characterized by

---

[36]"Los Alamitos High School," Los Alamitos High School, Anaheim, California, pp. 1–2.
[37]"Tupelo High School and the Team Teaching Approach," Tupelo Separate School District, Tupelo, Mississippi, pp. 1–6.

careful evaluation of the use of team members, instructional spaces, teaching materials, and measurement of student progress. Using these evaluative findings, team members have modified the program every year since 1960. Literature, spelling, and vocabulary were gradually correlated with the social studies program. After substantial in-service study, team members introduced the study of transformational grammar to their eighth graders.

Capitalizing on the teaching internship program at the Oregon College of Education, the Judson Junior High School principal made arrangements to have two interns (students in the final phases of their formal teacher education) join the team. One intern strong in English was assigned to assist the team leader to permit time for administrative work; the other intern, whose strength lay in social studies, had the responsibility to help team teachers in the total program. Interns thus extend the period of their induction into the teaching profession, the successful termination of which results in certification as well as the completion of the Master's Degree. Their compensation amounts to two-thirds of the beginning teacher's salary.

A secretary, a college graduate with an English major, serves as an integral part of the team, engaging in a range of semi-professional and clerical tasks. The team leader engages in preparatory work in August one week before the other team members arrive.

Included in facilities used in the project are three regular classrooms, a larger room for large-group instruction, the library as needed for independent study, the team office, and the faculty dining room. All facilities lie in close proximity to each other.[38]

Use of Instructional Specialists

"Team Planning in Syracuse, New York involves eleven Instructional Specialists assigned to thirteen schools within the City Public and Parochial School Districts. Of these, seven perform at the elementary level, four at junior and one at senior high levels. They meet with groups of teachers ranging in number from two to six on a fixed schedule. These planning sessions are organized generally by grade level or subject area . . . Opportunity is given for a sharing of ideas, methods, and techniques. In the interim period prior to subsequent meetings, teachers and Instructional Specialists continue to develop group plans, devise and gather pertinent supplementary materials for later use in classroom teaching. Techniques and innovations found successful in one school are shared with other schools by weekly reports and regular meetings of the team of Instructional Specialists."[39]

---

[38]A Report on the Judson Junior High School Team Teaching Project, 1960–1968," Salem Public Schools, Salem, Oregon, pp. 1–7 and pp. 14–19.
[39]"Team Planning: Special Projects," Syracuse City School District, Syracuse, New York, pp. 1–2.

Unit Specialization

Illustrative of the team approach calling for teacher specialization on one particular unit (or course segment) is the plan employed in the Long Branch, New Jersey High School. Three team members develop a high degree of specialization in the content and instruction of three different units of equal length. After the teaching of these different units is completed, each teacher again presents his special unit to another section of students. This rotation procedure is pursued until all sections have been exposed to the three units.[40]

A variation of the same general approach is described in an account of the Hurricane, Utah High School staff utilization project:[41]

> A rotation system was worked out so the teacher could prepare a unit of work in his special field [a previously designated area in language arts] which could be taught in about seven or eight weeks. He could then teach this unit the entire year, seven or eight weeks to each of five groups.
>
> When the teacher had only one eight-week unit to prepare, it made it possible to save a great deal of teacher preparation time and still give the teacher an opportunity to make a more thorough preparation than if he had to prepare five such units during the year.

Advantages of Team Teaching

Advocates of team teaching strongly believe that students taught by this method do as well as, and in some cases better than, students taught by the usual classroom method.[42] These supporters point out that team teaching has several basic advantages over the conventional teaching system using individual classroom teachers.[43]

1. Teaching teams can be organized in a number of different ways to meet the needs of the particular school and the course content.[44] Certain

---

[40]Clark and Starr, *Secondary School Teaching Methods*, p. 207.

[41]Matthew F. Noall and Maurice Nuttall, "Hurricane, Utah High School Ungraded English Project," *Bulletin of the National Association of Secondary-School Principals*, 46 (January 1962), pp. 187–188.

[42]Van Til, Vars, and Lounsbury, *Modern Education for the Junior High School Years*, pp. 216–217, provide an extensive list of team teaching advantages.

[43]Inlow, *The Emergent in Curriculum*, pp. 297–300, discusses in detail a few of the alleged advantages of team teaching.

Areas of concern with the traditional secondary high school program that led educators to initiate team teaching are discussed by Carl H. Peterson, "Team Teaching in the High School," *The Education Digest*, 30 (May 1965), pp. 3–10.

[44]Clark and Starr, *Secondary School Teaching Methods*, pp. 207–210, point out the controversy over the definition of team teaching and suggest the possibility of reducing wide-ranging definitions to three categories.

Leslie W. Kindred et al., *The Intermediate Schools* (Englewood Cliffs, New Jersey: Prentice-Hall, Inc., 1968), p. 131, indicate that Junior high school teaching teams are patterned after those commonly found in senior high schools, while teaching teams in the middle school reflect the elementary school influence.

content may best be learned through a teacher-centered approach in a large-group situation;[45] other content may be learned most effectively through interaction among students and teacher[46] or through individual study.

2. Individual students learn differently in groups of varying sizes; and team teaching, which usually provides for instruction in both large and small groups, can meet these individual student differences better than the usual classroom system.

3. The large-group instruction in team teaching gives both students and teachers a welcome break from the monotony of conventional small-group instruction.

4. Large-group sessions enable more students to benefit from instruction by the most skilled teachers.

5. Under team teaching students can beneficially be exposed to teachers with varying backgrounds and different areas of specialization.

6. When noncertified personnel and clerical aides are part of the team, the experienced teachers can be freed of nonprofessional, time-consuming tasks.[47]

7. Because team members must plan carefully and have the time in which to do so, the quality of instruction possible in a team project is often better than that possible in conventional classroom instruction. Team teaching also permits flexibility in organizing the teacher's time.

8. Team teaching provides the setting for more effective student participation in the teaching-learning process by means of small-group instruction. Under this system, students usually are given greater opportunity for self-directed study and independent research.

9. The content of different subjects may be coordinated more effectively in a team program than in a system where individual subjects are always taught in separate classes.

10. Team teaching allows for more efficient and economical use of building space and teacher personnel. Seldom-used auditoriums as well as small offices may be used to advantage, and team teachers not involved in actual instruction may spend a larger portion of their time on necessary nonteaching responsibilities.

---

[45]Advantages of large-group instruction as an essential part of team teaching are discussed by Davis and Tompkins, *How to Organize an Effective Team-Teaching Program*, pp. 45–48.

Purposes, preparations of the presentations, and logistical arrangements for large-group instruction are identified by J. Lloyd Trump and Delmas F. Miller, *Secondary School Curriculum Improvement: Proposals and Procedures* (Boston: Allyn & Bacon, Inc., 1968), pp. 275–279.

[46]*Ibid.*, pp. 281–287, provide a brief but meaningful chapter treatment of small-group instruction.

[47]Johnson and Hunt, *Prescription for Team Teaching*, pp. 4–5, define several terms— auxiliary personnel, paraprofessional, instructional assistant, intern, secretary, team clerk, teacher aide, community consultant, student consultant, resource personnel, and support personnel—commonly used to identify the nonleadership roles of specific team members.

Limitations of Team Teaching

Although team teaching has grown dramatically since the late fifties, it poses no real threat to the existence of the one-teacher classroom. Proponents of team teaching are quick to point out its strengths, but its opponents are just as quick to identify its limitations. Some of these limitations are listed here.[48]

1. Many teachers are not suited by training or disposition to engage in the cooperative planning and varied use of procedures, resources, and personnel that are essential in team teaching. In fact, it is often maintained that if a teacher is thoroughly competent in teaching his particular subject, team teaching is not necessary.

Some administrators—wishing to appear progressive—encourage faculty members to engage in team teaching although they may possess little inclination or aptitude for it. Members of a teaching team must possess special characteristics, and the variety essential to this type of teaching often taxes their ingenuity.

2. Team teaching calls for the use of special physical facilities. If these facilities are not available, they must be provided at considerable expense to the school district. Many older schools simply do not have the large rooms that are necessary for many team teaching situations.

3. Special planning periods must be scheduled at a time when all team members can meet. In order to make such meetings possible, the administrator sometimes must ask for concessions for team members or impose restrictions on nonteam members.

4. The per-student cost of team teaching is sometimes higher than the per-student cost of conventional teaching, because many teams are comprised of nonprofessional aides, paraprofessionals, and clerical assistants in addition to full-time certified teachers.

5. The necessary impersonality of large-group instruction hampers the emotional, social, and academic progress of certain students who need consistent, individual contact with their teachers. Team teachers seldom become well-enough acquainted with the individual students in the large group to be able to meet their needs effectively.

6. Planning essential to productive team teaching often becomes unduly complicated; the end result may not justify the expenditure of professional time and energy. If individualized instruction and instruction in both the small and large groups is not planned with great care, team teaching may be less effective than traditional classroom instruction.

---

[48]Jack R. Fraenkel and Richard E. Gross, "Team Teaching: Let's Look Before We Leap!" *Social Education*, 30 (May 1966), pp. 335–337, caution that wholesale acceptance of team teaching superiority in the absence of carefully structured and controlled research is dangerous.

Identifying the conditions that contribute to effective team teaching, Georgiades registers doubt about the validity of certain research studies. See William Georgiades, "Team Teaching: A New Star, Not a Meteor,"*NEA Journal*, 56 (April 1967), pp. 14–15.

Principles Related to Team Teaching

Examination of team teaching projects reported in professional literature reveals common principles basic to all projects. A number of these principles are listed below.

1. The chief purpose of team teaching is to improve the quality of instruction and learning by using the school staff as efficiently as possible.

2. The effectiveness of team teaching largely depends upon the variety of strengths of individual team members[49] and their ability to work together as a group. Team teaching permits teachers to capitalize on their particular strengths and to minimize their weaknesses.

3. Team teaching requires cooperative planning and capitalizes on group thinking.

4. Certain types of information lend themselves to different methods of teaching—independent study, small groups, or large groups.

5. In order to serve the needs of different instructional situations, teaching teams can be organized to teach the same subject to combined groups, to cross subject-matter boundaries, to take advantage of unique facilities and individuals within a community, or to individualize instruction as dictated by student needs.

6. Team teaching has inherent instructional flexibility possessed by no other teaching method. It may employ all types of audio-visual media, including television; a range of different teachers, each presenting the lesson he teaches best; and small or large blocks of time in teaching small or large groups of students.

7. Although team teaching may be used with marked success in one school, it may fail in another for several reasons: inability of teachers to plan effectively as a team, lack of interest on the part of the team members or the administrator, unrealistic expectations about team operation, insufficient time or space for planning, domination of team effort by one or more members of the team, or wrong team membership in view of instructional objectives.

8. Successful team teaching presupposes the team members' willingness to experiment and the availability of classrooms of varied sizes, conference rooms,[50] and a range of audio-visual aids.

Sound and Unsound Practices

Effective team teaching does not happen by chance; it is the result of careful planning. In team teaching the various segments of instruction

---

[49]Clark and Starr, *Secondary School Teaching Methods*, p. 206, support the assumptions that ". . . different levels of competence and training are needed for the various function that teachers now perform . . ." and that team teaching permits teachers to capitalize on individual strengths, interests, and capabilities.

[50]Pointing out that team teaching may flourish in properly adapted older school buildings, Beggs, III, *Team Teaching: Bold New Venture*, pp. 47–49, stresses the need for team planning areas, instructional space for large and small groups, and for resource centers for independent study.

taught by different participants have to be correlated. What happens when team teaching is not thoroughly planned is illustrated in the following examples.

THREE TEAM TEACHERS UNDERESTIMATE THE JOB

In February, Principal Ewell asked for volunteers to participate in the twelfth-grade English team experiment to begin the following year. Mrs. Bertha Smythe, Miss Bonnie Ruff, and Mr. Bertrand Diamond, three of the ten twelfth-grade English teachers, volunteered. Each teacher had three or more years of successful experience and appeared eager to try out the new procedure.

Mr. Diamond, the senior member of the team, was appointed chairman. Because the teachers assumed it was not necessary to rework units they had taught successfully before, they decided that planning could be deferred until one week before school started, when they would devote full time to the task. When school opened, the team members were still attempting to think through the methodological implications of team teaching. The principal set aside time for a common planning session in which the teachers could meet together three times each week. Large-group instruction for eighty-five students (three sections) was scheduled for twice each week.

The three team teachers soon found themselves planning and teaching on a day-to-day basis, hoping that somehow they would be able to reap some of the benefits of team teaching. In their insecurity they reverted to the traditional procedures in which they had confidence; unit planning geared to team teaching and utilizing the special abilities of team members was largely overlooked. Mr. Diamond, a dominant personality, assigned himself the major responsibility for teaching the large combined group, and the other team members yielded submissively.

The useful involvement of the administrator, librarian, and school secretary, as well as regular team members, is portrayed in the following account.

NONTEACHERS ARE MEMBERS OF A TEACHING TEAM

James Underwood, principal of Bryan Junior High School, strongly felt that a team approach might improve the quality of instruction in his eighth-grade English and history classes. After contacting the state Department of Education, he discovered that foundation money might be made available for such a team project if it were structured within certain limits. He consulted with the state representative of the foundation on several occasions before an acceptable project design was evolved. When the project was finally accepted, the foundation provided funds for (a) paying team teachers during workshops before and after the school year, (b) hiring a university curriculum consultant and a statistician, (c) buying certain needed audio-visual materials, and (d) purchasing standardized tests.

Because the school was small (300 students), all four eighth-grade teachers of English and social studies were invited to participate as members of the team. Because of his intense interest, the principal was frequently involved in team planning sessions. The librarian also met regularly with the four teachers, and the front office secretary gave clerical assistance whenever it was requested.

In the pre-school workshop, which began two weeks before the opening of school, the university consultant helped the teachers think through the type of planning most appropriate to the students and the content being taught. Specific ideas gradually took form:

1. Team teaching would consist of large-group instruction in which all sections (103 students) would participate as often as desirable. The auditorium would be available for their use at virtually all times.

2. Four small groups (sections consisting of approximately twenty-five students each) would meet under the direction of individual teachers. Students in individual sections would be grouped homogeneously on the basis of recorded I.Q. and past achievement.

3. Two eighth-grade subjects, English and United States history, would be correlated where possible and practical to lend added meaning to content.

4. Units correlating the two subjects would be worked out in rough form by team members during the daily planning periods. Each unit would be further refined by the librarian and then sent to the university consultant for his criticism. Necessary clerical work would be taken care of by the front office secretary under the direction of the librarian.

5. Audio-visual aids and resource persons in the community would be used extensively. The district superintendent promised to buy an overhead projector and a machine that would produce cell overlays quickly. A special room in the library would serve as a curriculum workroom and an audio-visual repository under the direction of the librarian. The art teacher and certain of his students would be asked to assist in producing special aids.

6. The university consultant would visit the school once each month for a two-hour conference with team teachers. It was decided that the meeting was not to be planned in advance but was to serve the immediate concerns of team members.

7. The two team members with English teaching majors had minors in history and sociology, respectively. The two teachers with history teaching majors had minors in English and journalism, respectively. The team members decided to capitalize on their areas of specialization and particular interest. One of the English teachers loved to make dramatic presentations of literary selections; she was to plan such a presentation for the large-group session. One history teacher had accumulated a number of slides of the battle sites of the Revolutionary War. He would develop, with the English teacher, a unit correlating the literature of this period with its historical content.

8. Evaluation procedures would consist of the following: (a) Students would be given standardized achievement tests in English and United States history at the beginning and end of the school year; both individual and average gains would be recorded. The same achievement tests would be administered to comparable eighth-grade students in two other schools of an adjacent school district; meaningful statistical comparisons

could thus be made by a competent statistician. (b) Twice during the school year, once in November and again in May, students would indicate in written form their likes and dislikes of team teaching. (c) Parents would also be asked to react twice. (d) Teachers would be interviewed individually by the university consultant during late October and again in May to determine their problems as well as their likes and dislikes of the program. (e) At the end of each unit team members would write a brief critique of the unit—and the teachers' criticisms would then be filed away for possible modification and use as a resource for the second year of the project.

At the end of the first year of team teaching, Principal Underwood could point with pride to the objective evidence of substantial student gains in subject-matter achievement in both history and English. Furthermore, his students had made somewhat better achievement scores than the students in the two control schools. Teachers, parents, and students were in general agreement that team teaching was an effective and interesting procedure.

Specific Suggestions

Although the newcomer to team teaching is apt to need particular guidance, both the inexperienced and experienced teacher may receive helpful direction from the following suggestions.

Recommendations

1. Prepare thoroughly before engaging in team teaching; be sure that the other team members also plan carefully.[51]

2. Select team members who possess specific qualities that contribute to team effort as well as to general instructional competence. Team teaching can only be as effective as the quality of the team members permits it to be.

3. Become informed on the current projects involving team teaching that are being tried throughout the nation.

4. During the planning phase of each unit identify the precise role each member of the teaching team is to play.

5. Make sure that the psychological principles of learning are not violated during large-group lectures.

6. Make sure that the necessary personal contact between team teacher and individual student is maintained in spite of large-group instruction.

7. Work for consistent improvement in team teaching even after one or two experimental years have been completed.

8. Be sure that the design for team teaching makes it possible to arrive at verifiable conclusions about its success or lack of success. Work out procedures for evaluating the efficiency of all aspects of team teaching.

---

[51]*Ibid.*, pp. 37–40, emphasizes the importance of in-service education for team teachers in addition to the provision of adequate time for planning.

Cautions

1. Don't assume that educational achievements are unimportant because they cannot be tested by paper-and-pencil tests. Student interest, teacher-student relationships, and appreciation for the subject—all of which may be positively affected by team teaching—are important educational gains that do not lend themselves readily to objective measurement.

2. Don't assume that all instructional experts are proponents of team teaching. Remember that the current evaluation of team teaching frequently is based on personal opinion.

3. Don't launch into an extensive program of team teaching unless the first experimental efforts prove to be unusually rewarding.

TELEVISION AND TEAM TEACHING IN REVIEW

Both educational television and team teaching have had a marked impact on instructional procedures and pupil learning since World War II. Educators have engaged in repeated experiments to determine how these tools can best be employed in instruction. Although educational television and team teaching are now established devices, all signs point to a continuation of testing in a search for their most effective use.

Because educational television makes use of both sight and sound, it can present natural phenomena and current events to the learners. Many school systems have employed educational television extensively, while others have used it only on a limited scale. Four major types of television facilities can be employed in education: (1) educational television stations, (2) commercial network educational programing, (3) closed-circuit production, and (4) low-power transmission by local commercial stations over UHF channels.

Team teaching consists of instructional procedures in which two or more teachers cooperatively work out a plan, carry it out, and evaluate its effectiveness as it relates to a specific group of students. Although many varieties of teaching teams are being experimented with, most such projects include large-group instruction under the direction of a team member, frequently a master teacher; small-group discussions in which each team member directs one group; special building and audio-visual facilities; and cooperative planning sessions at a specifically designated hour.

PROBLEMS FOR STUDY AND DISCUSSION

1. Identify and discuss briefly at least five major advantages of television instruction.

2. Identify and discuss at least five disadvantages of television instruction.

3. Explain the difference between ETV and ITV. Is the use of the two terms justified?

4. How is commercial television currently being employed for educational purposes?

5. Identify three new applications of television instruction. How can they be made to enliven classroom instruction in your teaching minor?

6. What is the current status of the MPATI program? Explain.

7. Discuss the nature of the programing on the educational television stations in your state.

8. What is closed-circuit television? What are its specific advantages?

9. List the specific ways television could best be used in your subject-matter area.

10. List the steps an administrator and teachers should take in preparing a presentation for closed-circuit television.

11. Discuss the specific advantages of immediate replay of videotapes with respect to either your teaching major or teaching minor.

12. What advantages does the classroom teacher have over the television instructor? Explain.

13. What do research studies reveal with respect to the relative advantages of television instruction over direct (non-television) instruction? How do you account for this?

14. What are the limitations of teaching skills by means of television?

15. Make eight key recommendations that would be of particular value to a new teacher anxious to use television effectively.

16. Identify five characteristics typical of all team teaching projects.

17. How do you account for the many types of team teaching programs?

18. Briefly describe the unique features of the team projects in each of the following schools: Meadowbrook Junior High School, Newton Center, Massachusetts; Los Alamitos High School, Anaheim, California; and Judson Junior High School, Salem, Oregon.

19. List six important principles underlying team teaching.

20. Through reading and inquiry determine what team teaching projects are currently being conducted in your state. Describe one of these projects in detail.

21. List and discuss briefly five reasons why your teaching major would or would not lend itself well to team teaching.

22. Describe the membership of four different kinds of teaching teams. Which do you prefer? Why?

23. What is meant by the *unit specialization* approach to team teaching?

19. *Recent Instructional Innovations*

The last five years have seen the emergence of many innovations and the extension of new instructional procedures classified as innovations a few years ago. Programed learning, instructional television, and team teaching may no longer be classified as new; however, a promising array of solidly anchored new branches are attached to the trunk of each of these practices. The next two chapters will examine briefly the most attractive of these branches.

Forward-looking, experimental schools often provide the setting in which a range of innovations may progress simultaneously. Seldom does a single promising practice stand alone in a school or school district; more often the *flocking* phenomenon is in evidence and related practices with sound promise tend to cluster around a central instructional concept. Hence, team teaching may involve the use of educational television, small and large groups, learning packages, and—in a few cases—computer-assisted instruction.

Chapters 19 and 20 will elaborate on some of the newer practices currently known to be in operation. Their relationship to parent practices will also be identified. This chapter focuses on recent innovations related to individualization, grouping, and their effect on instruction.

INDIVIDUALIZATION

The well-established fact that learning is an individual process has continued to modify the traditional concepts of class size, scheduling, and school building construction. Unfortunately, changes have been long in coming and have not moved with the speed desired by knowledgeable educators.

Among instructional procedures of the past decade aimed at individualizing instruction have been the use of programed learning, study carrels, and nongraded classes.[1] With continuing experimentation, each of these techniques has been modified and improved—in spite of the fact that many traditional secondary schools are aware of their benefits only through casual professional contacts and reading.

Programed Instruction

Widely used in many progressive schools throughout the country, programed instruction—now in its professional adolescence—has been subject to a range of experiments in virtually all content areas. Subjects often identified as *not* lending themselves to programing—literature, art, creativity, the social sciences—have been successfully programed, lending credence to the assumption of earlier programers that any subject may use digestable, sequentialized fragments to form a meaningful program.

In a three-year study, Parnes and his associates produced and tried experimentally auto-instructional materials capable of developing creative behavior in high school seniors.[2] Results of the investigation revealed that students in the experimental group (those who had taken the programed course either alone or with the aid of a teacher) made greater gains on eleven psychological *pre-* and *post-tests* than did students in the control group (those who received no training in creative behavior). Although

---

[1]*Final Report: Analysis of Instructional Systems* (Santa Monica, California: System Development Corporation, 1966), pp. 61–76, provides a range of tables indicating the frequency with which selected innovative schools employed specific innovations.

[2]Sidney J. Parnes, *Programming Creative Behavior* (Albany, New York: State University of New York Press, 1966), pp. iv–v.

such experiments are infrequent and need the confirming effect of replication, they indicate responsible, continuing interest in improving instruction in nonstructured curriculum areas.

A sizeable proportion of the experimentation with self-directive instruction has departed from the *stimulus-response-reinforcement* pattern. Seeking to effect a systematic and logical self-instructional pattern, many teachers have developed on their own programs to serve the needs of their particular subjects and students. Such programs usually identify a series of closely coordinated, sequentialized activities to be undertaken self-directively by the student. Using procedures carefully identified on a handout sheet, a unit of the Westward Movement, for example, might call for several activities in this order: reading the basic chapter from the textbook, viewing a special motion picture in the social science laboratory, reading a specified article from the *Encyclopedia Brittanica*, discussing basic unit-related dittoed problems with a group of four other students, working through a programed chapter on the Westward Movement, writing a short paper on a self-selected historical character, and taking a final essay examination.

The systematic use of such specific, sequentially-placed, learning tasks, sometimes confusingly identified as a program, should not be equated with programs involving the use of carefully worded stimulus-response frames. Although both procedures—reflecting systematic organization—may be included in the general category of programs, loose usage has tended to disturb the uninformed teacher. At the Brigham Young University Laboratory High School both programs were employed for several years. Certain English literature classes employed sequentially placed learning tasks while mathematics classes placed great reliance on the use of printed textbooks containing numbered frames.

Study Carrels

In no area of school housing has experimentation been more active and more varied than in the attempts to find practical and functional spaces for individual study. The six- and eight-foot partitions characterizing the carrels of the mid-fifties are no more; they were gradually reduced to heights varying from one to three feet. In many cases partitions were eliminated altogether, leaving students at conventional library tables. The elimination of partitions was based upon the assumption that a student ideally preoccupied with the study of content provided his own invisible barriers to distraction.

Many schools have chosen to provide a limited number of carrels— enough to seat 10 percent of the students in the room at any one time—placed in strategic positions along the walls of the room.[3] During

---

[3]"New Concepts in School Plant Design: An Accent on Accessibility," from the Conference on Accessibility (New York: Educational Facilities Laboratory, March 1969), p. 13, contends that "the most suitable space for mathematics learning consists of an area in which carrels are built around a perimeter. Mathematics more than any other subject lends itself to the use of carrels . . ."

study periods some students may elect to use the comparative seclusion of the confined area; other students with poor study habits may be assigned to such booths. Mobility is often assured through permanently mounted, lockable wheels. School furniture manufacturing concerns have also focused on flexible seating by producing student desks with two-foot, foldable extensions that may be used to supplement the writing or working surface, or to provide—when in upright position—an effective, view-blocking partition. Four seats so equipped may be placed in such a position that the view of each forward-facing student is shielded on two sides. Well-equipped school libraries often provide permanent, semi-soundproof carrels, closed on four sides in which students may type without disturbing others.

A limited number of schools have capitalized on the technological advances of the last half of this century to effectively equip carrels for instructional purposes. Expense, however, serves as a deterrent to the best laid plans, and few individualized study spaces are ideally equipped. Depending on the purposes to be served, such spaces may contain teaching machines; tape recorders for playing and recording; provisions for dial access to audio and visual tape banks; earphones; and small television receivers. Activities in an individualized study area may warrant particular equipment. Special wiring, gas, compressed air, or a typewriter may be essential for certain types of study.[4]

Special-purpose individual study areas have existed for many years in the form of welding booths, gas- and water-equipped science work areas, and individual woodshop benches. Perhaps the most sophisticated version of the individual work area is the computer terminal through which the advantages of programed instruction including *stimulus* (written word, graphic presentation, still pictures, movies, typewritten message, or oral communication), *response* (constructed answer, selection of a multiple-choice item, use of light pen, typed answers or oral response), and *reinforcement* (indication of correct answer or redirection to alternate frames) are made available.

Continuous Progress Programs

Instruction at its best calls for having each student achieve continuing success in terms of capacity. Overachievement and underachievement are scientifically excluded; psychological as well as grade-level barriers are eliminated.

In order to bring about optimum learning unhampered by grade structure or school organization, experimenters have tried a number of simplified and complex procedures—student self-direction, cluster grouping, individual projects, vertical and horizontal enrichment programs, frequent individualized teacher-student contact, teacher-developed mate-

---

[4] James W. Brown, Richard B. Lewis, and Fred F. Harcleroad, *AV Instruction: Media and Methods*, 3d. ed. (New York: McGraw-Hill Book Company, 1969), p. 77.

rials, and programed instruction. Such procedures, however, have met with varying degrees of success; none has been totally satisfactory. Simulation of continuing tutorial assistance has been approximated through the use of a combination of techniques with programed instruction serving as the central procedure.

High school level foreign-language instruction at the Brigham Young University Laboratory School was offered on a continuous progress basis. Salient features of the program called for:[5]

1. Encouraging students to progress at their own rate through curriculum and instructional techniques which encouraged continuous progress.

2. Dividing classes into cluster groups for instruction and laboratory work. Each cluster group progressed at a different pace.

3. Utilizing graduate assistants, student teachers, and regular teachers to instruct the various cluster groups.

4. Using the ALM materials in French and German.

5. Using a special Spanish text which instructors developed for individualizing instruction. It was complete with instructional slides, tapes, and tapes for testing.

6. Developing further materials in each language area for pilot use. These included texts, study guides, drill tapes, filmstrips, and teacher guides.

Emphasis on individualized instruction aimed at promoting continuous academic progress in the Theodore, Alabama High School calls for the use of four basic procedures—teaching based on three levels of difficulty, using study guides calling for maximum individualization, using programed instruction materials when assumed appropriate, and giving special assignments.[6]

By "individualized instruction", we mean that the plan for a course has been developed taking into account the unique differences of students within the class. Each student may progress independently of other members of the class and may receive teacher help as he needs it. Each student progresses at his own comfortable speed. Though in all subjects we do not accomplish individual progress to the same degree, our ultimate aim is to individualize the total instructional program, so that every teacher's plans and procedures will take into account the unique needs of each individual in the class. Teachers in different subject areas individualize their instruction in different ways.

For instance, in mathematics each student follows the same sequence and works through identical assignments. In history, however,

[5]Glen F. Ovard, Lowell Thomson, and Antone K. Romney, "Summary of Experimental Programs, Brigham Young Laboratory Schools," Brigham Young University, College of Education, 1965, p. 6.
[6]"Curriculum Guide for Individualizing Instruction," Theodore High School, Theodore, Alabama, 1964, pp. 5–6.

students will work on the same topics in the same sequence, but with individualized assignments. Smaller groups, at times the whole class, may be given the same assignment for survey and background study. These two subjects illustrate extremes.[7]

In the Nova High School in Fort Lauderdale, Florida a somewhat varied approach is employed to achieve continuous student progress.[8] Capitalizing on the most modern plant facilities available at the time of its construction, the high school was envisioned as the initial link in an educational complex extending from kindergarten through college and to be housed on the same campus. Because Nova is ungraded, it is possible for a seventh-year student to be studying mathematics with tenth-year students, science with ninth-year students, and social studies with students at his own grade level. The program is tailored to individual student needs and attempts to take each student as far as he can go. Implementation of this philosophy enables certain gifted students, aided by vertical acceleration, to complete, for example, an undergraduate college major in mathematics while still technically enrolled in high school.

Rejecting the concept of grade-level promotions, in each subject the school permits students to advance at their own pace through a series of achievement levels designated as units. Each unit must be completed before the student is permitted to move to the next unit; ladder-like progress is thus encouraged. In order to insure that students begin on the proper rung of the ladder, they are subject to area examinations at the time they enter school. Furthermore, students are encouraged to engage in independent study and research in each subject, and student freedom far in excess of that found in traditional schools is permitted.

Nova utilizes the most forward-looking educational techniques and media: team teaching involving large, medium, and small groups; subject-matter laboratories; schoolwide closed-circuit television; well-equipped resource centers; teaching machines, tape recorders, and microfilm readers; and overhead projectors in every room.

Self-Directed Learning

Emphasis on specific teaching and learning techniques to serve the media: team teaching involving large, medium, and small groups; subject-traditional teacher-centered procedures. Any method involving one-way communication—lecture, passive reading, or television instruction—that fails to elicit student response is subject to widespread criticism. Avoidance of passivity is encouraged if the student has a voice in selecting his

---

[7] *Ibid.*, p. 5.
[8] Burt Kaufman and Paul Bethune, "Nova High: Space Age School," *Phi Delta Kappan*, 46 (September 1964), pp. 9–11.)

own courses, the methods used to teach them, and the time and place to study them.

A large proportion of innovative, experimental secondary schools have provided for independent study (IS), especially those schools in which individual student schedules are provided through the use of the computer.[9] The typical arrangement calls for schedules that appear on individualized printout sheets showing the modules of each day devoted to specific classes and to independent study. Such schedules are similar to college-level variable schedules.

Use of self-directive study techniques has met with varying degrees of success. A sizeable proportion of the schools experimenting with such programs have overestimated student willingness and ability to use them effectively. Conditioned by years of authoritarian teaching, students were generally not trained to make efficient use of their own time. Some schools chose to grant students a larger proportion of independent study time with each successive grade level. Tenth graders, for example, might be restricted to using 10 percent of their total in-school time for self-directed study; eleventh graders might be allowed 20 percent and twelfth graders 30 percent of their school time for self-directed pursuits.

After two years of experimental effort at the high school level in the Brigham Young University Laboratory School, mathematics teachers concluded that instructional interests would be served best if students were placed in either 1) regular classes or 2) continuous progress classes when enough information was available to assess self-directive behavior. Continuous progress classes called for a large measure of student self-direction through the use of programed materials and independent study booths. Regular classes, on the other hand, called for traditional, high quality instruction in which student behavior could be controlled more effectively. Students were transferred at the discretion of the teacher from one type of class to another. The assumption held at the outset of the experiment—that bright students would be self directive—called for a reappraisal of student capabilities in this area. Although the more intelligent students were often capable of managing their own academic affairs, many conscientious but less gifted students of average and below average ability had somehow acquired the skills of self-direction.

Reaction to Teaching Styles

Adolescents have personal preferences in clothes, music, friends, and recreational activities—a fact that long has been used by educators to explain student behavior. However, only within the past few years have

---

[9]Thirteen specific accounts of instructional activities in nongraded schools are presented by David W. Beggs, III and Edward G. Buffie, eds., *Nongraded Schools in Action: Bold New Venture* (Bloomington, Indiana: Indiana University Press, 1967), chapters 7–19. The trend toward individualization, independent study, and student self direction is clearly discernible in these accounts.

psychologists begun to examine seriously the idea that individual preferences for certain kinds of instructional methods and teacher behavior
might strongly influence student achievement. Goldberg hypothesized
"that a pupil's learning is, in large measure, a function of the kind of
teaching to which he is exposed . . ."[10]

An increasing number of qualified researchers have focused attention
on what has come to be known as *teaching style*. Investigators have
probed into the direct influence (lecturing, giving directions, or criticiz-
ing) of teachers as contrasted with their indirect influence (clarifying,
lending encouragement, or accepting student ideas); into the teacher's
performance examined within the framework of classroom control, approach to teaching content, and creation of interpersonal climate; and
into the dimensions of teaching style, categorized in terms of personal
dimensions, task dimensions, and dynamic quality of the teaching
performance.[11]

GROUPING

Repeated attempts by educators to employ different grouping patterns
reflect the realization that tutorial instruction is too expensive for general
use and that the use of varied teaching groups can promote efficiency in
instruction. For decades the search for the optimum size group has
concerned educators. However, it was not until the early sixties that
Trump brought into sharp focus the desirability of using large groups as
well as small groups to serve the student's learning needs. Employment of
both large and small groups is now well entrenched as instructional
techniques in quality secondary schools.[12]

Large Groups

Large instructional groups of today are different from the large
instructional groups of a decade ago in that they are more varied and
numerous.[13] For example, combining the eight sections of the tenth grade
to listen to a special lecture on drug abuse is feasible. Under certain
circumstances all tenth grades in a large school district may be combined
by means of closed circuit television to listen to the same program.
Expanded still further, all students in a total school may join millions of

---

[10]Miriam L. Goldberg, "Adapting Teacher Style Pupil Difference: Teachers for
Disadvantaged Children," *Merrill-Palmer Quarterly of Behavior and Development*, 10
(1964), p. 162.

[11]*Ibid.*, p. 163

[12]Far-reaching international interest in grouping is reflected in a report sponsored
by the UNESCO Institute for Education in Hamburg, Germany: Alfred Yates, ed.,
Grouping in Education, (New York: John Wiley & Sons, Inc., 1966).

[13]Numerous examples of the use of large as well as small groups in implementing the
purposes of instructional teams are provided by David W. Beggs, III, *Team Teaching:
Bold New Venture* (Indianapolis: Unified College Press, Inc., 1964).

fellow students and people at large in viewing and listening to an educational commercial telecast or the launching of Apollo 11.

Infinite flexibility is now employed in the use of large groups. Teachers no longer feel restricted in varying the size of the large group if there is an educational justification for so doing. In some schools the combination of two sections of students, a scant 50 students, is viewed as large-group instruction. In others 500 may also be classified as large-group instruction and may employ essentially the same teaching techniques. Moreover, groups ranging in size from 50 to 500 may be justified where effective one-way communication is the essential concern. Using specially prepared video tapes projected on large screens, many universities are currently instructing groups ranging in size from 100 to over 1000 students.

Small Groups

Trump's original small group was fixed at twelve to fifteen students.[14] Since his widely heralded statement, however, teachers have gradually extended their experimentation to include groups ranging in size from three or four students to as many as twenty. The composition of small groups may also be advantageously controlled to promote participation, to encourage students to work to capacity, or to stimulate peer group thought. A recessive student who has not found courage to participate in the class-size group may blossom verbally in a small group composed of friendly peers. Further, the competitive, bright student who tends to monopolize class discussions may find himself challenged to maintain pace with a small group of teacher-selected students with intelligence equal to his own.

In the Shoreline and Shorecrest High Schools in Seattle, Washington, small groups of approximately seven students are employed to promote the free exchange of ideas among students who have listened to large-group lectures or who have studied common content.[15] Likewise, at the Tupelo, Mississippi High School the small group seminar is viewed as a follow-up experience. Here the large group is divided into smaller sections that meet with team members. Each of these sections is, in turn, subdivided into groups of three to six students who work under a student chairman in the preparation of projects, reports, and panel discussions.[16]

The pairing of students has often proven to be an effective instructional device. Foreign-language students frequently work in pairs while reciting dialogues. In many classes students with limited comprehension of a certain concept may find it more helpful to discuss it with another

---

[14] J. Lloyd Trump, *Images of the Future* (New York: National Association of Secondary-School Principals, 1959), p. 10.

[15] "The Year of the Non-Conference Demonstration Center," Shoreline School District No. 412, Seattle, Washington, 1966–1967.

[16] "The Approach to Flexible Scheduling in Tupelo High School," Tupelo Separate School District, Tupelo, Mississippi.

student who understands it thoroughly rather than to receive help from the teacher. The instructor is thus freed to pursue other needed tasks.

Individualization

Individualization is the antithesis of grouping and as such deserves consideration. The ideal learning environment is one in which each student is thoroughly interested, is motivated to maximum effort, and is working to his full capacity. The most significant recent changes in educational methodology, technology, and materials have been brought about by dedicated, inventive educators who have relentlessly pursued this ideal. Among these changes are the use of programed instruction, self-directive study, computer-assisted instruction, and dial access systems.

At the Waterford, New York High School the teacher in Basic Business chose to individualize instruction by developing, testing, and finally using a unit on automobile insurance. A programing technique involving branching was employed because it did not require the use of small steps; further, the programer was allowed to use mulitple-choice questions.[17]

Individual learning does not always mean individual study: sometimes the most fruitful motivation to efficient learning—always an individualized task—is meaningful interaction. The process (instructional technique) is a necessary means for fixing desired concepts in each individual learner—but the learning is uniquely his.

Grouping for Special Purposes

Grouping students to achieve nontypical educational purposes is an old practice; however, many of the purposes to be served are new. Among them are promoting social interaction through the formation of heterogeneous small groups, encouraging intellectual and social integration by not allowing minority-group students to sit together in a class, promoting academic excellence by assigning difficult joint projects to carefully selected bright students with common problems, and using special clubs— the Assistant Teachers Club, for example—to serve instructional purposes.

A work-study approach (STEP) is employed in New York State to serve the needs of students fifteen years of age or older who have been identified as potential dropouts. Using guidance techniques, teacher-coordinators meet daily with students in groups of twenty to twenty-five. Job placement as well as counseling are their central concerns.[18]

---

[17]Robert G. Gleig, "How to Develop a Unit Using Programmed Instruction," *Business Education World*, 45 (June 1965), p. 19.

[18]*Programs for Progress: Reaching the Disadvantaged* (Albany, New York: The State University of New York Press, 1968).

PROBLEMS FOR STUDY AND DISCUSSION

1. Should team teaching, programed learning, and instructional television be classified as innovations? Why?

2. Name five team-teaching related innovations of the past five years.

3. List five instructional innovations of the past half-decade directly related to the individualization of instruction.

4. What are the reasons for the slow acceptance of computer-assisted instruction in the public schools?

5. Why do innovations tend to cluster together in a given school or school district? Explain.

6. What does Parnes' study reveal with respect to the use of programed materials for the purpose of developing creative behavior?

7. Differentiate between stimulus-response-reinforcement programs and nonstimulus-response-reinforcement programs. What are the advantages of the latter?

8. Identify reasons for using the study carrel. How do you think it can best be used in your teaching major?

9. What are the advantages of a computer terminal over a conventional carrel?

10. Identify the characteristics of a continuous-progress program. Is such a program available to assist teaching in your teaching major?

11. List the steps involved in foreign-language, continuous-progress teaching at the Brigham Young University Laboratory School.

12. What are the basic procedures identified with individualized instruction at the Theodore Alabama High School?

13. In the Nova High School in Fort Lauderdale, Florida it is possible for a student with varying achievement levels in different subjects to work with three groups whose average ages are two or more years apart. Do you think this is wise? Why?

14. How effectively can self directed learning be employed among senior high school students of average academic ability? Clarify your response.

15. How essential is it for a teacher to have access to a wide range of audio-visual aids and other media? Explain.

16. What are the main problems encountered in introducing independent study into a traditional high school?

17. Explain why the following generalization is open to question: *Bright students are self-directive.*

18. If you accept the concept that styles of learning vary with each student in your class, how should this affect your teaching?

19. What is meant by large-group instruction? What teaching techniques are appropriate for teaching large groups?

20. What are the advantages of small-group instruction?

21. Name several procedures involving student self-direction. Which is most practical for use in teaching your subject specialty?

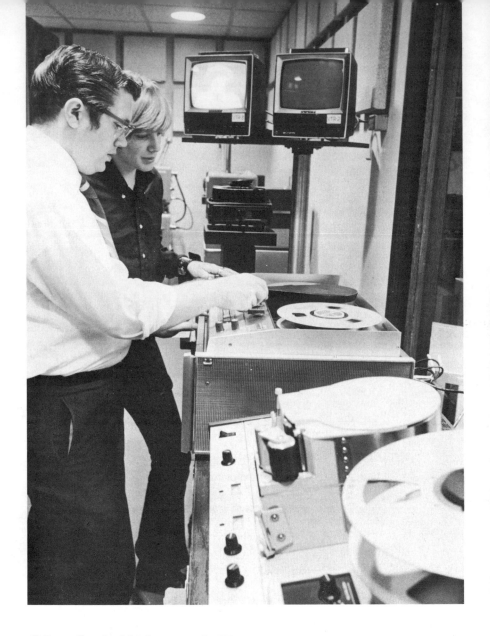

20. *Additional Recent Instructional Innovations*

Because educational innovations centered around technology and flexibility elicit the greatest general interest, they will be examined in this chapter. The most promising of the forward-looking practices in each category will be briefly discussed.

414

Scattered attempts at implementing some of the fascinating theories of a few years ago add excitement to the current educational scene. Computer-based education, novel instructional uses of television, new projection techniques, and unconventional uses of audio tapes are undergoing experimentation and rigorous evaluation. Greater instructional flexibility is being achieved through computer-assisted scheduling, classrooms with potential for changing dimensions, a variety of instructional personnel and aides, a systems approach to teaching, a wide range of nonconventional instructional materials, and the modification of the concept of student use of the library.

TECHNOLOGY

Perhaps technology has attracted greater instructional attention than it deserves; only the test of time will indicate whether the enthusiasm of the past few years has enduring merit. Educational history reveals short excitement-laden periods characterized by the most optimistic prediction of educational breakthrough—only to find that the assumed breakthrough is, within the span of a few years, absorbed into the already existing array of usable procedures.

Computer-Assisted Instruction

Few educational promises have glittered at the level of theory so enticingly and for so long a period as has computer-assisted instruction. Only within the past few years have large-scale, on-going experiments had an opportunity to confirm or refute oft-held assumptions.[1]

The Stanford University experiment in teaching arithmetic by means of the computer was highly revealing. Eight computer terminals were installed in an ordinary elementary school, permitting children to have daily contact with them. All students, with the exception of handicapped children, in grades three through six at the Grant Elementary School (located near Stanford University in the center of a middle-class, suburban community) were involved in the project. Each terminal was placed in a large book closet that opened into the classroom and made use of commercially available teletype machines. Functions controlled by the system made use of a medium-sized computer, the PDP-1.[2]

The program was conceived as a drill-and-practice system and was correlated with daily instruction. Concepts were arranged in blocks or units and sequentially placed to conform approximately to the order of topics in the textbook series, *Set and Numbers*.

---

[1]J. Lloyd Trump and Delmas F. Miller, *Secondary School Curriculum Improvement: Proposals and Procedures* (Boston: Allyn & Bacon, Inc., 1968), p. 353, provide a brief but optimistic assessment of the future of computer-assisted instruction.

[2]Patrick Suppes, Max Jerman, and Dow Brian, *Computer-Assisted Instruction: Stanford's 1965-66 Arithmetic Program* (New York: Academic Press, Inc., 1968), pp. 19–20.

Under computer control, each problem was completely typed out, including a blank for the response. The type wheel of the teletype was then positioned at the blank so that the response would be properly placed. . . . A correct response was reinforced by the appearance of the next exercise. When an incorrect first response was made, the word "wrong" was typed out and the exercise itself was retyped. A second error on the same exercise was followed by the message "wrong, the answer is _____," with the correct answer being displayed. The exercise itself was then retyped once more to allow for a correction response. An error on the correction response caused the correct answer to be given again, but whether the third response was correct or incorrect, the next exercise was presented. If a response was not given within a predetermined interval of time, usually ten seconds, the machine response followed the above pattern except that the words "time is up" were substituted for the word "wrong" at each step described above.[3]

The students took their lessons one at a time on each machine in the order prescribed by their teacher. The program began by asking the student to type his name. When the name had been correctly input, the lesson began as described above. . . . If a student failed to spell his name correctly, or gave a fictitious name (such as *Batman*), the program asked him to try again. An individual history was kept in computer memory for each student. When a student's name was input correctly, the proper lesson was selected, based on the branching criteria, and presented automatically. Students were free to sign on at any one of the machines in the school at any time during the day. It was also possible to take more than one lesson a day.

Lessons were designed to take from four to six minutes each, with an average of about five minutes, to allow each student in a class to take one lesson each day. The usual number of problems per lesson was 20. Following the lesson, a summary of the student's work was given . . . .[4]

Exhibiting amazing tenacity in a field of limited exploration—computer-assisted instruction—the University of Illinois has been involved, since 1960, in the development of an automatic teaching system called PLATO (Programmed Logic for Automatic Teaching Operations). The central concern of this long-range, complex experiment was related to determining how and to what extent individualized instruction could be automated.[5]

Over 300 programs have been written for the system using approximately sixty logics (rules governing the instructional process read into the

---

[3]*Ibid.*, pp. 26–27.

[4]*Ibid.*, p. 28.

[5]Elisabeth R. Lyman, *A Descriptive List of PLATO Programs*, 1960–1968 (Urbana, Illinois: Computer-Based Education Research Laboratory, University of Illinois, May 1968), p. 1.

central computer involving, among other approaches, tutorship, student-organized problem solving, a combination of visual presentations, problems to be solved, student responses, and student-computer intercommunication). These logics are scientifically planned to insure total individualization of instruction through computer use. One of the major purposes of project researchers has been to illustrate the flexibility of the system for teaching as well as for other educational research.

A team of interdisciplinary scientists and educators have worked for a decade on the troublesome problems associated with the project. In January of 1967, the sponsoring institution organized the Computer-based Education Research Laboratory for the PLATO project in the attempt to sharpen the focus of experimentation. With improvements in successive systems, lessons for PLATO I and PLATO II systems have become obsolete. However, many of these lessons have been rewritten, making use of the most recently developed software and hardware called for in the current version, PLATO III. Over the years a wide range of programs serving different instructional levels and purposes have been subject to experimentation.[6]

Projection Devices

Conventional use of all projectors has been streamlined and improved. This is true of projectors with a half-century of history as well as of the most recent devices.[7]

One of the chief concerns in the use of the *opaque projector* (now rapidly being replaced by the overhead projector) is the necessity for holding projected materials in place. To achieve this, roll-through material carriers have been developed, magnets attracted to metal plates are used, and masks for holding materials are employed. Moreover, projected pictures may be shown in a desired sequence and with a minimum of lost motion if they have been mounted in advance on long sheets of paper. Fully equipped projectors have a device for projecting an intensely illuminated pointer (usually an arrow) on any given spot on the screen.

The *overhead projector* has the advantage of providing a clear image in a fully lighted room. Its use has been considered so indispensable by many teachers that certain well-financed school districts have equipped classrooms with teacher desks featuring built-in overhead projectors. Properly trained teachers make the best use of this equipment by developing skill in lettering or drawing on plastic rolls or sheets.[8]

---

[6]*Ibid.*, pp. 1–5.

[7]James W. Brown, Richard B. Lewis, and Fred F. Harcleroad, *AV Instruction: Media and Methods* (New York: McGraw-Hill Book Company, 1969), pp. 529–574, provide a carefully illustrated section on audiovisual equipment designed for self-instruction.

[8]Reflecting widespread interest in the current use of the overhead projector, Herbert E. Scuorzo, *The Practical Audio-Visual Handbook for Teachers* (Englewood Cliffs, New Jersey: Prentice-Hall, Inc., 1967), chapter 3, provides a thorough discussion on projection and the production and use of transparencies.

Cartridge projectors provide a convenient means of storage for two-by-two-inch slides arranged in a most helpful sequence.[9] Although some machines are manually operated, automatic projectors have many attractive features that have increased their use. They may be remotely controlled, reversed, or focused at the whim of the user. Moreover, timing devices are included in some machines that provide for the automatic changing of slides at predetermined intervals. Synchronized sound-slide presentations are also possible by adapting an automatic projector to receive a signal pulse from a special tape recorder. A more sophisticated version of the automatic cartridge is found in the random-access slide projector. Using such a machine, the teacher may select any slide for viewing simply by dialing the slide number or by pressing the proper combination of buttons.

Ease in the use of the filmstrip has been enhanced by the development of the *Autoload projector*. Filmstrips contained in cartridges are easy to operate and have their own built-in storage.

The relative complexity of the sound-equipped *motion picture projector* has served as a deterrent to its deserved use, especially among teachers not mechanically inclined.[10] In order to help encourage more frequent use, manufacturers have produced self-threading projectors and have reduced mechanical operation to its simplest form. Sixteen millimeter projectors are currently being produced that can use either an optical or a magnetic sound track. Further, the magnetic soundtrack makes possible the recording of narration, music, or sound effects using the same procedures as the tape recorder.

Many educators have recently voiced a preference for *8mm projectors*. Because of their economy, ease of operation, and portability (both size and weight are reduced) as well as the development of new methods of packaging films, a substantial number of teachers have found them more practical than their 16mm counterpart.[11] One manufacturer has automated the 8mm projector to the point where the operator needs but properly insert the film cartridge, press the "on" button, and adjust the focus and volume control. Remote speaker outlets make it possible to set up the loudspeaker some distance away from the projector or to use earphones, a great advantage to the student operation of projection equipment when relative quiet is desired.

Creative Use of Projection Devices

The ingenuity of knowledgeable teachers aided by special equipment and facilities makes possible the creative use of projection equipment.

---

[9]*Ibid.*, p. 607, describes how a simulated field trip using two-by-two-inch slides can serve as an effective preview or review of the trip itself.

[10]*Ibid.*, chapter 2, refutes the idea of the assumed complexity involved in taking and showing motion pictures. A range of practical suggestions for motion picture use is included.

[11]Walter A. Wittich and Charles F. Schuller, *Audiovisual Materials: Their Nature and Use*, 4th ed. (New York: Harper & Row, Publishers, 1967), pp. 402–403, report the development and expanded use of 8mm films.

Instructional inventiveness is often expressed in the use of conventional devices.[12] When additional equipment is required for a given use, it is often made available for brief periods at little or no cost to the school.

Cartridge Films. Combination use of cartridge projectors, and tape recorders (cassette or other types) makes possible the preparation of valuable sight-sound presentations that may be used repeatedly for teaching groups or for student self-instruction. Synchronization of slides and recorded script may also be achieved through the use of simple attachments to tape recorders that permits automatic control of slide changes.

Rear-View Projection. The development of the cartridge-type 8mm projector used in connection with a rear-view projection screen has opened up exciting new opportunities for showing educational films. Because of its simplicity, this device can be operated by almost any student. Avoiding the tiresome tasks of threading and rewinding, the operator simply inserts the cartridge containing the film and turns on the projector. A single cartridge may hold from three or four minutes to over thirty minutes of color-sound film.

This projector affords meaningful instruction to groups of any size or to individual students interested in review or in forging ahead with new content. Further, it can be moved with ease to any position in the room that serves an instructional need. Capitalizing on the long-range conditioning of students, some manufacturers have produced machines that look like a television receiver. Use of the conventional movie screen is not necessary; the picture appears on the built-in screen, a picture that is incomparably better than the best available color television pictures.

Teacher-Made Films. A handful of classroom teachers have experimented with the production of their own instructional motion pictures. More frequently than not, such films are adaptations of television presentations that appear to have long-range value and are worthy of converting to a form usable in the motion picture projector. Occasionally short films are produced that teach a single concept or demonstrate a particular phenomenon.

The Single Concept Film. Effective instruction frequently entails presenting one idea—a single concept—with vividness, careful organization, and clarity. Such a concept may illuminate a range of related ideas. If it is misunderstood, it may thwart understanding in a sizeable content area. Inventive audiovisual specialists conceived the idea of presenting important concepts of this type in the form of short films, packaged in cartridges ready for insertion in the projector. Usually occupying three to four minutes, they may be seen repeatedly by the student until comprehension is complete.

---

[12]Suggestions for using creative activities following the showing of an educational motion picture are provided by *Ibid.*, pp. 442–444.

Ibid., p. 415, also identify the advantages of microphotography.

Full Courses by Film

During the past decade teachers in certain subjects have found it possible to teach entire courses through the use of carefully prepared, sequentially presented motion pictures. Known as *massed* films, they are usually brought into the classroom via some form of television. Films may be prepared in sufficient quantity to care for the needs of a semester or a full year. In the latter case, as many as 160 films may be used.[13]

Television

With the solid-state miniaturization of television receivers and related equipment came a reduction in costs and a willingness of classroom instructors to experiment. Fear of the electronic marvel gradually faded as its use became more commonplace. The assumption that it was to be used as an instrument of one-way communication gradually gave way under the realization that television equipment—cameras, and playback devices—could be operated with satisfactory efficiency by students with limited training.

Small, student-operated cameras were brought into the classroom. Teacher lectures, student reports, dramatic presentations, committee summaries, science demonstrations, or the comments of resource speakers could be recorded on magnetized tape. Visual as well as audio presentations could be captured for immediate replay.[14] The impact of personalized use was pointed, objective, and revealing.

At Stanford University the new technique was employed with marked success in teacher education under a program that came to be identified as micro-teaching. Students, teachers, and other students in the latter phases of their teacher education program were photographed as they taught specified content to small groups (five to eight students) for relatively short periods of time. Immediate replay of the recorded teaching performance provided supervisors as well as participating students an impact-laden review of strengths and weaknesses. Repeat performances gave budding teachers the opportunity to reteach identical content to another group after they had observed by means of video tape their own errors and had received the helpful comments of supervisors. The second performance—also frequently recorded—typically gave evidence of improved techniques. Further, the evidence of their improvement was available for observation.

Illustrative of classroom use of portable television is the videotaping of a carefully prepared report on the population explosion given by a three-student committee in an American Problems class. This is made possible through use of the mobile unit (camera, monitor, and recorder). Advance scheduling of equipment and student operators enables the

---

[13]Brown, Lewis, and Harcleroad, *AV Instruction: Media and Methods*, p. 270.

Wittich and Schuller, *Audiovisual Materials: Their Nature and Use*, pp. 434–436, examine some experiments involving teaching complete courses by motion picture.

[14]The effect of the development of the videotape recorder on classroom instruction is discussed by *Ibid.*, p. 467.

teacher to divest himself of problems related to mechanical operation. When the report is completed, major points are reemphasized through immediate replay. Further, if the report proves to be of superior quality, the teacher may choose to replay it for later sections of the same course.

FLEXIBILITY

The attempt to meet the needs of individual students has led many educators to assign high priority to flexibility—flexibility in scheduling, housing, instructional techniques, and teaching materials. This emphasis has struck terror in the professional composure of the traditional teacher, caused anxiety in the middle-of-the-roader, occasioned concern in the mildly progressive, and given rise to elation in only those teachers whose conversion was nearly complete. However, with the passing of each school year and emergence of a mounting number of educational success stories related to all aspects of flexibility, teacher anxieties have diminished.

Flexible Scheduling

The history of attempts to meet the individual needs of students has led to rotating schedules; classes assigned large blocks of time; classes before and after the regular school day; classes limited in size, offering, and types of student; and more recently, to computer-based flexible scheduling. Under this last approach, relevant information concerning each student is fed into the computer: which courses are required and which are optional; the priority of student preferences for elective classes; desired time for the taking of a given course; amount of time the student proposes to spend in independent study; and other information necessary to arrive at an effective school program for each student. Utilizing this information, the computer resolves conflicts, determines the most appropriate schedule in consideration of all factors, and records its findings on a printout sheet that becomes the student's official schedule.[15]

Flexible Housing

Basic to the effective use of instructional techniques developed in the sixties is a school plant that accommodates these innovations. The dramatic upsurge in team teaching, for example, has called for unconventional design in new school buildings as well as for the remodeling of older structures to make large group, small group, and individualized instruction possible.[16]

---

[15]A helpful discussion of the problems involved in the design of a computerized master schedule is provided by W. Deane Wiley and Lloyd K. Bishop, *The Flexibly Scheduled High School* (Englewood Cliffs, New Jersey: Prentice-Hall, Inc., 1968), chapter 6.

[16]The illustrated report of "New Concepts in School Plant Design: An Accent on Accessibility," from the Conference on Accessibility (New York: Educational Facilities Laboratory, March 1969), pp. 9–16, provides a stimulating discussion on the flexible use of instructional spaces.

Room Size

At the Cedar City, Utah High School a modern plant provides a range of fixed-wall rooms of varying size designed to serve different instructional needs. For example, small rooms for individual and small-group practice are located in the area of the large, riser-equipped, music ensemble room. Homemaking classes are taught in a large, open space that may be easily divided through the use of mobile partitions into two sizeable cooking and sewing areas in which team teaching can be effectively conducted. During inclement weather, track and football teams may utilize the large open space beneath the school for practice. Students conduct chemistry experiments on individual, mobile, counter-high stands. If a student does not finish an experiment by the end of the period, he leaves necessary equipment undisturbed on the stand which is then rolled into an adjacent storage area.

The Valley High School in Las Vegas, Nevada provides for flexibility in room size in part through the use of light-weight, movable partitions.[17] If teachers or administrators wish to change the size or shape of a given classroom, they may do so by unbolting partitions and moving them to meet the new instructional need. All such partitions are mounted on heavy duty carpeting.

Outdoor Spaces

For certain kinds of activities and in a variety of climates, the outdoors beckons with increasing strength as an arena in which realistic learning can take place. Long used for the purposes of sports events and the biological sciences, outdoor teaching has recently been extended to include selected segments of courses in mathematics, sciences, and the social studies. Many newly constructed schools make use of the school-based amphitheater for special musical and dramatic events, entertainment features, and graduation exercises.

With the new affluence of American society has come a general willingness of many school boards to purchase outdoor camps and recreation facilities remote to the schools themselves. Although the acreage, buildings, and equipment of such facilities vary a great deal, depending upon cost and location, they are usually designed for multipurpose use. Frequently they are scheduled months in advance by teachers and administrators responsible for students in grades four through twelve. Periods of usage may extend from one day (often on the weekend) to more than one week. Originally designed as fair weather recreational retreats, the outdoor school camp now provides a challenging environment for the teaching of certain aspects of physical education, health, biology, chemistry, social studies, and English. Moreover, its use has been

[17]"Valley High, Las Vegas: Approaching Individualization of Instruction," Clark County School District, Las Vegas, Nevada, November 1966.

extended by a number of school districts to utilize the facilities for the full calendar year including the winter as well as the summer months.[18]

Flexible Procedures

The attempt to meet the individual needs of students has been reflected in the use of a sizable array of new techniques in addition to existing proven methods. Among the novel procedures attracting the greatest attention are the expanded use of aids, the use of electronic devices, the use of nonprofessional personnel, and the use of a large variety of relevant procedures.[19]

Extensive Use of Aids

Use of instructional aids during the forties was characteristic of quality teachers. Today the extensive use of aids is viewed as a professional *must* for average teachers, and those who wish to excel are expected to use them with professional skill.[20] In the well-taught United States History class, it is not uncommon to find a seasoned instructor using the tape recorder, the slide projector, a brief segment of a motion picture, cell overlays, large wall maps, and dittoed handouts during one fifty-minute period. Effective planning and coordination of student and teacher efforts are essential in making such instruction possible.

Use of Electronic Devices

Novel use of existing electronic devices has added flexibility to teaching methods.[21] Television, for example, is now being employed by teachers and students to pinpoint weaknesses in a range of subjects; the in-class, student-operated television camera has become a financially feasible reality. Teacher-prepared and student-prepared audio tapes now serve a useful instructional purpose in foreign-language, social studies, English, recreation, and shorthand classes. Because they are individually made to meet specific student needs, they are often superior to commercially prepared tapes.

---

[18]Steven L. Barrett, "A Proposal to Establish an Outdoor Education-Recreation Center with the Cooperative Involvement of the Provo City School District and the Parks and Recreation Department of the City of Provo," unpublished Master of Education project, Brigham Young University, 1968, discusses the advantages of outdoor education and identifies the specific details of a feasible joint effort.

[19]Results of a survey of a wide range of innovative secondary schools through the United States are reported in *Final Report: Analysis of Instructional Systems* (Santa Monica, California: System Development Corporation, 1966), pp. 61–94. Names and locations of schools contacted are identified.

[20]Alvin C. Eurich, *Reforming American Education: The Innovation Approach to Improving Our Schools and Colleges* (New York: Harper & Row, Publishers, 1969), chapter 6, provides an insightful review of the development of educational technology and its impact on instruction and American education.

[21]*Ibid.*, pp. 219–265, describes a range of school practices involving the use of educational television.

Even the computer—wonder child of the post-World War II electronic era—has been subject to a variety of instructional uses. Using the letters and characters of the computer-attached electric typewriter, the student may call for programed responses (a word, frame, or brief message) that usually appear on a cathode ray tube as a result of pressing certain keys. Such responses are only possible when properly constructed programs, which spell out in machine language the precise tasks and sequences to be followed, are used to give human direction to the computer.

If an electronically-controlled, random-access slide projector is attached to the computer, graphic materials may also be presented on the picture tube as part of the instructional program. Further, capitalizing on the contributions of programed instruction, educators may make use of projected microtape frames to present one small concept or a full course of sequentially placed frames.

Use of Nonprofessional Personnel

The use of the first instructional paraprofessional was viewed by many threatened teachers as an act of heresy. However, the past few years have revealed an increasing teacher willingness to experiment with many varieties of nonprofessionals to assist in the process of education.[22] The clerical-stenographic aide has had a long history of use, but his role has more recently been given status through clarification and identification with the teaching team. Another frequently employed team member is the art specialist whose special talents are focused on preparing materials requested by senior members of the team. Often hired as a half-time, hourly employee, he makes charts, graphs, special drawings, bulletin boards, cell overlays, and special slides.

Use of noncertificated personnel to engage in certain restricted instructional tasks has tended to ease the burden of fully qualified classroom instructors. The correction of English compositions in high school—a continuous problem for the conscientious teacher—is sometimes taken over by a college graduate with an English major who lacks only formal certification. Because such a person can be employed for much less than the certificated teacher, this arrangement proves to be financially advantageous to the school district. Likewise, an individual without a college degree or teaching certificate but with known competence in mathematics may be assigned the responsibility of helping students with mathematics problems during a regularly scheduled study period or during the time devoted to independent study.

Much of the drudgery of calling the roll, recording grades, distributing handouts, giving and correcting prepared tests, and answering the noncontent-related questions of students is now assumed by teacher aides. This procedure is employed with particular effectiveness in large contin-

---

[22]David Street, ed., *Innovations in Mass Education* (New York: John Wiley & Sons, Inc., 1969), pp. 177–201, provides a useful description of the use of paid and voluntary nonprofessionals in five large city school systems.

uous progress classes or in independent study situations where detailed record keeping is essential to the success of the instructional program.

Use of a Systems Approach

Military and aerospace programs have focused attention on the value of the systems approach to solving problems, which has at its core ". . . the planned, evolutionary development of a unified information-process-ing system . . ."[23] Space-age use has largely concentrated on the employ-ment of extremely sophisticated hardware (high speed digital computers, for example) that may consist of interrelated but separate systems.

Many groups, including social scientists, have elected to extend the concept of systems analysis to include many nontechnological systems. Far-sighted educators have found value in this extension. Placing great reliance on automation and computerization, these professionals have also sought to give consideration to all human and mechanical variables and all alternative solutions to problems in arriving at the most nearly perfect use of instructional personnel, media, and techniques. All parts of a given system are designed to function with maximum effectiveness in relation-ship to all other systems in solving problems.[24]

Superimposed on classroom and nonclassroom instruction, the sys-tems approach concept means that the instructor first identifies precisely the goal he wishes to have his students achieve. He now carefully examines all factors that influence the teaching-learning process—student capacities, interests, desires, and achievements; teacher strengths and limitations in content, professional preparation, and basic insights; and the range of teaching techniques including the use of all media, instruc-tional materials, and automated devices. This examination enables him to single out the factors most relevant to the learning of each student. In consideration of the unique characteristics of each learner (as well as those of the teacher), he identifies the procedures best suited to helping the learner reach his goal efficiently. Such procedures may call for the use of conventional or nontraditional methods or a combination of both employed in proper sequence. A *systems* approach is thus effected that is superior to a single technique or a loosely coordinated combination of techniques.

Educational technology enables the systems approach to move closer to the elusive educational goal of maximum learning in the shortest possible time. A few publishing houses have sought to ease the teacher burden of identifying the necessary materials of instruction by producing systematized, interrelated multi-media instructional kits which may be easily assembled in the instructional media center.[25] In this systematically

[23]Don D. Bushnell and Dwight W. Allen, eds., *The Computer in American Education* (New York: John Wiley & Sons, Inc., 1967), p. 229.

[24]Matthew B. Miles, ed., *Innovations in Education* (New York: Teachers College, Columbia University, 1964), p. 13, defines *system* in a way that is meaningful in spite of its somewhat varied use in many differing fields and situations.

[25]Brown, Lewis, and Harcleroad, *AV Instruction: Media and Methods*, p. 17, provide an illustration of instructional materials that might be included in such a kit.

organized unit might be an encyclopedia set, text books for readers of differing ability, a filmstrip projector and appropriate films for student self-use, well-illustrated books dealing with unit content, commercially produced transparencies, a motion picture film, various devices for demonstration, and audio tapes and discs.

Flexible Use of Instructional Materials

Flexibility is a key concern in the enlightened use of teaching materials. The outdated view of a single textbook as the chief tool of the teacher is no longer valid. Whether used effectively or not does not negate the fact that a wide range of books is currently available for use at all grade levels and for virtually all subjects. Further, nontextbook materials have appeared in such abundance that even the well-organized instructor is hard pressed to determine what materials should be used and under what circumstances. The library itself—more often designated as the instructional materials center—has been relocated, reorganized, and redesigned in many schools to serve better the variable needs of students.

Textbooks

The functional concept that the textbook is a means and not an end, one tool among many, is finding widespread acceptance even among traditional teachers. Perhaps the most useful educational side effect of competition among publishing houses has been the production of vast numbers of books—basic texts as well as supplementary texts, anthologies as well as encyclopedias—which use vocabulary and present content at varying levels of difficulty. From this reservoir the individual teacher, the committee of teachers, or the school district may select those texts that serve best known student needs. Moreover, the trend toward the use of multiple texts has been enhanced by the expanding interest in individualizing instruction as well as by the general affluence of the past two decades.

Adding to the available teacher options have been a substantial number of programed texts in particular content areas. Mathematics, for example, has been especially favored. In heterogeneously grouped classes in which the teacher strives to achieve a degree of individualization for each student, well-chosen programed texts may be used with success. Often with respect to a specific student, a combination of programed and nonprogramed texts proves highly effective. Recent development of programed units (as opposed to course-length texts) has added much to the flexibility of their use.

The use of other nonconventional texts further expanded the range of options. Among these are found the simplified classics, profusely illustrated books, texts with cell overlays, identical concepts explained at different reading levels, oversized print for students with visual difficulties, special purpose workbooks, and teacher-produced texts designed to serve the needs of particular categories of students.[26]

Audio Materials

The social studies teacher in a school district with a well-equipped instructional materials center may plan to use the recorded voices of historical personalities of the recent past. Among them might be the voices of John F. Kennedy, Martin Luther King, Adolf Hitler, Franklin D. Roosevelt, Lyndon Johnson, Richard M. Nixon, or the astronauts who first set foot on the moon. He may systematize his approach to teaching by combining the best of available tapes and discs with current radio and television programs. Further, a large number of newly constructed secondary schools reflect the need for the latest audio equipment. In such schools listening centers are developed that maximize the use of available audio resources. "Many of them employ 'random access' circuitry to permit large numbers of students to listen at will to recordings stored in automated tape banks."[27]

A few large city school systems (New York, Chicago, Detroit, Cleveland, and Atlanta) for years have operated their own broadcasting stations which well-organized teachers have utilized effectively through classroom radios or public address systems. Moreover, through the combination use of tape recorder and radio, the best of the commercial programing may be brought into the classroom either as live or recorded presentations.

The telelecture is being used with increasing frequency in bringing the voice of national specialists into specific classrooms. Using voice amplification and long distance telephone lines, teachers are able to provide their students with timely, authoritative, and relevant comments. Cost factors encourage the use of interconnected classrooms in which students may simultaneously audit the live remarks of a respected authority. Student responses or questions are made possible through special hookups.

Visual Materials

In the absence of a real phenomenon, instructors have devised simulation devices to provide a close approximation of reality. Driver trainers—now in use in a substantial proportion of well-equipped high schools—provide a good example of such devices. Using simulators that look and respond like automobiles, students are confronted via motion picture with a series of critical and noncritical driving situations to which

---

[26]Wittich and Schuller, *Audiovisual Materials: Their Nature and Use*, p. 363, indicate that "a number of books have been published with illustrations on stereodisks (permitting three dimensional viewing), for which a folding plastic viewer is provided in the book along with the disks."

[27]Brown, Lewis, and Harcleroad, *AV Instruction: Media and Methods*, p. 342.

they must react quickly and intelligently. Errors are easily identified and brought dramatically to the attention of potential drivers.

Beehives, ant colonies, rats, hamsters, frogs, and snakes have long been employed to bring reality into the science classroom. More recently, teachers have used them for nonscience purposes in English composition. Some schools have developed museums of limited size to whet student interests in the biological, physical, and earth sciences.

Teaching displays have become more goal oriented and more attractive through the years.[28] Such displays are evaluated by the teachers from the point-of-view of the students who observe the finished product. To this end, careful planning is fundamental in all displays and bulletin boards. The ease of lettering through the use of precut letters, typewriters with giant-size letters, mechanical devices, and inexpensive felt-tip pens frequently results in displays with a professional look achieved by painstaking students as well as teachers.

The chalkboard, often assigned to the traditional category, is found to take on a new appeal through the use of lettering, sketching, a range of different templates, projectors, and pounce-pattern drawings. Magnetic chalkboards to which small objects with magnetized backing may be made to adhere provide a three-dimensional effect of great interest to teachers concerned with teaching dramatic art, history, geography, and team positions in physical education. Further, flannel board presentations have unusual potential for flexibility in placement of depicted items, for color, for general attractiveness, and for mobility.

Although the majority of teachers may give little evidence of true creativity in working with visuals, the majority of them may make attractive and instructive adaptations of pictures, bulletin boards, displays, and natural scenes. Depending on the purpose to be achieved in given classes, the production of visuals may often be justified as a team effort in which students become strongly involved participants. The making of puppets and the building of a puppet theater are commonplace creative activities in the dramatics class. Likewise, the construction of an accurate three-dimensional contour map in a geography class calls for the exercise of creativity.

Because of the reality of the still or motion picture, its use is often favored by students and teacher alike in virtually all subjects. Photographic records of important field trips spur accurate recall; foreign travel revivified through pictures provides an exciting afterglow of strange realities; motion picture closeups of extremely small objects breathe reality into the study of insects and leaves; and colored slides of social phenomena bring the student face-to-face with poverty, filth, and submarginal housing. The taking of all such photographs is well within the range of skills of students in a sizable senior high school.

Printed Materials
Riding the crest of the current emphasis on individualization, non-

---

[28]Wittich and Schuller, *Audiovisual Materials: Their Nature and Use*, chapter 7, provide a comprehensive treatment of the study display.

textbook materials are being used with increasing frequency. Newspapers and magazines—once relegated to the school library—are now used in the classrooms by teachers and students for a variety of purposes. A half dozen or more magazines with large national circulations provide relevant details in keeping students abreast of world affairs. Their pictures provide the essential materials for a bulletin board display; their articles are subject to classroom discussion; and their differing editorial comments may provoke student debate.

Although students still read the daily comic strips, they read the front page and the editorial columns as never before. Often the local newspaper is subscribed to and criticized soundly in the twelfth-grade American problems class, the ninth-grade civics class, and the eleventh-grade United States history class. In addition, the homemaking class clips out new recipes; the mathematics class files articles usable in their ongoing study of algebra; and the music instructor reads to the class the account of the New York Philharmonic's appearance in an adjacent city.

The United States Government is one of the chief suppliers of noncommercial, free materials. Packaged as small pamphlets, these brief accounts provide needed current information often not found in the textbook. In addition to the United States Government Printing Office, a majority of other government agencies issue information of interest to students. Materials sought most frequently stem from the Department of State, the Federal Bureau of Investigation, the Department of Agriculture, the Department of Transportation, and the Smithsonian Institute.

State agencies have also assumed the responsibility of supplying upon request information to students about the historical events and scenic wonders of the state. The various state departments supplement materials that are available locally through the chambers of commerce and local promotional agencies. Professional associations such as the National Education Association have long served as sources of inexpensive supplementary materials. Trade associations, private industry, and foreign embassies have also provided, usually at no cost, a range of well-illustrated but promotion-oriented educational materials.

Library

The most striking feature of the school library—now more properly designated as the *instructional media center*—is that it no longer serves as the repository for books alone. In the most modern sense, such a center is a multipurpose area often consisting of rooms of differing sizes that serve a range of purposes. Books are properly catalogued and shelved, to be sure, but a useful choice of nonbook materials—magazines, pamphlets, pictures, newspapers, and displays—are arranged on open shelves encouraging maximum student use. Electronic study carrels are made available to students in a separate room or in certain areas of the media center; materials and equipment—tape recorders, motion picture projectors, and overhead projectors—together with films and transparencies are stored in one room of the complex to which students have supervised access; and video tape recording equipment is occasionally located in the communication control and dissemination room. Conventional reference and card catalog areas are frequently adjacent to a small group discussion room or a lounge area furnished with comfortable furniture.

In short, the organization and structure of the forward-looking school library are designed to encourage student self-use or to insure that teacher-directed use meets with few obstacles.[29]

Student Self-Use

Students involved in a continuous progress program will find most of the tools of self-discovery at their fingertips in such a setting. They may discover relevant programed materials, learning packages, or encyclopedia articles that may be taken to individual study carrels for examination. Further, once in the carrel, they may have the option of dialing one of several audio or video tapes related to the content being studied.

If a motion picture film identified in the media center catalog proves to be particularly relevant to the subject, the student—serving as his own projectionist—may view in an adjacent dark room those portions that he feels serve his particular needs. Likewise, he may have access to a number of video tapes that are similarly used, assuming that he has competence in the operation of the video playback device. He assumes responsibility for finding in the card catalog or on open shelves those books that best illuminate his study. If he feels that small-group discussion would serve a useful purpose, he may arrange to meet several of his fellow students at a predetermined time in a small room of the library complex. Further, if he feels that a change of pace and location would result in more profitable learning, he may read in the comfort of an easy chair in the lounge area.

Teacher-Directed Use

Study prescribed by the teacher is often implemented in the educational media center where an ample number of supplementary nontextual materials—periodicals, encyclopedias, projection equipment—and other technological devices are available for use. Typically, the classroom teacher informs the librarian if a proposed assignment is likely to make special demands on library facilities. An ample supply of needed books can be made available to students needing them or alternate approaches to study may be worked out that will relieve instructional bottlenecks and reduce student frustrations. The wise teacher soon becomes aware of the limitations and strengths of the media center and gears his assignments accordingly.

Surrounded by the wealth of materials found in a well-financed, up-to-date instructional media center, the teacher is encouraged to avoid traditional textbook teaching. Here with a minimum of effort he may select from a wide range of available materials those that stimulate, simplify, and encourage maximum student effort.

---

[29]Trump and Miller, *Secondary School Curriculum Improvement,* pp. 266–267, stress two basic functions of the library in promoting independent study.

PROBLEMS FOR STUDY AND DISCUSSION

1. Identify at least three effective ways in which portable television might be employed in your subject specialty.

2. Describe two nonconventional uses of instructional television. What are their specific advantages?

3. How could dial-access to tapes stored in a central repository serve student needs in teaching your subject specialty?

4. What are the advantages of single concept films?

5. Focusing on your teaching major, describe five recent instructional innovations that can be used effectively during the same class period.

6. Describe the functions of at least three kinds of nonprofessional personnel.

7. Identify four different structural patterns in modern school buildings that come under the general category of flexible housing.

8. Describe five different ways to achieve flexibility through the use of instructional materials.

9. What were the main characteristics of the Stanford University experiment in teaching arithmetic by computer?

10. Describe the operation of the PLATO program developed by the University of Illinois. How does it differ from the Stanford University experiment in teaching arithmetic?

11. What are the advantages of having an overhead projector built into the teacher's desk?

12. Describe the advantages of a random-access slide projector. How does it differ from the typical automatic cartridge slide projector?

13. Why do many educators prefer the 8mm motion picture projector to the 16mm projector?

14. How practical are teacher-made motion pictures? Discuss.

15. Do you believe it would be possible to teach effectively your subject matter major by means of motion picture alone? Why?

16. Identify the basic provision for flexibility in room size at the Valley High School in Las Vegas, Nevada. Do you see any disadvantages in such a provision?

17. List five uses of media not currently employed by you that would enliven instruction in the area of your teaching minor.

18. Describe the characteristics of an up-to-date educational media center. Sensitive to your own teaching responsibilities, what would you include in such a center to enable you to teach more effectively?

19. What procedures would you employ to insure effective student self-use of the instructional media center?

20. Why is it important to have a range of nontextbook materials? Name several.

21. What is the most commonly used nonconventional textbook? What differentiates it from the typical textbook?

22. What is meant by a systems approach to teaching? Describe one such approach.

23. Differentiate between behavioral objectives and nonbehavioral objectives. Give examples of each.

24. Identify two ways in which outdoor spaces are being used to enhance instruction.

25. What is the telelecture and how is it best employed?

Bibliography

Alcorn, Marvin D., James S. Kinder, and Jim R. Schunert. *Better Teaching in Secondary Schools*. 3d. ed. New York: Holt, Rinehart & Winston, Inc., 1970.

Alexander, William M. and Vynce A. Hines. *Independent Study in Secondary Schools*. New York: Holt, Rinehart & Winston, Inc., 1967.

Alwin, Virginia. "Planning a Year of Units," *The English Journal*, 45 (September 1956), 334–340.

Ausubel, David P. *Educational Psychology: A Cognitive View*. New York: Holt, Rinehart & Winston, Inc., 1968.

Baller, Warren R. and Don R. Charles. *The Psychology of Human Growth and Development*. 2d. ed. New York: Holt, Rinehart & Winston, Inc., 1968.

Batchelder, Howard T., Maurice McGlasson, and Raleigh Schorling. *Student Teaching in Secondary Schools*. 4th ed. New York: McGraw-Hill Book Company, 1964.

Beck, William R. "Pupils's Perceptions of Teacher Merit: A Factor Analysis of Five Postulated Dimensions," *The Journal of Educational Research*, 61 (November 1967), 127–128.

Beggs, David W., III, ed. *Team Teaching: Bold New Venture*. Indianapolis: Unified College Press, 1964.

Beggs, David W., III and Edward G. Buffie, eds. *Nongraded Schools in Action: Bold New Venture*. Bloomington, Indiana: Indiana University Press, 1967.

Benyon, Sheila Doran. *Intensive Programming for Slow Learners*. Columbus, Ohio: Charles E. Merrill Publishing Co., 1968.

Berry, Elizabeth. "The Unit Process," *Educational Forum*, 27 (1963), 357–366.

Besvinick, Sidney L. "An Effective Daily Lesson Plan," *The Clearing House*, 34 (March 1960), 431–433.

Bigge, Morris L. and Maurice P. Hunt. *Psychological Foundations of Education*. 2d. ed. New York: Harper & Row, Publishers, 1968.

Bledsoe, Joseph C. and Iva D. Brown. "Role Perceptions of Secondary Teachers as Related to Pupils' Perceptions of Teacher Behavioral Characteristics," *The Journal of Educational Research*, 61 (May-June 1966), 422–429.

Bloom, Benjamin S., et al. *Taxonomy of Educational Objectives: Handbook 1, Cognitive Domain*. New York: David McKay Co., Inc., 1956.

Blount, Nathan S. and Herbert J. Klausmeier. *Teaching in the Secondary School*. 3d. ed. New York: Harper & Row, Publishers, 1968.

Borg, Walter R. "Teacher Effectiveness in Team Teaching," *The Journal of Experimental Education*, 35 (Spring 1967), 65–70.

Borger, R. and A. E. M. Seaborne. *The Psychology of Learning*. Baltimore: Penguin Books, Inc., 1966.

Boroughs, Homer, Jr., Clifford D. Foster, and Rufus D. Salyer, Jr. *Introduction to Secondary School Teaching*. New York: The Ronald Press Company, 1964.

Brethower, Dale M., et al. *Programmed Learning: A Practicum*. Ann Arbor, Michigan: Ann Arbor-Humphrey Science Publishers, Inc., 1967.

Briggs, Leslie J. "The Teacher and Programmed Instruction—Roles and Role Potentials," *Audiovisual Instruction*, 9 (1964), 273–276.

Broudy, Harry. *Paradox and Promise: Essays on American Life and Education.* Englewood Cliffs, New Jersey: Prentice-Hall, Inc., 1961.

Brown, James W., Richard B. Lewis, and Fred F. Harcleroad. *AV Instruction: Media and Methods.* 3d. ed. New York: McGraw-Hill Book Company, 1969.

Bruner, Jerome S. *The Process of Education.* Cambridge, Massachusetts: Harvard University Press, 1960.

Burton, William H. *The Guidance of Learning Activities.* 3d. ed. New York: Appleton-Century-Crofts, 1962.

Bushnell, Don D. and Dwight W. Allen, eds. *The Computer in American Education.* New York: John Wiley & Sons, Inc., 1967.

Calvin, Allen D., ed. *Programmed Instruction: Bold New Venture.* Bloomington, Indiana: Indiana University Press, 1969.

Carter, William L., Carl W. Hansen, and Margaret G. McKim. *Learning to Teach in the Secondary School.* New York: The Macmillan Company, 1962.

Clark, Leonard H. *Strategies and Tactics in Secondary School Teaching: A Book of Readings.* New York: The Macmillan Company, 1968.

Clark, Leonard H. and Irving S. Starr. *Secondary School Teaching Methods.* 2d. ed. New York: The Macmillan Company, 1967.

Cogswell, John F., et al. *Final Report: Analysis of Instructional Systems.* Santa Monica, California: Systems Development Corporation, 1966.

Coleman, John E. *The Master Teachers and the Art of Teaching.* New York: Pitman Publishing Corp., 1967.

Costello, Lawrence F. and George N. Gordon. *Teach with Television: A Guide to Instructional TV.* 2d. ed. New York: Hastings House, Publishers, Inc., 1965.

Cronbach, Lee J. *Educational Psychology.* 2d. ed. New York: Harcourt Brace Jovanovich, Inc., 1963.

"Curriculum Guide for Individualizing Instruction," Theodore High School, Theodore, Alabama, 1964.

Davis E. Dale. *Focus on Secondary Education: An Introduction to Principles and Practices.* Glenview, Illinois: Scott, Foresman and Company, 1966.

Davis, Frederick B. *Educational Measurements and Their Interpretation.* Belmont, California: Wadsworth Publishing Co., Inc., 1964.

Davis, Harold S. and Ellsworth Tompkins. *How to Organize an Effective Team Teaching Program.* Englewood Cliffs, New Jersey: Prentice-Hall, Inc., 1966.

Davis, Robert A. *Learning in the Schools.* Belmont, California: Wadsworth Publishing Co., Inc., 1966.

De Cecco, John P. *The Psychology of Learning and Instruction: Educational Psychology.* Englewood Cliffs, New Jersey: Prentice-Hall, Inc., 1968.

De Corte, D. A. *Television in Education and Training.* Amsterdam, Netherlands: Philips Technical Library, 1967.

Diffor, John W. and Mary F. Horkheimer. *Educators' Guide to Free Films.* Randolph, Wisconsin: Educators' Progress Service, 1969.

Douglas, Leonard M. *The Secondary Teacher at Work.* Boston: D. C. Heath & Company, 1967.

Draper, Edgar M. and Gordon Gardner. "How to Construct a Resource Unit," *The Clearing House,* 26 (January 1952), 267–268.

Dumas, Wayne and Weldon Beckner. *Introduction to Secondary Education: A Foundations Approach.* Scranton, Pennsylvania: International Textbook Company, 1968.

Durbin, Mary Lou. *Teaching Techniques for Retarded and Prereading Students.* Springfield, Illinois: Charles C Thomas, Publisher, 1967.

Ebel, Robert L. *Measuring Educational Achievement.* Englewood Cliffs, New Jersey: Prentice-Hall, Inc., 1965.

Esbensen, Thorwald. "Writing Instructional Objectives," *Phi Delta Kappan,* 48 (January 1967), 246–247.

Espich, James E. and Bill Williams. *Developing Programmed Instructional Materials: A Handbook for Program Writers.* Palo Alto, California: Fearon Publishers, 1967.

Estvan, Frank J. *Social Studies in a Changing World.* New York: Harcourt Brace Jovanovich, Inc., 1968.

Eurich, Alvin C. *Reforming American Education: The Innovative Approach to Improving Our Schools and Colleges.* New York: Harper & Row, Publishers, 1969.

The Evaluation of Teaching: A Report of the Second Phi Lambda Theta Catena. Washington, D.C.: George Banta Company, 1967.

Fallon, Belie J., ed. *Fifty States Innovate to Improve Their Schools.* Bloomington, Indiana: Phi Delta Kappa, 1967.

Faunce, Roland C. and Carroll L. Munshaw. *Teaching and Learning in Secondary Schools.* Belmont, California: Wadsworth Publishing Co., Inc., 1965.

Four Case Studies of Programmed Instruction. New York: The Fund for the Advancement of Education, 1964.

"Four Ways You Can Use Teaching Machines," *School Management,* (December 1965), 100–102.

Fraenkel, Jack R. and Richard E. Gross. "Team Teaching: Let's Look Before We Leap," *Social Education,* 30 (May 1966), 335–337.

Frandsen, Arden N. *Educational Psychology.* 2d. ed. New York: McGraw-Hill Book Company, 1967.

Franklin, Marian Pope. *School Organization: Theory and Practice.* Chicago: Rand McNally & Co., 1967.

Gagne, Robert M., ed. *Learning and Individual Differences.* Columbus, Ohio: Charles E. Merrill Publishing Co., 1967.

Garner, W. Lee. *Programmed Instruction.* New York: The Center for Applied Research in Education, Inc., 1966.

Georgiades, William. "Team Teaching: A New Star, Not a Meteor," *NEA Journal,* 56 (April 1967), 14–15.

Gladstein, Gerald A. *Individualized Study: A New Approach to Succeeding in College.* Chicago: Rand McNally & Co., 1967.

Glaser, Robert, ed. *Teaching Machines and Programmed Learning: A Source Book.* Washington, D.C.: National Education Association, 1965.

Gleason, Gerald. "Will Programmed Instruction Serve People?" *Educational Leadership,* 23 (1966), 471–479.

Grambs, Jean D., John C. Carr, and Robert M. Fitch. *Modern Methods in Secondary Education.* 3d. ed. New York: Holt, Rinehart & Winston, Inc., 1970.

Griffith, Leroy, Nelson L. Haggerson, and Delbert Weber. *Secondary Education Today*. New York: David McKay Co., Inc., 1967.

Gronlund, Norman E. *Measurement and Evaluation in Teaching*. Toronto: Macmillan Co., of Canada, Ltd., 1965.

Haga, Enoch, ed. *Automated Educational Systems*. Elmhurst, Illinois: The Business Press, 1967.

Hall, John F., ed. *Readings in the Psychology of Learning*. New York: J. B. Lippincott Co., 1967.

Harris, Ben M., Wailand Bessent, and Kenneth E. McIntyre. *In-Service Education: A Guide to Better Practice*. Englewood Cliffs, New Jersey: Prentice-Hall, Inc., 1969.

Haskew, Laurence D. and Jonathon C. McLendon. *This is Teaching*. 3d. ed. Chicago: Scott, Foresman and Company, 1968.

Hass, Glen and Kimball Wiles. *Readings in Curriculum*. Boston: Allyn & Bacon, Inc., 1965.

Havighurst, Robert J. *Human Development and Education*. New York: Longmans, Green and Co., 1953.

Heller, Melvin P. *Team Teaching: A Rationale*. Dayton, Ohio: National Catholic Education Association, 1967.

Hoover, Kenneth H. *Readings on Learning and Teaching in the Secondary School*. Boston: Allyn & Bacon, Inc., 1968.

Horrocks, John E. and Thelma I. Schoonover. *Measurement for Teachers*. Columbus, Ohio: Charles E. Merrill Publishing Co., 1968.

Huffman, Harry and B. June Schmidt. *Programmed Business Mathematics, Book I*. 2d. ed. New York: McGraw-Hill Book Company, 1968.

Hurlock, Elizabeth B. *Adolescent Development*. 3d. ed. New York: McGraw Hill Book Company, 1967.

Inlow, Gail M. *The Emergent in Curriculum*. New York: John Wiley & Sons, Inc., 1966.

Innovation in Education: New Directions for the American School. New York: Committee for Economic Development, 1968.

Jackson, Philip W. *Life in Classrooms*. New York: Holt, Rinehart & Winston, Inc., 1968.

Jeffries, A., et al. "Team Teaching Brings New Kind of Learning," *Pennsylvania School Journal*, 114 (May 1966), 420–423.

Jersild, Arthur T. *The Psychology of Adolescence*. 2d. ed. New York: The Macmillan Company, 1963.

Johnson, Robert H. and John J. Hunt, *Prescription for Team Teaching*. Minneapolis: Burgess Publishing Co., 1968.

Kaufman, Burt and Paul Bethune. "Nova High: Space Age School," *Phi Delta Kappan*, 46 (September 1964), 9–11.

Kemp, Jerrold E. *Planning and Producing Audiovisual Materials*. 2d. ed. San Francisco: Chandler Publishing Company, 1968.

Kinder, James S. *Using Audio-Visual Materials in Education*. New York: American Book Company, 1965.

Klausmeier, Herbert J. and William Goodwin. *Learning and Human Abilities: Educational Psychology*. 2d. ed. New York: Harper & Row, Publishers, 1966.

Koenig, Allen E. and Ruane B. Hill. *The Farther Vision: Educational Television Today*. Madison, Wisconsin: The University of Wisconsin Press, 1967.

Kork, Sister Mary Victor. "Positive and Negative Factors in Team Teaching," *The Mathematics Teacher*, 61 (January 1968), 50–53.

Kornrich, Milton, ed. *Underachievement*. Springfield, Illinois: Charles C. Thomas, Publisher, 1965.

Kuhlen, Raymond G., ed. *Studies in Educational Psychology*. Waltham, Massachusetts: Blaisdell Publishing Co., 1968.

Langdon, Grace and Irving W. Stout. *Homework*. New York: The John Day Company, 1969.

Lange, Phil G., ed. *Programmed Instruction: The Sixty-Sixth Yearbook of the National Society for the Study of Education, Part II*. Chicago: University of Chicago Press, 1967.

Lee, Florence Henry. *Principles and Practices of Teaching in Secondary Schools*. New York: David McKay Co., Inc., 1965.

Leedham, John and Derick Unwin. *Programmed Learning in the Schools*. New York: Longmans, Green and Co., 1965.

Lieberman, Myron. *Education as a Profession*. Englewood Cliffs, New Jersey: Prentice-Hall, Inc., 1956.

Lindeman, Richard H. *Educational Measurement*. Glenview, Illinois: Scott, Foresman and Company, 1967.

Lindgren, Henry C. *Educational Psychology in the Classroom*. 3d. ed. New York: John Wiley & Sons, Inc., 1967.

Lueck, William R., et al., *Effective Secondary Education*, Minneapolis: Burgess Publishing Co., 1966.

Lyman, Elisabeth R. *A Descriptive List of PLATO Programs, 1960–1968*. Urbana, Illinois: The University of Illinois Press, 1968.

McBride, Wilma, ed. *Inquiry: Implications for Televised Instruction*. Washington, D.C.: National Education Association, 1966.

McDonald, Frederick J. *Educational Psychology*. 2d. ed. Belmont, California: Wadsworth Publishing Co., Inc., 1965.

MacLean, Roderick. *Television in Education*. London: Methuen, 1968.

Mager, Robert F. *Preparing Objectives for Programmed Instruction*. Palo Alto: Fearon Publishers, 1962.

Markle, Susan Meyer. *Good Frames and Bad: A Grammar of Frame Writing*. New York: John Wiley & Sons, Inc., 1964.

Minnick, John H. and Raymond C. Strauss. *Structure of Arithmetic*. New York: Harper & Row, Publishers, 1966.

Mitzel, H. E. "Can We Measure Good Teaching Objectively?" *The National Education Association Journal*, 53 (January 1964), 34–36.

Moir, Guthrie. *Teaching and Television*. Oxford, England: Pergamon Press, Inc., 1967.

Monks, Robert L. "Team Teaching Tried in Tradition Schedule," *North Carolina Educator*, 49 (Spring 1968), 180–182.

Morphet, Edgar L. and Charles O. Ryan, eds. *Planning and Effecting Needed Changes in Education*. Denver, Colorado: Publishers Press, 1967.

Morse, William C. and G. Max Wingo. *Psychology and Teaching*. 2d. ed. Glenview, Illinois: Scott, Foresman and Company, 1962.

Mouly, George J. *Psychology for Effective Teaching*. 2d. ed. New York: Holt, Rinehart & Winston, Inc., 1968.

Murphy, Judith and Ronald Gross. *Learning by Television*. New York: Fund for the Advancement of Education, 1966.

Mussen, Paul Henry, John Janeway Conger, and Jerome Kagan. *Child Development and Personality*. 3d. ed. New York: Harper & Row, Publishers, 1969.

Nordberg, H. Orville, James M. Bradfield, and William C. Odell. *Secondary School Teaching*. New York: The Macmillan Company, 1962.

Oliva, Peter F. *The Secondary School Today*. New York: World Publishing Company, 1967.

Oliva, Peter F. and Ralph A. Scrafford. *Teaching in a Modern Secondary School*. Columbus, Ohio: Charles E. Merrill Publishing Co., 1965.

Otto, Wayne and Karl Koenke. *Remedial Teaching: Research and Comment*. Boston: Houghton Mifflin Company, 1969.

Ovard, Glen F. *Change and Secondary School Administration: A Book of Readings*. New York: The Macmillan Company, 1968.

Ovard, Glen F., Lowell Thomson, and Antone K. Romney. "Summary of Experimental Programs," Brigham Young Laboratory Schools, Brigham Young University, 1965.

Parker, Ronald K., ed. *Readings in Educational Psychology*. Boston: Allyn & Bacon, Inc., 1968.

Parnes, Sidney J. *Programming Creative Behavior*. Albany: State University of New York Press, 1966.

Peterson, Carl H. *Effective Team Teaching: The Easton Area High School Program*. Englewood Cliffs, New Jersey: Prentice-Hall, Inc., 1966.

Peterson, Carl H.: "Team Teaching in the High School," *The Education Digest*, 30 (May 1965), 22–24.

Popham, W. James. "The Performance Test: A New Approach to the Assessment of Teaching Proficiency," *Journal of Teacher Education*, 19 (Summer 1908), 210–222.

Programs '63: A Guide to Programed Instructional Materials. Washington, D.C.: Center for Programed Instruction, 1963.

Raths, James, John R. Pancella, and James S. Van Ness. *Studying Teaching*. Englewood Cliffs, New Jersey: Prentice-Hall, Inc., 1957.

Raubinger, Frederick M. and Harold G. Rowe, eds. *The Individual and Education: Some Contemporary Issues*. New York: The Macmillan Company, 1968.

Redl, Fritz and William W. Wattenberg. *Mental Hygiene in Teaching*. New York: Harcourt Brace Jovanovich, Inc., 1959.

Reid, J. Christopher and Donald W. MacLennan. *Research in Instructional Television and Film*. Washington, D.C.: U.S. Government Printing Office, 1967.

Resnick, Lauren B. "Programmed Instruction and the Teaching of Complex Intellectual Skills: Problems and Prospects," *Harvard Educational Review*, 33 (Fall 1963), 439–471.

Richey, Robert W. *Planning for Teaching: An Introduction to Education*. 4th ed. New York: McGraw-Hill Book Company, 1968.

Richmond, W. Kenneth. *The Teaching Revolution*. London: Methuen, 1967.

Ringness, Thomas A. *Mental Health in the Schools*. New York: Random House, Inc., 1968.

Rose, Homer C. *The Instructor and His Job*. Chicago: The American Technical Society, 1966.

Rossi, Peter H. and Bruce J. Biddle. *The New Media and Education*. Chicago: Aldine Publishing Company, 1966.

Sarri, Rosemary C. and Robert D. Vinter. "Group Work for the Control of Behavior Problems in Secondary Schools." In *Innovations in Mass Education*, ed. David Street. New York: John Wiley & Sons, Inc., 1969.

Saylor, J. Galen and William M. Alexander. *Curriculum Planning for Modern Schools*. New York: Holt, Rinehart & Winston, Inc., 1966.

Scurozo, Herbert E. *The Practical Audio-Visual Handbook for Teachers*. Englewood Cliffs, New Jersey: Prentice-Hall, Inc., 1967.

Sheviakov, George V. and Fritz Redl. *Discipline for Today's Children and Youth*. Rev. ed. Washington, D.C.: National Education Association, 1956.

Shimabukuro, Shinkichi. "Guideline for the Classroom Use of Programmed Courses," *The Journal of Teacher Education*, 16 (1965), 469–476.

Short, Jerry and Betty E. Haughey. *An Experimental Study of Sequencing Strategies*. Pittsburgh, Pennsylvania: American Institutes for Research, 1966.

Silverman, Robert E. *How To Use Programmed Instruction in the Classroom*. Cambridge, Massachusetts: Bolt Beranek and Newman, Inc., 1967.

Skinner, B. F. "Why We Need Teaching Machines," *Harvard Educational Review*, 31 (Fall 1961), 377–398.

Smith, Frederick R. and R. Bruce McQuigg. *Secondary Schools Today*. Boston: Houghton Mifflin Company, 1965.

Springhall, Richard C. and Norman A. Springhall, eds. *Educational Psychology: Selected Readings*. New York: Van Nostrand Reinhold Company, 1969.

Stolurow, Lawrence M. *Principles for Programming Learning Materials in Self-Instructional Devices for Mentally-Retarded Children*. Urbana, Illinois: University of Illinois Press, 1966.

Street, David, ed. *Innovations in Mass Education*. New York: John Wiley & Sons, Inc., 1969.

Strom, Robert D. *Psychology for the Classroom*. Englewood Cliffs, New Jersey: Prentice-Hall, Inc., 1969.

Suppes, Patrick, Max Jerman, and Dow Brian. *Computer-Assisted Instruction: Stanford's 1965–1966 Arithmetic Program*. New York: Academic Press, Inc., 1968.

Sylwester, Robert. *Common Sense in Classroom Relations*. Englewood Cliffs, New Jersey: Prentice-Hall, Inc., 1966.

Thorndike, Robert L. and Elizabeth Hagen. *Measurement and Evaluation in Psychology and Education*. 3d. ed. New York: John Wiley & Sons, Inc., 1969.

Trump, J. Lloyd and Delmas F. Miller. *Secondary School Curriculum Improvement: Proposals and Procedures*. Boston: Allyn & Bacon, Inc., 1968.

Van Til, William, Gordon F. Vars, and John H. Lounsbury. *Modern Education for the Junior High School Years*. 2d. ed. Indianapolis: The Bobbs-Merrill Company, Inc., 1967.

Vars, Gordon F. "Can Team Teaching Save the Core Curriculum?" *Phi Delta Kappan*, 47 (January 1966), 258–262.

Walton, John. *Toward Better Teaching in the Secondary Schools*. Boston: Allyn & Bacon, Inc., 1966.

Webster, Staten W. *Discipline in the Classroom: Basic Principles and Problems*. San Francisco: Chandler Publishing Company, 1968.

Wellington, C. Burleigh and Jean Wellington. *The Underachiever: Challenges and Guidelines*. Chicago: Rand McNally & Co., 1965.

White, William F. *Psychosocial Principles Applied to Classroom Teaching*. New York: McGraw-Hill Book Company, 1969.

Wiley, W. Deane and Lloyd K. Bishop. *The Flexibly Scheduled High School*. Englewood Cliffs, New Jersey: Prentice-Hall, Inc., 1968.

Wittich, Walter A. *Educators' Guide to Free Tapes, Scripts, and Transcriptions*. Randolph, Wisconsin: Educators' Progress Service, 1969.

Wittich, Walter A. and Charles F. Schuller. *Audio-Visual Materials: Their Nature and Use*. 4th ed. New York: Harper & Row, Publishers, 1967.

Woodruff, Arnold Bond and Shinkichi Shimabukura. *Studies in Individual Differences Related to Performance on Programmed Instruction*. Dekalb, Illinois: Northern Illinois University Press, 1967.

Woodruff, Asahel D. *Basic Concepts of Teaching; with Brief Readings*. San Francisco: Chandler Publishing Company, 1962.

Woodruff, Asahel D. "Cognitive Models of Learning and Instruction." In *Instruction: Some Contemporary View-Points*, ed. Laurence Siegal. San Francisco: Chandler Publishing Company, 1967.

Appendices

The following appendices are designed to encourage student and in-service teachers to evaluate themselves thoroughly and quickly with respect to a wide range of abilities and traits.

The material is classified under the five following categories:

Appendix A: Self-Scoring Instrument for Teaching Units

Appendix B: Confidential Evaluation of Self-Improvement Techniques

Appendix C: Innovations Awareness Checklist

Appendix D: Inventory of Student Unrest

Appendix E: How Relevant is your Curriculum for Students?

APPENDIX A

Self-Scoring Instrument for Teaching Units

The device presented here is designed to help the teacher—the experienced teacher as well as the beginning teacher—evaluate his own unit plans by assigning a specific numerical score to each of 205 relevant questions, grouped according to the areas involved in unit planning. This device may also be used to evaluate units obtained from other sources—teaching colleagues, school districts, and commercial publishing houses.

How to Score Your Unit[1]

1. Below is a graduated numerical scale descriptive of how well planning responsibilities have been discharged:

    5 . . . Cared for unusually well
    4 . . . Well cared for, only minor errors or omissions
    3 . . . Cared for moderately well
    2 . . . Given limited attention
    1 . . . Given token attention
    0 . . . Given no attention but recognized as being needed
    NA . . . Question has no application to this particular unit

---

[1]This scoring procedure was adapted from marking procedures used in the *Junior High School Evaluative Criteria* (Salt Lake City: Utah State Board of Education, 1960), p. 8.

2. Place your numerical response in the blank to the left of each question.[2]

3. Score the unit according to the above graduated numerical scale. If the responsibility called for in a specific question has been discharged unusually well, assign it a score of 5. If the responsibility has been overlooked, assign the question a score of 0. If the question does not apply to the particular unit, write NA (not applicable) in the adjacent space.

4. A properly organized unit will warrant a response to each question.

Questions for Evaluation
I. Basic Information
  A. Age and Grade Level
    _____ 1. Is the age level of the students expressed in terms of a range of ages?
    _____ 2. Is the grade level of the unit indicated?
  B. Length of Time for Unit
    _____ 3. Is the proposed duration of the unit indicated accurately?
  C. Relationship of Unit to Other Units in the Overall Plan
    _____ 4. Is the relationship of the teaching unit to the preceding and following units, as well as to other units in the overall plan, noted with sufficient clarity?
  D. Nature of the Class
    _____ 5. Is the I.Q. range of the students indicated?
    _____ 6. Is the students' average achievement in the subject area involved indicated?
    _____ 7. Is the social and economic status of the students included?
    _____ 8. Are students with particular mental, physical, emotional, or social difficulties identified?
    _____ 9. Is the proportion of boys to girls in the class noted?
    _____ 10. Are students who may cause classroom control problems identified?
    _____ 11. Is attention given to the range of experiential backgrounds represented by the different students in the class?
  E. Seating Chart
    _____ 12. Is there a seating chart giving the location of each desk in the room and its occupant?
    _____ 13. Are each student's level of achievement, I.Q., socio-economic status, and special problems noted in coded form on the seating chart?
    _____ 14. Is the code arranged to protect the confidential nature of the information?

[2]Another practical variation in the use of this instrument involves writing the specific numbers of questions and the accompanying scores directly on the unit being criticized.

_____ 15. Is the key to the code placed in a safe place where it can be referred to easily if necessary?

II. Enabling Objectives to Be Achieved[3]
   A. Objectives Stated as Concepts (Understandings) to Be Learned
      _____ 16. Are all conceptual objectives (understandings) to be achieved in the unit listed in this category?
      _____ 17. Are objectives that are frequently termed "mental skills" but that primarily involve concept formation classified as concepts?
      _____ 18. Is appropriate attention given to the conceptual aspect of learning skills or symbols (memorization)?
      _____ 19. Are concepts arranged in hierarchical order so that it is easy to see that the all-encompassing unit objective is composed of still smaller subobjectives?
      _____ 20. Are concepts stated in full-sentence form?
      _____ 21. Are concepts stated in the simplest form compatible with clarity and meaning?
      _____ 22. Have all procedural elements (methods) been eliminated from the statement of concepts?
      _____ 23. Are concepts above or below the range of possible achievement for the grade level and group involved?
      _____ 24. Have other sources (usually textbooks designed for student use) been consulted to determine whether desirable concepts have been omitted?
   B. Objectives Stated as Memorizations (Associations or Symbols) to Be Learned
      25. Are all names, dates, terms, phrases, or passages that should be memorized noted?
      _____ 26. Are the concepts underlying the symbols to be memorized listed as concepts to be learned?
   C. Objectives Stated as Skills (Involving Motor Functions Only) to Be Learned
      _____ 27. Do all the objectives listed as skills to be learned involve motor functions?
      _____ 28. Are the concepts related to the skills to be learned listed as concepts to be learned?
      _____ 29. Are skills broken down into the essential subskills?
      _____ 30. Are all skills and subskills stated meaningfully?
      _____ 31. Are all listed skills and subskills achievable in view of the physical and intellectual readiness of the class?
      _____ 32. Have textbooks been consulted to determine whether necessary skills have been omitted?

---

[3]Questions in this instrument do not focus directly on behavioral objectives; however, pages 59 through 64 provide extensive suggestions for the preparation and use of such objectives.

D. Objectives Stated as Tastes (Preferences) to Be Developed

   _____ 33. Is each major taste or preference to be developed during the teaching of the unit identified and classified properly?

   _____ 34. Is recognition given to the fact that positive tastes and preferences for a given subject or unit usually develop as the result of acquiring clear concepts of the content involved?

   _____ 35. When the subject is concerned directly with appreciation (music appreciation, art appreciation, etc.) are the preferences or tastes to be developed listed in this category?

E. Questions of General Concern Related to Objectives

   _____ 36. Is consideration given to the degree of student participation in determining certain unit objectives before the objectives are stated?

   _____ 37. Are the stated objectives attainable in view of the capabilities of the group being taught?

   _____ 38. Is there a clearly understood relationship between objectives and activities?

   _____ 39. Are all objectives stated with appropriate simplicity and clarity?

   _____ 40. Are the objectives comprehensive enough to cover adequately all major objectives and supporting objectives that should be treated in the unit?

   _____ 41. Do all supporting objectives bear a clear relationship to major objectives?

III. Activities in Which Students Will Engage to Achieve Objectives

A. Introductory Activities

   _____ 42. Is recognition given at the outset of the unit to the general and special interests of the group to be taught?

   _____ 43. Do the introductory activities avoid the commonplace?

   _____ 44. Are steps taken to insure that students will understand the objectives of the unit in terms of their individual experiences?

   _____ 45. Do the introductory activities encourage the students to identify themselves with the major purposes of the unit?

   _____ 46. Will the students have a satisfactory comprehension of the scope and significance of the unit when the introductory activities are completed?

   _____ 47. Is attention given to physically preparing the classroom for the introduction of the unit?

   _____ 48. Is the relationship between the unit being developed and other units of the Overall Plan clearly established in the introductory statement?

_____ 49. Are students permitted to share sufficiently in planning the various aspects of the unit?

_____ 50. Is a pretest (diagnostic test) provided if one would be useful?

B. Developmental Activities

_____ 51. Is the objective to which an activity relates clearly indicated in every case?

_____ 52. Are the developmental activities appropriate for the maturity of the class?

_____ 53. Is there an attempt to keep students aware of what has been achieved and what remains to be achieved?

_____ 54. Are lengthy study periods provided where desirable?

_____ 55. Is there appropriate use of group work?

_____ 56. Is attention given to building social cooperation during the developmental phase of the unit?

_____ 57. After examining the results of the pretest, does the teacher provide an appropriate study guide for the students?

_____ 58. Are developmental activities planned in considerable detail and in writing?

_____ 59. Is the number of activities to be covered during specific class periods indicated when this step is practical?

_____ 60. Is an appropriate variety of procedures used in the developmental activities?

_____ 61. Is the number of procedures used extensive enough to encourage efficient movement toward desired goals?

C. Concluding Activities

_____ 62. Do the concluding activities include some procedure of extreme interest to students that will clinch many of the basic points of the unit?

_____ 63. Is an exhibit of graphical representations or student-made items employed to conclude the unit where appropriate?

_____ 64. Are papers, themes, or articles used as concluding activities where appropriate?

_____ 65. Are practical problems used to help complete the unit where appropriate?

_____ 66. Are students given practice in applying generalizations to new situations?

_____ 67. Are students asked to make unit summaries when this would be a sound procedure?

_____ 68. Does the teacher review basic concepts, emphasize the important relationships between the concepts, and cite applications during the culmination of the unit?

_____ 69. During the final stage of the unit are students given the opportunity to relate details, search for larger meanings, establish closer relationships with other subjects, and integrate details into an expanded concept?

_____ 70. Is there appropriate variety in the concluding activities?

_____ 71. Does the plan include a procedure for summarizing the unit that is quite different from those employed in developing the unit?

_____ 72. Is provision made early in the unit for planning concluding activities?

_____ 73. Is a performance or exhibition used as a final activity where appropriate?

D. Questions of General Concern Related to Activities

_____ 74. Are recurring activities (those that are repeated at certain intervals) grouped together with an indication of their frequency?

_____ 75. Is it clear which activities are to be carried out by the teacher, which are to be the responsibility of the student, and which are joint responsibilities?

_____ 76. Is there appropriate differentiation between the types of activities designed to teach concepts, preferences, and skills?

_____ 77. Are activities arranged in proper sequence so that they provide a gradual unfolding of concepts?

_____ 78. Does the unit provide a suitable amount of pupil activity?

_____ 79. Are first-hand experiences employed where desirable?

_____ 80. When films, resource speakers, and special demonstrations are to be presented in class, is the length of time accurately stated?

_____ 81. Are activities unduly time consuming in proportion to their value?

_____ 82. Is particular attention given to the timing of introductory, developmental, and concluding activities?

_____ 83. Is there appropriate use of activities involving physical movements?

_____ 84. Is an appropriate variety of methods employed?

_____ 85. Are unusual activities placed where they are most psychologically and educationally valuable?

_____ 86. Are activities described in terms of specific things to be done, rather than as general procedures?

_____ 87. Is the teacher's ingenuity expressed in the types of activities chosen?

_____ 88. Will students be able to distinguish between activities and objectives?

_____ 89. Is the relationship between different activities clearly established?

_____ 90. Will the relationship between activities and unit objectives be clear to the students?

_____ 91. Are activities described in sufficient detail to provide a second teacher with a clear, well-rounded picture of what is to take place?

_____ 92. Has the teacher avoided scheduling too many activities to be successfully completed within the allowed time?

_____ 93. Are the activities practical in terms of the group and the circumstances in which the teaching must take place?

_____ 94. Will the activities be educationally sound as well as interesting to the students?

_____ 95. Is attention given to the preparation necessary to insure the success of the activity?

_____ 96. Is there an appropriate balance between individual and group activities?

_____ 97. Is there an appropriate balance between oral and written activities?

_____ 98. Is there an appropriate balance between teacher-centered and pupil-centered activities?

_____ 99. Is there provision for individual study supervised by the teacher?

_____ 100. Are activities related appropriately to the here-and-now?

_____ 101. Has the teacher avoided activities that, although of immediate interest to students, do not serve the basic purposes of the unit?

_____ 102. Do the activities planned aim at the formation of clearer concepts?

_____ 103. Are student activities sufficiently varied to maintain interest and to insure that individual differences are properly met?

_____ 104. Is sufficient flexibility built into the unit to accommodate unforeseen accelerations or slowdowns?

E. Activities Related to the Achievement of Concepts

_____ 105. To what extent do the activities follow the essential steps of (a) showing, (b) discussing, (c) memorizing, and (d) applying?

_____ 106. To what extent do the activities provide meaningful and vivid experiences for the learner?

_____ 107. Is sufficient attention given to procedures that promote an understanding of the concepts underlying new words and symbols?

_____ 108. Are activities sufficiently related to everyday life to promote maximum insight into the meaning of concepts?

_____ 109. Are the past experiences of pupils properly employed to add meaning to the concepts being taught?

_____110. Are concepts presented in concrete form before students are required to make generalizations?

_____111. Does the development of concepts within the unit move from the simple to the complex?

_____112. Is one carefully planned activity used to teach more than one concept when practical?

_____113. Are activities arranged in proper sequence to provide a gradual unfolding of concepts?

F. Activities Related to Memorization

_____114. Are the concepts underlying each word, phrase, term, or passage taught before the drill aspect of memorization is undertaken?

_____115. Is drill used sparingly or extensively, depending on the purpose to be served?

_____116. Is there appropriate differentiation between the degrees of memorization required for various purposes?

_____117. Are learning experiences grouped so that students are encouraged to form associations of symbols and concepts that are meaningful?

G. Activities Related to the Development of Skills

_____118. Is there provision for learning the concept related to the skill or subskill before it is tried?

_____119. Is emphasis placed upon practice under supervision?

_____120. Are performance errors quickly identified and corrected by the instructor?

_____121. Is practice continued under supervision until the desired level of proficiency is attained?

_____122. Are practice periods effectively distributed?

_____123. Is there appropriate use of activities involving physical movements?

H. Activities Related to the Development of Tastes and Preferences

_____124. Is the environment of the class consistently pleasant and conducive to the enjoyment of learning?

_____125. Do the activities stop when enjoyment is at its peak?

_____126. Is the learning experience satisfying to the student?

_____127. Are the conceptual aspects of an experience clearly formed, thus promoting satisfaction?

_____128. Are psychologically sound steps followed in developing tastes and preferences?

_____129. Do the activities used in developing tastes begin with the students' relatively limited appreciation of the course content?

IV. Materials and Resources

A. Teaching Aids

_____130. Are the pictures, models, or charts used sufficiently accurate to prevent the development of false concepts?

_____131. Are the unit teaching aids chosen for their educational rather than their entertainment value?

_____132. Is the use of educational radio and television programs coupled with other learning activities to clinch an understanding of concepts?

_____133. Are visual aids employed to help concept formation when it is impossible to provide first-hand experiences?

_____134. Are visual materials used to clarify abstract relationships?

_____135. Are models used in preference to pictures or verbal descriptions when the students' experiences make this desirable?

_____136. Are students properly briefed on what to look for in the filmstrip, movie, or field trip?

_____137. Are pupils stimulated to think about the relationships of ideas presented by the teaching aids?

_____138. Is the best possible aid chosen to accommodate the type of learning and the group involved?

_____139. Does the instructor have a first-hand knowledge of the content of records, filmstrips, or movies before they are used in class?

_____140. Is the availability of aids determined before a definite choice is made?

_____141. Does the teacher make his own visual aids to demonstrate unit objectives if appropriate aids are not otherwise available?

_____142. Does the value of a given aid in terms of its assistance to learning justify the amount of time spent in preparation, procurement, and/or use?

_____143. Are maps employed to develop proper concepts of location, direction, relative size, or topography?

_____144. Is an overemphasis on aids avoided?

_____145. Are all aids used properly as an aid to concept formation, not as ends in themselves?

_____146. Are some of the following aids used to achieve unit objectives?

Television	Films	Relics
Models	Microscopic slides	Exhibits
Chalkboard	Cell overlays	Globes
Bulletin board	Charts	Specimens
Pictures	Maps	Collections

_____147. Are some of the following projection devices used most advantageously?
Overhead projector
Opaque projector
Glass slides, filmslides, and microslides
Silent motion pictures

Sound filmslides

Sound motion pictures

_____148. Is there provision for determining whether the right concepts emerge from the use of aids?

_____149. Are visual aids used as a means for summarizing and clarifying relationships?

_____150. Are objects, specimens, and models used to teach concepts in preference to first-hand experiences when such materials are just as effective in concept development and when use of first-hand experiences calls for a greater expenditure of time and effort?

    B. Written Materials

_____151. Is all the reading material suitable in consideration of the maturity, vocabulary, and previous experiences of the students?

_____152. Are students informed about desirable supplementary sources of information relating to the unit?

_____153. Do students have access to a variety of reading materials (including programed texts) when these materials will assist in learning desired concepts?

_____154. Is the very best student text selected in terms of educational psychology, reading level of pupils, presentation, illustrations, and format?

_____155. Is a wide range of nontextbook material provided where it is appropriate to the learning undertaken?

_____156. Are encyclopedias and other reference books used effectively?

_____157. Does the unit plan include complete and exact references to the textbook and other sources to be used?

_____158. Are students encouraged to bring special items of information to class?

_____159. Are workbooks used as aids to develop concepts, not as ends in themselves?

_____160. Are hand-out materials prepared for distribution to students when they would be useful?

_____161. Is a study guide prepared to assist students in acquiring significant points, answering basic questions, and studying most advantageously?

V. Evaluation Procedures

    A. Tests and Examinations

_____162. Is a diagnostic test used as an introductory activity where appropriate?

_____163. Are quizzes given frequently when they would be useful?

_____164. Is there provision for reviewing tests with students?

_____165. Is a comprehensive test, covering the content of the entire unit, used as a culminating activity where appropriate?

_____166. Is there provision in the tests for measuring the progress of the brightest as well as the slowest student in the group?

_____167. Is a sample of the written unit test included as a part of the unit plan?

_____168. Are both subjective and objective tests used to advantage?

B. General Evaluation Procedures

_____169. Are various evaluation procedures used at intervals throughout the unit?

_____170. Are evaluation procedures sufficiently varied and extensive to provide a valid measure of pupil achievement?

_____171. Are evaluation procedures arranged to determine whether students possess true understanding of the material?

_____172. Are evaluation procedures for different phases of the unit weighted in proportion to the emphasis given to the objectives of the unit?

_____173. Do the evaluation procedures reflect the idea that the major purpose of evaluation is to assist in improving student behavior?

_____174. Are evaluation procedures organized so that they enable the teacher and students to determine whether stated goals have been reached?

_____175. Does the evaluation scheme help determine to what extent the student can apply what he is supposed to have learned?

_____176. Is there a procedure that enables the student to keep an accurate check on his progress at all times?

_____177. Is provision made for pupil evaluation of the teacher and the unit?

_____178. Is specific as well as general observation included among the evaluation procedures?

_____179. Where observation is employed as an evaluation procedure, is it so systematized that it provides maximum benefit for the student?

_____180. Is attention given to the capacities of individual students in the assignment of final grades?

_____181. Are themes and written work incorporated into the evaluation scheme where appropriate?

_____182. Is a notebook required where appropriate?

_____183. Are the pupils' study habits given proper consideration in the total evaluation procedure?

_____184. Are the undirected activities of students properly ap-praised in the total evaluation of the unit?

_____185. Where desirable and practical, are individual student conferences held?

_____186. Is a rating scale employed as an evaluation device where appropriate?

VI. Questions of General Concern to the Teaching Unit
  A. Form and Make-up

_____187. Are the objectives, activities and other positions of the unit clear enough that another teacher could teach the unit?

_____188. Does the write-up of the teaching unit avoid the danger of undesirable and unnecessary brevity?

_____189. Is more detail included in the unit plan than is necessary?

_____190. Is consistency in form maintained in the unit plan?

_____191. Is there a strong interrelationship of parts within the unit?

_____192. Is the title of the unit appropriate and descriptive?

_____193. If the title of the unit is to be used by the students, is it motivational, attractive, and interesting?

  B. English Usage

_____194. Is the teaching unit correctly punctuated?

_____195. Is an outline form employed in the various divisions of the unit so that relationships of major and minor parts are clearly indicated?

_____196. Is the unit written in correct and appropriate English?

_____197. Are the activities and procedures clearly stated?

  C. Miscellaneous

_____198. Is there provision for flexibility in the unit in terms of timing, individual differences, and possible activities?

_____199. Is planning sufficiently flexible to accommodate worthy student interests that vary to some extent from the unit plan?

_____200. Is duplication of content avoided?

_____201. Are there opportunities for student self-expression at appropriate times throughout the unit?

_____202. Is the relationship between (a) objectives, (b) activities, and (c) evaluation procedures clearly established in all cases?

_____203. Is appropriate attention given to the cohesiveness and interrelationship of the unit activities?

_____204. Is the unit organized logically or psychologically, as assumed most appropriate?

_____205. Does the unit planning avoid the commonplace?

APPENDIX B

•••

Confidential Evaluation of Self-Improvement Techniques

An honest response to the following questions will help to identify strengths and limitations in your self-improvement techniques. Unless you choose to share the findings of this survey, they will remain exclusively yours.

Insert the number (or letters) corresponding to the most appropriate answer in the blank space opposite each question. Possible answers are: Highly Effective—4, Effective—3, Moderately Effective—2, Ineffective—1, and Not Applicable—NA. No question should be left unanswered.

How effective are my self-improvement procedures with respect to:

SELF, COLLEAGUE, SUPERVISOR, AND STUDENT EVALUATION

Self-Evaluation

_____1.   Assembling a range of self-evaluation devices?
_____2.   Developing self-evaluation instruments suited to my particular needs?
_____3.   Responding thoughtfully to a carefully selected self appraisal instrument?
_____4.   Determining how often formal self-appraisal should be undertaken?

Evaluation by Colleagues

_____5.   Inviting colleagues to comment on my teaching after careful observation?
_____6.   Exchanging ideas with experienced, competent teachers whose subject matter specialization is the same as mine?
_____7.   Making innovative use of my fellow professionals in providing the type of criticism I need?

Supervisor-Teacher Rapport

_____8.   Establishing rapport with my supervisor?
_____9.   Inviting the supervisor to observe my teaching?
_____10. Frankly discussing my strengths and weakness with my supervisor?
_____11. Soliciting the suggestions of the supervisor with respect to what procedures would be most effective in improving my teaching?

Student Evaluation of the Instructor

dent opinions?

_____12. Determining what devices should be used in obtaining student opinions?

_____13. Soliciting student opinions as a practical means of helping me to improve?

_____14. Skillful use of student evaluation of my teaching?

_____15. Using special techniques in gaining anonymous student opinions about my teaching?

_____16. Using open-ended statements of what students like and dislike about my teaching.

_____17. Tabulating student responses concerning my teaching?

ESTABLISHING AND MAINTAINING TEACHER-STUDENT RAPPORT

Establishing Teacher-Student Rapport

_____18. Understanding students?

_____19. Liking students?

_____20. Being able to empathize with students?

_____21. Employing special techniques for communicating with students?

_____22. Evaluating the quality of student-teacher relationships?

Individualizing Instruction

_____23. Using the analysis of student strengths as a background against which individualized assignments are made?

_____24. Motivating different kinds of students using varied techniques?

_____25. Improving my ability to appraise correctly students' readiness for learning?

_____26. Using procedures varied to meet the needs of individuals?

_____27. Encouraging students to work to their capacities?

_____28. Identifying the learning problems of each student?

_____29. Assisting students to improve their study habits?

_____30. Pointing out to students the personal value of instructional tasks?

_____31. Encouraging each student to compete with himself in achieving what his potential will permit?

_____32. Being sure that individual student interests are considered in content treated and methods employed?

_____33. Insuring that each student understands the concepts necessary to the completion of his academic tasks?

_____34. Insisting each student evaluate his own work?

_____35. Holding private conferences with students as deemed necessary?

_____36. Making sure that individual students view school work as a pleasurable experience most of the time?

_____37. Providing a range of instructional experiences in which all students can find success?

_____38. Taking steps to insure that each student has a healthy self-concept?

_____39. Determining the effect of the teacher's personality on each student?

_____40. Helping students to establish desirable study habits?

_____41. Using a wide range of instructional techniques?

_____42. Suggesting work on individual projects that cater to individual interests?

_____43. Teaching certain students needed library study skills?

_____44. Developing individualized reading programs?

_____45. Determining that each student has needed first-hand experiences?

_____46. Analyzing the difficulties that students exhibit with respect to study techniques?

_____47. Helping students to become progressively more self directive?

_____48. Giving recognition to the desirable creative activities of students?

_____49. Using a range of different approaches (self-directive learning packages and special programs and textbooks) for presenting content?

_____50. Soliciting the help of other professionals as well as teacher aides in individualizing instruction?

_____51. Using special teaching materials?

_____52. Making full use of special plant facilities (carrels, subject-matter laboratories, and small group discussion rooms)?

_____53. Making full use of electronic equipment (computer terminals, portable television systems, and dial access systems) in individualizing instruction?

_____54. Insisting that the most effective study environment for each student be discovered and maintained?

_____55. Making full use of the instructional materials center in promoting individual study.

ANALYSIS OF TEACHER PERSONALITY

Determining Needed Personality Ingredients

_____56. Determining the areas of teacher personality that most strongly affect learning?

_____57.   Soliciting the help of others in analyzing my personality?

_____58.   Identifying the areas of greatest weakness in my teaching personality and taking positive steps to remedy them?

_____59.   Charting a course for continuing personality evaluation and improvement?

General Alertness

_____60.   Reacting quickly in emergencies?

_____61.   Using creativity in my teaching?

_____62.   Displaying a lively sense of humor that adds to my teaching?

Positive Projections of Personality

_____63.   Avoiding unreasonableness?

_____64.   Avoiding narrow-mindedness?

_____65.   Avoiding being old-fashioned in appearance or thought?

_____66.   Being considerate of others?

_____67.   Being sympathetic toward students with problems?

_____68.   Avoiding ridicule?

_____69.   Consistently shunning rudeness?

_____70.   Avoiding sarcasm?

_____71.   Avoiding the tendency to nag as a means of obtaining classroom control?

_____72.   Avoiding threatening or frightening students?

_____73.   Avoiding impatience in dealing with students?

_____74.   Avoiding the domination of students?

_____75.   Deferring judgment until all facts are available?

_____76.   Avoiding partiality to certain students?

_____77.   Being consistently approachable?

_____78.   Exhibiting friendliness on all occasions?

_____79.   Gauging my helpfulness to the specific needs of students?

_____80.   Being consistently fair?

_____81.   Creating a feeling of teacher sincerity?

Speech

_____82.   Avoiding speaking too softly or too loudly in the classroom?

_____83.   Avoiding monotonous speech?

_____84.   Speaking clearly and distinctly?

_____85.   Speaking correctly?

_____86.   Avoiding speech idiosyncrasies?

_____87.   Overcoming faltering speech?

ANALYZING AND PLANNING FOR INSTRUCTION

Planning for Instruction

_____88. Planning efficiently?

_____89. Planning for the use of specific methods?

_____90. Specific planning aimed at the individualization of instruction?

_____91. Planning for the school year?

_____92. Planning teaching units?

_____93. Daily lesson planning?

Developing Curriculum Materials

_____94. Modifying curriculum materials to meet the needs of the disadvantaged?

_____95. Developing certain materials not commercially available to serve the needs of specific students?

_____96. Keeping abreast of innovative curriculum developments in the area of my teaching major?

Analyzing Objectives

_____97. Using behavioral objectives to give specific direction to my teaching and to help students visualize goals more clearly?

_____98. Clearly differentiating the kinds of enabling objectives?

_____99. Matching objectives with procedures most effective in achieving them?

Analyzing Instructional Problems

_____100. Appraising the effect of school marks on in-class student behavior?

_____101. Analyzing the effectiveness of the relationship of each student to his peer?

_____102. Determining the degree of aptitude of each student for the subject I teach?

_____103. Determining student preferences for certain instructional methods?

_____104. Determining which of the teaching methods I prefer match the preferences of different students?

Analyzing Learning Problems

_____105. Determining which students are poor readers or nonreaders?

_____106. Identifying nonreading learning problems that affect student progress generally?

_____107. Identifying specific learning problems that hinder the academic gains of certain students?

_____108. Charting individualized programs to assist students whose learning problems have been identified?

_____109. Determining which students have poor study habits?

_____110. Determining which students have personality problems?

_____111. Determining which students are limited in capacity?

_____112. Determining which students would benefit by a change in instructional procedures?

INSTRUCTIONAL TECHNIQUES AND MATERIALS

Use of Innovations

_____113. Visiting innovative schools where a range of individualized practices are being employed?

_____114. Viewing carefully selected films that describe innovations?

_____115. Working with other teachers on innovative projects?

_____116. Making extensive use of electronic devices?

_____117. Using several kinds of projectors?

_____118. Devising and making use of a range of study spaces?

_____119. Adapting instructional innovations to serve my individual needs?

_____120. Reading about innovative efforts in professional periodicals and carefully selected books?

_____121. Using the instructional media center inventively?

_____122. Trying a few procedures that no teacher has tried before?

_____123. Scheduling classes on a flexible basis?

_____124. Using a systems approach in my teaching?

_____125. Using students in different ways to help others as well as themselves?

_____126. Obtaining the help of qualified volunteer helpers?

_____127. Preparing certain kinds of instructional materials?

Use of Sound Conventional Procedures

_____128. Insisting that each student measures up to his capacity?

_____129. Using a wide variety of reading materials?

_____130. Providing tutorial help for students with particular problems?

_____131. Allowing certain students free use of the library during class periods?

_____132. Arranging for one student to help another when it is psychologically sound?

_____133. Arranging for student-directed small group discussions?

_____134. Using appropriate methods for reaching a specific kind of goal?
_____135. Using methods that move students directly toward desired educational goals?
_____136. Supervising small-group discussions?
_____137. Selecting activities that are interesting for students?

Use of Instructional Materials

_____138. Using programed lessons, units, or full texts?
_____139. Using a wide variety of reading materials?
_____140. Using self-directive learning packages?
_____141. Being inventive in the use of teaching materials?

Effectiveness of Methods

_____142. Appraising the effectiveness of my methods?
_____143. Achieving an appropriate balance between individual and group activities?
_____144. Employing activities in the most productive sequence?

PROFESSIONAL STUDY AND INVOLVEMENT

Professional Study

_____145. Scheduling a specific period for professional study?
_____146. Submitting a professional article for publication?
_____147. Maintaining currency with respect to experimental teaching techniques related to my teaching major?
_____148. Reading widely in the teaching areas in which I have limited knowledge of content?
_____149. Taking graduate courses needed to round out my professional and subject-matter competence.
_____150. Listening to speakers of national reputation whose messages are relevant to my teaching specialization?
_____151. Carefully selecting professional reading?

In-service Training

_____152. Engaging in special in-service projects?
_____153. Taking advantage of optional in-service help offered by my school district?
_____154. Suggesting that needed in-service programs be conducted by my school or school district?

Formal Course Work

_____155. Taking a content class in the area of my teaching specialization?

_____156. Taking those graduate classes that afford the greatest promise of professional improvement?

Professional Organizations

_____157. Determining which professional organizations afford the greatest promise of helping me to improve?

_____158. Affiliating with professional organizations directly concerned with my subject specialization?

_____159. Attending professional conferences concerned with problems in the area of my specialization?

_____160. Holding membership in national professional organizations?

_____161. Holding membership in state professional organizations?

_____162. Holding membership in local professional organizations?

_____163. Serving in a leadership role in a professional organization?

Planning for Improvement

_____164. Assuming personal responsibility for self-improvement?

_____165. Identifying specific procedures that will lead to the improvement of my teaching?

_____166. Devising means for appraising my subject matter competence?

_____167. Following a specific plan designed to eradicate specific weaknesses in knowledge of content.

_____168. Audio or video tape recording my classroom presentations as a means of identifying particular problems?

_____169. Conscientious planning for improvement and implementation of self-improvement plans?

_____170. Determining what self-appraisal I can and should undertake?

Systematizing Improvement

_____171. Following a specific plan designed to eradicate weaknesses in knowledge of content?

_____172. Critical examination of specific instructional practices at regular intervals?

_____173. Using a systematic approach to identifying weaknesses in my teaching?

APPENDIX C

Innovations Awareness Checklist

How meaningful to you are the vocabulary, materials, equipment, and techniques of innovative educational practice? This checklist is designed to enable you to identify the ones that have attracted national attention and to indicate the degree of your acquaintance with each.

Directions:

A. Read the descriptive statements and related numbers printed below.
B. Indicate the degree of your acquaintance with each instructional process, device, or item listed under Innovations by placing the number identifying the most appropriate statement in the blank space to the left of each such procedure. (Higher numbers generally reflect a greater depth of understanding of specific practices.)

Descriptive Statements:
I have:

1. Never heard of it.
2. Heard of it.
3. Read at least one article about it.
4. Read extensively about it.
5. Observed its use at least once.

6. Observed its use repeatedly.
7. Tried it once.
8. Used it a few times.
9. Used it repeatedly.
10. Thorough understanding based upon consistent use.

INNOVATIONS

A. *Instructional Techniques*

_____Independent study
_____Student-made programs
_____Student responsibility for self-direction
_____Individualized programs
_____Inquiry training
_____Discovery learning

_____Game simulation

_____Weekly practicum sessions
_____Special grouping for laboratory work

_____Use of behavioral objectives

A.   *Instructional Techniques (Continued)*

_____Taped interviews
_____Community surveys
_____Released-time social ser-
vice internship

_____Sequentialized activities
_____Creativity training
_____Interdisciplinary teach-
ing
_____Training in generaliz-
ing, inventing, compos-
ing, and synthesizing

_____Power reading
_____Speed reading

_____Outdoor instruction

_____Speech therapy for
students with non-
standard dialects

_____Multiple motivation for stu-
dents from diverse ethnic
groups
_____Vocation-oriented
training cruises
_____Use of games to improve the
self-concept of disadvantaged
students

_____Cognitive tasks
_____Inductive teaching
_____Forced relationship associations
_____Levels of analysis

_____Complimentary computer in-
struction

_____Clinical approach to remedia-
tion

B.   *Instructional Personnel*

_____Paraprofessional
_____Student aide
_____Paid helper
_____Clerical aide
_____Teaching assistant
_____General aide
_____Technical aide

_____Noncertificated special-
ist
_____Learning resources mas-
ter
_____Staff specialists in spe-
cific skill fields
_____Master teacher
_____Skilled instructors teach-
ing large groups
_____Special consultants
_____Cooperative work of

teachers and noninstructional
specialists
_____Clinic of content specialists
_____Horizontal team
_____Multidisciplinary team
_____Team leader
_____Shared professional service
_____Shared decision making
_____Team evaluation of individual
student progress
_____Team selection of teachers to
work with special groups
_____Teaching intern
_____Shared instruction

_____Temporary teacher exchanges
_____Sharing by contiguous com-
munities of instructors with
scarce specialties

C. *Instructional Media and Technology*

_____Microfilm readers

_____Built in overhead projectors

_____Microbeam projectors

_____Microfiche cards

_____Instructor-developed teachers' manuals

_____Teacher-developed texts

_____Teaching machines

_____Multimedia facilities

_____Machine shorthand

_____Electronic video recording

_____Video tapes

_____Video playback unit

_____Multichannel tapes and playback machines

_____Simulation of real objects

_____Film loops

_____Massed films

_____Single concept films

_____Instructional film making by students

_____8mm film production

_____Student-made audio tapes

_____Teacher-made audio tapes

_____Dialog tapes

_____Disc recordings

_____Self-teaching machines

_____Machine-assisted drill

_____School-wide, closed circuit television

_____Intercommunication systems

_____COMSAT

_____Early Bird

_____Telstar

_____Communication satellites

_____Television-assisted classroom instruction

_____Teletypewriter

_____Two-way typewriter

_____Amplified (enlarged) television picture

_____System-wide instruction by television

_____Dial-access systems

_____Push-button Kinescope Libraries

D. *Computer-related Devices and Techniques*

_____Computer terminals

_____Computer-based teaching machines

_____Cathode ray tube

_____Computer-controlled electric typewriter

_____Light projecting pen

_____Touch sensitive screens

_____Random access devices

_____On-line terminals

_____Multi-terminal CAI system

_____Memory storage

_____Graphic display capability

_____Criterion branching

_____Lesson material storage and retrieval

_____Lesson prescription

_____Testing by computer

_____Interactive instruction

D. *Computer-related Devices and Techniques (Continued)*

_____Drill and review applications

_____Terminal behavior specifications

_____Cathode ray tube (CRT) display

_____Computerized grade reporting

_____Computer-assisted scheduling

_____Memory drum

_____Digital computer

_____Electronic banks

_____Data bank

_____Drill and review systems hardware

_____Teletype terminals

_____Storage capacity

_____Central processor

_____Printout sheet

_____CAI material houses

_____Hard copy output devices

_____Input-output relationships

_____Binary system

_____Information retrieval as a library function

_____Computer-based picture

_____Computer-generated display

_____Vocal response devices

_____Computer-student interaction

_____Time sharing

_____On-line computer use

_____Sign on

_____Sign off

_____Computational aid

_____Resource sharing

_____Statewide network of computer terminals

_____Cooperative use of computer terminals by several schools

_____Simulation

_____Computer use as part of a system

_____CAI languages

_____Man-machine communications

_____Alphanumeric information

_____Standard computer programming languages

_____CAI author languages

_____Conventional compiler languages

_____Interactive computing and display languages

_____COBOL

_____FORTRAN

_____PLANIT

_____COURSEWRITER

_____QUICKTRAN

_____Programers

E. *Housing*

_____Subject-matter laboratories

_____Teaching-materials workroom

_____Teaching-machine laboratory

_____Laboratories for the promotion of creativity

_____Laboratories for full-time use

_____Reading laboratory

_____Science laboratory

_____Language laboratory

_____Open laboratory

_____Multimedia laboratory

_____Skills development laboratory

_____School-land laboratory

E.   Housing (Continued)

_____Resource centers
_____Subject-matter work-rooms
_____Curriculum workroom

_____Classrooms of differing size
_____Small-discussion rooms
_____Electronics classroom
_____Sound-deadened rooms
_____Clusters
_____Independent study workrooms

_____Typing carrel
_____Television carrel
_____Electronic carrel
_____Small work cubicles
_____Soundproof cubicles

_____Instructional media center
_____Subject-matter learning center
_____Instructional resources center
_____Education service center
_____Field stations for curricular development

_____Demonstration, implementation and dissemination center

_____Schools for highly talented youth
_____Middle school
_____Low productivity schools
_____Nongraded school
_____"Special service" school

_____Foldable partitions
_____Bolted partitions
_____Lightweight partitions
_____Motorized partitions

_____Acreage for resident outdoor education
_____Facilities for outdoor education on school-owned property
_____Outdoor education center
_____Cooperative, multi-school, outdoor education center

_____School park
_____Education complex extending from kindergarten through graduate school

_____District spacemobile
_____Mobile exhibits
_____Rolling library

F.   Administrative techniques

_____Graduation based on work completed
_____Continuous progress without promotion
_____Non-grading
_____Ungrading

_____Flexible scheduling
_____Combining modules for specific instructional purposes

_____Blocks of time
_____Flexible time arrangements
_____Daily demand flexible scheduling

_____School attendance for a full calendar year with scheduled vacations
_____Organization of the school day into seven or more periods

F. *Administrative techniques (Continued)*

_____Advanced placement
_____Honors courses

_____Bussing students for a specific period to a school with special facilities

_____Coordination of educational purposes, program, and budget
_____Flexibility in grouping students
_____Use of the systems approach in solving problems

G. *In-service Training*

_____Special seminars
_____Interschool seminars
_____In-service minicourses
_____Inquiry workshop
_____Computer languages institute for high school teachers
_____Released-time in-service training for teachers of the disadvantaged

_____Mobilab unit with remotely-controlled television equipment for in-service training
_____Self-assessment in-service training
_____Action center for identifying, studying, evaluating, and visiting promising innovations

H. *Curriculum-related innovations*

_____Quest programs
_____Special programs for the highly gifted
_____Honors seminars
_____Advanced placement courses
_____Project Talent
_____Noncredit courses
_____Work-study programs
_____Prescriptive courses based on diagnosis
_____Courses in exotic foreign languages
_____Courses in computer programing
_____Computer programs to meet local specifications
_____High school space science and mathematics
_____High school inner space-marine biology

_____Bilingual theater
_____Junior high school earthspace computer science
_____Physics space-age applications
_____Chemistry space-age applications
_____Biology space-age applications
_____Correspondence courses
_____Student-tested courses

_____Continuous progress programs
_____Nongrading
_____Ungraded curriculum

_____Multi-track curriculum
_____Unipurpose high school
_____National curriculum
_____Packaged curriculum
_____Textbook curriculum
_____Ideas curriculum
_____Great books curriculum
_____Life-long learning

H.   Curriculum-related innovations (Continued)

_____Student-devised, teacher-approved programs
_____Teacher-developed curriculum

_____New physics program
_____New mathematics program
_____New English program
_____New foreign language program
_____New science program
_____Modern grammar
_____Modern biology
_____PSSC (Physical Science Study Committee)
_____SMSG (School Mathematics Study Group)
_____FLES (Foreign Language in the Elementary School)
_____UICSM (University of Illinois Committee on School Mathematics)
_____CHEM Study

_____Curricular offerings at earlier or later levels
_____Relocating existing curriculum content
_____Unification of concepts within a discipline
_____Integration of courses
_____Curriculum models
_____Analysis of content structure
_____Downward thrust of curriculum
_____Conceptual framework for loosely structured disciplines
_____Global framework for social studies
_____Replacing old content with new topics

_____Federation of disciplines
_____Interdisciplinary physics program
_____Multiple-subject classes
_____Exotic languages

_____Linear programs
_____Branching programs

_____Sequentialized nonframe programs
_____Sequentialized placement of concepts and skills
_____Curriculum sequences
_____Sequentializing behavioral objectives

_____Realistic curriculum for prospective dropouts
_____Programing according to student needs
_____After school programs
_____Week-end programs

_____Supplementary programed units (or lessons)
_____Manipulation units

_____Programed textbook
_____Teacher-prepared textbook

_____Special summer session to serve particular purposes
_____Basic education
_____Accelerated curriculum
_____Enrichment curriculum
_____Foreign language for a longer number of years

_____Behavioral objectives
_____Concept-oriented objectives
_____Performance criteria for behavioral objectives

APPENDIX D

• •

Inventory of Student Unrest

If the teacher can relate the symptoms of student unrest to basic causes before they escalate into major problems, he is in a favorable position to take timely and relevant action. How often do you take meaningful steps when you see evidence of budding problems as revealed by student behavior identified below? Indicate the frequency of your careful response to such behavior by inserting the appropriate number (5–Always, 4–Frequently, 3–Sometimes, 2–Infrequently, and 1–Never) in the blank space to the left of each numbered item.

ENVIRONMENTAL FACTORS

Peer-Group Influences

_____1. Consistent showing off in class

_____2. Baiting the teacher

_____3. Roughhousing in the classroom

_____4. Picking on certain classmates

_____5. Making unwarranted noises in the class

_____6. Frequent cheating

_____7. Seeking peer-group approval through socially unacceptable behavior

_____8. Voicing hatred of school authority

Nonschool Environment

_____9. Swearing and using obscene language

_____10. Continuing association with delinquents or near delinquents

_____11. Consistently using incorrect English

_____12. Being consistently impolite

_____13. Failing to maintain standards of cleanliness

_____14. Petty thievery

_____15. Minor acts of vandalism

_____16. Exhibiting general aggressiveness

_____17. Exhibiting growing submissiveness to peer group influences

Economic Limitations

_____18. Wearing shabby clothes

_____19. Having little or no spending money

_____20. Avoiding activities calling for financial outlay

_____21. Not being able to compete financially with members of the peer group

_____22. Telling falsehoods in explaining financial status to peers

ACADEMIC FACTORS

Curriculum Relevance

_____23. Having to take subjects inappropriate to perceived life goals

_____24. Inability to relate subject matter to current in-school activities

_____25. Inability to see the relevance of school attendance to nonschool activities

_____26. Inability to relate school attendance to post-school plans

Student Capacity

_____27. Finding content too difficult to grasp after a reasonable amount of teacher help

_____28. Finding content boringly easy

_____29. Inability of a few to grasp even the rudiments of the course

Failure

_____30. Consistent failure at academic tasks

31 Self - assumption that members of the peer group view him as a failure

_____32. Fear of the school, the teacher, and academic expectations

_____33. The student's perceiving himself as an academic failure

_____34. Infrequent opportunity for achieving academic success

Reading Ability

_____35. Inability to read textual material with needed speed and comprehension

_____36. Inability to read even simple printed materials

_____37. Inability to read rapidly but with adequate comprehension

_____38. Selecting reading materials that are consistently too easy

Underachievement

_____39. Working at a pace consistently below achievement potential

_____40. Working hard only as the mood strikes

_____41. Receiving grades consistently below what standardized tests and teacher opinion indicate the student should be able to obtain

Overachievement

_____42. Preoccupation with obtaining high grades to the exclusion of all other school activities

_____43. Dissatisfaction with grades and academic performance in spite of consistent hard work

_____44. Consistently achieving grades higher than warranted by capacity

Comprehension

_____45. Not understanding course content

_____46. Not understanding course content in spite of remedial help

_____47. Reflection of displeasure at having to gear pace to the less bright

_____48. Bluffing by insecure students who would suffer at having to disclose lack of understanding

_____49. Failure to understand after prolonged and extreme concentration

INSTRUCTIONAL FACTORS

Instruction

_____50. Domination of in-class activities by a small minority

_____51. General discontent with assignments

_____52. Student displeasure with little differentiation in instructional procedures to compensate for differing capacities, skills, and achievement

_____53. Student displeasure with lack of teacher sensitivity to student preferences for certain instructional activities

Teacher-Student Rapport

_____54. A general feeling of rejection of the teacher

_____55. Dislike of certain personality traits in the teacher

_____56. Being frequently discourteous to the teacher

_____57. Ignoring the teacher

_____58. Mimicking the teacher openly in class

Reading Level

_____59. Feelings of failure and frustration after trying to read teacher-assigned materials

_____60. Finding the generally assigned reading materials too simple for the majority

Methods

_____61. A general feeling that the teacher's methods are old-fashioned

_____62. Overt expressions of boredom with instructional methods employed

_____63. Suggestions and requests that other procedures be tried

_____64. General discontent with class assignments

_____65. Widespread feeling that assignments are of little value

PERSONALITY FACTORS

General Unfriendliness

_____66. General unfriendliness toward the teacher

_____67. General unfriendliness toward members of the peer group

_____68. Occasional overtly expressed hatred of all that relates to school

_____69. Unwarranted display of anger or fear

Defensiveness

_____70. Extreme sensitivity by some in the face of mild reprimand

_____71. Emotional reaction to an affront by the teacher or other students

_____72. Insistence on correctness of behavior in the face of evidence to the contrary

Aggressiveness

_____73. Obvious hatred between two members of the peer group

_____74. Overt expressions of dislike between two groups of students within the class

_____75. Minority-group students with "chip-on-the-shoulder" attitudes

_____76. Extreme verbal aggression on the part of one or more students in the class

Withdrawal

_____77. Consistent retreat from all competitive situations by a few students

_____78. Aggressive encouragement of withdrawal of certain disliked peers by dominant students

_____79. Excessive shyness on the part of some students in all social and academic situations

SOCIAL FACTORS

Peer-Group Acceptance

____80. Exclusion of certain peers from participation within the group
____81. Feelings of rejection by a limited number of students
____82. Inability to find accept-

ance among peers even after repeated attempts
____83. Social rejection of minority-group students
____84. Cliquishness among certain elite groups

Self-Acceptance

____85. Perception of oneself as an academic failure
____86. Perception of oneself as a social failure

____87. Withdrawal tendencies serious enough to seriously impair mental health

Teacher Acceptance

____88. The teacher's being viewed as not lending full acceptance to all students
____89. A general feeling that the teacher has favorite students

____90. A general feeling that the teacher rejects students with social or economic limitations

HABIT-RELATED FACTORS

____91. Consistent evidence of poor work habits
____92. Avoidance of hard study whenever possible

____93. Consistent misbehavior
____94. Failure to abide by reasonable standards of classroom control

COMBINATION FACTORS

____95. Desire to quit school at the earliest possible time
____96. Continuing pockets of disruption and malcontent

____97. Covert misbehavior under nearly all circumstances

APPENDIX E

How Relevant Is Your Curriculum for Students?

Curriculum relevance lies at the heart of the success or failure of many secondary school students. Questions contained in this instrument are designed to enable you to assess the relevance of the curriculum in the school in which you teach. Insert one of the letters A, B, C, D, or E—in the blank space to the left of each question indicating the degree to which you feel student needs are being met. The highest rating is represented by the letter A, the lowest by the letter E.

Curriculum Differentiation

_____1. Does the curriculum reflect the varied posthigh school goals of students?

_____2. Is an annual attempt made to modify the curriculum to meet the perceived needs of students?

_____3. Does the curriculum give consideration to all socioeconomic levels?

_____4. Are nonacademic students exposed to courses in which they can succeed?

_____5. Does the curriculum give consideration to the needs of each of the following groups: college-bound students, trade-oriented students, students seeking business occupations, and students whose posthigh school plans are indefinite?

_____6. Are programs prescribed for individual students reassessed at regular intervals?

_____7. Does homogeneous grouping help to place round pegs in round holes?

_____8. Are courses offered that are particularly appropriate for minority groups?

Low Achieving Groups

_____9. Does the curriculum reflect the specific needs of poor readers?

_____10. Does the curriculum reflect the specific needs of under-achievers?

_____11. Does the curriculum give consideration to students with I.Q.'s below 90?

_____12. Does the extra-curriculum provide a range of activities that are particularly attractive for the 50 percent of the students least likely to become involved in out-of-school activities?

_____13. Have special programs been established to serve the needs of potential dropouts?

Analysis of Curriculum Problems

_____14. Is a careful analysis made of the reasons for all school dropouts?

_____15. Is the curriculum modified after careful consideration of reasons for school dropouts?

_____16. Are pressure groups within the community permitted to exercise undesirable control over the curriculum or cocurriculum?

Expediting Communication

_____17. Are channels of communication available to students to express concern over course content and methods?

_____18. Have you adopted or devised systematic procedures for determining to what extent individual students believe that the curriculum is meeting their needs?

Guidance Procedures

_____19. Is a forward-looking program of guidance within the school realistically directing students into courses that reflect interest, capacity, achievement, and posthigh school goals?

_____20. Are students helped to determine the best courses for them?

_____21. Are students exposed to information on the basis of which they are encouraged to make correct curriculum decisions?

_____22. Do guidance procedures enable students to make logical decisions based upon a careful exposure to the available options?

_____23. Is it possible for students to change their goals for just cause without the teacher and parental censorship.

Methods

_____24. Is provision made for individualization of instruction?

_____25. Is consideration given to providing for instruction not involving class work?

_____26. Is consideration given to the learning styles of different students?

_____27. Does your teaching give consideration to the needed procedures used in teaching different kinds of enabling (cognitive, affective, and psycho-motor) objectives?

_____28. Are methods differentiated to conform to how individual students learn best?

_____29. Within each heterogeneously grouped class, are students with differing capacities and interests made to feel that this class is serving their needs?

_____30. Do instructional procedures enable the student to move (as slowly as he must or as rapidly as he can) at his own pace?

Index

A

Ability grouping, 290; grading in, 311–312

Activities, concluding, 92–95; in biological science unit, 135; in English unit, 145–146; examples of, 93–95; questions for evaluation of, 445–446; specific suggestions for, 95

Activities, developmental, 85–91; in biological science unit, 131–134; characteristics of, 85–86; in English unit, 140–145; examples of, 86–90; questions for evaluation of, 445; specific suggestions for, 90–91

Activities, introductory, 77–85; basic purposes of, 81–82; in biological science unit, 130–131; in English unit, 140; examples of, 78–80, 82–85; need for variety in, 80–81; questions for evaluation of, 444–445; specific suggestions for, 83–85

Activities, questions for evaluation of, 444–448

Activities, recurring, 89; in biological science unit, 131–132; in English unit, 140–141

Activities, sequential: in biological science unit, 132–134; in English unit, 141–145

Adjustment of the student, 24–26

Aids: community resources as, 104; extensive use of, 423; need for comprehensive list of, 106; questions for evaluation of, 448–450; special, 104; in specific subjects, 105–106. *See also* Audio aids; Materials and resources; Visual aids

Assignments, 110, 195–199; characteristics of, 195; individualization of, 195; for meeting individual differences, 288, 292–293; in specific subjects, 197–198. *See also* Homework

Audio aids, 99–100

Autobiographies, 225

B

Basic information, 43–51, 119, 222–223; in biological science unit, 122; in English unit, 137–138; examples of, 49–51; questions for evaluation of, 442–443; on seating chart, 46–49; about students, 43–46; about the unit, 46

Behavior, explaining adolescent, 3–8

Behavioral objectives. *See* Objectives

Bulletin board, 81, 100

C

Chalkboard, 81–82, 100

Classroom control, 20, 26–28; attention and interest related to, 252; in different subjects, 258–259; effect of adolescent needs on, 247–248; effect of curriculum on, 242; effect of environmental influences on, 245–247; effect of expectations on, 248–249; effect of goals on, 27–28, 252; effect of growth and development on, 243–245; effect of habits on, 72, 243, 256–258; effect of meaning on, 243; effect of motivation on, 250–252; effect of objectives and procedures on, 242–243; effect of planning on, 287; effect of readiness on, 249–250; examples of procedures in, 252–255; principles related to, 241–252; purpose of, 26; specific suggestions for, 259–262; successful experiences and, 251–252; the teacher and, 26–27, 246–247, 255–258

Classroom routine, 58, 256–258

Closed-circuit television, 101–102, 377

Code, for seating chart, 46–49, 225

Community resources, 104, 227–231

Computer-assisted instruction, 415–417; contrasted with lecture, 177; specific uses of, 294–295

Concept-centered subjects: classroom control in, 259; differentiating instruction in, 299; remedial teaching in, 305; the use of aids in, 105–106; the use of assignments in, 197; the use of television in, 387; the use of the textbook in, 193

Concepts: abstract, 13–14; concrete, 12–13; forming and using, 10–14; generalized, 13; levels of complexity in, 12–14; planning suggestions for, 54–55; questions to evaluate achievement of, 447–448; specific steps in teaching 68–69, 105–106; steps in planning for, 55; teaching of, 68–69. *See also* Objectives, conceptual

Conceptualization and meaning, 12

Concluding activities. *See* Activities, concluding

Conferences: parent-teacher, 224, 313;

teacher, 224; teacher-student, 114–115, 224

Contracts, student, 211, 232, 292

Control. *See* Classroom control

Crowderian programing, 346–350

Culminating activities. *See* Activities, concluding

Cumulative records, 224

Curriculum relevance, questions related to: analysis of curriculum problems, 474; curriculum differentiation, 473; expediting communication, 474; guidance procedures, 474; low-achieving groups, 473–474; methods, 474–475

D

Daily lesson plan. *See* Lesson plan, daily

Debates, 110, 206

Demonstrations, 106, 184–187; with lecture, 175, 177, 186; in special situations, 186; specific suggestions for, 187; types of, 185–186

Development. *See* Growth and development

Developmental activities. *See* Activities, developmental

Developmental tasks, 4

Differentiation and integration, 11–12

Discipline. *See* Classroom control; Student unrest, factors related to

Discussion, 110, 206; examples of, 208–209. *See also* Group procedures

E

Educational television. *See* Television instruction

Electronic devices, use of, 423

Emotional growth, 8, 223, 268, 270

Enabling objectives. *See* Objectives

English classes: classroom control in, 259; evaluation of a unit in, 111; example of a field trip in, 216–217; example of a unit in, 39; individualized instruction in, 213–214; motivation in, 282; programed materials for, 356, 358; teaching of memorization in, 71; the use of aids in, 104; the use of demonstrations in, 186; the use of the textbook in, 193

Environmental influences, 4–5; effect on classroom control, 245–247; and motivation, 18, 278; and remedial

teaching, 302. *See also* Family and home

Equipment, creative classroom, 417–421

Evaluation: nonunit-related, 114–115; of student knowledge, 112; of the teacher, 113, 322; of the unit, 113, 441–452, of value of student self-appraisal, 310

Evaluation procedures, 108–115, 120–121; in biological science unit, 136–137; in English unit, 111, 147–148; questions for evaluation of, 450–452

Expectations: effect on classroom control, 248–249; parental, 5, 248; peer-group, 6, 249; self, 6, 249; teacher, 5–6, 249

Experience units, 40

F

Family and home, 4–5, 45, 223, 224, 245–246, 383; expectations of, 5, 248; reporting pupil progress to, 312–314

Field trip, use of, 93, 215–219; example of, 216–217; principles related to, 215–216; in specific subjects, 218; specific suggestions for, 218–219

Films: cartridge, 419; massed, 420; single concept, 419; teacher-made, 419

Films and projections, 92, 100–102, 105–106, 233

Flexibility: housing, 421–423; procedures, 423–426; scheduling, 421; use of instructional materials, 426–430

Foreign-language classes: example of basic information for, 50–51; memorization in, 56; programed materials for, 358, 361; the unit plan and, 118; the use of demonstrations in, 186; the use of resource persons in, 229, 230; the use of teacher-prepared materials in, 234

G

Goals. *See* Objectives

Goals of students: effect on classroom control, 27, 251–252; and motivation, 18, 20, 279

Graduate work, importance of, 326
Group procedures, 206–211; examples of, 208–209; principles related to, 207–208; specific suggestions for use of, 209–211; types of, 206
Grouping for instruction: in class-size group, 207; through individualization, 207; in large group, 207; in small group, 207
Grouping innovatively, 410–412; using individualized learning, 412; using large groups, 410–411; using small groups, 411–412; using special groups, 412
Growth and development, 6–8; effect on classroom control, 243–245; emotional, 8; intellectual, 7, 244; physical, 7, 244–245; social, 7–8. *See also* Readiness
Guidance, 292

H
Habits, 57–58; categories of, 57–58; of classroom routine, 256–257; effect on classroom control, 243; teaching of, 72
Home. *See* Family and home
Homework, 199–203; controversy over, 199–200; examples of use of, 201–202; principles related to, 200; specific suggestions for use of, 202–203. *See also* Assignments

I
Improving instruction, 317–334; examples of procedures for, 328–331; principles related to, 326–328; specific practices for, 318–326; specific suggestions for, 331–333
Incentives, need for, 19–20, 279
Individual differences, 23–24, 287–301; administrative provisions for, 289–292; advantages of knowing, 287–289; in different subjects, 299; examples of procedures for meeting, 296–299; instructional provisions for, 292–295; in learning rates, 23; materials and, 232, 288, 291; methods and, 289; motivation and, 288–289; principles related to, 295–296; in readiness, 266–267, 268; specific suggestions for meeting, 300–301; in teaching techniques, 24; in unit

plans, 119, 121; within the learner, 24
Individualization, and planning, 36
Individualization, recent techniques, 212
Individualization through innovation, 404–410; using continuous progress programs, 406–408; using self-directed learning, 408–409; using study carrels, 405–406
Individualized instructional procedures, 211–215; and computer-assisted instruction, 212, 294–295; examples of, 213–214; and learning packages, 294; principles related to, 212–213; and programed learning, 212, 293; and programed materials, 273–274, 293; and self-directed learning, 212, 293; specific suggestions for, 215; types of, 211
Innovations, awareness of: administrative techniques, 465–466; checklist, 461–467; computer-related devices and techniques, 463–464; curriculum-related procedures, 466–467; housing, 464–465; in-service training, 466; instructional media and technology, 463; instructional personnel, 462; instructional techniques, 461–462
Innovations, instructional, 403–430; reflecting student reaction to teaching styles, 409–410; using continuous progress programs, 406–408; using grouping, 410–412; using individualization, 404–410; using programed instruction, 404–405; using self-directed learning, 408–409; using study carrels, 405–406
Instructional materials. *See* Materials and resources
Intellectual growth, 7, 222, 244, 267, 269–270
Interests of students, 20–21; effect on classroom control, 252; and motivation, 18, 277–278
Introductory activities. *See* Activities, introductory

L
Language arts classes, 175, 394
Learning, 10–11; of concepts, 10–14; effect of classroom control on, 240–255; effect of motivation on, 275–

284; effect of readiness on, 266–275; and experience, 10–11; transfer of, 28–29

Lecture, use of, 173–179; and demonstrations, 175, 177; examples of, 175–176; principles related to, 173–174; in special situations, 177; specific suggestions for, 177–179

Lesson plan, daily, 118, 151–166; essential parts of, 152–154; examples of forms, 154–157; in French, 166; in music fundamentals, 164; specific suggestions for use of, 165–168; suggested format for, 153; in U.S. history, 163; in woodshop, 162

M

Marking and reporting, 109, 306–315; with descriptive statements, 308–309, 313; with letter grades, 308; with numerical grades, 307–308; for parents, 312–314; principles related to, 309–311; purposes of, 306–307; specific suggestions for, 314–315

Materials, flexible use of: audio materials, 427; library, 429–430; printed materials, 428–429; textbooks, 426; visual materials, 427–428

Materials, instructional: student self-use of, 430; teacher-directed use of, 430

Materials, printed: nontextbook, 103; textbook, 103, 191–194

Materials, teacher-prepared, 104, 231–235; classification of, 231–233; principles related to, 233–234; special advantages of, 233; in specific subjects, 234–235; specific suggestions for use of, 235

Materials, written, questions for evaluation of, 450

Materials and resources, 98–108, 120; in biological science unit, 135–136; classification of, 99–104; in English unit, 146–147; examples of, 98–99; to meet individual differences, 288, 291–293; principles related to, 105; purposes of, 98–99; questions for evaluation of, 448–450; recommendations for use of, 107. See also Aids; Materials, teacher-prepared; Resource persons

Mathematics classes: classroom control in, 259; meeting the needs of individual students in, 273–274; programed materials for, 352–354, 358, 362–363; teaching of positive tastes in, 73–74; the use of demonstrations in, 186; the use of the lecture in, 176; the use of teacher-prepared materials in, 234

Memorization, 55–56; examples of, 56; questions for evaluation of, 448; specific steps in teaching, 71; teaching of, 71–72; understanding concepts related to, 55–56. See also Objectives, memorization

Misbehavior, teacher-caused, 255–256

Models, 101

Motivation, 17–20, 275–284; effect on classroom control, 250–251; effect on learning, 276–277; environment and, 18, 278; examples of use of, 281; extrinsic, 17, 276; goals and, 18, 279; incentives and, 279–280; intrinsic, 17, 276; to meet individual differences, 288–289; principles related to, 279–280; specific suggestions for use of, 282–284; student interests and, 18, 277–278; success and, 19, 278–279

MPATI, 374–375

N

Needs, adolescent, 3–4, 247–248

O

Objectives, 9–10, 119–120; effect on classroom control, 242–243; questions for evaluation of, 443–444; related to procedures, 9–10, 64–74; relating enabling to behavioral objectives, 124–129; types of, 8–9, 54–64

Objectives, behavioral: in biological science unit, 124–129; in daily lesson plan, 157, 160, 165, 167; definition of, 59–60; extent of use, 62; relationship to enabling objectives, 62–64; specific suggestions for, 64; specific uses, 61–64; stating with precision, 62; in teaching unit, 59–64

Objectives, conceptual: in biological science unit, 124–129; in English unit, 138–139; questions for evaluation of, 443. See also Concepts

Objectives, enabling: in biological science unit, 124–129; in English unit, 138–139; in health unit, 87–89; procedures for achieving, 64–74; for teaching unit, 54–58

Objectives, memorization: in biological science unit, 130; in English unit, 139–140; questions for evaluation of, 443. *See also* Memorization

Objectives, nonbehavioral: assumed limitations of, 60–61; restated as behavioral objective, 110–111

Objectives, skill: questions for evaluation of, 443. *See also* Skills

Objectives, taste: questions for evaluation of, 444. *See also* Tastes, teaching of

Observation, use of, 114, 225, 274

Overall plan, 35–38; examples of, 36–37; related to unit plan, 42–43, 82; steps in developing, 37–38

P

Panels, 206

Parents. *See* Family and home

Parent-teacher conferences, 224, 313

Peer group, 5–6, 26, 223, 240, 249

Personality, of the teacher, 34, 322–323

Personnel, nonprofessional, use of, 424–425

Physical education classes: classroom control in, 258; determining physical readiness in, 266, 269; determining skill objectives in, 57; the use of demonstrations in, 106, 186; the use of resource people in, 230; the use of television in, 387

Physical growth, 7, 22–23, 244–245, 250, 266–267, 269

Planning, 32–51; avoiding confusion in terminology in, 40; criteria essential to, 35; helping the teacher in, 8–10; need for, 33–34; objectives and procedures in, 9–10. *See also* Unit plans

Preassessment, 165

Procedures, 10, 120; for achieving objectives, 64–74; and classroom control, 242–243; flexibility in use of, 423–426; for meeting individual differences, 289–295; and motivation, 17–18; need for variety in, 66–68; relating objectives to, 65–66; selection of, 65–68, 79; student-centered, 190–220; teacher-centered, 172–188. *See also* Group procedures; Individualized instructional procedures

Professional organizations, 325–326

Programed instruction: advantages of 344–345; behavioral gains related to, 339; correct and incorrect use of, 365–369; current trends in, 341; definitions of, 337-339; as desirable substitute for lecture, 177; effective use of, 202; examples of uses of, 365–369; expansion of materials in, 200; generalizations about, 352–356; history of, 339–341; limitations of, 342–343; to meet individual differences, 272–273, 291; principles related to, 363–365; procedures with limitations in, 366–367; procedures with promise in, 367–369; specific suggestions for use of, 367–370; in subject areas, 356–363; teacher's questions related to, 342; types of, 345–352

Programed instruction, areas using: English, 358; foreign languages, 358; mathematics, 358; sciences, 356–357

Programed materials: example of effective use of, 298–299; textbooks, 337, 351–352; use by self-directive students, 278–279, 293

Programing: Crowderian, 346–347; Skinnerian, 346

Programs, in elementary science, 357; in English grammar, 347–348, 359–361; in German, 364; involving computers, 350–351; linear, 338; in mathematics, 353, 354, 362–363; for use in machines, 349–350

Projection devices: Autoload projector, 418; cartridge projector, 418; creative use of, 418–420; 8mm projector, 418; motion picture projector, 418; overhead projector, 417; rearview projector, 419

Projects, individual, 211, 292

Promotions, 22, 211–292, 300

Q

Questing, example of, 214

Questions, use of, 179–184; to meet individual differences, 293; purposes of, 179–182; specific suggestions for, 183–184

R

Readiness, 21–22, 265–275; conceptual, 22, 267; effect on classroom control, 249–250; emotional, 268,

270; intellectual, 267, 269–270; physical, 22–23, 266–267, 269; principles related to, 271-272; for self-direction, 270–271, social, 267–268, 270; for specific learning, 269–271; specific suggestions for using, 274–275; types of, 266–268

Reading assignments, 211

Record player, 100

Recurring activities. See Activities, recurring

Remedial teaching, 301–306; examples of procedures in, 303–305; goals in, 302; for meeting individual differences, 289–295; principles related to, 302–303; in specific subjects, 305; specific suggestions for, 305–306

Reporting pupil progress. See Marking and reporting

Resource persons, use of, 92, 104, 227–231; advantages of, 227–228; a card file for, 104, 227–228; examples of, 229; principles related to, 228; in specific subjects, 229–230; specific suggestions for, 230–231

Resource unit, 41

Role playing, 206

Routine in the classroom, 58, 89, 256–258

S

Scheduling, modular, 291

Science classes: concluding activities in, 93, 94–95; evaluation procedures in, 112; example of developmental activities in, 87–89; example of an overall plan in, 36; introductory activities in, 78–80; programed materials for, 356–357; teaching of concepts in, 68; team-teaching in, 391; the use of aids in, 105; the use of lectures in, 175; the use of resource persons in, 229; the use of teacher-prepared materials in, 234; the use of the textbook in, 193

Seating chart, 46–49; for biological science unit, 123; for English unit, 147

Self-directed learning, 408–409; and problems of classroom control, 256; teacher encouragement of, 197

Self-improvement, questions for evaluation of, 453–460; evaluation by others, 453–454; instructional techniques and materials, 458–459; planning for instruction, 457–458; professional study, 459–460; teacher personality, 455–456; teacher-student rapport, 454–455

Self-scoring instrument for teaching units, 441–452

Sequential activities. See Activities, sequential

Skill-centered subjects, 56–57; classroom control in, 258–259; differentiating instruction in, 299; remedial teaching in, 305; the use of aids in, 106; the use of assignments in, 198; the use of demonstrations in, 186; the use of resource persons in, 230; the use of television in, 386–387

Skills, 56–57; examples of, 56–57, questions to evaluate development of, 448; specific steps in teaching, 69; steps in planning for, 56; subjects related to, 56–57; teaching of, 69–71, 106. See also Objectives, skill

Skinnerian programing, 338, 346–348, 350

Social growth, 7–8, 225, 267–268, 270

Social studies classes: differentiating instruction in, 297–298; example of developmental activities in, 86–87; example of recurring activities in, 89; motivation in, 276–277, 281; programed materials for, 356; remedial teaching in, 304–305; teaching of memorization in, 71–72; the teaching unit and, 42–43; the use of lectures in, 175, 176; the use of television in, 387; variety in, 67

Sociometric devices, 225, 270

Standardized tests, 115, 269–270; lack of validity for disadvantaged, 269

Student, study of, 222–227; devices used in, 224–225; principles related to, 226; specific sugestions for, 226–227

Student unrest, factors related to: combination causes, 472; environment, 468–470; habit, 472; instruction, 470–471; social acceptance, 472; teacher personality, 471

Students: basic information about, 43–46, 222–223; capacity of, 43–44, 222; experiences of, 10–11, 222–223, 267; from minority groups, 247; opinions of, 113; self-evaluation of, 113, 182, 232; and skills in self-direction, 103, 256; socioeconomic status

of, 44; subject-matter achievement
of, 45–46, 222. *See also* Goals of
students; Interests of students; Motivation; Needs, adolescent
Study habits, 58, 302–303, 305–306
Study, self-directed, 293
Subject-matter units, 40
Success and motivation, 19, 251–252;
through use of programed materials,
278–279
Supervised study, 241, 211; to meet
individual differences, 292
Systems approach, use of, 425–426

T

Tastes, teaching of, 72–74; questions
for evaluation of, 448
Teacher: determining new criteria for
effectiveness of, 319–320; evaluation
of, 113–322; expectations of, 5–6,
249; materials prepared by, 231–
235; relations with parents, 312–
314; role in classroom control, 25–
27, 246–247, 255–258; role in determining readiness, 269–271; self-improvement, 317–326; understanding of minority groups, 247
Teacher-student conferences, 110,
114–115, 224
Teaching machines, 233, 337, 339,
349–350, 356
Teaching styles, effect on students,
409–410
Teaching unit. *See* Unit
Team teaching, 388–401; advantages
of, 394–395; definition of, 389–390;
development of, 389; examples of
procedures in, 397–400; facilities
for, 396; limitations of, 396; to meet
individual differences, 290; principles
related to, 397; sound and unsound
practices, 397–400; specific suggestions for, 400–401; variations of,
391–394
Technology, 415–417
Television, creative classroom use of,
420–421
Television instruction, 101–102, 373–
388; advantages of, 378–380; approaches to teaching, 375–378; and
closed-circuit production, 101–102,
377; and commercial programing,
101, 377; and differentiating ETV
and ITV, 378; and educational television stations, 101, 376; examples
of procedures in, 383–386; facilities
for, 380, 381; history of, 373–374;

and instructional television fixed service (ITFS), 377–378; limitation of,
380–381; and multistate cooperative
use, 374–375; new applications of,
382; principles related to, 382–383;
sound and unsound practices for,
383–386; in specific subjects, 386–
387; specific suggestions for use of,
387–388
Tests: diagnostic, 82; as evaluation
techniques, 109, 110, 112, 114; lack
of validity of culture-oriented, 269;
standardized, 115, 222, 269–271.
See also Evaluation procedures
Tests and examinations, questions for
evaluation of, 450–451
Textbook, use of, 37–38, 42, 103,
190–194; compared with formal lecture, 177; examples of, 192–193; to
meet individual differences, 288,
293; principles related to, 191–192;
in specific subjects, 193; specific suggestions for, 193–194. *See also* Programed materials
Threats of punishment, 256
Transfer of learning, 28–29

U

UHF (ultra high frequency), 377–378
Unit: in biological science, 122–137;
definition of, 38–39; determining
objectives for, 54–64; in English,
137–148; evaluation of, 108–109,
441–452; as learning package, 294;
planning for, 38–42; questions for
evaluation of, 441–452; related to
the overall plan, 42–43, 82; steps in
developing, 41–42; types of, 39–41
Unit plans: basic information for, 43–
51, 119; characteristics of successful,
118–121; evaluation procedures for,
108–115, 120–121; examples of,
118–148; materials and resources for,
98–107, 120; objectives for, 54–64,
119–120; procedures for, 64–74,
76–95, 120; steps in developing,
119–121

V

Visual aids, 100–102; inept use of, 102;
in team teaching, 397
Voice of the teacher, 99, 321–322

W

Whole-class discussion, 206, 209–210
Written composition, 211